AFRICA'S
INTERNATIONAL
RELATIONS

AFRICA'S INTERNATIONAL RELATIONS

Balancing Domestic & Global Interests

Beth Elise Whitaker
John F. Clark

LYNNE
RIENNER
PUBLISHERS

BOULDER
LONDON

Published in the United States of America in 2018 by
Lynne Rienner Publishers, Inc.
1800 30th Street, Boulder, Colorado 80301
www.rienner.com

and in the United Kingdom by
Lynne Rienner Publishers, Inc.
Gray's Inn House, 127 Clerkenwell Road, London EC1 5DB

Library of Congress Cataloging-in-Publication Data
Names: Whitaker, Beth Elise, author. I Clark, John F. (John Frank), author.
Title: Africa's international relations : balancing domestic and global
  interests / Beth Elise Whitaker and John F. Clark.
Description: Boulder, Colorado : Lynne Rienner Publishers, 2018. I Includes
  bibliographical references and index.
Identifiers: LCCN 2018016050I ISBN 9781626377349 (hardcover : alk. paper) I
  ISBN 9781626377370 (pbk. : alk. paper)
Subjects: LCSH: Africa—Foreign relations. I Africa—Politics and
government. I Security, International—Africa.
Classification: LCC DT31 .W45 2018 I DDC 327.6—dc23
LC record available at https://lccn.loc.gov/2018016050

British Cataloguing in Publication Data
A Cataloguing in Publication record for this book
is available from the British Library.

Printed and bound in the United States of America

The paper used in this publication meets the requirements
of the American National Standard for Permanence of
Paper for Printed Library Materials Z39.48-1992.

5 4 3 2 1

For our families

Contents

Acknowledgments

We would like to express our deepest gratitude to those who helped this book move from an idea to a reality over the period of several years. The book was a collaborative effort from the beginning, involving both coauthors and our supportive publisher, Lynne Rienner, who helped shape the scope and organization of its contents. Each of the two authors was responsible for the initial drafting of six of the main chapters of the volume; we leave it to the readers to guess who was the lead author of each! Each coauthor gave honest commentary to the other on the content, organization, and presentation of the other's work. Whitaker both conceived and wrote the volume's conclusion and took the lead in conversations with the publisher. She also undertook a number of more quotidian but time-consuming tasks, such as formatting the manuscript and editing the final drafts. As a result of her leadership in these areas, she is identified as the first author of this study.

Both authors are grateful to students who provided valuable feedback on early drafts of the chapters. These include especially Edward Dowling, Erin McNulty, Natalia Rivera, and Rachael Young at Florida International University (FIU), as well as Oluwatobi Kalejaiye, Anthony Lindsay, Isaac Setliff, and Koffi Charles-Hector Yao-Kouamé at the University of North Carolina at Charlotte (UNC Charlotte). Clark also wishes to thank the doctoral students he supervised while he was writing this book: Michael Aboagye, Fiacre Bienvenu, Serena Cruz, Zachary Karazsia (who was also his teaching assistant), Yonas Mulat, Ubba Kodero, and Tochukwu Madueke. Whitaker thanks doctoral students Katelin Hudak, Salma Inyanji, and Ada Uche. We learn a lot from our students, one of the joys of academic life, and this generation is uncovering exciting new knowledge about Africa and the world.

We are both indebted to colleagues in our respective departments. At FIU, Clark is especially grateful to Thomas Breslin for sharing his knowledge of China's activities in Africa, Ron Cox for providing refreshers on the neo-Marxian perspective, and Mohiaddin Mesbahi for answering questions about Islam in Africa. Markus Thiel provided useful materials on the European Union's activities in Africa. Clark has learned more than a few things about foreign policy analysis from his friend and former FIU colleague Paul Kowert, and some of that learning is doubtless reflected here. Erin Damman was a fantastic colleague and Africanist partner during her years at FIU, and she is missed. Clark is also grateful to those with whom he served while he was department chair: Kyle Mattes, Barry Levitt, Kevin Evans, Tatiana Kostadinova, Todd Makse, Julie Zeng, and Susanne Zwingel. At UNC Charlotte, Whitaker is grateful to be in a political science department that continues to value multiple methodologies and areas of focus, including the study and teaching of African politics. She thanks especially Gregory Weeks, Justin Conrad, James Igoe Walsh, and Jason Giersch for their support and collaboration, and Cheryl Almond and Jill Tucker for their valued assistance. These colleagues all provided indirect support through their professionalism and capability in their respective roles.

We are fortunate to be members of the African Politics Conference Group (APCG), a network of political scientists who study Africa. We are grateful to John Harbeson for founding the group in 2002 and honored to have been elected to serve as officers of the group as it grew (Whitaker as chair and Clark as vice chair). Indeed, it is through APCG that we first met and eventually developed a plan to write this book together. While preparing the manuscript, we had stimulating discussions with many Africanist colleagues, including Steve Burgess, Brett Carter, Nic Cheeseman, Christopher Day, Kim Yi Dionne, Kevin Dunn, Pierre Engelbert, Kevin Fridy, Jim Hentz, Jeremy Horowitz, Hye-Sung Kim, Loren Landau, Carl LeVan, Peter Lewis, Claire Metelis, Kennedy Mkutu, Mike Nelson, Jessica Piombo, Will Reno, Laura Seay, Leo Villalon, and Susanna Wing, among others. We are grateful for their insights, which have helped us better understand the complicated dynamics of Africa's politics and international relations.

Both authors would like to thank the people and organizations that have assisted us in conducting research in Africa over the years. Among them, Clark is grateful to the International Institute of Education (IIE) for providing him a Fulbright specialist grant to work at the Institute of Interdisciplinary Research and Training at the Mbarara University of Science and Technology in Uganda in summer 2014. The institute's director, Viola Nyakto, was a kind host and a stimulating interlocutor. Pamela Mbabazi, Charles Muchunguzi, Tom Ogwang, and Hannington Odongo were among some of the gifted scholars with whom he had the pleasure of working. Whitaker also thanks IIE for providing her with a Fulbright Scholar award to teach and conduct research at United States International University–Africa (USIU) in Nairobi, Kenya, in 2005–2006. She is grateful for the support and friendship of so many former students and colleagues at USIU, including Freida Brown, Mark Gaya, Rachel Gichinga, Patrick Kamau, Tallash Kantai, Norah Kiereri (and her wonderful family!), Naima Mohammed, Karega Munene, Macharia Munene, David Mwambari, Muthoni Ndonga, Moses Onyango, and Gitty van Middelaar, among others. She continues to be impressed with their enthusiasm for knowledge and their pursuit of their dreams, which have taken them in fascinating directions.

We both extend a hearty thanks to the American Political Science Association for funding the 2015 Africa Workshop in Nairobi on Conflict and Political Violence. We were co-leaders of the workshop, along with Kennedy Mkutu (USIU) and Pamela Mbabazi (now at the Institute for Peace and Security Studies in Addis Ababa), to whom we are ever grateful. We thank Andrew Stinson for making sure the workshop ran smoothly and all of the participants, from whom we learned a great deal. These include Jacob Dut, Tarila Marclint Ebiede, Kevin Greene, Ahmed Ibrahim, Zachary Karazsia, Kathleen Klaus, Aditi Malik, Kizito Sabala, William John Walwa, and Cori Wielenga, among others. Clark wishes to thank William John Walwa of the University of Dar es Salaam for hosting him in the summer of 2016 and introducing him to many Tanzanians knowledgeable about their country's foreign relations. Whitaker thanks Ahmed Ibrahim, Aditi Malik, and Cori Wielenga for organizing and including her in a workshop on Somali migration at the University of Pretoria in 2016 and for continuing to pursue publication of the papers delivered there.

We both wish to thank Lynne Rienner, who worked closely with us on the development of the book. In particular, we are grateful for her patience, as a variety of professional commitments delayed our research and writing. Her impact on the study of both Africa and international relations has been enormous. Two anonymous reviewers provided us with invaluable criticism and suggestions for improvement. We are grateful and made many changes as a result. We apologize to those whom we have neglected to remember here. We of course take full responsibility for any errors that remain and welcome any feedback.

Finally, we have enormous debts of gratitude to our families, who have been hearing us talk about this book for longer than we care to admit. Clark wishes to thank his wife, Esther Alonso, and their daughter, Samantha, for their patience and forbearance. Whitaker is especially grateful to her husband, Jason Giersch, and their children, Tessa and Colby, for fully supporting her career while always reminding her what is most important in life. Both families had amazing adventures together in Kenya in 2015. It is to our families that we dedicate this book.

1

Understanding Africa's International Relations

Understanding Africa's international relations is a daunting
challenge. The continent's fifty-four states and countless nongovernmental organizations are engaged in millions of daily interactions with
their citizens, with external partners and rivals, and with one another.
No one scholar or student can discern and follow more than a few of the
myriad patterns that one finds in these interactions. As a result, even
professional students of Africa often feel overwhelmed by the scope of
Africa's international relations. Only the immodest would claim any
kind of comprehensive knowledge of the subject.

Also striking is how regularly the political focus of Africa's international relations has shifted for Africans themselves and for outside
diplomats, scholars, and activists.[1] Beginning in the 1950s, both Africans
and outsiders were preoccupied with how Africans could end European
colonialism on their continent and what form the new international relations of Africa's new states should take. As formal colonialism came to
an end with the agreement of Portugal to liberate its colonies in the
mid-1970s, the emphasis for Africans shifted to the struggle to end
white minority rule in Rhodesia (now Zimbabwe) and South Africa.
This long struggle came to an end only with the election of Nelson
Mandela to South Africa's presidency in 1994. Overlapping with these
struggles, the Cold War between the United States and the Soviet Union
provided another context for Africa's international relations from 1960
to 1989. Finally, the intra-continental and external focus of Africa's
international relations since the early 1990s has been on two other
issues: the powerfully renewed role of China on the continent and the
role of outsiders in encouraging or battling various forms of radical

political Islam. Meanwhile, development has been perhaps the most constant preoccupation of both Africans and outsiders interested in the continent. Whether and how outside organizations, donors, states, and private capitalists can contribute to economic and social development in Africa remain as important today as in 1960. The stakes of these questions of independence, political alignment, autonomy, and development could not be higher for Africa's peoples.

Because of the wide scope of Africa's international relations, and the changing focus of the continent's major political challenges, this book makes recurrent use of several theoretical lenses. These theoretical lenses help us find our way through the intellectual thickets that Africa's complex and oft-changing international relations present. They help us explore how Africans have perceived their own problems in a global context. They also help us understand how and why outsiders have sought to shape Africa's political trajectories, profit from its resources, and imbue Africans with their economic ideologies, worldviews, and religious interpretations. The concept of "regime security," discussed later, is particularly valuable in understanding how African states engage with each other and with other global actors.

In keeping with these considerations, the remainder of this chapter proceeds in three sections. The first provides an overview of the scope of Africa's international relations; this section underscores the great challenge of finding persistent patterns in the relations of African states and peoples among themselves and with outsiders. The second section presents an overview of four theoretical approaches to international relations (realism, liberalism, constructivism, and neo-Marxism) and examines how they have informed the study of Africa over the years. At the end of that section, we introduce the concept of regime security as a motivating factor underlying various aspects of Africa's international relations. Finally, the last section outlines the remaining chapters of the book.

The Challenge of Understanding Africa's International Relations

The scope of Africa's international relations is strikingly wide. A traditional analyst of international relations might begin by noting the large number of independent African states on the continent: fifty-four in total, as recognized by the United Nations (UN), including forty-nine in sub-Saharan Africa.[2] Two other territories, Somaliland and Western Sahara, have sought recognition from the international community.[3] By comparison, Central and South America are composed of only twenty independent states, and the Middle East (delimited by

Turkey in the north, Iran in the east, Yemen in the south, and Egypt in the west) includes only eighteen independent states. Many of Africa's states have borders with a large number of neighbors; the Democratic Republic of Congo (DRC) has borders with nine African states, Tanzania with eight, and several other African states have four, five, or six neighbors. This fragmentation of political authority into so many different states multiplies the sheer number of possible interactions among African states, and between these states and their external interlocutors. It is one of the most important legacies of European colonialism in Africa (see Chapter 2).

Also distinctive is the great cultural and linguistic diversity of Africa's states and peoples. Whereas Arabic is the main language of the Middle East, and Spanish and Portuguese of Latin America, the official languages of Africa's states include four European languages (English, French, Portuguese, and Spanish) as well as Arabic, blended languages like Swahili and Afrikaans, and indigenous languages like Kinyarwanda. South Africa alone has eleven official languages. Even more striking is the large number of ethnic communities of many African states: Nigeria and the DRC have more than 250 distinctive ethnic groups, defined as peoples with a distinctive language and historical territorial home. Large percentages of the national populations of these countries do not speak or read the national languages of their own countries. In a great many cases, however, they do speak the languages of their kin and neighbors living on the other side of an interstate border, another legacy of colonialism.

More typical of other world regions, Africa also has a large number of subregional organizations. Some of the most important of these include the Economic Community of West African States (ECOWAS), the Economic Community of Central African States (ECCAS), the Southern African Development Community (SADC), the East African Community (EAC), the Intergovernmental Authority on Development (IGAD), and the Arab Maghreb Union (AMU). This basic set of subregional organizations overlaps with dozens of others, however, and many states belong to multiple organizations with nominally similar purposes. For instance, Tanzania belongs to both EAC and SADC, and Angola belongs to both SADC and ECCAS; several other states have similar overlapping memberships (see Chapter 6). In addition, two monetary unions, one for West Africa and one for Central Africa, control the currencies of the states that use the Communauté Financière Africaine (CFA) franc (the "Franc zone"). The activities of these two organizations overlap heavily with those of ECOWAS and ECCAS, respectively. Meanwhile, all of the independent states of Africa are members of the overarching African Union (AU). The interactions of these overlapping regional and subregional organizations further complicate Africa's international relations, viewed from a purely interstate perspective.

Also typical of other world regions, Africa's states have taken on new activities and faced new responsibilities over the successive decades. The heads of Africa's states naturally worry about the security of their regimes and the people they govern, just as they did in the early years of independence. The nature of African trade relations, on the other hand, has become far more complex than in the 1960s and 1970s. Economic globalization has increased the technical challenges of full and successful participation in the global economy. Likewise, the challenge of pursuing national economic development while simultaneously pursuing subregional integration has become far more complicated. Meanwhile, Africa's human population roughly quadrupled between 1955 and 2010, reaching approximately 1 billion in the latter year. Along with this remarkable expansion of population have come large waves of migration across interstate borders. For instance, hundreds of thousands of Africans migrated from Mali, Burkina Faso, and Guinea into Côte d'Ivoire from the 1950s to the 1990s. This challenge grows ever larger, and African states have managed changing migration patterns in different ways (see Chapter 9).

Other activities of African states are of a newer vintage. In the 1960s, African states had a relatively small role in global struggles against threats such as international drug trafficking, transnational terrorism, or global environmental degradation; their attention to these problems has necessarily increased in more recent decades as the threats posed by such phenomena have grown more urgent and apparent. HIV/AIDS, a disease that has now killed millions of Africans, imposed new responsibilities on many African states. Along with the rest of the world, African states have had to grapple with many new and unwelcome challenges in their international relations over the past thirty years. Yet most African states have had far less capacity to tackle these challenges than those in other regions.

Finally, the rise in power of many nonstate actors has further complicated the nature of Africa's international relations in recent decades. Newly empowered nonstate actors begin with individuals, like business leaders Mo Ibrahim and Aliko Dangote, many of whom are far more capable of international activity than they were in the 1960s. Along with the rise in the continent's population, the size of the middle class also has expanded in most African countries. These millions of modestly wealthier Africans have formed tens of thousands of nongovernmental organizations (NGOs), some of which are engaged in international activities. Many of them receive funding directly from NGOs or governments in the global North or Asia, and they use this funding to pursue a wide variety of agendas, from economic and social development to religious proselytization. As elsewhere in the world, the rise of nonstate actors in Africa has made international relations there more complicated than in the past.

These trends make it useful to look for broad patterns in Africa's international relations. Various theoretical approaches to the discipline or field of international relations (IR) help frame debates about Africa's international relations (the phenomena themselves) in several ways. First, they help us sort through a mass of different policies, behaviors, and relationships to identify patterns; unless we think theoretically, we may not "see the forest for the trees." Second, theoretical approaches to IR alert us to the different agendas of observers of Africa's international relations. These various observers come to the study of Africa with different political and intellectual sensibilities and thus look for different issues to study.[4] Third, using theoretical approaches to IR helps us to perceive Africa's international relations in a systematic way; insofar as each theoretical approach provides a distinctive and consistent view of specific problems, each may differ with other approaches on the same issues. Arguably, in studying the social world, our knowledge of the subjects we study advances only through the debates we have with one another. Theoretical approaches provide alternative explanations for the issues we find in Africa's international relations and thereby increase our understanding of them. In the next section, we outline four important theoretical IR traditions that are useful in understanding Africa's international relations. At the end, we introduce the notion of "regime security," a concept we find invaluable in making sense of much of Africa's international relations.

Theoretical Approaches to International Relations and Their "African Agendas"

The first and oldest approach to understanding international relations goes under the label "realism." A central aphorism for realism is that all political units seek survival and that this imperative leads to struggles for power. Most realists consider states to be the central actors in the international setting, and thus, for realists, international politics can most usefully be understood as a struggle for power among independent states. Since the global setting is anarchical, or without any supreme authority to make and enforce rules, the struggle for power often becomes violent. Domestic politics may be circumscribed by rules enforced by an accepted, legitimate authority, but international politics involve threats, broken promises, unstable periods of peace, competition, tragic misunderstandings, and violent encounters.

Arguably, the foundational text of realism in the twentieth century was Edward Hallett Carr's *The Twenty Years' Crisis: 1919–1939*, originally published in 1939 and appearing in a revised version in 1946. Carr blamed the emergence of Nazi Germany and the tragedy of World War II on "Utopian" ideas, such as the stabilizing influence of disarmament and institutions like the League of Nations. Ultimately more influential, especially in the United States, however, was Hans J. Morgenthau's classic study *Politics Among Nations: The Struggle for Power and Peace*. Morgenthau's text systematically covered the central problems of international politics of the era and made realism more systematic, reducing it to a number of specific "principles."

Two concepts are central to Morgenthau's work: the national interest and the balance of power. Yet Morgenthau used each concept in a way that undermined its explanatory value, namely, he used each both to describe international behavior and to prescribe how states ought to behave. In his analytical mode, Morgenthau insisted that states' pursuit of their national interests, "defined as power," was a signpost that "helps political realism find its way through the landscape of international politics" (Morgenthau 1973: 5). In his policy advisory mode, however, Morgenthau often insisted that leaders should eschew ideology or ideals in favor of the national interest, implying that national interest was not in fact always their guide.

In his descriptive mode, Morgenthau noted that weaker states regularly resist the imposition of hegemony (control) over them by their more powerful neighbors. Weaker states also make alliances with one another to resist the hegemony of a dominant state, both regionally and in the global setting. "Balances" of power, or roughly equal coalitions of states, thus typically emerge within regions and across the globe as a result of the natural tendency of states and groups of states to "check" the expansion of would-be dominators ("hegemons"). In his prescriptive mode, however, Morgenthau sometimes called upon leaders to pursue policies to check rising power, leading his readers to wonder whether the balance of power was the automatic mechanism in international relations he described.[5]

Alas, neither of these two central realist concepts from the midtwentieth century seems to have much to tell us about Africa's contemporary international relations (Clark 2001c). Within the African continent, no state has made any serious efforts to conquer and dominate its neighbors. Although South Africa did try to keep its antagonists at bay during the latter decades of apartheid, its efforts were more about trying to maintain its domestic system than to conquer its neighbors. The few interstate wars in Africa have been fought mainly over competing irredentist claims rather than for subregional or regional hegemony.[6] As a result, alliances designed to prevent subregional hegemony have not formed on the continent, except against South Africa in the 1970s and 1980s. It is open to debate whether "balances of power" have formed in intra-African international relations; Errol Henderson (2015) believes so, but others would demur. Likewise, it does not appear that African rulers have often pursued national interests at the expense of their neighbors. This is not surprising, since almost all African states are multiethnic polities rather than nation-states. In general, African rulers have been much more preoccupied with regime security than they have been with national interests (Clapham 1996; Clark 2001c), a point to which we return later.

Does this mean that "classical" realism makes no claims that can help us understand contemporary African international relations? Perhaps not. Realists like Niccolò Machiavelli of Renaissance Italy did not make the same stark distinctions between domestic politics and international politics as did the twentieth-century realists. For Machiavelli, domestic rulers pursued strategies designed primarily to secure themselves in power, and such strategies encompassed foreign as well as domestic policies. In cynical terms, state rulers often preyed upon their neighbors in order to seize booty and resources; these were used to reward domestic loyalists and to intimidate domestic rivals. In Machiavelli's era of Italian city-state politics, military force was used against domestic and "foreign" foes alike and without discrimination between them. Such strategies of power maintenance, involving both domestic repression and foreign adventure, would not seem at all alien to current and former African autocrats such as Omar al-Bashir (Sudan), José Eduardo dos Santos (Angola), Paul Kagame (Rwanda), or Muammar Qaddafi (Libya). In Italian city-states, rivals for power often hatched conspiracies from abroad, leading the princes, emperors, and dukes of that era to intervene in the affairs of their neighbors. This behavior, too, would be quite familiar to these rulers, and to many other African leaders as well.

One scholar of realism, Richard Ned Lebow (2003), has tried to argue for a continuity of this classical realist tradition, from the ancient Greek Thucydides to Morgenthau. Lebow claims that classical realists have consistently been interested in concepts that span the domestic-foreign divide. In both the foreign and domestic realms, he insists, prudent leaders have craved order and stability and tried to secure these values; they have tried to cultivate a sense of community with their fellow "statesmen" in search of such values; they have understood that interests cannot be defined without reference to values, and that credible claims of justice are crucial to successful foreign and domestic policies. Finally, realists from ancient times to the present have appreciated the dynamism of domestic and international politics; power relations within states can change rapidly due to shifts in public opinion, and power relations among states change due to differential rates of economic growth and to modernization.

Understood in this way, classical realism has a good deal to tell us about contemporary African international relations. African leaders, whether authoritarian or democratic, worry about getting and keeping power. In turn, some of the threats to their power come from rivals who may organize in neighboring states and sometimes launch insurgencies from across international borders. Such threats have led some African leaders to intervene in neighboring states. Meanwhile, foreign antagonists outside the African continent have posed related threats to the power of African rulers. Extra-continental antagonists can withhold aid from regimes that they dislike and provide both aid and encouragement to rivals. Yet extra-continental states and other actors can also provide useful support to African rulers. Such support ranges from rhetorical approval of domestic policies, to economic or military aid, to outright intervention against domestic rivals in times of crisis. External patrons have sometimes served as "guarantors" for the security of African regimes, past and present.

A more contemporary form of realism goes under the name "neorealism" or "structural realism." The foundational text of this form of realism is Kenneth Waltz's celebrated study *Theory of International Politics* (1979). Waltz argues not only for a strict separation between domestic and international politics but also for a sharp focus on the structure of the international system. Waltz begins by underscoring the fundamental anarchy of the global system. He then goes on to define varying systems in terms of the number of great powers, or superpowers, present in a given historical era. In essence, the international system may be either unipolar (under the hegemony of a single state), bipolar, or multipolar, with any number of relatively equal great powers. Waltz's theory is primarily about the likelihood of "central wars," or wars between great powers; in particular, he wishes to determine whether bipolar or multipolar systems are more likely to generate central wars. As such, neorealism would not seem to have much to say about the international relations of African states, which are all peripheral actors of the world political stage.

Yet neorealism does usefully direct our attention to how the structure of the international system might affect Africa's international relations. All African countries except Eritrea, Namibia, and South Sudan became independent during the Cold War, when the United States and the Soviet Union dominated world politics. By the time of the independence of Sudan (1956) and Ghana (1957), the two superpowers were involved in an intense competition for influence and clients in developing regions of the world, including Africa (see Chapter 3). In 1989, with the accelerating collapse of Soviet power at home and abroad, the Soviet Union withdrew from Africa politically, leaving its former clients with no patron. The former Marxist client regime in Ethiopia quickly fell apart in 1991 after the withdrawal of Soviet support in the previous year. For the next decade or so, the world was effectively unipolar, leaving African states little option but to seek the favor of the United States, its European allies, and the international financial institutions (IFIs) that it dominated. By the early 2000s, however, the People's Republic of China (PRC) had emerged as an important economic player on the continent (see Chapter 12). Although the nascent Sino-American rivalry in Africa is not yet as intense as the former Soviet-American rivalry, countries such as Sudan and Zimbabwe have effectively aligned themselves with China (see Chapter 12). If Sino-American hostility continues to mount, Africa could again become a setting for superpower rivalries to play out. Yet another possibility is that the world might become more obviously multipolar if other states (or the European Union [EU]) increase their power. In that eventuality, African states might enjoy more "freedom of movement" in their international relations.

Liberalism, a second major theoretical approach, is the main competitor to realism in IR. The aphorism of liberalism might be that "international relations is a struggle for freedom, justice, and prosperity." Liberalism assumes that all people want to live in freedom and prosperity and that we have enough will (or "agency") in the world to bring about these outcomes. Like realism, liberalism comes in two major variants: traditional liberalism, with an analytical focus on domestic politics and its consequences; and neoliberalism, which emphasizes the power of international interactions to shape and constrain behavior. The central claim of traditional liberalism is that democratic states do not fight one another militarily, although they may well go to war with nondemocratic states (Russett 1993; Doyle 2011). Rather than going to war, democratic states negotiate with their peers to resolve disputes peacefully; neither citizens nor governments of democratic states find it acceptable to engage in war with other democracies. Due to this phenomenon of the "democratic peace," communities of stable, war-eschewing democracies can evolve in world regions, including Europe and North America.

This approach had little relevance to continental Africa before the end of the Cold War. In 1989, there were only five multiparty democracies that held regular free and fair elections on the continent:

Botswana, Gambia, Mauritius, Senegal, and Zimbabwe.[7] From the 1960s through the 1980s, the de jure one-party state was the norm in African politics, though this situation did not lead to as many interstate wars as liberals might have expected. Since 1990, however, the picture has changed dramatically (see Chapter 5). In the early 1990s, a wave of political reform swept across the continent, transforming almost all African states into nominally multiparty states. Whereas the majority remained de facto dictatorships, with many of the old rulers surviving the change to "multipartyism," at least sixteen states had certifiable democratic transitions to new leaders and parties between 1990 and 1994 (Bratton and van de Walle 1997). In the following years, still other African states (like Ghana and Kenya) began experiments with multiparty democracy following transitions, while many of the early experimenters reverted to authoritarianism. As of 2014, only ten sub-Saharan African states were ranked "free" by the organization Freedom House (2014), whereas twenty were ranked "not free," and nineteen were rated "partly free." Despite this mediocre record of the spread of democracy in Africa over twenty-five years, one important Africanist scholar (Schraeder 2012) finds evidence that Africa's new democracies behave differently in their foreign relations than their authoritarian peers.

Neoliberalism focuses not on domestic politics but on how the nature of international institutions and states' participation in them affect interstate relations (see, e.g., Koremenos, Lipson, and Snidal 2003). Neoliberals assume that states want to collaborate for their mutual benefit—for instance, to engage in free trade—but are often stymied by "collective action problems." That is, each participant in various international "games" fears that its peers will cheat and obtain special advantages or that they will behave as "free riders" and not pay their fair share for collective goods, like an open trade regime, the orderly movement of citizens across international borders, a clean environment, or transnational infrastructure links. Neoliberals believe that the right kind of international institutions can lead states in a community to overcome such problems.

It is easy, then, to see what the main agenda should be for neoliberals who are studying Africa: to configure African regional and subregional institutions in such a way as to mitigate Africa's domestic and interstate problems. Africa has a plethora of subregional organizations, but their effectiveness in addressing regional problems is dubious. Africans were deeply disappointed in the performance of the Organization of African Unity (OAU, 1963–2002) and accordingly replaced it in 2002 with a more robust institution, the African Union. The two main purposes of Africa's regional and subregional organizations have been to resolve conflicts peacefully and to promote interstate economic integration. Recently, however, Africa's regional organizations have had to grapple with more specific problems such as transnational terrorist groups and insurgencies, the collapse of African states, the international consequences of domestic turmoil (including that caused by coups d'état), the trade in illicit drugs, and the spread of communicable diseases across borders. Most Africans, and neoliberals, believe that their regional organizations could do better in managing such problems.

The English School in IR could be seen as yet another variety of liberalism. Associated particularly with Martin Wight and Hedley Bull, this approach accepts the realist assumption that states are the main actors but is interested in the strength and quality of the norms that characterize "international society" at any historical juncture. Although Bull recognized that the balance of power and even war can be instruments for maintaining a (pluralistic) world order, his emphasis in *The Anarchical Society* (1977) is on international law and diplomacy. The level of commitment of diplomats to the norms of conduct embodied in international law and to the peaceful resolution of disputes through diplomacy corresponded to the strength of international society. When such common commitments were weak, the balance of power and war were the only other methods available for avoiding the domination of ambitious great powers.

Constructivism represents a third major theoretical approach in IR. In a broad sense, constructivism is not mainly a way to understand patterns of international relations; rather, constructivism is a position in the great debates over epistemology (the study of knowledge). To what extent can we demonstrate facts about the social world? To what extent can we be objective? To what extent are the concepts of the social world stable and comprehensible by all? Positivists are quite optimistic on these questions: they generally believe that we can objectively identify patterns that consistently characterize the social world. Positivists believe that change in the social world is predictable, in principle, based on the fundamental rationality of human beings. At the opposite end of the spectrum, post-structuralists are radically skeptical about our ability to separate ourselves from the social world or to identify any consistent patterns. They believe that all knowledge is socially constructed, as is human rationality. According to one trenchant view (Adler 1997), constructivism represents the middle ground between positivists and post-structuralists.[8] For constructivists in general, social knowledge is neither objective (as positivists believe) nor starkly subjective (as many post-structuralists believe), but rather "inter-subjective." That is, we human beings can agree among ourselves on the meaning of certain social concepts (consider "democracy" or "conflict"), though these phenomena cannot be defined objectively, or outside of the human experience. Fierce academic debates are currently ongoing within constructivism, mostly among those who lie closer to one end or the other of Adler's continuum. This is not the place to rehearse these debates.

Rather, let us draw out one application of constructivist epistemology to IR that has some utility in the study of Africa's international relations. Alexander Wendt applied constructivism to IR by insisting on the relative agency (free will) of the actors who create the normative context in which international politics take place. International structures do not force actors to behave in certain ways, but instead the choices of autonomous agents determine those structures. The title of a seminal Wendt article (1992) serves as an excellent aphorism for the approach: "Anarchy is what states make of it." That is, international actors are free to shape the fundamental anarchy of the global setting in ways that make violent conflict, among other outcomes, more or less likely. As a community of international actors interacts, chiefly through discussions, their communications create specific "cultures of anarchy," in Wendt's useful phrase. That is, they create varying kinds of communal norms and cultural patterns, which then shape future behavior. These cultures condition, but do not determine, the behavior of those who create them and their successors; moreover, diplomatic actors are perfectly capable of altering these cultures over time, through their actions and speech. Thus, Wendt's version of constructivist IR has a good deal in common with the English School, as others have noted (Lacassagne 2012).

Given these perspectives, English School thinkers and constructivists like Wendt are especially interested in norms within Africa and between African states and the external environment. One scholar (Pella 2014) has recently studied how interactions between European and African leaders beginning in the fifteenth century led to the development of new international norms that shaped future Euro-African relations. Studying the nature and quality of African diplomatic society at the continental level is an even more obvious agenda for such scholars. For instance, what critical norms and transnational identities emerged from the pan-Africanist conferences that took place during the colonial era (see, e.g., Persaud 2001)? What new norms emerged with the independence of the first African states and the inaugural meeting of new African leaders in Addis Ababa in 1963? What patterns of behavior governed the "society of African regimes" during the Cold War period (see, e.g., Clark 2011)? Has the culture of African diplomacy changed with the end of the Cold War, or with the foundation of the African Union in 2002? Further, how have recent developments in Africa's international relations changed the worldviews of Africans and their leaders? For instance, has Africa's recent economic growth changed ideas about the Western world or the global South? If we can document any such changes in attitudes, have they led to parallel changes in the international behavior of African states? Finally, how do we account for changing African attitudes about the critical issue of African states' interventions into one another's affairs? Whereas the OAU Charter did not countenance any interstate interventions among African states, the AU Constitutive Act does so, under specific circumstances (see Chapter 6). Constructivists want to know what critical encounters, declarations, or statements of principle lead to these changes of culture and norms.

Neo-Marxism is a fourth major approach in IR, and one with enduring relevance to Africa.[9] As with realism and liberalism, there are two distinctive traditions in neo-Marxist thought. The first follows Marx's own focus on the exploitative nature of capitalism but applies the logic to the global setting. Neo-Marxian materialists chiefly argue that underdevelopment in peripheral parts of the global economy is a function of capital accumulation and development in the global North. Their slogan might be, "Global politics is a struggle for economic justice and equality against the forces of capitalism." One early variant of this approach was the dependency theory of the 1960s. This theory blamed Latin America's relative lack of development on declining terms of trade[10] for developing countries, which exported mostly commodities, and the economic domination of industrialized capitalist countries (see, e.g., Frank 1967). Building on this approach, world systems theory made the scale of the analysis more global, notably including Africa in its exploration of the widening economic gap between the West and developing countries (see, e.g., Amin 1974, and especially Wallerstein 1979). These scholars predicted a full-scale global economic crisis of capitalism that has not yet come, despite such shocks as the Asian financial crisis of 1997–1998 and the Great Recession of 2008–2010.[11] They implicitly prescribed a revolution in the structure of the world economy and a radical redistribution of global wealth.

A second strand of neo-Marxists have focused their attention on the oppressive power of ideas and ideologies, following the Italian Marxist Antonio Gramsci. Among those studying Africa in particular, Frantz Fanon (1963) wrote the most powerful and enduring study of how Europeans used ideologies of superiority to oppress Africans, both before and after formal independence. There is nothing fundamentally contradictory about these two strands of neo-Marxist thought, and Marx himself was keenly attuned to the power of ideological indoctrination to reinforce the domination of the capitalist class.

Neo-Marxists have had to adapt their theories to important world developments since the late 1980s: the end of the Cold War and the collapse of the Soviet Union, the rapid rise of China and other East Asian economies, and the quickening pace of economic globalization. The first of these events was surprising to nearly everyone but did not especially perturb neo-Marxists, who typically viewed the Soviet Union as a "state capitalist" economy (Amin 1992). The rise of the East Asian economies was far more surprising for radicals, as they expected countries of the global periphery to become ever poorer, just as Marx expected the proletariat to become increasingly impoverished. When instead the East Asian economies showed they could outpace the industrial West in their growth over decades, neo-Marxists tweaked their theories to account for this unexpected development (Frank 1998). Neo-Marxists had an easier time incorporating the reality and language of globalization into their theories. For instance, Amin (e.g., 1997) rapidly assimilated the language of globalization into his analysis of global capitalism. To the extent that economic globalization involves a greater concentration and freer movement of global capital, materialist neo-Marxists can easily claim that globalization is precisely what their theories predicted. Likewise, the notable rise in global inequality in recent decades (see, e.g., Milanovic 2012) conforms neatly to the predictions of many neo-Marxists.

The relevance of neo-Marxist thinking to contemporary Africa is obvious. By the twentieth century, Africa was already the poorest continent in the world, even as colonialism was in its early years. The Atlantic slave trade and later the colonization of Africa (see Chapter 2) clearly disrupted the trajectories of African development ongoing before 1500 (Rodney 1972).[12] Moreover, following the first wave of independence of African states in the late 1950s and early 1960s, most Africans remained grievously impoverished. During the 1960s, many African elites, including some rulers, attributed the failure of Africa to experience a rapid takeoff in economic development to the residual influence of the former colonizers, who were accused of continuing to control African economies (Nkrumah 1965). This view accorded perfectly with the dependency school thinking prevalent in the era. By the 1980s, the focus of radical economic thinkers was on African debt and its consequences, namely, the structural adjustment programs of the International Monetary Fund (IMF) and the World Bank (see, e.g., Onimode 1989). The economic crisis of structural adjustment continued well into the 1990s for most African countries and remained a preoccupation of most scholars during that decade. From the 1960s through the 1980s, the scholarly agenda of the neo-Marxists seemed well-suited to explain Africa's relative economic stagnation, and their calls for a global economic revolution resonated with the African left.

Yet right around 1990 an acceleration in the average growth rate of African economies began. From an average of below 3 percent per year in the 1980s, the average rate of growth of African economies steadily rose to over 5 percent per annum by 2011, catching up to the average rate in Asia (*The Economist* 2011). Most of the improvement in growth rates was attributed to two key factors, neither entirely positive: the rise in the relative value of commodities on world markets, and rapid rises in Chinese trade and investment with Africa (Carmody 2010). In the fifteen-year period from 2000 to 2015, most African economies grew faster than those of Europe or North America. To some extent, this positive development muted the apparent relevance of neo-Marxist analysis to Africa. Along with faster economic growth, however, came growing investment from the outside world (especially in oil and minerals), and more important, rising inequality on the continent. These realities gave a new impetus to the research agendas of many radicals, encouraging them to again demonstrate how Africa was being exploited by the outside world, including China and the West (Bond 2006). Given the continuing destitution of millions throughout Africa and rising economic inequality fostered by the emergence of a larger middle class, the neo-Marxist economic research agenda for the continent is far from exhausted.

Although we draw insights in this book from each of these grand paradigms (realism, liberalism, constructivism, and neo-Marxism), we find the mid-level concept of "regime security" more consistently valuable in helping to understand Africa's international relations. Consistent with other scholars (compare Clapham 1996), we find that regimes rather than states are the right analytical focus. The history of Africa's international relations demonstrates that African rulers have considerable agency or ability to negotiate the terms of their international engagements. Further, the imperatives of domestic politics fundamentally condition the kinds of international engagements that African leaders seek. Above any other goals they may have, African rulers want to make their regimes, and themselves, secure in power. Unlike most Western leaders, they cannot take the security of their governments for granted. Most African leaders, even those who have achieved power through free and fair elections, face the dual threats of coups d'état from within their regimes and insurgencies from without (Roessler 2011). A related source of insecurity is popular dissent, which can lead to either civilian coups or electoral defeats. Although authoritarian regimes (and even some nominally democratic ones) usually try to manipulate elections, this becomes more difficult when outsiders are involved.

In general, all of these domestic risks can be mitigated by the right kind of international relationships. African regimes benefit from good relations with their neighbors (whence insurgencies may be organized) and from the patronage of powerful international partners, who may provide ideological support, domestic financing, arms, and explicit or implicit security guarantees. Whether negotiating the conditions of loans from lenders, developing subregional institutions to promote development, responding to violence in neighboring countries, or fostering ties with traditional Western powers or emerging ones like China, therefore, African leaders are motivated by the desire to sustain themselves in power. Although the specifics vary by country, this underlying need fundamentally influences the types of international actors with whom African leaders seek to partner and the terms of the resulting relationships.

The concept of regime security is related to classical realist ideas about the exigency of maintaining domestic power through favorable foreign relations, but we use it with deep awareness provided by other perspectives. Following classical liberalism, we acknowledge that the challenges of regime security are different for elected democratic regimes than for personalist dictatorships; we also take to heart the neoliberal idea that stronger regional and subregional institutions can mitigate the risks that African regimes face. Constructivism reminds us that identity politics are crucial for security at both the domestic and regional levels, and that the rhetoric of powerful leaders can shape the normative framework of Africa's international relations. Finally, we acknowledge that the global (capitalist) political economy is yet another framework within which African regimes operate. Regimes that defy international capital make powerful external enemies, but even those that align themselves with international capital may face greater domestic dissent when inequalities caused by development become too obvious.

The Plan of the Book

Part 1 of this book provides the historical context for Africa's international relations. Chapter 2 examines the transformation of Africa from a continent of diverse kingdoms, empires, and other political entities in the precolonial era to the system of independent states that was left behind after more than seven decades of European colonialism. Although the imposition of colonial rule was achieved with great brutality, and maintained with violence when necessary, many Africans cooperated with European colonizers to enhance their own power and influence at the local level. Nationalist leaders fought against colonialism not only to achieve self-determination but also to exercise control over their respective states thereafter. A case study of Africa's newest country, South Sudan, illustrates many of these points. Chapter 3 turns our attention to a critical aspect of Africa's international relations immediately following independence: the Cold War. Most African countries were officially nonaligned in the epic contest between the superpowers, but many embraced close engagement with the United States or the Soviet Union anyway. Some of these engagements fueled civil and interstate wars, as seen in the case study of Angola. Far from being pawns in the superpower struggle, African leaders often pursued these external alliances to secure the resources and support necessary to perpetuate their own regimes.

Part 2 explores the pursuit of freedom and development in Africa, and particularly the role of international actors in those quests. The question of foreign aid and its impact has been crucial in Africa from the 1960s to today, as examined in Chapter 4. In hopes of promoting economic development, though also motivated by their own political and economic interests, Western donors have provided billions of dollars in foreign assistance to African countries over the years. Despite the increasing imposition of policy conditions, critics note that Western aid has done little to promote the welfare of individual Africans, in part because many leaders have redirected these funds for their own purposes. Even so, recent economic growth in countries like Ghana gives reason for cautious optimism. Along similar lines, Chapter 5 examines external efforts to promote democracy and human rights in Africa. Such efforts have increased since the end of the Cold War and are fundamentally liberal projects, but even advocates realize that the consolidation of democracy will take more than the staging of one or two relatively free and fair elections. Excitement about democratic transitions in many African countries has been dampened by reversions in some, as illustrated by the case of Kenya, and authoritarian persistence in others. Chapter 6 explores the elusive quest for unity within Africa. Partly to reduce dependence on outside actors, African states created the Organization of African Unity (now the African Union) and various subregional bodies to promote economic development and political stability. Although these organizations generally have fallen short of their ambitious goals, at times because of the dominance of countries such as Nigeria, renewed enthusiasm for regional cooperation in recent years has spurred progress and innovations with respect to economic integration, trade and travel among African countries, and peacekeeping.

Part 3 explores security challenges in Africa, including causes and consequences of political violence. The regionalization of conflict, taken up in Chapter 7, reveals most vividly how African regimes try to protect their security at all costs. Domestic and interstate security concerns are inextricably interconnected as conflicts become regionalized through the sponsorship of insurgencies in neighboring states, the cross-border movement of refugees and militants, and the illicit smuggling of lucrative resources such as diamonds and gold, among other processes. A case study of the Democratic Republic of Congo illustrates the complicated dynamics of regionalized conflicts. Chapter 8 discusses humanitarian assistance and peace operations in Africa. Although generally designed to be neutral, such interventions often are motivated by political interests, including those of states that contribute troops, and can have very political consequences. In conflict situations, armed groups on all sides frequently seek to manipulate humanitarian interventions to their own benefit, as seen in the case of Liberia. Chapter 9 discusses the politics of migration, focusing especially on migration within the continent but also looking at the smaller numbers of Africans who migrate to other regions. The responses by African states often reflect regime interests, with leaders portraying migrants as a security threat and scapegoating them for economic problems. Meanwhile, African governments have sought to cultivate political and economic support from their own diaspora communities. Migration—both internal and external—has been central to the history of South Africa, as examined in this chapter's case study.

In Part 4 we turn to Africa's relations with external actors. Chapter 10 takes up the essential question of US policies in Africa and the relations that have resulted from them. Because of the nature of foreign policy making and the low prioritization of the region, US policy toward Africa tends to change only marginally from one presidential administration to another, as shown by an examination of various recent economic and security initiatives. It is typically only in crisis situations that Africa attracts high-level US attention, as with Somalia in the early 1990s and again more recently, but such attention does not necessarily benefit the target country. Relations between Europe and Africa are studied in Chapter 11. Former colonial powers have had complicated relations with African countries since independence. France has remained the most involved with its former colonies, often working to protect the regime security of its clients in the region. This has had long-term political implications, both within France and in countries such as Côte d'Ivoire, as explored in the case study. Chapter 12 examines Africa's international relations with emergent powers around the world, and China in particular. Other non-European powers with new or renewed interests in Africa include Brazil, India, Iran, and Turkey, among others. While these rising powers have provided African states with new sources of foreign aid and loans, contributing to a wave of infrastructure projects across the continent, their emphasis on economics over politics and relative lack of attention to democracy, human rights, and corruption have prompted criticism from human rights activists and growing political debate in countries such as Zambia.

In Part 5 we conclude the volume with a reflection on how domestic politics and international relations are intertwined for African states and people and a summation of key themes. All African regimes, even the more authoritarian ones, want to maintain their domestic legitimacy as a high priority. To do so, they strive to provide citizens with physical security, economic well-being, and a sense of national identity and purpose. Interstate wars in Africa have been rare, but cross-border support for rebel groups is all too common; these have threatened both African regimes and local communities. Many African regimes have tried to mitigate these risks through connections with extra-continental powers, including the United States, former colonizers, and more recently China. African regimes likewise look for markets in the larger global environment, improving their prospects for delivering economic sustenance to their people. Finally, Africans are no different from others in defining themselves in relation to others. Internally, identity politics have been salient in the African regimes that have opened their polities to political competition. In their international relations, too, Africans often have defined themselves in contradistinction with their neighbors, both near and distant. African regimes have used the construction of national identities, achieved through their rhetoric about the nature of the outside world, as an indispensable tool for the maintenance of legitimacy and power.

Notes

1. By contrast, it is striking how the questions of Palestine and the Israeli occupation of Palestinian territories have dominated the international relations of the Middle East since 1948. Although other political questions regarding the Middle East have surely been of great interest to the international community in the past seven decades, the failure to resolve this central question has given the study of the region a comparably more stable focus.

2. The five states of North Africa (Morocco, Algeria, Libya, Tunisia, and Egypt) are often treated as part of the Middle East. In this book, we focus on the forty-nine states of sub-Saharan Africa, while occasionally alluding to North African states. Unless otherwise noted, we use the label "Africa" to refer to sub-Saharan Africa.

3. The former of this pair enjoys de facto autonomy from any external control, whereas the latter is controlled by Morocco.

4. We have no single overriding political agenda, but we are acutely aware that many observers of Africa begin with strong ideological and intellectual convictions.

5. For a particularly trenchant critique of Morgenthau's use of the concept "balance of power," see Claude 1962: chaps. 2–3.

6. For instance, this is true for the clashes between Libya and Chad beginning in 1978, the Tanzania-Uganda war of 1979, the Ethiopia-Somalia war of 1977–1978, and the Eritrea-Ethiopia war of 1998–2000.

7. Two of these states (Gambia and Zimbabwe) subsequently devolved into authoritarian states.

8. Virtually all the cognoscenti in these epistemological debates will object to the exceedingly brief characterizations and labels of their schools of thought mentioned here; most of the terms associated with constructivism in IR, not to mention the meanings of positivism and especially post-structuralism, are highly contested and endlessly debated.

9. Neo-Marxists with a material focus also go under more generic labels such as "economic radicals" or "globalists," and those with a focus on the repressive power of ideas are usually called "critical theorists." We find the label that draws attention to Marx's original critique of capitalism ("neo-Marxist") as a system most useful and descriptive of the set, though we sometimes use the shorthand "radical" in the text.

10. "Terms of trade" refers to the relative value of commodities (including minerals, oil, and cash crops, like cotton) versus the value of manufactured goods. The claim of dependency theorists was that the relative value of commodities was in perpetual decline, trapping developing countries in a cycle of receiving ever less income for ever more commodity production.

11. Despite the severe impact of the Great Recession in Western Europe and the United States, gross world production declined in just one year, 2009, and then only by less than 1 percent.

12. This classic work, whatever its shortcomings and misperceptions, is one of the most widely read texts on the sources of Africa's underdevelopment in anglophone Africa, particularly in university settings.

PART 1

Historical Context

2

From Kingdoms to States

The study of international relations traditionally involves examining interactions among sovereign states in the international system, but how did we get to the current state system in Africa? This chapter explores the region's transition over two centuries from a continent with diverse political entities—ranging from empires to stateless societies—to the modern system of states with clearly defined borders representing more than one-quarter of the members of the United Nations. Although the colonial period was comparatively brief in Africa, from the 1890s to the 1960s in most countries, it had a lasting impact on the political and economic systems of the region. In many ways, the most obvious legacy of colonialism for Africa's international relations is the map; European powers drew borders creating the political units that would become today's sovereign states. The process by which those states were created and sustained has had important implications for both domestic politics within independent African countries and international relations among them.

Precolonial African States

Africa's precolonial political landscape was very diverse. Political institutions varied widely in their size, scope, and organization, and there was regular warfare among kingdoms, states, and communities. In some areas of the continent, large states emerged and conquered vast territories; other areas were dominated by stateless societies and nomadic groups with only loose connections among neighbors. Some societies were governed in a relatively consensual way, where elders collectively made decisions and people had a voice in the process, while others had authoritarian leaders with hierarchical and even militaristic institutions that implemented top-down decisions. It is worth noting that there were no true democracies as we currently conceive them in the world at this time, so Africa was no different in this regard. Much like in Europe, empire-building also was common during this period, especially in West Africa (where the Ghana, Mali, and Songhai empires dominated successively from the ninth century), northeastern Africa (home to ancient Egypt and the Kingdom of Axum), and southern Africa (where the Great Zimbabwe Empire ruled from the eleventh to fourteenth centuries). Historians, anthropologists, and archaeologists have provided ample scholarship about precolonial political organizations (Collins and Burns 2014; Connah 2001; Davidson 1969, 1998; Goody 1971; Iliffe 2017; Smith 1989; Vansina 2012), but several patterns are particularly important for understanding the subsequent transition to the modern state system in Africa.

The geographic borders of precolonial political entities were exceedingly fluid. On a vast continent with a relatively sparse population, states usually did not touch one another. There was rarely a clear line that delineated the area of control of one political leader from that of another. Instead, centers of political control were scattered around with vast areas of less control—and even no control—in between. Political leaders of each state exercised the most authority nearest their capital city, and the extent of that authority decreased as one moved away from the center.[1] Borders thus were not permanent lines on a map; they were flexible and overlapping depending upon the ability of leaders to extend their reach. The fluidity of borders in the precolonial period had two important implications. First, migration was common, as people moved away from some areas and toward others based on how state authority was exercised. A leader known for providing better protection might have attracted more subjects, for example, while one known for excessive taxation and repression might have driven people away. Also in this context, wars were more about controlling people (including captured slaves) and resources (including livestock) than they were about controlling specific territories (Thomson 2010).

Another pattern of the precolonial era was the importance of kinship (Thomson 2010). Societies were organized around clan and lineage networks that together formed broader ethnic groups. Using kinship connections as a justifying principle, leaders offered welfare and security to subjects in exchange for their loyalty. Marriage frequently was employed as a political tool to bring different kinship networks into the fold and to build alliances among states, much as it was among royal families in medieval Europe. Despite the importance of kinship for political organization during this period, such identities also were quite fluid. Much like the geographic borders among political entities, the boundaries among sociocultural groups were flexible and fuzzy. Depending on the context, which could be influenced by marriage, migration, war, and other changing circumstances, Africans often had multiple overlapping collective identities and moved among them to meet their needs. Rather than being primordial identities as European colonizers would subsequently assume, therefore, kinship and ethnicity in precolonial Africa were constantly being negotiated and renegotiated (Berman 1998; Southall 1970).

External influences also shaped Africa's history long before formal colonization of the continent by Europeans in the late nineteenth century. Back into the era of ancient Egypt (3100–332 B.C.E.), some precolonial African states were integrated into the global economy through trade with counterparts in the Middle East and across the Indian Ocean. In the century following the death of the prophet Muhammad in 632 C.E., these trading networks facilitated the spread of Islam from his home on the Arabian Peninsula throughout North Africa. From the ninth to eleventh centuries, Islam continued to spread through trade and conquest to the Horn of Africa, the East African coast, and across the Sahara to West Africa. Even today, many languages in these regions use words derived from Arabic for business and math concepts. These trading networks ultimately connected Africans with people as far away as East Asia, as evidenced by fifteenth-century Chinese artifacts recently discovered in coastal Kenya (Greste 2010).

Slavery was part of the Indian Ocean trade, though it differed from its transatlantic counterpart in important ways (Clarence-Smith 2006). The lack of detailed records and an emphasis among scholars on the Atlantic slave trade have hindered research about the Islamic slave trade (Clarence-Smith 1988). Efforts to quantify the number of slaves taken from Africa to countries around the Indian Ocean have been especially controversial, in part because they "began during the nineteenth century as part of an evangelical and colonialist assault upon Islam by contemporary Europeans" (Austen 1988: 21). More recent estimates suggest that the Indian Ocean slave trade increased in the 1800s, with more than a million slaves exported from East African ports during that century (Clarence-Smith 1988). Interestingly, though, this external trade was basically a by-product of a burgeoning internal trade, with millions more slaves captured and sold within East Africa (Austen 1988; Clarence-Smith 1988). In contrast to its Atlantic counterpart, there has been relatively little scholarship on the legacy of the Indian Ocean slave trade, whether internally or in destination countries.

Europeans began arriving along the African coast in the fifteenth century as the Portuguese set up trading posts on their way to more remote destinations in Asia. As Prince Henry the Navigator and his successors reached points farther south in Africa, thanks in large part to improvements in sailing technology, they traded goods and supplies with locals, spread Christianity, and captured slaves. Such activities were religiously sanctioned in 1452, when Pope Nicholas V authorized his followers to attack and subjugate pagans; Portugal exported 1,000 to 2,000 African slaves per year in the second half of the fifteenth century (Thornton 1998). Over time, as their naval capabilities increased, other European powers arrived on the scene. The British started establishing trading posts in Africa in the 1530s, reached the Cape of Good Hope in 1581, and chartered the East India Company in 1600. The Dutch East India Company was established two years later, and the French got in on the action as well, each setting up their own outposts along the coast. With their subsequent "discovery" and colonization of the Western Hemisphere, Europeans shifted their focus from east to west and became increasingly interested in exploiting Africa for its human capital. Slaving depots such as Elmina Castle in present-day Ghana, and Gorée Island in present-day Senegal, were established all along the African coast.

While the transatlantic and Indian Ocean slave trades are examined elsewhere (Austen 1988, 1992; Curtin 1969; Lovejoy 2012), two consequences are particularly relevant to Africa's international relations. First, the slave trades resulted in a huge loss of human capacity within Africa. During four centuries of the transatlantic slave trade, from the early 1500s to the late 1800s, roughly 12.8 million people were taken forcibly from Africa (Lovejoy 2012). Estimates for the Indian Ocean slave trade are similarly controversial but likely reached 11.5 million over thirteen centuries (650–1900 C.E.) (Lovejoy 2012). Given the population levels of the day, these numbers are not insignificant. In some areas of the Bight of Benin, for example, an estimated 3 percent of the population was exported as slaves each year in the first half of the eighteenth century (Reynolds 1985). Moreover, men and women in their most productive years were most likely to be captured into slavery, leaving some African societies with a severe labor shortage and disrupting local development (Iliffe 2017; Reynolds 1985; Rodney 1972). Second, as African elites came to recognize the profitability of selling captured slaves to Europeans (Pella 2014), the situation created additional incentives for conflict among precolonial African states. As in any region of the world, there were already plenty of wars among African societies prior to this period; however, the seemingly insatiable demand for slaves—and the use of imported technologies such as guns to capture them—increased the scope and intensity of these conflicts (Iliffe 2017; Reynolds 1985).

Even as the transatlantic slave trade declined in the early nineteenth century, particularly with the 1807 act abolishing the slave trade (but not slavery itself) in the British Empire, European interest in African territories increased. At the behest of European leaders, explorers started penetrating more deeply into the African continent. Larger-than-life personalities such as David Livingstone, Henry Morton Stanley, and John Hanning Speke gained fame and glory back in Europe as they searched for the source of various rivers, especially the mighty Nile, and gave European names to interior lakes and mountains (Moorehead 1960). As Africa's natural resource wealth became increasingly apparent, European powers were soon competing with one another in a massive "scramble" for Africa and its resources (Wesseling 1996). This paved the way for the Berlin Conference in 1884–1885, which led to the full-scale colonization of sub-Saharan Africa (though portions, especially in the south, had already been colonized).

The Colonial Experience

As Europeans intensified their exploration of Africa, they found themselves vying with one another for control over territories. When tension emerged over competing Portuguese and Belgian claims near the mouth of the Congo River, Germany's Chancellor Otto von Bismarck invited representatives from twelve European countries to negotiate a common approach toward the continent. At the Berlin Conference in 1884–1885, to which the United States also sent an observer, European leaders claimed their respective spheres of influence on a map of Africa. Focused on avoiding conflicts among their own armies (Herbst 1989), the Europeans paid little attention to the social and cultural realities of African peoples on the ground. The resulting borders were completely arbitrary, with 44 percent following latitudinal or longitudinal lines, 30 percent following geometric lines, and 26 percent following physical features such as rivers (Posner 2006). According to one count, 104 international borders in Africa dissected 177 distinct culture areas (Asiwaju 1985). This fragmentation would become a key part of Africa's colonial political inheritance, as explored later in this chapter.

After agreeing on their respective spheres of influence, the Europeans set out to establish "effective occupation" over them as required by the terms of the Berlin Conference. This process often took several decades, in part because of active resistance by Africans all over the continent, including the Ibo, Ashanti, Mandika, Herero, Zulu, Shona, and Ethiopians, among others (Davidson 1968; Isaacman and Isaacman 1976, 1977; Ranger 1967). Other African leaders, seeking to preserve their positions of power in a climate of rising insecurity, entered into protection agreements with Europeans, only to see those quickly erode into formal colonization (Pella 2014). Great Britain and France ultimately secured the largest empires in the region, with the former colonizing large chunks of eastern and southern Africa and parts of western Africa, and the latter taking control over vast areas of western and central Africa plus Madagascar. The Portuguese presence was predominantly in southern Africa (Angola and Mozambique), while the king of the relatively new country of Belgium convinced his counterparts in Berlin to give him a huge personal colony in central Africa (Congo). Spain secured rights to Equatorial Guinea and Western Sahara. Germany had a colonial presence in East Africa, South West Africa, Cameroon, and Togo until it was forced to give up its territories to other powers after losing World War I. The Italians gained colonies in Somalia and Libya but similarly lost all holdings in Africa as a result of World War II. By the 1910s, European powers had colonized nearly all of sub-Saharan Africa with three notable exceptions: South Africa became nominally independent from Great Britain in 1910 but remained under a white minority government until 1994; Liberia was established in the 1820s as a home for former American slaves and remained independent despite a close and dependent relationship with the United States; and Ethiopia was never formally colonized, though it was occupied by Italy during World War II. With the exception of a few settler colonies (including South Africa, Kenya, Zimbabwe, and Algeria), relatively few Europeans moved permanently to their governments' African territories.

The resources and effort required to establish a colonial presence in Africa raise the question of motivation. Why did European powers colonize Africa after 1885? From a realist perspective, European states were powerful—some more so than others—and African ones were weak, and the strong dominate the weak in international relations. In this context, the scramble for Africa was stimulated by competition among European powers and by the emergence of new and ambitious ones (Germany, Belgium) (Wesseling 1996). European colonization of Africa also was informed by prevalent ideologies at the end of the nineteenth century, which included a belief in European cultural and racial superiority and the notion that Europe was obligated to "civilize" Africa through the spread of Christianity. Imperialism was an acceptable strategy at the time for advancing European ideas and interests. And, as a Marxist might note, European countries needed raw materials for their industries and markets for their surplus production, so the commercial sector fully promoted the colonial project. Perhaps not surprisingly, there is some truth in all of these explanations for the European colonization of Africa.

Regardless of their motivations, Europeans kept tight control of their African colonies even as they adopted differing administrative approaches. The British were known for a system of indirect rule, in which they exercised authority through traditional African leaders such as chiefs. Laws were passed down from London or the colonial capital for local implementation. If a chief did not comply with colonial orders, he was replaced with another handpicked "traditional" leader who was more cooperative (Ranger 1983). The system was efficient and cost-saving from the British perspective but undermined the legitimacy of local leaders and was especially difficult to implement in societies that were not already organized hierarchically. France ruled its colonies more directly, deploying a large number of colonial administrators throughout its African territories though still relying on designated African chiefs at the local level. A unique aspect of the French system was its emphasis on assimilation, under which Africans could eventually become French citizens through education and acculturation. In practice, however, this was exceedingly rare and *évolués* were a small but privileged elite class (Oyebade 2002). At lower levels of colonial administration, both Britain and France hired a fair number of Africans drawn from the colonial education programs they established.

In comparison to the British and French systems, the administration of Portuguese and Belgian colonies in Africa involved an even higher degree of coercion and military force. In the Congo Free State under Belgium's King Leopold II (1885–1908), for example, colonial officials extracted rubber, ivory, and other resources through a brutal system of forced labor that included mutilation as punishment for not fulfilling production quotas; as many as 10 million people died during this period (Hochschild 1998). In such contexts, little effort was made to develop social services or train Africans for government positions, with the result that very few Africans earned secondary or university degrees. While these differences among colonial administrations help to explain some of the divergent experiences of African countries after independence, it is clear that colonialism on the whole was not a training ground for democracy or free market capitalism. In all cases, the colonial government restricted open political debate and intervened heavily in the economy, with long-term effects on Africa's political and economic development.

In the years after World War II, which turned out to be the waning years of colonialism, the European powers introduced various changes in their African colonies. Territorial assemblies were created with representatives elected by the colonial subjects, and suffrage was gradually extended to include more groups. Through a series of constitutional changes, France allowed African representation within its own National

Assembly. Several future leaders of independent African countries were elected to serve in the French parliament during this time, including Senegal's Léopold Senghor and Côte d'Ivoire's Félix Houphouët-Boigny. Many colonial administrations also eased penal codes, expanded social services, and in a few cases even drafted plans for decolonization. During the late colonial period, nationalist movements also gained momentum throughout Africa. In contrast to earlier resistance efforts, many of these movements were explicitly organized along national lines and brought together people from various ethnic and social groups. Others had a more pan-African focus and sought to build ties across colonially imposed borders. Faced with a common adversary, resistance movements of various types worked together toward the goal of ending European rule in Africa.

Much as the colonial experience varied throughout Africa based in part on which European power was involved, so too did the process of decolonization. After losing the jewel in the crown of its empire (India) in 1947 and brutally suppressing the Mau Mau uprising in Kenya in the 1950s, the United Kingdom (UK) finally recognized that the colonial era was coming to a close. In 1957, Ghana (formerly the Gold Coast) became the first sub-Saharan African country to gain independence. Decolonization was relatively peaceful in other British colonies as well, with the exceptions of Kenya, as mentioned, and Zimbabwe, where the 1965 unilateral declaration of independence by the white minority triggered a fifteen-year war during which the UK largely stood on the sidelines. Among the French territories, the bloody Algerian war of independence broke out in 1954 and was complicated by the presence of a million European settlers. The conflict had huge domestic political implications and led to the collapse of France's Fourth Republic. In 1958, to avoid similar uprisings elsewhere, France organized a referendum giving its African colonies a choice between limited self-government within the French Community or full independence. Led by the charismatic Sékou Touré, Guinea was the only one to vote for independence and was punished harshly when France cut off all aid. By 1960, though, another constitutional change allowed the other French colonies to assert their full independence as well, though many continued to work closely with the former colonial power (see Chapter 11).

Facing riots in Congo and a revolution by the Hutu majority in Rwanda in the late 1950s, Belgium sought to avoid an Algeria-like conflict of its own. It granted independence in 1960 to an ill-prepared Congo, which soon got caught up in Cold War politics (see Chapter 3), and left Rwanda and Burundi in 1962. Portugal was the only colonial power that fought hard to hold on to its African territories in the 1960s.

Anticolonial wars were fought by groups in Angola, Mozambique, and Guinea-Bissau with extensive casualties on all sides. With Antonio Salazar's authoritarian government having staked its reputation on holding on to the empire, it was not until 1974 that a coup in Portugal paved the way for the independence of its African colonies the following year. By 1980, nearly all of Africa was independent from European colonial rule, though white minorities controlled South Africa and Namibia until the early 1990s.

Why did Britain, France, and Belgium (if not Portugal) give up on colonialism in Africa around 1960? To some extent, European states were weakened by World War II and were no longer able to project their power internationally. The Cold War rivalry also increased the value of independent African countries that were able to align with East or West, and the dominant powers of the time, the United States and the Soviet Union, held anticolonial stances. Moreover, after fighting a world war ostensibly for values such as freedom and self-determination, and using soldiers from their African colonies to do so, the British, French, and Belgians could no longer justify colonialism morally. As the discourse of human rights expanded, Africans, too, demanded their rights. And European capitalists ultimately found colonialism too expensive, particularly given the level of repression required. If they could continue to exploit Africa's resources without maintaining colonies, as many would seek to do through neocolonial approaches after independence, they could reap the benefits of colonialism without the costs.

Legacies of Colonialism

Africa emerged from roughly seventy-five years of European colonialism with a system of sovereign, independent states that on paper looked much like those in other areas of the world. In practice, however, the newly independent African states behaved somewhat differently, in terms of both their domestic politics and their international relations. In many respects, this was due to the hybrid nature of African states, which were the result of having superimposed European-style states onto existing — and very different — systems of political and economic organization. Although it was lengthy and devastating in many countries, colonialism did not manage to destroy these precolonial patterns. Onto this template, European powers drew arbitrary boundaries, lumping together peoples of various cultural backgrounds, and established new political and economic institutions that were completely foreign in the local context. Though relatively brief in the overall scope of African history, colonialism transformed the continent in many ways and had long-lasting effects that continue to shape African politics today.

One legacy of the European colonial project was the weakness of Africa's political institutions. Imposed from outside and by force, the colonial regimes lacked legitimacy and popular support. The government institutions created by colonial powers were not familiar to the majority of Africans, nor did they build on preexisting power structures, except in superficial ways. Although the British and French hastily established elected legislatures in many African colonies after World War II, these institutions did not develop deep roots in society before independence. Thus, the government institutions inherited by African postcolonial leaders were regarded as foreign and irrelevant to many of the people whom they claimed to govern. Instead of working to enhance the legitimacy of these institutions, many African leaders undermined them and instead built up regional and ethnic bases of support. As theorized by Peter Ekeh, postcolonial African elites effectively functioned within two publics: the civic public, or the (illegitimate) institutions tied to the former colonial administration, and the primordial public, those linked to ethnic and cultural groupings. In this context, it was acceptable for leaders to take resources from the civic public in order to fulfill moral obligations to the primordial public, thus further weakening Africa's formal political institutions (Ekeh 1975).

Despite this weakness, the state was the primary source of wealth in colonial Africa. European colonialism was a system of resource extraction controlled largely by the government and, in some cases, well-connected private companies. The only path to economic advancement was through some sort of access to the colonial government. For Africans in particular, the primary avenue to privilege and wealth—at least as defined by Western standards—was to get an education in colonial schools and secure a job such as an interpreter or tax collector in the colonial administration. Some Africans got involved in politics, particularly after the post–World War II openings. At independence, with rare exceptions, these Western-educated African elites inherited control over the state institutions. Colonial parastatal companies were turned over to independent governments, and the private sector was tiny. With few opportunities to get rich outside of government, ambitious Africans sought to gain access to the state, by either working their way up within government institutions or taking them over by force. In this context, there was fierce (sometimes violent) competition to control state institutions. With such control increasingly associated with access to other resources like international aid (see Chapter 4), the economic primacy of the state had important domestic and international implications.

African countries also emerged from the colonial period in a position of economic weakness in the global economy. Established to make money for the mother country, African colonies exported low-profit primary commodities such as mineral resources and agricultural products and imported high-profit finished goods. In many cases, European powers developed the colonial economy around a single cash crop or mineral export. The colonial transportation infrastructure also was clearly designed for extraction; in most colonies, railroads and roads went straight from inland production areas to coastal ports, where goods could be loaded on ships bound for Europe. Few routes connected cities and countries in Africa's interior to one another. These patterns carried over into the postcolonial era, with most African countries relying on primary commodity exports despite periodic diversification efforts. Trade among independent African countries remained very low, in part because the existing infrastructure was not conducive, as explored later in the book. Given the poor terms of trade associated with exporting primary products and importing finished goods, postcolonial African leaders soon turned to external supporters for economic assistance, including the Cold War superpowers (Chapter 3), the international financial institutions (Chapter 4), the former colonial powers (Chapter 11), and eventually emerging powers such as China (Chapter 12). Even as the pace of globalization increased, Africa's economic marginalization proved exceedingly difficult to overcome.

Finally, perhaps the most obvious legacy of European colonialism in Africa, particularly from the international relations perspective, is the modern state system. European powers drew arbitrary borders on the map of Africa at the 1884–1885 Berlin Conference with the goal of reducing conflict among themselves. They then set out to establish control within their designated spheres of influence, and by 1914 the political map of Africa was virtually complete. As nationalist movements gained momentum in the late colonial period, their leaders promised to redraw the map of Africa after the Europeans left. Instead, in the early 1960s, the leaders of newly independent African countries decided to maintain the colonial borders. As explored more extensively in the next section, even in the few cases where international borders were changed, there has been pressure to return to the lines drawn on the map of Africa by Europeans.

The Durability of Colonial Borders

On the eve of independence in the 1950s, African elites frequently discussed the need to do away with the colonial borders. The ideals of pan-Africanism in particular called for bringing together peoples of African descent and erasing the borders that falsely separated them. Pan-Africanist leaders recognized that this process would not happen overnight but would start with smaller unions among former colonies. Within a few years, however, the rhetoric about Africa's borders changed dramatically. In 1963, the Organization of African Unity was formed among newly independent African countries. Chapter III of its charter called on member states to respect one another's sovereignty and territorial integrity and asserted the principle of noninterference. The 1964 Cairo resolution was even more explicit, declaring that "Member States pledge themselves to respect the borders existing on their achievement of national independence" (Organization of African Unity 1964). On these issues, the OAU was consistent with the principles of the United Nations, which independent African countries also joined. The new African leaders thus asserted the sanctity of the colonial borders, ensuring that the map of Africa would remain nearly unchanged.

What explains the durability of Africa's colonial borders? If the boundaries were so arbitrary, why would Africa's post-independence leaders decide to respect them? One obvious answer to this question is that newly empowered elites were protecting their own regime interests. Once they had power over their own small areas, as they did by the time they joined the OAU, they did not want to give it up. Independence was fought for the colonial states as drawn on the map, after all, and not for smaller (or larger) units. Leaders also could assure they would be relatively safe from cross-border attacks if they provided similar assurances to neighbors, thus increasing their international (if not domestic) security. After the experience of colonialism, African leaders also held as sacrosanct the norm of sovereignty and the principle of nonintervention, to the point that they did not intervene in members' affairs even when perhaps they should have done so (in situations of mass human rights violations, for example). Moreover, in part due to these norms more widely, it would have been difficult to obtain international recognition for a state that did not adhere to existing borders (Jackson and Rosberg 1982). In addition to these explanations, Jeffrey Herbst (1989) argues that preserving the colonial map was a cheap way for new African leaders to create and maintain borders without waging war and without having to establish a strong political presence throughout their territories. Just as the colonial powers had not wanted to fight each other or invest heavily in statebuilding, the same was true for African leaders. With no better way to draw borders based on geography, demography, or ethnicity, they found it easiest to stick with what they had inherited from their colonial predecessors (Herbst 1989).

As a result of these decisions by African leaders at independence, there have been very few changes to the map of Africa since that time. There were minor changes to the borders between Mali and Mauritania in 1963 and between Senegal and Gambia in 1975, for example, both by joint agreement between the countries involved. In the few cases where the African political map has been altered more significantly, however, there eventually have been pressures to revert to the colonial lines. These include Somalia and Tanzania, each of which resulted from the merger of two colonies, as well as Eritrea and South Sudan, where independence meant returning to colonial-era divisions. In many ways, as these examples demonstrate, the exceptions prove the rule with respect to the durability of Africa's colonial borders.

At independence in 1960, Somalia was a union of two colonies: British Somaliland (the northern portion along the Red Sea) and Italian Somaliland (along the Indian Ocean). During the colonial era, peoples of Somali ethnicity were divided among several colonies, including these two as well as French Somaliland, Kenya, and Ethiopia. Somali leaders longed for a Greater Somalia that would bring together all ethnic Somalis, and the alteration of the colonial map to create independent Somalia was a step toward the realization of that goal. But their irredentist dreams were dashed in 1963 when Kenya became independent with borders that included a predominantly Somali region, prompting the Shifta War, during which some of its inhabitants fought unsuccessfully to join Somalia (Branch 2014; Castagno 1964; Touval 1966). The presence of a large number of ethnic Somalis in Ethiopia also factored into conflicts with that country in the 1970s and 1980s that were exacerbated by Cold War dynamics (see Chapter 3). In 1977, in a further blow to Somali irredentism, French Somaliland became independent Djibouti.

Although the colonial map was changed just once in this case to bring together British and Italian Somaliland, events in more recent years have led to a reemergence of that earlier division. After the collapse of Somalia's government in 1991 and the intensification of the civil war (see Chapter 10), leaders of the former British colony in the north declared the independent Republic of Somaliland. As the rest of Somalia descended into a lengthy period of violence and statelessness, Somaliland created its own democratic system of government with regular multiparty elections and established relative peace and prosperity (Hansen and Bradbury 2007). It reinvigorated trading networks with other countries in the region and eventually managed to secure some international aid through indirect channels. Somaliland's leaders and supporters have waged an active campaign for international recognition (Schraeder 2006b), but the United States has left the question of independence up to the African Union (US Department of State 2008). Interestingly, a key aspect of Somaliland's claim to independence is the fact that it was a separate colony more than five decades ago. Thus, its recognition would represent the reassertion of one of the few colonial borders altered at independence.

Tanzania is another union of two former colonies: Tanganyika and Zanzibar. Originally German East Africa, Tanganyika became an internationally mandated territory under the United Kingdom after World War I. At independence in 1961, the country was led by Julius Nyerere, a former teacher who had helped form the main nationalist movement. Less than twenty-five miles off the coast in the Indian Ocean, Zanzibar was a separate British protectorate ruled by a cooperative Arab sultan. Its predominantly Muslim population included people who identified as Arab and others who identified as African, though there had been significant intermarriage over the years. In the late 1940s, Africans in Zanzibar started to protest their political and economic marginalization, and ethnic divisions deepened. In 1963, outgoing British authorities gerrymandered electoral districts so that an Arab alliance would retain power at independence (Rawlence 2005). African parties were frustrated at their underrepresentation in parliament and, in early 1964, staged a revolution and took over the government. Recognizing that his hold on power was precarious, the new president, Abeid Karume, reached out to Nyerere for assistance.

As a result of these negotiations, the United Republic of Tanzania was formed in 1964 as a merger between the two countries. Under the arrangement, Nyerere remained president and Karume became vice president, while Zanzibar retained some independent institutions (separate ministries of health and education, for example). In addition to electing their own representatives to the national parliament (roughly one-fifth of the total), Zanzibaris also elect their own house of representatives to legislate on nonunion matters. In a familiar twist, since the return to multiparty politics in Tanzania in the 1990s, a pro-Arab opposition party has emerged calling for more autonomy for Zanzibar and even possible independence from the mainland.[2] The Civic United Front (CUF) claims to have won Zanzibar's presidential elections in 1995, 2000, and 2005, but was blocked from taking power by the ruling Chama cha Mapinduzi (CCM), triggering several episodes of post-election violence. Under a new power-sharing system in 2010, the second-place presidential candidate (from the CUF) became first vice president of Zanzibar. Tensions escalated again in 2015, however, when the electoral commission canceled initial election results in Zanzibar because of alleged irregularities. Claiming it won the first time around, the CUF boycotted the rerun a few months later, allowing the CCM to get more than 90 percent of the vote. Although the Tanzanian union has survived for five decades, a vocal minority of the Zanzibari population would like to return to the colonial borders.

In two other cases, colonies that were merged during the colonial era have successfully fought for independence and been recognized by other African states based in part on having been separate colonies. The most recent is South Sudan's independence from Sudan in 2011, which is explored at length in the case study at the end of this chapter. The story of Eritrea is similar, with its independence from Ethiopia in 1993 representing a return to colonial borders (although Ethiopians claim that the territory was part of their precolonial empire). Eritrea became an Italian colony in 1890, but neighboring Ethiopia was never colonized. When Italy occupied Ethiopia in 1936, it created the short-lived Italian East African Empire. With Italy's defeat in World War II, the victorious Allies debated the future of Eritrea. In 1951, the United Nations made it an autonomous territory federated with Ethiopia. Over the next decade, with little international reaction, Ethiopia turned this federation into a full union, essentially governing Eritrea as another region within the country (Cliffe and Davidson 1988; Negash 1997). Eritreans responded by starting a decades-long guerrilla movement for independence (Pool 2001).

In 1977, the Eritrean People's Liberation Front (EPLF) managed to take over much of Eritrean territory, prompting the new military government of Ethiopia to respond with a massive invasion supported by Cuba and the Soviet Union (see Chapter 3). In the 1980s, an Ethiopian rebel movement against the Marxist regime joined forces with the Eritreans and promised a referendum on Eritrean independence if it came to power. In 1991, the combined rebels overthrew the Mengistu regime in Addis Ababa, paving the way for such a referendum. The people of Eritrea voted overwhelmingly in 1993 for independence, which was promptly recognized by the OAU, based in part on Eritrea's history as a separate colony. After the two countries later fought a war over their shared border (1998–2000), the Eritrea-Ethiopia Boundary Commission (EEBC) created by the peace agreement used a series of colonial-era maps to determine the border between them. One of the main disputed areas (Badme) was awarded to Eritrea, though Ethiopia continued to occupy it for more than a decade, contributing to ongoing tensions that were further complicated by domestic political dynamics within each country.

In the relatively few cases in which the map of Africa has been redrawn, as we have seen, the enduring legacy from the colonial inheritance often overrides other considerations. Rather than doing away with the European-drawn borders as pan-Africanist leaders proposed prior to independence, the trend has been to maintain them and even return to them in instances where they were altered, especially in the Horn of Africa. The epitome of this pattern is perhaps the EEBC's

archival search for original copies of Italian maps from the early 1900s
to resolve a border dispute between two independent countries a hundred years later. The willingness of African states to protect these borders and the desire to return to them in some cases suggest that the borders are anything but arbitrary in the current African context.

The Meaning of Borders

Over the past 150 years, as we have seen in this chapter, the political
landscape of the African continent has been transformed. In the precolonial era, myriad political entities with fluid boundaries and overlapping memberships populated the African landscape. Some areas were
controlled hierarchically while others involved loose alliances among
ethnic communities. There were vast areas of the continent where the
exercise of political control was uncertain or absent. Today, there are
fifty-four sovereign states in Africa with defined borders and governments that exert their authority therein. On paper at least, there are no
areas that lack political authority, though in practice there is wide variation in where and how such control is exercised. It was European colonialism in the intervening years that imposed on Africa the international
system of sovereign states, radically altering the continent's map and
leaving a lasting legacy of weak political institutions, intense competition, and global economic marginalization.

In many ways, African borders have become even more rigid since
independence. Colonial policies typically encouraged cross-border labor
migration, even among colonies of different European powers. Laborers
from Belgian-controlled Ruanda-Urundi frequently worked on sisal
plantations in British-controlled Tanganyika, for example, while South
African gold and diamond mines employed workers from colonies
throughout the southern region. In contrast, with few exceptions, postcolonial African governments typically have tried to stem the flow of
migrants and refugees. At various times over the years, countries such
as Tanzania, Chad, and Guinea have closed their borders to people fleeing insecurity in neighboring countries (despite previously having open-
door policies), while governments in Nigeria, Uganda, and Ethiopia,
among others, have expelled mass numbers of non-nationals. In recent
years, there has been an increase in hostility toward African immigrants
in many countries, including South Africa, Botswana, the Democratic
Republic of Congo, and Côte d'Ivoire (see Chapter 9). Itself a reflection
of broader political and economic causes, the rise of xenophobia at its
core suggests that many Africans have accepted the borders imposed
under colonialism and now see themselves as inherently different from
people originating across those lines.

Even so, these borders are not just barriers; they also provide opportunities. African peoples can cross international borders to avoid taxes, seek better services, or sell their goods for higher prices. Different regulatory policies in neighboring countries lead to lucrative smuggling networks for everything from oil and tobacco to livestock and mineral resources. Borders allow people to flee political repression and wars, and provide safe haven for rebel movements to organize to attack their home countries. Despite the permeable nature of African borders, therefore, they have meaning and importance to the people who live near them. From the coffee farmer who smuggles his beans across the border for a better price, to the mother who sends her children to stay with extended family in a neighboring country during a civil conflict, borders are not simply colonial creations that have no relevance to local peoples.

Moreover, borders are not just lines on a map. In many ways, they determine internal and external relations of power and are crucial to the very existence of African countries and their identities. Definitions of a state in the field of international relations typically include several criteria: control over a given territory, including a monopoly on the use of force; some degree of legitimacy among that territory's people such that they follow its rules; and international recognition of its right to exist (Jackson and Rosberg 1982). African states often fall short in several ways. Many African states do not exercise effective authority throughout their territories (whether because of weak capacity, rebellions, or other threats), and they frequently lack legitimacy among the local population (Herbst 2000a; Jackson and Rosberg 1982). Thus, their continued existence as states is due primarily to international recognition of their borders, both by neighboring states and by the broader international community. In this way, African states have juridical statehood (stemming from international law) but not empirical statehood (which would come from effective control and administration) (Jackson and Rosberg 1982).

In this context, international recognition of African states is crucial. According to norms that emerged in the mid–twentieth century, every state has a right to exist; the international community basically does not allow takeovers, ensuring that even very weak states survive (perhaps when they should not) (Herbst 1990). Because of the commitment among leaders to respect existing borders, African states also very rarely dissolve. Potential separatist leaders seek payoffs and accommodations to stay in existing states instead of breaking away without international recognition (Englebert and Hummel 2005). As this suggests, there is a huge benefit to being the internationally recognized government of an African state (Englebert 2009). In addition to freedom from external intervention, at least in principle, that government has access to international aid and institutional support (through the African Union and United Nations, for example) that rivals do not have. As a result, there is intense competition among African power brokers to gain and maintain international recognition. In the subsequent chapters of this book, we will see how this need for external recognition and support has affected Africa's international relations in the postcolonial era.

Case Study: The Durability of Borders in South Sudan

Prior to European colonialism, according to the limited historical record, the area now known as South Sudan was home to various agro-pastoralist communities, most of whom migrated there from other regions (Beswick 2016). During the colonial period, the area was combined with present-day Sudan, but the two were administered separately. Starting in 1898, both were included in the condominium of Anglo-Egyptian Sudan, through which Britain and Egypt exercised joint control over the Sudanese colony. Due in part to cultural differences between the predominantly Arab and Muslim north and the predominantly African and animist south, however, the north was administered through the arrangement with Egypt, while the south was governed through a system of indirect rule similar to the one used by Britain in its other sub-Saharan African colonies. From the 1920s, passports and permits were required for travel and trade between the two regions, and different official languages were established in each (Arabic in the north, English in the south). Christianity spread in the south, and British administrators there attended conferences with counterparts in East Africa instead of Khartoum. For all practical purposes, they were separate colonies (Collins 2008; Deng 2011).

In the 1940s, however, without consulting people in South Sudan, the British government changed its approach. In preparation for Sudanese self-rule, British authorities decided in 1946 to integrate north and south under a single government and in 1948 to create the Sudan Legislative Assembly with representatives from both (Collins 2008; Deng 2011). As British and Egyptian administrators started to pull out of Sudan in 1953, government positions throughout the country—including the south—were turned over to northern Sudanese almost without exception. Despite promises by leaders in Khartoum to develop a federal system, formal independence came in 1956 under a unitary government dominated by northern Sudanese.

Even before independence became official, war broke out. In August 1955, southern army officers who were unhappy about the south essentially being handed over to the north started a revolt, leading to the first

Sudanese civil war (1955–1972). As southerners fought for greater autonomy through federalism or even independence, the northern government cracked down, taking as many as 5,000 political prisoners. Northerners living in the south were also at risk, and many were killed during the fighting. In 1969, a coup d'état in Khartoum led by Jaafar Nimeiri paved the way for negotiations with the south, culminating in the 1972 Addis Ababa Agreement, which ended the first civil war. Under the power-sharing arrangement, southerners were integrated into the northern government and the south became self-governing. Arabic remained the official language, but English and local ethnic languages were permitted.

The ceasefire would not last. During what turned out to be a brief respite from the fighting, two major developments affected the future of the Sudans. In 1978, oil was discovered in southern Sudan, significantly increasing the resources at stake in controlling the territory. In addition, throughout the 1970s, there was increasing pressure on the Nimeiri government from Islamists in the north. Spurred on by the broader rise of Islamism in the region, and particularly the Islamic revolution in Iran in 1979, these groups pushed for a greater role for Islam in the governance of Sudan. In 1983, fearing his own removal from power, Nimeiri gave in to Islamist pressure and declared sharia (Islamic law) for the entire country, effectively ending southern autonomy and prompting the resumption of conflict (Collins 2008).

Led by John Garang, the Sudan People's Liberation Movement/Army (SPLM/A) was formed in 1983 to fight for southern autonomy, though there were also those within the movement who wanted independence. During the lengthy second Sudanese civil war (1983–2005), more than 2 million people died and at least twice as many were displaced, either internally or as refugees in neighboring countries (US Committee for Refugees and Immigrants 2001). The death toll was especially high in the late 1980s, when a drought produced a widespread famine in the context of the ongoing war; in one relief camp in Kordofan, for example, 7 percent of the population died each week over a nine-week period in 1988 (Keen 1994b). After an initial delay, humanitarian aid flowed into the country, where both SPLA troops and government-affiliated militias looted it and sold it for profit, making the situation even worse. During this time, more than 20,000 unaccompanied minors known as the "Lost Boys" fled their homes, crossing first into Ethiopia before settling in refugee camps in Kenya (Deng et al. 2005). More than 3,500 of this group were eventually resettled in the United States, where many have struggled to make new lives for themselves as they attend university and become citizens (Dau and Sweeney 2008).

Even as Sudan's civilian government was negotiating a peace plan with the SPLM in 1989, the situation was complicated by another military coup that brought to power Omar Hassan al-Bashir. Supported by the leading Islamist party, al-Bashir immediately faced opposition from a coalition of northern parties known as the National Democratic Alliance that would eventually join forces with the SPLM and rebel movements in other parts of the country (Collins 2008). Throughout the 1990s, as the political drama in Khartoum continued, there was a series of broken ceasefires between north and south. During this period, the United States accused the Sudanese government of supporting terrorism, including sheltering Osama bin Laden. Then, in August 1998, terrorist attacks on US embassies in Kenya and Tanzania killed more than 200 people. In response, the US government deployed cruise missiles, destroying a pharmaceutical plant in Khartoum that was allegedly producing chemical weapons. As Sudan's relations with the United States deteriorated, the SPLM raised substantial support from US civil society organizations, including some conservative Christians who saw Muslim oppression of Christians as the root cause of the war. Garang was happy to emphasize this narrative, and to downplay his movement's own divisions and weaknesses, in frequent public appearances in Washington, D.C., and other Western cities. When oil exports from Sudan began in 1999, the war escalated again in oil-producing areas, but so did the incentives to reach some sort of agreement.

Renewed political negotiations in the north and heightened international interest, especially from the George W. Bush administration after the terrorist attacks of September 11, 2001, on the United States, helped peace talks between the Sudanese government and the SPLM gain momentum in the early 2000s. Despite periodic skirmishes between the belligerents, negotiations eventually led to the Comprehensive Peace Agreement (CPA) in January 2005. The plan called for a six-year period of power-sharing and southern autonomy, after which a referendum would be held in the south on the question of independence. Garang became vice president of Sudan during that time, and oil revenues were split evenly between the government and the SPLM. Given the history of failed ceasefires in Sudan and ongoing conflicts in other parts of the country, many observers were skeptical that the plan would work. Along the way, in 2005, Garang died in a mysterious helicopter crash and was succeeded by his deputy, Salva Kiir. Later, in 2008, al-Bashir became the first sitting president to be indicted by the International Criminal Court (ICC) for his role in war crimes in Darfur (more on this later). Nevertheless, in January 2011, the referendum on southern independence was held as scheduled, and more than 99 percent of South Sudanese voted for secession (*BBC News* 2011). Perhaps even more surprising to many observers, Khartoum respected the results, and in July 2011 the Republic of South Sudan became independent.

South Sudan was promptly recognized by governments around the world, including member states of the African Union. Once again, as with Eritrea's independence from Ethiopia in 1993, a key factor motivating South Sudan's recognition by other African countries, many of which have faced their own separatist movements, was the fact that South Sudan had been administered separately during the colonial period. It soon became apparent, however, that the partition of Sudan along colonial-era dividing lines would not in itself resolve long-standing issues between Sudan and South Sudan, nor would it settle disputes within each of these independent countries. Both face significant challenges that will continue to affect domestic politics and international relations for years to come (Lyman 2017).

Among several unresolved post-secession issues is the exact demarcation of the border between Sudan and South Sudan. The oil-rich area of Abyei is a key focus of dispute, and a proposed referendum there has been repeatedly postponed. South Sudanese forces temporarily seized the border town of Heglig in April 2012, bringing the two countries close to all-out war, but they were quickly pushed back and the immediate crisis abated. There also are lingering disputes about oil revenues. At independence in 2011, South Sudan got 75 percent of combined Sudan's oil reserves; 98 percent of the budget of the new landlocked country came from selling oil, which had to be shipped out through ports in Sudan (de Waal 2013). In January 2012, after Khartoum dramatically increased its transit fees, the South Sudanese government suspended oil exports, forcing radical austerity measures and heavy borrowing to keep itself afloat. Oil exports resumed later that year after the two countries reached an agreement on transit fees; in 2016, they further agreed to adjust such fees based on prevailing oil prices (Dumo 2016). South Sudan eventually may be able to export its oil using planned pipelines in Kenya or Djibouti, but those are a long way in the future. In the meantime, renewed conflict between Sudan and South Sudan remains a real possibility until the belligerents reach a more permanent solution on these issues.

Ongoing rebellions in the southern part of Sudan are another source of tension with South Sudan. In the Nuba Mountains of South Kordofan and in Blue Nile state, rebels fought alongside the SPLA during the lengthy war. When South Sudan gained independence, per the terms of the CPA, these states remained in Sudan, but their future was to be determined through vaguely defined popular consultations. When such consultations were not held, the rebels renewed their fight against Khartoum, which accused Juba of providing military and logistical support and responded with massive air raids against the rebels. Between 2011 and 2012, intense fighting in these areas led to widespread displacement, including an influx of more than 114,000 refugees into South Sudan (Amnesty International 2012), further complicating development efforts in that new and very poor country.

The conflict in Darfur also affected relations between Sudan and South Sudan. During the lengthy war for South Sudan's independence, Khartoum recruited soldiers from predominantly Muslim Darfur to fight against the mainly Christian SPLA. In the early 2000s, when it became clear that the south would gain some degree of autonomy, African groups in Darfur wondered why their historically marginalized region in the west was not also getting a seat at the table. Two rebel movements emerged in 2003; in response, the government supported Arab militias known as janjaweed to put down the insurgency, destroying many African villages in the process. Estimates suggest that more than 300,000 people died (from both violence and preventable diseases) and 2 million were displaced during that time (Thomson Reuters Foundation 2014). What may have started as genocide soon evolved into a complicated multidimensional conflict as rebel groups splintered and started fighting one another in addition to the government, which made it difficult at times to determine which groups should be represented in periodic ceasefire talks (Prunier 2005).

As international attention shifted to Darfur, the conflict created significant challenges for relations between north and south, including the possibility of derailing negotiations entirely. The international community was reluctant to crack down too hard on the Sudanese government for fear that it would pull out of peace talks with the SPLM. When the CPA was finally signed in 2005, the continuing conflict in Darfur, and the eventual ICC indictment of al-Bashir for his role in war crimes there, made it difficult to extend promised rewards to his government (Lyman 2017). As the north-south peace process continued, international pressure on Sudan—and on its international allies China and Russia—led to the establishment in 2007 of the joint United Nations–African Union Mission in Darfur (UNAMID) for peacekeeping and humanitarian operations (see Chapter 8). The violence decreased and the government eventually signed peace agreements with most of the rebel factions, though tensions lingered. Looking at the conflict in Darfur, the long struggle for the independence of South Sudan, and periodic insurgencies in other parts of Sudan, a clear common denominator is the authoritarian nature of the government in Khartoum and its refusal to share power and to decentralize authority to groups in these marginalized regions.

As if these cross-border issues were not enough, South Sudan also faces myriad domestic challenges, including poverty, corruption, and insecurity. The most significant is a deadly civil war that has been waged since 2013, creating what the United Nations has labeled one of the worst humanitarian crises in the world (Parks 2017). In July 2013, concerned about power threats within his own government, South Sudanese president Salva Kiir abruptly dismissed the vice president, Riek Machar, and the rest of his cabinet. (Tension between the men was deeply rooted, with Machar having fought with Khartoum against the SPLA for a decade before returning to its ranks in 2002.) After an alleged coup attempt in December of that year, Kiir tried to arrest Machar and other opponents. Machar fled and mobilized his supporters from the Nuer ethnic community, while Kiir turned to his fellow Dinka, quickly transforming an elite power struggle into a broader war along ethnic lines (Roessler 2013). A shaky 2015 power-sharing agreement between Kiir and Machar collapsed in mid-2016, after which violence escalated and the crisis deepened. By mid-2017, at least 50,000 people had been killed in the conflict, 2.1 million were internally displaced, and another 2 million had fled as refugees (the majority of them children) to neighboring countries (Council on Foreign Relations 2017; *United Nations News Service* 2017). To make matters worse, warring parties prevented humanitarian aid from reaching nearly 5 million people (42 percent of the population) in South Sudan who lacked sufficient food, generating a human-made famine in which 2 out of every 10,000 people were dying each day (Parks 2017). With political leaders showing little will to resolve the situation, the people of South Sudan and their neighbors continue to suffer from this devastating crisis.

Despite the durability of colonial borders, therefore, the case of South Sudan demonstrates that simply reverting to old dividing lines does not eliminate fundamental power struggles on the ground. South Sudan was administered separately during the colonial era, only to find itself fully incorporated into Sudan by the British as independence approached in the 1950s. After fighting against Khartoum for decades, South Sudan became the world's newest country in 2011. Its prompt recognition by other African states was based in part on the separate status it had enjoyed during the early colonial era, similar to Eritrea's independence in 1993. Unfortunately, partition did not resolve all sources of tension between Sudan and South Sudan; in many ways, it just shifted the categorization of these tensions from domestic to international issues. In addition, the dramatic escalation of conflict along communal lines within South Sudan suggests that broader lessons were not learned about the need for power-sharing and the incorporation of diverse voices in government. At least for now, the return to colonial-era borders in South Sudan seems to represent a basic reorganization of power structures instead of a fundamental transformation in how power is exercised.

Notes

1. This pattern of state power dispersing away from centers of political control continues to this day, as discussed in Herbst 2000a.

2. Although rooted in pre-1964 divisions of race and class, the current political split in Zanzibar is driven largely by more recent developments, including widespread disappointment with the economic record of the ruling party and mobilization efforts by the opposition (Rawlence 2005).

3

Africa During the Cold War

From the middle 1950s to the end of the 1980s, the Cold War exerted a powerful influence on the nature of Africa's international relations. Although most African countries joined the Non-Aligned Movement (NAM) in the year of their independence or soon thereafter, several had de facto alliances with one of the two superpowers.[1] Since the main purpose of the NAM from its inception was to avoid domination by either superpower, and to assert independence from both, independent African countries that joined the organization were essentially rejecting superpower alignment. In practice, however, many African states were drawn into the orbit of either the United States or the Soviet Union. For many African rulers, close relations with one of the superpowers was a key element of their regime security. Further, several African regimes found that their ambitions to reorder regional power relations drew one or both of the superpowers into their foreign relations and internal politics alike.

Each superpower of course saw Africa through its own ideological lens. As for the Soviet Union, its ambitions in and for Africa were limited throughout the rule of Joseph Stalin (1922–1953). Stalin held racist views, and he saw little revolutionary potential in colonial Africa. Following Marxist orthodoxy (in this regard), Stalin believed that the economically advanced European countries, with their large proletarian classes, represented the best opportunity for spreading communism. Accordingly, Stalin had relatively little interest in Africa. Nikita Khrushchev, on the other hand, had quite different views (see, e.g., Bailer and Mandelbaum 1989). After consolidating his power over the Soviet state in 1956, Khrushchev was soon pursuing a more activist

47

policy in support of anticolonial, and also nominally Marxist-Leninist, movements in Africa. This shift in Soviet policy toward would-be African liberators coincided well with the rising strength of Africa's independence movements. For instance, Khrushchev was highly enthusiastic and supportive of Egyptian president Gamal Abdul Nasser's anti-imperialist rhetoric and activities in Africa, making him a "Hero of the Soviet Union" in 1964. Under Khrushchev, Soviet leaders began to aspire to make African states their partner in a broader "anti-imperial" struggle against the capitalist West.

For its part, the United States faced a dilemma in its policies toward Africa.[2] On the one hand, the United States benefited little from the economic domination of Africa by its European colonizers. Nor did most senior US officials believe that European colonization was morally or politically justified by the 1950s, widespread racism in the American political class notwithstanding. On the other hand, US officials were deeply worried that decolonization would allow the Soviet Union to gain allies on the African continent. Khrushchev's vigorous support for "radical" anti-imperialist leaders heightened these fears. Further, the United States did not wish to upset its European allies in the North Atlantic Treaty Organization (NATO, established 1949) or interfere in their processes of decolonization. Accordingly, the United States declined to push for African decolonization in the 1950s, despite its lack of interest in seeing colonialism continue.

Finally, African elites above all wanted to claim their dignity as autonomous leaders and succeed to power over the states defined by colonialism. Among these elites, some wanted to continue fulsome cooperation with their erstwhile colonizers as the best way of ensuring stability and development. Other African elites were more interested in the completion of the decolonization process and building African unity.[3] None wanted to suffer subservience to the Soviet Union, or continued domination by Europe, as much as some new African rulers admired European culture and values. Meanwhile, ordinary Africans had become conscious of their relative poverty vis-à-vis Europeans; they yearned for economic development and improvements in their standard of living. Most rulers aimed to fulfill these demands, though regime security was a more immediate priority. After the excitement of independence began to wear off for the new African leaders of the 1960s, it became clear to ordinary Africans that their economic circumstances would not change rapidly. At that point, regime security for rulers became trickier. In this context, the two superpowers made welcome partners for African rulers, providing both aid and, in some cases, explicit or implicit security guarantees.

In short, the process of decolonization beginning in the late 1950s created an environment that inexorably brought the two superpowers into Africa's international relations. An increasingly self-confident Soviet Union saw an opportunity to gain allies and thwart perceived US imperialist ambitions on the continent; the United States saw an opportunity to gain access to new markets, and the need to stem the advent of new Soviet allies in Africa; and African rulers saw an opportunity to use one superpower or the other as an instrument to serve their own ends. The results were often tragic for ordinary Africans, and the legacy of superpower intervention in several African conflicts persists to the present day.

Four broad generalizations are helpful in understanding how the Cold War shaped Africa's international relations. First, although the Cold War had a strong "framing" effect, African elites generally maintained their autonomy. In fact, differences among Africa's new leaders during the first wave of independence (1956 to 1964) helped draw the superpowers into African affairs. It was not simply the case that the superpowers imposed their will on Africa's newly independent weak states; rather, African leaders sought to use one or the other superpower for their own purposes, creating a contest for influence (Clapham 1996). Second, Africa was not a major priority for either superpower in the way that Europe, or even the Middle East, was. Whereas the two superpowers were committed to maintaining their respective European allies in power at the cost of a direct war between them in Europe, this was not the case in Africa. Third, and partly as a result, the nature of superpower competition in Africa took the form of low-grade influence-seeking, punctuated by a series of crises. These crises were usually occasioned by circumstances under which the succession of new African states gained their independence from European colonizers. Finally, one can discern the waxing and then waning of the attraction of Marxist ideologies and Soviet influence on the continent, as discussed later.

The remainder of this chapter is divided into three parts, followed by a case study of superpower involvement in the Angolan civil war. The next section identifies four aspects of the Cold War in Africa and issues one major caveat about it. The subsequent section traces some of the key developments in Africa's international relations driven by superpower competition from the mid-1950s to 1990. The nature of superpower competition on the continent evolved in line with the relative strength of each superpower over time. It also evolved in keeping with African opinions about which politico-economic models represented their best opportunities for stability and development. The third section offers differing interpretations of the superpower competition in Africa. Finally, the case study shows how superpower competition exacerbated and lengthened the Angolan civil war, which lasted from 1975 to 2002. From its inception through the late 1980s, the Angolan civil war seemed to mostly be a function of the Cold War in Africa. But its continuation after the end of the Cold War points to the indigenous roots of the conflict and makes our interpretation of external intervention there more difficult.

Aspects of the Cold War in Africa

The Cold War in Africa had two related but somewhat different dimensions. On one hand, there was the direct competition between the Soviet Union and the United States for political influence throughout the world, including in Africa. On the other hand, there was a broader clash of global ideologies between liberal, free market capitalism and one-party, state-managed socialism. The former prevailed in Western Europe, Japan, and the Americas, whereas the latter characterized not only the Soviet Union but also members of its Warsaw Pact, the People's Republic of China, and some nonaligned socialist states. As African states gained independence, most were inevitably caught up in these overlapping contests for loyalty and influence.

A first aspect of the Cold War in Africa was the de facto alignment of many African regimes with one camp or the other on political issues, despite some valiant efforts at neutrality. Almost all African states established formal diplomatic relations with both superpowers following their independence. Yet African states were divided on several political matters that arose in the context of Cold War competition. Such divisions are recorded, among other ways, in the votes of the United Nations on controversial issues of the day. For instance, in the midst of civil war in Congo in 1960 (discussed in more detail later), there was a controversy among African states at the United Nations over whether to recognize the government of President Joseph Kasavubu. Six African states that had become hostile to Western influence (Egypt, Ghana, Guinea, Mali, Morocco, and Togo) voted against seating the (pro-Western) Kasavubu representative; all of France's former colonies, all pro-Western except those just listed, voted in favor of the Kasavubu delegation; and another small set of African states either abstained or did not participate in the vote (Welch 1966).

Another issue on which one can perceive the "tilt" of many newly independent African states involved the appropriate representation of the Chinese people. Between 1949, the year of the Chinese communist revolution, and 1971, China was represented at the UN by the Republic of China (ROC) government, located in Taiwan, rather than by the People's Republic of China government in Beijing. During these years, the states of the Eastern bloc recognized the PRC government, whereas most Western states recognized the ROC government in Taiwan. Thus, African countries that achieved independence in the latter 1950s and early 1960s faced a choice of which Chinese government to recognize. The states with more strongly anti-imperialist or "socialist" regimes like Algeria, Ghana, Guinea, Mali, Tanzania, and Zambia recognized the PRC upon their independence or shortly thereafter. A group of more Western-oriented states, including most former French colonies, Congo-Kinshasa, Liberia, Nigeria, and Sierra Leone, all recognized the ROC government until 1971,[4] and some long after that date. Some other countries, including the Central African Republic (CAR) and Congo-Brazzaville, switched from recognition of one to the other as their internal politics changed over time.

The fundamental political split among African states in this era led to the formation of three groups with different attitudes about how to proceed in unifying Africa. As Chapter 2 records, some African leaders had to struggle hard, and even organized anticolonial military organizations, to achieve independence for their countries. Leaders such as Kwame Nkrumah (Ghana), Mobido Keita (Mali), and Sékou Touré (Guinea) defied their former colonial rulers and charted strongly independent postcolonial courses. These new rulers favored vigorous efforts to quickly liberate Africa's remaining colonies and then unify African states under a common political umbrella. On the other hand, many other African colonies had achieved independence through relatively peaceful political protests, without resort to all-out war; most of these favored more patient approaches to the liberation of French Algeria, the Portuguese colonies, and white-ruled southern African states. A bloc of twelve former French colonies met in Brazzaville in December 1960 to discuss cooperation among themselves that involved a loose confederation and fulsome cooperation with France.[5] In response, Morocco organized a meeting of the more radical African states (Egypt, Ghana, Guinea, Libya, and Mali, along with Algeria's provisional government) at the Casablanca conference in January 1961.[6] At this meeting, the representatives of these states took a strong anti-imperialist line, demanding independence for Algeria, the restoration of Patrice Lumumba to power in Congo, and the rapid unification of Africa's independent states (Welch 1966). In May 1961, several other relatively conservative African states, including Ethiopia, Liberia, Nigeria, and Sierra Leone, joined the Brazzaville bloc at Monrovia, Liberia, thus forming what became called the Monrovia Group. As a contemporary observer noted, "The Monrovia states consider that cooperation in practical matters comes first; political unity should follow, but may never reach the point of integration"

(Williams 1961: 119). Thus, the contrast between the Casablanca Group and the Monrovia Group mirrored divisions between the East and West in the larger global community: the former demanded immediate liberation, respect from the West, and radical social transformations; the latter favored patience, cooperation with the former colonizers, and gradual social reforms (on the resolution of the conflict between the Casablanca and Monrovia Groups, see Chapter 6).

In subsequent decades, several African countries became more explicitly aligned with one superpower or the other. The United States maintained Central Intelligence Agency (CIA) listening posts in Liberia and Zaire (now the Democratic Republic of Congo) during the height of the Cold War; the US base at Kagnew Station, Ethiopia (now Eritrea), began functioning as a radio communications site during World War II, and evolved into a small military base and listening post during the Cold War.[7] The United States also maintained close military cooperation with several other allies, such as Kenya. For its part, the Soviet Union consolidated its relations with certain allies through its signature "Treaties of Friendship and Cooperation." Beneficiaries of Soviet friendship included Angola, Benin, Congo-Brazzaville, and Ethiopia. This same set of countries received military assistance and implicit security guarantees for the nominally Marxist regimes in power.

A second aspect of the Cold War in Africa was competition between the Eastern bloc and the West to provide foreign aid. African regimes naturally desired to acquire as much aid as possible from all outsiders. Since the United States and developed Western countries had far more aid to give, they generally won this competition throughout the Cold War. The United States established significant economic aid programs for most of the West-leaning African states in the 1960s and increased this aid over time (Schraeder 1994). Although the Soviet Union was a far poorer patron than the United States and other Western states, its government did not need to submit to any legislative scrutiny of its aid programs. It provided substantial economic and military aid to a few radical regimes like those in Guinea, Mali, and Ghana (Legvold 1970). More important, the Soviet Union delivered considerable military aid to the liberation movements fighting against residual Portuguese colonialism and white rule in southern Africa. As with political alignment, African states were largely compelled to choose between East and West in the aid competition.

A third aspect of the Cold War in Africa comprised models of development, often explicitly adopted by various African states. Crawford Young (1982) identifies three ideologies that provided models for development in Africa: Afro-Marxism, African socialism, and capitalism. A number of African states, beginning with Congo-Brazzaville in 1970 and later joined by Somalia, Benin, Ethiopia, and Angola, declared themselves to be officially Marxist-Leninist. They adopted a nominally "scientific socialist" approach to development, focusing on industrial workers. The radical states of the Casablanca bloc, but also Algeria, Guinea-Bissau, and Tanzania, opted for a (theoretically) more authentic and local model for development known as African socialism, based on the notion of African communalism. A number of other states that aligned closely with either France, like Côte d'Ivoire, or with the United States (Kenya, Liberia, Nigeria, and Zaire) more or less explicitly embraced a capitalist model. Interestingly, however, Young did not find much difference in development performance among the categories, though the "capitalist" states did somewhat better during the 1960s and 1970s. Perhaps this is because the nominal differences were not entirely matched by real policy differences: all the African states of this period, including the "capitalist" ones, practiced heavy intervention in the economy.[8]

A fourth major aspect of the Cold War was forceful superpower intervention in several civil wars and interstate conflicts in Africa. These interventions went far beyond the kind of economic or even military aid provided to African states at peace. They involved efforts of the superpowers to bring to power client regimes, or at least to prevent their adversaries from putting sympathetic regimes in place. The competitive superpower interventions became most intense during three places and times: in the Congo crisis, between 1960 and 1962; in the Angola civil war, 1974–1975, as that country achieved its independence; and during the Ethiopia-Somalia war of 1977–1978 (Clark 1992). Low-grade, less dramatic, or one-sided superpower interventions took place during the Shaba invasions of Congo (1977 and 1978), during one critical juncture in the Chadian civil war of the 1970s, and during the struggles for majority rule in southern Africa. In the three main cases, however, both superpowers intervened on opposing sides in a competitive way. In these cases, each of the superpowers sent in advisers, arms, and troops from proxy or allied countries. Again, though, it is important to note that African actors maintained considerable agency during these struggles: in all cases, local belligerents were calling for the intervention of a superpower patron and their international partners. It is also worth noting that neither superpower intervened significantly in other African civil wars, including those in Nigeria (1967–1970) and in Sudan (1955–1972).

This section ends with a major caveat about Africa's international relations during the Cold War: other major external powers also had

strong interests in Africa during the Cold War, especially France and the
PRC. Further, neither of these countries aligned itself with the superpower whose politico-economic system matched its own. France did not
give up its ambitions to act autonomously of the United States after
joining the North Atlantic Treaty Organization in 1949. France tested its
own atomic weapon in 1960 and withdrew from NATO's integrated military command in 1966. Likewise, France did not give up its ambitions
to maintain an autonomous role in Africa. On the contrary, as discussed
in Chapter 11, France made major efforts to continue its influence in
Africa after 1960. Further, none of the major superpower crises in
Africa during the Cold War occurred in a former French colony. Savvy
rulers in francophone Africa did find ways to play off one Western
patron against the other, however.

As for the PRC, a political schism between it and the Soviet Union
had been brewing since the death of Stalin in 1953. The formal split
between the two communist giants became public at a congress of
world communist parties held in Moscow in November 1960; the split
was later recorded in official documents of the Soviet and Chinese
Communist Parties (Lüthi 2010). Thus, at the very moment when the
first group of African countries was gaining independence, the world's
two leading communist countries had become antagonists. As a consequence, the PRC pursued an independent path from that of the Soviet
Union in Africa. In particular, the PRC tried to present itself as the "natural" leader of developing countries and the NAM (see Chapter 12). As
with the subtle Franco-American rivalry in Africa, the Sino-Soviet split
gave African rulers more agency in playing the two communist powers
against each other, notably in the area of aid. Some of the states following an African socialist development model, especially Tanzania and
Zambia, aligned themselves more with China than the Soviet Union
(Bräutigam 2009). In the Portuguese colonies and Rhodesia, the Chinese competed with the Soviets by sponsoring rival liberation groups. In
Rhodesia, for example, China backed the Zimbabwe African National
Union (ZANU), while the Soviets backed the Zimbabwe African People's Union (ZAPU). The former prevailed against the white-ruled
regime and took power in independent Zimbabwe in 1980.[9]

Since both France and China followed independent policies in
Africa during the Cold War, African rulers exploited the resulting rivalries to extract more aid, weapons, political support, and security guarantees from all four external patrons. Other external players also pursued policies in Africa independent of the superpowers during the Cold
War: Portugal fought to maintain its colonial empire until 1975; India
and other nonaligned countries pursued independent economic and

political interests in Africa; and Cuba supported South Africa's African National Congress (ANC) and other liberation groups not as a pawn of the Soviet Union but for its own reasons. Meanwhile, the UN often struggled to mitigate the superpower rivalry and to find neutral solutions to Africa's crises, notably in the Congo crisis of 1960–1964 (more on this later). Finally, the Cold War context did not always determine intra-African relations in the ways that contemporary Soviet and US observers expected. In the 1970s, Benin was officially Marxist-Leninist, whereas neighboring Togo was closely aligned with France and the West—yet there were no serious interstate disputes between them. Likewise, "Marxist" Congo-Brazzaville got along quite well in its international relations with "pro-Western" Cameroon, Gabon, and Zaire. In short, although the Cold War provided one important context for Africa's international relations from 1956 to 1989, it hardly defined every aspect of African states' interactions with one another and with the larger world.

Africa's International Relations During the Cold War

During the Cold War, the level of superpower competition in Africa waxed and waned. In this regard, superpower competition in Africa can usefully be divided into three periods. The period from 1956 to 1965 was one of escalating superpower competition, peaking with the Congo crisis in 1960 and winding down with the installation of a US ally (Mobutu Sese Seko) in Congo. The key event of 1956 was the Suez crisis, in which Egypt's sovereignty over the Suez Canal was successfully asserted. In this crisis, the impotence of Britain and France in Africa was displayed by the failure of these two powers to reclaim their colonial-era influence over Egypt, by then ruled by Gamal Abdul Nasser. The Suez crisis thus marked "the beginning of the end" of British and French colonialism in Africa (Kyle 1991). Paradoxically, the Suez crisis also marked the beginning of superpower competition in Africa. The paradox lies in the fact that although both superpowers disapproved of the British-French-Israeli military effort to prevent Nasser from asserting Egyptian control over the Suez Canal, they had a major confrontation over how to resolve the crisis. The Soviet Union had provided arms to Nasser before the crisis began (Gaddis 1998) and then sent letters to anti-Nasser belligerents and to US president Dwight Eisenhower in the midst of the crisis threatening to intervene on Egypt's behalf (Kyle 1991). In response, the United States forced its allies out of Egypt but also adopted the Eisenhower Doctrine, which asked Congress "to agree in advance to military action in support of the territorial integrity and political independence of states in the Middle East, states who requested such aid 'against over armed aggression from any nation controlled by International Communism'" (Kyle 1991: 527).

In a subsequent period, from 1965 to 1974, the level of superpower competition was much lower. The United States began a major escalation of its war in Vietnam with the insertion of ground troops there in 1965, and it was preoccupied with Vietnam for the next eight years. Meanwhile, the Soviet Union was occupied by domestic issues during this period, as discussed later. After the United States withdrew its forces from Vietnam in 1973 and after President Richard Nixon's resignation in the wake of the Watergate scandal in 1974, US leaders remained uninterested in competition in Africa. Under President Gerald Ford and an anti-interventionist Congress, the United States declined to pursue vigorously its competition with the Soviet Union in Angola, and a Marxist, pro-Soviet regime came to power there (see case study at end of chapter).

A renewed period of Soviet-US competition in Africa began in 1975. Along with Angola, the other former Portuguese colonies, Guinea-Bissau and Mozambique, gained independence under Marxian regimes in that year. The 1970s were also the high tide of the ideological influence of official Marxism-Leninism in the developing world, including Africa. New rulers who came to power in Congo-Brazzaville (1968), Somalia (1969), Benin (1972), and Ethiopia (1974) declared official state Marxism in the years after they seized power in respective coups (none of which involved superpower intervention). US leaders began to entertain renewed fears of the spread of communism in Africa. In the superpower competition that marked the Ogaden War between Ethiopia and Somalia in 1977–1978, the Soviets emerged with the relative victory. Thus, in the first half of the final period of Cold War competition, the Soviets appeared to take the initiative.

The high tide of Soviet influence in Africa gradually began to wane after the inauguration of US president Ronald Reagan in 1981. Reagan adopted a policy, later called the Reagan Doctrine, of providing assistance to rebel groups fighting against Marxist regimes across the developing world, including Angola. Although these were partly opposed by a Democrat-controlled US Congress, the policy marked a return to US contestation of apparent Soviet gains. Meanwhile, the Soviet Union entered a tumultuous political period with the death of Brezhnev in November 1982. Following the deaths of two subsequent Soviet rulers, Mikhail Gorbachev emerged as the Soviet leader in March 1985. Gorbachev soon announced himself to be an advocate of "new thinking" in Soviet foreign relations, favoring a de-escalation of tensions between the Soviet Union and the United States (as well as advocating for perestroika and glasnost—economic reform and openness, respectively—in domestic affairs). With the world's leading communist country apparently questioning its own principles of "democratic centralism" (party dictatorship), the ideological appeal of Marxism began to wane in Africa by the late 1980s. The contemporary economic crises of Africa's Marxist-Leninist regimes deepened doubts about Marxism as a development approach. The end of the Cold War in 1989 spelled the end not only of Marxist ideology in Africa but of the de jure one-party state model, as well.

Before the drama of the Cold War in Africa ended, however, it shaped the continent's international relations for three decades. In the sub-Saharan part of Africa, the Cold War could be said to have begun in its ideological dimension in April 1957, at the time of the so-called West African wager (see Woronoff 1972). In that month two new West African leaders squared off against one another ideologically. Prime Minister Kwame Nkrumah of Ghana adopted a stridently anti-imperialist stance toward the former metropoles and the West in general. In neighboring Côte d'Ivoire, Félix Houphouët-Boigny, the president of the Territorial Assembly, took an opposing stand, pledging postcolonial collaboration with France. Each new leader boasted that his ideology and international stance would deliver more for his people (also see Chapter 11). The West African wager thus represented both differing development philosophies and positions in the ideological competition of the Cold War.

The Congo Crisis

The Cold War came to Africa in a dramatic fashion with the onset of the Congo crisis in 1960. This multidimensional affair brought each superpower into competing sides of a civil war, setting the stage for future competitions. The episode also served to remind African rulers how competitive superpower interventions could rob them of their autonomy. Further, the Congo crisis became a critical reference point for the generation of African leaders who took power in the first wave of independence, from 1957 to 1964, in both domestic and international policies.

The Congo crisis actually entailed many overlapping elements, including four major ones discussed here. The superpowers became involved in all four over the 1960–1964 period. The first element was contestation over the purposes of the United Nations Operation in the Congo (ONUC), which began in July 1960. Under the terms of Congo's independence from Belgium, achieved on June 30, 1960, Belgian officers remained in Congo in command of the Congolese army, and Belgium retained access to two military bases in the country.[10] When the Belgian army commander addressed Congolese noncommissioned officers on the day after independence, he told them that nothing had changed and that Belgium was still in charge. Mutinies soon broke out at military bases and in cities across the country. Some of the rebellious Congolese troops began assaulting European (mostly Belgian) expatriates living there.[11] On July 8, Belgian forces began counterattacks on the mutinous Congolese troops, quickly deploying many of the 2,500 Belgian troops already in the country and flying in more from Belgium. Congo's new leaders, President Joseph Kasavubu and Prime Minister Patrice Lumumba, were aggrieved, feeling that Congo's former colonizers were reasserting their control. The two leaders then jointly sent two successive telegrams on July 12 and 13 to United Nations Secretary-General Dag Hammarskjöld, asking for UN intervention in Congo to help expel Belgian troops. The second of these telegrams clearly specified the reason for the request:

> The Government of the Republic of the Congo requests urgent dispatch by the United Nations of military assistance. This request is justified by the dispatch to the Congo of metropolitan Belgian troops in violation of the treaty of friendship signed between Belgium and the Republic of the Congo on 29 June 1960. Under the terms of that treaty, Belgian troops may only intervene on the express request of the Congolese Government. No such request was ever made by the Government of the Republic of the Congo and we therefore regard the unsolicited Belgian action as an act of aggression against our country.[12]

The Security Council responded with unusual rapidity, authorizing the use of UN troops in Congo the very next day and then actually dispatching the first troops on July 15, 1960. Although the motivation for the Congolese request for UN intervention was clear, the actual resolution (S/4387) that authorized ONUC was less clear; it spoke vaguely of helping Congo's national security forces "to meet fully their tasks." Indeed, the resolution was intentionally left vague so as to gain the agreement of the permanent members of the United Nations Security Council (UNSC). In their attempt to create a neutral mission for Congo, however, UN diplomats opened the way for superpower competition over ONUC. US officials generally took the view that the main purpose of ONUC was to restore order in Congo, and particularly to protect Europeans there. For the Soviets, on the other hand, the main purpose of ONUC was to help the Congolese expel Belgian troops, and also to restore Congolese authority in Katanga (see later and Clark 1992).

Each side tried to push Secretary-General Hammarskjöld and the successive special representatives reporting to him in opposite directions. By September 1960, Khrushchev was so angry that he proposed that the UN revise its charter to replace the single secretary-general with a troika of three representatives, representing the West, the Eastern bloc, and neutral countries, respectively. Various African countries were divided over the ONUC mission; Guinea, Ghana, and Egypt took a position close to that of the Soviets, and others took a pro-US view. The UN was generally more responsive to Western concerns than to those of the Soviets and Eastern bloc and intervened on behalf of pro-Western forces (Schmidt 2013). As a result, many African leaders became deeply suspicious of the UN, and no further UN missions were dispatched to the African continent until 1988 (in Angola), as the Cold War wound down.

A second element of superpower contestation in Congo was the clash over how to deal with the attempted secession of Katanga province. In the midst of the disorder caused by the rebellion of Congolese soldiers, Moïse Tshombe, the governor of Katanga, declared the province independent on July 11, 1960. Katanga was the center of copper and cobalt mining in Congo, and Belgian troops assisted the nascent government of the province to (briefly) establish its independence. Belgium hoped that it might maintain a neocolonial presence in Katanga, even if it lost influence in the remainder of Congo (Gibbs 1991). The Soviet Union, on the other hand, wanted ONUC and the international community to provide immediate aid to Congo to reassert its authority in Katanga and expel the Belgians there. Indeed, the Soviet Union dispatched military aid to the Congolese government at the secret request of Prime Minister Lumumba in August 1960 (Hoskyns 1965; Kalb 1982). As for the United States, it preferred a negotiated settlement to the secession, brokered by Hammarskjöld or other international mediators, but not a military assault on Katanga. Most important, US officials were thoroughly alarmed when they learned that the Soviets had secretly sent military aid to Lumumba in Congo to help reintegrate Katanga (Devlin 2007). That mission was finally achieved with UN support in 1962 (O'Brien 1962).

A third element of contestation in the Congo crisis revolved around the gulf that opened between President Kasavubu and Prime Minister Lumumba, and the two superpowers took sides. The two leaders had different personalities, and different worldviews: Kasavubu was quiet, deferential to authority, and quite open to collaboration with the West, if not Belgium; Lumumba was a fiery orator, a militant anti-imperialist, and a fervent advocate of autonomous African development, possibly with Eastern-bloc aid. Although the two had responded jointly at the outset of the crisis, Kasavubu was subsequently alarmed by Lumumba's strong anti-Western rhetoric. When he learned of Lumumba's secret overtures to the Soviets for aid, he announced that he was dismissing Lumumba as prime minister on September 5, 1960. In the National Assembly, however, Lumumba's National Congolese Movement (MNC) and its allies held a plurality of seats, and he was generally more popular. Not lacking in confidence, Lumumba rejoined that *he* was then dismissing Kasavubu, a political move not permitted under the constitution. When Kasavubu then sent police to arrest Lumumba, UN forces protected him, leaving him effectively under house arrest. In this standoff and the general split of the Congolese government that ensued, the United States supported Kasavubu and other pro-Western forces, whereas the Soviets supported Lumumba and his allies. When the US diplomats and CIA agents based in Leopoldville began to perceive that Lumumba would ask for massive intervention, they began to develop plans for an assassination attempt (Devlin 2007; Schmidt 2013). However, Lumumba escaped from his house arrest (and UN protection) in November and was arrested by forces loyal to Kasavubu. According to one source (de Witte 2002), Lumumba was shortly thereafter transferred to the custody of Belgian and Katangan security forces in the Katanga region, where he was tortured and then murdered on January 17, 1961.[13]

The fourth element of conflict in Congo concerned a succession of rebellions over the following year. Once again, the superpowers supported competing sides. Following the arrest of Lumumba, many of his supporters attempted to set up an alternative government in the eastern city of Stanleyville (now Kisangani). The Soviet Union provided some modest support to this alternative government (Kalb 1982: 169). The United States backed a succession of new prime ministers named by Kasavubu over the next several years, including Justin Bomboko, Joseph Ileo, and then Cyrille Adoula (1961–1964), including with considerable military equipment (Devlin 2007). Congo faced another major crisis beginning in January 1964, when pro-Lumumba rebels of a different political party (the Parti Solidaire Africain) took over a large portion of eastern Congo, including Stanleyville. Belgian troops brought to Stanleyville on US Air Force planes were eventually used to put down this rebellion in November 1964. In the midst of this crisis, Adoula was actually replaced as prime minister by none other than Tshombe, a political eventuality most unlikely in the absence of Belgian and US intervention.

In November 1965, Colonel Joseph Mobutu, later Mobutu Sese Seko, took power in a coup d'état. Although the American CIA station chief denies orchestrating the coup, he did admit a close personal friendship with Mobutu going back to 1960, when Mobutu briefly took power (Devlin 2007). Mobutu remained a client of the United States for the next twenty-five years, until the end of the Cold War, receiving military and financial aid on a regular basis. Although both sides had intervened in the Congo crisis, the United States was the more aggressive intervener in the critical early years, and it brought its client to power. Mobutu did not go on to rule in a liberal fashion, either politically or economically; rather, he created a one-party state and nationalized all major foreign business enterprises. Mobutu *posed* as a grassroots African politician, renaming the country (as Zaire) and the country's major cities (the capital became Kinshasa). He also developed relatively close relations with the PRC and outwardly adopted some Chinese-style symbols, such as his famous *abacos* form of dress, even while he always turned to the United States for support in times of crisis.[14]

Africa's Cold War International Relations, 1965–1974
The decade following the end of the Congo crisis was one of relative quietude in Africa's international relations, despite the struggle to end white rule in southern Africa. Each of the superpowers appears to have been sobered by the potential for conflict in Africa, given that the strategic stakes for both were minimal. Meanwhile, African rulers surely witnessed the dangers of involving the superpowers in their domestic disputes. A large majority of African rulers were more interested in making themselves secure in power than they were in serving as pawns in a global superpower struggle. African states reached a sort of modus vivendi among themselves at the Addis Ababa summit in 1963, allowing for the formation of the Organization of African Unity. The signature of the OAU Charter signaled a reconciliation of the Casablanca and Monrovia blocs that had formed earlier. The PRC began its Great Proletarian Cultural Revolution in 1966 and was thus largely preoccupied at home; it was also effectively estranged from both superpowers during this time. France deepened its ties with all of its former colonies (save Guinea) during this period, providing domestic stability to most of them, while also engaging in economic exploitation and cultural imperialism. These practices at least served to minimize superpower competition in the former French colonies.

To begin with the Soviet Union, there was a major shift in that country's orientation toward Africa beginning with the ouster of Premier Nikita Khrushchev in October 1964. Khrushchev was overthrown by his colleagues, led by Leonid Brezhnev, in large part because of Khrushchev's perceived adventurism in foreign affairs. Khrushchev had failed to make the Western allies abandon Berlin in 1958–1959, he failed to bring a pro-Soviet government to Congo in 1960–1961, and he was then forced to withdraw Soviet missiles from Cuba following a US ultimatum in 1962. As for his African policies, Khrushchev's Soviet colleagues "doubtless suspected that he had misjudged the revolutionary potentiality of states like Ghana and Mali and oversimplified the formidable problems involved in any genuine socialist revolution in Africa.

[Accordingly], their decision to abandon Khrushchev's ideological gambit was the first notable feature of the new leadership's Africa policy" (Legvold 1970: 227). On the ground in Africa, Sékou Touré of Guinea proved to be an unreliable ally, zigzagging between state-socialist and market-oriented domestic policies, while alternatively courting donors in Europe and then the Eastern bloc. All of the states to which the Soviets had loaned money in West Africa came seeking debt relief in 1964 and 1965. The Soviets were closest by then to the Nkrumah regime in Ghana, but this country's economy was in shambles. When the Ghanaian foreign minister visited Moscow in early 1965, the Soviets refused to provide scarce hard currency to the regime (Legvold 1970). In 1966, Ghanaian coup-makers ousted Nkrumah from power with apparent US backing and without significant Soviet reaction.

As noted earlier, neither the Johnson nor the Nixon administration had much interest in Africa, except to minimize Soviet influence there. Given that the Soviets had begun exercising more caution under Brezhnev, the United States had little interest in Africa during this period beyond avoiding crises. Meanwhile, the United States became increasingly focused on the war in Vietnam at the start of this period. In March 1965, the United States sent its first ground combat troops into Vietnam, beginning a rapid escalation of forces whose numbers surpassed half a million by 1968. Economic investment in a few selected countries was the main US activity in this period, and there was a "flourishing American trade with South Africa and the Portuguese territories" in the mid-1960s (Lake 1976: 62). In 1965, moreover, the United States invested $650 million in white-ruled South Africa (Lake 1976: 62). Oil production in Angola began a steady climb in the late 1960s as foreign investment flowed in from Gulf Oil, a US company. Likewise, the United States maintained substantial investments in Liberia, ruled by a black Americo-Liberian minority, particularly in rubber production. The United States tried to present a kindly face to its African partners through modest foreign aid programs, including the Peace Corps, beginning in 1961.

Among African states, the perpetuation of Portuguese colonialism on the continent and white minority rule in southern Africa was the primary preoccupation during this period. In November 1965, the government of Ian Smith in Rhodesia made its famous Unilateral Declaration of Independence (UDI) from Great Britain under a white minority government.[15] Portugal refused to give up its African colonies (Angola, Guinea-Bissau, and Mozambique) in the early 1960s, when other European colonizers did so. By the mid-1960s, the Portuguese military was involved in open military confrontation with liberation groups in all three countries. South West Africa (now Namibia) remained a legal possession of South Africa, going back to the end of World War I. Even before the formation of the OAU, however, Africa's independent states had already begun to condemn apartheid (minority white rule) in public resolutions; after the advent of the OAU, the organization passed condemnatory resolutions against apartheid in nearly every year through 1991 (African National Congress 2017). The OAU regularly condemned colonialism in the Portuguese colonies until 1975 and white minority rule in Rhodesia (now Zimbabwe) until its end in 1980. Although independent African states were divided on a number of issues, they were united in their desire to end colonialism and minority rule in the remainder of the African continent.

The United States was generally ambivalent about the situation in southern Africa and Guinea-Bissau. On one hand, the United States had no interest in the perpetuation of either Portuguese colonialism or whites-only rule in southern Africa. Indeed, the US ambassador to the United Nations under President Lyndon Johnson, Arthur Goldberg, helped craft the UN Security Council Resolution (UNSC 217) that condemned the UDI in 1965 (Lake 1976). The United States duly levied economic and military sanctions against the new white regime in the following years; the United States also observed the international arms embargo against South Africa beginning in 1964. On the other hand, a series of concerns stayed the US hand in coming out forcefully for the liberation of southern Africa and Guinea-Bissau: first, in its military efforts against the Soviet Union in Europe and the Middle East, the United States relied heavily on its military bases on the (Portuguese) Azores Islands (Lake 1976); second, many of the liberation movements in southern Africa had Marxist political orientations or, like the African National Congress, alliances with communist parties; third, the United States regarded South Africa as a reliable ally in its anticommunist efforts; and fourth, the United States had some substantial business interests in southern Africa and was responsive to the rather reactionary positions of private capital interests.

The balance between these competing views of US interests shifted with the advent of the Richard Nixon administration in 1969. After coming to office, Nixon put together an interdepartmental group of African policy specialists from the State Department (a progressive domain), the National Security Council (a conservative bastion), and other agencies tasked with reviewing US policy in Africa. The interdepartmental group's work ended with a report laying out five options, ranging from the full normalization of relations with the whites-only regimes to a complete severance of relations with them in protest of their discriminatory policies (Lake 1976). After a review, the administration chose the second option, which permitted greater contact with these regimes and a "relaxation of American measures against the white regimes" (Lake 1976: 128). This new US policy of greater engagement with the white minority and colonial regimes continued throughout the Nixon and Ford administrations.

If the Nixon administration felt it was taking a stronger anticommunist line in southern Africa, the Soviet leaders correctly perceived an opportunity in the new policy. In the early 1970s, Soviet leaders began to substantially increase the amount of aid that they were providing to liberation movements in southern Africa (Schmidt 2013). Although Brezhnev and his colleagues did not put Africa near the top of their concerns,[16] they clearly saw an opportunity to benefit at the expense of their Cold War adversary. It was clear that the United States was failing to realize its objectives in Vietnam in the 1960s, and in 1973 the United States withdrew from Vietnam, allowing Ho Chi Minh to unite Vietnam under communist rule in 1975. The result showed both the lack of US resolve and the pluckiness of determined insurgent forces battling regimes deemed to be "colonial." In addition, the tide of history was clearly against both colonialism and white minority rule; both practices were condemned with increasing vehemence in international forums by the early 1970s. Moreover, Marxist insurgencies, ideologies, and regimes were in vogue in the early 1970s, from Asia to Latin America to several new regimes in Africa. Finally, China threatened to fill the void if the Soviets failed to provide more aid to African insurgencies (Schmidt 2013). In Africa, anticolonial insurgencies and their supporters were heartened by the evolution of international rhetoric and increased support from the Soviet Union and China.

Africa's Cold War International Relations, 1975–1988

Beginning with the Angola crisis, the level of superpower competition in Africa once again escalated. In the decade that followed President Nixon's resignation from office, a majority of African states favored Soviet (and Chinese) policy on the continent over that of the United States. The beginning of this period marked the end of Portuguese colonial rule in Africa and the advent of new Marxist regimes on the continent. Thereafter, pressure on the white minority regime in Rhodesia became intense. The Lancaster House Agreement, signed in December 1979, facilitated a ceasefire in the war there and a transition to majority rule. A number of African states beyond southern Africa opted for Marxist governments during this period of time. At the United Nations, apartheid in South Africa became a perennial issue for discussion. In the annual votes against apartheid, the Soviet Union was aligned with majority African opinion, favoring nonviolent and violent struggle against the discriminatory practices. Meanwhile, Jimmy Carter's anti-apartheid policies, adopted in 1977, did not go nearly far enough for most African countries; the constructive engagement policy of President Ronald Reagan was even less popular. Thus, the Soviet Union was far more "aligned" with Africa during this decade than was the United States.

The armed struggles of the anticolonial insurgency groups in Portuguese Africa put increasing pressure on the neofascist regime in Portugal by the early 1970s. In April 1974, a group of progressive, anticolonial Portuguese military officers staged a coup, and Portugal's African empire quickly began to unravel. In Guinea-Bissau, the leader of the main independence movement, Amilcar Cabral, had been assassinated in a plot organized by the Portuguese secret police (Schmidt 2013), but the country acceded to its independence peacefully in 1974. Mozambique, Cape Verde, and then Angola all acceded to their independence in the following year (Schmidt 2013). Unfortunately, Angola and Mozambique subsequently became arenas of fierce superpower struggle, with interventions on both sides of their respective civil wars. In both cases, officially Marxist-Leninist regimes came to power, and both were contested by rebel groups who claimed to have a different ideology, though each was just as distinguishable by its ethno-regional base. The civil wars in both countries continued until after the end of the Cold War. The complex case of Angola is explored at the end of this chapter.

As the civil wars of southern Africa continued, one of the Cold War's most bizarre developments soon unfolded in the Horn of Africa. Following the overthrow of Ethiopian emperor Haile Selassie in 1974, politics in the country grew increasingly bloody and chaotic under the Derg (meaning "military committee" in Amharic) government led by Haile Mengistu Mariam. At this time, Ethiopia was still aligned with the United States, going back to the 1950s; the putatively Marxist regime in Somalia run by Siad Barre, meanwhile, had acquired Soviet backing and arms in return for allowing the Soviet Union to build a naval base at Berbera, among other considerations (Schmidt 2013). Meanwhile, Somalia had irredentist claims over parts of the Ogaden region of Ethiopia, populated largely by ethnic Somalis. Taking advantage of the growing chaos in Ethiopia, Siad Barre ordered tens of thousands of Somali troops into the Ogaden to support a liberation front for ethnic Somalis in July 1977. In response, and in the face of advancing Somali troops, the leftist Derg quickly called upon the Soviets for military assistance. After trying and failing to reconcile its existing ally with its potential new one, Soviet leaders faced an intriguing problem: whether to continue backing their established ally (Somalia) or to come to the assistance of the revolutionary Derg in Ethiopia. Realizing that Ethiopia was ultimately a more powerful partner, and perhaps led by a more reliably Marxist regime, the Soviets opted to aid Ethiopia. Beginning in September 1977, the Soviets began airlifting $1 billion worth of arms and supplies, some 1,000 Soviet military personnel, and later 18,000 allied Cuban soldiers and advisers into Ethiopia (Schmidt 2013).[17] After the end of the war in 1978, the United States later began to provide military aid to the Barre regime in Somalia and gained access to the erstwhile Soviet naval bases there. Thus, "by 1978, Somalia and Ethiopia had effectively switched sides in the Cold War" (Schmidt 2013: 150).

Although the late 1970s marked the pinnacle of Soviet power in Africa, Soviet influence there proved short-lived. Soviet expenditures abroad were one cause of a prolonged stagnation of economic growth at home from 1975 to 1985. By the time Gorbachev came to power in 1985, the country was virtually broke. Under his rule, the Soviet Union sought to reduce its foreign obligations, reach accords with the United States, and undertake domestic reforms. In that context, the Soviets began to negotiate with the United States on how to end superpower support for the competing sides in the ongoing civil wars in southern Africa. In December 1988, the two superpowers were parties to an agreement in which each side pledged to reduce its commitments in the Angolan civil war (see later), effectively marking the end of the Cold War in Africa. By 1990, Namibia had at last gained independence, and Nelson Mandela had been freed from prison in South Africa. By 1992, none of the nominally Marxist-Leninist regimes in Africa remained.

Interpreting the Cold War in Africa

Recalling the theoretical approaches to international relations reviewed in Chapter 1, realism seems an obvious candidate to help us understand the Cold War in Africa. Each of the two superpowers quite clearly feared the gains that the other might make on the continent. Both wanted to deny the other access to strategic shipping lanes, raw materials to feed industrial complexes, and ideological allies. The latter were particularly important in international forums such as the UN, where African states represented a major voting bloc. During the Cold War, scholarly analysts implicitly aligned with their own national governments and warned of the dangers represented by the other side.[18] Toward the end of the Cold War, some scholars (e.g., Laïdi 1990) began to interpret superpower competition in Africa from the outside. For their part, African regimes were able to play on superpower fears to gain both economic and military assistance. Such assistance was valuable not only in their rivalries with one another, such as that between Ethiopia and Somalia, but also for domestic political reasons: many African rulers sought external support to bolster their regime security (David 1991; Clark 2001b), fearing both military coups and rebellions.

United Nations Secretary-General Dag Hammarskjöld embodied the liberal view at the start of the Cold War in Africa: he sought to restore order there (as the United States wanted), to have the Belgians depart quickly (as the Soviets wanted), and to have Katanga peacefully reintegrated into the country. Many US policymakers essentially had a liberal view of Africa during the Cold War, even if these views were tempered by fears of a Soviet advance. For instance, G. Mennen Williams (1969) and Anthony Lake (1976) were typical liberals in the policymaking establishment. Williams (1969) called for an early end to Portuguese colonialism whereas Lake called for tougher sanctions against South Africa in protest against apartheid. Lake, Williams, and many others like them hoped that Africa could establish independence from outside powers, start along a path of autonomous development, and develop multiparty political systems like those in the West. They believed that Western engagement could help African states realize such ends.

Neo-Marxist views of the Cold War in Africa deem US policies to have been essentially harmful to the economic welfare and political ambitions of the continent. Although the likes of Lake or Williams could be critical of specific US policies, they never questioned America's basically good intentions. Critical thinkers in IR, however, made much deeper critiques of US policy. For instance, George White (2005) argued that US policies in Africa, especially into the 1960s, were essentially a reflection of domestic racism within the United States, including in its policymaking establishment. David Gibbs (1991) criticized the West from a political economy perspective, arguing that both the United States and Belgium had their economic interests foremost in mind while pursuing their policies in the Congo. Ebere Nwaubani (2001) combines an analysis of both American domestic racism and its economic interests in Africa to explain the failure of the United States to push its European allies to grant independence to their African colonies in the 1950s, points of view that could equally be applied to later periods.

In addition to these views, constructivist accounts of both superpower and African attitudes toward one another are valuable to our understanding. The normative consensus that African rulers achieved at the founding of the OAU on principles such as nonintervention and the need for the complete liberation of Africa from foreign and white minority control shaped how they saw superpower activities in Africa. The Soviet model of development, based on the transformation of industrialized economies, had little relevance to newly independent

Africa. Yet the Soviets strongly supported African autonomy from the West and the completion of liberation from colonialism. These stances gave the Soviet Union more leverage in Africa during the 1960s and 1970s than its modest ability to support economic development would otherwise have. Both the United States and the Soviet Union had self-identities as pro-liberation countries, just as each perceived—or "constructed"—its adversaries as an embodiment of imperialism. These identities allowed each superpower to pursue its goals in Africa in a self-righteous and ideological fashion. As for the interests that realists perceived each superpower to have in Africa in the 1970s, constructivists would counter that these "interests" were in fact normative constructions of foreign policy establishments. In this view, the superpower interests defined as the denial of space to the adversary would evaporate instantly with the end of the Cold War.

Case Study: Angola in the Cold War

The first phase of the Angolan civil war (1975–1990) had all the ingredients of an African Cold War conflict. These included a stubborn colonizer (Portugal) that was unwilling to give up power; multiple contestants to take power after the colonizer could be driven out; multiple ethnic constituencies on whom these contestants could draw for support; African state sympathizers, whose regimes perceived an interest in the outcome of the contest; and, of course, external superpowers with the willingness to intervene in the conflict. While the epic Soviet-US rivalry was ongoing, the civil war in Angola was often depicted in the scholarly literature as a Cold War conflict carried out through local proxies, both within and contiguous to Angola. In reality, the roots of the Angolan civil war lay within the country itself (Guimarães 1998).[19] The intervention of the superpowers in Angola, as well as that of other interested parties, only served as accelerants to the flames that engulfed the benighted country even before its independence.

The roots of the Angolan civil war lie in the three national liberations movements that emerged. First to appear was the Movement for the Popular Liberation of Angola (MPLA) in 1959 or 1960, though a fabricated official history claimed that the movement was created in 1956 (Guimarães 1998). The MPLA had an ethno-regional base in the capital city, Luanda, and its hinterlands, notably among the mixed-race (*mestiço*) population and the Mbundu ethnic group living in the area. Some *assimilados* ("assimilated") Angolans of other ethnicities living near the capital also adhered to the MPLA beginning in the 1950s. Agostinho Neto, medical student and poet, emerged as the group's leader after his escape from a colonial prison in 1962. The second liberation group to emerge was the National Front for the Liberation of Angola (FNLA), formed in March 1962, replacing the defunct Union of Angola Peoples (Guimarães 1998). The FNLA had an ethnic base among the Bakongo people of northern Angola, the group from which its leader, Holden Roberto, hailed. In 1964, the FNLA's foreign minister, Jonas Savimbi, resigned from the movement, and in 1966 he formed the National Union for the Total Liberation of Angola (UNITA). UNITA had an ethno-regional base among the Ovimbundu of southern Angola, the country's largest ethnicity, of whom Savimbi was a member. Savimbi claimed to be disillusioned with the FNLA's lack of practical action against the Portuguese.

As Fernando Guimarães notes (1998), it was not the case that ethnic difference led to the formation of three different liberation groups; rather, three competing leadership sets exploited different ethno-linguistic constituencies for their own ends. Further, the basis of competition among the three leaders and their parties was more personal than ideological. All three movements were anti-imperialist and nationalist in orientation, although each was subsequently shaped by its external patrons. The MPLA's officially Marxist orientation corresponded with its constituency basis in urban areas, whereas UNITA's original Maoist orientation reflected its rural constituency in the south. From the FNLA, Roberto's anti-imperialist credentials were as strong as those of Neto or Savimbi, though he was influenced by his friends in Leopoldville, Congo, which had a pro-Western government by 1962.

Indeed, patronage from the outside had a major influence on the orientation and direction of the three liberation groups. Neto undertook a tour of the United States in 1963 in search of political support, but he was essentially rebuffed (Guimarães 1998). The MPLA received arms and aid from "radical" African regimes like those in Ghana, Morocco, and later Congo-Brazzaville, which has a border with the Angolan enclave of Cabinda. According to the US State Department (cited in Marcum 1978), the Soviet Union and its Warsaw Pact allies gave the MPLA approximately $63 million between 1964 and the start of the Angolan civil war in 1975. Independently, Cuba established links with the MPLA leadership in 1965 and began to provide military training, arms, and advice (Guimarães 1998). Meanwhile, the FNLA's Roberto had established ties with the United States and received limited financial support (the amounts were the subject of controversy) throughout the 1960s, possibly into the 1970s. After being abandoned by the Nixon administration, Roberto's organization began to receive military training and weapons from China in 1973. At this time, despite being a US ally, Mobutu was also friendly with China, and Chinese aid was channeled through Kinshasa. As for Savimbi, he also tried to cultivate Chinese aid, albeit with less success than Roberto up until 1974 (Guimarães 1998).

The April 1974 coup in Portugal set off a chain of events in Angola involving a civil war and far more overt foreign intervention. Following a period of turmoil in Portugal, its new ruler, Antonio de Spínola, announced on July 27, 1974, that all of the country's foreign territories would be granted independence. Since Angola had three competing liberation parties, Portugal was forced to negotiate with all three to provide a modality for independence. The result was the Alvor Accords of January 1975. These accords arranged for a transitional government including a troika presidency representing the three groups and elections for a new government. The country was to gain independence on November 11, 1975.

Instead of orderly elections, however, fighting among the three groups ensued, accompanied by escalating foreign interventions. The local Portuguese high commissioner, Silva Cardoso, claimed that the government could not intervene in the fighting under the terms of the Alvor Accords; local Portuguese troops, feeling resented by all, refused to enter the fray without orders; and the metropolitan Portuguese government was undecided about how to respond (Guimarães 1998). This confusion encouraged the belligerents to increase their attacks upon one another.

Meanwhile, the foreign backers of the three liberation groups began scaling up their assistance. China was the first to step up aid, sending over a hundred military advisers to Kinshasa to support the FNLA military in May 1974, followed by 450 tons of arms in August (Guimarães 1998). The Soviet Union, perhaps in response, began channeling increased aid to the MPLA through the OAU's Liberation Committee in the same month. In October, the Soviets began delivering large-scale arms caches directly to the MPLA via Brazzaville. By March 1975, the Soviets were delivering huge shiploads of arms, including armored vehicles, directly to Angolan territory.[20] Meanwhile, "between April 1974 and January 1975, Washington did not intervene in any significant way in Angolan political affairs" (Guimarães 1998: 189). The CIA did approve a $300,000 grant to support the FNLA in the latter month, but this support reached the FNLA only belatedly (Guimarães 1998: 189). The FNLA received far more support from the Mobutu regime in Zaire. Unlike in the Congo crisis of 1960–1961, then, the United States was by far the more timid intervener. Further, UNITA was not receiving any substantial outside support at this stage.

In Pretoria, South Africa's apartheid government watched events in Angola with alarm. Since the end of World War I, South Africa had ruled neighboring South West Africa (Namibia) as a colony. In 1960 a group of Namibia liberation leaders created the South West African

People's Organization (SWAPO) to contest South African rule. The apartheid government (correctly) feared that SWAPO would receive aid from the nascent Marxist regime in Luanda. Thus, the Angolan civil war entered a new phase in August 1975 when South African ground troops moved into southern Angola, ostensibly to protect a joint South African–Portuguese hydroelectric project there (Hanlon 1986).[21] South Africa began passing large quantities of weapons to UNITA and training UNITA troops. In October 1975 a large South African armored column, accompanied by UNITA and mercenary forces, began advancing from southern Angola, pushing to within 200 miles of Luanda by the end of the month (Guimarães 1998). In response, Cuba began flying in troops (on Soviet aircraft) to Luanda on November 7, beginning with a "crack battalion" of 650 troops.[22] These troops helped the MPLA hold on to the capital city of Luanda until the country's scheduled independence day. Accordingly, the MPLA was able to declare Angola independent with itself as the legal government on November 11. Cuban troops and Soviet arms continued to flow steadily into the country over the following months. By February 3, 1976, the MPLA was supported by 14,000 Cuban troops and equipped with Soviet arms including armored cars, tanks, MiG aircraft, and helicopters. The FNLA was soon routed by these Cuban troops and MPLA fighters, and the remnants retreated to Zaire. In February 1976, three further events sealed the MPLA's victory: South Africa (temporarily) withdrew its forces, and UNITA retreated to the country's southern periphery; the OAU officially recognized the MPLA as the legitimate government of Angola; and the United States cut off all further aid to its Angolan allies under the Clark Amendment. Thus, the MPLA prevailed in this Cold War contest for power with the help of its Cuban and Soviet allies.

Alas, for the Angolan people, 1976 was hardly the end of the civil war.[23] In the following years, South Africa provided arms and training to the UNITA rebels in southern Angola. It repeatedly sent military expeditions into the country and attacked MPLA/Cuban elements from the air (Hanlon 1986). In response, the number of Cuban troops continued to increase, ultimately reaching a peak of some 50,000, always backed by Soviet advisers and equipment. Without the presence of these Cuban troops, South African forces would have surely overrun the MPLA government in Luanda. The war dragged on for more than a decade, with South Africa periodically launching incursions into Angolan territory from Namibia. In turn, the Angolan army periodically launched unsuccessful offensives aimed at a final defeat of UNITA forces. Neither side had any real hope of defeating the other. The MPLA government of Eduardo dos Santos proved itself to be a deeply authoritarian regime, whereas UNITA engaged in diamond smuggling and indiscriminant murders against anyone thought to be supporting the MPLA.

Finally, in 1985, the US Congress repealed the Clark Amendment, which had blocked US aid to the FNLA in 1976. The Ronald Reagan administration quickly resumed its aid to UNITA, portraying Savimbi as an anticommunist freedom fighter. This move bolstered UNITA politically and raised the fears of the MPLA that UNITA would be revitalized and pose a major threat to MPLA control of the country. The MPLA government, backed by its communist allies, decided to make one last push to break UNITA's power and capture Savimbi. After several months of preparation and rearmament by the Soviet Union, Angolan government and Cuban forces launched a major offensive from the city of Cuito Cuanavale against UNITA forces concentrated in the southwestern Angolan town of Jamba in August 1987 (Polack 2013). The South Africans responded by mobilizing forces already in southwestern Angola and northern Namibia in a major counterattack. As UNITA forces backed by South African arms and air power approached Cuito Cuanavale, the Cubans committed more of their troops to the battle, and the Soviets more arms. The series of offensives and counteroffensives that ensued became known as the Battle of Cuito Cuanavale, a military confrontation that ground to a stalemate by March 1988.

By this juncture, the Soviets had grown tired of funding the Cuban presence and faced their own internal financial problems; in the United States, the Reagan administration had become embroiled in the Iran-Contra affair and was ready for a symbolic victory in Angola (Pazzanita 1991). In fact, negotiations for the removal of Cuban troops from Angola in exchange for concessions from South Africa had begun in late 1987, even as fighting raged in southeastern Angola. After one year of negotiation, the result was the Angola-Namibia Peace (also "Tripartite") Accord of December 1988, signed by Angola, Cuba, and South Africa. Under the terms of the accord, South Africa was to withdraw its troops from Angola and organize elections in Namibia leading to its independence. In return, Cuba and Angola were to arrange the phased withdrawal of Cuban troops over a thirty-month period. All parties kept to the agreement, the first phase of the Angolan civil war ended, and Namibia gained its independence in March 1990. A UN mission, the United Nations Angola Verification Mission (UNAVEM), oversaw the process, verifying that each party was keeping its part of the agreement. Thus ended superpower involvement in the deadliest Cold War conflict in Africa.

Subsequent events, however, serve to reinforce the notion that the conflict in Angola was not primarily ideological or a pure creation of superpower competition. As the international parties were implementing their respective obligations under the Tripartite Accord, negotiations between representatives of the MPLA and UNITA were meeting under Portuguese mediation. In May 1991, the parties reached the Bicesse Accords (named for the Portuguese city where they met), providing for an integrated Angolan army and national elections to be held within one year. The accords were to be supervised by a follow-on UN mission, UNAVEM II, whose mandate was later expanded to elections supervision. When the elections took place, in September 1992, President dos Santos prevailed by a margin of 49.6 percent versus 40.6 percent for Savimbi. Under the electoral law, there should have been a second round. Instead, Savimbi rejected the results of the first round and then refused to go to the Angolan capital to negotiate; MPLA supporters were soon murdering Ovimbundu citizens in Luanda (Rothchild 1997), and a return to war shortly ensued. Tens of thousands more Angolans perished in this renewed fighting as first UNITA and then gradually the MPLA government seized control of the country's major cities. During this fighting, the Angolan government depended upon its oil revenues to provide the funding to buy arms that it had once received from the Soviet Union. For its part, UNITA depended largely on the revenues of diamonds smuggled out of the country, with the willing complicity of the international diamond trade (Global Witness 1999). When neither side could ultimately take control of the country, they returned to the bargaining table and eventually agreed to the Lusaka Protocol, which essentially returned to the principles of the Bicesse Accords. UNAVEM III was established to implement this agreement.

Despite this agreement and the new UN mission, the two parties were again soon at war. Both the United States and United Nations gradually turned against UNITA, imposing various sanctions on the organization. In April 1997, the Angolan government and UNITA agreed to a government of unity and national reconciliation, but each side remained in sole possession of various towns and territories within the country. Nonetheless, in June 1997, the UN allowed the mandate of UNAVEM III to expire, replacing it with a token observer mission. The new unity government quickly ceased to function, and war between the parties began once again, each side continuing to depend upon oil and diamond revenues, respectively, to finance their arms purchases. UNITA increasingly behaved like a terrorist organization, firing on the aircraft of humanitarian agencies like the World Food Programme, and kidnapping individuals for ransom. The Angolan government meanwhile became distracted when it intervened in the wars of Congo-Brazzaville and the DRC (see Chapter 7). In 2001, fighting once again intensified between the two belligerents.

Finally, the Angolan government gained the upper hand and killed Savimbi in a gun battle in the eastern province of Mexico in February 2002. Soon afterward, the leadership of UNITA began to bicker among themselves, and the organization sued for peace. In October 2002 UNITA finally agreed to disband its armed forces, and it declared itself a political party. The MPLA has prevailed in all of the elections subsequently held in Angola, including those in 2002, 2008, and 2017. After his forty years in power, dos Santos did finally give up power to a successor, João Lourenço, after the elections of August 2017.

Notes

1. The NAM continues to exist, with a rather different focus since the end of the Cold War. Indeed, every single contemporary African state (except South Sudan) is a member of the organization. For one positive assessment of the achievements of the NAM, see Morphet 2004.

2. For one representative view (from an establishment, liberal Democrat), see Williams 1969. For a critical view of US policy, emphasizing American racism and US indifference to decolonization in West Africa, see Nwaubani 2001. Ebere Nwaubani's book reopened a debate over the extent to which the United States supported decolonization in the 1950s.

3. In particular on this divergence of views among new African elites, see Woronoff 1972.

4. In 1971, the PRC replaced the Republic of China (Taiwan) on the United Nations Security Council as the official representative of China.

5. In September 1961, these twelve states became the founding members of the Union Africaine et Malgache, an organization that maintained close relations with France.

6. Morocco's government was not particularly radical in 1961, nor has it been since. At the time, however, Morocco was hoping to enlist any potential friends in its contemporary efforts to annex Mauritania, following that country's liberation from French colonial rule.

7. It was closed at the request of the Ethiopians in April 1977, after they aligned themselves with the Soviet Union (Ottaway 1982).

8. Modern socialism would require a well-developed industrial economy, including the formation of a bourgeoisie independent of the state and a class of industrial workers (i.e., proletariat). In the 1960s, no African state except South Africa was industrialized. Accordingly, both the proletariat and the bourgeoisie were tiny (the "political class" being much larger than the capital-owning class). Rather, the large majority of Africans were peasants, while the wealthier "classes" were indigenous authorities or those connected with service in the postcolonial state.

9. ZANU later forcibly incorporated ZAPU under its umbrella, creating the ZANU–Popular Front (ZANU-PF).

10. Such arrangements were not unusual for France's former colonies, many of which provided for the continuing presence of French aid workers and military officers after independence.

11. Catherine Hoskyns's (1965) early work on the Congo crisis is one of the best and also most neutral accounts of the beginning of the Congo crisis. On the events recounted here, see pp. 85–92 in her book in particular.

12. UN Security Council Document S/4382, available at http://www.un.org/en /ga/search/view_doc.asp?symbol=S/4382.

13. Although Ludo de Witte's account of Lumumba's demise seems compelling and is broadly confirmed by Larry Devlin's account (2007), there remains some controversy over the exact circumstances of Lumumba's apparent murder.

14. *Abacos* is a shortened version of the French expression "Á bas le costume," literally meaning "down with the business suit." The style is similar to the so-called Mao jacket adopted in China. Mobutu's close relations with China suited the times by the early 1970s. After President Nixon's visit to China in 1972, the United States and the PRC were broadly aligned in their opposition to the threat of Soviet expansionism.

15. Smith declared the independence of Rhodesia under minority white rule at this time because Britain was beginning the process of organizing Rhodesia's independence under majority rule.

16. See Andrew 2006; note the scant attention given to Africa and its placement in the analysis of the study.

17. For an excellent full account of the Ogaden War, see also Ottaway 1982. East Germany also provided some support troops, and North Korea and South Yemen provided other forms of assistance to Ethiopia.

18. See, for instance, Klinghoffer 1980 and Tarabrin 1980, respectively.

19. This section relies significantly on the neutral summary of Fernando Guimarães (1998). Arthur Klinghoffer (1980) provides a more pro-American and anti-Soviet view; Joseph Hanlon (1986) provides a view sympathetic to the cause of black African liberation in southern Africa.

20. For details on the Soviet escalation of arms shipments, see Clark 1992.

21. See this same work, Hanlon 1986, for other instances of South African interventions against the so-called Frontline States during the 1970s and early 1980s.

22. Most analysts now agree that Cuba was already planning to send additional military assets, including advisers and arms, to Angola before the South African intervention (Guimarães 1998).

23. For a reasonably neutral account of the remainder of the Angolan war, see Weigert 2011.

PART 2

The Pursuit of Freedom and Development

4

Foreign Aid and Economic Conditionality

Despite the continent's abundant natural resources and human capital, many African countries remain heavily dependent on foreign aid nearly sixty years after independence. Having steadily risen over three decades to nearly $30 billion in 1994, according to the World Bank's *World Development Indicators* (2017b), official development assistance[1] (ODA) to sub-Saharan Africa declined markedly in the late 1990s. It increased again after 1999, dropped during the global recession in 2007–2008, and climbed slowly thereafter to about $45 billion in 2016.[2] Africa receives more aid as a percentage of gross national income (3.03 percent in 2016) and more total ODA than any other region. Sub-Saharan Africa is second only to the Middle East and North Africa with respect to aid per capita ($43 in 2016). By almost every measure, therefore, sub-Saharan Africa is the world's most aid-dependent region, though there is significant variation by country.[3] In contrast, the region received just 1.7 percent of total global foreign direct investment in 2016, vastly disproportionate to its share of the world's population (13.9 percent) (World Bank 2017b).

Africa's dependence on foreign aid has both international and domestic political implications. Although most of this chapter explores how African states and peoples experience foreign aid, one cannot ignore the fact that the donors have nonhumanitarian motives, some more explicit than others. In promoting the development of African economies, many donor governments aim to create larger markets for their country's own exports. International aid is a big industry in some countries, as evidenced by the large number of contractors (or "beltway bandits") in the Washington, D.C., area. There are commercial interests at stake too, with a significant portion of aid from countries like France and the United States tied to the purchase of goods and services from those countries. And, of course, foreign aid reflects donor political considerations, including the need to recruit allies and win votes at the United Nations. As a result of these incentives, there is a significant domestic constituency in many countries lobbying for the continuation of foreign aid. Even so, foreign aid constitutes a relatively small portion of most donor-government budgets. Opinion polls consistently show that Americans think the US government spends more than one-quarter of its budget on foreign aid, but the real figure is less than 1 percent (Rutsch 2015).

On the African side as well, there are clear motives for perpetuating this relationship. In many countries, foreign aid constitutes more than 50 percent of government revenues, making it crucial to the delivery of services such as education and healthcare. Even where governments have managed to reduce this dependence by increasing tax collection and revenues from other sources, foreign aid pays for programs that might not otherwise receive funding. Aid also provides African governments with a buffer, reducing the pressure on leaders to cut expenditures or change policies even when doing so might make economic sense. More worrying, foreign aid can allow illegitimate regimes to survive when they might otherwise collapse.[4] To put Africa's dependence on foreign aid in perspective, the post–World War II Marshall Plan at its peak provided Western Europe with about 2.5 percent of its gross domestic product (GDP) (Moyo 2009). Aid to sub-Saharan Africa reached 7 percent of GDP in the 1990s, though it has since dropped to around 3 percent as income has increased (World Bank 2017b). Although the short-term Marshall Plan was different in many ways, not least because it was for rebuilding instead of building (Moss 2004), tough questions remain as to why Africa does not have more to show for the decades of aid it has received (Lancaster 1999; Moyo 2009).

Over time, for a variety of reasons including but not limited to the desire to increase aid's effectiveness, donors attached a growing number of conditions to their overseas development assistance. Starting in the 1980s, donors increasingly required recipient governments to implement a range of neoliberal economic policies in order to keep the aid flowing. As explored in this chapter, such economic conditionality was intended to jump-start stagnant African economies, generate increased growth, and ultimately reduce reliance on foreign aid. The long-term effects were mixed, however, and varied among countries and individuals, resulting in diverse economic trajectories throughout the continent. Moreover, many of the effects—both negative and positive—that have been attributed to this process of structural adjustment took place in the context of major global economic changes, making it impossible to isolate a single cause. In the 1990s, as the Cold War ended, Western donors also started applying political conditions to their aid, requiring recipient governments to legalize opposition parties, allow independent media, and the like. This increasing use of political conditionality is the focus of Chapter 5. Despite the various conditions applied to aid, and at times because of them, there continues to be heated debate about the effectiveness and desirability of foreign aid to Africa.

The Pursuit of Development

African countries emerged from the colonial period as marginal players in the global economy. In addition to being exporters of raw materials, African economies were predominantly agricultural. The majority of African people made their living off the land using low-tech farm tools and machetes. Although these patterns were true earlier, colonialism ushered in a number of changes that set the stage for subsequent developments. In many areas, European officials sought to replace food crops with cash crops such as cotton, tea, and tobacco so that the colonies would cover their own administrative expenses. Colonial authorities exacted taxes that had to be paid in cash, forcing farmers to move away from subsistence production and making them more vulnerable to broader economic fluctuations (a family cannot eat tobacco if the market drops, after all). This contributed to the commercialization of land and labor in much of Africa as well, increasing the competition for control over such resources (Bates 1974).

Colonialism also established the government as the major player in each colony's economy. From the early development of state-owned enterprises and government monopolies to the provision of social services during the late colonial period, the European-run state intervened heavily in economic markets, establishing a system that would be inherited by independent African leaders. Marketing boards were established as the sole legal purchaser of crops in many colonies, for example, presumably to stabilize prices paid to farmers but also to regulate prices and production levels. An example is the Gold Coast Cocoa Marketing Board, which was established by the British in 1947 after a decade of volatility in the cocoa market that prompted unrest among farmers (Milburn 1970). There was also increasing social differentiation during this period between urban and rural areas and between the peasant majority and those involved in government, state-run enterprises (parastatals), and the small commercial sector. In some cases, based largely on connections to the colonial state, emerging class divisions reinforced existing ethnic divisions (Bates 1974). In Nigeria, for example, Ibo and Yoruba elites played up ethnic distinctions in an effort to capitalize on their positions of authority under the colonial system (Ekeh 1975). Such dynamics would complicate politics and governance for years to come.

In the context of these economic legacies of colonialism, national development was a key goal of African leaders after independence. Frequently with advice from Western economists, governments pursued various development approaches. In the 1960s and 1970s, many countries in Africa (and elsewhere) adopted a policy of import substitution industrialization (ISI), which was designed to increase the domestic production of manufactured goods that otherwise had to be imported. Policymakers taxed imports and subsidized local producers, though there was variation in the extent to which production was by private or state-run enterprises. Although ISI had some success in other parts of the world (especially India and Brazil), its impact in Africa was limited, and few countries achieved significantly higher levels of industrialization through their adoption of this policy. One reason was that Africa's relatively small domestic markets could not buy enough of the new manufactured goods to sustain those industries. This challenge spurred on efforts toward regional integration throughout the continent, as examined in Chapter 6, though politics and other factors thwarted many of those plans too.

In line with ISI policies, many African governments also overvalued their exchange rates during this period. By pegging their currencies to global currencies at rates that failed to reflect their actual values (17 Tanzanian shillings per US dollar in the mid-1980s, for example, when someone could get more than five times that amount per dollar from illicit currency traders), governments effectively made imports cheaper and exports more expensive. (In contrast, present-day China has been accused periodically of undervaluing its currency in order to promote exports.) Overvalued exchange rates were advantageous for elites who wanted to import cars, wine, and other products, and for manufacturers who wanted to import equipment, but undermined exports by making them more expensive on the global market.

With the push for industrialization in the 1960s and 1970s, many African governments neglected the agricultural sector. Smallholder farmers are the backbone of most African economies, but production of food crops was discouraged by government pricing schemes, poor infrastructure, minimal investment in agricultural research and extension services, and forced attempts at collectivization in some countries. As explained by Robert Bates in his classic *Markets and States in Tropical Africa,* agricultural policy was determined by political instead of economic rationales. To appease urban consumers, who posed the greatest political threat to existing leaders, policymakers kept food prices artificially low by overvaluing exchange rates (reducing the cost of imported food) and perpetuating the colonial system of marketing boards as the sole legal purchaser of farmers' crops (allowing the boards to set prices). These policies reduced incentives for producers (Bates 1981). There is some debate between Bates and another superstar in the study of African politics, Goran Hyden, as to whether African farmers sold instead to informal markets or simply withdrew to the pre-capitalist subsistence economy (Hyden 1980), but it is clear that government policies during this period undermined the agricultural sector as a potential engine of economic growth.

Although there were some efforts at diversification, including the ISI approach discussed earlier, most African countries continued to rely heavily on one or two export crops or minerals for the vast majority of their export earnings. Whether it was crude petroleum in Angola, diamonds in Botswana, cocoa in Côte d'Ivoire, coffee in Rwanda, or copper in Zambia, countries continued to be extremely dependent on the world market price for a single commodity. Unable to influence the world price due to the presence of many other global producers, many African economies rose and fell based almost entirely on fluctuations in that price. The dependence on a single commodity was particularly problematic for nonrenewable mineral resources, which cannot be sustained over the long term, and for crops such as coffee, for which there is a lengthy wait between planting trees and harvesting exportable beans.

Despite these many economic challenges, newly independent African governments made significant improvements in social service delivery. African leaders were under pressure to provide education, healthcare, and other services to their populations, and many invested a significant portion of government expenditures in these areas. School enrollment went up and rural health facilities were built, though the quality of such services varied. Unfortunately, these investments were expensive, particularly as improved healthcare led to reduced mortality and higher rates of population growth. As other areas of African economies stagnated, the investment in social services could not be sustained.

Overall, as we have seen, African governments pursued a variety of development strategies in the two decades after independence. Most sought to extract a surplus from the large agricultural sector in order to promote industrialization, though they often ended up undermining both sectors in the process. As in many contexts, policy decisions were not always motivated by economic efficiency and often reflected political priorities. Even so, many of these policies were recommended by Western economists and adopted in countries throughout the developing world. Over time, as agriculture was squeezed and industry faltered, the economic growth of African countries slowed and in some cases even went into reverse.

The Lost Decade of the 1980s

By the early 1980s, most African economies were in a state of crisis. After an initial period of expansion that led to growth rates averaging 4.1 percent a year in sub-Saharan Africa from 1961 to 1969 and an impressive 6.4 percent a year from 1970 to 1974, that figure dropped to just 2.3 percent on average between 1975 and 1979 (see Figure 4.1). With population growth hovering around 2.8 percent a year during the 1970s, per capita income actually decreased (World Bank 2017b). In five countries (Chad, Ghana, Madagascar, Zaire, and Zambia), GDP per capita in constant dollars fell by more than 15 percent from 1970 to 1980 (World Bank 2017b). Due largely to the challenges discussed earlier, agriculture had negative growth rates and production declined. In the late 1970s throughout most of Africa, trade and investment dwindled, living standards dropped, basic services deteriorated, and poverty spread. Earlier optimism about Africa's economic potential faded into the shadows as the focus shifted to basic survival.

Figure 4.1   Annual GDP Growth Rates for Sub-Saharan Africa, 1968–2016 (annual percentages)

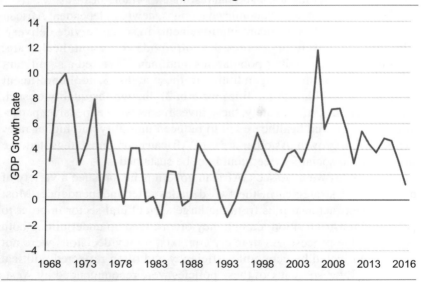

Source: World Bank 2017b.

What explains Africa's economic crisis? At the time, two highly publicized reports focused on very different sets of factors. In 1980, the Organization of African Unity released the *Lagos Plan of Action for the Economic Development of Africa,* which emphasized external obstacles to African development. These included the poor terms of trade faced by African countries as commodity exporters, their vulnerability to market fluctuations, and the drop in world prices of many commodities. The report also blamed the 1973 oil shock, when the Organization of Petroleum Exporting Countries (OPEC) reduced supply to drive up prices in response to Western support of Israel. Another price spike was triggered by the 1979 Islamic revolution in Iran, which generated fears about oil supplies. The dramatic increase in transportation costs associated with these shocks slowed growth in many countries. Interestingly, the spike in oil prices also created a huge surplus of "petro-dollars" from oil exporters, which banks sought to lend to any government that needed cash. This situation contributed to the dramatic increase in sub-Saharan Africa's external debt stocks, from $2.1 billion in 1970 to $60.7 billion just ten years later (World Bank 2017b). Although Africa's oil producers (Angola, Nigeria, Gabon, etc.) benefited from oil price hikes, they also managed to acquire unsustainable debt during the 1970s. There were thus a number of external sources of Africa's economic malaise.

The World Bank's 1981 *Accelerated Development in Sub-Saharan Africa* (commonly known as the Berg Report after its lead author, Elliot Berg) painted a very different picture of the roots of the African economic crisis. It focused almost exclusively on internal factors, and particularly on inefficient economic policies adopted by African governments. The report blamed currency overvaluation for discouraging exports and price controls for reducing incentives for agricultural production. Tariffs and other protectionist policies were allowing inefficient African producers to make subpar products, the report argued, rather than forcing them to compete with imports. On the budgetary side, governments were spending money to expand the civil service, increase armed forces, and dole out patronage, all of which increased loyalty and reduced threats to the incumbent regime but did little to promote growth. According to the Berg Report, therefore, solutions to Africa's economic situation would come through domestic policy changes.

In actuality, of course, the causes of Africa's economic crisis were not nearly as one-sided as either the Lagos Plan or the Berg Report implied. The crisis was caused by a combination of internal and external factors, including some the reports did not even explore. In seeking to explain Africa's slow rate of growth well into the 1990s, recent studies continue to blame internal and external policies while also examining the role of "destiny,"[5] or characteristics about African countries that cannot be changed (because of their geography, for example). Such factors include their tropical climate (and associated disease threats), poor soil, low population density, high diversity, and small markets. The continent's sixteen landlocked countries face additional costs and challenges as they seek to get their goods to global markets (Collier 2007; Gallup, Sachs, and Mellinger 1999). There is no simple explanation for Africa's economic crisis of the early 1980s; therefore, nor were there to be simple solutions.

By 1985, the overall GDP of sub-Saharan Africa in current dollars was below its level in 1960, and per capita income had dropped to $479 (World Bank 2017b). With such appalling official economic numbers, how did Africans survive? Many people disengaged from the formal economy and retreated into the informal (or parallel) economy, where transactions were not regulated or taxed by the government. Instead of seeking formal sector employment, people started their own income-generating businesses—selling vegetables on a local corner, smuggling fuel across an international border, hawking umbrellas on rainy days, peddling secondhand clothing, and the like. In the face of overwhelming obstacles, people devised creative ways to eke out a living (MacGaffey 1991). Vastly underrepresented in the formal sector, women were especially drawn to informal activities due to low barriers to entry and flexible work schedules (Jiggins 1989). A Tanzanian woman with little education could tie her baby to her back and sell home-cooked *mandazi* (doughnuts) outside an office building at lunch, for example, raising much-needed money for food, healthcare, and other household expenses.

Although accurate numbers are unavailable almost by definition, the informal economy probably was two to three times larger than the formal economy in many African countries during the 1980s. The relative importance of the informal economy in countries such as Zaire (now the Democratic Republic of Congo) led one scholar to call it the "real economy" during this period (MacGaffey 1991). Although many unregulated economic activities were technically illegal, few participants were arrested or punished, often because of government complicity. Many ground-level police officers and border patrol agents benefited from such activities—by demanding payments to avoid harassment, for example, or developing their own side businesses. In addition, the success of the informal economy took some pressure off top-level leaders to deliver stronger rates of growth and development in the formal economy. The flourishing informal economy undoubtedly allowed more people in Africa to survive, but official economies remained in a state of crisis with chronic and growing budget deficits. In this context, African governments were forced to look externally for assistance.

The Donor Prescription

One by one through the 1980s, African leaders sought economic assistance from international financial institutions, particularly the International Monetary Fund and the World Bank. Especially after 1982, when Mexico became the first in a series of countries to default on its international debt, private banks disappeared from lending markets and governments around the world could get loans only from the "lenders of last resort." From this powerful position, the IFIs advocated a process of structural adjustment to generate renewed economic growth in struggling economies. Using an approach known as conditionality, the IFIs required recipient countries to implement certain policies in order to receive loans. Funds were distributed in portions (*tranches*) to ensure that the policies were sustained over time. Structural adjustment was guided by neoliberal economic assumptions that said that free markets, trade, and investment were the recipe for growth. Governments were thus told that they had to reduce intervention and liberalize markets to receive external loans.

Structural adjustment was initially envisioned as having two main phases (Callaghy and Ravenhill 1993). The first, known as stabilization and often administered through an agreement with the IMF, involved restoring macroeconomic stability and getting inflation under control over a period of one to two years. The second, administered through the World Bank, aimed to revitalize production and restore economic growth over three to five years. In actuality, however, these were not simple processes and took much longer than anticipated in most African countries (and elsewhere around the world). During the 1980s, thirty-six sub-Saharan African countries entered into structural adjustment programs (SAPs) through the IMF and World Bank (van de Walle 2001). Despite the promise of renewed growth, in part through aid and investment, most were still undergoing structural adjustment reforms more than a decade—and often two—after initiating the process (van de Walle 2001).

Structural adjustment through the IMF and World Bank involved four broad sets of policy conditions (Clapham 1996). The first was currency devaluation, through which exchange rates were meant to more accurately reflect the underlying value of a country's currency. Because currencies had been deliberately overvalued, the process of devaluation would effectively increase the price of imports, including oil, but would also make the country's exports cheaper and thus more attractive to buyers. On paper at least, currency devaluation was an easy process and could often be done with the stroke of a pen, meaning that it was among the first reforms implemented in many countries. Some governments opted to devalue by simply changing the amount to which their currencies were fixed; in 1994, for example, the CFA franc used by fourteen African countries was devalued from 50 CFA per French franc to 100 CFA per French franc. Other governments floated their currencies, allowing forces of supply and demand to determine their values against other major currencies. After Tanzania floated its shilling in 1993, the value dropped from 505 shillings to the US dollar in 1994 to 791 in 2000 (and 1,325 ten years later) (OANDA n.d.). Currency devaluation initially generated inflation as prices adjusted to the new exchange rates, but price levels typically stabilized within a few years.

Another requirement of structural adjustment was for African governments to balance their budgets by reducing costs and increasing revenues. Among the policies advocated by the World Bank and IMF to reduce costs was downsizing the civil service, which had become bloated in many African countries. Throughout the 1960s and 1970s, university graduates were essentially guaranteed government jobs, thus ensuring loyalty among people who were most likely to pose a political threat. With structural adjustment, the promise of a career in the civil service for new graduates disappeared as governments slowed the growth of hiring. Some existing civil service positions also were eliminated, though not as many as governments initially promised (van de Walle 2001). The IFIs also advocated cuts in military spending to reduce deficits, but few African states took that advice. On the revenue side, and quite controversially, the IFIs encouraged governments to impose "user fees" to recover some costs of delivering social services. These fees were typically quite low by Western standards (about $1.50 for a year of primary school in Tanzania in 1996, for example), but posed considerable hardship for poor families trying to care for their children. Many families were forced to make tough choices about which children to send to school, sometimes choosing to educate boys but not girls. Fees also were imposed for health services and for public secondary schools and universities.

A third set of structural adjustment policy conditions focused on trade and price liberalization. The core idea was to reduce government intervention in the economy and to allow market forces to determine prices and distribution. African governments were required to reduce tariffs that had been used to protect domestic producers and open their markets to outside goods. This forced the products of domestic manufacturers to compete with imported goods, though devaluation helped counteract this effect some by effectively making imports more expensive. Governments also had to eliminate subsidies to domestic producers and get rid of price controls. On the whole, trade and price liberalization were more complicated than some of the other required reforms and involved many different policies. Given the vested interests, many African states resisted making these reforms (van de Walle 2001). As a result, they took longer to implement than planners at the World Bank and IMF had anticipated.

Last, structural adjustment required African governments to privatize state-run portions of their economies. Going along with the price liberalization just discussed, governments were forced to dismantle the marketing boards that they (or their colonial predecessors) had established as the sole legal purchasers of various crops. Instead, private purchasers were allowed to enter the market and could compete with one another to buy farmers' crops. No longer required to sell to the state-run commodity board, farmers could sell their produce to the purchaser that offered the best price. The privatization of agricultural marketing reduced the ability of African governments to tax cash crops by paying farmers substantially less than world market prices, as the commodity boards had done. It also prevented policymakers from keeping food prices artificially low in cities, as discussed earlier. While beneficial to farmers in many ways, the elimination of marketing boards also ended existing systems through which farmers had obtained subsidized fertilizer and other inputs on credit to be paid with a portion of their harvest.

Another component of privatization required governments to sell off state-run companies, also known as parastatals. In many African countries prior to this time, railroads, airlines, industries, and even tourist hotels were owned by the government and run by public employees (often politically connected ones). Even countries like Kenya, Nigeria, and Côte d'Ivoire that adopted comparatively more capitalist approaches to development had a large number of state-run companies. Like governments, parastatals often had bloated staffs and were economically inefficient; many lost money. With structural adjustment, governments were required to sell these companies to private investors, who often laid off staff and tried to turn them around. A key challenge in Africa was the shortage of internal investors with enough capital to buy a large company; instead, foreign investors frequently swooped in and bought up key parts of the economy, raising concerns about where any profits would go. In other cases, neither local nor foreign investors were interested in buying indebted, overstaffed parastatals, leading to their liquidation. Such concerns slowed the process of privatization, which is still ongoing in many African countries. Recently, some countries have moved to the stock market to facilitate privatization and preserve some element of local control in the face of foreign investment (Lavelle 2004). Kenya, for example, attracted hundreds of thousands of new investors through initial public offerings of shares of the Kenya Electricity Generating Company (KenGen) in 2006 and Safaricom (a telecommunications subsidiary) in 2008.

Seeking to balance domestic political interests with global policy demands, African governments responded in a variety of ways to the structural adjustment prescription advocated by Western economists. In the 1980s, some leaders tried to avoid or delay economic reforms for as long as possible. Despite a severe crisis in Tanzania, for example, then-president Julius Nyerere resisted free market reforms that went against his long-standing ideology of *ujamaa* (African socialism). Eventually recognizing that policy changes were necessary, but not wanting to make them himself, Nyerere voluntarily resigned as president in 1985 and paved the way for his successor to implement a sweeping reform package. Interestingly, the delay may have made the reforms more palatable to Tanzanians as the economic situation became so dire that it demanded some sort of relief (Lofchie 1993).

Another group of African leaders took the opposite approach, embracing the structural adjustment process and going all out on the implementation of economic reforms. After coming to power in 1981 and 1986, respectively, Ghana's Jerry Rawlings and Uganda's Yoweri Museveni soon adopted full-scale structural adjustment programs. (Rawlings initially took a populist stance, but a drought and deep economic crisis by 1983 prompted him to reverse course and embrace the free market approach.) By the mid-1990s, both countries' economies were growing rapidly (though quite unevenly), causing them to be held up as success stories of structural adjustment by the World Bank. From the beginning, Rawlings and Museveni may have found it easier to implement structural adjustment than some of their counterparts. Ghana and Uganda were each coming off years of civil war that had disrupted existing economic systems. As new leaders who came to power through military means, Rawlings and Museveni were not beholden to the same types of vested political interests, enabling them to implement tough economic reforms without fear of alienating their support bases.

Somewhere between these poles, the most common response among African leaders was to accept the conditions of structural adjustment loans but drag their feet on implementation, particularly of the most politically unpopular reforms (Moss and Resnick 2018; van de Walle 2001). Leaders such as Daniel Arap Moi in Kenya made the policy changes that were minimally necessary to get the next *tranche* of funds from the World Bank or IMF and often blamed any slippage on pressure from disgruntled citizens. Indeed, there was limited public support among Africans for structural adjustment. The losers of these reforms included laid-off civil servants and parastatal employees, university students facing higher fees and reduced job prospects (particularly in government), urban consumers paying more for food, and rural populations whose services were cut or made more costly. Facing immediate losses, many of these groups were concentrated in urban areas, allowing them to organize large protests against structural adjustment. In contrast, people who had the most to gain from these reforms over the long term (but often not immediately) were more spread out and less organized. They included farmers getting better prices for their crops, exporters who benefited from devaluation, and entrepreneurs who could take advantage of privatization. Due largely to political pressure, therefore, consistent and successful implementation of structural adjustment programs in Africa was rare. In the 1990s, as pressure increased for political reform (see Chapter 5), African leaders often abandoned unpopular economic reforms to increase their chances of winning the next election.

It is difficult to assess the results of structural adjustment in Africa, in part because of incomplete implementation. To some extent, nearly forty years later, the process is still ongoing, as many countries continue to move hesitantly toward greater economic liberalization and privatization. Supporters claim that structural adjustment has helped African economies, while critics argue that inappropriate economic policies made the crisis worse. It is clear that the economic turnaround in African countries was slower than expected, if it happened at all. From 1990 to 1994, sub-Saharan Africa's economy grew at just 0.4 percent per year on average (see Figure 4.1). Annual regional growth rates improved to 3.4 percent on average from 1995 to 1999, jumped to 5.5 percent from 2000 to 2009, and dropped back to 3.9 percent from 2010 to 2016. With population growth rates steady around 2.7 percent annually, the region's GDP per capita grew by an average of just 2.1 percent per year from 2000 to 2016 (World Bank 2017b).

Moreover, economic trajectories have varied widely among African countries (Moss and Resnick 2018). Eight economies had average annual growth rates above 7 percent in the late 1990s and twelve surpassed that impressive threshold from 2003 to 2008 before the global recession. From 2010 to 2016, just four countries had average annual growth rates above 7 percent: Ethiopia, Ghana, Rwanda, and Zimbabwe (World Bank 2017b). Counterbalancing these are other African countries whose economies have stagnated or declined, often as a result of political crises. For example, the economy of Côte d'Ivoire, once a star economic performer in West Africa, shrunk during a civil war in the early 2000s and again during the post-election crisis of 2010–2011 (see Chapter 11) before rebounding to notable growth rates above 8 percent since 2014. Countries still experiencing political violence have seen no such bounce. The economy of South Sudan, since the country gained independence in 2011 and descended into civil war two years later, has shrunk by an average of more than 8 percent annually (World Bank 2017b).

There are various reasons for the mixed results of structural adjustment in Africa. Free market reforms exposed African economies more fully to global fluctuations, contributing to growth in boom periods but making it difficult to avoid recessions. Structural adjustment focused on policy changes but did little to address other problems hindering African development, including poor infrastructure, primary-commodity dependence, tropical diseases, and soil quality. Perhaps most important, global investors did not live up to their end of the "implicit bargain" of structural adjustment: if policymakers reformed their economies, foreign direct investment (FDI) would be forthcoming (Callaghy 1993). In contrast to Asia and Latin America, countries in Africa that embraced structural adjustment did not see the promised increase in foreign investment. Instead, Africa's share of global FDI decreased dramatically in the 1990s as investors gravitated toward new opportunities in Eastern Europe and Latin America. In 1995, for example, Colombia and the Czech Republic each received more FDI than all of sub-Saharan Africa combined (Bräutigam 1998). The failure of foreign investment to materialize discouraged the few African leaders who had implemented sweeping reforms and gave additional excuses to the many who were dragging their feet.

Regardless of development outcomes, one clear result of structural adjustment across Africa was a huge increase in external debt. This was diametrically opposed to the original intent of these programs, which aimed to reduce the debts that governments had amassed during the global economic crisis of the 1970s. But structural adjustment was promoted by the World Bank and IMF through loans that governments were ultimately expected to pay back. When African economies did not turn around as quickly as economists had predicted, governments struggled to stay current on loan payments. By the mid-1980s, the region was paying out more money each year to service its huge debt than it was receiving in aid and new loans. Sub-Saharan Africa's total external debt stocks increased from $60.7 billion in 1980 to $213.4 billion in 2000 (World Bank 2017b). Instead of reducing African debt, then, structural adjustment exacerbated the problem. As critics blasted structural adjustment and defenders argued that African economies would have been even worse without it, attention increasingly shifted to how these countries would emerge from the massive debts they had accumulated over several decades.

Dealing with Debt

As the structural adjustment process continued throughout the 1980s, there was a growing realization in some circles that the external debt of developing countries in Africa, Asia, and Latin America was becoming unsustainable. Early on, no one wanted to talk about the debt issue, especially creditors who assumed they would get their money back. By the late 1980s, however, due in part to pressure from Catholic campaigners in Latin America, bilateral creditors under a negotiating umbrella known as the Paris Club started rescheduling the debts they were owed. This move benefited countries in Latin America and Asia more than Africa, where more external debt was to multilateral creditors like the World Bank and IMF. By 1995, for example, an average of 44 percent of African countries' debts were to multilateral creditors, compared to 32 percent in Latin America; in seventeen African countries, including Burundi, Ghana, Malawi, and Uganda, multilateral debt constituted more than half of the total (World Bank 2017b). Moreover, rescheduling debt meant simply changing the terms of payment plans, not reducing the total amount of debt stock owed. The assumption remained that structural adjustment would generate renewed growth and ultimately allow countries to repay their debts in full.

In the 1990s, as the full promise of structural adjustment failed to materialize, especially in Africa, and external debt continued to grow, activists dared to start talking about debt forgiveness. Drawing on the Old Testament tradition of jubilee, under which debts were forgiven every fifty years, a creative public relations campaign known as Jubilee 2000 pushed creditors to forgive developing countries' debts at the new millennium, allowing for a fresh start. The movement attracted support from both the left and the right, including U2 lead singer Bono, retired boxer Muhammad Ali, Pope John Paul II, and several conservative Christian leaders. Activists highlighted the economic need for developing countries to come out from under massive external debts but also focused on the moral imperative. As more developing countries held multiparty elections during this period, debt relief advocates drew special attention to the problem of "odious debt" that had been accrued by corrupt authoritarian leaders who were no longer in office and yet their countries were still required to pay it back. As popular support for debt relief increased in the early 1990s, several donor countries, including the United States, the United Kingdom, and France, started to forgive portions of their bilateral debt. This paved the way for multilateral creditors to develop similar programs (Moss and Resnick 2018).

The World Bank and IMF launched the Heavily Indebted Poor Country Initiative (HIPC) in 1996 and revised it three years later because of initial slow progress. Countries are determined to be eligible for HIPC if they qualify for World Bank and IMF assistance, have a track record of sound reform policies (i.e., structural adjustment), and face an unsustainable debt burden (calculated as a complicated ratio of debt to export earnings). Of the forty-one original HIPC-eligible countries, thirty-three are in sub-Saharan Africa.[6] Once deemed eligible, countries must maintain their policy track record, develop a poverty reduction strategy (PRS), and agree on a plan to clear their arrears with creditors. At the decision point, countries get some initial debt relief, but creditors reserve the right to reverse course if policy changes do not continue. The IFIs also agree with the government in question on certain triggers to reach the next step, such as fighting corruption and developing transparent budgeting processes. If the policy record continues, the PRS is implemented for a year, and the agreed triggers are achieved, a country reaches the completion point, at which a portion of its debt stock is irrevocably canceled.

Ten years after HIPC was launched, the World Bank and IMF supplemented it with the Multilateral Debt Relief Initiative (MDRI). Under this program, at the completion point, a country gets 100 percent cancellation of its debt to specific units within the IFIs (the International Development Association, which is the World Bank's concessional loan arm, the African Development Fund, and the IMF). Creditors initially resisted the idea of 100 percent forgiveness due to concerns about moral hazard: if a country's debt is totally canceled, what will stop leaders from running up debt again in the hopes of similar forgiveness in the future? Pressure from activists like Bono turned the tide in favor of 100 percent forgiveness, but only to certain creditors. Policymakers also were influenced by the experience of some early countries to reach the HIPC completion point such as Uganda and Mozambique, which closely followed IFI prescriptions and received some debt relief but still faced onerous debt obligations. By 2017, thirty African countries had reached the completion point and received significant relief under these programs; three others (Eritrea, Somalia, and Sudan) were still eligible, but their respective governments were doing little to move toward relief (International Monetary Fund 2016b, 2017b).

Through HIPC and the MDRI, debt stocks of completion countries were reduced by 90 percent and debt service obligations were cut by 44 percent by 2013. The programs have provided more than $116 billion in debt relief, which is substantial (International Monetary Fund 2016b).

Even so, there are lingering concerns. Although the intent is for countries to use their savings from debt relief to fight poverty, it is unclear whether the process is having any significant impact on poverty levels. In addition, several African countries—most notably Nigeria—are not eligible for HIPC because their export earnings are too high (though it has received some relief through related programs). Many countries continue to face bilateral debt, for which there has been some relief (especially from Paris Club members) but most need more. Finally, with the global recession of 2008–2011, which saw increases in fuel and food prices, many African countries that received debt relief through HIPC and the MDRI started taking on additional loans. Indeed, recent data show that debt service obligations are creeping upward again in HIPC countries (International Monetary Fund 2016b), suggesting that the problem of external debt is likely to trouble African countries for years to come.

The Nongovernmental Sector

Over time, an increasing share of foreign aid has been channeled through nongovernmental organizations working in target countries. By the late 1990s, for example, roughly a third of US development assistance was going through NGOs (Lancaster 2000). This shift toward NGOs has been due primarily to donor concerns that governments in recipient countries are not using aid resources as effectively and efficiently as possible, even squandering them in some cases. NGOs can be an attractive alternative because they tend to focus on service delivery, particularly in underserved communities, and they typically have people on the ground implementing grassroots programs. Even so, as critics have noted, the assumption that NGOs necessarily make better use of aid funds than government agencies is simplistic and may reflect a romanticized notion of such organizations (Makumbe 1998).

Millions of aid dollars each year are directed through international NGOs with headquarters in cities like Washington, D.C., New York, London, and Paris. Indeed, some international aid organizations such as CARE, the International Rescue Committee, and Save the Children get more than a third of their revenues from donor governments. These NGOs have offices in countries around the world, with staff typically a mixture of expatriates and locals. There is thus an entire industry focused on the pursuit of international development (Hancock 1989; Moyo 2009). Channeling donor funds through these organizations has several advantages. Many people involved in development work have built up a wealth of experience and are able to apply lessons learned in one context to challenges in another. More broadly, some organizations have developed expertise in specific sectors (Oxfam with water, for example) that they can implement across a variety of settings. NGOs typically move more quickly than government bureaucracies, due in part to less red tape, and can be involved more readily in emergency relief work (in times of drought or conflict). Finally, international NGOs especially have additional funding streams (individual contributors, private foundations, etc.) that supplement the funds they get from donor governments and broaden the reach of their work.

Not surprisingly, however, there are concerns about channeling aid through international NGOs. Observers question the motives of these organizations (Murdie 2014), which make millions of dollars and support thousands of employees with money intended to bring about development in poor areas of the world. If they are effective in their work, development-focused NGOs in particular should essentially put themselves out of business, an eventuality they do not always appear to be pursuing (Hancock 1989). Given the amount of money NGOs get from donor governments, there also are concerns about the extent to which they are truly independent of the foreign policy objectives of those donors. In many situations, they work more like private contractors than autonomous nongovernmental bodies (Mills 2005). Unlike democratically elected governments, NGOs are not accountable to citizens of either the donor country or the recipient country through elections. Although some NGOs have incorporated beneficiaries into program evaluation processes, there continue to be serious power imbalances and concerns about who should have the final say on development projects (de Waal 1997a). Empirical analysis of the effects of international NGOs around the world shows that they tend to be more successful in promoting basic human rights than in pursuing broader economic development, and that they are most effective when they have support from the host state and society (Murdie 2014).

In addition to this network of international NGOs, there has been an explosion of local NGOs and community-based organizations (CBOs) in African countries in recent years. The number of registered NGOs in Tanzania, for example, increased from 224 in 1993 to 8,360 just four years later (Tripp 2000). Among the factors contributing to the exponential growth of the NGO sector have been the availability of money from international donors, development needs created by Africa's economic crisis and structural adjustment, openings for civic activity facilitated by political liberalization since the 1990s, and challenges associated with the region's HIV/AIDS epidemic (Tripp 1994). In a context where governments were unable or unwilling to meet growing development needs, private citizens came together to form NGOs and CBOs—ranging in size from a few people to thousands—to fill in the gaps. Over time, some organizations, especially those with entrepreneurial leaders who can put together solid grant proposals, have managed to secure funding for their work from international donors. Perhaps even more so than with international NGOs, donors are attracted to local NGOs that are seen as working most directly with community members who will benefit from aid projects.

Once again, though, it is important not to romanticize the work of these local African NGOs and CBOs. Many organizations have limited capacity to implement their proposed development projects. Indeed, there are many examples of people who write great proposals to get funding but have little to show for it in the end. Like their international counterparts, many local NGOs are not internally democratic and often are run in a hierarchical manner. In some cases, the founding president of an organization remains in that position for years and even decades. Often with little awareness among donors, local NGOs sometimes promote sectarian agendas along ethnic or religious lines, seeking to assist members of their own group while neglecting others (Makumbe 1998). Though there are also many examples of local African NGOs bridging ethnic and religious divides (Tripp 1994), there continue to be concerns about their accountability. Many of these organizations are also highly dependent on donor funding, raising questions about whether their agendas are driven by local or outside interests (Makumbe 1998). As substantial portions of foreign aid are channeled through both international and local NGOs, therefore, it is necessary to evaluate each organization and assess the extent to which it is actually meeting local development needs.

The Debate About Aid Continues

In the late 1990s, as US policymakers debated the African Growth and Opportunity Act (AGOA) (see Chapter 10), a new mantra emerged with respect to African development: "trade not aid." Aid would simply perpetuate Africa's dependence, proponents argued; long-term growth could only be achieved through international trade and investment. Critics like Nelson Mandela countered that Africa needed both trade *and* aid, and that the playing field of international trade would not be level without continued aid. Regardless, few questioned the need for Africa to increase its exports and attract foreign investment to facilitate economic growth. Due in part to concerted efforts by policymakers and financiers, sub-Saharan Africa's share of global FDI increased (though still not to a level proportionate to its population, as mentioned at the beginning of this chapter) and stock markets throughout the continent grew.

Even as Africa's attractiveness to investors increased, concerns remained about the extent to which international trade could bring about broad-based sustainable development. Foreign investment in the region is still driven largely by natural resources, especially oil, although there is evidence of growth in service sectors (Ernst and Young 2014). The discovery of oil in places like Ghana, Uganda, and Kenya has raised hopes for more investment and income in those countries, as well as concerns that they could face governance challenges similar to some of the region's traditional oil exporters (Nigeria, Angola, Equatorial Guinea, etc.). Among other consequences, heavy reliance on mineral extraction can cause serious environmental damage and health problems, and the profits typically are not shared among the population. With the possible exception of diamonds in Botswana (which itself is not without critics; see Good 2008, 2010; Taylor and Mokhawa 2003), mineral extraction has rarely generated widespread development in Africa. Many oil companies such as Chevron and British Petroleum have development accounts that fund local education and health projects, but these are often ineffective public relations schemes that cost peanuts compared to the billions of dollars the companies earn from Africa's resources. If mineral resources continue to be the main focus of foreign investment in the region, the potential to raise living standards for the majority of Africans is limited.

Looking beyond minerals to agriculture, African countries can do little to influence world market prices for most commodities because there are so many producers. Profits are minimal and many farmers struggle to cover costs, again raising questions about whether trade in this sector can generate long-term development. Hoping to address some of these challenges, the growing "fair trade" movement seeks to get farmers better prices for their products and to invest some profits in grassroots projects. Under various certification schemes, farmers agree to conditions such as using organic inputs or not using child labor and are guaranteed higher prices. Their products are then certified as fair trade and sold around the world, often at premium prices. With encouragement from groups like Fair Trade USA and the World Fair Trade Organization, retailers in wealthier countries carry everything from fair trade coffee, chocolate, and tea, to fair trade cotton sheets, lip balm, and cut flowers. Some large retailers such as Walmart and Target have even started their own fair trade product lines.

However well-intentioned, there is some debate about the value of fair trade programs (Fridell 2007; Raynolds, Murray, and Wilkinson 2007). They raise the incomes of participating farmers only slightly and fund small-scale projects, but they cover just a tiny fraction of Africa's farmers, mainly because of low demand for higher-priced fair trade products. The vast majority of coffee, cotton, and cocoa is still produced and marketed through traditional mechanisms. Perhaps more important, these programs typically work through existing supply chains where decisions are made outside of Africa and thus do not fundamentally transform the power imbalances faced by farmers (Bassett 2010). (Indeed, a much more dramatic—but politically difficult—way to increase prices for *all* West African cotton farmers would be to eliminate US subsidies to its cotton farmers, which drive down the world market price; see Heinisch 2006; Watkins 2002.) Although fair trade programs may not be able to drive Africa's development, they do have some positive effects. In West Africa, they have increased women's participation in cotton cultivation, improved quality, and facilitated the diffusion of organic farming techniques (Bassett 2010). More broadly, fair trade programs provide consumers with choices and raise awareness about the challenges faced by African farmers, perhaps ultimately helping to bring about policy changes that will provide better opportunities.

In the long term, economic development in Africa seems most likely to be generated by international trade and private investment in minerals, agriculture, and the growing industrial and service sectors, not by highly publicized government development projects funded by foreign aid. Such projects are important in providing the human capital and infrastructure to support other economic activities. Businesses need an educated and healthy workforce, for example, as well as reliable roads, ports, electricity, and telecommunications networks. Governments also have a role in reconciling competing political interests to determine regulatory frameworks that will help ensure any development is broad-based and sustainable. Foreign aid may help enhance the capacity of African governments in some of these areas, but it is the resources, innovation, and human capital within Africa that will determine economic results over the long term.

More than at any time since the end of colonialism, then, African countries are on diverse economic trajectories. Some economies (Rwanda, Uganda, Ghana, Tanzania, Ethiopia) are moving in a fairly positive direction with comparatively high growth rates, increased diversification, and rising living standards, though they face lingering problems of poverty and inequality. Other economies have stagnated or even declined, often in association with political instability (the Central African Republic, South Sudan, Somalia). Clearly, structural adjustment and other donor-prescribed development policies have not generated consistent results across the continent. Many countries continue to grapple with high external debt and low levels of foreign investment. Even some of the region's established middle-income economies (Botswana, Namibia, South Africa) continue to rely on foreign aid in certain sectors, especially health.

Whether in the form of grants, projects, or concessional loans, African countries have received billions of dollars in foreign aid since independence, and most will continue to need foreign aid for years to come. And yet what does Africa have to show for all of this? The latest round of the long-standing debate over the effectiveness of aid to Africa was sparked by the 2009 publication of Dambisa Moyo's *Dead Aid: Why Aid Is Not Working and How There Is a Better Way for Africa*. In her book, the Zambian-born economist describes a long list of negative effects of systematic aid to Africa (which she distinguishes from humanitarian and charity-based aid): it prevents bad governments from falling; it encourages corruption; it creates bureaucracy and red tape; it undercuts local producers by providing free products like mosquito nets and food; and it brings in foreign currency, which can cause inflation and distort exchange rates.

In line with these critiques, many economic studies find no significant correlation between foreign aid and economic growth, or a positive relationship only under very specific conditions (Burnside and Dollar 2000; Collier and Dollar 2002; Dalgaard, Hansen, and Tarp 2004; Easterly 2003; Mallik 2008). Moreover, the priorities of international donors do not always match those of beneficiaries, resulting in projects that fail because of insufficient local support. Despite the billions of dollars donors have put toward fighting HIV/AIDS in Africa, for example, resources have been squandered and redirected, in part because most Africans are more concerned about clean water and education than they are about this particular disease (Dionne 2012; Dionne, Gerland, and Watkins 2011). For a variety of reasons, therefore, foreign aid has not always achieved its claimed objectives in Africa.

Nevertheless, as argued most forcefully by economist Jeffrey Sachs, foreign aid has had some successes in Africa. Sachs leads the Millennium Villages Project, which uses a multisector aid approach to promote sustainable development in fifteen target villages in ten African countries. In a series of attacks on Moyo's book (Sachs 2009; Sachs and McArthur 2009), Sachs notes that critics of foreign aid have themselves benefited from government scholarships and other assistance programs. More substantively, he lists many improvements in Africa since independence, especially in health and education: child mortality has declined, adult literacy has increased, and primary school enrollment is up. These are real benefits for real people. Foreign aid has helped achieve these goals, Sachs claims, even if the cycle of aid dependency in Africa has not yet been broken (due in part to other problems such as tropical diseases and the lack of a green revolution). Supporters thus acknowledge that foreign aid has often been inefficient and ineffective, but they say reform is the solution, not ending aid altogether.

As the debate continues, there are few signs that foreign aid to Africa will stop anytime soon. Many players have a vested interest in perpetuating the current system, including African leaders wanting to balance their budgets (and stay in power), aid workers pursuing careers in this field, development organizations applying for government contracts, donor governments seeking to win diplomatic support at a relatively low cost, and indeed local beneficiaries who want their school renovated or a water project built with external support. As we have seen in this chapter, conditionality has become increasingly common, with donors requiring specific economic reforms from recipient countries. A key question moving forward in Africa is whether the current system can survive the growing presence of China, which offers significant funding to African countries with few policy conditions (see Chapter 12). While African leaders clearly are attracted to aid with few strings attached, most continue to seek funding from traditional Western donors. The jury is still out on whether China will find the need to impose more conditions on its aid, or whether Western donors will loosen their requirements. For now, the systems exist side by side, and African leaders have more options from which to seek their desired foreign aid.

Case Study: Economic and Political Reform in Ghana

As the first sub-Saharan African country to gain independence, Ghana (the former Gold Coast) was a center of euphoria and optimism in 1957. Its pan-Africanist leader, Kwame Nkrumah, gained a reputation throughout the region for promoting independence from colonialism and decreased reliance on foreign aid. A nominal Marxist, Nkrumah embraced his version of African socialism and increasingly turned to Eastern-bloc countries for support. Despite some early gains, including in the important cocoa sector, his economic policies ultimately failed to deliver as promised and his political style became increasingly authoritarian. While on a state visit to China in 1966, Nkrumah was overthrown in a military coup d'état and lived out his life in exile as the personal guest of Guinean president Ahmed Sékou Touré. Ghana descended into a fifteen-year period of political instability, marked by a series of military coups against short-lived civilian governments, during which the economy declined dramatically.

In 1981, two years after he turned over power to a civilian government, Flight Lieutenant Jerry Rawlings staged his second coup d'état and took power for the long term. At first, he pursued the same economic approach as his predecessors, which involved heavy government intervention and a large number of government-run enterprises. Continued economic decline and threats to his power soon led Rawlings to shift gears, however, and in 1983 his government implemented a sweeping program of economic liberalization with support from the IMF and World Bank. The Ghanaian cedi was devalued, price controls were gradually eliminated, and government expenditures were slashed, all with the goal of allowing market forces to work. Although many reforms were politically difficult, and provoked widespread protests among Ghanaian citizens, Rawlings was relatively new to power and did not face the same network of entrenched interests as some of his counterparts elsewhere in Africa. Despite the opposition, Rawlings was able to maintain power and stick with the tough economic reform process. By the 1990s, whether due to the reforms or simply because the country had finally experienced a sustained period of political stability, Ghana's economy made a turnaround with growth rates averaging more than 4.25 percent a year (World Bank 2017b).

Ghana often has been held up as a success story of structural adjustment, but critics note that the macroeconomic numbers do not accurately describe the economic situation of all Ghanaians (Konadu-Agyemang 2000). As market forces were introduced, the gap between rich and poor grew substantially; while some Ghanaians indeed have benefited from economic growth, there are still millions of people living in poverty who have seen few gains. Ghana's Gini inequality index increased from 35.3 in 1987 to 42.2 in 2012, the latest year for which this measure is available (World Bank 2017b). This may seem marginal, but it is clearly moving toward greater inequality. In addition, the country continues to rely on external aid and, despite some relief through HIPC and the MDRI, faces a large external debt. Even as Ghanaians celebrated the start of oil exports in 2010 and the emergence of a successful information technology sector, the government once again started taking out new loans. Economic growth is welcome, therefore, but has not dramatically transformed conditions for many Ghanaians.

Interestingly, the political results of structural adjustment in Ghana may be more pronounced than its economic effects. Starting in the 1980s, people upset about difficult economic reforms protested against the Rawlings government and lobbied for political change, setting off a series of events that would lead to Ghana becoming one of the most democratic countries in Africa. Faced with ongoing domestic opposition and increased international pressure for democracy in the 1990s, Rawlings converted his support base into the National Democratic

Congress (NDC) and held multiparty elections in 1992. Despite being known for free market reforms, Rawlings drew on earlier populist roots and positioned the party slightly to the left of center. In part because under-resourced opposition parties had little time to organize, Rawlings won, buying more time for his programs and for the economy to grow. He was reelected for another four-year term in 1996, after which he faced constitutional term limits and duly stepped aside to become an elder African statesman.

In 2000, the NDC presidential candidate was defeated by John Kufuor of the right-of-center National People's Party (NPP). The NPP government continued implementation of the economic reforms started under Rawlings and pursued debt relief through multilateral programs (HIPC, MDRI). Although the movement against Rawlings had started in opposition to structural adjustment, he was ultimately replaced—through popular elections—by a party that embraced the free market approach even more. After Kufuor and the NPP won reelection in 2004, the 2008 election was very close once again. In a runoff between the presidential candidates of the same two parties, which have deep roots in the country (Whitfield 2009), the NDC's John Atta Mills (who had been vice president under Rawlings) won with 50.3 percent of the vote compared to 49.7 percent for his opponent. Despite the razor-thin margin, the NPP candidate accepted the results and power was transferred peacefully.[7] With two successful transitions from one party to another through elections, observers celebrated Ghana's democratic consolidation. Just a few months later, to recognize this achievement, newly inaugurated US president Barack Obama chose Ghana as the site of his first visit to sub-Saharan Africa as president (see Chapter 10).

As the process of economic reform in Ghana continued, political changes helped facilitate a rise in foreign investment from about $100 million per year in the 1990s to more than $3 billion per year since 2011. This huge increase was spurred in large part by the discovery of offshore oil in 2007 and its export beginning in 2010, raising some concerns about potential political implications down the road (Gyimah-Boadi and Prempeh 2012). For now, though, the two-party system appears to be holding. In 2012, when President Mills died in office, Vice President John Dramani Mahama stepped in and was reelected as president later that year. When he ran again in 2016, Mahama was defeated in the first round by the NPP's Nana Akufo-Addo, whose campaign focused on economic issues and unemployment. This led to a third peaceful transition from one party to the other through elections (2000, 2008, 2016), cementing Ghana's status as one of the continent's most consolidated democracies. With rising foreign investment and diaspora remittances, Ghana's economy has benefited substantially from more than three decades of political stability, a pattern that Ghanaians hope will continue.

Notes

1. Measures of official development assistance include grants, concessional loans, food aid, training and technical assistance, and support to nongovernmental organizations.

2. Numbers here are in constant 2015 US dollars.

3. In 2016, for example, official development assistance represented more than 20 percent of gross national income in six African countries (Liberia, the Central African Republic, Burundi, Malawi, Sierra Leone, and Somalia), while that number was below 1 percent in nine other countries (Equatorial Guinea, Angola, Gabon, Mauritius, Seychelles, South Africa, Botswana, Nigeria, and Sudan). Notably, most of the countries that are most dependent on foreign aid are recovering from (or still experiencing) conflicts, while many of those that rely minimally on aid earn significant income from natural resources such as oil or diamonds.

4. In her 2009 book *Dead Aid: Why Aid Is Not Working and How There Is a Better Way for Africa,* Zambian economist Dambisa Moyo spells out many of these critiques about the impact of aid in Africa. While she could be criticized for cherry-picking evidence (Sachs and McArthur 2009), and many of her arguments are not new (Easterly 2006; Hancock 1989; Riddell 1987), she makes a convincing case against large-scale government-to-government aid projects and offers more in the way of proposed solutions than many previous authors have.

5. For a useful review of existing research along the dimensions of external versus internal and policy versus destiny, see Collier and Gunning 1999.

6. The exact number of HIPC-eligible countries has varied slightly over time as political and economic situations in the countries have changed.

7. Although there has been relative stability at the political center in Ghana, there are long-simmering conflicts surrounding land and power in several northern regions that often are overlooked.

5

External Pressures for Political Reform and Human Rights

During the late years of the Cold War, the de jure one-party state had become the norm in African politics. Only a handful of African countries permitted multiparty political competition between the late 1960s and the late 1980s. Some of these countries, like Ghana and Nigeria, oscillated between rule by military regimes and by civilian regimes that came to power through multiparty elections (see Chazan 1988; Diamond 1988). Often, the charismatic presidents who came to power through free, multiparty elections gradually began to behave in an autocratic fashion. This behavior, along with the poor economic performance and corruption of their regimes, was frequently the pretext for military coups d'état, as was the case in both Ghana (1966) and Nigeria (1966 and 1983). A handful of other African states allowed multiparty competition and regular elections but were dominated by the parties that came to power at independence. These included Gambia (from 1965 to 1994) and Botswana (from 1966 to present). None of these passed the test of alternation of parties in power, the indicator of consolidated democracy proffered by Samuel Huntington (1991). The large majority of African states were more or less stable single-party states through the 1980s.

Interestingly, most African states started off their post-independence histories as multiparty democracies. After ruling their respective African colonies for seventy-five years or more as dependent states, most European colonizers (ironically) organized relatively free and competitive elections before granting their erstwhile colonies independence. Thus, most of the first generation of African rulers came to power through competitive elections. Indeed, this was the case for all African countries except those like Algeria, Angola, Guinea-Bissau, and Mozambique that had to fight wars of liberation against their colonizers. Those coming to power in these free elections subsequently either converted their multiparty constitutions to single-party ones or were overthrown in military coups. Although the limited democratic experiences of African states in the 1960s, 1970s, and 1980s provided little freedom for their people, they were crucial reference points for the renaissance of democracy in the 1990s (Lindberg 2006).

For most African states, politics in the 1970s and 1980s was focused on nation building rather than on building multiparty democracies (see, e.g., Kpessa, Béland, and Lecours 2011). That is, rulers preferred to focus on creating a sense of national consciousness rather than allowing multiple parties to compete for power on the basis of differing ideologies. Of course, this favored the interests of the rulers, who in fact were more interested in their regime security than fostering multiparty competition. Reducing ethno-regional tensions and creating a national consciousness reduced the number and scale of the threats to their power. Some African historians argued that proto-democratic institutions in precolonial Africa were a myth (Simiyu 1988). African leaders essentially echoed this sentiment when they claimed that the one-party state resonated better with African traditions than Western-style democracy.

Others argued that while multiparty competition might be fine for economically developed Western societies, it did not work for the economically underdeveloped, multiethnic states created by colonialism. After coming to power in Uganda in 1986, President Yoweri Museveni instituted what he called "no-party democracy." He argued that his country would not be ready for multiparty competition until class divisions had become more important than ethno-regional divisions (Museveni 1997). It was not until 2005 that the constitution was amended to allow multiparty competition, though another amendment also removed presidential term limits, permitting Museveni to run for (and win) another term.

During the thirty years between 1960 and 1990, most outside countries did exceedingly little to promote political reform in Africa. As noted in Chapter 3, many African regimes were effectively clients of one of the two superpowers, while others were essentially clients of France (see Chapter 11). The Soviet Union explicitly promoted the adoption of one-party constitutions, namely, Marxist-Leninist ones. China favored one-party states with a slightly different (peasant-oriented) emphasis. For their part, the United States and France were scarcely more interested in promoting multiparty competition in Africa. From a realist perspective, this could be explained by the fact that free and fair elections might well have supplanted some of the client regimes in power; from a liberal perspective, the Western powers may have agreed with the paternalistic argument of Museveni that African countries were not ready for democratic competition. Some Western leaders no doubt agreed with Museveni that "pre-mature" liberalization would lead to conflict in African states, rather than the deepening of democracy over time.

In fairness to the Western states and their peoples, they did make some limited efforts to promote both good governance and human rights in Africa. The United States and Europe took some steps to stem corruption in Africa, especially insofar as corruption impeded economic reforms. French officialdom occasionally tried to reinforce an *état de droit* (the rule of law) in their client states (even though they undermined the same principles in fomenting coups d'état and other nefarious acts). Meanwhile, both Western states and nonstate groups tried to promote human rights in Africa. Perhaps the most famous nonstate human rights group, Amnesty International, was founded in London in 1961. It soon began to campaign for the rights of prisoners of conscience, as well as for an end to discriminatory policies like those of apartheid in South Africa. Another group, Human Rights Watch, emerged in Europe after the Helsinki Accords were signed by the United States, Canada, and thirty-three European states in 1975. This group eventually organized an Africa Watch division to "name and shame" egregious abusers of human rights on the continent. Meanwhile, US president Jimmy Carter created a Bureau of Human Rights and Humanitarian Affairs in the State Department in 1977. This bureau subsequently has produced annual human rights reports on all countries of the world, including African states. These reports document the extent to which various states respect the political and civil rights of their citizens, as well as "rights of the person," such as protection against arbitrary arrest, physical mistreatment, and violations of due process. The EU also began to promote human rights abroad seriously beginning in the 1970s (see Chapter 11). During the 1970s, almost all states of the world supported the decolonization of the Portuguese colonies and Namibia, and an end to white minority rule in southern Africa. These positions were the most elemental form of human rights promotion in Africa.

Despite these earlier efforts, it was the end of the Cold War that put political reform squarely on the agenda of most African societies. By the end of the 1980s, the single-party states of Africa had been largely discredited by their economic underperformance; African economic growth in the 1980s had been less than population growth (e.g., Leibfritz and Flaig 2013). Likewise, the single-party states of Eastern Europe had been unable to deliver either personal freedoms or economic development. The political revolutions that swept away the communist states of

Eastern Europe delegitimized the single-party model in general. Following upon the success of anticommunist opposition groups in Eastern Europe, labor unions, church groups, and all manner of civil society organizations in Africa began to mobilize against the old one-party regimes. As the contemporary French minister of cooperation, Jacques Pelletier, colorfully put it, "The wind from the east is shaking the coconut trees [in Africa]" (cited in Epstein 1990).[1]

Indeed, by the time these words were uttered, Benin had already held a sovereign national conference[2] in February 1990 that had stripped former dictator Mathieu Kérékou of power. The sovereign national conference subsequently became the model for other states across francophone Africa (Clark 1994), leading to multiparty transitions in several states.[3] Zambia was the leader among the one-party states of anglophone Africa. Following a period of unrest, the Zambian president Kenneth Kaunda suddenly called snap elections in July 1990 (VonDoepp 1996), perhaps hoping to preempt the further organization of opposition groups. In October 1991, the leader of the (main opposition) Movement for Multiparty Democracy, Frederick Chiluba, was elected president in a multiparty election. He thus supplanted Kaunda, who had ruled Zambia since independence in 1964. Between 1990 and 1994, a full sixteen African countries experienced a formal transition from de jure one-party rule to a new regime and leader (Bratton and van de Walle 1997). Most of the remainder experienced political openings that allowed multiparty competition, and many had multiparty elections in which incumbents were returned to power.

The remainder of this chapter explores the international relations of political reform and human rights in Africa since this historic democratic opening, beginning with a theoretical examination of the prospects for democracy promotion in Africa. It next examines the prospects for promoting political reform in light of these theories and the strategies that governments and nonstate actors have pursued to promote liberalization in Africa. The chapter also assesses the record of these efforts and draws attention to the many dilemmas of promoting political reform. This analysis is followed by a case study of Western and domestic efforts to promote political reform in Kenya since the early 1990s.

Perspectives on the Democratic Opening and Its Trajectory

In examining the theoretical views of political reform in Africa, let us begin with the view that is most skeptical of promoting democracy in Africa: realism. Unlike the other theoretical perspectives in international relations, realism does not have a well-developed theory of domestic politics. Mainly, it expects people to crave order, as Thomas Hobbes claimed, and for regimes to reinforce their grip on power, as Machiavelli stressed. Insofar as political reform was about reducing regime power and bringing about justice (both involving a good deal of political *dis*order), many realists found the sudden advent of political reform efforts in Africa surprising. Yet realism does provide one compelling explanation for this phenomenon, namely, the virtual eclipse of the Soviet Union from the global political scene beginning in 1989. In the absence of their erstwhile patron, all of the Afro-Marxist states experienced political openings between 1989 and 1992, and all but Angola and Mozambique underwent political transitions. Ironically, these developments brought pressure on the other outside patrons of African regimes, the United States and France, to deepen their own commitments to democracy. Whereas realism does not explain this behavior on the part of the external patrons, it does explain the African response: African regimes that were dependent upon foreign aid had little choice but to "play the democratic game" and adopt multiparty constitutions. At this juncture, China was not yet the alternative external partner that it would later become (see Chapter 12).

If realism has little to say about why Western powers would begin to promote political reform in Africa, realists attuned to domestic politics do have a view about the subsequent trajectory of political reform. Realists would expect African regimes to engage in the pretense of political reform while continuing to reinforce their grip over their domestic societies in more subtle ways. Indeed, many of the old African rulers of the single-party era, like Félix Houphouët-Boigny of Côte d'Ivoire, Omar Bongo of Gabon, and Blaise Compaoré of Burkina Faso, did retain power after the democratic opening. It is notable that all three of these regimes were close to France, whose policies in Africa did not change as much as those of the superpowers.[4] As for their relations with one another, realists would not expect "regime type" to play a significant role in the behavior of African states on the continent. Indeed, one realist analyst of relations among African states (Henderson 2015) has taken precisely this view, positing a model of African interstate relations (neopatrimonial balancing theory) that dismisses significant differences in behavior based on regime type. In general, realists would not expect African rulers to undertake real political reform except under duress, and they would not expect external great powers to promote political reform, except in the specific circumstances when it served their interests. The rise of China in Africa may have created such circumstances. Realists have not been surprised by the many democratic reversals in Africa.

Neo-Marxists have generally been equally skeptical about the authenticity of the democratic opening in Africa and its prospects. Many saw the advent of political reform springing chiefly from the imposition of harsh economic conditionalities on African states in the context of structural adjustment (e.g., Fatton 1990, 1995; also see Chapter 4). In fact, even many liberals attributed the sudden animation of existing political reform movements to the economic crises then gripping most African states (e.g., Clark and Gardinier 1997; VonDoepp 1996). Another neo-Marxian view saw the advent of multipartyism in Africa as a function of the West's desire to impose its ideology on Africa in an essentially imperialist fashion (e.g., Akindès 1996; Mappa 1995). Thus, far from being organic or authentic, political liberalization represented another assertion of Western ideology on the African political space.

Neither neo-Marxists of a materialist orientation nor those of an ideological bent perceived the sudden fetish for multiparty politics as liberating or productive of real human rights. The program of radicals was one of socioeconomic revolution and economic redistribution to the disenfranchised social classes (e.g., Fatton 1990). The real source of oppression in Africa was the concentration of wealth in the hands of a narrow class of elites. The advent of multiparty political competition within this political class, especially when wedded to a fulsome embrace of free market capitalism in the economic domain, could hardly improve the lot of the African masses or expand rights for the large majority.

Liberals have celebrated the democratic opening in Africa most vigorously and advocated for policies promoting continued political reform. Liberals analyzed Africa's democratic opening as stemming chiefly from a failure of authoritarian regimes—often tyrannical ones—to deliver political and civic rights but also to create conditions for the satisfaction of people's economic and social needs. As long as the one-party states of Eastern Europe persisted, Africa's dictators could plausibly echo the lie that the one-party model provided social equality and a buttress against the predations of Western imperialists. Yet many African peoples, like those of Eastern Europe, yearned for human rights, dignity, and individual freedom. Opposition movements, once they received encouragement from the West to do so, gradually succeeded in instituting new, multiparty constitutions and in some cases brought about regime transitions (Clark and Gardinier 1997). Liberals in the West naturally sought to encourage such outcomes in Africa.

The constructivist interpretation of Africa's opening overlaps with that of liberals but emphasizes the diffusion of human rights norms and changes in political culture. For Francis Fukuyama (1991), the competitive liberal model of politics and economics had triumphed over the latest

ideology of oppression, Marxism-Leninism. More typically, constructivists would attribute the democratic opening more to the gradual adoption of a global discourse of human rights than to the collapse of the
Soviet Union per se. As Beth Simmons (2009) has shown, states that
adhere to international human rights conventions usually encourage
human rights activists within their states to press for more human rights.
These activists become the local agents of both political reform and better respect for human rights. At the international level, the implicit norm
among the great powers that each had to respect the autonomy of other
great powers' client regimes similarly lost credibility. In terms of culture,
African domestic political cultures were suddenly shaken up with the
political openings in Benin and Zambia. The "big man" politics in which
the state and its leader served as patron to the people (Schatzberg 2001),
deeply ingrained in the consciousness of millions of Africans, was suddenly brought into doubt. That politico-cultural change has allowed democratic experiments to survive and even thrive in some African states.

Strategies for Political Reform in Africa

This section discusses the strategies and prospects for outsiders to promote political reform in African polities. "Outsiders" include African
expatriates living in states other than those that face the possibility of
reform at a given moment. The section begins with a brief description
of the types of actors who may seek to promote reform from without. It
then discusses some of the strategies that outsiders have tried to adopt
in promoting liberalization. Third, it highlights some of the dilemmas of
democracy promotion in Africa. The final section of the chapter assesses
the prospects for political reform in Africa.

Actors Promoting Political Reform

A wide range of actors has sought to promote political reform in Africa.
Intergovernmental organizations (IGOs) like the UN, the World Bank,
and the EU all try to promote political reform in Africa, both directly
and indirectly. (For more on the UN in Africa, see Chapter 8. For more
on the EU in Africa, see Chapter 11.) Their efforts parallel the limited
steps that have been taken by the African Union. Among IGOs, the
World Bank's International Development Association (IDA), the EU,
and the African Development Bank are the three leading donors (Organization for Economic Cooperation and Development 2015). The latter
is funded by all of its members, including the EU, individual Western
states, China, Japan, Saudi Arabia, and Turkey. Of these, however, only
the EU is directly interested in promoting political reform in Africa,
though the IDA is interested in good governance, a related concept.[5]

The British Commonwealth observes elections and occasionally imposes sanctions on authoritarian regimes, including some in Africa. The AU's African Commission on Human and Peoples' Rights tries to set guidelines and establish frameworks within which elections monitoring and human rights organizations can operate on the continent.

International nongovernmental organizations (INGOs) are another important category of actors that have tried to promote democracy in Africa. They do so by strengthening opposition political parties, drawing attention to authoritarian practices by governments, promoting an independent media, and other ways (more on this later). In the United States, the National Democratic Institute and the International Republican Institute, two party-affiliated groups, support such goals; based in Germany, the Friedrich Ebert and Konrad Adenauer Foundations are parallel party-affiliated groups that support human rights and democracy in Africa. Aside from these quasi-official NGOs, others are fully independent of governments. Freedom House provides scores for civil liberties and political rights around the world. In the area of human rights, Amnesty International, Human Rights Watch, Global Rights, and the International Federation of Human Rights perhaps lead the field. Myriad other organizations such as the International Foundation for Electoral Systems and the Carter Center monitor elections, as do the bodies of the AU and EU. Many other INGOs try to promote civil society in Africa, which is a longer-term method of promoting political reform. Such INGOs often partner with local human rights, civic education, and election reform NGOs to support their work. Although INGOs do not officially serve the interests of foreign states or groups of states (like IGOs), their levels of funding and influence are comparatively low.

Finally, there are the bilateral donors to African states. In 2013, among members of the Development Assistance Committee (DAC) of the Organization for Economic Cooperation and Development (OECD), the largest bilateral donors to Africa, in order of importance, were the United States, the United Arab Emirates, the United Kingdom, France, Germany, and Japan (Organization for Economic Cooperation and Development 2015).[6] Their aid budgets to Africa for that year ranged from about $2 billion from Japan to $9 billion from the United States. On the other hand, the five Western donors noted earlier are all consolidated democracies, as are all member states of the EU. All of the bilateral donors and the EU have declared themselves to be interested in the promotion of political reform in Africa. Moreover, the disproportionate percentage of the development assistance they provide to African states and subregional and regional entities gives them considerable leverage over the internal politics of African states. Accordingly, we focus the remainder of this section on these donors and their efforts to promote political reform.

Approaches to Political Reform in Africa

For those who believe that promoting Western-style, multiparty democracy is desirable and possible for donors to undertake, and possible for African states to achieve, the next question is how such a result can be accomplished. Among advocates for multiparty democracy in Africa, there are a number of debates. Should the donors try to focus on democratic transitions (in the near term), or should they try to create the conditions for long-term democratic consolidation, assuming that transitions will eventually come? Should they emphasize material incentives for progress toward democracy, or should they try to expand awareness of the human rights that Africans and all others can claim? Should they focus on building institutions of a democratic state or changing the consciousness of African populations at the grassroots?

Given their perceptions of the situation, liberals and liberal-constructivists favor an active promotion of democracy in Africa. Yet they do so in somewhat different ways, which are reflected in the range of policies that have actually been pursued by the donors; in general, liberals are more focused on institutions and constructivists on culture. Those of a constructivist mind-set would highlight the possibilities of transforming culture, norms, and identities in Africa. That is, they would seek to change the culture of politics from one that often treats longtime rulers as "fathers" (Schatzberg 2001) to one that values fair and regular competitions for office; they would seek to reinforce norms of behavior that favor the alternation of parties in power and term limits for executives; and they would prefer that individual Africans take on an identity of rights-holding citizens rather than subjects of authoritarian postcolonial regimes. Such changes can only be brought about by changing civil society and political culture, as discussed later.

Classic liberals believe that people respond to material incentives, carrots and sticks, in a rational fashion. Accordingly, they favor using aid, debt relief, and trade incentives as inducements for proto-democratic regimes to deepen their democratic commitments. Likewise, they favor the use of various economic sanctions to punish authoritarian rulers who ignore the rule of law, limit the rights of opposition movements to organize, or manipulate election results to remain in power. Economic sanctions include suspensions of aid programs, arms embargoes, trade sanctions, and restrictions on the financial transactions of leading regime figures.

A classic case of the use of sanctions against recalcitrant authoritarian regimes is that of EU and US sanctions against Robert Mugabe's regime in Zimbabwe. Mugabe took power in Zimbabwe at independence in 1980 and became increasingly authoritarian during the 1990s. In 2000, he sought to consolidate his presidential powers in a public referendum, but the measure was defeated by a margin of 55 to 45 percent.[7] With legislative elections scheduled for June of that year, Mugabe organized regime militants to threaten, intimidate, and attack the political opposition. As a form of political cover, he insisted that these militants were war veterans who were chiefly on a mission to seize the land of Zimbabwe's remaining white population. The real purposes of Mugabe's campaign were not lost on either the opposition or Zimbabwe's human rights community. As a report of the Zimbabwe Human Rights NGO Forum (2001) documents, the chief victims of the campaign were not white landowners but partisans of the opposition Movement for Democratic Change (MDC), media figures, witnesses to violence, and those challenging elections results. The official results showed that Mugabe's Zimbabwe African National Union–Popular Front (ZANU-PF) had won 48.6 percent of the vote to the MDC's 47 percent, but few outsiders accepted these figures as legitimate. More electoral violence followed the presidential elections of 2002, which Mugabe officially won with 56 percent of the vote. Although some observers from other African states endorsed these results, leading Zimbabwe political figures described the elections as having been hijacked (Makumbe 2002). The head of the EU electoral observation mission was expelled from Zimbabwe shortly before the elections took place.

In response to the electoral violence perpetrated by the Mugabe regime, the EU imposed targeted sanctions on President Mugabe and his inner circle in 2002 (Evans-Pritchard 2002). The sanctions included visa bans for Zimbabwean officials wishing to travel to Europe, a freezing of assets held in Europe, and a ban on the export of weapons and police equipment. Eventually, the United States imposed similar sanctions on Mugabe and seventy-six other Zimbabwean government and ZANU-PF officials (US Government Printing Office 2003). These sanctions against Mugabe and his close lieutenants remained in effect through several more disputed elections until he was finally overthrown in November 2017. During this time, the US embassy in Harare emphasized on its website that US aid to Zimbabwe had not decreased. To the contrary, a chart on the webpage showed that US aid to Zimbabwe rose from less than $50 million in 2001 to over $300 million in 2008 (US Embassy–Harare 2015). Nonetheless, Mugabe mocked these attempts at Western pressure and denounced them as a racist effort of Western states to reimpose their will on the country.

The counterpart to punishing authoritarianism is to reward the perception of political reform. Mamoudou Gazibo (2005) has argued that robust economic aid to liberalizing states at critical moments can lead to democratic consolidation. One case where the approach has been tried is the Democratic Republic of Congo since the end of the Cold War. In 1986, the DRC (then Zaire, a US ally) received $132 million in US foreign aid, but this figure dropped to $1 million in 1992, following the end of the Cold War. US aid then remained below $2.5 million for every year through 1997, the year of Mobutu's departure from power.[8] During Laurent Kabila's three years in power, from 1998 through 2000, US aid to the DRC rose only modestly to $27.2 million per year. Kabila, however, never made any effort to open the political space of the country, or to move toward elections, and received only token humanitarian assistance.

Following Kabila's assassination in January 2001, his son, Joseph, took power. The younger Kabila negotiated a treaty (completed in December 2002) with the rebels who had started a war against his father in 1998, and he formed a unity government with representatives of the major rebel groups. Joseph Kabila subsequently worked to organize elections in the DRC, seeking and receiving assistance from an International Committee to Support the Transition (de Goede and van der Borgh 2008).[9] The younger Kabila was rewarded with increasing amounts of foreign assistance during the transition and, after, for his liberalizing behavior. Official development assistance to the DRC from OECD countries increased from $245 million in 2001 to $1.12 billion in 2002 to $5.45 billion in 2003 (World Bank 2015). US development assistance also followed this pattern, reaching a peak of $410 million in 2011. In 2010, Joseph Kabila received a much larger reward: the IMF announced that the DRC would receive $12.3 billion in debt relief under the Highly Indebted Poor Countries Initiative and Multilateral Debt Relief Initiative programs (International Monetary Fund 2010). By the end of 2010, Congo's total external debt was down to $5.77 billion, compared to $12.28 billion in 2009 (World Bank 2012).

A related but more specific way in which the donors try to promote democracy is by assisting African countries in organizing their elections. Successful elections in contemporary states, after all, require careful preparation and execution if they are to be credible, even when the authorities do not seek to manipulate them. Among the many elements of successful elections are accurate census-taking and voter registration exercises, partition of the polity into acceptable administrative constituencies, the provision of balloting materials, the training of poll workers, credible observation of the polling process, and the preparation of transparent vote-tabulating systems following the elections. Organizations like the International Foundation for Electoral Systems and the Carter Center in the United States are among those that assist with the organization of elections and monitor the polling. The EU has had its own highly trained and well-funded election observation program since 2011, working under the umbrella of the European External Activities Service. Technical assistance is generally available to African countries from the United States, the European Union, and the NGOs that they fund. Elections observation missions from the same organizations, as well as the African Union, are always on hand when they are invited. South Africa's Electoral Institute for Sustainable Democracy is a key institution on the continent, building capacity in parliaments, strengthening political parties, and helping to organize elections.[10]

When elections are organized in conflict or postconflict situations, the international community can become heavily involved. The 2006 elections in the DRC are a good example. Concerning these elections, Britain's Department for International Development claimed, "It is safe to say that the elections would not have nor could have taken place without this involvement [of Congo's foreign partners]. The financial, logistical, and security support provided by the international community were massive and ultimately successful" (UK Department for International Development n.d.). The report continues by noting that the international community provided a "basket fund" of $267 million to support the elections, and that the government of the DRC paid less than one-tenth the total cost. It seems most unlikely that the DRC could have organized credible elections in 2006 without this support. Further, the 2006 elections were regarded by all major members of the international community, including African observers, as being remarkably free and fair, given the still chaotic conditions then prevailing in the DRC.

As in the DRC, UN peacekeeping missions often have been involved in efforts to promote democracy in Africa. As of 2018, the UN had completed twenty-three peacekeeping missions in Africa and was actively engaged in another eight (see Chapter 8).[11] Although many of these were designed simply to keep an existing domestic or international peace agreement, several of them became deeply involved in efforts to organize free and fair elections following violent civil conflicts. Among these were UN missions to Angola (1991–1995), Mozambique (1992–1994), Liberia (1993–1997), and Sierra Leone (1999–2005). Although these efforts do not always succeed, they represent the efforts of the international community, particularly those who shoulder the cost of UN peacekeeping operations, to promote political reform in Africa.

When peacekeeping operations lead to new constitutions, and then successful elections, nascent institutions emerge. These often include new forms of legislatures, or at least legislatures populated with new legislators. Other new institutions can include electoral oversight commissions, ministries in charge of civil society, and government bodies charged with information services. Many of the IGOs and NGOs described earlier are involved in strengthening the capacity of these new institutions. Among other things, they frequently lack trained staff, computer and communications equipment, and even basic supplies. Such needs frequently have been met, if inadequately, by the foreign partners of specific African states. Likewise, in postwar contexts, judicial institutions have been weak or even collapsed. In such cases, organizations like the International Bar Association and the US Agency for International Development (USAID) have provided assistance in rebuilding them. These institutions serve both to protect human rights and to balance the often overweening power of African presidencies. When these institutions are strong, they support the consolidation of democracy.

Another strategy for bolstering political reform in Africa has been to support the strengthening of African organizations. As voluntary associations involving people in groups larger than families, civil society organizations include media outlets, human rights groups, professional societies, labor unions, development organizations, social clubs, and a wide variety of other nongovernmental bodies set up for specific social purposes. In Western political theory, a vibrant civil society has long been thought to be the basis for both democratic transitions and democratic consolidation. Famously, Alexis de Tocqueville identified the vibrant civil society in the United States in the nineteenth century as the foundation of the country's durable democracy. Following this lead, many Western social scientists have regarded a vibrant civil society in African states to be key to political liberalization there (e.g., Barkan 2003; Harbeson, Rothchild, and Chazan 1994; VonDoepp 1996). In keeping with this view, donors have contributed billions of dollars and launched hundreds of programs to promote civil society in Africa.[12] Support for civil society organizations has the added attraction that it does not confront ruling African regimes head-on with the donors' desire for liberalization. Rather, it tries to create underlying conditions that can lead to either eventual democratic transition or consolidation. In the information technology age, information-sharing organizations like Ushahidi, launched in Kenya in 2009, have been particular targets for donor support.

Another important, if indirect, way of supporting both respect for human rights and political reform has been to seek justice against individuals who are alleged to have committed war crimes and crimes against humanity. This short-term strategy against human rights violations serves the longer-term process of political reform by acting as a deterrent against either rebels or rulers who might resort to political violence against civilians in the future. In the sense that it seeks justice, it could be described as a liberal strategy, and in the sense that it seeks to reinforce norms against political violence in Africa, it could be seen as a constructivist approach. Insofar as the AU Constitutive Act already condemns such crimes, it is worth emphasizing that the international community seeks only to bolster existing African norms.

Two major types of judicial bodies have sought justice against the perpetrators of war crimes and crimes against humanity in recent decades. One type is the local judicial tribunal, often established with the support of the United Nations to deal with cases in a specific situation. Two such courts in Africa have been the International Criminal Tribunal for Rwanda, set up in 1995 in Arusha, Tanzania, and the Special Court for Sierra Leone, set up in Freetown in 2002. As of the end of 2017, the former had indicted ninety-three individuals and sentenced sixty-two and the latter had indicted thirteen individuals and convicted nine (Burchfield and Dorchak 2017). One of those convicted was former Liberian president Charles Taylor, who is currently serving a fifty-year sentence in Britain for his involvement in war crimes in Sierra Leone. Some other alleged perpetrators of human rights crimes have been prosecuted by the courts of individual states with the support of the African Union. Notably, former Chadian president Hissène Habré has been held in Senegal since 2005, and in 2012 the Senegalese parliament agreed to having him tried in a special court (Fessy 2012). Other domestic institutions set up to seek justice for human rights abuses have received less explicit external support. South Africa's Truth and Reconciliation Commission was widely lauded for helping victims and perpetrators move beyond the abuses of the apartheid era, whereas Rwanda's *gacaca* courts have been the object of considerable international criticism for their shaky legal rules and perceived emphasis on just one group of perpetrators.

The International Criminal Court, established in 2002 and located in The Hague (Netherlands), represents a second type of judicial body, existing by virtue of the accession of 123 countries to the Rome Treaty (as of 2018). These countries voluntarily joined the Court and agreed that their citizens indicted for war crimes and crimes against humanity can be tried there. Most African states were initially enthusiastic about the formation of the ICC, and most are signatories of the Rome Statute. Further, as of 2018, nine of ten "situations" investigated by the ICC have been in Africa, and all of the twenty-five cases of those wanted by the Court have involved African nationals.[13] In 2009, the ICC issued an arrest warrant for Sudanese president Omar al-Bashir on charges of torture, murder, other war crimes, and genocide (International Criminal Court 2015a), making him the first head of state to be indicted by the Court.

Like many of the strategies outlined earlier, the strategy of changing political culture is a controversial one. Yet, essentially, this is the purpose of the many "civic education" programs that donors support across Africa. Such programs typically involve training community leaders—often the heads of important NGOs—on their political rights and duties as citizens of their countries. Paternalistic though such programs appear, it is useful to note that a large number of African states have ministries of civic education (often joined with the portfolios for youth or information), nominally devoted to similar purposes. Moreover, some scholars (e.g., Finkel and Smith 2011) have found that such programs have changed the attitudes of citizens over time. Like civil society programs, civic education programs do not confront African authoritarianism head-on but rather try to create social conditions for political reform over the long term.

Implicitly, rhetorical and diplomatic efforts to recognize "good" democratic behavior serve the same purposes. For instance, the notion that the United States would support freedom around the world was the key theme of President George W. Bush's second inaugural address in 2005.[14] It is easy to be cynical about such rhetorical statements, but they do sometimes powerfully signal the intentions of major powers. Even if foreign leaders do not take them very seriously, foreign citizens may do so. A year after Bush's inauguration speech, Secretary of State Condoleezza Rice visited Cairo, where she met with dissidents in addition to President Hosni Mubarak. In June of 2009 President Barack Obama was in Egypt, trying to reconcile Muslims to US policy, but also again spreading a message in favor of freedom and liberalization. Obama's speech has sometimes been connected with the start of the Arab Spring democracy movements that began the following year in Tunisia. In July 2009, Obama made his first foreign trip to sub-Saharan Africa—namely, to Ghana. There can be little doubt that the US president wished to signal his approval and support for the success of democratization so evident in Ghana at that time.

The Dilemmas of Promoting Political Reform in Africa

Unfortunately for those seeking to promote political reform in Africa, each strategy discussed here is connected with dilemmas, difficulties, and even dangers. With respect to the use of sanctions against regimes that employ violence to maintain power, such sanctions consistently have failed to bring about democratic transitions. Consider the case of Zimbabwe, raised earlier. Following the imposition of donor sanctions against the Mugabe regime in 2002, the wily Zimbabwean president continued both his divide-and-rule strategy and his use of violence against the opposition. In the 2008 elections, he actually lost in the first round against his chief rival, Morgan Tsvangirai, who did not reach the 50 percent threshold needed to claim the office. Thus, a second round of elections was required to determine a president. However, Mugabe unleashed terrific violence against the opposition and its supporters, leading Tsvangirai to withdraw from the second round of voting. Eventually, the opposition leader joined a power-sharing government later in 2008, but the violence did not end. Moreover, state security agents were not held accountable for abducting and torturing human rights activists and opposition party officials (Human Rights Watch 2011b). Again, there was a great international outcry, yet Mugabe remained in power. When Mugabe was finally forced to resign in November 2017, it was not because of international sanctions, but because he had sacked his vice president, Emerson Mnangagwa, and was plotting to put his wife in power. Sanctions levied against Sudanese president Omar al-Bashir following genocidal violence in Darfur in the early 2000s did just as little to bring about a transition in power. Both the al-Bashir and Mugabe regimes reinforced their partnerships with China after being targeted with sanctions (see Chapter 11).

Another danger of putting pressure on authoritarian regimes to liberalize is that the result may be civil war, state collapse, or even mass killing, rather than political transition. Although the one-party African regimes of the 1970s and 1980s were surely authoritarian, many were relatively stable. For instance, authoritarian regimes in Congo-Brazzaville and the Central African Republic were stable in the 1980s, but the opening of the political space to competition in the early 1990s led to repeated episodes of political violence (see Clark 2005 and Mehler 2005, respectively). In Somalia, the withdrawal of US support for the Siad Barre regime and pressures for democratization led to state collapse, from which the country has still not recovered (see Chapter 10). Most shocking of all, the opening of the political space in Rwanda in 1990 led first to civil war and ultimately to the genocide of 1994. Many diplomats are painfully mindful of these terrible experiences when they are called upon to pressure authoritarian regimes to allow more political competition.

Providing assistance to transitional regimes is fraught with a different kind of danger: unintentionally supporting authoritarian consolidation instead of democratic consolidation. Many of the freely elected regimes that came to power between 1991 and 1995 in Africa did not prove themselves to be truly democratic in character (Villalón and VonDoepp 2005). Rather, many of the new leaders focused on dividing the opposition and consolidating their power instead of building the institutions associated with a new, multiparty order. The regime of Joseph Kabila, discussed earlier, may well be a case in point. Following Kabila's free election in 2006, most of the political and economic reforms that the donor community tried to promote in the DRC in the following years failed (Trefon 2011). Worse still, the next national elections in the DRC, held in 2011, did not meet international standards for freeness and fairness. The Carter Center (2011) report on the elections, based on its robust observation mission in the country, found that the elections lacked credibility, citing a long list of shortcomings, including the disappearance of the ballots from 2,000 polling stations in Kinshasa. President Kabila let the scheduled date for the next elections in 2016 come and go without taking steps to organize them. He subsequently violated an agreement he made in December 2016 to leave office by the end of 2017. Thus, aid that was intended to help consolidate political competition in Congo unintentionally helped consolidate a new authoritarian regime there.

Peacemaking missions represent yet another dilemma for the establishment of democracy in Africa. The presence of the world's largest peacekeeping operation in the DRC, with over 22,000 personnel since 2008, did not affect the reality of Kabila's authoritarian consolidation of power. Massive and widespread human rights abuses also occurred in the presence of the UN mission there (see Chapter 7). A succession of UN missions to Somalia also have failed to restore order to the country or help bring to power a legitimate government, much less start a process of political reform. In other cases, however, like Liberia, the UN has been more successful in creating the conditions for political reform (see Chapter 8).

The pursuit of justice against the perpetrators of war crimes and crimes against humanity also has done little for political reform, at least in the short term. Notably, al-Bashir remains the president of Sudan ten years after the ICC issued a warrant for his arrest. In the interim, he has visited over twenty foreign countries, including seven that are ICC members, without being arrested (*Nuba Reports* 2016). Neither he nor his co-conspirators in the violence in Darfur have been brought to justice. A more troubling case for the OECD donors is that of Kenyan president Uhuru Kenyatta. In 2011, the ICC issued summonses for Kenyatta and two other Kenyan individuals to appear on charges related to electoral violence in the country following the December 2008 elections there (International Criminal Court 2015b). In 2013, however, Kenyatta was elected president of the country, and the charges against him at the ICC soon became a dilemma for the Western donors (see case study at end of this chapter). Moreover, African opinion now seems to have turned decisively against the ICC, if not against the notion of individual responsibility for human rights violations in general. In October 2013, an extraordinary session of African Union leaders decided that all cases against sitting incumbent heads of state would have to be deferred; there was general dismay at the apparent targeting of African figures at the ICC by the African heads of state there (*Africa Research Bulletin* 2013). In late 2016, Burundi, Gambia, and South Africa announced their intention to withdraw from the ICC, though only Burundi followed through (see Chapter 6).

Support for civil society organizations (CSOs) in Africa from abroad also generates a profound dilemma. What makes CSOs effective in their struggle for political reform and human rights in any country is their authenticity. That is, they must represent and advocate for the local constituencies from which they emerge on the specific issues for which they were created. When donors step into the picture, however, the leaders of CSOs and development NGOs become quite responsive to the logic of those external donors (Abrahams 2008). In that sense, when indigenous CSOs seek and receive funding from outside, they can quickly lose responsiveness to their local constituents. Meanwhile, African regimes have become extraordinarily adept at co-opting the leaders of CSOs and harnessing them to their own purposes. In Rwanda, for instance, the state has created a troubling organization, the Rwandan Governance Board (RGB). The purposes of the organization are to "Monitor the practices of good governance; Coordinate and support media sector development; Document and assess Home Grown initiatives; [and] Register, empower and monitor civil society organizations" (Rwandan Governance Board 2015).[15] Essentially, the RGB seeks to harness the activities of Rwanda's civil society organizations to the purposes of the state, whatever these are, while also monitoring and constraining them. As a result, any donor aid channeled to Rwanda's civil society ultimately ends up reinforcing the power of the Rwandan state over society, exactly the opposite of what liberals hope to achieve in aiding CSOs.

Finally, turning to the transformation of political cultures, this may well be the most permanent method of ensuring the success of political reform in Africa in the long term. The findings of Steve Finkel and Amy Smith (2011) notwithstanding, other scholars are skeptical that such programs will change political attitudes in the absence of economic development. For instance, Ronald Inglehart and Christian Welzel (2005) made a profound case that the only thing that ultimately changes the values of a population is sustained economic development. Further, these changes are witnessed only over generations, as younger cohorts of citizens grow up in an environment of economic security. In cases of sustained economic development, populations eventually acquire "self-expression values," which allow them to tolerate both social differences and free contestation for power. If these scholars are correct, then donors should logically focus on economic development, not political liberalization, at least in the short term. Indeed, the donors are in fact often focused on development, handsomely rewarding regimes like that in Ethiopia that have demonstrated their developmental prowess. Alas, in the short term, Ethiopia's Freedom House scores have gone in the opposite direction of its GDP as the regime there has become increasingly repressive. Thus, policies that may bring about economic development and changes in authoritarian cultures in the long term may put money into the pockets of increasingly authoritarian regimes in the near term.

Prospects for Political Reform in Africa

Before examining its prospects, we must ask whether donors really want to bring about political reform in Africa. Both realists and radicals are intuitively skeptical of such claims. For instance, some important African scholars of a critical bent (e.g., Ake 1996) have doubted the intentions of the West to spread democracy in Africa. Moreover, some empirical scholars who detach themselves from large theoretical approaches have found that Western aid levels are not linked to political liberalization efforts. For instance, studying the record of the United States from 1992 to 1996, Steven Hook finds that "contrary to the government's pledges, democratic and democratizing states have not received a greater share of aid. Instead, the distribution has been closely linked with security concerns—a pattern consistent with the Cold War record—and US economic self interests have also been evident" (1998: 151). Other empirical scholars, however, have found that Western donors do in fact try to reward and encourage political liberalization in Africa (e.g., Goldsmith 2001). The analysis of Thad Dunning (2004) suggests that Western donors did not try to support liberalization through aid during the Cold War, but they have done so since, confirming and extending the finding of Goldsmith. Stephen Brown (2005) also agrees with this finding.

We are surely aware that Western donors have many interests in Africa other than the aspiration for democracy. For instance, Beth Whitaker (2007) has shown how the George W. Bush administration encouraged some African states to adopt anti-terrorism policies in the wake of the terrorist attacks of September 11, 2001. In turn, the regimes governing these states often used these laws to throttle local democratic movements. We are likewise well aware of the many economic interests that Western donors have in Africa that may conflict with their stated goals of promoting political reform (see Chapters 9 and 10). In the short term, such fears and interests do often undermine efforts to promote democracy. Yet it is also the case that the interests of states, including the Western donors, cannot be fully defined without reference to the values and cultures of their peoples. In the case of the Western donors, democracy is central to the identity of the political classes. As a result, the desire to promote democracy abroad finds its way into their understanding of their own interests. We thus conclude that promoting political reform is on the agenda of the Western donors, if not always near the top of the list.

The prospects for political reform in Africa depend largely on the kind of goals one has for African states. Consolidated democracy is an ultimate goal that can only be achieved in the long term, if ever; democratic breakdown is also entirely possible, even for developed countries (Linz and Stepan 1978). As John Clark has suggested elsewhere, the terms "political reform," "liberalization," and "democratization" represent progressively more ambitious concepts on the menu of liberal aspiration (1997: 24). Political reform is the broadest, and hence the one chosen for this chapter: it could entail as little as more choice of candidates within a single-party context, a goal once considered progressive. Political reform could also refer to an expansion of the freedom of association, a freer press, and the protection of certain individual liberties. Opening the political space to competition among multiple political parties represents a further, and crucial, step in the spectrum of political reforms. In the liberal view, the ultimate liberalization of political party activity is the essential step needed to ensure the progressive realization of human rights and democratic deepening. Multiparty political competition is hardly enough, however; critically, it must be accompanied by regular, free, and fair elections in which multiple parties compete. Otherwise, a likely result is electoral authoritarianism, a regime type characterized by de jure multipartyism but the de facto domination of one party or ruler through savvy manipulation of political processes (see Schedler 2006). Some left-of-center liberals have condemned the "fallacy of electoralism," or the idea that regular elections ensure that citizens are truly empowered vis-à-vis their own governments (Bratton 1998).

Leaving aside the sobering notion that even free and fair elections do not lead to real democracy, few African states have yet achieved Huntington's "two-turnover test" since the return of political competition to Africa. Only a handful of states like Benin, Ghana, Nigeria, and Zambia have thus far seen a second change of power through the ballot box following democratic transition. As noted earlier, even Botswana, once considered a model for democracy in Africa, has been ruled continuously by the Botswana Democratic Party since its independence in 1966. Moreover, it has recently been criticized for growing authoritarianism. Likewise, the robustness of South Africa's democracy has yet to be tested by a real challenge to the dominance of the African National Congress, despite internal battles within the party. Many other African states are essentially governed by personalist rulers (Sudan), one-party regimes (Eritrea), or monarchs (Morocco and Swaziland). The influential NGO Freedom House rated only ten of sub-Saharan Africa's forty-nine states as "free," with twenty-one scoring "not free" (Freedom House 2015). Thus, the political opening of the early 1990s has hardly led to rapid democratic transitions and then democratic consolidation (a second change of power) across the continent.

Nonetheless, Africa is inarguably freer than it was during the 1970s and 1980s. Tanzania is an example of a country that has not had a democratic transition but has made clear progress on multiple fronts. First, its founding president, Julius Nyerere, resigned from power in 1985, well ahead of the wave of political reform that soon came to Africa. In 1992, the country lifted the ban on the existence of opposition parties. In the competitive elections of 1995, 2000, 2005, and 2010, the ruling Chama cha Mapinduzi continued to dominate the National Assembly, and its presidential nominees won every contest. In 2010, however, the opposition Chadema party won a record 27 percent of the vote, signaling the CCM's loosening grip on power. According to Freedom House, "The October 2010 presidential and legislative elections were considered the most competitive and legitimate in Tanzania's history."[16] In the 2015 elections, the CCM margin of victory in the legislative elections was further reduced to only 55 percent, versus 32 percent for the leading opposition party; the opposition presidential candidate, Chadema's Edward Lowassa, won 40 percent.

Tanzania's respect for political and human rights has also gradually improved. Freedom House ranks countries on a scale of 1 to 7 for political rights and on the same scale for civil liberties; the best combined score for freedom and rights is thus a 2, and the worst is a 14.[17] In 1994, Tanzania garnered a combined Freedom House score of 12, scoring a 6 in each category and rating "not free" overall. Over the subsequent two decades, Tanzania's scores gradually improved with some ups and downs. By 2005, its combined score had dropped to a 7; its score dropped to 6 in 2015, earning the country a "partly free" ranking by Freedom House, but its score was again 7 in 2017.[18] Tanzania is thus a country that seems to be on a trajectory of political liberalization, albeit without (yet) experiencing a political transition.

The second question relevant to the prospects for the promotion of political reform is whether African norms about democracy and human rights are changing, in response to outside encouragement or otherwise.

One development leading us to think so is that African leaders have embraced the rule of law (if not democracy in a wider sense) as a norm of governance. In particular, Africa's leaders took a small step in favor of political reform with the signature of the African Union's Constitutive Act in 2000. Article 4(p) of the act identifies one of the AU's principles as "condemnation and rejection of unconstitutional changes of governments," and Article 30 stipulates that "governments which shall come to power through unconstitutional means shall not be allowed to participate in the activities of the Union." This language is a kind of code signaling disapproval of military coups d'état in Africa by African leaders. In practice, African regimes that have come to power through coups have usually not been excluded from participation in the AU for very long. Their suspensions are usually lifted as soon as new elections are staged, at latest. Nonetheless, the embrace by African leaders of the norm of the rule of law gives constructivists, in particular, reason to believe that democracy has a future in Africa.

Case Study: Pressure for Liberalization in Kenya

The case of Kenya illustrates many of the dilemmas that external donors have faced in trying to promote political reform in African countries. There is no doubt that the OECD donors wished to promote political reform in Kenya at the beginning of the 1990s, following the wave of enthusiasm for democracy that swept the continent starting in 1989. Donors put considerable pressure on President Daniel arap Moi after 1990 to reform Kenya's single-party constitution and allow multiparty competition. Yet they were not certain whether or how quickly Kenya could make a transition to full-scale multiparty democracy. Many diplomats from donor countries feared that a rapid transition might lead to ethno-political violence in the country. Another way of characterizing this dilemma is that it was between promoting gradual political liberalization for the long term or pressing for an immediate transition. A second dilemma, emerging especially after 2001, was that between the exigency of cooperating with the Kenyan government against terrorism or continuing to push for deeper political reform. A third dilemma, particularly after 2007, was that between the demand for justice in the face of grave human rights violations and respecting the outcome of a democratic process in Kenya. Thus far, donors have broadly been helpful to the process of political reform in Kenya, though the outcomes speak as much to the commitments and patience of the Kenyan people as they do to the efforts of outsiders.

During the Cold War, Kenya maintained a relatively open, free market economy and close relations with Western democracies. It had a particularly close relationship with the United States and engaged in modest military cooperation with it. The US Navy called regularly at Kenya's port of Mombasa, and a good number of Kenyan officers received training under the Pentagon's International Military and Education Training (IMET) program. Between 1975 and 1985, Kenya received annual military aid from the United States (US Federal Budget 2015b), unlike most other African countries. At the end of the Cold War, Kenya was one of the more prosperous African countries and enjoyed good trade relations with Western European states and the United States.

Meanwhile, Kenya's political trajectory mirrored that of other African states of the era: founding president Jomo Kenyatta banned the country's only opposition party (the Kenyan People's Union) in 1969 and Kenya became a de facto one-party state. Vice President Daniel arap Moi succeeded Kenyatta upon his death in 1978. In 1982, Kenya became a de jure one-party state when the parliament changed the constitution to make the Kenyan African National Union (KANU) the sole legal party. Throughout the 1980s, and especially after an apparent military coup attempt in 1982, Moi's regime became increasingly authoritarian, cracking down on local democracy activists and arresting and torturing political opponents. Despite such threats, Kenyan civil society and church leaders continued to push hard for democratic political reforms and greater respect of human rights.

With the end of the Cold War, donors quickly began to pressure President Moi to change the constitution to allow the formation of opposition parties. According to Stephen Brown, "donor conditionality forced Moi to allow multipartyism in 1991 and donors provided encouragement to opposition parties" (2001: 725). Although Kenya's debt was still modest in the late 1970s, its economy had begun to slow down, and it signed the first of nine structural adjustment program agreements with the World Bank in 1980. Four more structural adjustment agreements dealing with specific aspects of the economy followed between then and 1989 (World Bank 2000). Under their terms, the Kenyan government accepted increased aid and debt relief in return for promising liberalizing economic reforms. World Bank (2015) data show that Kenya received economic assistance exceeding $1 billion a year in 1989 and 1990. As a side effect, Kenya became especially susceptible to the pressure exerted by Western donors when the era of political liberalization arrived. Under President George H. W. Bush, US ambassador Smith Hempstone was an outspoken critic of Moi, calling on him to allow the Kenyan opposition to organize and compete for power, using unusually blunt terms for a diplomat (Hempstone 1997).

Moi responded to pressures for political reform from his own population, supported by those of the diplomatic community, in the fashion of autocrats of his era. On one hand, he arranged for KANU to repeal the provision of the Kenyan constitution banning opposition parties at a meeting in December 1991. He duly allowed opposition parties to form and began to make preparations for multiparty elections in 1992. On the other hand, he took steps to maximize his prospects for maintaining power: he stacked the Kenyan electoral commission with KANU party loyalists who wanted him to remain in office; he promoted electoral laws that would increase KANU's chances of controlling the parliament; he limited his opponents' media access; he stimulated ethnic tensions and violence between the large ethno-regional constituencies that supported a fragmented opposition; and, when it was finally necessary, he rigged the counting of ballots to ensure that he won the count, if not the vote (Brown 2009). As a result, he prevailed in the 1992 election despite receiving just 36 percent of the vote.

Donors were seemingly ambivalent about how to respond to Moi's tactics and the general trajectory of Kenyan politics. Moi did not suffer a major decline in foreign aid revenues either immediately before or after the elections of December 1992 (World Bank 2015). Moi's opening of the political space to the opposition apparently went far enough for most donors. According to Brown, "From 1992 onwards donors as a whole actually discouraged measures that could have led to more comprehensive democratization. They did this by endorsing blatantly unfair polls and subverting domestic efforts to secure wide-ranging reforms" (2001: 731). Thus, while donors wanted the Moi regime to have a political opening, they were not willing to use sustained pressure to force the regime to relinquish power. Throughout this period, Kenya remained a key Western ally in the region; Kenya was especially important as a staging location for the international military intervention in Somalia from 1992 to 1995 (see Chapter 10).

In the five years between the 1992 and 1997 elections, there was no more appreciable liberalization in Kenya (Brown 2001). Moi concentrated (successfully) on dividing the political opposition and manipulating the political process to favor KANU and his personal candidacy in the forthcoming elections. Moi's behavior again created conditions that led to low-level political violence and several dozen deaths during 1997. The donors did respond to this trend, citing corruption and poor governance rather than political repression. Nonetheless, "mentions of accountability and good governance were widely interpreted as expressing dissatisfaction with political governance as well." In sum, bilateral and multilateral donors suspended over $400 million in aid (Brown 2001: 732). Moi's government responded with minor concessions and modest political reforms passed through the parliament between August and November 1997. The donors responded by easing the pressure on Moi and even pressuring the opposition to proceed with the elections peacefully. Moi went on to win a plurality in the December 1997 contest (with 40 percent of the vote), and KANU won a very narrow majority in the parliament (107 of 210 seats). Official assistance to Kenya did fall in 1997 and remained at low levels for the remainder of his final term in office (World Bank 2015).

Unlike some other African rulers, the seventy-eight-year-old Moi opted to respect constitutional term limits and stand down from the presidency in 2002.[19] Moi endorsed Uhuru Kenyatta, the son of Kenya's founding president, to be his successor and run on the KANU ticket. Moi's selection of a young, relative newcomer to politics (despite his family name) over several KANU loyalists who had been waiting in the wings for years caused fissures within the party, prompting several high-ranking members to join the opposition. In part because of this development, for the first time in the multiparty era the opposition rallied behind a single opposition figure, Mwai Kibaki, whose Democratic Party was the linchpin of the National Rainbow Coalition (NARC). In the December 2002 elections, Kibaki beat Kenyatta 62 to 31 percent. The NARC also won a solid majority in the parliament (132 of 224 seats). In interpreting this result, Samuel Barkan (2003) attributed it to several internal developments: the election of a new generation of younger members of parliament, many of whom challenged Moi; the rapid growth and activism of Kenyan civil society; and the establishment of several new institutional checks on the power of the Kenyan executive. According to Barkan, all of these changes led to a decline in the patronage system and an overdue democratic transition. Yet Figure 5.1 provides some prima facie evidence that donor patterns also may have influenced Kenya's political trajectory. The level of aid going to Kenya hit a long-term low in 1999 and was consistently at very low levels through Moi's last term. US aid to Kenya followed the same pattern, hitting historically low levels in the late 1990s and then increasing rapidly after 2002 (US Federal Budget 2015b). The meager aid given to Kenya during Moi's last term mostly went to the NGO community. Hence, outside aid patterns seem to have reinforced the domestic changes identified by Barkan.

Even as Kenyans celebrated their democratic transition, the priorities of Western donors, and especially those of the United States, were shifting. The issue of terrorism factored into US-Kenyan relations from 1998,[20] but it became an overriding concern of US policy after the September 11, 2001, attacks on New York and Washington, D.C. US officials pressured governments around the world to adopt

Figure 5.1   Official Development Assistance to Kenya, 1989–2016 (constant 2015 dollars, millions)

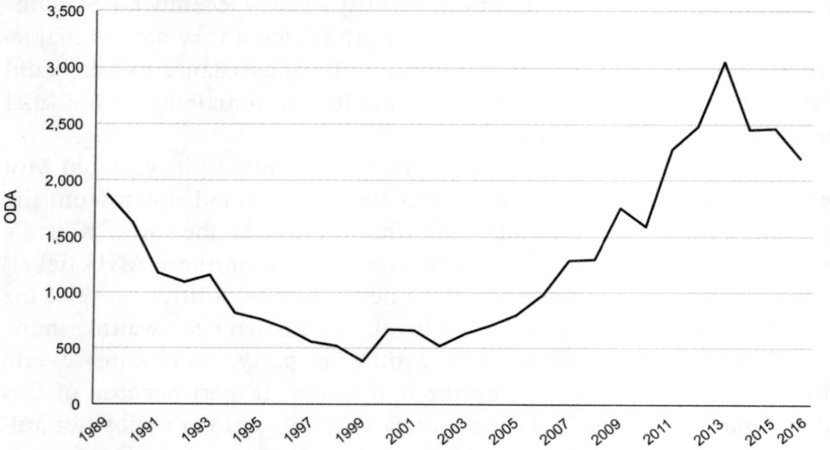

Source: World Bank 2015.

strict anti-terrorism legislation and cooperate in going after terrorist cells; often, political reform became a secondary concern. Having finally experienced a democratic transition in 2002, though, Kenya initially resisted US pressure to enhance government surveillance powers and security institutions, though the Kibaki administration cooperated closely with US officials behind the scenes (Whitaker 2008). Eventually, faced with a growing threat from al-Shabaab in neighboring Somalia (see Chapter 10), Kenya enacted strong counterterrorism legislation and increased security cooperation with foreign partners, including the United States and Israel.

Kenya's next elections, held in December 2007, provoked a crisis for the Kenyan people and presented donors with another dilemma. In these elections, Kibaki ran for a second term against a veteran politician, Raila Odinga, and his Orange Democratic Movement (ODM). Odinga had endorsed Kibaki in 2002, and his support was crucial to the NARC victory that year, but he split with Kibaki in subsequent years over cabinet appointments, a failed constitutional proposal, and an alleged commitment to serve just one term. Although opinion polls before the 2007 election were close, evidence from the early returns and from the parliamentary elections (where the ODM beat Kibaki's coalition by 102 to 78 seats) strongly suggests that Odinga won (Dercon and

Gutierrez-Romero 2012). Nonetheless, on December 30, more than twenty-four hours after the electoral commission stopped releasing precinct-level results, its chair announced that Kibaki had won reelection; hours later, he was inaugurated for a second term. Odinga refused to accept the results, which many domestic and international observers regarded as fraudulent, and called on his supporters to engage in public protests. Very quickly, and fueled by a complex history of election-related conflicts, land disputes, marginalization, and displacement, violence escalated between supporters of Odinga (mostly from the Luo and Kalenjin ethnic communities) and those of Kibaki (mostly Kikuyu). In the weeks that followed the contested election, more than a thousand people were killed and another 300,000 were displaced.

As the violence increased, a succession of African mediators traveled to Nairobi to seek a political solution. These included South Africa's Archbishop Desmond Tutu, rapidly followed by the former heads of state of Tanzania, Mozambique, Botswana, and Zambia. US assistant secretary of state Jendayi Frazier joined these African leaders in early January in an attempt to stimulate negotiation between Kibaki and Odinga (Lindenmayer and Kaye 2009). From that starting point, the mediation passed successively from African Union chairperson John Kufuor (Ghana's president) and then to former UN secretary-general Kofi Annan. The latter, backed by the United States and European donors, negotiated a power-sharing agreement at the end of February, under which Odinga became the prime minister of Kenya through 2013, the remainder of Kibaki's term. Both sides also agreed to adopt a new constitution and to bring to justice the perpetrators of the post-election violence. In the mediation efforts following the 2007 elections, therefore, Western donors faced a stark dilemma: they could join Odinga's protest against the flawed elections and seek a thorough judicial account, or they could seek an immediate solution to the electoral violence in the aftermath of disputed elections; they opted for the latter.

For several years following the agreement, the power-sharing government essentially buried the issue of culpability for the violence, disappointing those who favored justice for the crimes of incitement (Hansen 2013). Eventually, as promised, Annan turned over evidence he had collected as mediator to the ICC. After further investigations, the ICC indicted six high-profile Kenyans for their roles in the violence, conveniently three on each side. The most well-known were Uhuru Kenyatta and William Ruto, longtime politicians who were on opposite sides of the 2007–2008 violence. Both announced plans to run for president in 2013. Even as the ICC charges were pending, the two men joined forces as running mates on a single ticket with Kenyatta at the top.

Instead of being harmed by the pending criminal cases, Kenyatta and Ruto campaigned against the ICC, bashing it as a neocolonial institution that was digging up old animosities when Kenyans wanted to focus on the future (Malik 2016).

The 2013 election once again posed a dilemma for donors, this time between justice for human rights violations on one hand and respect for democracy on the other. Although the Kenyan population was aware that Kenyatta had been indicted by the ICC, he was elected narrowly with 51 percent of the vote. The result allowed him to avoid a runoff against Odinga under the new majority system laid out in the 2010 constitution. Perhaps as a result of ongoing fears stemming from the earlier post-election violence, the 2013 elections were marked by fewer irregularities and less controversy than any since 2002. Accordingly, donor governments joined Africa's states in quickly recognizing Kenyatta's victory after the elections. Kenyatta was also supported by his African peers in insisting that he should not face interrogation before the ICC until after his term ended.[21] Donors not only accepted the election results but also lavished an all-time high amount of aid on the Kenyan state in 2013. Kenyatta was also bolstered by the 2015 visit of President Barack Obama, who had avoided visiting his father's homeland earlier in his presidency because of the marred 2007 election. The visit underscored the close political and military relations that have developed between the United States and Kenya in the battle against Somalia's al-Shabaab (see Chapter 10),[22] despite lingering US concerns about the role of Kenya's president and vice president in the earlier post-election violence (Whitaker 2013). In August 2017, Kenyatta defeated Odinga in another election marred by irregularities. Even as donor countries quickly accepted the outcome, Kenya's high court nullified the results and required the presidential election to be held again two months later. Concerned about the lack of meaningful reform to the electoral commission, Odinga and his supporters boycotted the October rerun, guaranteeing Kenyatta a second term and allowing donors to avoid the dilemmas that could have resulted from another contested outcome. Thus, state interests played a significant role in the conflicting imperatives of justice and democracy in this case.

Notes

1. This observation is very widely attributed to Gabonese president Omar Bongo, both in Africa and in the West, but it was originally stated, apparently, by this French minister.

2. These conferences were essentially constitutional conventions that replaced single-party constitutions with new, multiparty constitutions.

3. According to most theories of democratization, "transition" from authoritarian rule to a democratic experiment is the initial phase of the process. Transitional democracies must then undergo "consolidation" before they become stable, democratic polities.

4. Mobutu Sese Seko of Zaire became much closer to France after 1990, when he was essentially abandoned by the United States, and survived in power for seven more years.

5. "Good governance," a term popular in the early 1990s, refers to the quality of government decisionmaking and implementation rather than the processes of how those who govern are chosen. It entails the rule of law and the limitation of corruption in government operations.

6. China and most other Arab states, including Saudi Arabia, are not members of the DAC or the OECD, and their levels of aid are hard to gauge. In any case, none of these countries is a democracy, and few if any are specifically interested in democracy in Africa, though each may advocate for some elements of good governance.

7. Data on Zimbabwe's elections can be found on the African Elections Database at http://africanelections.tripod.com/zw.html.

8. All figures on US aid to the DRC in this paragraph are taken from US Federal Budget 2015a. The figures are adjusted for inflation and are in 2015 US dollars. On the advent of the Mobutu regime, see Chapter 3.

9. This committee was composed of the ambassadors of fifteen countries and intergovernmental organizations (the European Union) in the DRC, including those from some African countries (Angola and South Africa) as well as from China.

10. This organization also provides invaluable electoral analysis through its *Journal of African Elections,* available at https://eisa.org.za.

11. Information on all past and current UN peacekeeping operations may be found on the website of the UN Department of Peacekeeping Operations at https://peacekeeping.un.org/en.

12. For the work on the US Agency for International Development on civil society in Africa, for instance, see its website at https://www.usaid.gov/africa-civil-society.

13. Three of those wanted by the Court were from Libya (North Africa). These twenty-five cases include ones in which those wanted never have been apprehended, ones in which charges were dropped (notably, against Kenyan president Uhuru Kenyatta), ones in which trials led to convictions and sentences, and ones in which trials led to acquittals. See the following page on the ICC website: https://www.icc-cpi .int/Pages/cases.aspx.

14. The text of the address may be found at https://georgewbush-whitehouse .archives.gov/news/releases/2005/01/20050120-1.html.

15. We thank Fiacre Bienvenu for drawing our attention to this organization.

16. For more information, see https://freedomhouse.org/search/Tanzania.

17. To illustrate, in 2015, Canada and France both scored a combined rating of 2, whereas Sudan and North Korea each scored 14.

18. Data for the earlier years were taken from a spreadsheet titled "Freedom House World Rankings, 1990–2005," downloaded in 2006. The figure for 2015 was taken from Freedom House 2015.

19. As a result of the constitutional changes in 1992, the two-term limit applied to subsequent elections. Thus, despite having been in office since 1978, Moi was permitted to serve two five-year terms thereafter.

20. On August 7, 1998, a car bomb exploded outside the US embassy in downtown Nairobi, killing more than 200 Kenyans and 12 Americans. The incident, and the sense that Kenya was targeted due in part to its long friendship with the United

States, temporarily reduced the pressure that US officials put on the Moi administration for political reform.

21. Not long after the election, the ICC cases against Kenyatta and Ruto were
suspended, due in part to the fact that several witnesses recanted their testimony.

22. The United States has apparently been operating a de facto military facility
in coastal Kenya, called Camp Simba, since 2006 or earlier (see Barnett 2007). This
facility no doubt supported US operations against the Islamic Courts Union, Somali
pirates operating in the Indian Ocean, and later al-Shabaab (see Chapter 10).

6

The Elusive Goal of African Unity

As soon as their countries gained independence, Africa's new leaders sought to build diplomatic and economic ties with others in the region. In 1963, leaders of thirty-two sovereign states established the continent-wide Organization of African Unity. Despite the pleas of Ghanaian president Kwame Nkrumah for a stronger union, the OAU was formed as a relatively weak intergovernmental organization. Other countries joined as they emerged from colonial rule in the ensuing years, and smaller intergovernmental organizations were formed throughout the continent.[1] Broadly speaking, these regional and subregional institutions represented an effort to support mutual development and liberation and to reduce Africa's dependence on the outside world, even as leaders continued to cultivate external partners and pursue more self-serving interests behind the scenes. The OAU focused from the beginning on political goals but has adopted a more ambitious economic agenda in recent years, especially since its 2002 transition to the African Union. In contrast, most subregional organizations were created initially to pursue economic goals, particularly growth and development. Over time, though, they have been drawn increasingly into the political and security concerns of their member states.

This chapter examines the quest for unity in Africa at both the regional and subregional levels. We start by looking at continent-wide cooperation, including the strengths and weaknesses of the OAU, the reasons behind its transition to the AU, and the organization's record since then in collectively managing the various challenges facing African member states. Next, we turn more specifically to the question of economic integration, discussing the motivations behind various initiatives at the subregional level and the obstacles they have faced over the years. Through an exploration of several cases (East African Community, Economic Community of West African States, and Southern African Development Community), it becomes clear that economic integration in Africa remains as elusive today as it was half a century ago. The chapter ends with a case study of Nigeria, whose status as the largest country in Africa has influenced intergovernmental cooperation at both the continental and subregional levels.

Continent-Wide Cooperation

When the newly independent states of Africa created the Organization of African Unity in 1963, it had two main stated goals. The first was to end colonialism and white minority rule on the continent. At the time of the OAU's founding, many Africans were still fighting for independence from European colonial rule. The OAU and its member states provided financial and diplomatic support to liberation struggles throughout Africa, typically recognizing a single nationalist movement in each colony.[2] Over time, country after country became independent, joining the OAU themselves,[3] though the struggle against white minority rule in southern Africa took longer. Eventually, with the installation of African majority governments in Zimbabwe (1980), Namibia (1990), and South Africa (1994), the process was complete and colonialism in Africa was over. With respect to this key goal, then, the OAU could claim ultimate success.

The second stated goal of the OAU from its founding was to collectively resolve conflict and pursue economic development. In these areas, much less progress was made in the three decades after the organization's creation. Even today, most African countries linger near the bottom of the list on standard measures of economic development. Africa remains the world's most aid-dependent region (see Chapter 4), and economic integration efforts described later in this chapter have failed to counteract this marginality. On resolving conflict, the OAU record was arguably even worse. Through the 1980s, with the exception of a short-lived Nigerian-led peacekeeping mission in Chad in 1981–1982, the organization did little to address conflicts throughout the continent: Mozambique, Angola, Burundi, Uganda, Ghana, Nigeria. Even after the 1992 creation of the OAU Mechanism for Conflict Prevention, Management, and Resolution, large-scale wars in Somalia, Rwanda, Sudan, Liberia, and Sierra Leone highlighted the impotence of the OAU in this area (see Chapter 7).

A key reason for the inability of the OAU to achieve its economic and political goals, especially in the area of conflict resolution, was its prioritization of the principle of noninterference. This goes back to its origins as an organization for countries that had just gained independence after years of colonial domination. The OAU's founding fathers relished their newfound sovereignty and did not want to subject their countries— or their own regimes—to any form of foreign domination, whether from outside the continent or within. They also wanted to preserve the status quo in terms of territorial borders, as discussed at length in Chapter 2. The founders thus filled the OAU Charter with language about sovereignty, noninterference, and respecting the territorial integrity of member states.[4] When domestic power disputes turned violent, therefore, the prescribed role of the OAU was not to intervene. This principle was so sacrosanct that the OAU denounced Tanzania's 1979 invasion of Uganda as a violation of sovereignty, despite the initial attack into Tanzania by Idi Amin's troops, and forced Tanzania to pay the costs of the war (Taylor 2013). As realists would have anticipated, the OAU was an organization of sovereign states that took action only on the rare occasions when it served their collective interests.

In the 1990s, with the OAU's failure to do anything in crisis after crisis, some Africans started calling for change. A generation after colonialism ended in most countries, they were less concerned about blindly respecting sovereignty and sought an organization that would be able to better address emerging conflicts. They also wanted to jump-start economic growth by working toward continent-wide trade deals and integration efforts. By the end of the decade, these ideas had worked their way into discussions in the halls of the OAU headquarters in Addis Ababa, Ethiopia, and among officials in various corners of the continent.

The push to reform the OAU, and ultimately to transform it into the African Union, was driven in large part by the leaders of three regional powers: South Africa's Thabo Mbeki, Nigeria's Olusegun Obasanjo, and Libya's Muammar Qaddafi (Tieku 2004). Mbeki and Obasanjo were each elected president of their respective country in 1999. Mbeki had been deputy president under Nelson Mandela, who chose to serve just one term, and had dreams of an "African renaissance" in which his newly liberated country would play a leading role (Mbeki 1998). In addition to promoting South Africa's commercial interests in the rest of Africa,[5] he sought to transform the image of the OAU as a "dictators' club" (Tieku 2004). Obasanjo, a retired military leader, was elected president in Nigeria's first multiparty elections in nearly two decades. He also had hopes that Africa was turning a page on its past and sought OAU support for his proposed Conference on Security, Stability, Development, and Cooperation in Africa. In contrast, Qaddafi had been in power since 1969 and had meddled frequently in sub-Saharan African affairs, including in Liberia (see Chapter 8) and Chad, but his diplomatic

focus had been on building bonds among Arab countries. After his relations with the League of Arab States soured in the late 1990s (Sturman
2003), Qaddafi increasingly turned to Africa, where his country's oil
wealth bought him significant influence.

At an extraordinary summit in Sirte, Libya, in 1999, Qaddafi surprised African leaders with his proposal for a "United States of Africa,"
which competed with proposals already circulated by South Africa and
Nigeria. Delicately avoiding a direct rejection of their host, delegates
voted instead to develop a new institution that would replace the OAU.
The resulting Constitutive Act of the African Union, signed in Lomé,
Togo, in 2000, drew heavily on the ideas of Mbeki and Obasanjo (whose
representatives were involved in its drafting) while rebuffing Qaddafi's
more radical and ambitious plans. A disappointed Qaddafi came to the
inaugural meeting of the African Union in 2002 with proposed amend-
ments, including one for a single African army, but was prevented from
introducing them because he had not circulated them in advance (Tieku
2004). Qaddafi pushed for greater AU authority until his ouster from
power in 2011, but he never gained as much influence as he had hoped.

Even without his more radical ideas, the new African Union had
ambitious plans. In seeking to promote peace, security, and development through continent-wide cooperation and integration, it developed
a range of new institutions. Several began operating within a few years
of the AU's creation: the Pan-African Parliament, now based in South
Africa; the fifteen-member Peace and Security Council, with three
rotating members from each of Africa's five geographic regions; the
African Court of Justice, based in Tanzania; and the AU Commission,
essentially the secretariat, based in Ethiopia. The AU also has plans for
the creation of an African Central Bank, which would eventually regulate a common currency throughout the continent.

Perhaps the most important change in the transition from the OAU to
the AU is the abandonment of the principle of nonintervention. Instead,
Article 4(h) of its Constitutive Act gives the AU the right to intervene in
a member state "in respect of grave circumstances, namely war crimes,
genocide and crimes against humanity." In practice, and per the requirements of the United Nations Charter, the AU has sought UN Security
Council authorization for its military interventions and has not intervened without the consent of the host government (Williams 2011). In
early 2016, for example, the AU scrapped plans to send 5,000 peacekeepers to contain escalating violence in Burundi when President Pierre
Nkurunziza (whose bid for a third term triggered the violence) likened
such action to an invasion. Although this move was criticized as a missed
opportunity to protect victims of a long-simmering conflict (International

Crisis Group 2016), the Constitutive Act clearly reflects a shift in attitude with respect to the expected role of the AU when violence erupts, and it provides the organization more legal authority to act.

In seeking to prevent, manage, and resolve conflicts throughout the continent, the AU's Peace and Security Council is supported by the Continental Early Warning System, which provides information and analysis about potential problem spots, and the Panel of the Wise, whose members are meant to facilitate communication between parties to a conflict. In practice, funding shortfalls and political arguments have limited the effectiveness of these bodies (Williams 2011), though their efforts continue. The AU's African Peace and Security Architecture (APSA) also includes the African Standby Force (ASF), which will ultimately include 25,000 troops who can deploy rapidly when conflict prevention fails. Political and logistical challenges delayed ASF implementation (Williams 2011), but it started successful training exercises in 2015 (Rees 2015). The ongoing development of these various AU peace and security initiatives aligns nicely with broader rhetoric about "African solutions to African problems," which has circulated both within Africa and beyond since the 1990s.[6]

Since its creation in 2002, the African Union has authorized several peacekeeping operations around the continent, most notably the African Union Mission in Burundi (AMIB, 2003–2004), the African Union Mission in Sudan (AMIS, 2004–2007), which was replaced by the hybrid United Nations–African Union Mission in Darfur (UNAMID, 2008–present), and the African Union Mission in Somalia (AMISOM, 2007–present). Between 2006 and 2008, the AU also conducted three operations in Comoros to monitor and support elections there and to oust an unconstitutionally elected leader from the island of Anjouan (Williams 2009). Debates about peacekeeping are discussed more extensively in Chapter 8, but in general these operations represent a growing commitment among African leaders for the AU to take a lead role in addressing conflict and insecurity within the region. Indeed, as part of its fiftieth-anniversary celebrations in 2013, the AU endorsed a vision of "silencing the guns" in Africa by 2020. While the goal of ending conflict is laudable (if somewhat unrealistic), insecurity is only one of many challenges facing the continent (Schünemann 2014).

On the economic side, the AU also includes a new approach to regional cooperation. Launched in 2001 and later folded into the AU umbrella, the New Partnership for Africa's Development (NEPAD) aimed to promote sustainable development, good governance, respect for human rights, and the integration of Africa into the global economy. It was spearheaded by South Africa, Nigeria, Algeria, Senegal, and Egypt, whose leaders were offering various competing economic plans at the time. From its inception, NEPAD aimed to cut poverty in half by 2015, which was also perhaps unrealistic but a worthwhile goal nonetheless. It actively pursued an agreement (or partnership) with the world's wealthiest countries to provide new aid and investment if African governments implemented desired economic and political reforms, prompting critics to blast it for promoting a neoliberal agenda (Taylor 2010).

As NEPAD garnered headlines in the early 2000s, especially in South Africa, whose President Mbeki was its strongest proponent, many wondered what was so "new" about it (de Waal 2002). In many ways, it was an effort to gather and promote best practices without creating a lot of new institutions, which was seen by some as a strength. The key difference from previous continental initiatives such as the OAU and AU, however, was that NEPAD did not automatically include all African countries. Instead, AU members had to meet certain economic and governance standards to be admitted into NEPAD and thus have access to resources secured through its partnership with donor countries (de Waal 2002). The selective nature of NEPAD was a source of some controversy within the AU but moved in the direction of the European Union in terms of requiring countries to meet certain standards to join.

Another unique feature of NEPAD was its African Peer Review Mechanism (APRM), established in 2002. After first doing a self-assessment, signatory countries agreed to be evaluated by a panel of eminent Africans with respect to their human rights, governance, and economic records. This innovation reflected Mbeki's philosophical commitment to the notion of Africans regulating themselves, but the process was fraught with challenges from the beginning. Its voluntary nature meant that there was tension between setting the bar low enough for leaders to be willing to subject their countries to peer review and high enough to satisfy donors. One of the first countries to undergo review—Rwanda—exemplified these problems, starting with the release of a "rosy" self-assessment that "inadequately addresses a number of serious political problems in Rwanda" (Jordaan 2006: 333). When the report from the panel of eminent persons basically accepted Rwanda's self-assessment with a call to keep working on governance matters (Stultz 2006), critics questioned the value of the process altogether. Similar concerns emerged regarding the peer review of Kenya, which was described as a "model of best practice" and a "bastion of stability" (Stultz 2006), despite rampant corruption and widespread political mobilization along ethnic lines, among other challenges (see Chapter 5).

As the APRM process faced criticism about its rigor, donor funds dried up due to the global recession starting in 2008, and as key drivers such as Mbeki and Obasanjo ended their terms in office, it became increasingly clear that NEPAD would not meet its initial goals with respect to poverty reduction and economic growth. Skeptics worried that NEPAD was doing little more than legitimizing authoritarian governments in the eyes of donors by providing them with a regional stamp of approval. Although "NEPAD has died a death, for all practical purposes" (Taylor 2010: 64), there were renewed efforts at the AU Summit in January 2016 to revive the APRM process (Adebajo 2016). The goal of having a selective international organization with clear criteria for membership and a rigorous process of peer review remained intriguing to observers who ultimately want to see an EU-like structure within Africa.

In recent years, the AU has developed other innovative programs, particularly with regard to financing operations. In 2012, it created a risk-pooling insurance mechanism for natural disasters known as African Risk Capacity (ARC).[7] Participating member states[8] pay premiums each year; when a country experiences a natural disaster, it receives a payout to assist affected households (Runde 2015). The program focuses on droughts but aims to cover floods and other natural disasters too. Another innovation seeks to address the chronic shortfall of funds, especially for peace and security operations. In 2016, member states agreed to impose a 0.2 percent levy on eligible imports, with the revenue to go to AU operations and its Peace Fund. The goal is to generate at least 25 percent of AU funding from internal sources instead of relying on external donors.[9] In 2017, Ghana, Kenya, and Rwanda became the first countries to implement the AU import levy (Dogbevi 2017), though others are expected to do so soon.

Most recently, in early 2018, the AU adopted a protocol promoting the free movement of people within Africa and eventually residency rights. Building on the successes of subregional organizations with regard to visa-free movement among citizens of member countries (see later), the AU protocol calls on members to grant visas on arrival to all Africans by the end of 2018 and to eliminate all visa requirements for fellow Africans by 2023. Several countries, including Seychelles, Ghana, Rwanda, Nigeria, and Kenya, already grant visas on arrival to citizens of African countries, but others have significant obstacles to entry. Even as governments move toward greater freedom of movement within the region, many migrants continue to face hostility, discrimination, and violence in other African countries (see Chapter 9).

Despite renewed energy and innovation behind continent-wide cooperation, there are reasons to question the extent to which the African Union represents a real turning of the page in African international relations. The heads of state chosen to chair the AU in its first sixteen years included some democratically elected leaders (South Africa's Mbeki, Nigeria's Obasanjo, Ghana's John Kufuor, Malawi's Bingu wa Mutharika), to be sure, but also some of the continent's longest-serving authoritarian rulers: Denis Sassou Nguesso (Congo-Brazzaville), Qaddafi (Libya), Teodoro Obiang Nguema Mbasogo (Equatorial Guinea), Idriss Déby (Chad), Robert Mugabe (Zimbabwe), and Paul Kagame (Rwanda). The selection of leaders such as these suggests that the African Union is no more committed to democratic principles than was its predecessor. Furthermore, the organization's attempt in 2011 to mediate a resolution to Libya's civil war was seen by many outsiders as an (ultimately unsuccessful) effort to prevent the overthrow of Qaddafi. In 2016, the decision not to send peacekeepers into Burundi because of its president's refusal begs the question of whether the AU will employ the right to intervene outlined in Article 4(h) as intended.

The bias toward protecting one's own members has been obvious once again in recent debates about African membership in the International Criminal Court. In January 2016, the AU approved the development of a road map for African countries to withdraw from the ICC's governing Rome Statute. Although African leaders initially celebrated the ICC's creation in 2002 and most countries became state parties to its statute, they now accuse it of focusing only on war crimes in Africa and ignoring those in other regions (Taylor 2015). As evidence, they point to the fact that all forty-one people indicted by the ICC as of late 2017 were African, though investigations were under way in other regions. But African leaders themselves requested many of these investigations, and several offending regimes in other regions (Syria, for example) are not signatories to the Rome Statute, making the reasons for the emphasis on Africa more apparent (Cronin-Furman 2015). Nonetheless, there is a growing perception among African leaders that the ICC is biased (Mills 2012). Critics see the movement for African countries to withdraw from the ICC, especially without any clear alternative plan to seek justice for war crimes, as an effort to protect wrongdoers and perpetuate a long-standing culture of impunity.

Leading the charge against the ICC in the African Union has been Kenyan president Uhuru Kenyatta, who was indicted by the Court for his alleged role in post-election violence in early 2008;[10] his case was dropped later when witnesses refused to testify against a sitting president (see Chapter 5). Another ICC critic, Sudanese president Omar al-Bashir, has traveled to at least four other African countries freely despite an outstanding warrant for his arrest on war crimes charges (Keppler 2012; Mills 2012). But Burundi, South Africa, and Gambia were the first AU members to announce plans to leave the ICC, in

October 2016. The leaders of Burundi and Gambia were facing potential ICC investigations, and the government of South Africa was the
subject of intense criticism for not having arrested al-Bashir during a
2015 summit in Johannesburg. South Africa's decision prompted an
outcry from human rights activists, who brought a case in court, and a
strong rebuke from Botswana, which has emerged as the leading
African defender of the ICC (*This Is Africa* 2016). In an interesting
twist, both Gambia and South Africa revoked their withdrawals in early
2017, the former after its long-standing leader was ousted in an election and the latter after a court ruled the decision unconstitutional. In
October 2017, Burundi became the first African state to formally leave
the ICC.[11] Even as the AU seeks to move forward on security and
development, therefore, debates such as the one regarding African
membership in the ICC generate doubts about the organization's ability
to move beyond legacies of the past.

The Logic of Integration

Economic integration has been an ideal since the pan-African movement
of the early 1900s and gained strength during anticolonial struggles in
the 1950s, but few leaders in postcolonial Africa have been committed to
making it a reality. Despite the appeal of bringing African countries
together into regional and subregional groupings, diplomatic wrangling,
economic obstacles, and a basic lack of political will are among the
many challenges that have come in the way of achieving anything close
to the level of integration seen in other regions of the world, especially
Western Europe. Even so, integration remains a long-term goal for many
African peoples, if not always their leaders (Bach 1999).

Economic integration typically proceeds in stages. The first stage
often is a free trade area, in which member countries drop tariffs and
other restrictions on trade with one another. A free trade area may then
become a customs union, in which member states impose a common set
of external tariffs on goods coming from nonmember countries. In some
cases, customs unions redistribute revenues from these tariffs among
members according to an agreed formula. The next step is a common
market, which allows for the free movement of labor and capital among
countries within the grouping. Eventually, some regional organizations
form a monetary union in which they share a common currency regulated by a central bank, thus requiring members to give up control over
their own fiscal policies (Mirus and Rylska 2001). Because most states
are reluctant to cede power to supranational organizations, as realists
would predict, few regional bodies have achieved that level of integration. Higher levels of economic integration often are accompanied by

some level of political integration, as in the European Union. Indeed, political integration has been the ultimate goal for various African leaders going back to Nkrumah and Nyerere, even if they differed over the recommended pace of change.

Integration in Africa is appealing for many reasons. Most obvious, the integration of African countries into larger regional and subregional groupings could serve to counteract the political, social, and economic fragmentation that resulted from the imposition of arbitrary borders by European colonial powers. As discussed in Chapter 2, colonial borders frequently dissected existing cultural areas, leaving some groups divided between multiple colonies and lumping together other groups who previously had not lived within a single political entity. Precolonial patterns of trade and migration also were disrupted as European powers sought to control movement across these borders. When African leaders opted to preserve the colonial boundaries after independence, regional integration offered a less radical alternative that would allow for more cross-border trade, cooperation, and migration without completely changing the map of Africa, and with it the organization of power on the continent.

Many African countries have small populations, limiting the size of the market to which local producers can sell their products. Seven sub-Saharan countries have populations under 1 million people, and another twelve countries have populations under 5 million. Regional integration is especially appealing to small countries because it expands the size of the market to which local producers can sell their products without facing tariffs and other tax restrictions, allowing them to realize economies of scale.

For the sixteen landlocked countries in sub-Saharan Africa, regional integration is particularly appealing. Governments of countries such as Niger, Uganda, and Botswana must negotiate with their neighbors for access to railroads and shipping ports to export their products. This process can become highly politicized. During the apartheid era in South Africa prior to 1990, for example, many governments in southern Africa sought alternative routes to avoid paying transit costs to the white minority government there. More recently, only a year after South Sudan won a decades-long struggle and gained independence from Sudan in 2011, a dispute about the transit fees imposed by Sudan for using its oil pipeline forced South Sudan (one of the poorest countries in the world) to suspend oil production for several months (see Chapter 2). Facing such challenges, landlocked countries often view regional integration as a way to negotiate more consistent access to export routes from their neighbors in exchange for the larger market they can provide.

Building on these economic incentives within Africa, regional integration also has the potential of helping African countries counteract their marginality within the global economy more broadly. Larger regional markets can attract foreign investors who are seeking to reach as many consumers as possible with their investment dollars (or euros or yuan). Investing in a country with a domestic market of fewer than 5 million people may not be very attractive to a foreign businessperson, but calculations may change dramatically if that country is part of a tariff-free regional grouping that includes 50 million potential consumers. Regional integration in Africa thus offers the promise of increased foreign direct investment. If managed properly, more FDI can mean less dependence on aid and other forms of development assistance (Moyo 2009). When African countries are permitted to negotiate as one or more regional groupings in international economic talks, their bargaining power also may be enhanced.

Last, regional integration in Africa has been motivated by the success of such processes in other parts of the world. Although African leaders have taken some inspiration from the North America Free Trade Agreement (NAFTA) and the Association of Southeast Asian Nations (ASEAN), they have been especially focused on the process of integration in the European Union. There are obvious differences between the EU and the AU, not least being that the former sets clear criteria for membership and aspiring countries must go through a lengthy review process before admission. Even so, the notion that a negotiated economic agreement among six countries (the European Coal and Steel Community of 1951) can grow into a continent-wide economic union with supranational political institutions gives hope to Africans who eventually want to see similar levels of integration across their own continent.

Despite these many appeals of regional integration, it has had limited success in the African context. At least fifteen subregional organizations have been established since independence (Scott 2011), most of them with explicit economic goals, yet few have gone beyond creating a free trade area by limiting tariffs and quotas among members. Plans to establish common external tariffs (customs unions) or adopt a common currency (monetary unions) generally have fallen short. As a result, intra-regional trade in Africa remains quite low. In 2014, for example, just 17.7 percent of African countries' exports went to other countries within the region, compared to 27.3 percent that went to Asia and 36.2 percent to Europe (World Trade Organization 2015). Although these figures do not include unrecorded trade outside of official channels, which can be significant (Kennes 1999), intra-regional trade is lower in Africa than in nearly every other region.[12] In addition, there has been limited progress on plans to facilitate the movement of capital, services, and workers within such groupings. Whereas some subregional organizations have made renewed progress toward their goals in recent years, as discussed later, others are little more than a series of promises on paper.

Why has regional integration had such limited success in Africa? The most important obstacle has been the lack of political will among leaders who are not willing to give up control over economic levers that allow them to dole out patronage in exchange for loyalty. Personal rivalries among leaders also have hindered collaboration in some regions, while tensions between governments with different approaches to economic policy (especially socialist versus market-oriented policies during the Cold War) have thwarted efforts in others. The divide between francophone and anglophone countries has been a fault line at times in West Africa. In theory, such challenges can be overcome if leaders are sufficiently committed to the process and goals of integration. In practice, however, African leaders have jealously guarded the prerogatives of sovereignty and have allowed these tensions to block integration efforts.

Another obstacle to regional integration has been domestic politics in member countries. The prevalence of civil conflict in particular has forced leaders of regional organizations to focus on trying to achieve political stability before they can work toward economic integration. When people are dying, the terms of a negotiated free trade area or customs union do not warrant the same level of attention. This shift was most obvious for the Economic Community of West African States, which got into the peacekeeping business in the 1990s in response to civil wars in Liberia, Sierra Leone, and Guinea-Bissau. Indeed, most regional organizations in Africa that originally were formed with economic goals have eventually found themselves dealing with member states' domestic political issues.

Economic factors also have hindered the regional integration process in Africa. Although the goal of increasing intra-regional trade is attractive, in reality there are limited benefits to trade among African countries, many of which produce and export similar products. Despite diversification efforts over the past few decades, most African economies remain heavily dependent on a handful of primary commodities.[13] Countries within a given region of the continent often produce very similar agricultural and mineral products, limiting opportunities for specialization within regional groupings. There is little benefit in exporting Kenyan coffee to Tanzania, for example, as it produces and exports its own coffee. Until African economies are diversified enough to develop comparative advantages in certain areas, it is unlikely that there will be sufficient complementarity to dramatically increase intra-regional trade.

Another obstacle to increasing economic activity among African countries is the continent's poor infrastructure. During the colonial era, most roads and railways were designed with the purpose of getting raw materials from the interior to the coast for exporting to Europe. Even where infrastructure has been built to facilitate travel and trade among African people in the interior, it has been poorly maintained (Kennes 1999) and does not use modern technology that would sufficiently reduce the cost of transport. While recent Chinese investment in the continent's infrastructure has the potential of facilitating more trade among African countries (or of reinforcing the existing emphasis on natural resource extraction) (see Chapter 12), for now most movement of goods continues to be within individual countries.

Where regional organizations have been established in Africa, the benefits of cooperation often have been uneven, as illustrated by the first iteration of the East African Community (see below). Although multiple countries within a regional grouping may agree to open their economies to competition with one another, some may benefit disproportionately, perhaps because they have better infrastructure or policies that are more attractive to foreign investors, or simply because they have more people. Under such circumstances, other member states often become resentful and decide that the costs of collaboration are not worth the uneven benefits.

The fact that regional integration in Africa is both appealing and challenging is perhaps best evidenced by the multiplicity of organizations that have been founded since independence. There are subregional bodies in varying stages of integration throughout Africa, and many countries are members of several agreements. This has generated a confusing network of subregional organizations with overlapping memberships, complicating integration efforts within each and creating tensions among them (Kennes 1999). Leaders at times have to choose between obligations to two or more different subregional organizations. Tanzania, for example, has struggled to meet its commitments on tariff rates and other policies to both the East African Community and the Southern African Development Community (Mashindano, Rweyemamu, and Ngowi 2007), prompting calls for it to choose one or the other. Kenya and Uganda are members of the Intergovernmental Authority on Development and the EAC, while the Democratic Republic of Congo has obligations to SADC and the Economic Community of Central African States.

This tension between the desirability of economic integration and the challenges posed by too many integration efforts led African leaders to sign the Abuja Treaty in 1991, establishing the African Economic Community (AEC). With a long-term goal of creating a continent-wide economic and monetary union by 2028, the AEC sought first to harmonize and coordinate activities of existing and new regional economic communities (RECs) that would serve as its building blocks. Under the African Union, the AEC has made a more concerted effort to push each country into just one of eight designated RECs; the 2007 Protocol on Relations Between the African Union and Regional Economic Communities specifically sought to address the issue of overlapping memberships. Even so, integration efforts are proceeding quickly in some RECs and are virtually nonexistent in others, and no REC fully achieved the AEC's intermediate goal of having a free trade area and customs union by 2017. The promise of integration has been further complicated by the complex legal web of treaties and agreements that have been created and the blurring of the line between economic integration and political unification (Oppong 2010).

Although the record of economic integration in Africa has been relatively weak and the process continues to face many obstacles, there are signs that the situation could be changing in some regions. The recent successes of some RECs, including those discussed in the next section, and the strong involvement of the African Union, have raised hopes that more progress will be made toward economic integration in the coming decades.

Experiences with Subregional Integration

While some regional economic communities have been formed recently, others have long and complicated histories. As the AEC moves toward its goal of establishing a continent-wide economic and monetary union, it is useful to examine the experiences of three RECs that have made more progress than some others at the subregional level: the East African Community, the Economic Community of West African States, and the Southern African Development Community. Two lessons emerge from the following sections. First, integration efforts often proceed in fits and starts, depending on a variety of factors, including leader personalities, economic conditions, and the global context. Second, economic integration is inherently political, at both the international and domestic levels. Political dynamics shape everything from the terms of agreements to the chances that provisions will be implemented. Without recognition of these realities, it is hard to imagine continent-wide integration efforts moving forward as smoothly as plans suggest.

East African Community

Kenya, Uganda, and Tanganyika shared collaborative institutions for decades under British colonial rule. Starting in the 1890s, East African postage stamps were used in Kenya and Uganda. The East African shilling was used throughout the subregion from the 1920s.[14] Transportation and shipping were facilitated by East African Airways, established in 1946, and by the East African Railways and Harbours Corporation, formed by a merger of the Kenya/Uganda railway and its Tanganyikan counterpart in 1948. The three colonies also shared a telecommunications network. These regional institutions continued to operate jointly under the East African Common Services Organization after independence in Tanganyika (1961), Uganda (1962), and Kenya (1963). Each country issued its own currency in 1966, but they were on par with one another and were regulated by a shared currency board.

The formation of the East African Community in 1967 was thus an effort to build upon existing institutions and to promote deeper regional integration through a common market and a customs union, with a goal of increased economic development for all three countries. Despite a long history of collaboration and lofty plans for the future, however, this iteration of the EAC fell apart within a decade. By 1977, not only were newly created EAC structures defunct, but preexisting collaborative institutions also were dismantled. The shared currency board, for example, gave way to separate central banks by 1968. East African Airways was liquidated, and each country established its own national airline (Kenya Airways, Uganda Airlines, and Air Tanzania). Railroads, ports, and postal networks met a similar fate. The leaders of Kenya, Uganda, and Tanzania decided to go their own ways, at least for the time being.

Why did the EAC fall apart after just ten years? If any regional economic grouping could have been expected to succeed, it would presumably be one with a long history of collaboration among member states. In reference to the integration challenges discussed earlier, there were two main reasons for the swift collapse of the EAC: political rifts among leaders and uneven gains of cooperation. When the EAC was first negotiated, the three countries were led by founding fathers who had been active in the anticolonial movement: Julius Nyerere in Tanzania, Jomo Kenyatta in Kenya, and Milton Obote in Uganda. All three were pursuing mixed economic policies that included a combination of state-run enterprises and private sector investment.

Even before the final EAC agreement was signed in December 1967, however, Nyerere started laying out a different economic course for Tanzania. In his Arusha Declaration earlier that year, Nyerere outlined the principles of *ujamaa,* or African socialism, and called for a policy of self-reliance. As these principles worked their way into policies over the coming years, the balance shifted in favor of government-run economic institutions and reflected an underlying distrust of the private sector. Like some other countries in Africa, Tanzania also moved away from the West and cultivated relations with a wide range of donors, including Scandinavian countries, China, and the Soviet Union. Kenya's Kenyatta, on the other hand, continued to implement mixed economic policies and to encourage foreign investment. His government remained close with Britain and developed strong ties with the United States. Over time, the conflicting economic approaches of the EAC's two larger economies became harder to reconcile, creating tensions that contributed to the regional agreement's collapse.

Perhaps even more important than the ideological divide between the Kenyan and Tanzanian leaders, however, were the dramatic changes of power in Uganda. After first relying on his military in a power struggle with a traditional king, Obote moved to undermine the growing popularity of his chief of staff, Idi Amin. In January 1971, while Obote was overseas, Amin seized power. The coup d'état was initially welcomed by some Ugandans concerned about economic woes and corruption, and by Western leaders, who thought Obote was moving toward socialism. But Amin's authoritarian nature and paranoid personality soon became apparent, as his forces violently attacked any sources of opposition to his rule. In one of the bloodiest periods in the country's troubled history, as many as half a million people were killed and thousands more imprisoned. Uganda's economy also was destroyed by Amin's policies, including the forced expulsion of Asians (many of them businesspeople of Indian descent) in 1972. Amin also nationalized many industries and expanded the public sector.[15] From Tanzania, where Obote was living in exile, Nyerere was a frequent critic of Amin's human rights abuses. With Uganda in a state of disarray and the economy there shrinking, there was no love lost between these two leaders when the EAC fell apart in 1977.[16]

Beyond these dramatic rifts among East African leaders, another reason for the EAC's collapse was the perception among people in Tanzania and Uganda that Kenya was benefiting disproportionately from the collaboration. Kenya entered into the agreement with the largest of the three economies, and its industrial sector in particular was much stronger. In addition, Kenya had better infrastructure, a more welcoming climate (especially in its capital city of Nairobi), and economic policies that encouraged private investment. It is not surprising, then, that many companies invested in Kenya and took advantage of EAC policies to sell their products throughout the subregion. With no system in place to compensate Tanzania and Uganda for these disparities, leaders and citizens in these countries became increasingly resentful. In light of these various challenges, it was no surprise when the EAC disbanded in 1977.

The most interesting aspect of the EAC's history, however, is its revival since 2000. Leaders of the three countries started discussing renewed cooperation in the early 1990s and signed a treaty in 1999 to reestablish the EAC the following year. In late 2001, the East African Legislative Assembly and the East African Court of Justice started operations in Arusha, Tanzania, with equal representation from the three countries. As initial steps were taken toward planned milestones — including a customs union, common market, monetary union, and eventual political federation — neighboring countries expressed interest in joining. Burundi and Rwanda became full members of the EAC in 2007, and South Sudan joined in 2016, despite its many troubles (see Chapter 2). Somalia's 2012 membership application remains on hold for now, though it is poised to become the EAC's seventh member soon.

Even as the EAC expands, it has continued to make progress toward some of its integration goals, such as harmonizing tariffs among members. One of the most obvious developments for people on the ground has been an agreement to allow member state citizens to travel within the community using their national identification cards instead of having to obtain costly passports and entrance visas. In 2017, EAC member states started replacing their national passports with East African passports, which are embedded with an electronic chip and valid for international travel. Kenya, Rwanda, and Uganda also started issuing an East African tourist visa that allows outsiders to visit all three countries on a single visa.

There are reasons to believe that the EAC could be more successful this time around, not least because it has already lasted several more years than its first iteration and neighboring countries have actively sought admission. Under the umbrella of donor-sponsored structural adjustment programs (see Chapter 4), the governments of the three largest EAC economies — Kenya, Uganda, and Tanzania — have been pursuing similar free market economic policies since the 1990s. The ideological divisions that undermined the EAC forty years ago no longer exist, and successive leaders of these countries also have gotten along with one another far better than did their predecessors. Recent growth of the Tanzanian and Ugandan economies and more welcoming policies toward foreign investment mean that they are in a better position to compete with Kenya now. The fact that the EAC integration process is moving slowly also gives hope that it can be done in a manner that satisfies all member states and that stays on track.

Nevertheless, there are still plenty of reasons to doubt that the EAC will fully achieve its integration goals. The organization already has failed to implement most planned milestones by the initial target dates, and Tanzania especially is wary of moving too quickly (Golooba-Mutebi 2013). Economic disparities among member countries remain, with Kenya's gross domestic product roughly equal to that of Tanzania and Uganda combined and its per capita income nearly five times as large as Burundi's. Perhaps most worrisome for a community that plans a political federation are the governance woes throughout the region, particularly the ongoing civil war in South Sudan and the recent escalation of political violence in Burundi. Uganda and Rwanda are led by authoritarian presidents who are reluctant to give up power, and Tanzania has had the same ruling party for five decades. Despite many flaws, Kenya is arguably the most democratic country in the region but has experienced election-related violence and terrorist attacks in recent years. Without resolutions to the many political challenges of its member countries, the EAC will continue to face obstacles in the integration process.

Economic Community of West African States

The Economic Community of West African States was founded in 1975 with a treaty among fifteen member states: Benin, Burkina Faso, Côte d'Ivoire, Gambia, Ghana, Guinea, Guinea-Bissau, Liberia, Mali, Mauritania, Niger, Nigeria, Senegal, Sierra Leone, and Togo. Cape Verde joined within two years, giving the organization sixteen members until Mauritania withdrew in 2000. ECOWAS thus encompasses francophone, anglophone, and lusophone countries. With a population of roughly 175 million, Nigeria has more people than the other members combined; seven ECOWAS member states have populations under 5 million people.

From the beginning, as implied by its name, ECOWAS was focused on economic issues. It sought to promote development in the region through an ambitious fifteen-year process of integration, moving from a free trade area with no restrictions on trade among members to a customs union with a common external tariff. The next step was to permit the movement of people and capital among members in a common market before establishing a full economic union with a shared currency throughout West Africa. To avoid distribution problems like those experienced in the EAC (which was collapsing when ECOWAS was established), the Fund for Cooperation, Compensation, and Development (FCCD) was designed to offset the uneven benefits of trade liberalization by compensating smaller countries for their losses (Ojo 1999).

More than four decades later, ECOWAS has barely moved beyond the first stage of its planned integration. Indeed, in 2015, Nigeria finally launched the implementation of the common external tariff, with other member states scheduled to implement it over a five-year transitional period. Plans for a common market and a full economic union are far from being realized. As with other efforts at regional integration in Africa, ECOWAS has experienced a variety of challenges since its creation.

A key reason for the slow progress of economic integration within ECOWAS is tension among member states, especially the anglophone and francophone blocs. This is less of a logistical issue than it is a problem of different approaches emerging from different colonial experiences. One example of this is the close relationship that many former French colonies such as Côte d'Ivoire and Senegal have had with their former colonial power (see Chapter 11). As a legacy of that relationship, seven former French colonies and one former Portuguese colony (Guinea-Bissau) in ECOWAS share a common currency known as the CFA franc, whose value is guaranteed by the French treasury.[17] These eight countries have sought to promote integration among themselves through the West African Economic and Monetary Union (UEMOA). Meanwhile, six other ECOWAS countries (five former British colonies plus Guinea, which dropped the CFA franc at independence in 1960) have been trying to establish a rival currency since 2000 through the West African Monetary Zone. Although the plan is to eventually merge these two currencies into one, periodic trade and policy disputes between and within the two groupings have hindered the broader integration process.

Another obstacle to the realization of ECOWAS goals has been fears of domination by the community's largest member state, Nigeria. Despite having received small amounts of compensation through the FCCD over the years, smaller countries have been resentful of Nigeria's economic strength and concerned about the competitiveness of their own economies. The fact that Nigeria is a major oil exporter and other ECOWAS members are net oil importers has only heightened these concerns. Although most other ECOWAS members have some level of suspicion of Nigeria, the francophone countries—the most influential of which are Côte d'Ivoire and Senegal—have been particularly adamant that the grouping not be dominated by a single state. They have sought at times to block Nigerian proposals and to alter their implementation (Adebajo 2002a).

The fact that many ECOWAS member states have been chronically delinquent in paying their dues is a small indication of perhaps the largest obstacle to regional integration in West Africa: many countries have other more important priorities. Foremost among these is the ongoing problem of conflict and political violence in the region. In the 1990s, the emergence of large-scale conflicts in several countries shifted the focus of regional leaders from economic issues to security concerns. A civil war in Liberia starting in 1989 had regional implications (see Chapter 8), as did

Sierra Leone's own deadly conflict in the 1990s. In 2002, a conflict in Côte d'Ivoire revolved around identity issues related to long-standing patterns of regional migration (see Chapter 10). Beyond civil wars, other forms of insecurity have plagued West Africa in recent years, including terrorist attacks by al-Qaeda in the Maghreb (AQIM) in Mali and Burkina Faso, and by Boko Haram in Nigeria and Niger. As ECOWAS states often deal with basic issues of insecurity and violence, economic integration is not always a top priority.

As the economic side of ECOWAS's mission stalled, members sought to address security concerns through the organization. The group negotiated a mutual defense assistance protocol in 1981. Then, in 1990, the ECOWAS Ceasefire Monitoring Group (ECOMOG) was created to intervene in Liberia's civil war (see Chapter 8). Reflecting regional divisions, it was led by Nigeria with the support of anglophone countries over the objections of the francophone bloc. ECOWAS also sent ECOMOG troops into Sierra Leone in 1997 to suppress a rebellion and into Guinea-Bissau in 1999 in response to a civil war. Each ECOMOG intervention was complicated by concerns about the dominance of Nigeria, which was a military dictatorship throughout the 1990s, and by divisions among ECOWAS members, some of whom supported competing sides in the conflicts. Such problems often exacerbated instead of alleviating underlying conflicts (Adebajo 2002a). Even so, in 1999 ECOWAS created its Mechanism for Conflict Prevention, Management, Resolution, Peacekeeping, and Security to consolidate ECOMOG's achievements with respect to conflict resolution (Economic Community of West African States 1999).

These peacekeeping operations receive more attention in Chapter 8, but the point here is that security challenges within the region forced ECOWAS as an organization to put its economic goals on the back burner. Increasingly, ECOWAS also has involved itself in the political affairs of member states, often under the auspices of its Supplementary Protocol on Democracy and Good Governance (2001). In response to military coups d'état in Togo (2005) and Burkina Faso (2015), for example, ECOWAS sent representatives to pressure officials to hold elections.[18] Since 2006, ECOWAS also has deployed teams of observers to monitor multiparty elections in various member countries. Even as progress toward the original economic goals of the organization has been delayed by persistent tensions and challenges, therefore, ECOWAS has moved in new directions—especially with regard to security and politics—and continues to be the most important regional grouping in West Africa. Like the EAC, ECOWAS may also be on a path toward expansion; in 2017, Morocco formally applied for membership and

Mauritania signed a cooperation agreement to allow the movement of goods and people and to strengthen security operations in the region.

Southern African Development Community

When nine southern African countries (Angola, Botswana, Lesotho, Malawi, Mozambique, Swaziland, Tanzania, Zambia, and Zimbabwe) initially formed the Southern African Development Coordination Conference (SADCC) in 1980, their underlying aims were to disengage from South Africa and reduce dependence on the white minority regime there. South Africa had the largest and most diverse economy in the region, with a mixture of industry, mining, and agriculture. Many countries in southern Africa relied heavily on trade with their powerful neighbor, typically exporting to South Africa raw materials and buying its finished goods, and often using its highways, railroads, and ports to ship products beyond the region. This was especially true for landlocked members, including Botswana, Zambia, Zimbabwe, and Malawi. Moreover, South Africa continued to be controlled by a white minority government under a system of segregation known as apartheid, which reserved nearly all political, economic, and educational opportunities for the small white minority and left the majority African population poor and powerless (see Chapter 9).

In order to counteract this economic dependence on the regional power, SADCC sought to facilitate cooperation on regional development projects and the allocation of international aid. Using a less centralized structure than the other regional organizations discussed earlier, each member state was assigned responsibility for coordinating SADCC efforts in a different sector: Angola for energy, Zambia for mining, Tanzania for trade, Zimbabwe for food security, and so on. An advantage of this dispersed structure was that coordination efforts were managed by existing ministries within each country and regional meetings were inter-ministerial instead of at the head-of-state level. In other words, the people who met to negotiate regional agreements were the actual ministers responsible for overseeing those sectors. A disadvantage perhaps was that the limited involvement of heads of state reduced the visibility of coordination efforts.

Despite these plans, SADCC made limited progress throughout the 1980s, in part because it was difficult to find technocratic solutions to structural problems. There were tensions among members at times, primarily with regard to how to handle changing circumstances in South Africa. Most SADCC governments[19] were among the so-called Frontline States (FLS) working to end minority rule in the region. They provided support and safe haven to South African freedom fighters from the African National Congress, allowing them to establish training camps within their borders (Lodge 1987). Longtime Malawian president Hastings Banda, in contrast, maintained diplomatic ties and advocated dialogue with the apartheid regime, a policy for which other SADCC leaders often criticized him, at one point even threatening an economic blockade (Klotz 1999). Although part of the FLS, Botswana initially opted for a nonconfrontational approach but joined Lesotho, Zambia, and Zimbabwe in rejecting South African demands for a nonaggression pact in the early 1980s (Dale 1987).

More than internal divisions about how to handle South Africa, however, the primary obstacle to SADCC's efforts was South Africa. Throughout the 1980s, its military launched a program of "regional destabilization" designed to punish neighboring countries for their support of the ANC (Martin and Johnson 1989). South African forces bombed and attacked key infrastructure in SADCC countries, including roads, bridges, rail links, and even health facilities (Cliff and Noorma-homed 1988). The apartheid government also periodically blocked migration of people from those countries seeking to work in South African mines, depriving their home economies of much-needed remittances. The scale of violence was especially high in Angola and Mozambique, where South Africa fomented outright civil war (Ramphele and Wilson 1987), but Botswana, Zambia, and Zimbabwe also suffered from periodic attacks. The human toll of South Africa's destabilization campaign was severe (Ramphele and Wilson 1987), and costs to the regional economy were estimated at $4 billion per year (Klotz 1999). These actions by the apartheid government highlighted the need for reduced economic dependence on South Africa, therefore, but also made that process more difficult.

The end of apartheid in the 1990s and the election of ANC leader Nelson Mandela as president in South Africa's first democratic election in 1994 dramatically changed both the composition and the goals of SADCC. In 1992, at a summit in the newly independent country of Namibia,[20] existing members and their host country transformed the grouping into the Southern African Development Community. The new organization sought to promote economic development in member countries through greater regional integration. Over the next several years, six new members (Democratic Republic of Congo, Madagascar, Mauritius, Namibia, Seychelles, and South Africa) joined the community, bringing total membership to fifteen countries. The most notable of these, of course, was South Africa, which in 1994 joined an organization originally formed to counteract its economic dominance. South Africa continues to have the largest economy in the region, and has

become a dominant player within SADC, but it now works in cooperation with other members instead of thwarting their integration efforts.

Since its transformation in the 1990s, SADC has made more
progress toward its economic goals. Under a new institutional structure
with offices in Botswana, SADC negotiated legally binding protocols in
traditional sectors of interest, including energy, fisheries, forestry, mining, and trade. It also moved into other areas (gender equality, environmental protection, corruption, and the free movement of people) and led
the formation of a fifteen-year regional development plan.[21] Perhaps
most important, SADC entered a new realm with its 1996 creation of
the Organ on Politics, Defense, and Security Cooperation. This body
authorized a joint military intervention in Congo-Kinshasa in 1998, giving legal cover for Angola, Namibia, and Zimbabwe's participation in
that war (see Chapter 7). SADC has continued to play an important role
in mediation efforts there, and SADC members Malawi, Tanzania, and
South Africa have been the primary contributors of 6,000 troops to the
Force Intervention Brigade (FIB), which has helped to reduce violence
in eastern Congo (Mutisi 2016). Most recently, in late 2017, SADC
launched a peacekeeping mission in Lesotho to address ongoing political instability after a series of political assassinations. Like ECOWAS,
therefore, SADC has moved into new areas beyond its initial economic
focus and is gaining strength in many ways.

Nevertheless, SADC's efforts continue to be hindered by two main
issues. The first is the existence of other subregional groupings whose
memberships overlap with that of SADC. For example, eight SADC
members including Zambia, Zimbabwe, Malawi, and Congo are also
members of the Common Market for Eastern and Southern Africa
(COMESA), a free trade area that stretches north to Egypt, while Tanzania is part of the reinvigorated EAC. In addition, five SADC members
are part of the long-standing Southern African Customs Union (SACU),
which has a common external tariff and shares revenues according to an
agreed formula. Making matters more complicated, twelve SADC members have been trying to create a SADC free trade area since 2008 while
also working with COMESA and the EAC toward a larger African free
trade zone. The competing objectives and overlapping memberships of
these different initiatives raise serious doubts as to whether any can
meet their planned milestones.[22]

SADC also has been criticized for not playing a more active role in
addressing recent economic and political crises in Zimbabwe, where President Robert Mugabe was in power from 1980 until 2017. His controversial politically motivated land reform process in the early 2000s forcibly
displaced many farmers (including members of the white minority) and

led to a huge drop in agricultural production, triggering a rapid economic decline. A series of contested elections, some of which turned violent, further undermined Mugabe's legitimacy. As most of the international community condemned Zimbabwe and applied targeted sanctions to its leaders, SADC pursued a policy of "silent diplomacy." Even as Zimbabwean citizens flocked to neighboring countries, and Botswana's President Ian Khama briefly advocated a more critical stance, SADC as an organization did nothing to punish Mugabe's behavior. This inaction may have been due to Mugabe's status as a leading anti-apartheid activist and a founding member of the organization, or to South Africa's concerns about its own unfinished process of land reform.

In late 2017, when ninety-three-year-old Mugabe appeared to designate his fifty-two-year-old wife as his successor, the Zimbabwean military stepped in, holding them both under house arrest until the aging president finally resigned. With the apparent blessing of military leaders and international allies, including South Africa and China, Mugabe's former vice president, Emmerson Mnangagwa, assumed the presidency and promised to hold elections within a year. While Zimbabwe's political future is far from certain, Mugabe's sudden downfall has removed a long-standing source of embarrassment for SADC that drew attention to the organization's limited capacity to deal with political challenges within key member countries.

Whither Regional Integration in Africa

As the African Union works toward greater continent-wide cooperation and subregional organizations redouble their integration efforts, now under the AU/AEC umbrella, the key question is whether they will succeed where predecessor organizations failed. As we have seen, the AU is different in important ways from the OAU, particularly with respect to having a right to intervene in member states under grave circumstances. It has taken a lead in addressing conflicts in places like Darfur, Somalia, and Burundi, where the OAU likely would have done little. The AU also seeks to play a greater role in coordinating economic integration efforts, in part by streamlining and removing duplication among the subregional bodies. Meanwhile, several subregional organizations have made more progress toward economic integration and have sought to address insecurity in member states. These developments give observers hope that the African Union and the continent's RECs will do more to address ongoing challenges on the continent.

At times, however, the AU runs the risk of looking like the OAU of old. A lingering perception of the continental body as little more than an "old boys' network" has been reinforced during recent debates about intervention in Libya and Burundi, and about African membership in the ICC, among other matters. At the 2016 AU Summit, Chadian president Idriss Déby (who has been in power for nearly three decades) complained, "Our organization acts as it has for the past 20 or 30 years: we meet often, we talk too much, we always write a lot, but we don't do enough, and sometimes nothing at all" (Adebajo 2016). Indeed, the African Union has few obvious successes when it comes to its conflict resolution and development goals.

Realists would not be surprised at all by the lack of progress toward regional integration in Africa. African leaders seek to protect their sovereignty and sustain their own domestic regimes, making use of regional and subregional organizations when doing so serves their purposes and ignoring them when it does not. On this logic, there is no inherent tension in the fact that a military government in Nigeria led the 1997 ECOMOG intervention to restore a democratically elected government in Sierra Leone (see case study at end of chapter) because democracy was not the issue. Indeed, African rulers often use subregional organizations to pursue regime interests. Another example would be Zimbabwe's participation in the SADC intervention in Congo (see Chapter 7), which allowed Mugabe to keep troops busy and divert domestic attention away from his government's many shortcomings. In this sense, then, realists would not expect African intergovernmental organizations to alter regime behavior in any meaningful way.

Even so, liberals may take hope in the fact that new institutions have been developed with more authority than in the past. They would acknowledge disappointment in the failed potential of the AU to expand freedoms and to promote development through larger markets, but would point to the emergence of legally binding protocols in SADC and the EAC as a sign that regional organizations can in fact constrain government behavior in important ways. The very fact that Zimbabwe and Nigeria seek SADC or ECOWAS authorization to intervene in another member state instead of just invading on their own suggests a role for such bodies. Along similar lines, constructivists would be encouraged that democratic norms have taken root in more countries, particularly among the peoples (if not the leaders) of Africa, and that the rules for regional organizations are changing. This is reflected most obviously in the change of language from the OAU Charter to the AU Constitutive Act, particularly the removal of the nonintervention principle. In the end, at least for the time being, it may be more realistic to expect small successes from cooperation at the subregional level, especially in the economic arena. These may lay the groundwork for more widespread cooperation and integration at the continental level, particularly if leaders can recognize mutual benefits.

Case Study: Nigeria as a Regional Power

As the most populated country on the continent and the seventh most populated country in the world, Nigeria has always been a key player in African international relations. Its role as a regional power, however, has frequently been undermined by its own turbulent history. Ever since independence in 1960, the country has experienced serious domestic challenges—regional and ethnic tensions, corruption, military dictatorships, ill-fated attempts at democracy, and violent insurgencies—that have affected its international reputation. Although there is hope that Nigeria has recently turned a corner, particularly with respect to democratization, ongoing challenges linger with implications for other countries in West Africa and beyond.

Nigerians have been divided along regional lines ever since the British colonial period, when authorities developed different administrative structures for the three main regions. There are more than 250 ethnic groups in Nigeria, but the dominant ones are the Hausa-Fulani in the arid and dry north, the Yoruba in the fertile southwest, and the Ibo in the rainy and densely populated southeast. Ethnic identities coalesced along these lines as people sought to access resources through the colonial administration; this pattern of tapping into public coffers to benefit one's own ethnic group continued after independence (Ekeh 1975). Religious differences between the predominantly Muslim north and the mostly Christian and traditionalist south helped to fuel additional tensions that also fell along regional lines. Despite these divisions, a strong nationalist movement emerged in the 1940s and 1950s to challenge British colonialism.

The 1956 discovery of oil in the southeastern Niger Delta radically altered the calculus of governance just before the country gained independence in 1960. Under a parliamentary system, with the British monarch as head of state until 1963 and then a nonexecutive president, Nigeria was plagued by rampant corruption, economic mismanagement, escalating tensions among ethno-regional political parties, and a controversial census during which many areas were accused of overcounting to boost their political representation. As the political situation became increasingly unstable, a military coup d'état by Ibo army officers in January 1966 was initially welcomed by many Nigerians, but a counter-coup by northern military officers six months later and a campaign of anti-Ibo retribution threw the country into further disarray.

In May 1967, the southeast declared independence as the Republic of Biafra, prompting the military government to fight to hold on to this oil-rich region. During the ensuing war, which lasted until secessionist leaders surrendered in January 1970, the Nigerian military established a blockade around Biafra, cutting it off not only from military equipment but also from food and medical supplies. An estimated 1 million Nigerians died, mainly from famine and disease. International responses to the conflict were mixed. Within Africa, just Tanzania, Zambia, Côte d'Ivoire, and Gabon recognized the independence of Biafra (Clapham 1996); most other African leaders seemed reluctant to endorse secessionism for fear of what might happen in their own countries (see Chapter 2). The former colonizer, Britain, backed Nigeria as it fought to retain the southeast, an important source of oil. Although the federal government ultimately won and Nigeria held together,[23] the conflict generated tensions and resentment that linger to this day.

After having been relatively inward-focused through the 1960s, post–civil war Nigeria sought to establish itself as an international power (Aborisade and Mundt 2002). Under General Yakubu Gowon, it joined the Organization of Petroleum Exporting Countries in 1971 and was active (including as OAU chair in 1973–1974) in negotiations between European and African, Caribbean, and Pacific (ACP) countries that led to the first Lomé agreement in 1975 (see Chapter 11). But Nigeria's primary focus was on West Africa, where it wanted to increase its own influence and reduce the role of France. Gowon's success in the Lomé negotiations allowed him to approach several small francophone countries (Togo, Benin, Niger) about the possibility of a wider regional organization, effectively undermining the emerging francophone-only Economic Community of West Africa (CEAO), led by Côte d'Ivoire and Senegal (Aborisade and Mundt 2002; Bach 1983). Nigeria's vision eventually prevailed, resulting in the 1975 formation of the Economic Community of West African States. The organization's main objective was economic integration, at least on paper, but it was as much about Nigeria wanting to shape its external environment (Bach 1983).

Just two months after the signing of the Treaty of Lagos, in the face of rampant corruption in his administration, Gowon (a military ruler) was overthrown in a coup d'état. As the new ECOWAS organization struggled to make progress toward its initial goal of freezing tariffs among members, Nigeria's reputation and leadership role suffered from the continued dominance of its military in domestic affairs. Nigeria's second attempt at democracy in 1979—the Second Republic—was plagued once again by corruption and regional divisions. A global drop in oil prices led to a serious economic crisis. When the 1983 elections were marred by irregularities, the military took over yet again. As other African countries moved toward multiparty competition in the 1990s (see Chapter 5), a series of increasingly brutal military rulers in Nigeria gained a reputation for widespread human rights abuses, corruption, and repression. Elections were held in 1993 for a Third Republic, but the military prevented the winners from taking power because it did not like the results.

The continued dominance of the military undermined Nigeria's role in West Africa, especially as other countries within the region moved haltingly along a path of political liberalization. This included key francophone rivals like Senegal, where existing multiparty elections became more competitive, and Côte d'Ivoire, which opened to multiparty competition in 1990. Even Ghana's Rawlings, who had come to power through a military coup, subjected himself to multiparty elections in the 1990s (see Chapter 4). In this context, Nigeria's dominant role in ECOWAS and its leadership of military interventions under the ECOMOG umbrella raised eyebrows. In 1990, for example, existing connections between Nigeria's military leader and Liberian president Samuel Doe generated doubts about the neutrality of the ECOMOG intervention from its outset (Clapham 1996) (see Chapter 8). Similarly, suspicions about Nigeria's motivations ran high when it led the 1997 ECOMOG mission to restore an elected president to power in Sierra Leone. The irony of a military government intervening to restore democracy was not lost on critics, who noted that Sierra Leone was rich in natural resources, especially diamonds. The perpetuation of military rule in Nigeria thus did little to help overcome fears within ECOWAS about that country's dominance.

After a strange twist of fate in 1998, when both the incumbent military leader and the presumed winner of the aborted 1993 elections suddenly died, the new military leader agreed to hold elections for the Fourth Republic. In 1999, Olusegun Obasanjo won the presidential election. A retired military leader who had turned over power to an elected civilian government twenty years earlier, Obasanjo was seen as a bridge between military and civilian leadership and thus as less likely be overthrown. Even so, Obasanjo faced plenty of other challenges during his eight years in office,[24] including corruption, ethnic clashes, and religious tensions after democratically elected legislatures in several northern states adopted sharia (Muslim law). In the oil-rich southeast, the Movement for the Emancipation of the Niger Delta (MEND) staged attacks and took hostages to draw attention to the negative consequences of oil extraction. Its leaders eventually reached an amnesty deal with the government, though the resulting disarmament, demobilization, and reintegration (DDR) program has done little to alter existing power structures or address underlying grievances in the region (Ebiede 2017).

Under Obasanjo, Nigeria once again became a dominant regional player. While still fully involved in ECOWAS, Obasanjo focused much of his energy on reforming intergovernmental organizations at the continental level. Even before he was elected president, in the early 1990s Obasanjo spearheaded the development of a proposal for a Conference on Security, Stability, Development, and Cooperation in Africa that would be more effective than the OAU at addressing the continent's security and development challenges (Deng and Zartman 2002). After 1999, as president of the most populated country in the region, Obasanjo was able to promote this proposal more forcefully among his peers, and many of its elements found their way into the final documents that transformed the OAU into the African Union in 2002 (Tieku 2004). Nigeria also played a leading role in the development of NEPAD and other recent initiatives and is one of the leading financial contributors to the AU, providing about 13 percent of its annual budget (*Premium Times Nigeria* 2014). At the individual level, many Nigerians serve as senior officials in AU bureaucracies, and a large delegation of doctors and nurses participated in the AU response to the Ebola outbreak in West Africa in 2014.

While Nigeria's reputation and leadership within Africa certainly have improved since military rule ended in 1999, the country has continued to face serious governance challenges at home. In a 2006 move that was seen as a victory for democracy, the Nigerian senate rejected an effort by Obasanjo's supporters to change the constitution to allow a third term. In 2007, his handpicked successor, Umaru Musa Yar'Adua, won a flawed and probably rigged election that turned violent in many places, but the situation stabilized over time. When Yar'Adua (a Muslim northerner) died in office in 2010, his vice president, Goodluck Jonathan (a Christian southerner), took charge. Despite some controversy within the ruling party about whether it should put up another northerner based on an internal north-south alternation agreement, Jonathan ultimately stood as the party's presidential candidate in 2011 and won.

During this time, an insurgent group known as Boko Haram launched a series of attacks in the northeast part of the country and the capital city of Abuja. Informed by a broader radical Islamic ideology but rooted in local grievances related to the northeast's long-standing marginalization (Dowd and Raleigh 2013), the group gained international attention when it kidnapped nearly 300 schoolgirls from Chibok in April 2014, prompting a social media campaign calling for their release. Over time, presumably in an effort to recruit more fighters, Boko Haram linked up with other radical groups in the region and beyond, to the point of swearing allegiance to the so-called Islamic State in May 2015. As Boko Haram gained control over more territory and even launched attacks into neighboring countries, many Nigerians and others started to question Jonathan's resolve and tactics to defeat this threat. The refusal by some military officers to fight until they got better equipment further undermined domestic and international confidence. After a temporary delay due to security concerns, presidential elections were held in March 2015. Challenger Muhammadu Buhari won and, perhaps most important, Jonathan accepted the results. For the first time in the history of Nigeria, there was a peaceful transition of power from one party to another through elections. Although Boko Haram did not disappear with the election of a new president, as highlighted by ongoing sporadic attacks and another mass kidnapping of schoolgirls in early 2018, a renewed international military campaign has scored some key victories and reduced the amount of territory under the rebel group's control.

Nigeria always has been an important player in the African region, if only due to its massive population. As described earlier, it has played a lead role in ECOWAS for many years, often prompting resentment and suspicion among other member states. Since emerging from the shadow of military rule in 1999, Nigeria's leaders have been in a better position to seek a prominent role for their country in regional and international bodies. Obasanjo especially pushed for reforms to the OAU, and many of his proposals are now in the structures of the African Union. At times, Nigeria also has expressed an interest in holding a permanent seat on the United Nations Security Council if it were to be reformed to allow representation from more regions. Nigeria's case to be a leading regional power is probably enhanced by the 2015 election, which established it as one of relatively few countries in Africa to have undergone a democratic transition from one party to another. Although it continues to face immense challenges, including from Boko Haram, this was a shining moment for a country that had long been criticized for focusing too much on other countries' troubles and not enough on its own.

Notes

1. Institutions with member states in specific parts of Africa often are known as subregional organizations (to distinguish from a regional organization such as the African Union). Since the early 1990s, though, they have been recognized as regional economic communities (RECs) within the larger African Economic Community, as explored later in this chapter. Here, we typically use the term *subregional* to avoid confusion.

2. This pattern was challenged in Angola (see Chapter 3), where Cold War divisions led to a split among OAU members about whether to recognize the MPLA or the FNLA. Unable to reconcile the movements, the OAU recognized both as authentic liberation movements. At Angola's independence in 1975, OAU members split again about which group to recognize as the government but eventually backed the MPLA when the military situation shifted in its favor.

3. The Sahrawi Arab Democratic Republic was admitted into the OAU in 1982, even as its Polisario Front was still fighting against Morocco for control of Western Sahara. This decision prompted Morocco to withdraw from the OAU in 1984. Although the dispute over Western Sahara has yet to be resolved, Morocco returned to the continent-wide organization, by then known as the African Union, in 2017. Western Sahara remains a member of the AU as well and continues to have many supporters among its member states.

4. Article III of the 1963 OAU Charter reads as follows: "The Member States . . . solemnly affirm and declare their adherence to the following principles: 1. the sovereign equality of all Member States; 2. non-interference in the internal affairs of States; 3. respect for the sovereignty and territorial integrity of each State and for its inalienable right to independent existence; 4. peaceful settlement of disputes by negotiation, mediation, conciliation or arbitration; 5. unreserved condemnation, in all its forms, of political assassination as well as of subversive activities on the part of neighboring States or any other State; 6. absolute dedication to the total emancipation of the African territories which are still dependent; 7. affirmation of a policy of non-alignment with regard to all blocs."

5. South Africa had been prevented from investing in many other African countries during the apartheid era (see Chapter 9).

6. Scholar George Ayittey reportedly coined this phrase in 1993, though it has been widely used without attribution since. For an interesting discussion of its intended meaning compared to how it has often been used instead, see https://kasieconomics.com/2014/01/02/african-solutions-for-african-problems-the-real-meaningby-george-ayittey.

7. Updated information about African Risk Capacity can be found at the agency's website: http://www.africanriskcapacity.org.

8. Eight African countries have participated in ARC as of 2017: Burkina Faso, Gambia, Kenya, Malawi, Mali, Mauritania, Niger, and Senegal. As Kenya and Malawi chose not to participate in 2016–2017, Risk Pool III included only West African countries, raising some concerns about the ability to pay out if a drought were to affect that particular region. The program works best at pooling risk if members from different regions participate.

9. More information about this Financing the Union initiative can be found on its website: https://au.int/en/financingau.

10. Kenyatta and his running mate, William Ruto, successfully used the pending ICC charges against them as a selling point in the 2013 elections by rallying against Western intervention and neocolonialism (Malik 2016; Mueller 2014).

11. Less than two weeks later, the ICC opened an investigation into crimes against humanity in Burundi in the two years prior to its departure from the organization.

12. The exception is the Middle East, where exports to other Middle Eastern countries constitute just 8.8 percent of the total. In contrast, intra-regional trade is 68.5 percent in Europe and 52.3 percent in Asia. Data come from World Trade Organization 2015.

13. An exception to this general pattern is South Africa, whose moderate climate, mineral deposits, and comparatively high level of industrialization have generated a much more diversified economy.

14. Tanganyika was originally a German colony but became a British territory during World War I. It became Tanzania in 1964 when it merged with Zanzibar after independence.

15. Another noteworthy incident during Amin's tenure as president of Uganda was his decision in 1976 to allow Palestinian hijackers to land an Israeli plane at the

airport in Entebbe. Israeli forces eventually raided the airport and rescued the hostages, humiliating Amin and prompting retaliation against airport employees.

16. This was not the end of the tensions between Nyerere and Amin, though. In late 1978, Amin's forces invaded the Kagera Salient, a piece of land south of the straight-line Uganda-Tanzania border and north of the Kagera River that Amin claimed rightfully belonged to Uganda. Nyerere's troops responded quickly and forcefully, pushing Ugandan troops back across the border and marching on to Kampala, where they removed Amin in 1979 and restored Obote to power. Amin lived the rest of his life in exile in Saudi Arabia.

17. The CFA franc includes two different currencies (the West African CFA franc, used by these eight ECOWAS members, and the Central African CFA franc), but the two are equal to one another in value and are essentially interchangeable. When France converted to the euro in 1999, its treasury continued to guarantee the value of the CFA franc against a fixed value of the euro.

18. When Togo's Gnassingbé Eyadéma died in 2005 after thirty-eight years in office, the army quickly named his son Faure Gnassingbé as successor, prompting widespread criticism and protests. ECOWAS sent a delegation to pressure Togolese officials to hold elections. Gnassingbé won easily in what was widely seen as a fraudulent election, and security forces cracked down on opposition protestors. ECOWAS action thus did little more than provide a false veil of democratic legitimacy to an authoritarian regime. The outcome was different in Burkina Faso in 2015, when military officials loyal to former president Blaise Compaoré ousted the transitional government that replaced him after popular protests against his twenty-seven-year rule. A high-level ECOWAS team convinced the presidential guard to step down and get the transition back on track, paving the way for the country's first free and fair elections in more than three decades in November 2015. Although he was elected democratically, President Roch Marc Christian Kaboré's connections to the previous regime have raised some concerns among observers.

19. The exceptions were Lesotho and Swaziland, whose geographic locations surrounded by South Africa made strong anti-apartheid resistance difficult, and Malawi.

20. Until 1990, Namibia was known as South West Africa and was a colony of the white minority government of South Africa.

21. For more information about recent SADC protocols and other activities, see http://www.sadc.int.

22. COMESA and SACU have been fairly successful at establishing a free trade area and customs union, respectively, and COMESA is one of the AEC's eight recognized RECs. There is not space here to cover the history of integration efforts in all of these organizations.

23. A lesser known international consequence of the conflict was the establishment of Doctors Without Borders, under its French name Médecins Sans Frontières. It was started by French doctors working for the International Committee of the Red Cross in Biafra who were frustrated by the organization's refusal to speak out about the murders and starvation of civilians by the Nigerian blockade (Weiss 1999).

24. Despite accusations of authoritarian tactics, Obasanjo was reelected in 2003.

PART 3

The Challenges
of Security

7

The Regionalization
of Conflict

With the end of the Cold War, most observers thought
that conflict would likely diminish in Africa, as elsewhere in the world.
Instead, the incidence of violence actually increased, partly because the
end of the one-party state opened up the political space in African polities
(see Chapter 5). Moreover, many of the post–Cold War conflicts became
regionalized with the intervention of neighboring states. This is not to say
that regionalized conflicts are a wholly new phenomenon in Africa. As we
saw in Chapter 3, the long Angolan civil war that lasted from 1975 to
1991 drew in outside actors from both within Africa (Zaire and South
Africa) and beyond (most importantly Cuba, with Soviet support). The
long struggle against apartheid in South Africa also generated a regional
conflict in southern Africa more broadly: the Frontline States supported
the African National Congress, and South Africa responded with periodic
attacks on its neighbors (see Chapter 9). Indirectly, however, these conflicts were connected with the final stages of Africa's liberation from
colonialism and white minority rule. Outside of southern Africa, outright
military intervention in the civil wars of African states (as in Chad) by
their neighbors was uncommon, though rhetorical or material support for
rebels in neighboring countries was not unusual (as in Sudan's first civil
war, 1955–1972). Since the end of the Cold War, however, the continent
has been wracked by a rising number of regionalized conflicts.

Millions of Africans have perished as a direct or indirect result of
these wars.[1] Millions more have suffered assault, dislocation from their
homes and families, illness, forced service in armies, and the psycholog-
ical traumas that these phenomena entail. The life possibilities for millions of people have been foreshortened by the dislocation, trauma, and

lost opportunities for education that they have endured. Africa's regionalized conflicts have distracted African leaders from the focus on economic development that all agree should be the continent's first priority. Regionalized conflicts, then, are a matter of human development, as well as one of security.

Although states and diaspora communities outside of Africa are implicated in all of these conflicts, their principal drivers are to be found within the continent. Africa's long-term economic decline that began with the debt repayment crises of the late 1970s was not meaningfully addressed by the structural adjustment programs that these crises provoked (see Chapter 4). Even before the end of the Cold War, Africa's economic problems led to a crisis in the patronage politics that characterized many authoritarian African states. According to William Reno (2011), this crisis in patronage politics gave rise to new kinds of African rebel leaders, namely, "warlords" and then "parochial rebels." These new types of insurgent leaders were driven not by ideological motives but rather by economic greed and ethno-regional grievances. The withdrawal of superpower support from former superpower client regimes (see Chapter 3) encouraged such rebels. Their emergence was possible due to the growing weakness of African states, but their insurgencies accelerated the process of state failure in Africa.[2] A vicious cycle of state decline and rebellion developed in a number of African states: state decline led to increasing grievances against the central authorities, as well as opportunities for predation, which led to more intensive insurgencies; these in turn led to a further contraction of state-provided security and welfare.

This analysis raises the question of how so many of these internal conflicts became regionalized wars. The reasons are complex but are related to the trends just described. In the Cold War years, outsiders feared to intervene directly on the territory of superpower clients, knowing that these outside patrons would likely come to their clients' defense.[3] The end of the Cold War removed such constraints. Further, rebels interested in liberation or reform (see Reno 2011) had a strong internal focus in their activities. Those interested in looting or rallying their ethnic kin, however, often crossed interstate borders in pursuit of their goals. Neighboring states have been driven both by fear and by a sense of opportunity in intervening in neighboring states. In some cases, African leaders appear to have been drawn into conflicts virtually against their will; in others, they have seized opportunities to enhance their regime security, or to enrich their domestic clients who keep them in power.

Another kind of regionalized conflict in Africa has been exacerbated by the activities of transnational terror groups. These have generally begun within various African states and then later spread to neighboring states in response to the pressures that they have faced. As with the regionalized civil wars of Africa, non-African states and nonstate actors have supported or battled against these terrorist groups. Again, however, their roots are to be found primarily in the domestic politics of the countries in which they have emerged (Dowd and Raleigh 2013).

The next section addresses the question of causation for the regionalization of African conflicts. It divides the causal elements into permissive conditions, "efficient" causes, and facilitators of conflict.[4] The subsequent section outlines a number of Africa's regionalized conflicts that erupted or grew more severe after the end of the Cold War. The listing is not comprehensive, but it includes the deadliest regionalized conflicts as well as some other examples that illustrate specific ways in which African conflicts become regionalized. These cases illustrate the wide range of different forms of outside intervention that stoke regionalized conflict. They also show how certain conditions make regionalized conflicts more likely, but also that the actions of specific agents were the proximate cause. The case study explores the deadliest and perhaps most complicated regionalized conflict in Africa, that of the Democratic Republic of Congo since 1996.

Causes and Interpretations of Regionalized Conflict

This section discusses the debate over the causes of regionalized conflict in Africa and how to interpret these causes. We are skeptical of a general theory of regionalized conflicts in Africa; that is, we do not believe any single variable accounts for the proliferation of regionalized conflicts or for specific instances. The permissive conditions for the regionalization of conflict do allow us to see more easily some of the broad patterns of regionalized conflict. To some extent, we endorse Paul Williams's notion of "recipes" (2011) for African regional wars, even if one often can identify a "main ingredient" in the recipes. In this formulation, each conflict has a somewhat different set of variables that have caused conflict to erupt, become regionalized, and then either endure for a long time or be settled.

Permissive Conditions of Conflict Regionalization

Permissive conditions are those structural features of the social environment that allow a phenomenon to occur. In the example of Kenneth Waltz (1959), the fundamental anarchy of the international environment is what allows interstate war to take place. Although states (or state leaders) may still need specific reasons to launch wars or to defend themselves, the absence of a global state allows for, or permits, the phenomenon of war between or among sovereign states. In the presence of a global state, there might well still be conflict, but it would have to be defined as something else, not interstate war. Even without a global state, a global hegemon might be able to prevent sustained conflict among nominally sovereign states. Given the fundamental anarchy of the international system that he identifies, Waltz goes on to ask what kinds of global power configurations (namely, bipolar or multipolar) make the system more prone to war.

Turning to the African regional level, one might likewise ask what structural conditions of the region have permitted the increase in regionalized conflict on the continent. From a realist perspective, two features of the African international political landscape are key. First, with the end of the Cold War, no external powers have any longer exercised significant constraint over the transnational behavior of African states. During the Cold War decades, beginning in the late 1950s, France, the Soviet Union, and the United States developed strong patron-client relations with various newly independent African states (see Chapters 3 and 11). These external great powers often exploited their clients economically while also providing security to the specific regimes in power. More subtly, however, their external patrons also constrained client regimes from interfering in the disputes of their neighbors. It is true that the Soviet Union channeled arms through its African allies (like Angola) as the United States did with its own allies (like Zaire). Yet neither superpower wished to fight proxy wars in a region of the world that each regarded as peripheral. As a second-tier power, France could afford to antagonize neither its major ally nor a major adversary in Africa. The end of the Cold War and France's decline as an African power (see Chapter 11) have reduced these constraints on the impulse of African regimes to interfere in neighboring states. Meanwhile, as China has expanded its investment and trading presence in Africa (see Chapter 12), it has not made the same kind of security commitments on the continent previously made by these external powers.

The decline of great power influence in Africa during the 1990s also had an important indirect effect on regional security there. The withdrawal of great power support for a number of regimes on the continent has led to a weakening of many states, in some cases leading to state failure or collapse. Two former American clients, Somalia and then the DRC, successively experienced state failure during the 1990s. The territories of these two states have in turn become "ungoverned spaces"[5] in which insurgent and even terrorist groups have subsequently organized their activities. Arguably, these situations have drawn in neighboring states that perceive their interests to have been imperiled by the lawlessness existing on their borders. Sudan, site of other regionalized conflicts, represents a more complicated case. Although the Sudanese state has never "failed," and has actually been relatively strong compared to the African standard, the country did enjoy close relations with the United States until 1989. During the 1980s, Sudan consistently received the most US foreign aid in Africa, more than close US allies such as Liberia and Zaire (US Federal Budget 2015a). Since 1989, China has gradually emerged as Sudan's major external sponsor, yet China has failed to provide the same security assistance. The gradual weakening of Sudan after 1989 may thus account for the rise in insecurity in the country and the tendency of its neighbors to intervene. In the French sphere of influence, the decline of the Malian state in the face of Islamist influences reflects France's diminished ability to help preserve order in the former French clients. Indeed, the realist perspective suggests that weak and failing states become power vacuums that attract the attention of neighbors, who both prey upon and fear the consequences of their weakness.

Another permissive condition of regionalized conflict from the realist perspective is the inability of sub-Saharan Africa's regional powers to play a hegemonic role in the continent's subregions. Regional powers in any world region can potentially prevent the regionalization of conflict by deterring outside powers from intervening in domestic conflicts. More rarely, they may be able to impose their own preferred order on the internal belligerents in foreign states.[6] If Africa had regional powers that were able and willing to play such roles, regionalized conflict might emerge less often. According to one website that attempts to assess the relative military power of states (Global Firepower 2015), the five leading military powers of sub-Saharan Africa are (in order) South Africa, Nigeria, Ethiopia, Kenya, and Angola. Yet these states have generally been unable or unwilling to impose solutions to conflicts in their respective subregions. South Africa faces too much internal division to act in a coherent way on the continent, despite the global role as an African leader that it enjoys playing (Clark 2016). Nigeria made some efforts to impose order in Liberia and Sierra Leone in the 1990s through the mechanism of ECOMOG, but had only limited success (see Chapter 8). For its part, Ethiopia has a large and formidable military, and yet it had difficulty defeating tiny Eritrea in the war of 1998–2000. Nor have its interventions in Somalia been decisive in that country. As for Kenya, that country's successive rulers have been more interested in economic influence over its neighbors than in subregional military hegemony. In short, the absence of subregional hegemons in Africa is another permissive condition for the occurrence and persistence of regionalized conflicts.

If realists focus on the absence of regional hegemons, then liberals would focus on the absence of strong regional institutions. The African Union was created to supplant the old Organization of African Unity, which had failed to bring about the unity to which its founders (in principle) aspired. Since the year of its founding, the AU has been at work putting in place an African Peace and Security Architecture,[7] designed, in the first instance, to prevent new conflicts from emerging through deterrence. Failing that, the APSA is designed to resolve conflict, preferably through mediation but by force if necessary. Its institutions include a Peace and Security Council, an African Standby Force, a Continental Early Warning System, and a Panel of the Wise. An enormous number of academic analyses and policy papers have been written on various elements of the APSA.[8] Yet honest liberals would have to admit these institutions are not yet functioning in a significant way, despite over fifteen years of effort. The academic and policy analyses have mostly been discussing what "will happen" in the future, for more than a decade. For instance, the date for the African Standby Force to attain its full operational capacity has been a moving target since the idea was first mooted. Like the UN more broadly, the APSA has done little either to prevent conflict in Africa or to end it once it has begun. The intriguing case of the AU intervention in the Comoros in 2008, however, may signal a change in the AU's willingness to restore peace and unity in some cases of African conflict.[9]

If liberals are perhaps puzzled, and frustrated, by the incapacity of the AU to live up to the hopes of its supporters, constructivists are far less so. Constructivists generally believe that institutions are only the outward manifestation of the collective norms, cultures, and identities that underlie them. Thus, the "failures" of the AU in the realm of conflict prevention and resolution are not to be found in the institutional nature of the AU and its associated organs, but in the normative and cultural unity that connects African leaders with one another—or that fails to do so. One can perceive both changes and continuities in the norms and culture of African diplomacy. To illustrate the power of the norms of diplomacy, consider Article 30 of the AU Constitutive Act: "Governments which shall come to power through unconstitutional means shall not be allowed to participate in the activities of the Union." Despite this provision, however, the AU has elected as its leaders such individuals as Denis Sassou-Nguesso of the Republic of Congo, Muammar Qaddafi of Libya, Teodoro Obiang Nguema of Equatorial Guinea, and Robert Mugabe of Zimbabwe. None of these four individuals is highly regarded for their commitment to constitutional government. Yet the choice that these leaders represent reflects the culture of diplomacy in

Africa. With whom do African leaders identify most closely? Is it with members of their own ethnicity? With citizens of the countries that they lead? Or with the larger African community of peoples? If African rulers identify strongly with members of their own ethnicity or country, but only weakly with the entire African community, they are most likely to put the welfare of those former groups ahead of the latter. In short, changing norms of diplomacy represent another structural context in which the regionalization of conflict has taken place.

Finally, the "liberation" of international capital from any constraints is arguably another permissive condition for the regionalization of conflict in Africa. According to some neo-Marxists (e.g., Bond 2006; Okpalaobi 2014), economic globalization has intensified the global competition to secure the supply of natural resources. It has simultaneously removed the few existing restraints of international capital to interfere inside African states to gain access to these resources. According to Pádraig Carmody (2010), the influx of global capital in support of oil pipelines in Chad/Cameroon and in Sudan exacerbated existing conflicts in the two respective areas. In this view, the liberalization of African markets and the liberation of Western capital have created an environment for a new proliferation of African conflicts, including regionalized conflicts.

Proximate or "Efficient" Causes of Regionalized Conflict

If these are some of the putative conditions that permit the regionalization of African conflicts, what then are some of the proximate causes (or "efficient" causes, in the language of Waltz)? Perhaps the most compelling proximate cause of intervention by neighboring states is the imperative of regime security. Unlike the well-institutionalized states of the global North, many African states do not have strong political institutions that are widely accepted by their populations. As a result, African rulers, particularly those who did not come to power through free or fair elections, are vulnerable to being overthrown. As one scholar has observed (Roessler 2011), African authoritarian rulers face dual threats of being overthrown in coups d'état, chiefly by regime insiders, or by losing power to insurgent groups who begin rebellions in remote areas. Africa's authoritarians spend a good deal of their time thinking about how to avert these threats. One of the threats they face is an insurgency that can be supported from outside their own state borders. Thus, it is the rulers of neighboring states whom African leaders must try to cultivate or otherwise deter from allowing insurgencies to operate from their territory. Once an African ruler has supported rebels operating in a neighboring state, however, he or she can expect the neighbor to reciprocate. Errol Henderson (2015) refers to these

reciprocal interventions as "neopatrimonial balancing," which he identifies as a central pattern in Africa's international relations.

This pattern of tit-for-tat support for rebel groups operating in contiguous states is more likely when one or both of the two states are
experiencing civil war, as quantitative scholarship has shown (Gleditsch, Salehyan, and Schultz 2008). Insurgents fighting wars against
incumbent regimes often seek sanctuary in a neighboring state whose
government is sympathetic to their cause. The regimes governing the
host states then often provide assistance to such insurgents who have
sought sanctuary abroad. If there is no insurgency ongoing in the host
state, its neighbor may be tempted to stimulate a civil war there.

Such a pattern of support for rebels by rival regimes can be observed
in the relations between Uganda and Sudan. At the time that President
Yoweri Museveni seized power in Uganda in 1986, the civil war in
neighboring Sudan had resumed more than two years before. By the late
1980s, the Museveni regime was facing its own major insurgency in
northern Uganda in the form of the Lord's Resistance Army (LRA).
Museveni was gradually able to improve the performance of the Ugandan
army and began to pressure LRA forces, headed by Joseph Kony, forcing most of them across the border into southern Sudan in 1993 and
1994 (Cline 2013). At that time, the Sudanese government had managed
to split the SPLA rebel group into a number of factions, one of which
pledged loyalty to the government in return for certain favors. In this
context, the Sudanese government decided to use Kony's LRA forces
for its own purposes in southern Sudan. Kony went to live under
Sudanese protection in the town of Juba. The LRA was allowed to
establish a camp, where it received food and arms from the government,
as well as training from the Sudanese army. Gérard Prunier (2009) estimates that this support allowed the LRA to increase the number of its
fighters from only about 300 to over 2,000 from 1993 to 1994. According to Lawrence Cline, "certainly one of the key factors in the early survival of the LRA was its support by the Sudanese government" (2013:
142). In due course, Museveni responded in kind by passing arms and
supplies to the SPLA rebels operating in southern Sudan, and some
SPLA militants were allowed to live and train in Uganda.[10] For the
remainder of the 1990s, the governments of Sudan and Uganda were
sponsors of rebel forces on the other's territory.[11]

Another case of tit-for-tat support for rebel groups was the behavior
of Chad and Sudan in the early 2000s. Chadian president Idriss Déby's
support for rebels in Darfur in 2002 was almost certainly what led
Sudanese president Omar al-Bashir to sponsor anti-regime Chadian
rebels. (More on this case is included in the next section.)

Likewise, the even more aggressive Angolan invasion of Congo-Brazzaville follows a similar logic. In that case, the Angolan regime had been fighting against the UNITA rebels since before independence (see Chapter 3). After the end of the Cold War, however, a peace process began in Angola, and it was not one that worked to UNITA's advantage. Following the contested elections of September 1992, UNITA went back to war with the MPLA government of Angola. Meanwhile, after his own election in 1992, newly elected president Pascal Lissouba of Congo-Brazzaville made the ill-fated decision to allow UNITA to open an office in the Congolese city of Pointe Noire. As the resumed civil war in Angola grew more intense, this office, from which UNITA arms were passed into Angola, became a threat to the MPLA's regime security. This largely explains why Angola intervened in the Congolese civil war of 1997 on behalf of Denis Sassou-Nguesso, whom Angola effectively put back in power (Clark 2008).

As these cases show, the pathways by which an African ruler may come to support anti-regime insurgents targeting the rulers of neighboring African states are variable. In the case of Sudan's support for the LRA rebels who crossed into southern Sudan, the Sudanese government did not initially have any antipathy for the new Museveni regime in Uganda. Rather, after coming to power in 1989, the al-Bashir regime began using the LRA for its own local purposes against the SPLA. But its support to the LRA soon turned Museveni against the al-Bashir regime, causing him to provide aid to the SPLA. In turn, the al-Bashir regime later increased its support to the LRA, and also created the Allied Democratic Forces (ADF) in Zaire to menace Uganda's western frontier. In the case of the pairing of Angola and Congo-Brazzaville, a similar logic applies. It is actually unclear to outsiders why President Lissouba maintained cordial relations with Cabindan separatists[12] and allowed the UNITA rebels from Angola to establish an office in Pointe Noire. One of Central Africa's leading specialists only had this to say: "Lissouba had had [in 1997] a long-running relationship with both UNITA and the Cabindan FLEC (Frente de Libertação do Enclave de Cabinda, an anti-MPLA guerrilla group, closely allied to UNITA), several of whose members had been active in his entourage" (Prunier 2009: 168). A report of the UN's information service (Integrated Regional Information Network 1997) asserted that UNITA's Jonas Savimbi had moved his headquarters to Brazzaville and then Pointe Noire in May 1997, after the fall from power of Mobutu Sese Seko in Zaire. Permitting this move proved to be a fatal mistake for President Lissouba as it reinforced the animosity of the Angolan government toward him.

The observation that ruling regimes of African states could be drawn into the civil wars of neighboring states should not be a surprise, as these examples suggest. Yet this observation does not explain to us why or how regimes are led to intervene against their neighbors. Realists generally point to alliances or antagonisms between states as a cause for support to an incumbent regime or aid to insurgents in an adversary state. Such alignments follow the logic that "the enemy of my enemy is my friend";[13] in Africa, this applies more to regimes than to states.[14]

One example of this phenomenon is the competition between Ethiopia and Eritrea in Somalia. Eritrea had to fight a long liberation struggle, from 1961 to 1993, to gain its independence from Ethiopia. The enmity between the two countries was reinforced by their border war of 1998 to 2000. On another front for Ethiopia, Somalia posed another threat to the regime's security and the country's territorial integrity. Somalia had already invaded Ethiopia once (see Chapter 3), and then Somalia collapsed as a state in 1991. Ethiopia intervened first covertly and then openly in Somalia in 2006 against the Islamic Courts Union (ICU) and in support of a weak secular government (see Chapter 10). Ethiopia enjoyed the implicit support of the United States in these interventions. For Eritrea, however, the successor organization of the ICU, al-Shabaab, was the "enemy of an enemy"—that is, the enemy of Ethiopia—and, therefore, a "friend," and so it received support from Eritrea. In late 2009, the UN Security Council passed Resolution 1907, imposing sanctions on Eritrea for its aid to al-Shabaab. Thus, the regionalization of the conflict in Somalia was exacerbated by the presence of two nearby antagonists, one of which (Ethiopia) had the support of the United States.

The references in this analysis to states beyond the two primary antagonists show that wider "alliance systems" sometimes drive a dyadic rivalry. These alliance systems are often connected with extra-African actors, as the reference to US-Ethiopian relations shows. In the mid-1990s, following the Rwandan genocide of 1994, a sort of francophile versus anglophile antagonism emerged in central Africa (compare Schraeder 2000). The new ruler of Rwanda after the end of the genocide there was Paul Kagame, a Rwandan who had grown up in exile in Uganda (speaking English, among other languages). The old regime in Rwanda, that of Juvénal Habyarimana, meanwhile, had been closely allied with France, which took Habyarimana's side in the Rwandan civil war (1990–1994) (Prunier 1997). France had also taken up the cause of Mobutu after he was essentially abandoned by the United States. Meanwhile, US relations with the al-Bashir regime in Sudan had been deteriorating rapidly. For one, Sudan had supported Saddam Hussein's invasion of Kuwait in 1990, unlike the majority of other

African and Middle Eastern states. Further, Sudan decided in the early 1990s to give refuge to a number of known international terror suspects, including Abu Nidal and Osama bin Laden. As a result, the United States designated Sudan as a state sponsor of terrorism in 1993. In that context, Uganda became a key US ally in East Africa, serving, along with Ethiopia, as a source of pressure on the Islamist government in Khartoum. Thus on the eve of the Congo wars, analyzed in the case study at end of this chapter, France supported Mobutu and the Rwandan regime of Habyarimana until its demise, and the United States supported Museveni, and by extension Kagame, who eventually seized power in Rwanda. Some realists simply take such alliance systems for granted or consider them the results of serendipitous events beyond the control of agents, whereas others (e.g., Henderson 2015) see them emerging as a result of the exigencies of neopatrimonialism. That is, much of leaders' decisionmaking is driven by their need for financial resources with which to "buy off" leading political opponents and military figures to ensure regime security.

The personal relationships that often evolve between the rulers of neighboring states in Africa can sometimes be another proximate cause of regionalized conflict. In Africa, many (not all) regimes continue to be defined by the personalities of the rulers rather than by ideology. In Africa's personalist regimes, personal relations often explain a good deal about the foreign relations of African states. Rulers who stay in power over several decades may develop strong feelings about one another. In turn, the personalist regimes that they head rely less on the institutionalized input of foreign ministers, military officials, legislative leaders, and other state agents (Clark 2011). Personal relationships of amity or enmity that affect the affairs of state easily develop and evolve over time. For instance, Gabonese president Omar Bongo was married to the daughter of Congolese president Denis Sassou-Nguesso in 1990, and the two rulers were partners in a number of Central African initiatives when they overlapped in power. Further, both rulers were essentially clients of French patronage. The personal relationship of Bongo and Sassou-Nguesso cannot be discounted in helping to understand why Bongo allowed French agents to transport arms to the latter during the Congo civil war of 1997 (Clark 2008). On the other hand, consider the mutual suspicion that surely characterizes the personal relations of al-Bashir and Museveni, two leaders who engaged in periodic episodes of aggression since the former came to power in 1989, nearly three decades ago.

Religious and ethnic identities also play a role—if sometimes an unconscious one—in the development of relations between neighboring states. In the civil war in Côte d'Ivoire that erupted in 2002, the insurgents who took up arms were northerners, mostly Muslim, many of whom traced their origins to Mali or Burkina Faso. In that context, Burkina Faso's support of these rebels could easily be seen as a form of ethnic and religious solidarity with their oppressed brethren across the interstate frontier. The same logic applies to Museveni's support for the SPLA in Sudan: the large majority of the residents of South Sudan are black-skinned Africans and non-Muslims, either Christian or animist. Meanwhile, Islamic law (sharia) has applied in Sudan since the 1960s, but it was significantly strengthened in 1991, following al-Bashir's rise to power. The practice of enslavement by (Arabized) northern Sudanese soldiers of (black) southerners during the civil war was an affront to the sensibilities of blacks and Christians worldwide.[15] Such practices surely added to the hostility between rulers like al-Bashir and Museveni, who presents himself as a serious Christian. Ethiopian support for the SPLA can be understood according to the same racial and religious solidarity with black Christians. To give a final example, the hostility between Idriss Déby and al-Bashir can again be explained by the same logic: Déby is a dark-skinned member of the Zaghawa ethnic group, a group that dominated one of the rebel groups in Darfur (Flint and de Waal 2005) and that was targeted by janjaweed militias supported by Khartoum. Such ethnic, racial, and religious links are clearly relevant to the mutual interventions undertaken by ruling regimes.

A more dubious proximate cause of conflict may be the desire of one regime to spread its governing ideology to a neighboring state or states. In the 1970s, the West worried that Afro-Marxist states would try to spread their ideology to their neighbors, and the conflicts between such states and their neighbors were sometimes depicted this way (see Chapter 3). In reality, though, there is no record of any Afro-Marxist state exporting its ideology through force to a neighboring country: various Afro-Marxist states like Angola, Benin, Congo-Brazzaville, and Ethiopia got on perfectly well with moderate neighbors like Zambia, Togo, Gabon, and Kenya.

In the 1990s, a narrative spread in policy circles that a new generation of leaders had come to power in Eritrea (Isaias Afwerki), Ethiopia (Meles Zenawi), and Uganda (Museveni) (Ottaway 1999). These new leaders were allegedly committed to statebuilding and development in a way that the old leaders who had come to power in the 1960s and 1970s were not. In explaining Uganda's policies in first Rwanda and then the DRC, Ugandan officials have often referred to Museveni's ideology as the source of his foreign policies in these neighboring countries, though the logic of such claims is exceedingly weak (Clark 2001a). More recently, two other African states, Libya (under Qaddafi) and Sudan, were sometimes thought to have been attempting to spread Islamist ideology in Africa, in particular to Chad. Again, however, such claims are dubious. In the late 1970s, Libya's Qaddafi published *The Green Book,* expressing vague and contradictory commitments to socialism, direct democracy, and inchoate forms of nationalism. Yet it is difficult to discern how Libya's erratic foreign policy under Qaddafi can be connected with the "ideology" of *The Green Book.*

Another possible proximate cause for the regionalization of conflict in Africa might be the desire to loot or gain access to resources in neighboring states. "Lootable" resources are clearly an element in many of Africa's regionalized conflicts, though it is less certain that the desire to loot is a primary cause of conflict. Further, lootable resources do not figure in all regionalized conflicts: Somalia is not known for possessing any easily lootable resources, though it has been the target of much external intervention since 1991. In fact, the theft of resources may serve different economic and political ends. To the extent that the revenues from lootable resources are channeled into statebuilding, the theft of resources could be seen as part of a process of strengthening states vis-à-vis both the societies they govern and against neighboring states. More commonly, however, outsiders have interpreted the theft of resources as a private activity of elites rather than for the public purpose of statebuilding. Some activists also have connected the theft of resources in African conflicts with the economic needs of global companies headquartered in both Western and East Asian states (e.g., Prendergast 2009). In this way, the theft of resources in regionalized African conflicts has been connected with the needs of global capitalism and the blame placed on those making profits from the sale of products dependent upon mineral projects found in African conflict zones.

Facilitators of Conflict

Another part of the "recipe" of African conflicts are those factors that can be understood as the facilitators or drivers of regionalized conflict. Indeed, some of the variables described earlier could be seen as drivers rather than efficient causes. Consider again the presence of easily lootable resources in an African state whose government has failed and that has become the target of intervention. Although it is hard to show that the looting of mineral resources was an original reason (efficient cause) for states to intervene across borders, the revenues from looted minerals surely facilitate conflicts, making them bloodier and longer. Indeed, the possibility of looting is likely a reason why states stay in a conflict (see case study), if not an original cause.

Likewise, the diffusion of modern small arms into the hands of nonofficial civilians has facilitated violence in all African conflicts (see, e.g., Mkutu 2008). Some forms of violent conflict are certainly possible in the absence of small arms. But the ready availability of small arms and light weapons makes conflicts far bloodier and longer. The relative ease of transporting light arms across interstate borders leads more specifically to the regionalization of conflict. The smuggling of light arms across borders usually involves communities on both sides of an international frontier and often brings state actors into local conflicts.

The escape of refugees across interstate borders is a third example of a facilitator of conflict. Idean Salehyan and Kristian Gleditsch (2006) have shown statistically how the flow of refugees fleeing a civil war in one state increases the likelihood of conflict in host states, though the overall risk of conflict in such situations is still very low. Refugees do not necessarily cause conflict, but their presence in the fragile states of Africa raises the likelihood of civil war in states that host them, sometimes against their will. Comparative case studies suggest that the likelihood of conflict in refugee-hosting situations depends on the political cohesion of the refugees (Lischer 2003, 2005) and the existing political context in the host state, including the level of politicization of ethnic identities (Whitaker 2003).

Finally, as a fourth example, let us consider the extra-continental support that certain regimes in Africa receive from the outside great powers. The al-Bashir regime in Sudan could have mobilized forces for ethnic killing in Darfur without any external support, but the international backing that it received from China gave it protection while doing so. For instance, China was in a position to weaken the UN Security Council resolutions against Sudanese state terror that arose in the early 2000s. Similarly, the implicit or explicit backing of the United States could be seen as a facilitator of Ethiopian, Rwandan, and Ugandan intervention in several of the regionalized African conflicts described in this chapter.

Conclusion on the Causation of Regionalized Conflicts

This section shows that there are at least three aspects to the analysis of regionalized conflicts. Permissive conditions make the regionalization of conflict possible. During the Cold War, there were many structural constraints on the regionalized conflict, and southern Africa was the main location of sustained cross-border intervention and war. Ironically, the end of the superpower rivalry in Africa and France's pullback from the support of its allies made interstate conflict more common. Arguably, changing African norms at the continental level also made cross-border conflict more likely (Clark 2011). Even when conditions are ripe for regionalized conflict, however, there must still be specific reasons, or efficient causes, several of which have been discussed here. Most neighboring African states get along with each other quite well, resolving the inevitable disputes that arise peaceably. Consider mineral-rich Zambia and its neighbors: since the end of white minority rule in Zimbabwe, Zambia has had no militarized disputes with its neighbors. Finally, the facilitators of conflict make regionalized wars longer and more violent. Like civil wars, regional conflicts are dynamic. Even after the original reasons for the start of a conflict are nearly forgotten, the new realities of conflict, including the displacement of persons and the exploitation of minerals, often keep them going. A deep understanding of the cases of regionalized conflict depends upon an awareness of all these analytical elements.

Some Regionalized African Conflicts Since the Cold War

In this section we briefly discuss five regionalized conflicts in Africa, bringing to bear the analysis of the previous section. All of the conflicts discussed here had essentially local origins, but all became regionalized over time, drawing in neighboring states. This set, which is far from exhaustive, suggests how common regionalized conflict has become in recent decades. The increase in the incidence of regionalized conflict suggests that structural changes have had an impact. Yet the details of these cases also show that the dynamics of conflict regionalization are quite distinctive. In the cases here, we attempt to identify one or two elements of the regionalization of conflict that seem central to us.

The case of the second Sudanese civil war, beginning in 1983, highlights the importance of shifting local alliances with global actors.[16] Over time, this Sudanese war attracted far more outside intervention than the first (see Chapter 2 case study). At the start of the war, the SPLA's leading figures soon took refuge across the border in Ethiopia, and the movement subsequently enjoyed the support of Haile Mengistu Mariam's regime for the next eight years. SPLA forces also used northeastern Zaire as a sanctuary, and in response Zairian president Mobutu Sese Seko allowed Sudanese forces to pursue them on Zairian territory (Prunier 2009). Despite Nimeiry's nominal adoption of Islamic law, he in fact enjoyed a "close relationship" with the United States in the Cold War context (Lesch 1987: 807), just as Mobutu did. Mengistu, on the other hand, had aligned his country with the Soviet Union (see Chapter 3). Another supporter of the SPLA (and enemy of Nimeiry) was Libya's Muammar Qaddafi (Lesch 1987). During this period, then, support for the SPLA broadly followed a Cold War logic: the United States generally supported the Sudanese government, whereas the Soviet Union had an explicit alliance with Ethiopia and a cordial relationship with Libya, both SPLA supporters. In the mid-1980s, however, neither superpower wished to engage in proxy conflict in northeastern Africa.

In the late 1980s, these alliances began to shift, and the Soviet Union began to withdraw from the political scene. Uganda's Museveni gradually became a partner of the United States, as did the new Meles Zenawi regime, which took over in Ethiopia in 1991. The United States was optimistic that this new generation of leaders would restore order to their respective countries. Meanwhile, as the Cold War ended, the United States became much more concerned about radicalization of political Islam in Africa (see Chapter 10). In this context, the United States began to perceive Sudan as a major threat to US interests on the continent, as al-Bashir used local Salafi leaders for his own purposes.[17] As the United States distanced itself from Sudan, al-Bashir soon began to cultivate China as an outside partner, culminating with a major oil deal in 1996 (James 2011). In this way, the United States came to be friendly with the allies of the SPLA and hostile to the Sudanese government. The tit-for-tat support of rebels between Sudan and Uganda was described earlier; al-Bashir's and Museveni's needs for regime security were proximate causes of the regionalization of this conflict.

Three further cases seem to suggest the centrality of ethnic fealty and migration of refugees to the regionalization of conflict. One of these is the Darfur conflict, which began within Sudan but became more regional in scope. Just as negotiations to end the second Sudanese civil war were getting under way, rebel groups began attacking government installations in Sudan's Darfur region in 2002 (Flint and de Waal 2005; also see the case study in Chapter 2). Full-scale conflict and then genocide soon ensued.[18]

Although this conflict was less regionalized than the second Sudanese civil war, it did reflect mutual interventions by the governments of Chad and Sudan into one another's politics. It also stimulated even more dramatic interventions. Many of the anti-regime fighters were representatives of the Zaghawa ethnic group, which happens to be the ethnicity of Chadian president Idriss Déby. As Zaghawa citizens began to take refuge across the Chadian border, the Déby regime began to provide assistance to the anti-regime rebels in 2005. In response, the al-Bashir regime began to support rebel groups in Chad who were determined to overthrow Déby and take power for themselves (de Waal 2008). In April 2006 and again in February 2008, Chadian rebels backed by Sudan attempted to take control of the capital, Ndjamena. After the first instance, Chad unilaterally broke diplomatic relations with Sudan, though these were restored by the end of the year. In the second battle for Ndjamena, in 2008, the Déby regime was saved only by the intervention of 1,250 French troops against the Sudan-backed rebels (*Africa Confidential* 2008). Libya, still then under Muammar Qaddafi, also came to the defense of the Déby regime at this time (Hansen 2011). On the Sudanese side, China and Russia were both selling arms to Sudan during the conflict in Darfur and while Sudan was interfering in Chad. These sales facilitated the conflict but were not a deep cause of the war.

Identity politics and migration also played central roles in the civil war in Côte d'Ivoire (2002–2011), including its regional aspects. Following the death of founding president Félix Houphouët-Boigny in 1993, the country's new leaders struggled to find a basis for legitimacy. Ahead of the country's competitive, multiparty elections of 1995, Henri Konan Bédié began to promote the concept of *Ivoirité,* or Ivorian nationalism defined as Christian and southern. Through this mechanism he sought to exclude people from the predominantly Muslim north, as well as immigrants. Ruling party leaders pushed through a law requiring presidential candidates to demonstrate not only their own Ivorian citizenship but also that of both parents. The law was specifically designed to disqualify a leading contender for the presidency, Alassane Ouattara, whose father was reportedly from Burkina Faso (Whitaker 2005).[19]

Following a coup d'état in 1999 that ousted Bédié, a retired general named Robert Guéï was put in power by the mutinous soldiers. Unlike his two predecessors, Guéï was not of Baoulé ethnic origin but rather was a Yacouba from the west. Deciding to run for president in 2000, Guéï found it convenient to maintain the presidential citizenship law, thus again preventing Ouattara from running (Akindès 2004; Whitaker 2005). Guéï was defeated by a longtime opposition politician from the south, Laurent Gbagbo, who was able to claim power only after street protests prevented Guéï from rigging the results. Gbagbo, another southerner of Bété ethnicity, continued the xenophobic rhetoric against Ivorians from the north, many of whom were assumed to be foreigners or to have foreign parents.

Before there could be any further elections, northern troops in the army began a mutiny and then a coup attempt in September 2002 against the Gbagbo regime. Although the coup attempt failed, the rebel forces soon consolidated their control over the northern half (roughly) of Côte d'Ivoire. Eventually the rebels became known as the New Forces of Côte d'Ivoire (FNCI) and created a political party called the Patriotic Movement of Côte d'Ivoire (MPCI). According to most sources (e.g., Bovcon 2009), the government of Burkina Faso was implicated in protecting the northern rebels, and also in passing arms to them to support their fight against the Gbagbo regime. Burkina Faso was sympathetic to the northern Muslims of Côte d'Ivoire, many of whom had migrated from Burkinabé territory in past decades, and by extension, favorable to the FNCI. Meanwhile, two new rebel groups sprang up in western Côte d'Ivoire, the Movement for Justice and Peace (MJP) and the Ivorian Popular Movement of the Great West (MPIGO). Then–Liberian president Charles Taylor "contributed greatly to the creation, arming and military training of the members" of these forces (Bovcon 2009: 6). Taylor hoped to play upon the loyalty of these Ivorian westerners to Guéï's memory to gain influence in the country. It is thus clear that the politics of identity and migration played a central role in Côte d'Ivoire's first civil war. Ouattara finally gained power only with the help of outside intervention, chiefly from France (see Chapter 11 case study).

Somalia is at the center of another regionalized conflict in which the key ingredients are both ethnic and politico-religious identity. Together, Djibouti, Eritrea, Ethiopia, and Somalia form a "regional security complex"[20] in the Horn of Africa, connected by the perceived threats emanating from the power vacuum in Somalia. It is surely true that the collapse of the Somali state has been a permissive condition of regionalized conflict there: no proper, internationally recognized political regime has controlled the territory of Somalia since the demise of the Siad Barre regime in 1991 (see Chapter 10). This fact has two consequences: first, there is no central authority that might control the organization of militant groups of various political orientations in Somalia; second, the absence of a central Somali state allows outsiders to enter Somali territory with no fear of deterrence by a Somali state army. Were it not for the insecurities caused by politicized ethnicity and religion, however, Somalia would not necessarily have become a site of regional contestation.

Ethnicity makes Somalia regionally problematic because of the Somali ethnic communities who live in neighboring Ethiopia and Kenya, and because of Somalia's history of ethno-nationalism.[21] These communities do not pose any threats to neighboring states simply by virtue of their ethnic identity: diverse ethnic communities live cheek-by-jowl across Africa with little if any ethnic strife. In the case of Somalia, however, the country's invasion of the Ogaden region of Ethiopia in 1977 (see Chapter 3) has made its neighbors leery of revived Somali unity and power. The presence of Somali refugees in neighboring countries exacerbates these fears.

The rise of Salafi (fundamentalist) Islamic movements in Somalia since the late 1990s is the other reason why the Somali conflict has become a regional one. Ethiopia and Kenya are secular states but with large minority Muslim populations. Ethiopia has been ruled by Christians for centuries, and Kenya since independence. Again, religious difference is far from an automatic source of conflict: interfaith conflict has been decidedly muted in other regional countries, such as Tanzania and Uganda. But the rise of Salafi movements in Somalia has made the governments of Ethiopia and Kenya fearful that their own Muslim populations might be radicalized. Kenya has been the target of a succession of high-profile terrorist attacks, including by al-Qaeda (the US embassy bombing in 1998) and more recently by al-Shabaab-related militants (the Westgate Mall attack in 2003 and the Garissa University attack in 2015). The presence of large numbers of Somali refugees in northeastern Kenya has raised the country's fears of further terrorist attacks. As noted in the case study in Chapter 10, both countries have undertaken interventions in Somalia provoked by fears that terrorism would originate from Somali territory.

Across the continent, in West Africa, the key ingredient of another regionalized conflict was warlord politics. At the heart of this regional conflict was a pair of domestic conflicts, the first civil war in Liberia (1989–1997) (see Chapter 8 case study) and the civil war in Sierra Leone (1991–2002). The leaders of the two key rebel groups were Charles Taylor of the National Patriotic Front of Liberia (NPFL) and Foday Sankoh of the Revolutionary United Front (RUF) in Sierra Leone. Each movement had indigenous roots in its respective country, but the two rebel leaders both received training in Libya in the 1980s and made a tactical alliance: "Sankoh and his group would help Taylor 'liberate' Liberia, after which he would provide them with a base to launch their armed struggle" (Abdullah 1998: 220–221). The contiguity of the two countries made this alliance practical. When Taylor launched his invasion of Nimba county, Liberia, from a base in Côte d'Ivoire in December 1989, he enjoyed support from Sankoh and other Sierra Leoneans, both before and after the start of the invasion (compare Abdullah 1998 and Peters 2010). By June 1990, Taylor's forces were closing in on the capital of Monrovia, which they were prevented from taking only by the intervention of an ECOMOG force staffed chiefly by Nigerian soldiers (see Chapter 8). Taylor and the NPFL continued to control much of the country, however, until 1997, when Taylor was elected president. Meanwhile, in March 1991, Sankoh's force entered Sierra Leone's Kailahun district from neighboring Liberia with the support of NPFL special forces and arms funneled through the group (Peters 2010).

Upon gaining power in 1997, Taylor proved to be as ruthless as a ruler as he had been as a rebel, committing untold atrocities against the Liberian people. He was finally forced out of power by the second Liberian civil war (1999–2003) and went into exile in Nigeria in the latter year. In 2006, Taylor was arrested while trying to flee Nigeria and was transferred first to Liberia, then to Sierra Leone, where he faced charges before the Special Court for Sierra Leone. In 2012, after a lengthy trial in The Hague, Taylor was finally convicted of war crimes and crimes against humanity, and he was given a fifty-year sentence. Sankoh died of a stroke in 2003 in Sierra Leone after having been arrested there in 2000 and subsequently charged with war crimes. The nefarious partnership of these two warlords was at the heart of these conflicts, and Libyan support was a facilitating factor. The fact that Taylor ultimately faced justice in a court for Sierra Leone reflects the regionalization of the two linked civil wars.

This set of cases reveals much about the complexity of the idea of the regionalization of conflict. First, like conflicts in general, the regionalization of conflict often involves a "recipe," but analysts can usually identify one or two primary ingredients. Second, in every case, there was some form of domestic, or internal, conflict that tempted or (possibly) compelled outsiders to intervene. In some cases, the rulers of neighboring states felt that their regime security was at stake; in others, they may have seen an opportunity to undermine a historical adversary or bolster an ally. Second, these cases show that many forms of outside intervention are possible. Although the barebones descriptions here emphasize military interventions, the "menu" of interventions is long. The list of kinds of intervention begins with rhetorical support for rebels or condemnation of ruling regimes; more aggressive forms of intervention include the passage of arms to insurgent or rebel groups or the infiltration of armed sympathizers. Outright invasion by the official state forces is only the most visible and blatant form of intervention by neighboring states. Finally, many of the regionalized conflicts described here also involve support or intervention from extra-continental actors. The support of external great powers (like China and the United States) or of multilateral institutions (like the UN or the EU) is frequently a permissive condition or stimulant to regionalized conflicts.

Case Study: The Congo Wars as a Regionalized Conflict

The Congo conflicts merit particular attention due to their deadly and debilitating qualities. In 2007, the International Rescue Committee (IRC) estimated that 5.4 million "excess deaths" had occurred as a result of the Congo conflicts between August 1997 and April 2007 (International Rescue Committee 2007).[22] The IRC's estimates were based on a series of five household-level surveys of mortalities experienced across the DRC. Fewer than 10 percent of these "excess deaths" were due to violence; the bulk were the result of diseases caused by exposure to the elements, hunger and malnutrition, the exertions of displacement, and lack of proper medications. Other organizations have suggested that the actual number of excess deaths is much lower, perhaps even fewer than 1 million (see Williams 2011). Yet there is no doubt that the Congo conflicts have been exceedingly deadly, and also that millions of people have suffered assaults, displacement, theft of their property, denial of schooling opportunities, hunger, humiliation, and myriad other forms of suffering. The epidemic of sexual assault, in particular, has seized the attention of the Western press and scholarly communities (Autesserre 2012; Freedman 2016).

The multifaceted conflicts that have wracked the DRC since 1996 represent a classic case of regionalized conflict in Africa, involving successive conflicts at multiple levels. The first of Congo's modern conflicts (i.e., excluding the 1960–1964 civil war) involved the displacement from power of President Mobutu, who had originally gained power in 1965 (see Chapter 3). By the mid-1990s, Mobutu was slowly losing his grip on power after he had opened the political space to multiparty competition in 1990 (see Chapter 5). Although he allowed the opposition to come into the open, Mobutu manipulated them to ensure his continuation in office between 1990 and 1996 (Nzongola-Ntalaja 2002). During this interim, the genocide unfolded in neighboring Rwanda, and as the war ended there, over 1 million refugees, mostly Hutu, fled across the border into the neighboring North and South Kivu regions of Zaire (as it was still known). Among these refugees were some who were implicated in the genocide (*génocidaires*) and former members of the Rwandan Armed Forces.

These individuals soon reorganized themselves as the de facto masters of the sprawling refugee camps and gained the forbearance of Mobutu, who had a close relationship with former Rwandan president Juvénal Habyarimana. In October 1996, Rwandan forces entered Zaire under the cover of a nascent insurgent group, the Alliance of Democratic Forces for the Liberation of Congo (AFDL), led by Laurent Kabila.[23] Rwanda, Uganda, Angola, Burundi, and, to a lesser extent, several other African states soon formed a loose coalition against Mobutu, contributing support to the AFDL and other anti-Mobutu rebels. In May 1997, these rebels marched into Kinshasa as Mobutu fled the country for exile in Morocco. Kabila became the country's first new president in thirty-two years and renamed it the Democratic Republic of Congo.

The Second Congo War,[24] also known as the Great African War (Reyntjens 2009), proved to be longer and more complex. It involved several levels of conflict, many of which represented wars within the war. Even the origins of the war can be traced to three different levels. Months before the war began, tensions were rising, and low-grade violence was escalating between the Banyamulenge population[25] of South Kivu and local militia groups known as the Mayi-Mayi. These local tensions had their roots in long-standing disputes over land and citizenship (Whitaker 2003) but were exacerbated by tensions between President Kabila and his erstwhile foreign patrons, the Rwandan Patriotic Army of Paul Kagame (Prunier 2009). Kabila was caught between the demands of his own Congolese population to assert his independence from his foreign backers and the demands of the Rwandans that he protect the Banyamulenge population of eastern Congo. During this time, the chief of staff of the Congolese Armed Forces (FAC) was James Kabarebe, a Rwandan general who had played a key role in the First Congo War. After Kabila dismissed Kabarebe on July 27, 1998, mutinies against the Kabila government broke out throughout Congo but were centered in the Kivu regions. Rwandan troops began pouring across the border in support of the rebels; on August 4, the first of several Rwandan planes landed at the Kitona airbase on the other side of Congo, bearing more Rwandan troops, commanded by James Kabarebe himself (Prunier 2009). Thus, the start of the Second Congo War had a local element (tension in the Kivu regions between Banyamulenge and other groups), a national element (dissatisfaction with Kabila for his apparent subservience to Rwanda), and an interstate element (the rising tensions between the rulers of the DRC and Rwanda).

Rwandan and Ugandan intervention would almost certainly have led to the overthrow of Laurent Kabila but for the counter-intervention of his new Southern African Development Community allies, Angola and Zimbabwe. The Second Congo War soon bogged down into a conflict that lasted for several more years. Rwanda quickly organized a rebel group and political party, the Rally for Congolese Democracy (RCD), while Uganda created another rebel group, the Movement for the Liberation of Congo (MLC). Each of the politico-military organizations assumed control of sizable portions of north-central and eastern Congo.[26] The Kabila government and its foreign allies maintained control over southern and western regions of the country. The war was at a stalemate, while much violence unfolded within the occupied zones of the country, particularly against ethnic groups considered to be hostile or political opponents of the occupiers. All sides were intransigent about ending the conflict.

In January 2001, President Kabila was assassinated under mysterious circumstances, perhaps by representatives of his own child soldiers, or perhaps as a result of an Angolan conspiracy (Dunn 2002). Kabila's son, Joseph Kabila, was quickly able to consolidate power following the assassination. Peace negotiations brokered by South African president Thabo Mbeki soon ensued, and in December 2002 the major parties to the conflict reached an agreement to withdraw their troops from Congolese territory the following year.[27] This also led to a transitional government with Joseph Kabila as president; four vice presidents, three of whom represented the opposition; and the merging of state and rebel armies. Regional conflict continued within Congo under this peace agreement, and the record of achievement of the transitional government was limited. Nonetheless, the peace held enough for the country to hold largely fair and peaceful elections in July (first round) and October (second round) of 2006. In the second round, President Kabila prevailed with 58 percent of the vote, defeating Jean-Pierre Bemba of the MLC. Unfortunately, fighting continued in the eastern part of the country even after the elections, as the Kabila regime was unable to suppress the main rebel groups operating there. Rwanda and Uganda were implicated by the UN in supporting these rebel groups with money, arms, and troops. The Congolese army never became strong and well-organized enough to defeat the rebel groups or to enforce order in the east. In 2013, a special UN military unit, the Force Intervention Brigade, was deployed with more offensive capabilities and helped to disband one particularly troublesome rebel group, the March 23 Movement (M23). Even so, periodic violence continued in parts of eastern Congo, and instability increased throughout the country as Kabila stayed in power past the constitutionally mandated end of his second term in 2016.

Clearly, the Congo conflicts are not one conflict but many related ones. After the start of the Second Congo War, the Rwandan army and Tutsi-dominated militias hunted down and killed tens of thousands of Hutu refugees. Later, in the Kivus, Tutsi-dominated rebel groups (like M23) fought against the Mayi-Mayi and other organizations dominated by other ethnic groups. Rwanda interfered in this conflict, supporting the Banyamulenge. In the Ituri province of Orientale region, rebel groups dominated by Hema and Lendu political entrepreneurs fought ongoing battles over land and control from 1999 to 2003, goaded on by both Rwandan and Ugandan interveners. Meanwhile, the Congolese state tried to suppress these conflicts but without success. Following the disputed Congolese elections of 2011, in which Joseph Kabila was reelected in a deeply flawed set of polls, violence against the regime broke out in the west of the country before being suppressed. The kaleidoscope of conflicts begs the question of how we can understand the apparently never-ending disorder of the benighted central African state.

Paul Williams's earlier-discussed recipe metaphor is valuable in helping us to understand Congo's complex conflicts. Many ingredients have gone into the toxic stew that has ended so many lives and stunted the hopes of so many survivors. It is useful to begin with the permissive conditions that allowed Congo's conflicts to erupt, spread, and fester for two decades now. Among these conditions, the collapse of the Congolese state, beginning in the 1970s and culminating in the 1990s (Young 1994; Clark 1998), is a useful place to begin the story. Under the venal rule of Mobutu, the Congolese state progressively lost the ability to project the authority of the state into the country's far-flung regions. The virtual privatization of the country's economy for private economic gains and its ensuing collapse progressively robbed the Congolese state of its ability to perform even the most basic functions (Schatzberg 1988). The opening of the political space to opposition parties in 1990 accelerated the social dissatisfaction and allowed opposition groups to organize. In the early 1990s, ethnic conflicts broke out in several places and could not be suppressed by the authorities. The gradual implosion of the Zairian state under Mobutu meant that the state lost the capacity to respond to other internal rebellions or external interventions.

One could point to two other permissive conditions that allowed for foreign intervention from neighboring states, and even noncontiguous ones (like Zimbabwe). First, African regional norms about interstate intervention were beginning to change around the time that the Cold War ended (Clark 2011). Intervention in one another's internal affairs became more acceptable among African states following the withdrawal of the previously restraining influences of the superpowers and (to a lesser extent) of France (see Chapter 11). Related to this same point, US and British support to the regimes in power in Uganda and Rwanda was another permissive condition of those countries' interventions in the DRC. If the United States, in particular, had signaled its opposition to the Rwandan and Ugandan intervention that sparked the Second Congo War, it likely would never have happened. The arms and financial support that the Kagame and Museveni regimes, respectively, received from the United States greatly enhanced their ability to invade their large neighbor. In turn, Anglo-American support could be interpreted through either a realist or a constructivist lens. From the realist point of view, Anglo-American support for these regimes was driven by a common interest in containing Sudanese influence in the region, and as payback for Rwandan and Ugandan participation in African peacekeeping missions (Damman 2015). From a constructivist point of view, Anglo-American support for Rwanda was driven as much by "genocide guilt" as by specific interests. That is, Britain and the United States were among the countries that stood idly by during the 1994 genocide, taking no real action until after the massive killing was done (Melvern 2000). Arguably, this genocide guilt made these two countries tolerant of Rwandan intervention in eastern Congo, which was partly in pursuit of the *génocidaires* of 1994. According to the United Nations Office of the High Commissioner for Human Rights (2010), the Kagame regime committed its own round of mass murders in eastern DRC.

As for the efficient causes of the Congo wars, one has to look to the motivations of individual ethnic-group leaders, would-be rulers of Congo, and foreign heads of state. Before the start of the Second Congo War, the leaders of various ethnic communities in eastern Congo acted out of both fear and lust for power to mobilize militias from among their respective communities. They hoped both to protect their ethnic communities and also to position themselves as local authorities or warlords. Rwanda and Uganda appear to have had rather different motives for intervening at the start of this war; the Kagame regime quite clearly wanted to increase its security by dispersing the Hutu-dominated militias operating in eastern Congo and to replace Laurent Kabila with a more pliable neighboring ruler (Longman 2002). Uganda's motivations for intervention in Congo are more obscure (and remain contested) but may have to do with Uganda's long-standing alliance with Rwanda (Clark 2001a; compare Reyntjens 2009). Angola intervened on behalf of Kabila because of its calculation that the Kabila regime had been and would continue to be a reliable partner in its war against the UNITA rebel group (Turner 2002). In between the local ethnic leaders and the foreign interveners were those Congolese politicians who hoped to be able to take control over their state. The two most important were Jean-Pierre Bemba of the MLC and Azarias Ruberwa of the RCD, both of whom ran against Joseph Kabila for president of Congo in 2006. The motivation of these individuals was to take power over the DRC, but such ambitions would have been entirely moot were it not for the foreign intervention in the country, which essentially created the militia groups that each ran.

Two other variables, refugees and mineral resources in Congo, are best seen as facilitators of conflict, despite the critical role that they have played. Had it not been for the many hundreds of thousands of Hutu refugees in eastern Congo, it is not at all clear that the Rwandan regime would have attacked, sparking the First Congo War. The former *génocidaires* and revenge-minded Hutu elements among these refugees represented an existential threat to the new Tutsi-dominated regime (of which Kagame was only vice president and defense minister until 2000). Since most innocent Hutus returned to Rwanda after the First Congo War, and since most of those suspected of genocide were either murdered or jailed, however, refugees played a much smaller role in the Second Congo War. This war proved far longer and deadlier. The presence of Congolese Hutu populations (i.e., not refugees but nationals) was a bigger source of concern for the Rwandan regime in launching the Second Congo War.

The presence of "lootable" minerals in eastern Congo, including casserite, coltan, gold, and tantalum, was only arguably an original stimulus for foreign intervention in Congo, particularly that of Uganda. As documented in several UN reports, Ugandan army officers quickly got involved in the illegal extraction and evacuation of minerals from Congo. What is less clear is whether the promise of exploiting Congolese minerals was an original motivation for Ugandan intervention (Clark 2001a). In any case, it is inarguable that the exploitation of minerals became a tremendous motivation for Uganda to remain in Congo after its intervention in 1998 since so many Ugandans profited from the illicit trade. Rwanda also engaged in mineral exploitation in eastern Congo, allegedly for the purpose of funding its military occupation. After the implementation of the 2002 peace agreement for Congo, Rwanda and Uganda officially withdrew their armies[28] and became less involved in mineral exploitation. This practice then came to be associated with the many rebel groups operating in eastern Congo, including those sponsored by Rwanda or Uganda. Thus, the presence of exploitable minerals in eastern Congo served to perpetuate the conflict at the local level, just as they had done at the interstate level.

As suggested by Williams, then, no single cause explains the Congo wars, but the ingredients we find in the "recipe" of the Congo wars help us to understand them. Certain ideological and political conditions that emerged in the 1990s made foreign intervention in Congo "thinkable" for the country's neighbors. The illegitimacy and inefficacy of the Mobutu regime in its twilight years encouraged a range of different kinds of rebels to take up arms against both neighboring communities and the state. Still other variables have perpetuated conflict in Congo for two decades. Ending the Congo wars more conclusively will also likely require a recipe: firm commitments from key members of the international community; the support, or at least acquiescence, of Congo's immediate neighbors; and, not least, patient mediation of land and other disputes at the local level among various ethnic communities, as called for by Séverine Autesserre (2010). Only once Congo's most serious conflicts are ended can the country's rulers turn their full attention to the urgent issues of policy reform and development so craved by the Congolese population.

Notes

1. In fact, most war-related deaths have been indirect. Indirect deaths occur, for instance, when civilians are forced to flee their homes and become refugees or internally displaced persons. Such persons are highly vulnerable to disease, hunger or starvation, and nonpolitical (criminal) predation. Most of the "excess deaths" of the Congo wars have been the result of such situations.

2. On both the concept of state failure and the causes of state failure in Africa, see in particular Bates 2015.

3. France, too, was an implicit "guarantor" of some client regimes (Decalo 2008).

4. The distinction between permissive conditions and efficient causes is taken from the work of Kenneth Waltz (1959).

5. This is a controversial term. Large parts of the territories of these two states have been ungoverned by an internationally recognized state; this is not to say, however, they are not governed by local or unrecognized political forces.

6. On this issue see Godehardt and Nabers 2011 and Prys 2010, among other sources.

7. For an overview of the APSA, see in particular Vines 2013. A wider analysis of African efforts to resolve conflicts through peacemaking and peacekeeping can be found in Chapter 8.

8. For a representative survey, see the edited collection Engel and Porto 2010.

9. In this case, the AU authorized African states to assist the government of Comoros to reincorporate the island of Anjouan, whose leader sought to secede from the country. Senegal, Sudan, and Tanzania sent troops to assist Comoros in successfully undertaking this mission. For more on peacemaking in general, see Chapter 8.

10. When John Clark taught at Makerere University in 1999 and 2000, a number of southern Sudanese enrolled in his classes. One of them explained that he was an SPLA fighter who had been wounded several times in the second Sudanese civil war.

11. In fact, in the mid-1990s, the Sudanese Secret Service allegedly created another armed group, the Allied Democratic Forces (ADF), operating from Zairian territory, to attack Uganda. According to Gérard Prunier, the ADF was "forced into emergency action" against Uganda in 1996 as the war in eastern Congo got under way (2009: 120).

12. Cabinda is a geographical enclave, controlled by the government of Angola and previously the Portuguese colonial state in Angola. It is physically separated from the main territory of Angola by the territory of the DRC and is contiguous along much of its border with the territory of Congo-Brazzaville. It is the site of a large portion of Angola's petroleum and is thus jealously protected by the Angolan state. A liberation group has operated on its territory since the 1960s.

13. This realist aphorism is generally attributed in international relations to the ancient Indian philosopher Kautilya, though the notion behind it is so elemental that it might have any number of original sources.

14. When new regimes come to power in African states, the prior alignments are frequently reoriented (as outlined later).

15. For one view on this problem, see the website of Christian Solidarity International at http://csi-usa.org/slavery.

16. The first Sudanese civil war, from 1955 to 1972, was not really regionalized, despite some modest outside support for southern Sudanese rebels. One useful map can be found in the work of Samuel Totten (2015).

17. Sudan was a host of al-Qaeda leader Osama bin Laden from 1991 to 1996, during which time al-Qaeda undertook its bombing of the World Trade Center (in 1993).

18. The killing was so indiscriminate and indifferent with respect to the distinction of combatants and noncombatants that it was labeled "genocide" by US secretary of state Colin Powell (Kessler and Lynch 2004) and many other international observers. The map in Totten 2015 shows the location of Darfur within Sudan.

19. Due to French colonial policies and economic enticements, millions of Ivorians trace their family origins to the poorer Sahelian countries of Burkina Faso and Mali (Bovcon 2009).

20. On the concept of the regional security complex, see Buzan and Wæver 2004.

21. The majority of the population of another Somali neighbor, Djibouti, is actually ethnic Somali, and the government is heavily influenced by a Somali clan. Paradoxically, these demographic and political realities, as well as US and French support, make Djibouti less fearful of a reunited Somalia than is Ethiopia or Kenya.

22. Others, including Paul Williams (2011), claim that the real number is probably far lower.

23. Kabila had tried many times previously to rebel against Mobutu but without success. This time, his insurgency benefited from the support of the new, Tutsi-dominated regime in Rwanda, of which Paul Kagame was the vice president but de facto ruler.

24. This labeling of the 1998–2002 conflict as the "second" war does not take account of Congo's 1960–1964 civil war.

25. The Banyamulenge are Congolese people of Rwandan descent, most of them Tutsi, who fled the Rwandan statebuilding project in the precolonial era and settled in Congo in the mid-nineteenth century, well before colonial borders were drawn (Newbury 1997).

26. One useful map that shows rebel- and government-controlled areas soon after the start of the conflict can be found at https://www.thoughtco.com/second-congo-war-battle-for-resources-43696.

27. The cumbersome name of this accord was the Global and Inclusive Agreement on Transition in the Democratic Republic of Congo, signed in Pretoria. While Rwanda and Uganda withdrew their formal military units according to the agreement, both countries continued clandestine and low-level interventions in the DRC.

28. Each maintained clandestine forces in eastern DRC.

8

Humanitarian Assistance and Peace Operations

As elsewhere, conflicts in Africa often are associated with significant suffering among civilian populations, including displacement, abductions, sexual violence, human trafficking, famine, and death. Some people seek safety across international borders, becoming asylum-seekers and refugees,[1] while others become internally displaced persons (IDPs) within their own countries. Natural disasters (drought, floods, earthquakes, etc.) also can cause significant harm, particularly where infrastructure is already weak. In some cases, but certainly not all, civilian suffering associated with such situations receives international media attention and generates public sympathy around the world. Conflicts and natural disasters in Africa have long attracted an international humanitarian response, but the scale of response has increased in recent years, due in part to the pace with which images of human suffering travel around the globe.

In these situations, there are several ways in which the world can respond. At a minimum, people, organizations, and governments within and outside of Africa typically provide *humanitarian assistance* in the form of food, healthcare, and other aid to civilian victims. Traditionally, humanitarians are expected to abide by the core principles of independence, neutrality, and impartiality, though there are inevitably political challenges,[2] as explored later. In some cases, the international community undertakes joint action motivated by the desire to protect civilians. Such *humanitarian intervention* can take several forms: economic sanctions, whether targeted at specific leaders or broader restrictions; diplomatic punishment, including rhetorical condemnation, suspensions from international organizations, and expulsions of ambassadors; and military intervention, which can involve air strikes, arms embargoes, or the deployment of peacekeeping troops, as discussed in this chapter.[3] Lastly, *peacebuilding* efforts include brokering peace agreements and bringing perpetrators of violence to justice, though there can be significant tension between the goals of peace and justice, as shown later.

Regardless of the form that the response takes, humanitarian action is typically presumed to be neutral and above politics. In actuality, any sort of external intervention, even if it is "humanitarian" in nature, has political effects and can at times make the conflict worse. In this chapter, we examine the politics surrounding the provision of humanitarian assistance in African conflicts and natural disasters, the deployment of peacekeeping operations in the region, and the efforts of international actors to broker peace and seek justice. Moving beyond inherent debates about responsibilities, rights, and resources, we explore the risks of humanitarian action and the ways in which external interventions can at times prolong and exacerbate the conflicts they seek to ameliorate. Finally, we consider how simplified understandings of many conflicts in Africa further undermine efforts to seek solutions. A case study of Liberia at the end of the chapter illustrates many of the challenges of humanitarian action.

Humanitarian Assistance

Often the first external response to a conflict situation or natural disaster comes in the form of food, water, medical care, and other essentials to civilian victims, including injured survivors and those forced to flee their homes as IDPs or refugees. Local people and organizations do what they can to help, sharing what they have and at times risking danger themselves, until humanitarian assistance from farther afield makes its way to the area. How quickly and how much aid arrives depend on a variety of factors, including the accessibility of the area, the extent of international media coverage, and the existence of other crises around the world at the time. There often is a surge of humanitarian assistance during the initial emergency phase, followed by a significant drop-off as the media spotlight moves elsewhere.

A great variety of actors are involved in the delivery of humanitarian assistance. When a significant number of people are displaced, as is common in many conflicts, the United Nations High Commissioner for Refugees (UNHCR) usually plays a leading role. Although officially responsible for people who have crossed international borders, thus becoming asylum-seekers and refugees, the UNHCR increasingly has become involved in situations of internal displacement. The World Food Programme (WFP) is typically responsible for providing food, most of which comes from cash and in-kind donations from Europe and the

United States.[4] Depending on the context, the United Nations Children's Fund (UNICEF), the World Health Organization (WHO), and other international agencies also provide humanitarian assistance. The efforts of these various UN agencies are coordinated through the Office for the Coordination of Humanitarian Affairs (OCHA).

In most emergencies, UN agencies contract with nongovernmental organizations as "implementing partners" to do everything from food distribution to "vector control" (killing insects and rodents that spread diseases). International NGOs such as the International Rescue Committee and Doctors Without Borders typically are more experienced and better funded, but local NGOs often win major UN relief contracts as well. Local Red Cross and Red Crescent societies also mobilize their volunteers and resources. The involvement of national and local governments in providing humanitarian assistance depends on the political context, as gaining access to civilian victims in rebel-controlled areas can sometimes require delicate negotiations. Civilian victims are a key part of any humanitarian operation, though they are rarely empowered to determine assistance priorities and oversee distribution to the extent that they could be.

On the surface, humanitarian assistance may not sound particularly controversial or politically charged. After all, most people would agree that civilian victims of a conflict or disaster should receive food, temporary shelter, and medical assistance. In practice, however, even the most basic decisions about the provision of humanitarian assistance can become quite contentious. Take, for example, the number of people who are affected. This information is necessary to determine how much aid to send, from food rations and tents to medical supplies and doctors. But it can be difficult to get an accurate count of the population needing assistance. At times, the situation is too dangerous or inaccessible to do a thorough survey of needs. In other cases, officials have incentives to overestimate or underestimate the number of people affected. Governments typically do not like to appear as if they cannot protect their own populations, so officials may underestimate the number of refugees who have crossed into another country. On the other side of the border, the host government may inflate refugee figures to get more aid. Similarly, government officials might want to discredit a domestic rebel group by claiming it has killed or wounded more people than it has. In the case of natural disasters, government officials may overestimate the number of people affected to increase the amount of aid. Thus, even determining the number of people needing humanitarian relief can trigger controversy.

More debates often emerge in determining who qualifies for humanitarian assistance. Do all residents of an affected village receive food rations, for example, or only those whose houses and farms were destroyed? Should scarce resources be spent trying to deliver aid to remote regions, or should agencies focus on more populated areas even if the needs are not as great? When people flee into another country, should they receive aid only if they have officially registered as refugees? What if the host government perceives them as economic migrants instead of victims of conflict (see Chapter 9)? Should civilians still receive aid if they are providing moral and material support to armed rebels or to an abusive government? In theory, the humanitarian principles of neutrality, independence, and impartiality are meant to guide decisionmaking on such issues; in practice, emergency situations are complex and fluid, and these decisions must be made quickly by people who often are living in dangerous contexts.

Then, of course, there is the question of who pays for humanitarian assistance. If a conflict or disaster attracts international media coverage, the humanitarian response can be massive, as people around the world do what they can to help by donating to relief agencies. But most funding for humanitarian relief operations comes from donor governments, especially the United States, the European Union, and Japan. The willingness of these governments to donate humanitarian assistance depends on the extent of their interests in the affected countries and the level of support among their domestic populations. Many Western governments will contribute heavily to humanitarian relief efforts in a conflict-affected area, even as they avoid military and diplomatic involvement to resolve the conflict. This allows them to claim to be doing something about the conflict without undertaking a more extensive commitment. Over time, if a conflict continues, the international spotlight moves to new crises elsewhere in the world, and funding for humanitarian relief declines (see Chapter 10 case study of Somalia).

Manipulation of Humanitarian Assistance

Decisions about humanitarian assistance can become contentious in any emergency, but this is especially true in situations where warring parties seek to manipulate relief efforts for their own benefit. Indeed, one of the greatest risks of providing humanitarian assistance is that it will empower or embolden violent actors within a conflict, potentially making the situation worse. This possibility has led to a growing body of literature exploring the complicated ethical dilemmas involved in providing humanitarian relief (see, among others, Anderson 1999; Barnett and Weiss 2013; Branch 2009; de Waal 1997b; Keen 1994a, 2008; Kennedy 2011; Lischer 2005; Menkhaus 2012; Rieff 2002; Terry 2002; Weiss 1999; Wheeler 2000).

One way to manipulate aid is by using political instead of humanitarian considerations to determine its distribution. A government might do this by directing aid agencies to provide relief in some areas and not others, rewarding supporters of the regime and punishing opponents. In this way, however unintentionally, humanitarian aid can further the political interests of those in power. During the famine in Ethiopia in the mid-1980s, for example, as much as one-third of the population in need of immediate food aid was in Tigray, yet the northern region received only roughly 5 percent of the relief food that came into the country (de Waal 1997b). The Ethiopian government directed aid agencies to focus their efforts on other geographic areas, claiming that it could not guarantee their security in the north. Not coincidentally, Tigray was the stronghold for a rebel movement that was gaining ground against the government, eventually coming to power in 1991. Government officials effectively denied much-needed food aid to regime opponents and sent aid agencies instead to areas experiencing less severe shortages that were more supportive of the regime. Concerned about security and their continued authorization to work in the country, aid agencies opted to follow Ethiopian government directives on where to operate.

A related strategy to manipulate humanitarian aid is to divert it to support military causes. African leaders—whether government or rebel—often turn a blind eye when troops under their command steal deliveries of humanitarian aid and sell them at exorbitant prices to supplement their meager salaries. (Prices for basic supplies, especially food, often skyrocket in conflict situations because of shortages.) Some rebel groups in Africa have generated significant amounts of funding by capturing and selling humanitarian aid, thus converting international goodwill into money to purchase weapons and recruit soldiers. As David Keen (1994a) documents extensively, both Sudanese government soldiers and rebel forces from the Sudan People's Liberation Army benefited greatly from the famine in southern Sudan in the late 1980s as they seized incoming food aid and sold it to desperate people (see Chapter 2). Traders and raiders also got in on the action, taking advantage of severe shortages to increase their own profits. Similar dynamics were at work during the 1991–1992 famine in Somalia, where troops of various warring parties stole food aid shipments and controlled their distribution (see Chapter 10). In such situations, aid agencies are faced with a dilemma of whether to continue providing relief, knowing that it is being diverted to military causes. By continuing to send aid, some aid workers reason, the food makes it to the market, though its distribution is based on ability to pay instead of need. If food aid is cut off entirely, many more people could starve.

At times, militants hide among civilian victims in order to benefit from international humanitarian aid. The influx of food, medicine, and other necessities provides them with the means to survive while they organize and train for military operations. In some cases, civilian populations support the militants' cause and willingly share the aid; refugee women may cook food for rebel soldiers, for example. In other cases, militants essentially hold civilians hostage, preventing them from leaving for fear of losing their steady stream of supplies. A good example of this intermixing of militant and civilian populations was the Rwandan refugee camps in Tanzania and the Democratic Republic of Congo (then known as Zaire) from 1994 to 1996. Among the refugees who fled the genocidal violence in Rwanda in 1994 were some (unknown) number who actively participated in the killing. Militants received aid in the camps, which at their peak cost the international community about $1 million per day, while they actively prepared for an attack to take back power in Rwanda. To be sure, many refugees supported the militants' cause, but there is also evidence of violence being used to prevent civilians from returning home (Whitaker 1999). Eventually, this threat along the border prompted Rwanda to attack the camps in eastern Congo in 1996 (see Chapter 7), causing some residents to return home and others to flee deeper into Congo, where they continued to organize and train.

Warring parties may use humanitarian aid to win populations over to areas they control, potentially shifting the balance of power within a conflict. To the extent that any conflict is about controlling both territory and people, the migration of people into an area suggests a greater level of legitimacy and support for the group that controls the area (and less for its opponent). In Mozambique in the late 1980s, for example, humanitarian aid was concentrated in areas controlled by the Mozambique Liberation Front (FRELIMO) government. Only the International Committee of the Red Cross (ICRC) provided aid in areas held by rebels from the Mozambican National Resistance (RENAMO). Aid agencies justified the decision to concentrate on one side because of human rights abuses committed by RENAMO and resulting insecurity during that period. In search of much-needed assistance, especially with a drought in the early 1990s, people fled rebel-held areas and relocated to the government side. The aid-induced population displacement and inability to access starving populations in rebel areas helped put pressure on both sides to reach a peace agreement in 1992 (Barnes 1998).

At times, governments use their control over aid distribution to legitimize their approach to counterinsurgency. In situations where the government wants to concentrate people in closely guarded areas and monitor their activities, they may mandate that aid be distributed only in those locations. Such was the situation in northern Uganda, where the government forced a significant portion of the Acholi population to reside in IDP camps. The official justification was that the camps were necessary to protect people from attacks by the Lord's Resistance Army, but many saw the camps as a counterinsurgency strategy to control the population and ensure they did not aid the rebels. Many people wanted to return to homes in more remote areas, but the government prevented humanitarian aid from being provided anywhere outside of the camps, ensuring that most of the population would stay (Branch 2009, 2011). As in many other situations, aid agencies were faced with the tough choice of following government regulations, thus legitimizing its policy, or providing no assistance whatsoever.

In these ways and others, then, warring parties in a conflict often manipulate incoming humanitarian aid to advance their own cause and undermine their opponents. Aid workers typically are quite aware of how their assistance is being captured or abused, but the alternative of not providing it at all is often less desirable. Periodically, an aid agency takes a principled stand by leaving a situation instead of providing aid under questionable ethical circumstances, but invariably another organization steps in to do the job. In Tanzania in late 1994, for example, the French branch of Doctors Without Borders pulled out of the Rwandan refugee camps to protest the abuse of humanitarian aid by people responsible for genocide (Terry 2002). Other aid agencies respected the group's decision but quickly submitted bids to secure the contract to take over its work.[5]

Is the manipulation of humanitarian assistance new? The short answer is no. From Afghan mujahidin training in refugee camps to fight the Soviet occupation to the Khmer Rouge's control over Cambodian camps in Thailand (Terry 2002), humanitarian aid has been abused by militants for years. Even so, such dilemmas have received increased attention from academics, practitioners, and policymakers since the 1990s, in part because they have become more complex. During the Cold War, external donors and aid agencies perceived many conflicts through the lens of superpower competition. Western aid agencies often accepted the abuse of humanitarian aid if it was for the side they favored in that broader struggle (as with the Afghan refugees, for example). The end of the Cold War removed this externally imposed lens and prompted aid workers and others to raise more questions about the political impact of humanitarian aid. In addition, armed groups—both government armies and rebels—have become more sophisticated in their manipulation of assistance. Moreover, due in part to the effect of twenty-four-hour global news coverage, the magnitude of the humanitarian response in many conflicts is unprecedented. Thus, the problem of manipulating humanitarian assistance is not new, but efforts to prevent aid from exacerbating violent conflicts may require some creative thinking.

Peacekeeping in Africa

Unlike humanitarian assistance, humanitarian intervention has become common only more recently in African conflicts. After an ill-fated United Nations mission in Congo in the early 1960s, Cold War dynamics and suspicions among African leaders prevented the deployment of any further UN missions to sub-Saharan Africa until Angola in 1988. The Organization of African Unity's emphasis on the principles of sovereignty and nonintervention (see Chapter 6) similarly hindered the deployment of any regional peacekeeping operations during that period, with the exception of a short-lived mission to Chad in 1981–1982.[6]

Since the end of the Cold War, there has been a dramatic increase in the number of multilateral peacekeeping operations in Africa, with some led by the United Nations and others by regional bodies. Nearly thirty UN missions have been deployed to twenty African countries since 1988; as of early 2018, there were eight ongoing UN peacekeeping operations in the following countries: Western Sahara, Liberia, Sudan (Darfur and Abyei), the Democratic Republic of Congo, South Sudan, Mali, and the Central African Republic.[7] Since replacing the OAU in 2002, the African Union also has deployed missions around the continent, specifically to Burundi, the CAR, Comoros, Darfur (Sudan), and Somalia. As discussed in Chapter 6, subregional organizations have gotten involved in peacekeeping too. The Economic Community of West African States has undertaken interventions in Liberia (see case study at the end of chapter), Sierra Leone, Côte d'Ivoire, and Guinea-Bissau; the Southern African Development Community has authorized joint member-state interventions in Congo-Kinshasa. Add to these the involvement of European countries in places like Mali, Somalia, and the CAR, and it is clear that humanitarian intervention has become common and multifaceted in African conflicts (Renwick 2015).

As the primary body responsible for maintaining international peace and security under the UN Charter, the Security Council authorizes intervention in member states. This includes military intervention, economic sanctions, arms embargoes, and similar actions. The mandates, or authorized responsibilities, of peace operations typically fall under one of two sections in the UN Charter. Chapter VI covers traditional peacekeeping operations in which warring parties reach a peace agreement and peacekeepers monitor its implementation. Chapter VII, often described as peace enforcement, has been invoked increasingly by the Security Council to authorize military intervention and the use of force in situations that threaten international peace and security but where agreements between warring parties are not holding. Similar missions by regional and subregional organizations must be authorized by the Security Council, as per Chapter VIII. Beyond traditional peacekeeping and peace enforcement, the Security Council also authorizes observer missions (often intended to report back on any violations of tentative accords) and election monitoring in some postconflict contexts.

The Politics of Peacekeeping

In theory, peacekeeping is impartial, consensual, and humanitarian in nature.[8] The term itself — *peacekeeping* — implies that there is an agreement among warring parties and that foreign soldiers are there to ensure its terms are respected. Indeed, the promise of peacekeepers is often used to overcome commitment problems in negotiations and help warring parties reach an agreement. In practice, however, peacekeeping is fraught with politics from the moment that international intervention is considered through the withdrawal of an operation. Even before getting into the specific factors of a given conflict, the most basic questions about peacekeeping operations often fuel complicated international debates over responsibilities, rights, and resources: Should someone intervene? If so, who? How does one know when an intervention is done?

The question of whether someone should intervene arises whenever there is a conflict with major humanitarian consequences such as population displacement, food shortages, and loss of life. People watching horrible images on their television screens may find it obvious that something should be done to stop the humanitarian crisis, but diplomats typically resort to military intervention only after exhausting other options (sanctions, arms embargoes, etc.). Even once military intervention is on the table, the criteria for determining whether it is warranted are unclear. The circumstances that constitute a "threat to international peace and security," the existence of which gives the UN Security Council authority to act, can be defined broadly or narrowly, depending on the interests of those involved. Factors may include the intensity of the conflict (death toll, refugee numbers), geographic location (including proximity to powerful countries), economic interests, international alliances, and the level of public attention (often determined by media coverage), among others, but their relative importance depends on the situation. The ideological leanings of leaders in prominent UN member states also can play a role, as some leaders are more willing to intervene than others (Hildebrandt et al. 2013).

There inherently is some tension between the principle of sovereignty and the idea of humanitarian intervention. While recognizing the sovereignty of member states, the UN Charter allows the possibility of external intervention when a situation constitutes a "threat to international peace and security." But what happens when the threat is domestic? In the 1990s, after the United Nations failed to address situations of genocide in Rwanda and ethnic cleansing in the Balkans, critics started pushing for a reconceptualization of sovereignty that would allow for external intervention in such situations. The result of these discussions was the principle of the responsibility to protect (R2P), which was eventually endorsed by United Nations member states in 2005.[9] Under this norm, a sovereign state has the responsibility to protect its own citizens from human rights violations and other atrocities. If it fails to do so, the Security Council may authorize the use of force as a last resort. Although still controversial in some circles, the endorsement of R2P by member states was a victory for human rights activists seeking to empower the United Nations to do more about mass atrocities.

Another challenge related to the decision to intervene in a conflict is that there is no legal framework for how to deal with situations in which the Security Council is incapable of acting, often because a permanent member threatens to exercise its veto power for political reasons (perhaps to protect a key ally). Such stalemates were common during the Cold War but also have occurred more recently. The deployment of a UN peacekeeping mission to Darfur, Sudan, for example, was delayed for nearly two years—from 2005 to 2007—because Russia and China insisted it be acceptable to the Khartoum government, which they supported. Only after it was converted into the joint United Nations–African Union Mission in Darfur did Khartoum accept and the Security Council approve the mission.

Ultimately, the decision by the international community to intervene in a given conflict in Africa or elsewhere must be weighed against the option of not intervening at all. As discussed further later, there is a risk that humanitarian intervention will make the situation worse instead of better. If peacekeepers become parties to the conflict, for example, as Nigerian troops under the first ECOMOG mission were accused of doing in Liberia (Adebajo 2002b), their presence can increase hostilities and exacerbate human suffering. Similarly, while the United Nations Operation in Somalia (UNOSOM) of the early 1990s increased access to food aid and ameliorated famine, the activities of foreign troops fueled hostilities that limited the effectiveness of international efforts there for years to come (see Chapter 10). In many cases, the decision to intervene depends on whether any internal actors are calling for intervention.

Even after a decision is made to intervene, the question of who should do so remains problematic. Although the United Nations Security Council has the power to authorize peacekeeping operations, it does not have a standing force of trained peacekeepers. Despite discussions in the early 1990s about the need for such a force that could more rapidly respond to crises (de Jonge Oudraat 2000), there has not been sufficient support to make this idea a reality. Instead, the Security Council relies on member states to contribute troops and funding for each intervention it authorizes. This process takes time and results in some missions being significantly better resourced than others. The UN Organization Mission in the Democratic Republic of the Congo (MONUC), for example, launched in 1999, suffered repeatedly from deployment delays and troop shortfalls. Moreover, the Security Council often underestimates the number of troops needed in order to more easily meet targets, often leaving operations without sufficient peacekeepers to deal with unexpected security challenges (Williams 2011).

In the absence of a standby force, the United Nations or the African Union must provide incentives for member states to contribute troops to participate in peace operations. For many countries, that incentive is financial. Countries that contribute troops to UN missions currently are reimbursed more than $1,300 per soldier per month;[10] rates are typically lower for regional peace operations. Even after paying soldiers their salaries plus deployment bonuses, governments are left with additional funds to use as they please. Financial incentives help explain why developing countries—including many in Africa—often contribute troops. For UN operations as of June 30, 2017, six of the top ten troop-contributing countries were African: Ethiopia (1), Rwanda (5), Egypt (7), Burkina Faso (8), Senegal (9), and Ghana (10).[11] The remaining four were in South Asia (India, Pakistan, Bangladesh, Nepal). Given the relative population sizes of these countries, the African troop contributions are especially noteworthy.

Beyond financial incentives, governments may contribute troops to humanitarian operations because they have an interest in the outcome of the conflict, want to prevent refugees from reaching their borders, or face pressure from a domestic interest group to intervene, among other reasons. Although these motives are not necessarily bad, they can create risks with respect to the dynamics of the conflict, as discussed later. It can be difficult to find countries to intervene that are clearly neutral and have no interest in the conflict, especially when fund-raising for an operation falls short. Within Africa in particular, there are no "benign hegemons," and there are not usually enough resources to buy "disinterested intervenors" (Herbst 2000b), so intervention is more likely to be undertaken by countries that have a motive.[12] There is thus significant self-interest involved in contributing troops to peacekeeping operations, and such decisions often reflect domestic political considerations as much as humanitarian need in the target country. At different times over the years, for example, governments in Nigeria, Uganda, and Zimbabwe have been accused of intervening in other African countries as a way to keep troops busy and distract citizens from their own political and economic shortcomings.

Since the 1990s, there has been an effort to "Africanize" peacekeeping operations on the continent (Herbst 2000b). As discussed in Chapter 6, subregional organizations led the way with the deployment of several operations, most notably the first ECOMOG mission, in Liberia (1990–1997); the second ECOMOG mission, in Sierra Leone (1997–2000); and SADC's Operation Sovereign Legitimacy in Congo-Kinshasa (1998–2002).[13] Since its creation in 2002, as noted earlier, the African Union has authorized operations in Burundi, the CAR, Comoros, Darfur (including a hybrid operation with the UN), and Somalia. And SADC countries have been the primary troop contributors to the UN's Force Intervention Brigade in Congo (see Chapter 7). In addition to helping make up for the reluctance of Western countries to contribute troops to peace operations in Africa (Williams 2011),[14] these efforts fit nicely with the growing emphasis on "African solutions to African problems" (see Chapter 6). The United States, France, and other donors have sponsored programs to train and equip African peacekeepers, and some African countries have become top troop contributors globally. Even so, the challenge of recruiting "disinterested intervenors" remains (Herbst 2000b), especially because regional and subregional peacekeeping operations are perennially short on funds. In late 2015, the first training exercises were held for members of the African Standby Force, which will eventually draw about 25,000 troops from five regional blocs. Leaders hope this will allow the African Union to respond more rapidly to security crises on the continent, but the ASF will continue to rely heavily on external actors for funding and logistical support (Williams 2011).[15]

How does one know when a humanitarian intervention is done? If the mandate of a peace operation is clear, and if everything goes relatively smoothly, the organization involved should be able to tell when its objectives have been accomplished and end the mission. For example, despite some delays, the two-year United Nations Operation in Mozambique (ONUMOZ) withdrew troops in late 1994 after helping to disarm warring parties, facilitate refugee repatriation, and oversee a democratic election. At times, instead of ending completely, regional interventions pave the way for larger United Nations operations, such as when the African Union Mission in Burundi (AMIB) monitored the implementation of a tentative agreement until the deployment in 2004 of the United Nations Operation in Burundi (ONUB).

In many cases, however, there are significant challenges along the way. It is not unusual for the agreement whose implementation a peace-keeping operation oversees to fall apart. When belligerents start fighting again, the status of an operation comes into question and peacekeepers can be at risk. The most dramatic example may be the United Nations Assistance Mission in Rwanda (UNAMIR), which was deployed in 1993 to oversee the implementation of a peace agreement ending a three-year war between the Hutu-dominated government and the Tutsi-dominated Rwandan Patriotic Front (RPF) rebels. In 1994, when the president's plane was shot down and hostilities resumed, the Security Council famously reduced UNAMIR's troop contingent because there was no longer a peace to keep (Barnett 2002). With no deterrence, Hutu militias waged a massive campaign of genocidal violence during which approximately 800,000 Tutsis and moderate Hutus were killed before the RPF seized power (des Forges 1999).[16] The UN decision to reduce UNAMIR's force prompted years of criticism (des Forges 1999; Power 2001, 2002a) and soul-searching among those involved (Barnett 2002; Dallaire 2009).

More recently, hostilities resumed in Mali, despite the deployment of 15,000 international peacekeepers. In early 2012, a Tuareg separatist group, the National Movement for the Liberation of Azawad (MNLA),[17] joined forces with several transnational Islamist armed groups[18] to attack government bases in northern Mali. Disagreements over how to handle the rebellion led to a military coup d'état in March 2012, prompting an ECOWAS-led mediation and the installation of a transitional government. As the insurgents advanced and took over northern Mali in January 2013, the government requested assistance from France, which linked its Operation Serval to broader counterterrorism efforts (Wing 2016). French troops were joined in February by the African-led International Support Mission in Mali (AFISMA); together, they helped the transitional government reestablish control over most towns in the north. After a tentative peace agreement in June 2013, the United Nations Multidimensional Integrated Stabilization Mission in Mali (MINUSMA) assumed responsibility for peacekeeping operations, and elections were held.[19] Unfortunately, despite the additional resources provided by the transition to a UN operation, the tentative agreement soon fell apart, and violence resumed. After an escalation of fighting in early 2015, renewed international pressure led to a new agreement among the government, its armed allies, and the main rebel coalition in June 2015. Despite lingering distrust on all sides and a spotty implementation record, the agreement mainly held, although sporadic terrorist attacks continued to target civilians and peacekeepers.[20]

Even when underlying agreements do not fall apart, peace operations in Africa face plenty of other challenges to fulfilling their mandates. They frequently suffer from troop shortages and coordination problems among actors. They operate under complex mandates that often involve building democratic institutions, which can be difficult— if not impossible—to achieve (Williams 2011). There may also be disagreements regarding the objectives of an intervention, thus making its completion even harder to determine. This was perhaps most obvious with the United Nations Operation in Somalia in the early 1990s, when US and UN officials disagreed about whether the objective was to end the famine (which the mission did) or to resolve the conflict that created the famine (which it did not) (see Chapter 10). There has been more attention in recent years to the need for an "exit strategy" in any military intervention, though circumstances on the ground are not always conducive to implementing such plans without leaving the situation worse.

The Risks of Humanitarian Intervention

Beyond inherent political debates involved in any deployment of foreign troops for humanitarian purposes, there are risks that military intervention will not resolve the situation or even will make it worse. Third-party intervention can in fact lengthen conflicts or exacerbate the level of violence. According to Richard Betts (1994), this is especially likely when interventions are "limited" in terms of military commitment and "impartial" with regard to supporting a side, as is generally true of traditional humanitarian interventions. In such contexts, the presence of foreign troops keeps warring sides from defeating one another but does not stop them from trying. By this logic, a neutral humanitarian intervention can be successful only if it is so strong militarily that it can impose a settlement (Betts 1994). Empirical analyses of more than 150 conflicts support these claims, showing that third-party interventions of all types prolong conflicts, and neutral interventions (such as humanitarian ones) prolong conflicts more than do one-sided interventions that help one party win (Regan 2002; Regan and Abouharb 2002).

Humanitarian intervention also can prolong conflict by applying inappropriate solutions and failing to address underlying sources of violence. In the Democratic Republic of Congo, for example, the existence of a peace agreement (however problematic) at the national level led the United Nations to treat it as a postconflict context, even as local-level conflicts over land, identity, and other issues continued to simmer and fuel violence, especially in eastern parts of the country (Autesserre

2009). By operating as if the conflict was over and failing to address the root causes of lingering resentment and hostility at the grassroots, MONUC struggled to deal with violent incidents and human rights violations for years after the national-level peace agreement. This top-down approach to peacebuilding and the insistence on categorizing into conflict and postconflict situations can limit the ability of peacekeepers to understand and address deeper sources of conflict within a country (Autesserre 2010).[21]

Another risk is what Alan Kuperman (2008) calls "the moral hazard of humanitarian intervention." Drawing on the idea that having insurance can lead people to engage in risky behavior, Kuperman argues that the growing norm of humanitarian intervention leads people to expect the international community to send troops whenever a government is engaged in massive human rights abuses. Thus, some people may start a rebellion even when they know the government will retaliate with overwhelming force because they assume that the United Nations or another body will send troops to protect them. Such expectations may have emboldened rebels in Darfur to take up arms against the Sudanese government in 2003 and to reject an initial peace agreement in 2006 (Kuperman 2008). The intervention assumption seems especially bold in Africa, where United Nations powers typically have not been anxious to intervene, but the point is that a pattern of frequent intervention could encourage new rebellions that might otherwise not take the risky step of starting an armed struggle against the government.

There are other risks associated with humanitarian intervention as well. In some cases, participation in an intervention can represent a diversionary strategy, with leaders contributing troops as a way of distracting their own citizens from domestic policy failures. By sending troops to participate in SADC's Operation Sovereign Legitimacy in Congo-Kinshasa from 1998 to 2002, for example, Zimbabwean president Robert Mugabe may have sought to rally support and keep his troops active (perhaps to avoid a coup d'état) as his domestic popularity was falling sharply in the face of a political and economic crisis. Countries also may contribute troops to humanitarian operations as a way of generating funds to cover military budgets, raising questions about their true level of commitment to mission objectives. And the deployment of thousands of foreign military personnel as peacekeepers tragically has been associated with severe misconduct, including corruption, sexual assault, and human trafficking (Williams 2011) in places such as the Central African Republic, Congo-Kinshasa, Somalia, and Liberia. In late 2016, the Kenyan commander of the United Nations Mission in South Sudan (UNMISS) was dismissed after a report showed that forces under his command had abandoned their posts and ignored calls for assistance from aid workers who were under attack (Quinn 2016).

As has become clear from this discussion, then, humanitarian intervention rarely resolves the target conflict and runs the risk of making the situation worse. In recent years, concerns about the ineffectiveness of humanitarian intervention have prompted calls for "robust peacekeeping" that empowers intervenors to disarm specific militant groups or otherwise impose a desired outcome (Guéhenno 2009). The logic behind these calls led to stronger peace enforcement mandates for UN peacekeeping operations in the CAR, the DRC, and Mali (Karlsrud 2015; Tull 2009), among other countries. In the DRC in particular, the UN's Force Intervention Brigade was authorized to engage in offensive operations against M23, a rebel group with a brutal human rights record (see Chapter 7). Working together with Congolese army troops, and with an agreement from Rwanda to stop supporting the rebel group, FIB forces helped bring about the demise of M23. Before concluding that all humanitarian interventions should have stronger mandates, though, one must consider that "robust peacekeeping" raises important concerns about the role of the UN and other organizations as impartial mediators and the willingness of member states to put their troops in harm's way (Karlsrud 2015; Tardy 2011).

Peacebuilding in Africa

In addition to providing humanitarian assistance and supporting intervention in various forms, the international community often is involved in efforts to build peace in countries experiencing conflict. The peacebuilding process usually involves both peacemaking, or facilitating negotiations that lead to a settlement among the warring parties, and establishing institutions that will help to avoid further conflict in the future. The latter can include supporting disarmament, demobilization, and reintegration programs for ex-combatants (to prevent them from returning to fighting); organizing democratic elections (despite concerns that elections themselves can foment violence); and holding people accountable for atrocities committed (under the assumption that the pursuit of justice will make for a more sustainable peace).

In recent decades, peacemaking has focused primarily on negotiating an agreement that allows the warring parties to share power, at least for a transitional period (Williams 2011). Under prevailing international norms, in which war and the associated suffering should be avoided at all costs, it is no longer acceptable to suggest that belligerents fight it out until one side wins (Herbst 1990). The international community often is not comfortable choosing a winner unless there are clear interests involved. Moreover, governments are no longer accorded special status (Williams 2011); armed actors—both state and nonstate—have equal standing in most peace negotiations (Clapham 1998). Under such circumstances, power-sharing is generally seen as the only way to give all warring parties at least some of what they want, paving the way for them to lay down their weapons and work toward a future together.

The Politics of Negotiating

Although the involvement of external actors—both from within Africa and beyond—in efforts to build peace may be motivated by humanitarian goals, there are plenty of political debates involved in any negotiation. Who should mediate? There can be significant disagreement among the parties involved in a conflict with respect to which external actors are neutral enough to serve as mediators. In the late 1990s, for example, President Pierre Buyoya and other members of the Tutsi minority in Burundi questioned the neutrality of former Tanzanian president Julius Nyerere in his role as facilitator of the peace process.[22] Although Nyerere was respected internationally and had been one of the few to speak out against the killing of Tutsis in neighboring Rwanda, many saw him as favoring the Hutu majority in Burundi, in part because of the large number of Hutu refugees who had fled to Tanzania over the years (Wolpe 2011). It was not until after his death in 1999 and the assumption of the role of facilitator by former South African president Nelson Mandela that an agreement on Burundi was reached with the 2000 Arusha Accords.

Who should be at the table? While it is generally assumed that the government of a country in conflict should be represented at the negotiating table, there can be heated debates about which rebel leaders to include. Moreover, rebel groups often split into factions, even as negotiations are ongoing, in part because every ambitious person wants to get some share of power in a final agreement (more on this later). In the Burundi negotiations just mentioned, the absence of two key rebel groups from peace negotiations proved disastrous, as they continued to fight even after an agreement was signed (Wolpe 2011). Similarly, although there are plenty of reasons to criticize the actions of the Sudanese government in Darfur (see Chapter 2), Khartoum had a legitimate complaint when it came to the question of which rebel groups should be represented at peace negotiations. As the two original rebel groups (the Justice for Equality Movement and the Sudan Liberation Army) splintered into nearly twenty factions, fighting one another at times and making hasty alliances at others, there were doubts about whether any agreement at the negotiating table could reduce violence on the ground. The refusal of some factions to participate in negotiations has complicated the search for a long-term solution to the conflict in Darfur for years.

Related to this question of who should be represented in peace negotiations are concerns about the emergence of what might be called "professional negotiators" in some long-standing conflict situations. In places like Sudan and Somalia, where conflicts—and negotiations— have gone on intermittently for decades, there are some people who have essentially made their living by representing one group or another in peace talks. Negotiations typically are sponsored by the international community in peaceful cities like Addis Ababa, Nairobi, and Arusha, where delegates are housed in up-scale hotels and given generous per diem allowances. They live comfortably, even as the people they claim to represent continue to suffer. This dynamic has raised questions among observers about how committed some delegates are to truly making peace.[23] In an almost comical example, more than six months after negotiations in Nairobi resulted in the creation of a transitional federal government for Somalia, the Kenyan government stopped paying delegates' hotel bills to force them to return home to Somalia instead of continuing to govern from the relative safety and comfort of Kenya (Integrated Regional Information Network 2005).

Who should vote in a referendum? At times, peace agreements require that the terms be approved in a popular referendum or that a referendum determine the outcome. In theory, this is meant to ensure that any deals made between the government and rebels during the negotiations are supported by citizens who are not part of the process. If one side is perceived as gaining too much, people can reject the deal.[24] In practice, the requirement of a referendum can create additional debates, to the point of derailing the process entirely. Since a ceasefire in 1991, the agreed solution to the status of Western Sahara has been to hold a referendum on whether it should be independent, a goal for which the Polisario Front has been fighting since the 1970s, or continue to be controlled by Morocco. The ongoing United Nations Mission for the Referendum in Western Sahara (MINURSO) even includes the plan in its name, but the sticking point has been the question of who should be allowed to vote. Since 1975, Morocco has encouraged hundreds of thousands of its own citizens to settle in Western Sahara, to the point that they now outnumber local Sahrawi two to one (Shefte 2015). Morocco wants these people to vote in the referendum and Polisario does not, which has left the situation unresolved for decades.

Challenges of Peace Agreements

Although peace agreements are usually seen as preferable to fighting until one side wins, they inevitably face challenges that can threaten the sustainability of the agreement, at best, and exacerbate tensions and generate more conflict, at worst. The recent emphasis on power-sharing in particular as the most common approach to peacemaking carries with it inherent risks. Even as the international community continues to promote and sponsor negotiations for various conflicts around the world, the underlying assumption that it is possible for warring parties to sit together and negotiate a lasting end to their conflict faces increasing scrutiny.

A common criticism of negotiated peace agreements, and of power-sharing agreements specifically, is that they rarely work. Of thirty-five power-sharing deals signed in Africa between 1990 and 2008, more than half fell apart, and the target countries experienced renewed violence (Williams 2011). South Sudan is the latest country to see a series of power-sharing agreements collapse, with devastating consequences for the civilian population. Globally, empirical analyses also demonstrate that negotiated settlements are less likely to prevent conflict from recurring than other war-termination strategies such as one side winning (Licklider 1995; Toft 2010). Nevertheless, Caroline Hartzell and Matthew Hoddie (2003) show that the more dimensions of power-sharing (political, territorial, military, economic) that are included in a peace agreement, the more likely peace will endure. This suggests that the specific terms of an agreement can make a difference.

There are various reasons why peace agreements fall apart. In some cases, belligerents may think they can get more than they got in the agreement by resuming their armed struggle. UNITA's Savimbi acted as such a "spoiler" in Angola (see Chapter 3) when he resumed fighting after losing the 1992 election (Stedman 1997; Greenhill and Major 2007). I. William Zartman (1989) argues that conflicts are not "ripe" for resolution until all sides experience a "mutually hurting stalemate," such that no side sees a benefit to resuming violence in this way.[25] There also may be frustration about the terms of the agreement, with perceptions that one side got more than it deserved. The Tutsi-dominated RPF in Rwanda was seen as getting more than its share of military officer positions in the 1993 power-sharing agreement, for example, fueling resentment among Hutu militants that helped reignite the violence in 1994 (Newbury 1995). In Sierra Leone, the 1999 Lomé Accord controversially gave control of mining operations to Foday Sankoh, leader of the Revolutionary United Front rebel group, which raised funding for its brutal campaign of violence by exploiting the country's diamonds. That agreement also did not last.

Often peace agreements do not work because they are essentially a pact among elites—armed elites at that—and do not involve society more broadly (Mehler 2009; Williams 2011). As such, they are designed primarily to get armed actors to stop fighting with one another and rarely address underlying grievances over land, resources, and other issues that are crucial to any effort to build a long-lasting peace (Autesserre 2009, 2010). More often than not, these elite agreements leave power concentrated in the hands of a few people, often the president and his inner circle, and avoid devolving any true decisionmaking authority to other actors.

Beyond the concern that peace agreements will not hold is the chance they will actually spark more rebellions. This is a critique especially of power-sharing, which involves bringing to the negotiating table all armed actors in a conflict and giving them some share of power in exchange for laying down their weapons. As seen in Darfur, the very process of holding negotiations can cause rebel groups to break into factions, with each faction leader wanting a seat at the table (and hopefully a share of power in whatever agreement is reached). In this sense, the effort to include all warring parties creates a "power-sharing trap" (Spears 2000) as more and more parties emerge. Moreover, the current popularity of power-sharing as an approach to peacemaking has a powerful demonstration effect elsewhere in Africa. When would-be leaders see that armed rebellion is a way to win a share of power, they may choose that path over more peaceful alternatives, thus reproducing insurgent violence in other contexts (Tull and Mehler 2005). The most obvious example of this pattern is in Sudan, where the government has repeatedly demonstrated (in the south, in Darfur, and in Kordofan more recently) that the only way to get a piece of power is by taking up arms and fighting.

Another controversial aspect of peace agreements is the extent to which they involve the pursuit of justice. Should militants receive amnesty for crimes they committed during the war? If punishment is pursued, should all perpetrators be charged or only leaders who orchestrated the violence? Although peace and justice are often seen as going hand in hand, the reality is that the pursuit of justice can make it difficult to reach peace. Peace negotiations often break down over the question of amnesty, and some belligerents refuse to come to the table. In Uganda, for example, Museveni's government asked the International Criminal Court to investigate the actions of LRA rebel leader Joseph Kony, which resulted in an indictment and arrest warrant. Although Kony previously had participated in periodic peace talks, he refused to sit down at the negotiating table thereafter for fear that he would be arrested (Apuuli 2006). In this case, then, the pursuit of justice against Kony reduced the ability to end the conflict. The tension between peace and justice also has been apparent in Kenya (see Chapter 5), where the 2013 election of President Uhuru Kenyatta and Vice President William Ruto led to the suspension of ICC cases against them for alleged crimes during the 2008 post-election violence after witnesses recanted their statements. There is a tentative peace, but the pursuit of justice has been abandoned.

There are obviously many problems with peacemaking, therefore, and especially with the dominant power-sharing approach, but it is not clear that the international community has many other options when it comes to resolving conflicts in Africa. Should external observers let warring parties kill one another, and potentially hundreds of thousands of civilians, until one side overpowers the other? Should they support one side over others and help it come to power, even when it is not known what the people of the country want? Some point to Rwanda as an example of where one side (the Tutsi-dominated RPF rebels) eventually won the conflict, resulting in a period of relative peace and economic growth. But the one-sided peace that has been imposed there and the alleged human rights violations committed by the authoritarian government raise serious doubts about advocating that approach in other contexts (Lyons 2016). Given the lack of better alternatives, the pursuit of negotiated settlements continues.

Moving Beyond Simple Narratives About African Conflicts

Even when pursued with the best of intentions, which is not always the case, as we have seen, humanitarian operations can fall short of achieving their objectives or even exacerbate the conflicts they seek to address. As this chapter has shown, humanitarian assistance programs, peacekeeping missions, and peacebuilding efforts inherently involve contentious decisions about rights, responsibilities, and resources. The governments that are often involved in such decisions—those both in Africa and outside— are influenced by a range of factors, including relations with the government of the conflict country and their own domestic political environments. Moreover, armed groups can be creative in their attempts to manipulate humanitarian aid and agencies to their advantage, often changing the course of the conflict or delaying its resolution. In these complex emergency situations, humanitarian actors and journalists reporting on their operations frequently find themselves at risk of attack.[26]

As the international community continues to search for resolutions to African conflicts, policymakers and others tend to rely on simplified interpretations of the conflicts. As Séverine Autesserre (2012) argues, "dominant narratives" often emerge with respect to a conflict's causes, consequences, and solutions. These are driven in part by aid workers who are seeking funding for their operations and journalists who are expected to cover complex situations in as little airtime or newspaper space as possible. According to such narratives, for example, the cause of the conflict in Congo-Kinshasa was the exploitation of mineral resources, the consequence was sexual abuse of women and girls, and the solution was extending state authority (Autesserre 2012). These simple narratives bring attention to far-off emergencies, which can be helpful in motivating a more concerted response, but they also can lead to oversimplified solutions. In the Congo case in particular, the emphasis on extending state authority failed to recognize the corrupt and predatory nature of that state in the eyes of many Congolese (Autesserre 2012). Similarly, calls to stop the purchase of "conflict minerals" from Congo led to a US law that reduced demand for the country's exports, eliminating much-needed mining jobs even as violence continued (Seay 2012). Another example of the global spread of an oversimplified narrative about African conflict is *Kony 2012*, a video that went viral after being released in March 2012 by a US nongovernmental organization known as Invisible Children. It provided a simplistic and outdated interpretation of the conflict in northern Uganda against Kony's LRA and proposed a militaristic response that neglected the Ugandan army's own shortcomings. The video prompted substantial backlash among academics and activists around the world.[27]

Ultimately, conflicts in Africa—as elsewhere—are complex. They are not driven by a single cause, nor do they have simple solutions. The responses offered by the international community, both within the region and outside, must be similarly complex. At whatever level of intervention—providing humanitarian aid, establishing peacekeeping operations, or facilitating negotiated settlements—external actors should be aware of the potential consequences of their actions and avoid reinforcing existing divisions, emboldening armed groups, or exacerbating the violence. At a minimum, as Mary Anderson (1999) argues, aid workers should "do no harm," which might require creative strategies and approaches. Over the years, there has been increasing realization among scholars and practitioners of the ethical dilemmas involved in humanitarian action. Even so, recent debates about how to assist famine victims in Somalia, displaced people in South Sudan, and abducted children in northeastern Nigeria demonstrate that we are still searching for ways to intervene without making conflicts worse.

Case Study: Conflict and Intervention in Liberia

Founded in the 1820s as a home for freed American slaves as part of the "back to Africa" movement, Liberia became independent in 1847. Despite their own history of oppression, African American settlers and their descendants, known as Americo-Liberians, established themselves as the political and economic elite over indigenous ethnic groups already living in the area. For years, they excluded indigenous people from the rights of citizenship, resulting in a de facto one-party state under the True Whig Party, and implemented systems of forced labor. The remaining 95 percent of the population greatly resented the dominance of the America-Liberian minority, who managed to keep power in part by maintaining close ties with the United States. This relationship also protected Liberia from European colonization, though its claims to more territory were constrained. In the twentieth century, US interest intensified as demand for rubber increased and the Firestone company started a massive rubber plantation in Liberia.[28]

After more than 150 years of America-Liberian rule, including almost three decades under William Tubman and nine years under William Tolbert Jr., many indigenous Liberians initially welcomed the 1980 coup d'état by Master Sergeant Samuel Doe, a member of the indigenous Krahn ethnic group. His People's Redemption Council included junior officers from several indigenous groups, and his government secured large amounts of foreign aid from the United States in the context of an escalating Cold War. Within a few years, however, Doe purged his regime of alternative voices, surrounding himself mainly with Krahn supporters, and blatantly rigged elections to stay in power (Adebajo 2004). By the late 1980s, Liberia's economy was in shambles, there were reports of widespread corruption and human rights abuses, domestic opposition was rising, and relations with the United States were strained.

It was in this context that the National Patriotic Front of Liberia launched an attack into Liberia from Côte d'Ivoire on Christmas Eve 1989. The NPFL was led by Charles Taylor, a colorful figure who previously served in Doe's regime but fled the country after being accused of embezzlement. He had been awaiting extradition from the United States when he mysteriously escaped a Boston prison and thus was a fugitive when the war started.[29] The NPFL gained support among indigenous groups in the northeast, especially the Gio and the Mano, who were punished harshly by Doe's predominantly Krahn forces. By mid-1990, the NPFL controlled most of Liberia, with the exception of Monrovia, even as competing rebel factions emerged. In September, the faction led by Prince Johnson captured Doe and brutally tortured him to death, as shown on a widely circulated video. Taylor, Johnson, and at least one other rebel leader each declared himself president, and violence escalated among their troops, many of whom were young boys armed with machine guns and mind-altering drugs. Hundreds of thousands of refugees streamed across the border into neighboring countries (Adebajo 2004).

As the situation in Liberia deteriorated, ECOWAS tried to broker an agreement among the armed groups. It negotiated the creation of an interim government, led by Amos Sawyer, and authorized a peacekeeping mission known as ECOMOG. Often accused of having hegemonic goals within West Africa (see Chapter 6), Nigeria pushed strongly for the intervention and eventually provided 80 percent of the troops and 90 percent of the funding (Adebajo 2004). Francophone countries, including two that supported Taylor's rebellion (Côte d'Ivoire and Burkina Faso), objected to the military intervention, but other ECOWAS members had interests in supporting it (Adebajo 2004). The first ECOMOG troops were deployed to Liberia in August 1990.

Far from being perceived as a neutral humanitarian intervention, ECOMOG quickly became embroiled in the conflict. Many Liberians saw ECOMOG troops as just another armed faction and accused them of looting the country, leading to the nickname "Every Car or Moving Object Gone" (Gaviria et al. 2014). Having established an alternative regime in areas under his control,[30] Taylor targeted the peacekeepers as an occupying force. As ECOMOG fought the NPFL on behalf of an interim government that never controlled much more than Monrovia, leadership contests and ethnic tensions resulted in the emergence of even more armed factions. Escalating violence resulted in massive casualties and widespread human rights abuses, including abduction and rape, and made the delivery of humanitarian assistance difficult. Taylor also sponsored a brutal rebel incursion into neighboring Sierra Leone, exploiting that country's diamonds and other resources.[31] Eventually, after twelve failed peace accords, the warlords—including Charles Taylor—reached an agreement in 1995 that paved the way for elections in 1997 (Abdullah and Rashid 2004). With many Liberians fearing that he would resume fighting if he did not win,[32] Taylor received 75 percent of the vote and finally achieved his goal of becoming president of Liberia. By then, approximately 150,000 of a total population of 2.1 million had been killed and 850,000 had fled the country as refugees.

The relative stability did not last. Even before the final ECOMOG troops withdrew in October 1999, a new insurgent group attacked Liberia from Guinea. Backed by diaspora Liberians and the Guinean government, the Liberians United for Reconciliation and Democracy (LURD) sought to remove Taylor from power. Liberia returned to war, though LURD avoided breaking into countless factions as rebels had done in the earlier conflict. It was joined in 2003 by the Movement for Democracy in Liberia (MODEL), which attacked from the south with support from Côte d'Ivoire. By July 2003, as the world was preoccupied with the US invasion of Iraq, Liberian rebels were on the outskirts of Monrovia and Taylor's forces were surrounded.

The African and international communities once again called upon ECOWAS to broker an agreement, resulting in the resignation of Taylor as president in August 2003 and his transfer to exile in Nigeria. West African peacekeepers deployed in September under the ECOWAS Mission in Liberia (ECOMIL), which was replaced the following month by the United Nations Mission in Liberia (UNMIL). UNMIL eventually deployed 25,000 troops, making it one of the largest peacekeeping operations in the world. Free and fair elections were finally held in 2005, bringing to power Ellen Johnson Sirleaf, Africa's first elected female head of state and a US-educated economist who had worked previously for the United Nations and the World Bank. Under pressure from various constituencies, Sirleaf requested the extradition of Taylor from Nigeria to the Special Court for Sierra Leone, which had indicted him for war crimes in that country. After a drawn-out legal process, Taylor was found guilty in 2012 and is currently serving a fifty-year sentence at a prison in the United Kingdom.

While peace has prevailed in Liberia since 2003, it has not been without challenges. Rebuilding the country after decades of war has not gone as quickly as many had hoped, even with a massive influx of funding from international donors and diaspora Liberians and an extensive — if flawed—DDR program for ex-combatants (Jennings 2007, 2009). Despite some disappointment with her leadership, Sirleaf won reelection in 2011 just days after being recognized as a co-recipient of the Nobel Peace Prize. In 2014, Liberia was hit by another crisis: Ebola. It took months for an international operation that included medical professionals from around the world and the construction of health clinics by the US military to contain the virus; nearly 5,000 people died in Liberia, along with another 6,500 in Sierra Leone and Guinea.[33] Even with these setbacks, the political situation in Liberia has stabilized. In 2016, UNMIL officially ended its mission and withdrew the majority of its peacekeepers, though some Liberians still worried about the ability of domestic security personnel to maintain the peace (Pailey and Jaye 2016). In December 2017, with Sirleaf constitutionally barred from seeking a third term, her vice president was defeated in a runoff by retired international soccer superstar George Weah. In an interesting twist that has raised concerns in some circles, Weah's vice president is Jewel Taylor, ex-wife of the former rebel-turned-president.

Touching on themes discussed earlier in this chapter, the conflicts in Liberia were complex, involving multiple armed groups that crossed international borders. It was difficult to find external actors to intervene who did not have their own interests in the conflict, especially in the 1990s. West African peacekeepers, led by Nigeria, were seen as pursuing their own interests and became targets of violence. The disintegration of the rebels into various competing factions both escalated the violence and made it more difficult to negotiate a peace agreement. When

222 The Challenges of Security

one was reached in 1995, it did not last, largely because it did not address underlying grievances and was simply an accommodation among warlords with guns. Not long after Liberians begrudgingly elected Taylor as president, longtime rivals reemerged to seek his ouster. Lessons learned during the first conflict helped shape the international response to the second, including the decision to negotiate Taylor's resignation and to deploy a massive UN peacekeeping operation. Even so, it is impossible to know whether the relative success of that operation was due to its design or simply to the fact that Liberians were sick of years of war. As Liberians look toward the future, their country faces many challenges of rebuilding and reconciliation that cannot be achieved overnight and will continue to require outside support.

Notes

1. People who cross international borders are considered "asylum-seekers" until they are formally recognized as "refugees" by the host-country government. In some cases, refugee status determination is done individually, person by person, and can take months, if not years. In certain situations of mass influx, refugee status determination is at the group level, with the host government recognizing anyone who came from a given country during a given time period as a refugee. The complex situation of refugees and other migrants is discussed further in Chapter 9.

2. For an important discussion of how these humanitarian principles often come into conflict with political realities, see Weiss 1999.

3. Humanitarian military interventions are distinct from other military interventions that are not motivated by humanitarian concerns.

4. The United States and the European Union are the biggest contributors of food aid, but their approaches are quite different. The EU tends to provide cash so that the WFP can purchase food directly in or near the affected region. This allows relief to reach victims more quickly, though care must be taken not to artificially drive up food prices with large-scale purchases. The United States, on the other hand, provides the vast majority of its support to the WFP in kind—that is, in the form of food. Although it can take six months for food to reach affected populations, US farmers benefit significantly from their sales to the US government. In the early 2000s, for example, food aid accounted for an estimated 10–20 percent of all US wheat and rice exports (Clapp 2015). US farmers have lobbied aggressively to preserve this system and to resist efforts by both Republican and Democratic presidents to allow for greater "monetization" of food aid. The Agricultural Act of 2014 (also known as the Farm Bill) increased the cash portion of US food aid from 13 percent to 20 percent, well below President Obama's proposed 45 percent. At the time of writing, deliberations about the 2018 Farm Bill were just beginning in the US Congress. For more information on this debate and others related to international food aid, see Clapp 2015.

5. This information comes from interviews one of the authors (Whitaker) conducted with aid workers in western Tanzania in late 1996.

6. In the most detailed analysis available of the OAU mission in Chad, Terry Mays (2002) characterizes it as a Nigerian-led intervention, motivated by that country's own regional interests, with backing from France and the United States.

7. Information about historical and ongoing UN peacekeeping operations can be found at https://peacekeeping.un.org/en.

8. The three principles of UN peacekeeping are "consent of the parties," "impartiality," and "non-use of force except in self-defence and defence of the mandate." For more information about each, see https://peacekeeping.un.org/en/principles -of-peacekeeping.

9. For more information about the responsibility to protect, including the 2005 World Summit Outcome Document language, see http://www.responsibilityto protect.org.

10. For current reimbursement rates and more information about financing peacekeeping, see https://peacekeeping.un.org/en/how-we-are-funded.

11. For updated totals, see https://peacekeeping.un.org/en/troop-and-police -contributors.

12. There has been some discussion over the years of hiring private military companies, or military contractors, for peacekeeping operations, especially when member states do not volunteer enough troops. This option is highly controversial, as explored elsewhere (Bures 2005), not least because private military companies operate in an international legal vacuum and are explicitly driven by profit motives instead of humanitarianism. Private military companies have been used in military interventions in Iraq and Sierra Leone, among other countries, but these were not peacekeeping operations.

13. Laurent Kabila came to power in the Democratic Republic of Congo in 1997, and his country soon joined SADC. In 1998, when Congo was attacked by rebels with backing from Rwanda and Uganda (see Chapter 7), Kabila called on his new SADC allies for support. The controversial operation was supported by Zimbabwe, Angola, and Namibia, which all sent troops, but was opposed by other members of the subregional organization.

14. From 2001 to 2009, the United States, the United Kingdom, and France together contributed fewer than 300 peacekeepers to UN peacekeeping operations in Africa, less than 0.5 percent of the total (Williams 2011: 197).

15. Even the new AU import levy discussed in Chapter 6 is expected to only cover a fraction of the organization's peace operations.

16. For a concise explanation of the complex social, economic, and political factors that led to the horrifying genocide in Rwanda, by an expert who lived in that country for many years, see Newbury 1995.

17. There is a long history of separatism among the semi-nomadic Tuareg population of northern Mali. The current iteration was spurred on by the return to Mali of hundreds of Tuaregs who had been living in Libya and fighting on behalf of its longtime dictator, Muammar Qaddafi. When Qaddafi was overthrown in 2011, they returned home with stockpiles of his weapons and revived the call for the independence of Azawad.

18. These include al-Qaeda in the Islamic Maghreb (AQIM), Ansar Dine, and the Movement for Unity and Jihad in West Africa (MUJAO).

19. Up-to-date information about MINUSMA, including troop deployment levels and contributing countries, can be found at https://peacekeeping.un.org/en/mission /minusma.

20. As of January 2018, there had been 158 fatalities in the MINUSMA operation. Fatality statistics for UN peacekeeping operations are available at https://peace keeping.un.org/en/fatalities.

21. For an interesting debate among country specialists about whether Congo's insecurity is driven by local or state-level factors, see Autesserre 2017a, 2017b; Stearns et al. 2017.

22. The 1993 assassination of the first democratically elected president (a Hutu) and the 1996 military coup that returned to power a former Tutsi president

exacerbated hostilities and led to an escalation in violence, prompting the international community to sponsor negotiations to try to avoid a genocide like the one in neighboring Rwanda.

23. We are grateful to Kizito Sabala, a Kenyan academic and practitioner who has been involved in multiple regional peace negotiations, for pointing out these dynamics.

24. This happened in Latin America with an August 2016 peace deal between the government of Colombia and the Revolutionary Armed Forces of Colombia (FARC) rebels. After more than five decades of violence, voters apparently felt that the agreement did not punish the FARC enough and rejected the deal in a September referendum. Government and FARC negotiators reached a revised deal in November 2016; it was ratified by both houses of the Colombian congress instead of being subjected to referendum.

25. Although the logic makes sense, it is difficult to operationalize in practice; when a peace agreement holds, the conflict was apparently "ripe," and when it does not, the conflict was not ready to be resolved.

26. In 2005, as attacks on aid workers increased, an organization known as Humanitarian Outcomes started the Aid Worker Security Database (see https://aidworkersecurity.org). It records incidents of violence against aid workers going back to 1997.

27. For a widely circulated critique by Ugandan blogger Rosebell Kagumire, see https://youtu.be/KLVY5jBnD-E.

28. For a fascinating examination of Firestone's experiences in Liberia, especially during the civil war in the 1990s, watch the PBS *Frontline* documentary "Firestone and the Warlord" at http://www.pbs.org/wgbh/frontline/film/firestone-and-the-warlord (Gaviria et al. 2014).

29. When Taylor was eventually tried by the Special Court for Sierra Leone for his involvement in that country's war, he claimed that the US Central Intelligence Agency helped him escape the Boston prison. Though the CIA denied this claim, it later confirmed that Taylor worked as a CIA informant starting in the 1980s (*BBC News* 2012).

30. Taylor's "Greater Liberia" included the Firestone plantation in Harbel, Liberia, and the company paid taxes to Taylor for his protection (Gaviria et al. 2014).

31. The Revolutionary United Front, led by Foday Sankoh and sponsored by Taylor, attacked Sierra Leone from Liberia in 1991, starting a civil war there that lasted for more than a decade. While the details of that conflict are covered elsewhere (see, for example, Adebajo 2002a; Adebajo and Rashid 2004), the RUF was especially known for its brutal practice of forced amputations and for its exploitation of the country's diamond resources. A former child soldier in Sierra Leone, Ishmael Beah, provides a firsthand account of his experiences in *A Long Way Gone: Memoirs of a Boy Soldier* (2007).

32. In 1997, Taylor famously campaigned on the slogan, "He killed my ma, he killed my pa, but I will vote for him."

33. Detailed data about the 2014 Ebola outbreak in West Africa are available from the US Centers for Disease Control and Prevention at https://www.cdc.gov/vhf/ebola/outbreaks/2014-west-africa/case-counts.html.

9

The Politics of Migration

Sub-Saharan Africa has a long history of migration, both within the region and beyond. For centuries, African peoples have migrated to other areas in search of better economic and political opportunities. Linguistic evidence shows similarities among languages spoken by people who now live thousands of miles apart, suggesting patterns of migration and trade that predate historical records. In the modern era, and with the benefit of technology and more rapid transportation, thousands of Africans migrate annually to other countries, either temporarily or permanently. As much attention as is given to the "waves" (Kainz 2016) of African migrants trying to reach Europe in rickety boats crossing the Mediterranean, there are many more Africans who cross borders into neighboring countries or find their way to other countries within the continent. Indeed, about two-thirds of the nearly 20 million Africans living outside their home countries in 2013 were elsewhere within sub-Saharan Africa (Gonzalez-Garcia et al. 2016).

As is true elsewhere in the world, there are various factors that motivate Africans to leave their families, friends, and homes and start lives in new geographic areas. Some flee individual persecution[1] or generalized violence[2] and seek protection elsewhere, either as refugees in another country or as internally displaced persons within their own. Others migrate in search of better economic opportunities than they can find at home. In the past, temporary labor migration was common, and people traveled to other areas within their country or even to other countries to work on farms or in mines. The increasing regulation of international borders in many places, however, often has meant that people who manage to cross a border even for short-term work tend to stay in their new areas for longer periods, in part because they fear they will not be able to cross the border again in the future. Environmental and climatic changes also have led African populations to move over time as deserts expand and water sources dry up or change course. And although most groups these days are rooted to some geographic place, there continue to be semi-nomadic populations throughout Africa who migrate seasonally to find better grazing lands for their livestock, often crossing international borders to do so.

Despite the prevalence of migration within Africa, this issue often has been overlooked by political scientists. People who study comparative politics tend to focus on institutions and patterns within African countries (democratization, identity politics, etc.), while international relations scholars concentrate on relations among states and conflict dynamics. Because migration involves the movement of individuals across international borders, it sits at the nexus of international and comparative politics and warrants examination by scholars in both subfields. Moreover, as Africans continue to cross borders in large numbers, the issue of migration is becoming increasingly important in African international relations, in terms of both the interaction among states as well as how states (home and host) treat migrants. Indeed, for many African leaders over the years, the presence of large numbers of migrants on their territory has been an issue of regime security.

In this chapter, we examine recent trends in African migration patterns, looking at both refugees and economic migrants (and the fuzzy line between them) and their impact on host communities. We then explore the escalation of hostility toward migrants in some African countries, including the rise of anti-immigration attitudes and the development of more restrictive government policies. Shifting angles, we subsequently investigate the ways in which African governments are reaching out to their own citizens living abroad and seeking their involvement in economics and politics at home. Throughout these sections, it becomes clear that political competition plays an important role in shaping responses to migration with respect to both immigrants and emigrants. We conclude the chapter with a case study of South Africa, which has experienced complicated waves of in- and out-migration for decades.

Trends in African Migration

Over the past three decades, the number of Africans living outside their home countries has doubled. A recent report published by the International Monetary Fund uses data from the World Bank and the United Nations High Commissioner for Refugees to examine trends in African migration during this time period (Gonzalez-Garcia et al. 2016). Several patterns are noteworthy. First, even as the number of African international migrants has increased from fewer than 10 million in 1990 to nearly 20 million in 2013 (the most recent year for data used in the report), the proportion of Africans living outside their own country has remained fairly stable at about 2 percent. This suggests that the upward trend in migration numbers is driven largely by the rapid growth of Africa's population, which also has nearly doubled over this period, rather than by some greater proclivity to migrate. In fact, Africans remain considerably less likely to migrate than people in other regions; in the rest of the developing world, an average of 3 percent of citizens live outside their home countries (Gonzalez-Garcia et al. 2016). Despite these continental averages, emigration is especially important for certain African island nations; about one-third of Cape Verde's population and one-tenth of the populations of Mauritius, São Tomé and Príncipe, and Seychelles live in other countries (Gonzalez-Garcia et al. 2016).

Second, most sub-Saharan African migrants move to other countries within Africa, not to wealthier Western countries as is often assumed. Many go to neighboring countries, though some move on to regional economic hubs. In 2013, the top receiving countries in Africa were Côte d'Ivoire and South Africa, with each hosting 2 million or more immigrants from other African countries. Nigeria was home to nearly 1 million African immigrants, while Burkina Faso, Cameroon, Tanzania, and Uganda each hosted about half a million (Gonzalez-Garcia et al. 2016).[3] Even so, the proportion of African migrants who leave the region has risen over the past three decades, from about a quarter of the total in 1990 to about a third in 2013. Most Africans who live outside Africa are in Europe and North America. Indeed, estimates suggest that one-half of the total sub-Saharan African diaspora population lives in just three countries: France, the United Kingdom, and the United States. Other popular destinations include Portugal, Italy, Australia, Canada, and Saudi Arabia (Gonzalez-Garcia et al. 2016). Although the number of African migrants to Europe certainly has increased since 2014, as highlighted by recent media reports, far more people migrate within the continent.

A third trend in African migration is a relative decline in the number of refugees.[4] In 1990, about 50 percent of Africans who left their home countries were fleeing violence or persecution. By 2013, that number was down to 10 percent, as the vast majority of Africans left their countries instead for economic reasons (Gonzalez-Garcia et al. 2016). The drop in the proportion of refugees is a fortunate by-product of the decline of conflict in the region, though the recent escalation of violence in places like South Sudan and the Central African Republic threatens to reverse this trend. Nevertheless, the distinction between "economic migrant" and "refugee" is overly simplistic. Africans leave home for a variety of reasons (as do people in other regions), frequently including economic *and* political factors. Moreover, the lack of economic opportunity often is a result of political problems. This point is illustrated by the fact that Eritrea, Zimbabwe, and Equatorial Guinea have been among the top sending countries of migrants in Africa over the past decade. Recent economic recessions in these countries have been driven partly by the self-interested policies of their respective governments, whose authoritarian leaders have avoided responsibility by insisting that anyone who leaves is doing so for economic and not political reasons. Meanwhile, leaders of destination countries cling to this convenient fiction of purely economic migration because it provides an acceptable reason for denying entry (Connell 2017).[5] The interconnection between economics and politics thus makes it difficult to draw a clear line between migrants and refugees (Whitaker 2017), despite the efforts of government officials and international bureaucrats to do so.

With the number of African migrants on the rise, both within the continent and to other regions, there is considerable debate about the impact of such population flows on receiving countries. As in other regions, politicians in Africa often blame immigrants for everything from crime and unemployment to disease and social breakdown, but it can be difficult to determine the precise impact of the presence of immigrants when they are interspersed throughout host communities. Increases in immigration to a country or geographic area typically also are accompanied by various other demographic, economic, and social changes, making it nearly impossible to isolate the effects of immigrants in particular. Moreover, assessments of the impact of immigrants are generally loaded with political debates and influenced by the desire to make a case either for or against immigration, leading people on the other side to discount them entirely. In Africa especially, the lack of detailed and reliable local-level data about immigration and related variables has contributed to a dearth of empirical research on this topic.

In situations that involve a massive influx of refugees concentrated in a single geographic area, the impact on host communities can be more obvious, and even more controversial. Over the decades, as discussed elsewhere in this book, conflicts in various African countries (the DRC, Rwanda, Liberia, Somalia, Sudan, etc.) have generated large-scale refugee flows into neighboring countries. As a result of their proximity to conflict zones, Ethiopia, Kenya, Uganda, Tanzania, Guinea, Chad, and Sudan are among the African countries that have hosted the largest number of refugees since the early 1990s. In most host countries in Africa, refugees live in large camps that are assisted by the UNHCR and an array of international and local nongovernmental organizations. The host government determines where refugees settle and typically concentrates them in large camps close to the border to attract international aid, prevent integration in local communities, and facilitate easier repatriation if and when circumstances change in the country of origin (Crisp and Jacobsen 1998; Kibreab 1985).

The influx of refugees and humanitarian assistance can be both a burden and a resource for host communities (Jacobsen 2002). Costs associated with hosting refugees include environmental damage; shortages of resources like clean water and firewood; disease outbreaks such as cholera from the close concentration of people; labor competition, as refugees compete with locals for jobs; social problems (crime, alcoholism, prostitution) that tend to come with any sudden increase in population; and security concerns, at times including attacks from the home country if the refugees are considered a threat (Whitaker 1999, 2002). At the same time, however, there are benefits that can come from hosting refugees. Local people often gain access to humanitarian aid through the camps, including food rations and healthcare, even if doing so sometimes requires them to "pass" as refugees. Infrastructure such as roads and government buildings (including schools and health clinics) frequently are upgraded with international funding, a benefit that lingers even after refugees leave. The population increase also generates greater business activity, better-paying jobs with internationally funded organizations, and an opportunity for locals to hire cheap refugee labor (Whitaker 2002).

An important point here is that the costs and benefits associated with a refugee influx are not evenly distributed among the host population. Some people benefit more than others. Locals who are better educated or have experience are more likely to get jobs with aid agencies, for example, and those with spare capital can invest in expanding their businesses or starting new ones. Meanwhile, locals who rely on casual labor to pay their bills find themselves competing for work with refugees, who can charge less because they receive food rations and other basic needs in the camps (Whitaker 2002). Interestingly, because of the divergent impact of refugees on local hosts, politicians from these areas often are guarded in their public statements. In western Tanzania in the 1990s, for example, parliamentary candidates avoided taking a stance for or against the presences of refugees from Rwanda and Burundi for fear of alienating those who were benefiting or those who were negatively affected (Whitaker 1999).

An influx of refugees and international aid also has implications for statebuilding in Africa. On one hand, the situation provides resources to the host government, which adopts policies to maximize the benefits by concentrating refugees in camps, for example, and lobbying for increased foreign aid. Security concerns associated with a refugee influx also provide a rationale for the state to strengthen its control over remote border areas where it previously may not have had a significant presence (Jacobsen 2002). On the other hand, the involvement of international aid organizations with a refugee influx provides people in border areas an alternative structure through which to access resources for socioeconomic development, particularly in the areas of health, education, infrastructure, and the environment. With African governments often unable to provide quality services in these sectors, international aid agencies can become a sort of substitute for the government, potentially creating challenges to regime security over the long term (Whitaker 2001). In the end, the implications of a refugee situation for host states can work in both directions, as local people may both feel more connected to their national government and also develop competing relations with nonstate entities (Landau 2003).

It is clear, then, that migration in Africa is on the rise, at least in terms of sheer numbers. Although the issue has attracted global attention recently because of the growing proportion of African migrants arriving on European shores, the majority of the region's migration still takes place within the continent. The movement of large numbers of people across international borders has implications for relations among African states, particularly when such migration patterns are determined at least in part by state activities. Moreover, particularly with the spread of multiparty competition in Africa (see Chapter 5), migration has become a focus of domestic political debates in many countries. While some African governments have responded to these dynamics with increased restrictions and border controls, others have remained relatively open to cross-border migration. The variation in responses to African migration among people and governments is explored more thoroughly in the next section.

Responses to African Migration

Immigration Attitudes and Policies Within Africa

As migration has increased in recent years, anti-immigrant hostility has become widespread in much of sub-Saharan Africa, and government policies on immigration have become more restrictive. While there has been resentment at times toward non-African immigrants, including large Indian, Lebanese, and Chinese diasporas in some countries, there is a broader pattern of antipathy toward Africans from other countries within the region (for more on the involvement of China and other emerging powers in Africa, see Chapter 12). From Johannesburg to Nairobi and Windhoek to Abidjan, African migrants and refugees have been subject to suspicion, discrimination, negative rhetoric, exclusionary policies, and at times violence.

Survey data from the World Values Survey and the Southern African Migration Project in the early 2000s revealed high levels of anti-immigrant sentiment in many African countries (Crush and Pendleton 2004; World Values Survey 2017).[6] Even so, this trend was not uniform throughout the continent. Opposition to immigration—measured as the proportion of survey respondents wanting to "place strict limits on the number of foreigners who can come here" or "prohibit people coming here from other countries"—varied significantly among respondents in the fifteen countries covered by the two surveys (see Table 9.1). Opposition was highest in Namibia, Botswana, and South Africa, whereas respondents were less opposed to immigration in places like Mali, Burkina Faso, and Rwanda. On the surface, this may seem to be a difference between in-migration and out-migration countries, but many factors contribute to anti-immigrant attitudes, and demographic patterns often are less influential than one might expect. Although evidence from Western countries suggests that

Table 9.1   Opposition to Immigration in Surveyed African Countries

Surveyed Country	Survey (Year)[a]	Percentage of Respondents Opposed to Immigration[b]
Namibia	SAMP (2001)	92.7
Botswana	SAMP (2001)	78.7
South Africa	WVS (2005)	76.4
Tanzania	WVS (2001)	71.8
Swaziland	SAMP (2001)	68.4
Mozambique	SAMP (2001)	61.5
Zambia	WVS (2005)	58.7
Ghana	WVS (2005)	42.6
Uganda	WVS (2001)	41.4
Zimbabwe	WVS (2001)	35.7
Ethiopia	WVS (2005)	31.6
Nigeria	WVS (2000)	30.9
Mali	WVS (2005)	20.0
Burkina Faso	WVS (2005)	11.8
Rwanda	WVS (2005)	10.5

Sources: World Values Survey 2017; Crush and Pendleton 2004.
Notes: a. SAMP = Southern African Migration Project; WVS = World Values Survey.
b. Proportion of respondents choosing "place strict limits on the number of foreigners who can come here" or "prohibit people coming here from other countries" in response to a question about preferred government immigration policy.

refugees face less hostility than economic migrants (O'Rourke and Sinnott 2006), this distinction is less obvious in a region where the line between refugee and economic migrant frequently is blurred.

As anti-foreigner attitudes have increased, governments throughout the region have imposed more restrictive immigration policies. Such policies have affected both immigrant admission (the ability to come into a country) and integration (their ability to live and work among citizens). In various countries, border closures and deportations have been used to reduce the number of immigrants (and discourage more from coming), and restrictions have been placed on the rights and naturalization prospects for immigrants already living there. In Botswana, for example, the government has conducted mass deportations and constructed an electrified border fence, while adhering to very narrow guidelines on the determination of refugee status and the movement of migrants within the country. The Tanzanian government, which once embraced an open-door policy, has forcibly repatriated hundreds of thousands of refugees and imposed strict limits on the mobility of others still in the country, even as it has granted citizenship to some long-standing refugees from Burundi and Somalia (Whitaker 1999). Despite enduring insecurity in Somalia, Kenyan officials have threatened repeatedly to close massive camps along the border and rounded up Somalis living outside of camps; construction of a border wall is under way (Whitaker 2016). While many African countries permit naturalization in theory, few make it easy in practice, and several governments have added language, ethnic, and other requirements for immigrants seeking citizenship (Manby 2009). On a continent with a long history of cross-border migration, earlier hospitality seems to have given way to hostility.

In some African countries, tensions between citizens and foreigners have escalated to the level of violence. The 2008 xenophobic violence in South Africa that killed more than sixty people (mostly immigrants from Zimbabwe and Mozambique) and displaced thousands of others drew international attention to the problem there, but that country is hardly alone. In the Democratic Republic of Congo, land disputes involving a longtime immigrant group and the political manipulation of these tensions by power-hungry leaders have fueled a lingering civil war that has claimed millions of lives since 1996 (Whitaker 2003). In Côte d'Ivoire, the exploitation of xenophobia by political opportunists and the characterization of some citizens as foreigners generated a bloody conflict from which the country only recently emerged (Whitaker 2015). At times, the cross-border movement of people also has contributed to international conflict, including Rwanda's military involvement in Congo and Kenya's intervention in Somalia.

Although there is a sense in much of the research and media reporting that anti-immigrant hostility in Africa has increased, it is not clear that African countries were ever as hospitable as conventional wisdom suggests. Even countries like Côte d'Ivoire and Tanzania, known in the 1970s and 1980s for welcoming millions of foreigners, were motivated by self-interest to adopt the policies they did. The decision by both governments to allow foreigners to vote in national elections, for example, was strategic under one-party systems in which there was little threat to regime security and additional votes simply enhanced the tally for the ruling party. Each country also benefited from immigrants' involvement in the production of cash crops, which were sold through marketing boards at a significant profit to the government. For decades, therefore, immigration policies have been determined by national interests, leading some to question the notion of "traditional African hospitality" (Kibreab 1985). Similarly, mass immigrant expulsions are not new in Africa and have in fact been relatively frequent since independence (Adida 2014; Peil 1971, 1974), often driven by domestic political considerations. Whether anti-immigrant hostility is new in Africa or not, it is getting more attention now than in the past.

As with any region of the world, there are numerous factors influencing attitudes and policies toward immigration in sub-Saharan Africa. Empirical research on immigration attitudes and policies in Europe and North America often draws on cross-national survey data and other quantitative measures that are widely available in such contexts. With a few exceptions (Adida 2014; Whitaker and Giersch 2015), most studies about hostility toward immigrants and other migrants in Africa are based on specific countries or, at times, comparative case analyses. The majority of these are qualitative in nature, although survey and other quantitative data are becoming more widely available in some countries, especially South Africa (Claassen 2016; Fauvelle-Aymar and Segatti 2011; Gordon 2015, 2017; Gordon and Maharaj 2015). Together, these lines of research point to several factors influencing anti-immigrant hostility, though the relative importance of these factors varies across countries and over time.

Attitudes and policies toward immigration can be shaped by demographic factors, including the relative size of the immigrant community compared to the local population. Sharp increases in the number of immigrants can generate hostility among hosts who feel threatened by outsiders. If those outsiders are noticeably different from locals (in terms of race or religion, for example), this sense of threat may intensify. Interestingly, cross-national quantitative studies of African countries find no statistically significant influence of immigrant population size or growth on attitudes and policies (Adida 2014; Whitaker and

Giersch 2015), although it is clear that rapid increases in the number of migrants have been important in some situations. The steady flow of migrants from Zimbabwe amplified anti-immigrant hostility in South Africa, Botswana, and other neighboring countries, for example, while large-scale influxes of refugees into places like Kenya and Tanzania have been a factor in shifting policies there.

Regarding cultural differences between immigrants and hosts, studies from Western countries suggest that immigrants who are more culturally similar to their hosts are better received (Brader, Valentino, and Suhay 2008; Ford 2011; Hainmueller and Hangartner 2013). Evidence from West Africa challenges this conventional wisdom, however, showing that cultural similarities actually can exacerbate relations between hosts and migrants by driving community leaders on both sides to highlight distinctions between them in order to maintain their influence (Adida 2011, 2014). Indeed, cultural differences often are constructed and perpetuated by both sides, resulting in perceptions of immigrants as strangers who do not belong (Whitehouse 2012). Interestingly, countries with high levels of ethnic diversity are not necessarily more welcoming to immigrants, who bring additional diversity, perhaps because they already face resource struggles among different groups. Opposition to immigration is significantly higher in more ethnically diverse African countries (Whitaker and Giersch 2015), and governments in such countries are more likely to expel large numbers of immigrants (Adida 2014). These findings suggest that demographic and cultural factors do not in and of themselves cause anti-immigrant hostility, though some threshold level of migration may be necessary to trigger other factors.

Economic variables also shape immigration attitudes and policies. Tension can result when more people compete for their share of the economic pie, especially if that pie is not growing as quickly as the population. In Africa, the exclusion of foreigners often has coincided with economic downturns (Adida 2014) and with uncertain processes of liberalization that generate debates over what groups "belong" to the national polity (Ceuppens and Geschiere 2005; Geschiere 2009). The need to satisfy growing demands for collective resources has given rise to strategies that differentiate between "deserving" and "undeserving" populations (Nyamnjoh 2006; Peberdy 2001), with migrants typically lumped in the latter category. In a region where a large percentage of people still make their living from agriculture, efforts to exclude those perceived as outsiders—whether foreigners or migrants from other regions within the same country—frequently occur in the context of disputes over land (Jackson 2006; Leonhardt 2006; Socpa 2006). Even so, recent increases in hostility toward immigrants in Africa are not driven solely by economic scarcity, which has existed in the region for a long time. In fact, one cross-national study finds that opposition to immigration is higher in wealthier African countries, not poorer ones (Whitaker and Giersch 2015). This is consistent with case study findings from Botswana, where xenophobia is driven in part by "strong desire to preserve the 'fruits' of economic prosperity for citizens alone" (Campbell 2003: 71).

Another factor fueling anti-immigrant hostility is the use of exclusionary political rhetoric. Politicians in countries around the world seek scapegoats for complex social and economic problems, and foreigners are a common target. Xenophobic rhetoric among elites gives nonelites a focus for their frustrations and legitimizes any underlying prejudices they may have. In Africa, anti-immigrant hostility has increased in the context of broader political liberalization, which has been under way in many countries since the 1990s. The adoption of competitive party systems leads politicians to develop strategies to deflect blame and win support, which can be done by targeting immigrants, suggesting that democracy has a darker side. In countries as diverse as South Africa (Landau 2005, 2006, 2010; Mosselson 2010; Neocosmos 2008, 2010), the Democratic Republic of Congo (Jackson 2006), Cameroon (Geschiere 2009), and Côte d'Ivoire (Whitaker 2015), politicians have fueled xenophobic attitudes in their effort to gain power and have promoted the perception of migrants as a threat. A recent study found that opposition to immigration was higher among respondents in African countries that were more democratic and when the survey was conducted closer to a national election, providing evidence that political competition helps fuel xenophobia (Whitaker and Giersch 2015). Even so, not all politicians embrace anti-immigrant rhetoric, and some reject such messages outright. In Ghana, for example, several recent incumbent and opposition candidates have sought support from immigrant communities as they tried to assemble winning electoral coalitions (Whitaker 2015).

Immigrants often are viewed as a security threat (Adamson 2006), with fears that they may carry out violence within the host country or make it otherwise vulnerable to attack.[7] Security concerns have long shaped the policies of African governments toward refugees (Jacobsen 1996; Whitaker 1999), especially when refugee influxes are large and relations between home and host countries are contentious. For decades, government officials in Kenya have depicted Somali refugees as a security threat (Lochery 2012). This message has been underscored in recent years with the rise of al-Shabaab attacks in response to Kenya's military intervention in Somalia, though no evidence has been produced showing that refugees were involved. Even so, Kenyan officials have used the climate of insecurity to justify harassment of ethnic Somalis (Balakian 2016) and to defend plans to close refugee camps (Whitaker 2016). Security concerns also motivated the 1996 forced repatriation of Rwandan refugees from Tanzania, where officials worried about a possible attack by Rwanda similar to the one in Congo (Whitaker 1999, 2003). Increasingly, nonrefugee immigrants are seen as posing a similar threat. The level of vitriol directed toward Muslim immigrants in Western countries suggests that security fears fuel xenophobia. Africa is not immune to this pattern, as terrorist incidents in Nairobi, Kampala, and elsewhere have generated reprisals against noncitizens.

Finally, international norms influence African policies toward immigrants, though not always in the way one might expect. On one hand, international legal agreements can obligate governments to extend certain rights to refugees and migrants (Jacobsen 1996), providing some minimal protections. On the other hand, African leaders often highlight the exclusionary policies of Western countries to deflect criticism of their own. In Tanzania in the late 1990s, for example, policymakers compared their crackdown on Rwandan refugees to exclusionary policies in the United States toward Haitians (Whitaker 1999). In justifying recent plans to close Somali refugee camps, Kenyan officials similarly have pointed to the increasingly restrictive migration policies of Western countries. In the context of growing hostility toward migrants in many countries around the world, African migrants and their supporters should be concerned about evidence that governments historically have modeled their immigration policies after those adopted by global economic leaders (Timmer and Williams 1998).

Many factors have contributed to rising hostility toward immigrants in Africa, therefore, including demographic changes, cultural dynamics, economic uncertainty, political competition, security concerns, and diffusion effects. The interaction and relative balance among these factors shape attitudes and policies in different countries, with the result that some are more welcoming to migrants than others. Although we have emphasized examples of hostility, some countries in Africa remain surprisingly generous toward migrants. As host of nearly 1.3 million refugees, Uganda stands out in recent years. Since 2013, when the brutal civil war began in neighboring South Sudan, more than 800,000 refugees have fled into northern Uganda.[8] In early 2017, an average of 2,000 refugees arrived every day, and more than 60 percent were children (United Nations High Commissioner for Refugees 2017). Despite these numbers, the Ugandan government continued its policy of providing land and education to refugees and allowing them to work and move around the country (Patton 2016). This approach has been praised for generating better economic outcomes for refugees and hosts (Betts et al. 2017), but not all refugees benefit from such opportunities (Kigozi 2017). Although there are signs that Uganda's policy may be under strain as the influx from South Sudan continues, the government deserves praise for admitting hundreds of thousands of refugees while other governments were closing their doors (Associated Press 2017).

Responses to African Migration Beyond the Region

When it comes to hostility toward immigrants, of course, African countries are hardly alone. Over the past several years, an escalation in the number of people migrating from the Middle East and Africa has contributed to renewed calls for restrictive immigration policies in Europe and North America. As populism surged and xenophobic rhetoric circulated, immigration became a crucial issue in several elections, including the 2016 referendum on British membership in the European Union ("Brexit"), the 2016 presidential election in the United States, and the 2017 presidential election in France. As in Africa, though, policy responses to such sentiments have varied. Hungary, Slovenia, Austria, and Bulgaria hastily built fences along their borders, while Germany admitted hundreds of thousands of asylum-seekers. Under Donald Trump, the United States has stepped up deportation proceedings and imposed controversial new limits on immigration, including dramatically reducing refugee admissions and banning travelers from several countries in Africa and the Middle East; most, but not all, of these measures have been blocked temporarily by US courts. Meanwhile, Canada has dramatically ramped up efforts to resettle refugees, especially those from Syria. Many of the same factors shaping African responses to immigration resulted in similar variations elsewhere.

In Europe in particular, African migration receives significant attention due to the large number of migrants and refugees trying to make the perilous journey across the Sahara and the Mediterranean Sea. News media frequently report on unscrupulous smugglers who overload rickety boats with desperate and vulnerable migrants in North Africa and abandon them in international waters. The fortunate migrants are picked up by one of the many rescue boats plying these waters and taken to Italy or Spain, from which those who are not deported often try to work their way toward France, Germany, or the United Kingdom; thousands of migrants who are not fortunate enough to be rescued drown at sea. Migrants have been crossing the Mediterranean for decades, but numbers have increased recently. Nearly 72,000 migrants reached Italy in the first six months of 2017, 28 percent more than the same period a year earlier; roughly 2,100 migrants died trying to cross (Searcey and

Barry 2017). If periodic accounts of people drowning were not harrowing enough, video evidence emerged in late 2017 of modern-day slave markets in Libya, a transit point on the way to Europe, with African migrants being auctioned off as laborers to the highest bidder. Media coverage prompted a global outcry and calls for something to be done to end such abuses. Despite the extreme risks, many young African men and women continue to attempt the journey for a chance at a better life.

For years, European policy responses to African migration have focused on three "solutions," none of which has effectively reduced the number of migrants (de Haas 2008). First, through a series of agreements with North African transit countries, the European Union has essentially "externalized" border control (de Haas 2008), requiring people to provide proper documentation before leaving African soil. Ironically, by tightening controls at traditional transit points, such restrictions led to a diversification of migration routes and the professionalization of human smuggling (de Haas 2008). Even so, more recently, European governments have established centers to process asylum requests within Africa in the hopes that those whose applications are rejected will not attempt the dangerous journey. Second, European donors have invested heavily in African development, providing billions of euros to migrant-producing and transit countries in the hopes that enhanced economic opportunities will discourage people from leaving (Macdonald 2015). But economic growth actually is associated with higher levels of out-migration (de Haas 2007, 2008), in part because more people can afford the costly journey; indeed, migration to Europe has risen over the past decade as many African economies have grown (Whitaker 2017). A third approach has been to publicize in Africa the risks of the journey and the challenges of life in Europe (de Haas 2008), but such campaigns have done little to discourage people from migrating in that direction. As European policymakers continue to grapple with these challenges, the migration issue has become a recurring theme of European-African relations (see Chapter 11).

Engaging the African Diaspora

While African governments continue to debate policies toward immigrants, many also have developed policies toward their own emigrants living in other countries. For decades, African citizens who migrated elsewhere—whether to neighboring countries in the region or to Europe or beyond—maintained connections to their home countries in various ways. They stayed in touch with family and friends, sending money and visiting whenever possible, and engaged in home-country politics and culture from afar. Technological developments facilitated such contacts, allowing migrants to transfer money with a click on their phones, for example, but these ties remained relatively informal and personal. Indeed, government officials often viewed migrants with suspicion for having fled the country and contributing to "brain drain" (Mohan 2008). This was particularly true when migrants went into exile for political reasons, as with the large number of South Africans who fled apartheid from the 1950s through the 1980s (see case study at the end of this chapter). Working from abroad to end the abuses of authoritarian governments at home, exiles can constitute a unique and powerful threat to the regime security of some African leaders.

In recent years, however, many governments in Africa (and other regions) have developed initiatives to institutionalize relationships with diaspora populations, actively seeking their economic and political participation at home. Driven by political and economic restructuring in the context of globalization, official efforts to cultivate a "diaspora abroad" have important implications for our understanding of international relations (Varadarajan 2010).

When it comes to African countries' connections with their modern diasporas,[9] most attention has focused on economic ties, particularly remittances sent home by migrants living abroad. In 2015, sub-Saharan African countries received an estimated $35 billion in remittances (World Bank 2017a), probably higher after accounting for transfers through informal networks (such as travelers carrying cash). This compares to about $45 billion in official development assistance that same year, according to World Bank data. Remittances thus are nearly as important as foreign aid to the economy of the region as a whole, and more important to the national economies of certain countries. In addition, remittances are a more consistent source of foreign exchange than official aid or private investment, which both tend to fluctuate depending on donor-country politics, economic recessions, commodity prices, and other factors. Recent research provides quantitative evidence that remittances to African countries reduce poverty, promote savings and investment, and enhance economic growth at the macro level (Anyanwu and Erhijakpor 2010; Baldé 2011; Fayissa and Nsiah 2010; Gupta, Pattillo, and Wagh 2009). Interestingly, though, household-level findings suggest that African families who send people abroad become dependent on their remittances and do not exert as much effort to earn income locally as families without such international connections (Azam and Gubert 2006). To some extent, then, foreign aid and remittances both risk leading to dependency.

Given the role of remittances in an uncertain global economic environment, African governments increasingly have been seeking ways to "harness" such transfers toward national development (Leblang 2017;

Mohan 2008). One of the most aggressive policies has been pursued by the government of Eritrea, which imposed a 2 percent tax on its diaspora population soon after independence from Ethiopia in 1993. Most diaspora Eritreans willingly paid the tax at first to facilitate national reconstruction after a decades-long war, and then again during renewed conflict with Ethiopia from 1998 to 2000. However, critics in the diaspora now argue that the tax is serving only to perpetuate a corrupt authoritarian regime in Asmara, helping that government get around international sanctions, and many have stopped paying (Hirt 2015).

Other attempts to harness remittances have been more voluntary. The Nigerians in Diaspora Organisation (NIDO) was formed in 2000 and has chapters around the world. It has been recognized by the government as an umbrella body through which individuals can channel their support for national development (Nigerians in Diaspora Organisation UK 2016). In 2017, the Nigerian government also issued its first diaspora bond, which was portrayed as an opportunity for Nigerians abroad to contribute to the country's development; it raised $300 million in a week (Kazeem 2017). With funding from private companies, the Ghanaian government has organized homecoming summits, most recently in 2017, to "harness capital for development purposes by encouraging Ghanaians abroad to invest in Ghana" (Ghana Diaspora Homecoming Summit 2017). The Ghana Investment Promotion Center, established by the government in 2013, also focuses heavily on recruiting diaspora funds. In Kenya, the government announced a diaspora policy in 2014 that calls for the creation of a national diaspora council and seeks to "empower Kenyans abroad to effectively make a greater contribution to the development of the country" (Kenyan Ministry of Foreign Affairs and International Trade 2014). Similar diaspora initiatives have been launched by other African governments, and not only at the national level. In Senegal, Ghana, and Nigeria, among other countries, local governments have linked up with hometown associations abroad to raise funds for area development (Mohan 2006, 2008). At the continental level, the African Union has sought to involve diaspora representatives in programs since recognizing the diaspora as Africa's "sixth region" (in addition to five within the continent) in 2003 (Kamei 2011).

Recent outreach efforts by African governments to their citizens living abroad have been strongly encouraged by external donors. Often under the "diaspora for development" rubric, the World Bank, International Monetary Fund, International Organization for Migration, and various bilateral donors (including the US Agency for International Development) have organized conferences, published reports, and solicited grant proposals to develop and circulate best practices for recruiting diaspora input into national development efforts. While these opportunities have been welcomed by diaspora organizations and home-country governments alike, it is worth noting that any effort to boost remittances and investment by diaspora populations takes some pressure off international donors to provide development aid. This is particularly attractive to bilateral donors like the United States that face domestic political pressure to reduce foreign aid, despite its constituting only a tiny fraction of government budgets. Even with these concerted internal and external efforts to channel diaspora contributions toward national development projects, most remittances still go directly from citizens living abroad to personal connections (family and friends) back home. This leads to the creation of a "remittance class" in some communities of people with diaspora connections, which can have implications for class relations and politics at the local level (Obadare and Adebanwi 2009).

While there is a clear focus on economic contributions, African governments increasingly allow citizens living abroad to engage in home-country politics as well. For years, political candidates from Senegal, Ghana, Zimbabwe, and Kenya, among others, have made frequent visits to diaspora communities in Europe and North America to raise money for their campaigns (Whitaker 2011). In fact, data from 1990 to 2005 show that remittances to countries around the world increase in election years, especially when the election is competitive (O'Mahony 2013). But since 2000 especially, the political involvement of African diaspora populations has moved beyond contributions to political campaigns. More than half of all African countries now permit dual citizenship, allowing their nationals to maintain legal connections to their homeland even after becoming citizens of other countries (Manby 2009; Whitaker 2011). In addition, forty-one of fifty-four African countries have passed measures to allow citizens living abroad to participate in home-country elections, though implementation has been slow in many cases (Jaulin and Smith 2016). Several governments, including those in Benin, Mali, and Ethiopia, have created ministerial-level offices for diaspora relations, while Angola, Cape Verde, Mozambique, and Senegal allow for diaspora representation in parliament (*Africa Research Bulletin* 2017; Ellis et al. 2007).

Several factors, including the rise of remittances, have driven African governments to adopt diaspora empowerment policies such as dual citizenship and external voting. The lengthy, and often flawed, process of political liberalization in many countries since the early 1990s and the associated development of new constitutions have created opportunities for citizens living abroad to push for greater recognition and inclusion (Lafleur 2015). International norms also have started to emerge around these issues, with countries around the world more likely to allow external voting when neighboring countries also do so (Turcu and Urbatsch 2015). In this broader context, African diaspora leaders have lobbied actively for emigrant rights, including dual citizenship and the right to vote. Diaspora Kenyans, for example, pushed hard to get these rights included in the 2010 constitution and have gone to court repeatedly since then to push for implementation (Whitaker and Inyanji 2016). Similarly, South Africans living abroad have taken the government to court on several occasions to seek voting rights (Wellman 2016). Emigrants from Senegal, Nigeria, and other countries also have lobbied for political rights at home.

African emigrants emphasize their economic contributions as a justification for receiving political rights, though they are unlikely to stop sending remittances if such rights are not realized. Perhaps recognizing this conundrum, governments often grant such rights on paper but are slow to implement them in practice. There are legitimate logistical challenges to the implementation of dual citizenship and diaspora voting, but delays often result from negotiations and competing interests that are largely political in nature (Lafleur 2015). The extension of rights to Ghanaians living abroad has been hindered by their perceived leanings in support of one of two major political parties, for example, prompting the other party to resist implementation. Ghanaian law now permits both dual citizenship and diaspora voting, but dual nationals are blocked from holding high-level public office (Whitaker 2011), and external voting has yet to be implemented more than a decade after its passage (Ghana Web 2017). Even when the partisanship of emigrants is less clear, as in Kenya, politicians' concerns about the unpredictability of the external vote can delay implementation (Whitaker and Inyanji 2016). Diaspora voting clearly generates questions about the potential impact on election outcomes, though it is only in Cape Verde that diaspora votes are seen as having tipped an election, in this case in favor of the incumbent president (Turcu and Urbatsch 2015). There is initial evidence that diaspora Kenyans are less likely to vote along ethnic lines than their counterparts at home (Whitaker and Inyanji 2016). As African emigrants increasingly engage in home-country politics, more research is needed on their influence on election outcomes and broader political dynamics.

For countries experiencing violent conflict, the involvement of diaspora populations can be particularly controversial (Sheffer 2003; Adamson 2006; Lyons 2006). At times, diaspora residents promote conflict resolution by encouraging warring parties to come to the negotiating table and providing remittances for postconflict reconstruction (Bercovitch 2007; Collier, Hoeffler, and Rohner 2008; Shain

2002; Smith and Stares 2007). In other situations, however, diaspora populations can exacerbate or lengthen conflict by providing financial and other support to rebel groups and undermining government legitimacy (Collier, Hoeffler, and Söderbom 2004; Miller and Ritter 2014). Diaspora populations generated by out-migration from long-standing conflicts can be especially reluctant to compromise on politics at home. In 2005, for example, parts of the Ethiopian diaspora pushed opposition-party members to boycott parliament after controversial elections, prompting a series of arrests and violent clashes (Lyons 2007). In places like Liberia, Rwanda, and Somalia, some residents have come to resent the financial support provided to warring parties by citizens living abroad, where they are protected from day-to-day violence and do not experience the consequences of prolonged conflict. Tensions between people who stay and those who flee also often intensify after a conflict ends, when some members of the diaspora return and seek political power. This was perhaps most pronounced in Rwanda, where genocide survivors accused members of the ruling Rwandan Patriotic Front, many of whom were returnees from places like Uganda, of capitalizing on the memory of the genocide for their own political gain without actually having experienced its horrors themselves (Reyntjens 2013).

Finally, the political engagement of Africans in the diaspora does not focus exclusively on their country of origin. Increasingly, diaspora residents also engage in the politics of their host countries, often in an effort to influence policies toward their home country. In 2004, for example, refugees from South Sudan (which was then still fighting for independence from Sudan) participated in marches across the United States calling for the George W. Bush administration to do something about the rising violence against civilians in Darfur. Many of them spoke about their own experiences living under the repressive Sudanese government. These demonstrations helped push then–secretary of state Colin Powell, and later President Bush, to apply the term "genocide" to the situation in Darfur. Similarly, Ethiopians in the United States lobbied congressional representatives, especially those from districts with large diaspora communities, for passage of the Ethiopia Democracy and Accountability Act of 2007 (Lyons 2007), which called for the Ethiopian government to negotiate with opposition groups and release political prisoners. For Africans living abroad, therefore, it is not a choice between participating in home-country politics or host-country politics; many engage in both. This transnational nature of diaspora politics has clear and yet unexplored implications for international relations among African states and with countries around the world.

Migrants as Political Actors

Although African peoples have been on the move for centuries, migration is often overlooked in studies of contemporary African politics and international relations. The movement of people across international borders affects relations among African governments, especially in large-scale refugee situations, and with other countries around the world, particularly Europe, where the influx of African migrants has become a key focus of policymakers. The issue of migration also highlights the fact that international relations are shaped not only by interactions among governments but also by the decisions and actions of individual migrants—from the choice of where and when to migrate in the first place to efforts to engage in home-country development and politics from afar. Last, this chapter has emphasized the importance of domestic politics in shaping responses to African migration, including the use of anti-immigrant political rhetoric to win support in the context of multiparty competition and the emergence of debates about whether to allow diaspora populations to participate in home-country elections. These themes have played out in various ways in recent discussions about immigration and emigration in South Africa, which is the focus of the following case study.

Case Study: Migration in South Africa

From the precolonial era to the present, migration has been a central theme of the history of South Africa.[10] Archaeological and linguistic evidence suggests that African speakers of Bantu languages moved into the area now known as South Africa from about 500 to 1500 C.E., pushing indigenous Khoisan populations farther south. Soon thereafter, Europeans started arriving along the coast as they sailed around Africa on the way to Asia. In 1652, the Dutch East India Company established a permanent settlement at the Cape of Good Hope, forcibly displacing Khoisan peoples living there and importing slaves from their colonial holdings in present-day Indonesia.[11] The Cape Colony expanded quickly, attracting settlers not only from the Netherlands but also from Germany, France, and elsewhere in Europe. Over time, the mixture of European, African, and Asian peoples led to the emergence of a new derivative of the Dutch language—Afrikaans—and the growth of a mixed-race population known as "coloureds."

In the early 1800s, Great Britain invaded and took over the Cape Colony, prompting thousands of farmers (known as Boers) to migrate east and north to establish three autonomous republics. A foundational moment for Afrikaner nationalism, the so-called Great Trek of the 1830s and 1840s, put these white populations in direct conflict with African populations, particularly Zulu and Ndebele peoples, and led to many deadly battles.[12] Even as these conflicts continued, the discovery of diamonds in 1866 and gold in 1886 motivated British interest in the Transvaal region and led to two wars with the Boers (1880–1881 and 1899–1902). Britain's eventual victory paved the way for the 1910 merger of the four colonies into the Union of South Africa, which became a fully independent member of the Commonwealth in 1931. Under an electoral system in which only whites could vote,[13] the main political fault-line of the new country was between English-speaking Anglos, who tended to be better educated and wealthier, and Afrikaners, who traced their heritage to the early Dutch settlers and farmers.

The Afrikaner-dominated National Party won a majority of seats in the 1948 parliamentary election, despite losing the popular vote.[14] Under pressure to address a perceived problem of increasing African urbanization, which many linked to rising unemployment among working-class whites (Bakker, Parsons, and Rauch 2016; Beinart 2001), the new government moved quickly to implement a formal system of racial segregation, though discrimination and racial stratification had been around for centuries. Under apartheid, people were classified into four racial categories (white, coloured, African, and Indian) that determined everything from whom they could marry to where they could live. Millions of nonwhites were removed from areas reserved for whites; Africans in particular were forced into ethnic homelands, several of which were nominally independent but were never permitted to exercise autonomy. Nonwhites over the age of sixteen were required to carry passbooks and to obtain permits to live or work outside of their designated areas. As wealthy white South Africans (many of them Anglo) still wanted people to work in their homes and businesses, though, it was impossible to relocate all nonwhites to remote areas, leading to the rapid growth of townships around the periphery of urban centers. There were separate townships for each nonwhite racial group, and government services were poor to non-existent both there and in the homelands.

Although migration was severely restricted under apartheid, South Africans were surprisingly mobile. Some found ways to get around the pass laws to secure better housing and employment opportunities outside their designated areas (Reed 2013).[15] Others left the country altogether to escape apartheid, often finding jobs as teachers or civil servants elsewhere in southern Africa as more countries gained independence from European colonizers in the 1960s and 1970s. Many fled the country as exiles and worked from abroad to try to end the white minority regime at home. In addition, despite the brutality of apartheid, South Africa's mines and factories continued to attract migrant labor from countries throughout the region. Immigrant laborers were subject to similar discriminatory laws and restrictions as nonwhite South Africans and often were able to visit family in their home countries only once a year. Thus, despite the goal of apartheid to keep diverse populations separated in clearly defined spaces, there continued to be a fair amount of both internal and external migration during these decades.

In the face of long-standing domestic opposition and growing international pressure (including economic sanctions and bans on South African participation in international sporting events), the apartheid system finally started to crumble in the 1980s. The enforcement of pass laws was discontinued in 1986, resistance leader Nelson Mandela was released after twenty-seven years in prison in 1990, and multiracial elections were held in 1994. As a sign of reconciliation, Mandela invited his former prison guards to his inauguration as president (Mandela 1994). After years as an international pariah, suddenly South Africa was open for trade and investment. Not surprisingly, South Africans had high expectations of the new African National Congress government, though the economic and social problems created by centuries of discrimination, segregation, and repression could not be solved overnight. In the years after 1994, Mandela and his successor, Thabo Mbeki, set about to try to dismantle the remnants of apartheid, pursue economic growth, enhance access to education, reduce inequality, and rebuild international relationships, while also addressing emerging challenges such as the spread of HIV/AIDS.

With the end of apartheid, limitations on internal migration were lifted and people were on the move. Given that the vast majority (around 90 percent) of whites, Asians, and coloured South Africans already lived in cities, the rapid rise in urbanization rates in the 1990s was driven primarily by the influx of Africans from the countryside (Bakker, Parsons, and Rauch 2016). Even so, as is true elsewhere in Africa, many of these city dwellers continued to maintain family ties and homes in rural areas (Posel 2004). Meanwhile, the end of apartheid in South Africa in the 1990s coincided with an increase in conflicts and political crises elsewhere in Africa, including Rwanda, Somalia, Congo, and Zimbabwe, generating an increased flow of refugees and migrants to the wealthiest country in the region. As spaces in which South African migrants and foreign migrants converged, Johannesburg and other cities became sites for competing perspectives on what it meant to belong, with the former emphasizing a community rooted in national citizenship and the latter portraying a context of permanent transit (Landau 2006).

Over time, as South Africans came to realize that the promises of a post-apartheid socioeconomic order would not be fulfilled immediately, frustration was channeled increasingly toward immigrants, especially other Africans. The rise of xenophobia in South Africa has been well documented,[16] particularly since the outbreak of violence in May 2008 that left sixty-two people dead, most of them foreigners. Periodic attacks against Mozambicans, Zimbabweans, Somalis, Congolese, and Nigerians, among others, have created a climate of fear in immigrant communities and affected South Africa's relations with home-country governments. An escalation of xenophobic violence in 2015, including the murders of seven foreigners, prompted Nigeria to recall its top diplomats (Associated Press 2015) and people in neighboring countries to boycott South African music and products (*BBC News* 2015). In early 2017, another series of anti-foreigner attacks led to reprisals against South African businesses in Nigeria (Gaffey 2017). Despite efforts to counter xenophobia in South Africa by civil society organizations, human rights groups, and some government programs (especially before hosting the 2010 World Cup), anti-foreigner sentiment remains widespread and all too frequently rises to the point of violence.

Explanations for the rise of xenophobia in South Africa are multi-faceted. Demographic and economic factors, as discussed earlier in this chapter, created a context in which immigrants could become a target of hostility. The number of foreign-born individuals living in South Africa rose from just over 1 million in 1990 to more than 3 million in 2015 (United Nations Department of Economic and Social Affairs 2015). This rapid increase in the number of immigrants, and their concentration in urban areas, made the country's demographic changes highly visible. The competition among diverse social groups for scarce resources also played a role, as sluggish economic growth, high unemployment, and persistent inequality in the 1990s generated widespread disappointment and frustration. Interestingly, growth rates improved after 2000, even as reported incidents of xenophobic violence increased, but dropped again with the 2009 recession and have failed to recover since (World Bank 2017b).[17]

Beyond these common demographic and economic explanations, though, a unique constellation of historical and political factors has contributed to the prevalence of xenophobia in South Africa (Neocosmos 2010). Having been denied the rights of citizenship for decades, nonwhite South Africans are anxious to finally get some benefit from living in one of the continent's wealthiest economies. The lack of sustained equitable growth has dashed their hopes, leaving many searching for answers. In this context, politicians—seeking to hold on to power they only recently acquired—have sought scapegoats, with immigrants becoming a frequent target. Political elites have blamed foreigners mainly for taking jobs and for competing with South African–owned small businesses (especially informal convenience stores known as *spaza* shops), but also for everything from crime and insecurity to the spread of HIV/AIDS.

Xenophobic rhetoric among South African political elites has helped to channel general frustration into a belief that immigrants are a source of the country's many problems. Indeed, the escalation of xenophobic attacks in early 2015 was widely attributed to comments by Zulu King Goodwill Zwelithini calling for foreigners (whom he called "criminals") to "pack their bags and go home," though the South African Human Rights Commission ultimately ruled that his words did not constitute hate speech (Human Rights Watch 2017). Moreover, the use of extralegal practices by police and other government officials when dealing with immigrants has shown that normal rules do not apply (Landau 2010; Mosselson 2010). In this context, then, South Africans who continue to feel excluded from the economic rights of citizenship periodically have turned to violence to fight against a perceived source of their problems and assert their own rights. While South Africa clearly is not alone among African countries in witnessing anti-immigrant hostility (Whitaker and Giersch 2015), its unique history of migration from near and far and the legacy of forced exclusion of various social groups make the situation especially complicated and undermine ongoing efforts to reduce xenophobia and violence in that context.

Even as South Africa continues to grapple with challenges posed by immigration, old and new, it also faces the question of how to deal with emigration. This has been most pronounced since the end of apartheid with respect to the question of whether South African citizens living in the diaspora should be permitted to vote. As explained by Elizabeth Wellman (2016), politics and the legacy of apartheid have been key factors behind fluctuating policies on diaspora voting. In the country's first democratic election in 1994, significant resources were devoted to opening polling stations around the world. After its long struggle against white minority rule, the ANC was adamant about making the election as inclusive as possible, especially given the large number of Africans living in exile. With permissive rules allowing anyone with South African identity documents to vote, 100,000 people cast their ballots in seventy-eight countries (Wellman 2016).

After Mandela and the ANC came to power in 1994, the nature of emigration changed. As black South African exiles flocked back to the country in large numbers, many white families left, often permanently. Their departure was perceived by many South Africans as a rejection of the ANC and, more broadly, of democracy and majority rule (Wellman

2016). In this context, and with the ANC in firm control of parliament, the 1998 Electoral Act abolished diaspora voting, with seemingly little reaction among emigrants. In the 1999 and 2004 elections, only South African diplomats and military personnel overseas were permitted to vote. In 2009, however, just three months before the next election, several South Africans living abroad filed court cases claiming that their constitutional right to vote was being denied. By then, emigration patterns had shifted again, as more South Africans of all races moved abroad temporarily for education and employment. Just six weeks before the election, the Constitutional Court ruled in favor of the claimants, effectively forcing the government to reinstate diaspora voting. With a short time frame for implementation, just 10,000 people in the diaspora voted in 2009; that number increased in 2014 but only to about 18,000. With low turnout, and the vast majority of diaspora votes going to the opposition Democratic Alliance, ANC leaders have been reluctant to devote more resources to expand overseas voting and have rejected all efforts by the Democratic Alliance to do so (Wellman 2016). For now, South African emigrants continue to have the right to vote, but their impact on electoral outcomes likely will remain limited.

Thus, migration has shaped the entire history of South Africa, from the early settlement of Khoisan and Bantu populations and the later arrival of peoples from Europe and Asia, through forcible policies to exclude and separate different racial groups during the colonial and apartheid eras, to ongoing tensions between those who have been marginalized for far too long and more recent arrivals hoping to build better lives. Although South Africa's history within Africa is unique, the country is currently facing many of the same challenges with regard to immigration and emigration as others in the region. Immigration is the subject of significant debate in countries such as Côte d'Ivoire, Kenya, Tanzania, and Botswana, with human rights groups often at the forefront of fighting against widespread hostility and restrictive policies. Meanwhile, governments throughout Africa, including those of Kenya, Ghana, Nigeria, and Ethiopia, have been reaching out to citizens living abroad, seeking their economic contributions and, somewhat more cautiously, their political participation at home. Leaders of these countries will continue to watch South Africa, one of the largest economies in the region and a key player in international negotiations, as it addresses migration and related challenges.

Notes

1. The 1951 United Nations Convention Relating to the Status of Refugees defines a refugee as "a person who owing to a well-founded fear of being persecuted

for reasons of race, religion, nationality, membership of a particular social group or political opinion, is outside the country of his nationality and is unable or, owing to such fear, is unwilling to avail himself of the protection of that country." To be recognized as a refugee under this convention, asylum-seekers generally have had to demonstrate evidence of an individual fear of persecution.

2. The 1969 OAU Convention Governing Specific Aspects of Refugee Problems embraced the 1951 UN Refugee Convention definition while adding the following: "The term 'refugee' shall also apply to every person who, owing to external aggression, occupation, foreign domination or events seriously disturbing public order in either part or the whole of his country of origin or nationality, is compelled to leave his place of habitual residence in order to seek refuge in another place outside his country of origin or nationality." Under this expanded definition, many African governments granted refugee status to people fleeing generalized violence without requiring them to prove an individual fear of persecution.

3. Updated 2015 numbers from the United Nations show that there were more than 3 million people of foreign origin living in South Africa, 2 million in Côte d'Ivoire, and 1 million each in Ethiopia, Kenya, and Nigeria (United Nations Department of Economic and Social Affairs 2015).

4. One factor underlying the drop in the number of refugees has been the shift by many African governments from "group status determination" of refugee status using the 1969 OAU expanded definition presented earlier, to "individual status determination" of refugee status using the 1951 UN definition emphasizing an individual fear of persecution.

5. International law makes it more difficult to deny entry to people who are fleeing political persecution and seeking asylum, though recent border closures in Europe and elsewhere are calling these norms into question.

6. Unfortunately, the widely used Afrobarometer has not included a cross-national question about immigration attitudes in any of the six rounds of its public opinion survey, and the most recent round of the World Values Survey dropped the most relevant question. The relative absence of cross-national data on immigration attitudes has limited the ability of researchers to examine these trends more systematically (Whitaker and Giersch 2015).

7. Although such threats sometimes are exaggerated, there is evidence that large refugee influxes can increase the risk of conflict in host countries (Salehyan 2008; Salehyan and Gleditsch 2006), at least under certain conditions (Lischer 2005; Whitaker 2003).

8. Uganda also hosts smaller numbers of refugees from the Democratic Republic of Congo, Burundi, Somalia, Rwanda, and other countries.

9. There is a significant body of literature on the historical dimensions of the African diaspora going back to its roots in the enslavement of people from the continent and their forced transfer to other regions of the world (see, for example, Akyeampong 2000), but the current discussion focuses on present-day connections between specific African countries and their citizens who have migrated elsewhere.

10. For much more detailed accounts of South African history, see Beinart 2001; Comaroff and Comaroff 1991; Davenport and Saunders 2000; and Thompson 2001.

11. This population came to be known in South Africa as Cape Malays.

12. The Voortrekker Monument in Pretoria was built in 1949 to commemorate the Great Trek and celebrate Afrikaner nationalism. Since the end of apartheid, its displays have been updated to provide a more balanced portrayal of the impact of these movements on other peoples in South Africa, particularly Africans with whom the Boers fought.

13. The exception was in the former Cape Colony, where suffrage had long been based on wealth and education instead of race, thus permitting segments of the coloured and African populations to vote. In the former Boer/Afrikaner colonies of Natal, Orange River, and Transvaal, suffrage was limited to white males (Lewsen 1971).

14. The National Party dominated in rural areas, where constituencies had smaller populations, while the opposing United Party was especially popular in more populated urban centers.

15. Comedian Trevor Noah (2016) writes in his autobiography about growing up in South Africa as the product of an illegal relationship between a black woman and a white Swiss man. At one point, his mother, who earned a small but steady income as a secretary for a multinational company, convinced a German acquaintance to rent her an apartment in a designated white area in his name. She lived there and paid the rent, wearing a maid's uniform when coming and going, though she periodically was arrested and fined for violating pass laws.

16. See, for example, Crush 2001; Crush and Pendleton 2004; Gordon 2015, 2017; Hassim, Kupe, and Worby 2008; Landau 2011; McDonald and Jacobs 2005; Mosselson 2010; Neocosmos 2010; and Nyamnjoh 2006.

17. The lack of economic recovery in South Africa is due at least in part to a series of political crises and corruption scandals under former president Jacob Zuma, who was finally forced by ANC party leaders to step down in February 2018. The new president, Cyril Ramaphosa, is less controversial within the party; more broadly, recent infighting has raised questions about the future of the ANC's grip on power.

PART 4

Engaging with External Actors

10

Africa and the United States

In the early 1990s, there was renewed hope about the possibilities for peace, democracy, and development in sub-Saharan Africa. The end of the Cold War in particular meant that conflicts on the continent could be put in their proper context instead of being seen as episodes in a larger superpower confrontation. However, the withdrawal of the major powers—the United States and the Soviet Union—also led to Africa's marginalization as interest in the continent declined and other regions (especially a changing Eastern Europe) attracted attention. This waning interest was reflected in US economic and military assistance to sub-Saharan Africa, which declined from $2.4 billion in 1992 to $1.7 billion in 1996 before rising again thereafter (US Agency for International Development 2017).[1] Throughout the 1990s, the United States, and the international community more broadly, engaged in Africa primarily on humanitarian grounds and with limited economic initiatives, developing reluctant and belated responses to serious crises. External interest in the continent rose once again after 2001 with the realization that terrorism was a global threat, but this renewed attention also had its drawbacks.

Most observers mark 1988—the year of the tripartite agreement that led to the withdrawal of foreign troops from Angola (see Chapter 3)— as the end of the Cold War in Africa. For several years thereafter, US policy in the region focused primarily on wrapping up Cold War conflicts in Mozambique and the Horn, advocating for an end to apartheid in South Africa, and promoting democracy more broadly (see Chapter 5). When Somalia's Siad Barre was overthrown in 1991 and the country deteriorated into civil war, therefore, it was the first real test of US policy toward Africa in the post–Cold War era. In an era of international optimism following the Gulf War, as explored in the case study at the end of this chapter, the Somali famine prompted a multilateral military intervention. While initially successful at getting food to starving people, peacekeepers soon became targets in the conflict. The shooting down of a US Black Hawk helicopter in October 1993 and the videos of Somalis dragging the bodies of American troops through the streets led to the complete withdrawal of US forces in early 1994, followed by UN forces a year later. For many, Somalia became a symbol of failure for both the United States and the United Nations in Africa.

For several years after the Somalia intervention, the United States was wary of any involvement in Africa. Just a month after the last American troops left Somalia, violence escalated in the Central African country of Rwanda. On April 6, 1994, the Hutu president's plane was shot down, triggering a massive campaign of organized violence against members of the minority Tutsi ethnic group and moderate Hutus who supported an earlier power-sharing agreement.[2] By July, when a Tutsi-dominated rebel group took power in Kigali, roughly 800,000 people had been killed and 2 million displaced (des Forges 1999). The situation was met with complete inaction by the international community (Melvern 2000; Power 2001). The United States downplayed the violence, and a State Department spokesperson famously avoided using the term "genocide" (presumably to sidestep any obligation to intervene). On April 21, 1994, with US support, the UN Security Council voted to withdraw peacekeepers from Rwanda, leaving only 264 behind. One month later, the Clinton administration issued Presidential Decision Directive 25, setting clear criteria for US involvement in peacekeeping operations—criteria that were not met by the situation in Rwanda.

There has been significant debate among scholars about why the United States did not do more about the genocide in Rwanda. Alan Kuperman (2000) argues that the killing was too rapid and that US policymakers did not have enough information about the situation in time to prevent most of the deaths, though this lack of information claim has been strongly disputed (des Forges 2000; Power 2001, 2002b). Even taking Kuperman's argument at face value, though, a minimum intervention at the time he says US policymakers had enough information could have saved 75,000 lives, which is not an insignificant number. Samantha Power (2002b) offers a more convincing explanation for the US inaction in Rwanda: there was little, if any, domestic political pressure to do anything about the genocide. In the aftermath of the Somali disaster, few Americans contacted their representatives or the White House to demand action. Most had never heard of Rwanda and few perceived

US interests there. With no pressure from below, policymakers saw no reason to be drawn into another African conflict. Several months later, then-senator Paul Simon said, "If every member of the House and Senate had received 100 letters from people back home saying we have to do something about Rwanda, . . . then I think the response would have been different" (quoted in Power 2002a: 377). Whatever the reasons, the United States seemed to avoid Rwanda—and most of the rest of Africa—for several years after Somalia.

It was not until President Clinton's 1998 visit to six African countries that his administration started laying out a new policy toward the region and aid started rising. The visit included a short layover at the airport in Kigali, Rwanda, where Clinton gave a speech to genocide survivors. He did not explicitly apologize for international inaction four years earlier but admitted that "we did not act quickly enough" and called on "civilized nations to strengthen our ability to prevent and, if necessary, to stop genocide" (Clinton 1998). During and after this visit, the Clinton administration launched several initiatives toward Africa focused around economic and security concerns. They were accompanied by a strong rhetorical commitment to engage more in Africa, though more substantive commitments did not always follow. Policy announcements were full of references to partnership with African countries and leaders, but inherent power imbalances limited the realization of that approach. In describing this period as one of "virtual engagement," one scholar notes that the motivating themes of US policy in the region were the same as they had been for many years: "extractive commercial, limited security and selective humanitarianism" (Alden 2000: 368). Even so, US economic and military assistance to sub-Saharan Africa rose to its highest level since 1985, reaching $2.7 billion by 2000 (US Agency for International Development 2017).

Throughout the 1990s, therefore, there was no overarching ideology in US policy toward Africa. Attention to stated priorities such as democracy promotion and humanitarian relief was inconsistent at best. Countries like Kenya were under significant pressure to embrace multiparty reforms, even as US investment in oil-rich dictatorships in Nigeria and Angola increased dramatically. The US military intervened to stop the famine in Somalia, but did nothing while nearly 800,000 died in Rwanda. This lack of consistency and vision for US policy in the region was frustrating to many observers, including Africans. The Cold War may have caused havoc in Africa and elsewhere, but at least US interests and goals were clear and predictable during that era. Even Clinton's embrace of what his administration called a "new generation of African leaders" in Uganda, Rwanda, and Ethiopia (Ottaway 1999) proved to be shortsighted, as Yoweri Museveni, Paul Kagame, and Meles Zenawi, respectively, turned out to be little different from their authoritarian predecessors. In many ways, the Africa policy of the United States in this era was characterized by a sort of "Band-Aid" approach, by which officials tried to patch up large cuts (and often gaping wounds) only once they were bleeding, and sometimes not even then. The uncertainty of this period also revealed the importance of building a domestic constituency to lobby on Africa-related issues, a topic discussed later in this chapter.

When terrorists attacked the World Trade Center and the Pentagon on September 11, 2001, US foreign policy immediately gained a new overarching ideology. In fact, counterterrorism had been a priority in Africa since August 7, 1998, when nearly simultaneous bombs destroyed the US embassies in Kenya and Tanzania, killing more than 200 people. The bombings prompted a US cruise missile attack on a pharmaceutical plant in Sudan that was allegedly producing chemical weapons. It was the attacks on US soil in 2001, however, that motivated a renewed focus on security threats around the world during the George W. Bush administration. Instead of countering the threat of communism, as it sought to do during the Cold War, US foreign policy emphasized the need to counter the threat of international terrorism, particularly by al-Qaeda and related groups. Even as most Africans agreed with the broader goal of counterterrorism, many expressed concerns about the securitization of US policy in the region and the prioritization of terrorism over issues such as human rights, democracy, and development. Instead of changing under President Barack Obama, as many Africans hoped, security issues continued to dominate the policy agenda. The rhetoric may have been different, as discussed later, but the core policies remained unchanged.

The remainder of this chapter examines the Africa policy of the United States since the end of the Cold War. We start by discussing the actors involved in making US policy toward Africa and the tendency for policies to change only incrementally from one presidential administration to another. Aid levels to Africa do not vary systemically between Republican and Democratic administrations, for example, and policy initiatives developed under one president generally continue under subsequent presidents, sometimes with little more than a name change. To illustrate this relative consistency in US policy, we then examine a series of US economic and security initiatives toward Africa since the 1990s, as well as African responses to them, and discuss how they have changed (or not) over time. We give particular attention to US-African cooperation in fighting terrorism, which has been a key focus of this relationship in recent years, and the tension between security concerns and other priorities like democracy and development. Although Africa generally has been relegated to the margins of US foreign policy debates, there have been several efforts over the years to build an American constituency to support Africa-related issues, as explored toward the end of the chapter. Finally, the case study examines US policy in Somalia, where US involvement over the past three decades often has been a source of debate. Although the Somali case is hardly typical, it demonstrates the perils of both too much attention and too little attention, and US experiences there often have shaped its policies elsewhere.

Making US Policy Toward Africa

Some areas and countries of the world—China, the Middle East, Europe, Russia, Cuba—get significant attention in US policymaking circles. They are frequently mentioned during political campaigns and are the subject of regular discussions among foreign policy elites. Political candidates debate the merits of different policies in these regions, sometimes tossing out popular soundbites and at other times offering substantive proposals. Some of these countries and regions even factor into debates at the state and local levels.[3]

The same cannot be said about Africa. US policy toward countries in the region rarely attracts widespread attention, and few policymakers focus specifically on the region, unless and until there is some sort of crisis. The relative lack of attention to Africa among high-level US policymakers helps to explain the general continuity of US policy toward Africa from one presidential administration to another (Schraeder 2001). In exploring where US policy toward Africa is made, Schraeder focuses on three concentric circles at the federal level. Within the White House inner circle, the main incentive during a president's first term is to get reelected, which typically means focusing on domestic affairs. (Note that the Rwandan genocide, as discussed earlier, happened during Clinton's first term in office; US inaction during that period did not appear to hurt his 1996 reelection.) Foreign policy may get more attention in a second term, but often with the hopes of establishing some long-term legacy (peace in the Middle East, for example) rather than addressing more day-to-day concerns. Foreign policy experts in and around the White House tend to focus on Africa only when a crisis arises.

Similarly, in the congressional outer circle, members are focused on reelection or at times on seeking higher office (Schraeder 2001). Except in certain constituencies (with high numbers of immigrants from a particular country, for example), these goals generally are not aided by focusing on foreign policy. Members of the House of Representatives are up for election every two years, making them especially focused on local issues (and fund-raising). The six-year time horizon of senators allows somewhat more time for foreign affairs, but members of Congress and their staffs rarely have expertise on Africa-related issues. The Africa subcommittees in the House and Senate are low on the list of desirable assignments, though they have had a few very knowledgeable members over the years.[4] In this context, it can be difficult to get Africa on the congressional agenda. Perhaps even more so than the White House, therefore, Congress typically deals only with African countries when there is a crisis.

Because of these dynamics, responsibility for making US policy toward Africa rests primarily with bureaucrats in the Department of State and other executive branch departments. These are usually career civil servants (as opposed to political appointees) who remain in their positions even when new presidents take office. There are several implications of Africa policy being developed mainly at this level: consistency over time regardless of administration, fragmentation due to the lack of coordination at higher levels, and a resistance to change that characterizes almost any bureaucracy (Schraeder 2001). As a result, US policy toward Africa changes only very slowly over time, a process that Peter Schraeder (1994, 2001) terms "incrementalism." This pattern characterized the transitions from the Clinton administration to the George W. Bush administration and later to the Barack Obama administration. Indeed, with the exception of the renewed focus on security after 2001, there has been significant continuity in US policy toward Africa since the early 1990s. The recent neglect of the State Department under the Donald Trump administration has led to funding shortages and a large number of staff vacancies; many political appointments remain unfilled and career diplomats are leaving the department. Under these conditions, and with Africa even lower on the priority list than under previous administrations, dramatic new US policy initiatives toward the continent are very unlikely.

Continuity and Change in US Policy Toward Africa

Building on the arguments in the previous section about the overarching consistency in US policy toward Africa from one presidential administration to another, the following sections examine several US initiatives in Africa since the 1990s and the ways in which they have evolved—or not—over time. As we will see, the most obvious change has been the increased emphasis since 2001 on security over other stated US priorities in the region. Reflecting this shift in focus, we start by discussing early economic and health initiatives before focusing on more recent policies to counter perceived security threats in Africa.

African Growth and Opportunity Act

In the mid-1990s, US policymakers started discussing a new economic approach to Africa. Under the mantra of "trade not aid," the idea was that African economies could better achieve sustainable long-term growth by increasing exports to outside markets rather than relying on foreign aid. The argument had its critics, perhaps most notably then–South African president Nelson Mandela, who contended that Africa needed both trade *and* continued aid to help level the playing field for fair market exchange. Even so, the "trade not aid" philosophy resonated with many policymakers and economists concerned about the perceived ineffectiveness of foreign aid and looking to expand global markets (Moyo 2009). President Clinton's visit to Africa in 1998 provided an opportunity to pitch this approach to African leaders, though it remained US-driven, and the initiative gained momentum.

In May 2000, during his last year in office, Clinton signed the African Growth and Opportunity Act; it was subsequently revised or extended four times (2002, 2004, 2006, and 2015), making its terms valid until 2025. The law provides eligible African countries duty-free access to the US market for more than 7,000 designated products. Eligibility is based on conditions that include free market reforms, political pluralism, efforts to combat corruption, protection of intellectual property rights, respect for human rights, and the elimination of barriers to US trade and investment. This last point should not be overlooked; indeed, a key factor driving support for the law within the US business community was the opportunity to gain greater access to new overseas markets. Among various details of this trade legislation, perhaps the most complicated were provisions—pushed especially by lawmakers from historically textile-producing states—limiting the amount of apparel (clothing) that could be made in Africa from non-US-sourced fabric, yarn, and thread.[5] AGOA also supports an annual US-Africa Trade Forum that brings together trade officials from participating countries.

When AGOA was enacted, many African business leaders lobbied their governments to meet eligibility criteria. Local media covered negotiations and announced with excitement when their country's exports became eligible for duty-free access to US markets. More than forty sub-Saharan African countries have been declared AGOA-eligible since 2000, though some (Burundi, the Democratic Republic of Congo, Gambia, Guinea-Bissau, Mali, South Sudan, Swaziland) have lost eligibility for periods of time, typically as a result of political problems at home.[6] In the wake of the law's passage, exports from AGOA-eligible countries to the United States nearly quadrupled, from a total value of $22 billion in 2000 to $82 billion in 2008.[7] Apparel exports doubled, and it became common to find US retailers selling clothes made in places like Botswana, Lesotho, Mauritius, Ethiopia, and Kenya.

Enhanced access to US markets did not dramatically transform African economies, however. Despite special attention to textiles, which many hoped would become an engine of development for Africa, oil and other commodities continued to account for the majority of trade under AGOA. Indeed, much of the increase in the value of African exports to the United States between 2000 and 2008 was due to the rise of oil prices during that period. Moreover, in 2005, the end of the Multi-Fiber Agreement under the World Trade Organization (WTO) lifted all textile quotas, meaning that the United States could no longer limit textile imports from any particular country. As a result, low-cost textiles flooded into the United States from China, Taiwan, and elsewhere. Even with duty-free access, emerging African textile producers could not compete; many went out of business and employment in this sector dropped. In addition, due largely to the elimination of trade barriers required by AGOA, US exports to eligible countries continued to rise even as imports from those countries declined. After reaching more than $64 billion in 2008 (when oil prices were especially high), AGOA countries' trade surplus with the United States was down to just $2 billion in 2015 (when oil prices had dropped). The global recession did not help; two-way trade between the United States and AGOA countries dropped to $36 billion in 2015 from $100 billion in 2008.

After some promising results in the early years, therefore, the effectiveness of AGOA has been hindered by other developments in the global economy, including the recession, trade agreements, and oil price fluctuations. Although the initiative has not lived up to its initial promise, US lawmakers have seen no reason to end eligible countries' duty-free access to US markets, especially because it has come with greater access to African markets for US companies. On the African side, concern about the declining trade surplus has not undermined support for some of AGOA's benefits, and governments continue to seek to maintain their eligibility. AGOA was initially signed into law by Clinton; Bush and Obama signed bills supported by bipartisan majorities in Congress to revise its provisions and extend their duration. AGOA is not expected to be extended again beyond 2025, but it is clearly an example of continuity in US policy toward Africa from one presidential administration to another.

President's Emergency Plan for AIDS Relief

Of the roughly 35 million people globally who have died from AIDS-related causes since the HIV virus was identified in the 1980s, roughly three-quarters have been in sub-Saharan Africa.[8] The region accounts for almost 70 percent of the 37 million people currently living with HIV, only a fraction of whom receive antiretroviral drug therapy to suppress the virus. The overall rate of HIV infection among adults in Africa is under 5 percent, but prevalence is much higher in southern Africa, particularly Swaziland (27.2 percent in 2016), Lesotho (25 percent), Botswana (21.9 percent).[9] With a 2016 estimated prevalence of 18.9 percent of a much larger population, South Africa has the highest number of people living with HIV in the world.

The spread of HIV/AIDS has had a significant impact on African societies. In many countries, life expectancies have dropped dramatically and the number of orphans has increased.[10] Women and girls have been especially hard-hit, both because of their traditional role as caretakers for sick relatives and because they are biologically more likely to contract the virus from an infected partner. Nearly 60 percent of African adults living with HIV are women. African countries' economic growth rates have been reduced by 2 to 4 percent per year because of the decline in productivity associated with HIV and AIDS (Dixon, McDonald, and Roberts 2002), though the most obvious losses have been at the micro level in households affected by the sickness and death of income earners (Bachmann and Booysen 2003; Rugalema 2000).

The political impact of the pandemic has been somewhat less evident. Concerns about security risks due to the large number of orphans and high prevalence in African militaries led to a special session on HIV/AIDS at the United Nations Security Council in January 2000, but such fears have not materialized. Similarly, predictions of a governance crisis (de Waal 2003) have been avoided, at least for now, due in part to denialism among African leaders[11] (and among opposition politicians who would otherwise critique their policies) and the success of international activists in advocating for antiretroviral treatment (de Waal 2007). Despite the huge social and economic impact, especially in the southern part of the continent, AIDS and related policies have not become a real election issue in any country. Survey data show that most respondents—even those who are HIV-positive—view other problems as more pressing for their communities (Dionne 2012; Dionne, Gerland, and Watkins 2011). African leaders, especially those with short-term time horizons, tend to allocate resources to those other problems first (Dionne 2011).

As the scale of the pandemic in Africa became clear, pressure mounted on world leaders to respond. In 2002, the Global Fund to Fight AIDS, Tuberculosis, and Malaria was created to finance prevention and treatment efforts around the world. Then, in January 2003, President

George W. Bush surprised many observers when he announced the President's Emergency Plan for AIDS Relief (PEPFAR) during his State of the Union address.[12] The plan included $15 billion of funding over five years, including $10 billion in new allocations (beyond what had already been earmarked for the Global Fund) for prevention and treatment of HIV/AIDS in fifteen countries, twelve of which were in Africa. Perhaps even more surprising in the context of growing polarization in Washington was the level of bipartisan support the initiative received, bringing together progressives who often advocated for increased foreign aid and conservatives responding to a call from Christian leaders to assist victims of HIV/AIDS. Congress provided nearly $19 billion to PEPFAR in its first five years, well above the initial request. When it reauthorized the program for another five years in 2008, Congress allocated $48 billion total to PEPFAR and the Global Fund. With these contributions, the United States provided roughly 30 percent of global resources to fight the HIV pandemic and more than doubled its aid to sub-Saharan Africa.

There is no doubt that PEPFAR has had an impact on the ground in Africa. Especially in target countries, HIV testing and counseling are widely available. Clinics are highly visible, and some of the stigma of going to them has declined. As a result of PEPFAR and various other government and foundation programs, millions of HIV-positive people are receiving antiretroviral treatment and living relatively normal lives. According to the initiative's own data,[13] in fiscal year 2015 alone PEPFAR facilitated antiretroviral treatment for 9.5 million people, supported 8.9 million voluntary male circumcision procedures,[14] provided care for 5.5 million vulnerable children, trained 190,000 new healthcare workers, and supported testing and counseling for 68.2 million people, including 14.7 million pregnant women. These numbers have increased nearly every year since PEPFAR started and have contributed to a reduction in fatalist attitudes in many African countries where contracting HIV is no longer perceived as a death sentence.

In order to maintain bipartisan support and to reach these numbers, PEPFAR had to overcome early critiques. When PEPFAR was first announced, for example, skeptics worried that the Bush administration was developing a unilateral alternative to the multilateral Global Fund. Though the two programs continue to exist independently, they collaborate on the ground and the United States has remained a significant contributor to the Global Fund. Another early critique of PEPFAR was that it required the purchase of brand-name antiretroviral drugs instead of cheaper generic alternatives, presumably as a result of lobbying from the pharmaceutical industry. This pushed up costs and limited the number of people who could receive treatment. Over time, as more generic drugs were tested and as governments and foundations negotiated better prices on brand-name drugs, PEPFAR dramatically escalated its purchases of generics, helping to increase the number of people receiving treatment. Under the Bush administration as well, pressure from conservative groups led to a requirement that 33 percent of funding be spent on promoting abstinence programs. Although most critics agreed that abstinence should be part of any prevention program, implementing agencies on the ground found it difficult to spend a full third of their budgets on such programs. Simply put, abstinence promotion does not cost much money, and there are only so many billboards and flyers that can be made. This requirement was relaxed under the Obama administration, freeing up implementing partners to allocate funds more strategically. Last, the number of countries covered by PEPFAR has been expanded, with support now being provided in sixty-five countries around the world, including twenty-seven in Africa. More so than many other US government initiatives, therefore, PEPFAR has demonstrated an ability to adapt and to respond effectively to a crisis situation.

In contrast to some other Bush administration policies in Africa, as discussed later, PEPFAR was widely perceived as a foreign policy success. Indeed, during Bush's farewell visit to five African countries in February 2008, he focused on highlighting public health cooperation while downplaying concerns about his security policies. When Barack Obama came into office the following year, his administration embraced PEPFAR and requested more funding but made changes around the edges consistent with its policy preferences. This is a clear example of the incremental way in which US policy toward Africa changes from one presidential administration to another (Schraeder 2001). A 2017 proposal by President Donald Trump to cut foreign aid by 32 percent, including PEPFAR by 17 percent and US contributions to the Global Fund by 25 percent, sparked backlash even among congressional representatives from his own Republican Party, suggesting that actual cuts would be much more modest (Torbati 2017). Even as PEPFAR continues to support important prevention and treatment in Africa, the program does little to address underlying causes of the spread of HIV, including poverty and limitations on women's empowerment. Some women resort to sex work to feed their children, for example, while others find it difficult to get their wandering husbands to wear condoms. Related to these challenges, it is also important to remember that fighting HIV/AIDS is not generally a top priority for most Africans, even in highly affected regions (Dionne 2012). While PEPFAR has been an important US initiative, therefore, other initiatives often attract greater attention from people in the region.

African Peacekeeper Training Programs

During the 1990s, the phrase "African solutions to African problems" became popular. African leaders seized on it as a call for less dependence on the outside world and more homegrown approaches, though the definition of what constituted an "African solution" was open to debate. For Western leaders, use of this phrase was both supportive and convenient. They could appear to be soliciting more African input into resolving issues on the continent while at the same time avoiding deeper commitments of their own (Williams 2008). In the aftermath of the Somalia intervention in the early 1990s, there was little interest in getting involved in other African conflicts, and the idea of Africans seeking solutions to regional conflicts was appealing. In this context, the British, French, and US governments developed programs to increase peacekeeping capacity within African militaries (see Chapter 8).

In 1997, the Clinton administration launched the Africa Crisis Response Initiative (ACRI) to train troops from selected African countries for humanitarian and peacekeeping missions. Each contingent trained through the program also received nonlethal equipment, mainly communications technology to facilitate coordination in case of deployment. Initially a five-year program, ACRI was restructured by the Bush administration in 2002 as African Contingency Operations Training Assistance (ACOTA), which added training for offensive engagement in hostile environments. The program was folded into the Global Peace Operations Initiative (GPOI), launched in 2004, and continued under both Obama and Trump, though there are indications that funding will drop under the latter. Once again, then, there were marginal changes from one administration to another, including a name change, but the general thrust remained the same: train African militaries to respond to humanitarian crises and conflict situations within the continent. Since 1997, ACRI and ACOTA have trained more than 250,000 peacekeepers from twenty-five African countries.[15] These countries sent peacekeeping contingents to United Nations and African Union missions in Sudan, the Democratic Republic of Congo, Sierra Leone, the Central African Republic, Ethiopia-Eritrea, Côte d'Ivoire, Liberia, Burundi, Somalia, and Chad. US-trained contingents also deployed for humanitarian relief in Mozambique and for peacekeeping operations outside of Africa (Kosovo and Lebanon).

While the motivations and impact of peacekeeping and humanitarian operations in Africa are discussed at more length in Chapter 8, the United States has supported their Africanization through training programs like ACOTA and by funding and providing logistical support to various missions on the continent. Even so, it is not clear that there are benign regional powers in Africa, and there are typically not enough resources to buy disinterested intervenors (Herbst 2000b). As a result, intervention is more likely by African countries that have a motive for getting involved in a particular context, whether because they want one side to win or because they have other interests on the ground. This situation raises questions about whether US support through these programs will ultimately help resolve African conflicts or could at times make their resolution even more complex due to the number of actors involved.

US Africa Command

In 2007, the Bush administration announced the creation of the US Africa Command (AFRICOM) within the Department of Defense. Officials argued that it was a bureaucratic move designed to have a single command overseeing US military operations in nearly all of Africa (excluding Egypt) instead of dividing African countries among three unified commands.[16] By embedding State Department personnel within the hierarchy, the reorganization also would allow better coordination of US government programs in the region, bringing together security, governance, and development efforts (Piombo 2015). Beyond the relatively innocuous official justification, observers saw the creation of AFRICOM as motivated by underlying strategic concerns (Volman 2007). With rising oil prices and continuing instability in the Middle East, the United States was getting greater amounts of oil from Africa, especially Nigeria and Angola. Meanwhile, as explored in Chapter 12, the increasing involvement in Africa of China, driven in part by the need for oil to fuel its economic expansion, raised the possibility of direct competition with the United States. And the growing threat of international terrorism in Africa, discussed further later, was attracting significant attention and resources from US security officials.

AFRICOM was created in October 2007 and became operational a year later. Its creation prompted an immediate backlash among political leaders, academics, and journalists in both Africa and the United States. To some extent, the negative reaction reflected frustration that African leaders had been neither consulted nor involved in discussions (Burgess 2009; Forest and Crispin 2009). More substantively, though, critics had concerns about what AFRICOM meant for US policy in the region. The inclusion of development and humanitarian relief under the AFRICOM umbrella raised fears about the militarization of US policy and the dominance of security interests (Menkhaus 2009). Many Africans also had concerns about the US approach to counterterrorism, which was seen as a key motivating factor behind AFRICOM (Menkhaus 2009; Whitaker

2010b). Even beyond specific policies, many African leaders and publics worried about US hegemony in the international system (Burgess 2009). South Africa and other regional powers in particular saw AFRICOM as a threat to their own influence and sought to balance against that threat (Whitaker 2010b). An analysis of African news reports found that less aid-dependent countries with high economic growth were more critical of AFRICOM, suggesting that some leaders had more latitude to resist than others (LeVan 2010). Notably, there also was opposition to AFRICOM within the US government, especially the State Department, which had previously taken a lead on US policy toward Africa. More than just a turf war with the better-resourced Department of Defense, many career diplomats had spent years living in African countries and felt they had a better understanding of realities on the ground (Menkhaus 2009).

Bush administration officials clearly had not anticipated such a backlash and launched a "strategic communications" campaign to generate support for AFRICOM. Through a series of meetings and workshops with leaders, journalists, and academics, officials sought to reassure critics that AFRICOM was about partnership with African countries and did not seek to control them militarily. Even so, the message was vague and muddled at times, which did not help win support (Burgess 2009). Anti-AFRICOM rhetoric continued in Africa, with leaders in South Africa and Nigeria especially vocal, and country after country refused to host AFRICOM's headquarters. Among the few supporters was Liberian president Ellen Johnson Sirleaf, who circulated an opinion piece describing the initiative as an opportunity for Africa. Most other African leaders were defiant in their resistance. In May 2008, the Bush administration abandoned plans to put AFRICOM's headquarters in Africa and made permanent the location in Germany.

When Barack Obama came into office in early 2009, he went ahead with AFRICOM as planned, despite hopes in some circles that his administration would change course. Over time, with the decision not to locate a large US military headquarters within Africa and the realization that AFRICOM was not going away, resistance died down and African leaders began to accept the new command. With the exception of South African officials, many of whom remained suspicious and critical, leaders of many other African countries started to cooperate with AFRICOM and send their militaries to participate in its programs. Diplomatic outreach and basic pragmatism may have helped bring African leaders around to supporting AFRICOM (Burgess 2009), but the change of presidential administration likely also played a role. With his Kenyan roots and his first visit to the continent less than six months after being inaugurated,[17] Obama appeared to have a more cooperative approach than that of his predecessor. Once again, then, any policy changes from one presidential administration to another were incremental, even if perceptions among African leaders and publics shifted markedly.

Although the debate over AFRICOM has disappeared from headlines, some initial concerns expressed by its critics have started to materialize. Most obvious, the US military presence in Africa has increased dramatically. A 2015 report identified more than sixty US military outposts, port facilities, and access points in at least thirty-four African countries, though AFRICOM officials publicly acknowledged just eleven cooperative security locations along with the long-standing military base at Camp Lemmonier in Djibouti (Turse 2015). US military personnel are heavily involved in the fight against terrorist groups across the Horn of Africa and the Sahel region. In response to public demand in 2012 to "do something" about Joseph Kony and his Lord's Resistance Army, 100 US special operations forces were sent to the Central African Republic to advise Ugandan troops in their effort to capture members of that rebel group. The US military even got involved in the response to the 2014 Ebola epidemic in Liberia. Although many of these operations are supported by African governments and people, they have received relatively little attention from the American public. An ambush of US troops in Niger in October 2017 and the resulting deaths of four American soldiers garnered international headlines and prompted congressional and media investigations of US operations in the region. Indeed, as others have argued since even before the most recent tragedy, the increased involvement of the US military in Africa and the complex relationship among its security, government, and development goals warrant sustained monitoring and analysis (Piombo 2015).

The Global War on Terror

After terrorist attacks on the World Trade Center and the Pentagon on September 11, 2001, US foreign policy immediately adopted a new focus. In what became the most visible foreign policy initiative of the George W. Bush administration, the global war on terror at first concentrated on the Middle East, especially Afghanistan and Iraq, but second fronts soon opened in the Sahel and Horn of Africa. To be clear, African countries had been victims of international terrorism even before 9/11, including the 1980 bombing of the Norfolk hotel in Nairobi, Kenya,[18] and coordinated bombings of the US embassies in Kenya and Tanzania in 1998. Even so, instead of focusing on Africans as potential victims, the United States was primarily concerned about Africa as a possible breeding ground for terrorist activity that would threaten its interests around the world. As President Bush declared, "Every nation, in every region, now has a decision to make. Either you are with us, or you are with the terrorists" (Bush 2001).

In the context of the war on terror, US policymakers portrayed Africa as a region with high levels of poverty, weak and failed states, and growing mobilization of Muslim populations, all of which were seen as contributing factors to terrorism. This portrayal of Africa was oversimplified, however, and did not reflect the diversity of political and economic situations throughout the continent. Moreover, the underlying premise that these factors would cause terrorism was not subjected to greater scrutiny. If poverty causes terrorism, for example, we would expect much higher levels of terrorist activity in some of the poorest countries in the world, many of which are in Africa. It also is not clear that terrorists would prefer operating in countries with failed states given their need for a basic level of communications and transportation infrastructure to organize attacks. Perhaps most important, the reasons for the political mobilization of Muslims in many African countries have not been fully understood. In most cases, Muslim populations started to mobilize politically in response to local-level grievances, including historical economic and political marginalization. Hesitant moves toward democratization provided more political space for their mobilization. Over time, though, often for strategic expedience, leaders of some groups cultivated ties with broader terrorist networks and embraced radical ideologies (Dowd and Raleigh 2013). As the governments they were fighting gained US support, their adversaries also sought external backing. In some ways, then, Bush's "you're either with us or against us" pronouncement became a self-fulfilling prophecy.

Indeed, there was extensive pressure on African governments to cooperate with the United States in its war on terror (Whitaker 2007, 2010a). Policymakers were pushed to pass anti-terrorism legislation that would criminalize terrorist acts and make it easier for law enforcement and intelligence agencies to investigate possible terrorist cells. African governments also were pressured to share intelligence with the United States and to implement higher levels of screening at border crossing points. Moreover, as the US military presence increased around the world, leaders in Africa and other regions were pushed to sign bilateral immunity agreements that would protect US service members from being brought before international courts for war crimes. The US government promoted cooperation in these areas using a variety of incentives, including diplomatic pressure, public relations campaigns, and threats to suspend aid.

To support counterterrorism efforts in Africa, the United States launched several new programs starting in the early 2000s. Headquartered at the US military base in Djibouti since 2002, the Combined Joint Task Force–Horn of Africa (CJTF-HOA) supports militaries in that sub-region through training and short-term assistance in emergency situations. In a model that later was absorbed into AFRICOM, CJTF-HOA operations also included drilling water wells, building schools, and upgrading medical facilities in remote areas. The East Africa Counter-Terrorism Initiative, launched in 2003, provided funding and technical assistance to strengthen border security, enhance the counterterrorism capacity of police and judicial institutions, and promote counterterrorism financing legislation in six target countries. It was replaced in 2009 by the Partnership for East Africa Regional Counterterrorism (PREACT), which involves twice as many countries in these same activities and additionally supports efforts to reduce the appeal of radical ideologies. Since 2005, the Trans-Sahara Counterterrorism Partnership (TSCTP) has supported similar objectives in eleven countries in West Africa.

The response within Africa to US counterterrorism programs has been decidedly mixed.[19] Some leaders have embraced US counterterrorism efforts, particularly when facing their own opposition from terrorists or groups that could be labeled as such. Soon after 9/11, for example, Uganda's Yoweri Museveni pushed through counterterrorism legislation and successfully lobbied the US Department of State to add two Ugandan rebel groups to its list of designated terrorist organizations. Taking advantage of the opportunity to foster closer ties with the United States, his government contributed troops to the US-led coalition that invaded Iraq in 2003 and later to the US-backed African Union Mission in Somalia. In power since 1986, Museveni faced little opposition in a parliament stacked with supporters and even used counterterrorism measures to crack down on domestic political opponents (Whitaker 2010a). While Uganda's government may have been the most enthusiastic African supporter of the war on terror, authoritarian governments in Ethiopia, Sudan, and Rwanda, among others, also offered substantial cooperation, often with similarly mixed motives.

Some other African countries were more reluctant to cooperate with the United States in its war on terror. Leaders of South Africa, Kenya, Nigeria, Senegal, and Tanzania were among those who resisted key demands of US counterterrorism efforts, including passing anti-terrorism laws and signing bilateral immunity agreements. Interestingly, these countries were more democratic on average than others in the region, and their leaders often were responding to domestic political pressure (Whitaker 2010b). Many Africans were concerned that providing increased surveillance powers to police and security forces would undermine recently won democratic gains. They also worried about growing

US hegemony around the world. Some did not see terrorism as a major threat in the region and questioned the apparent prioritization of counterterrorism above issues like democracy and development. Elected leaders found support in resisting US demands in such contexts but often cooperated with US efforts behind the scenes. In Kenya, for example, the government resisted US pressure to pass an anti-terrorism bill for many years, even as it shared intelligence and investigated terrorist cells (Whitaker 2008). It was not that these countries supported terrorism, therefore, but rather that they advocated a different approach to counterterrorism than the one pursued by the Bush administration.

If Africans were hoping for an end to the war on terror when Barack Obama was inaugurated in 2009, they got it, if only in the name. The new administration adopted the term "overseas contingency operations" but continued to pursue similar policies to strengthen security forces, investigate and pursue terrorist groups in the region, and prevent radicalization. Under Obama, counterterrorism operations extended into more African countries, partly in response to the growing threat of groups such as al-Shabaab, al-Qaeda in the Maghreb, and Boko Haram. The tone of US policymakers changed and the language of partnership was embraced more often, but the underlying approach was the same. Whether because of the new tone or the increased threat, some previously reluctant countries became more interested in cooperating with US counterterrorism efforts. Among these was Kenya, which sent troops into Somalia to go after al-Shabaab in 2011 and passed counterterrorism legislation in 2012. Ironically, by then, the United States was less interested in working closely with Kenya because of pending international charges against its elected president for his alleged involvement in earlier post-election violence (Whitaker 2013). On the whole, though, the Obama administration received fairly strong counterterrorism cooperation from African governments, and the same has generally been true so far under the Trump administration.

Despite international attention to fighting terrorism since 2001, the threat in Africa has only increased. Two examples from West Africa illustrate the complexity of the problem, and Somalia's experience is discussed at the end of this chapter. In Mali, long-standing grievances among the semi-nomadic Tuareg community led to a renewed insurgency in the northern part of the country in 2007. It continued at a low level until 2011, when the overthrow of Libya's Muammar Qaddafi prompted the return to Mali of Tuareg fighters who had supported his regime and were now ousted along with their weapons. The perceived ineptness of the elected Malian government in dealing with this threat led to a military coup d'état in March 2012 and, after international and domestic pressure, the installation of an interim government a month later. In this context of uncertainty, two militant groups captured significant chunks of territory in the north: AQIM, an al-Qaeda affiliate that until then had operated mainly in Algeria, and Ansar Dine, a new group with roots in previous Tuareg rebellions but with connections to AQIM. When these groups seized half the country in January 2013, France (with US support) responded to Mali's request for military intervention and pushed back the extremists. French troops were replaced by a UN peacekeeping mission in July 2013, and elections were held soon thereafter, leading to a new round of talks with Tuareg separatists and a 2015 peace agreement. Although the situation has stabilized, the underlying grievances of people in northern Mali have yet to be fully addressed, and opportunistic militant groups continue to operate in the area. Several recent attacks, including against peacekeepers, demonstrate the continued threat of terrorism in Mali and neighboring countries. In 2017, with donor support and UN endorsements, the governments of Burkina Faso, Chad, Mali, Mauritania, and Niger launched the Group of Five Sahel Joint Force to work together to address ongoing instability and terrorism in the region.

A similar dynamic has played out in Nigeria. Motivated initially by political and economic grievances in the marginalized northeastern part of the country, Boko Haram rose to prominence in 2009 with a series of attacks on civilian targets in that area and in the capital city of Abuja. The most famous was in April 2014, when the militant group kidnapped more than 300 schoolgirls in Chibok, prompting a global social media campaign (#bringbackourgirls). Boko Haram became the most deadly terrorist organization in the world, causing more deaths in 2014 than the Islamic State of Iraq and Syria (ISIS) (Institute for Economics and Peace 2015). As the Nigerian military went after Boko Haram, eventually collaborating with Chad, Cameroon, and Niger under the Multinational Joint Task Force, the group's leadership fostered connections with other terrorist organizations like AQIM, presumably in an effort to recruit fighters and mobilize resources. In March 2015, Boko Haram leader Abubakar Shekau pledged allegiance to ISIS.[20] The Nigerian government's apparent inability to deal with this threat was a key reason for President Goodluck Jonathan's defeat in the March 2015 election, which was delayed for six weeks due to insecurity (see Chapter 6). Under successor Muhammadu Buhari, a former military officer who campaigned on a security platform, and with intensified regional cooperation, Boko Haram has lost territory but continues to mount periodic attacks, including another mass kidnapping of schoolgirls in early 2018.

In each of these cases, then, unaddressed grievances at the grassroots led to the emergence of a militant group that later reached out to international terrorist networks for recruits and support, often adopting their ideologies in the process. Importantly, this is not the typical narrative about terrorism in Africa put forth by many journalists and analysts (Dowd and Raleigh 2013). The more common narrative describes a global Islamist threat to Western interests that seeks to operate in ungoverned territories providing a safe haven for extremism. This focus on a global threat is promoted by US policymakers, whose primary concern is US security, but is also convenient for African leaders, who blame groups like al-Qaeda and ISIS for violence in their countries instead of acknowledging the shortcomings of their own administrations in addressing political and economic woes (Dowd and Raleigh 2013). There are clear parallels to the Cold War era, when African leaders often attributed insurgencies to a global communist threat, thus attracting US military and economic support, instead of addressing the underlying complaints that contributed to anti-government mobilization. As the current situations in Mali, Nigeria, Somalia, and elsewhere demonstrate, local grievances often create the context for rebel mobilization, while international networks can provide the tools, resources, and ideologies to further insurgent aims, and to fight against them. Once again, Bush's categorization of global actors into terrorists and their opponents seems somehow prophetic.

Even as the United States and African countries continue to deal with the threat of terrorism, there are risks associated with counterterrorism activities. Just as elsewhere in the world, African governments, including those in Uganda, Kenya, and Nigeria, have been accused of violating people's civil liberties in the pursuit of terrorist connections. People have been detained without charge, prevented from seeing lawyers, and harassed for wearing certain types of clothing. Leaders in Uganda and Zimbabwe have used anti-terrorism laws to go after domestic political opponents who have no credible connection to militant organizations (Whitaker 2007). Much like during the Cold War, the emphasis on counterterrorism has led the United States to collaborate with authoritarian governments that would otherwise face pressure to embrace democratic reforms. Uganda and Ethiopia, for example, are strong allies in US counterterrorism efforts but have authoritarian leaders who restrict civil liberties and punish opponents. US counterterrorism officials even have cooperated at times with Sudan, whose leader faces international charges for crimes against humanity. In the meantime, some of Africa's more democratic countries have been reluctant to cooperate in the US approach to counterterrorism despite shared interests and values. As the United States is emphasizing counterterrorism and security even more so under the Trump administration, many Africans continue to be concerned about the perceived neglect of other important priorities like democracy and development.

Although policies toward Africa have changed only marginally from one administration to another, African views of the United States have varied under different presidents. Many Africans supported Clinton, despite his administration's effective disengagement from the continent for several years, most egregiously during the 1994 Rwandan genocide. In contrast, George W. Bush was accused of securitizing US policy with programs such as AFRICOM, even as critics overlooked his administration's massive investment in public health. These core policies did not change under Obama, particularly the emphasis on counterterrorism, though he supplemented them with initiatives to train young African leaders[21] and promote electrification, and he hosted the 2014 United States–Africa Leaders Summit.[22] These low-cost, high-profile programs had an outsized impact on perceptions, and Africans were generally supportive of the first US president with African roots. Although the Trump administration has not articulated a clear policy toward Africa, there has been more emphasis on the military and less on human rights and democracy (Page 2017), provoking criticism among civil society actors in Africa.

Arguably, what changes more than policy from president to president is rhetoric. Both Clinton and Obama had a way of addressing African audiences that built a sense of connection, while Bush's "you're either with us or against us" philosophy rubbed many the wrong way. The effects were perhaps most obvious in African opposition to AFRICOM, which decreased once Obama came into office. Given Trump's own reputation for harsh rhetoric, with little regard for diplomatic consequences, it was only a matter of time before one of his statements (or tweets) provoked controversy in Africa. One such moment came in January 2018, when it was widely reported that Trump had described nations in Africa as "shithole countries" in a meeting about immigration with several members of Congress. African leaders briefly expressed outrage and demanded an apology, but weeks later, during a visit to the region by Secretary of State Rex Tillerson, said the statement was history and they were focusing instead on areas of cooperation. This pattern suggests a lesson for all US presidents: just as important as policy details is how a policy is packaged. To the extent that Africans can be made to feel respected and included, they are more likely to support US policy and work toward common goals.

Shaping US Policy Toward Africa

Over the years, in part to counteract the crisis-oriented approach to US policy in Africa, some groups have sought to build a constituency for the region in the United States. Recognizing the success of similar constituencies for Israel and various European countries (Ireland, Armenia) in shaping US policy in those places, these organizations have lobbied US officials for favorable policies and resources and launched public education campaigns to raise the profile of Africa in policymaking circles. Early efforts to build a pro-Africa constituency started even before independence in most African countries but encountered controversies at home. The Council on African Affairs was created in 1937, for example, but disbanded during the McCarthy era in 1956 after being accused of "subversive activities." In the 1960s, the American Negro Leadership Conference on Africa fell apart less than five years after its creation when rumors circulated of connections to the Central Intelligence Agency.

Several Africa-related organizations have roots in the global movement against apartheid in South Africa. Three such groups—the American Committee on Africa (ACOA, 1953), the Africa Fund (1966), and the Africa Policy Information Center (1978)—came together in 2001 under the umbrella of Africa Action, which sought to lobby policymakers and raise public awareness about issues in the region. An offshoot of ACOA with ties to several Christian denominations, the Washington Office on Africa similarly monitored congressional bills and promoted favorable legislation on Africa. In recent years, these organizations have faced fund-raising challenges that have limited their operations and visibility,[23] though activists in their networks continue to lobby on African issues.[24] Two other long-standing organizations mobilized African Americans to support African causes: Africare (1971) is an African American–led nonprofit organization that continues to support development projects throughout the continent, while TransAfrica (1977) is an advocacy organization that brings together diaspora groups broadly defined to influence US policy toward Africa and the Caribbean.

In the 1990s, efforts such as the Constituency for Africa (1990) and the Corporate Council on Africa (1992), among others, sought to broaden the base of support for Africa and to strengthen commercial ties. This was a shift from earlier organizations, which were focused primarily on human rights and sustainable development. Starting in 1997, the National Summit on Africa organized a series of regional meetings to discuss US policy toward the region, culminating in a high-profile event in Washington, D.C., in 2000 that attracted multiple heads of state and thousands of participants. These organizations made the case that the United States has clear economic interests in Africa and successfully lobbied for the AGOA legislation. Even so, critics were concerned about the top-down nature of these groups and the heavy influence of corporate interests, especially as compared to earlier Africa-related advocacy organizations that were dominated by left-leaning activists. The sponsorship of companies like Exxon Mobil, Chevron, and Daimler-Chrysler in particular raised questions about the prioritization of extractive industries over other economic sectors in Africa.

Efforts to build a constituency for Africa in the United States face many challenges, including fund-raising, organization, and duplication of efforts. Groups compete with one another for donations and involvement from the relatively small portion of the American public who care about Africa, and their interests often are competing. Few Americans have traveled to the continent or learned a lot about it in school. In addition, unlike a single country such as Israel or Armenia, the diverse continent of Africa lacks a "natural constituency" within the United States. African Americans have historical ties to the region, but those connections were centuries ago and the brutal institution of slavery did not allow people to maintain contact. Moreover, relations between Africans and African Americans are fraught with misunderstanding, suspicion, and stereotypes generated mainly by media portrayals of both groups. Like other Americans, many African Americans do not understand or want to associate with the problems they hear about in Africa.[25] On the other side, African immigrants to the United States often distance themselves from African Americans, whom they associate with various social ills.[26] While it is important to mobilize a diverse group of activists on Africa-related issues, therefore, it is not clear that the constituency will ever be as large or as focused as the pro-Israel lobby. And given the complications that can emerge when the United States becomes more interested in a country or a region, as illustrated by Somalia in this chapter's case study, there is some question as to whether supporters should advocate more US attention to Africa.

In the end, as shown throughout this chapter, US policy toward Africa is motivated by a mix of factors. Security remains a top priority in the region and helps explain both the decline in US engagement in the 1990s, after the communist threat disappeared, and renewed attention to Africa in the 2000s, as the terrorist threat increased. More recently, China has emerged as a key player in Africa (see Chapter 12), driving a sense of competition for influence and resources that has motivated US initiatives such as AFRICOM (Campbell 2008; Carmody and Owusu 2007). The United States has not given up on the quest for freedom and democracy in Africa, however, even if this often takes a backseat to security concerns. US involvement in multilateral interventions in Somalia, imposition of targeted sanctions against Zimbabwe's leaders, and support of democratic institutions in places like Kenya, among other examples, reflect a belief in international cooperation to pursue these goals. US policy toward Africa also is shaped by commercial interests, especially the demand for oil and other minerals, which leads to inconsistent application of policy preferences depending on a country's resource endowments. Finally, the tone with which US policies are implemented shapes African reactions and willingness to collaborate. Instead of relying on a single theory to understand US-African relations, therefore, it is important to consider the range of factors that influence interactions on both sides.

Case Study: US Policy in Somalia

After more than twenty years in power in Somalia, Siad Barre was overthrown in 1991 in the context of a broader civil war. In the ensuing power vacuum, various strongmen (or "warlords") competed for control over territory and people. An ill-timed drought during this conflict led to widespread famine by early 1992 and the use of food as a weapon of war with which armed groups rewarded supporters and punished opponents. Horrifying media images of starving children and dead bodies led to mounting calls for the international community to respond. Having been the third largest recipient of US aid throughout the 1980s, Somalia posed the first real test of US policy in Africa after the Cold War. The crisis came on the heels of the creation of safe havens in northern Iraq to protect the Kurds in 1991, which generated optimism about the potential for multilateral cooperation to address humanitarian crises. In April 1992, the Security Council authorized the United Nations Operation in Somalia, which transitioned from observers to the deployment of Pakistani security personnel in October.

In early December 1992, under Operation Restore Hope, the United States sent 25,000 troops into Somalia to work with UNOSOM under a Unified Task Force (UNITAF). The mission was authorized by President George H. W. Bush, who no longer had to worry about the domestic political implications of a foreign intervention, having lost his bid for reelection the previous month. Soon after his successor, Bill Clinton, took office on January 20, 1993, the UNITAF operation in Somalia reached its peak, with 37,000 troops controlling roughly 40 percent of the country's territory (UN Department of Public Information 1997). Food was getting to people once again and the worst of the famine was over, but continued insecurity and violence raised questions about what would happen once foreign troops left. Under strong pressure from UN Secretary-General Boutros Boutros-Ghali, Clinton—an idealistic former governor with little foreign policy experience—soon endorsed a nation-building mission to restore peace and stability and to prevent future suffering. In May 1993, UNOSOM II was launched to establish a secure environment for the delivery of aid by disarming militants and seeking reconciliation among the various factions (United Nations Department of Public Information 1997).

As the peacekeeping operation shifted focus, attitudes in Somalia toward the presence of foreign troops changed. Militant groups had opposed the intervention from the onset, but civilians also started to believe that UN and US troops were becoming combatants in the broader civil war. Many were concerned that foreign troops failed to understand Somali society, particularly the high respect given to elders. On June 5, 1993, UN peacekeepers were attacked by troops of militant commander Mohammed Aidid, and twenty-four Pakistanis were killed. The next day, the United Nations Security Council authorized the arrest of Aidid, prompting an intense manhunt. On July 12, US helicopters fired missiles into a compound where Aidid was believed to be hiding, killing more than fifty people. Many of the dead were Habr Gidr clan elders, including some who were complicit in attacks on UN peace-keepers and others who opposed such actions (Bowden 2000). Aidid was not at the meeting. This tragic mistake had the effect of solidifying opposition to the UN operation among Somalis in Mogadishu (Bowden 2000). Aidid's forces increased their attacks on US targets, resulting in several deaths and injuries.

It was in this context that US forces launched a mission on October 3, 1993, to arrest two of Aidid's lieutenants. In an incident that became widely known as Black Hawk Down, thanks to a detailed book (Bowden 1999) and a subsequent movie (Scott 2001), two US helicopters were shot down by rocket-propelled grenades. US and UN troops were sent to res-cue the dead and wounded as Somalis angry with the presence of foreign troops rushed toward the crash sites. In the ensuing Battle of Mogadishu, eighteen Americans were killed, along with one Pakistani and one Malaysian, and one American was taken prisoner by Aidid's forces. Hun-dreds of Somalis were killed, including both militants and civilians.

Just as important to US policy as the tragic battle was its aftermath, during which photos emerged of jubilant Somalis dragging the dead bod-ies of two American soldiers through the streets of Mogadishu. As these images circulated internationally through the media, the backlash in the United States was swift and severe, with everyone from members of Congress to average citizens questioning US involvement and strategy in Somalia (Lyons and Samatar 1995). The United States immediately stopped pursuing Aidid and put in motion plans to withdraw forces from Somalia by March 1994. Secretary of Defense Les Aspin was forced to resign. The United Nations followed a year later, withdrawing the last of its troops in March 1995. UNOSOM II was officially over, with its goals of reconciliation and democracy far from being realized.

Somalia was left alone in the second half of the 1990s, with no for-eign troops and minimal attention from an international community still reeling from its involvement there. Despite the absence of a central government and periodic violence between rival militant groups, the overall security situation was much better and there were few civilian deaths. The main reason for this relative stability was a complex network of formal and informal institutions at the local level, creating a situation of "governance without government" (Menkhaus 2006). As commercial opportunities increased, leading Somali businesspeople refused to pay protection money to the warlords, instead buying out their militiamen and putting them under the control of sharia courts. By the early 2000s, the most powerful militias in Somalia were private security forces controlled by businesspeople (Menkhaus 2006). Driven in part by lack of regulation and an influx of cash from the Somali diaspora, many of whom had fled as refugees, Somalia's economy flourished: Coca-Cola opened a bottling plant, private universities were established, and cell phone companies developed one of the most competitive markets in the region.

US attention to Somalia rose again after September 11, 2001, with the fear that the stateless country would provide a safe haven to terrorists like Osama bin Laden. A renewed peace process hosted in Kenya led to the 2004 creation of a transitional federal government, though its officials initially refused to move to Mogadishu because of rising insecurity, opting instead for the smaller town of Baidoa. As a rival network of Islamist leaders gained strength in many areas of Somalia, officials of the new transitional government sought support from international allies, including their connections in Ethiopia. In a move that caused tension within the US government, the CIA backed an ill-conceived alliance of warlords against the Islamists instead of the newly established transitional government (Lyman 2009). As State Department officials had warned, this decision sparked renewed anti-American sentiment, generating further support for the Islamists.

In June 2006, the Islamic Courts Union took power in Mogadishu, even as fighting continued in the countryside. ICU control was welcomed by many Somalis, who appreciated the restoration of law and order after years of insecurity and violence (Barnes and Hassan 2007). The ICU resumed long-neglected services such as trash collection and reopened the Mogadishu airport and seaport. It did not take long, though, for frustration to grow over the group's draconian social policies, including bans on alcohol and khat (a stimulant plant chewed by many Somalis). Divisions also emerged within the ICU, which was little more than a loose alliance of sharia courts brought together by their opposition to the transitional government. Over time, hard-liners within the ICU leadership prevailed and used the language of jihad to call on supporters to help realize irredentist dreams of a greater Somalia (see Chapter 2).

Their anti-Ethiopian rhetoric tapped into long-standing tensions between the two countries and attracted new recruits.

As threats to its territory and interests increased, neighboring Ethiopia responded. In December 2006, Ethiopian troops invaded Somalia and ousted the ICU from Mogadishu. The move was supported by the United States, which was concerned that some ICU hard-liners had terrorist connections. As ICU leaders and militants fled the capital city, the US military bombed their locations in southern Somalia and pursued high-value targets. Some people were later caught by Kenyan authorities and reportedly rendered to Ethiopia for covert interrogation by US intelligence officials (Human Rights Watch 2008). The United States called for a regional peacekeeping operation to support the weak Somali government. The African Union Mission in Somalia was authorized by the UN Security Council and deployed in March 2007 with troops from Uganda and Burundi and funding mainly from the United States.

Although the ICU fell quickly, its most extreme elements soon regrouped and launched an insurgency known as al-Shabaab ("the Youth"). The militant group has waged a brutal war against the Somali government and its AMISOM backers since 2007. Shifting from its initial anti–foreign nationalist stance to a more universal jihadist agenda, al-Shabaab attracted a steady stream of followers, including some young Somalis from the diaspora. By 2011, when the region was once again afflicted with severe drought, al-Shabaab controlled more than half of Somalia. Its obstructionist policies, coupled with the reluctance of humanitarian agencies to work in al-Shabaab-controlled areas,[27] prevented famine relief from reaching huge parts of the country, contributing to the shocking death toll of more than 250,000 people (Menkhaus 2012). During these years, piracy off the coast of Somalia also reached a peak, though there is little evidence of al-Shabaab involvement. Even so, the general climate of poverty and insecurity in Somalia likely drove many young men to seek opportunities with piracy operations or the militant group.

In late 2011, in response to rising attacks within its borders, Kenya sent troops into Somalia to join the fight against al-Shabaab.[28] Soon thereafter, the leaders of al-Shabaab pledged allegiance to al-Qaeda, presumably in an effort to garner resources and recruits.[29] Even as the group lost territory to the AMISOM-backed transitional federal government, al-Shabaab staged several high-profile terrorist attacks, most notably a 2010 attack on World Cup watchers in Kampala, Uganda; a 2013 attack on Westgate Mall in Nairobi, Kenya; and a 2015 attack on a university in Garissa, Kenya. The decision by al-Shabaab to take the struggle into Kenya provoked heated debate in that country about the military intervention in Somalia and reignited long-standing tensions between the government and Muslim communities (Anderson and McKnight 2015). The situation came to the fore again in 2016 when Kenyan officials announced plans to close all Somali refugee camps due to security concerns and send home nearly 300,000 Somali refugees, some of whom had been in Kenya for thirty years (Whitaker 2016). Although the camp-closure decision was later blocked by Kenya's high court, the situation remains precarious for Somalis living there.

Meanwhile, in Somalia, the conflict simmers while citizens try to carry on their lives. Some Somalis from the diaspora have returned to help rebuild, while others remain outside and send millions of dollars in remittances. In 2012, the transitional federal government was replaced by a permanent federal government, whose president was elected by a diverse parliament. Hassan Sheikh Mohamud's government included several moderates from the ICU and enjoyed support at home and abroad. Many countries restored diplomatic ties and reopened embassies. Continuing insecurity thwarted plans to hold national popular elections in 2016, resulting in the use of a complicated electoral college system in early 2017. The incumbent president was defeated by challenger Mohamed Abdullahi Mohamed, a diaspora returnee with dual US-Somali citizenship, and turned over power peacefully. Despite these promising developments, periodic attacks on civilians, government officials, and AMISOM troops are a constant reminder that peace has not yet been realized. This point was made abundantly clear in October 2017 when a massive truck bomb in a crowded area of Mogadishu killed more than 500 people, putting Somalia back in international headlines. An offshoot of al-Shabaab has pledged allegiance to ISIS (Kriel and Duggan 2015), raising the prospect of increased and more severe attacks as the factions compete for attention and recruits (Conrad and Greene 2015). As Somalis continue to search for solutions, foreign actors—including the United States—cannot ignore the role they have played in undermining stability in Somalia. If the late 1990s are any indication, Somalia may be better off when the United States and the international community more broadly keep their distance.

Notes

1. Totals here are in constant 2015 US dollars.
2. For a thorough yet concise explanation of the various factors that led to the violence in Rwanda, see Newbury 1995.
3. US policy toward Cuba is a constant subject of political debates in southern Florida, for example, even at the local level.
4. Seven-term Michigan congressman Howard Wolpe had a PhD in political science with a focus on Africa and published two books in this field before entering politics. He chaired the Africa Subcommittee of the House Foreign Affairs

Committee for ten years. Other Africa subcommittee chairs who took a special interest in the region were Senator Russ Feingold of Wisconsin and Congressman Donald Payne of New Jersey.

5. Under a special rule in subsequent iterations of AGOA, designated less developed African countries can use fabric manufactured anywhere in the world unless it is in "abundant supply" within sub-Saharan Africa.

6. In 2017, Seychelles "graduated" from AGOA and was no longer eligible for benefits because its per capita income put it in the category of high-income countries as defined by the World Bank.

7. Extensive data about US trade with AGOA-eligible countries, both in total and individually, can be found on the AGOA website at http://www.agoa.info.

8. Up-to-date data about HIV/AIDS globally and within Africa can be obtained from the World Health Organization at http://www.who.int/topics/hiv_aids/en, and from the Joint United Nations Programme on HIV and AIDS (UNAIDS) at http://www.unaids.org. These are the sources of the statistics provided here.

9. Prevalence rates are more reliable now than they were in the early years of the HIV/AIDS crisis, when they were based primarily on tests at antenatal clinics (among a population who were obviously sexually active, thus likely inflating the estimates). Even so, the rates should still be treated with caution. UNAIDS prevalence rates are extrapolated from a small sample population and are presented as an estimate within a wider range.

10. Note that most studies count a child as orphaned after losing just one parent.

11. Former South African president Thabo Mbeki and his health minister in particular attracted widespread criticism for questioning the link between HIV and AIDS and for suggesting that antiretroviral drugs were toxic (Mbali 2004; Nattrass 2007). In a country with the highest number of HIV-positive individuals, his administration's rejection of scientific evidence was seen as irresponsible and deadly, and it likely contributed to the further spread of the virus.

12. Bush had not previously shown much interest in the issue of AIDS in Africa. Some people saw the announcement as an effort to build bridges with African American leaders who were critical of his domestic policies.

13. Up-to-date data on PEPFAR's results are available at http://www.pepfar.gov.

14. After research demonstrated that noncircumcised men were significantly more likely to contract HIV, many countries in eastern and southern Africa started promoting voluntary male circumcision in communities that do not traditionally engage in this practice.

15. Up-to-date information about ACOTA and other programs under the GPOI can be found at https://www.state.gov/t/pm/gpi/gpoi/index.htm.

16. Before AFRICOM, the US European Command was responsible for US military operations in West Africa, the US Central Command was responsible for East Africa, and the US Pacific Command was responsible for island countries in the Indian Ocean.

17. President Obama visited Ghana in July 2009 and gave a speech to the parliament there that was covered around the continent and world. Although most Africans were excited to have a US president visit their continent so early in his presidency, many Kenyans were disappointed that he did not choose his father's native country.

18. The 1980 attack on a Kenyan hotel by Palestinian militants was seen by some observers as revenge for Kenya's support of a 1976 Israeli military raid on the airport in Entebbe, Uganda, where Palestinian hijackers were holding hostage more than a hundred passengers from an Air France plane they had diverted a week earlier. Most of the hostages were freed and most of the hijackers were killed in the raid.

19. Despite increasing use of the language of partnership over time, these clearly have been US-led programs.

20. In August 2016, ISIS announced a new leader for Boko Haram and then Abubakar Shekau claimed to still be in control, suggesting some sort of leadership battle within the group.

21. More information can be found about the Young African Leaders Initiative (YALI), which seeks to train Africans in leadership, entrepreneurship, and professional development, at http://yali.state.gov.

22. The 2014 summit in Washington, D.C., was seen as a direct (if delayed) US response to the Forum on China-Africa Cooperation (FOCAC), which has held six high-profile meetings between Chinese and African leaders dating back to 2000 in Beijing. In his remarks at the 2014 summit, President Obama implied that the United States is a better partner than China to Africa (Sun 2015).

23. For more on the history of Africa Action and its component organizations, and its more recent struggles to raise funding, see https://africaactiontransition.com.

24. The independent *AfricaFocus Bulletin*, for example, grew out of Africa Action and continues to provide regular email updates to more than 5,000 recipients on pressing issues in the region.

25. For a fascinating and controversial articulation of such sentiments, see Richburg 1997. As a reporter for the *Washington Post*, Richburg was posted in several African conflict zones during the 1990s.

26. For a fictional account that describes the warnings many African immigrants get from their family members, see Oguine 2000.

27. Even where al-Shabaab granted access, aid agencies were hesitant to provide relief for fear of being charged under US laws with assisting a terrorist organization (Menkhaus 2012).

28. The Kenyan invasion of Somalia was initially a unilateral move, but its troops soon joined AMISOM, which was approved by both the African Union and the United Nations.

29. Al-Shabaab reportedly tried to become an affiliate of al-Qaeda even earlier but was rejected by Osama bin Laden for being too brutal against the Somali population.

11
Africa and Europe

The great complexity of relations between Africa and Europe reinforces the notion that Africa's international relations can usefully be studied only through a theoretical lens. The contemporary European Union has twenty-eight member states, but the region of Europe also includes Norway, Sweden, the non-EU Balkan states, and Slavic Eastern European countries. The former colonizers have deeper interests and obligations in Africa than other European states. Africa, meanwhile, is organized into fifty-four independent states, grouped into both subregional organizations and the African Union. Aside from the sheer number of possible state-to-state and intergovernmental relationships, countless nongovernmental organizations on the two continents work both below and through bilateral relationships, bringing social change to both world regions. Likewise, private business organizations operating across the Mediterranean divide sometimes draw upon state support but just as often try to avoid it in their pursuit of profits.

Realists focus on the interests of regimes and states of the two continents, inevitably favoring the analysis of bilateral relations between African and European states. Neo-Marxists (e.g., Bond 2006) just as predictably emphasize private capital interests in the more developed region (Europe) and how these reinforce the marginal status and poverty of Africa. The liberal perspective on Afro-European relations is paradoxical: this perspective surely underlies the most visible European initiatives undertaken in Africa, including development through international aid, the promotion of multiparty democracy and human rights, and encouragement for regionalization of African continental affairs. Yet the liberal perspective is nearly always implicit rather than explicit in the

285

ever-increasing number of policy statements on Africa arising in Europe. From an African perspective, the embrace of liberal-oriented policy prescriptions is also paradoxical: some African leaders and citizens remain skeptical about the universality of the multiparty political model, the promise of foreign aid and investment to stimulate sustainable development, and even the preeminence of human rights above other goals. As for subregional and regional integration, this is a preoccupation more of elites than of ordinary African citizens, who are concerned chiefly about the material circumstances of their lives. Despite doubts from both regions, then, a liberal agenda of democratization, development through cooperation, and regional integration undergirds Afro-European relations.

A constructivist perspective is perhaps most valuable in helping understand the essence—if any such thing exists—of Afro-European relations. One can make a strong case that the legacy of colonialism remains a critical variable in the identities of both Africans and Europeans more than sixty years after decolonization began (in Sudan) and more than twenty years after the process ended (with South Africa's liberation from minority rule). The centuries-long slave trade followed by seventy-odd years of European colonial exploitation continues to bear heavily on the normative responsibilities felt in both Africa and Europe. Europeans surely see their extension of aid and cooperation to Africa as the repayment of an obligation created by their exploitation of Africa; Africans, in general, feel just as strongly that Europe owes them a debt for the same reason.[1]

There is strong ambiguity on both sides of the Mediterranean in terms of identity. Africans see themselves both as victims of European imperialism and economic exploitation and as self-liberators who fought hard to win their independence. Europeans surely bear the burden of being past oppressors, yet they also see themselves as Africa's benefactors and protectors. This paternalistic, if subconscious, identity is a continuation of attitudes from the colonial era, when the "civilizing mission" figured significantly in European justifications for domination. The liberal projects that Europeans pursue in Africa, especially human rights promotion, reflect the Enlightenment culture. Even today these animate Europe's historical sense of mission. On the African side, a sense of cultural distinctiveness and pride tempers Africans' willingness to cooperate with Europe on the terms of the donors, yet many also express a frank admiration for European culture (e.g., Achebe 2012).

The special relationships that the ex-metropoles have long sought to maintain with their former colonies are the most obvious manifestation of the colonial legacy. Such relationships are reinforced by the use of English, French, Portuguese, or Spanish as official languages in all the countries of sub-Saharan Africa.[2] France, in particular, has long sought to maintain economic and political influence over its former African colonies through a series of arrangements. Britain's efforts were considerably more halfhearted, as discussed later. Britain has, however, employed the Commonwealth as an umbrella organization under which it has sought to group all its former colonies, including those in Africa. The other former European colonizers were all supplanted as the external patrons of their former colonies because they lacked the economic wherewithal to play the role of external benefactor.

At independence Africans clearly felt ambivalent about the residual colonial aspects of these special relationships. On the one hand, newly independent African countries clearly needed the continuation of European cooperation after independence. Most had only a handful of university graduates and lacked the trained civil servants to run modern states. Individual African elites had also developed strong affinities with the metropolitan capitals, where many had lived and trained. On the other hand, African populations and elites yearned for de facto as well as de jure independence from European colonizers. The retention of European military officers, public officials, private capitalists, and landowners following independence was naturally irksome to Africa's newly independent populations. Yet only in one extreme case—that of Guinea under Sékou Touré—did an African country immediately cut all ties with the former metropole following a peaceful accession to independence. Links also were cut by the former Portuguese colonies following their respective long liberation wars. Most African countries tried to build up their local cadres before gradually reducing the European presence in their administrations. Some others, notably many former French colonies, maintained fulsome cooperation with the former metropole. Large expatriate European communities also remained after decolonization in a few countries, like Côte d'Ivoire and Kenya.

One broad trend in Afro-European relations has been a decline in the special relationships between European countries and their former colonies over time. Even pro-Western African states sought to diversify their European partners. The Scandinavian states, Germany, and other European partners also began to offset the beneficial influence of the former colonial metropoles. Tanzania, notably, developed a close aid relationship with Denmark, Norway, and Sweden. From the late 1960s through the end of the 1980s, many African states sought economic and military aid from the formerly communist Eastern-bloc states and China (see Chapters 3 and 12). Moreover, France and French corporations have developed significant political and business interests in countries like Nigeria and Angola, which are not former French colonies. Likewise,

Britain has developed significant relationships with Rwanda and Mozambique and other historically non-anglophone African states. These patterns have expanded the autonomy of African states, giving them more choice in their sources of foreign aid and investment.

A second long-term trend in Afro-European relations is the general reduction in European influence in Africa. This development owes to a number of historical developments. The two superpowers competed for influence in Africa from the late 1950s through the late 1980s. US political and economic interests in many parts of the continent have since persisted, supplanting some of Europe's former influence. During the height of the structural adjustment era in the 1980s (see Chapter 4), an outsized US stake in the International Monetary Fund and World Bank amplified US influence in Africa. The successive rise of Japan, then China, and more recently India has given Africa a new set of economic partners (see Chapter 12). China's economy had grown from the fifth largest in the world in 1960 to the second largest by 2010, and its influence in Africa has increased accordingly. By comparison, the economies of European states excepting Germany have been relatively stagnant, diminishing their potential for aid and investment. Despite the common perception to the contrary, African countries have been developing at significant rates since the 1990s. They thus need European assistance less than in the past. The debt crisis of the 1980s has now mostly passed, and the development of human capital in Africa has recently accelerated.

A third trend in Afro-European relations tends to reinforce the previous two: the gradual regionalization of European aid, cultural influence, and political engagement. Most significant, an ever-greater portion of foreign aid from Europe is given through the machinery of the European Union rather than as bilateral aid from states. The percentage of total European aid (bilateral and multilateral) disbursed through the EU institutions has increased from less than 1 percent in 1960 to 19 percent in 2000 to 48 percent in 2016. Further, a growing portion of aid given by individual EU states flows through African multilateral institutions. Aid given by EU states and institutions through the African Development Fund and the African Development Bank increased from less than $10 million in 1973 to about $1.17 billion in 2016, representing about 9 percent of total European bilateral and EU aid (Organization for Economic Cooperation and Development 2018). The EU is taking the lead in other areas as well. The European Instrument for Democracy and Human Rights (EIDHR) (and its predecessors) has promoted its titular values in Africa and elsewhere since the 1990s. For 2014–2020, the organization has a budget of $1.84 billion (European Instrument for Democracy and Human Rights 2017).[3] In Africa, the organization has taken the lead in monitoring elections for Europe and supports a host of local human rights, civic education, free press, and other civil society organizations. As a result, individual European countries feel less need to support such programs in Africa.

Several of these themes are developed in the remainder of this chapter. The first section examines the bilateral relations between specific European states, especially the former colonizers, and Africa's newly independent states and South Africa. It explores the evolution of the policies of individual European states over time, and how African leaders have reacted to these policies. The second section outlines some elements of the European Union's relations with Africa. African leaders have grown accustomed to dealing with the EU as its importance has steadily grown compared to that of individual European states. Even when individual European countries take a leading role in Africa, they prefer to have the approval of the EU. This section demonstrates both that Europe's agenda for Africa has grown wider and that Africa has gained more assurance in negotiating with Europe. The case study examines the role of France in Côte d'Ivoire from independence to 2011, when France was directly implicated in the displacement of Ivorian president Laurent Gbagbo from power. The case shows that the historical interest of former colonizers in Africa remains in place, but also that the EU and the AU have taken a larger role in mediating the activities of the former metropoles in Africa.

Bilateral Engagements Following Decolonization

For most African states, bilateral relationships with the former metropoles and other European countries represented their most important foreign contacts in the first years after independence. Exceptions to this generalization included Liberia and Zaire,[4] which both developed close relations with the United States after 1960. Other exceptions included the African states that officially adopted Marxism-Leninism in the 1970s, though even most of these continued to receive most of their economic foreign assistance from Western Europe. Most former British and French colonies remained dependent upon their former metropoles for technical, economic, and security assistance. As Britain's importance for anglophone African states faded beginning in the 1960s, the gap was filled increasingly by other European countries and the United States. The remainder of this section is divided into four parts. The first two deal with the approaches of Britain and France, respectively; the third deals other individual European countries, including other former colonizers; and the fourth categorizes the varying approaches of independent African countries to managing their European relationships.

Britain in Africa

As of the 1950s, the United Kingdom had the most colonies in Africa, including several of the largest in terms of population (Nigeria, Sudan, Tanzania, Kenya). Accordingly, one might well have expected Britain to have the greatest impact on African affairs following the advent of independence, but this was not to be. Instead, Britain rather quickly divested itself of most responsibilities for the development or security of African states that it had formerly colonized. By 1965, aid from the United States to sub-Saharan Africa ($248 million) had surpassed that of Britain ($210 million) and approached that of France ($258 million). Ten years later, British aid to sub-Saharan Africa ($132 million) was less than one-third that of France ($591 million) (Organization for Economic Cooperation and Development 2018). Britain also minimized its military and political role in the region, except for in Zimbabwe, as discussed later.

Britain's devolution of power to local authorities in Africa during decolonization was characterized by two paradoxes. First, Britain had accepted the inevitability of granting independence to its colonies, and yet for various reasons it attempted to suppress most nationalist movements. As one sympathetic interpreter recalled, Britain had a long experience with decolonization beginning with the American Revolution and accelerating after the end of World War I in the Middle East (Nielsen 1969). He claimed that "once India, Pakistan, and Ceylon became independent [after World War II], British administration urgently began to consider guidelines for the decolonization of Africa and methods for controlling its pace" (1969: 32). Indeed, British internal debates about decolonization after World War II were about the timing and modalities. The fact that Britain's African colonies had become a financial liability by the 1950s reinforced British attitudes about decolonization.

The main consideration for the British was that a Western-educated cadre of new leaders and functionaries would be available to take over the practical aspects of governance before independence was granted. Since colonial rule had not theretofore produced such cadres in sufficient numbers, Britain accelerated its training efforts during the postwar period. Two other considerations moderated Britain's sincere desire to liquidate its African colonial holdings. First, Britain accorded serious concern to the interests of white settlers where they were implanted in large numbers, chiefly Rhodesia and Kenya. Second, it preferred not to grant independence to "impoverished scraps of territory such as Zanzibar and the Gambia" (Nielsen 1969: 32) since it regarded these as economically unviable. As a result, Britain found itself resisting independence in some cases. For instance, in 1948 Britain arrested the Sudanese nationalist Ismail al-Azhari, later Sudan's first prime minister, on charges of subversion and imprisoned him for a year. Kwame Nkrumah of Ghana was arrested in 1948, and again in 1950, both because he was implicated in anticolonial rioting and because his independence efforts were thought premature. Kenneth Kaunda, Zambia's independence leader, was imprisoned twice, first in 1955 (for two months) and again in 1959–1960 (for nine months), before he became the country's first president. Britain had hoped that Zambia (then Northern Rhodesia) would join with Zimbabwe (then Southern Rhodesia) in a postcolonial union, which Kaunda opposed. In Kenya, Jomo Kenyatta served by far the longest prison sentence of any, nine years between 1952 and 1961, because he was (falsely) implicated in the Mau Mau uprising against British landholders. The British employed their most brutal suppression efforts in response to the Mau Mau, including mass detention camps, gruesome torture, massacres, and even judicially authorized capital punishment. Although controversy remains about the numbers killed, they are to be counted in the tens of thousands (Elkins 2005). In most other cases, however, Britain did not resort to violence in suppressing nationalist movements. Its former colonies of Botswana, Gambia, Malawi, Nigeria, Swaziland, Tanzania, and Uganda, for instance, achieved independence with little violence or repression of nationalist leaders.

A second paradox of decolonization of British-ruled Africa was that Britain made systematic plans for decolonization, but the reality proved to be contingent and messy (Nielsen 1969). Britain had envisioned the establishment of legislative councils, then the gradual incorporation of African subjects into these councils, and ultimately independence. For various reasons, though, Britain was not able to follow its plans for decolonization and instead ended up reacting to events on the ground. Some nationalist movements (as in Ghana) moved more quickly than Britain would have preferred; in other cases (as in Kenya and Zimbabwe), the interests of white settlers impacted the transferal of authority; in still others (British Cameroons, British Somaliland, Sudan, Zanzibar, and Zambia), there were strong debates about the incorporation of colonies into larger political entities. The independence of Britain's African colonies began in 1956 with the independence of Sudan and ended in 1968 with Swaziland. Zimbabwe (Rhodesia) was a special case, as discussed later.

Following independence, Britain attempted to exercise political influence in its former colonies through the British Commonwealth. In general, the goals of Britain were vague and their impact was limited. At the domestic level, Britain set up Westminster-style parliament institutions in most of its former African possessions as part of the decolonization process and organized founding elections. By the end of the 1960s, however, these institutions had not taken hold anywhere. Several former colonies (notably Ghana and Nigeria) had experienced coups d'état and were enduring military rule. Most others had become de jure one-party states under revised constitutions. Executive presidents replaced the prime ministers who had been bound to the new parliaments during the 1960s. This was the case even in the two countries (Botswana and Gambia) where multiparty political competition survived. Swaziland reverted to being an autocratic monarchy rather than the constitutional one Britain had hoped. Britain could not and did not seriously attempt to redirect such trends after its military interventions of the mid-1960s.

As for the Commonwealth, Britain had hoped to use this multi-racial grouping of countries to coordinate the activities of its former colonies, to resolve internal conflicts, and to maintain British influence around the world. In Africa, the existence of the Commonwealth did help to ease the anxieties of independence for both Britons and Africans, but its purposes and procedures were vague (Nielsen 1969) and remain so today. All of Britain's former colonies except Rhodesia, South Africa, and Sudan were members of the Commonwealth as of the late 1960s, the former two having been excluded on the grounds of their discriminatory racial policies. Indeed, the Commonwealth was deeply split by the 1965 Unilateral Declaration of Independence from Britain by the white minority government of Rhodesia; whereas Britain hoped to negotiate some accommodation for Rhodesia's 200,000-odd whites, the African members simply wanted the Commonwealth to come out unequivocally for (black) majority rule. Thus, the Commonwealth did not prove to be a viable vehicle either for continuing British influence in Africa or for the collective influence of anglophone African countries on the world stage.

By far the most fraught case of British decolonization was that of Rhodesia. The UDI that was issued by the white government in 1965 came as Britain attempted to negotiate decolonization on terms that could satisfy both the black and the white subjects of the country. Britain rejected the declaration as one of rebellion but failed to act decisively to end it. As Josiah Brownell noted, "Competing demands for either conciliation or stern action resulted in successive British governments of both parties adopting a muddled middle approach which was both ineffective and unpopular" (2010: 472). Indeed, British action after the UDI was ambiguous. On the one hand, Britain sponsored a series of resolutions in the UN Security Council placing sanctions on Rhodesia's exports and domestic industries. On the other hand, Britain did not close Rhodesia House, the country's diplomatic mission in London, until 1969. As a result of Britain's ambiguous policies, several African states temporarily broke diplomatic relations with

Britain (Pallotti 2009; Nielsen 1969). Ultimately, however, Britain was instrumental in mediating the standoff between the white government and Zimbabwe's two main opposition forces. In particular, the mediation of British foreign minister Peter Carrington was essential (Novak 2009). The 1979 Lancaster House Agreement, negotiated by Carrington, provided the framework for a ceasefire, followed by elections, and then finally independence for the state of Zimbabwe in 1980 (see White 2015: chap. 10). British diplomacy was later far less significant in ending white rule in South Africa in the 1990s.

Britain's military presence in Africa was sharply reduced in each former colony as it achieved independence, and it declined further after the mid-1960s. At independence, Britain planned modest support for the militaries of its erstwhile colonies, including training programs and facilities, technical support, funding for the purchase of arms and equipment, and officer training in Britain. Only in Kenya did Britain undertake a long-term military commitment to army bases and overflight rights for the Royal Air Force (Nielsen 1969). Rather unexpectedly, Britain was called upon by three successive governments to provide assistance against internal rebellions, all in January and February 1964. Britain obliged, and the rebellions in Tanzania, then Uganda, and then Kenya were quelled. Ironically, though, the rebellions were fueled by resentment over both poor pay and the continuing presence of British officers. As a result, Britain thereafter accelerated its military withdrawal from Africa with the encouragement of the host governments. As of 2017, Britain's only significant base in Africa is at Nanyuki, Kenya, home of the British Army Training Unit Kenya, where British forces regularly exercise; Britain also maintains two small training centers in South Africa and Sierra Leone (British Army 2017).

The next unilateral British military intervention in Africa did not come until twenty-six years later, in Sierra Leone. Britain's intervention unfolded in the context of a brutal civil war between the government of Sierra Leone and the Revolutionary United Front, a vicious rebel group sponsored by Liberian warlord Charles Taylor (see Chapters 7 and 8). In January 1999, the RUF took Freetown and engaged in a massacre of some 5,000–6,000 persons, causing the multilateral ECOMOG force in the country to begin its withdrawal (Williams 2001). The ECOMOG force was then replaced by the United Nations Mission in Sierra Leone (UNAMSIL), which also was unable to enforce peace in the country and protect civilians. In May 2000, the British government took the decision to intervene in order to evacuate its citizens from the country, bolster the weak UN mission there, protect Sierra Leonean citizens, and try to impose a political settlement (Williams 2001). The mandate of the 1,300

British troops sent into Sierra Leone evolved from evacuating foreigners to military engagement with the RUF. Although sent in unilaterally, the British mission had broad international support. It provided essential support to the UN mission and began retraining the Sierra Leonean army. British intervention proved critical to ending the war by January 2002 and restoring to power an elected (and then deposed) Sierra Leonean civilian politician, Ahmad Tabbah. Although judged positive by almost all outside observers, this British intervention proved to be a onetime event.

Britain's economic relationships in Africa, and especially British-African trade, have been of declining significance since the onset of independence in the late 1950s. Even at its height in 1960, Africa collectively was not a major trading partner for Britain, representing less than 9 percent of total British trade. Further, the percentage of British trade conducted with Africa declined to less than 2 percent by 1980 and to less than 1 percent by 1990 (International Monetary Fund 2016a). South Africa has been Britain's largest trading partner in Africa by far; the amount of Britain's African trade conducted with South Africa has ranged from 34 to 56 percent of the total (International Monetary Fund 2016a). Interestingly, South Africa was Britain's largest African trading partner both during and after the troubled years of apartheid.

Britain also has not dominated the trade patterns of its former colonies, as some dependency theorists might expect. Rather, Britain's former colonies have all steadily diversified their trading partners around the world. During the 1960s and into the 1970s, Britain did remain the leading trading partner for many of its former colonies, but the percentage of their trade with Britain steadily declined (International Monetary Fund 2016a). The pattern held for different kinds of African economies, including agricultural commodity exporters (like Kenya), large petroleum exporters (like Nigeria), and the continent's one industrial economy (South Africa). In the first two decades after independence, most of Britain's former colonies diversified their trade relations by increasing commerce with other developed countries, like the United States, Japan, and West Germany; after 2000, China rapidly increased its trade with African states (see Chapter 12). By 2010, China was the single largest bilateral trading partner of economically important former British colonies like Kenya, Nigeria, and South Africa.

British investment in sub-Saharan Africa declined as a percentage of the total along with its trade figures. During the first half of the 1960s, British investment in sub-Saharan Africa was still increasing, going up about one-third between 1960 and 1965 to $2.24 billion (Nielsen 1969).[5] About half of this investment was in South Africa, still under white minority rule. After a peak in the late 1960s, British investments in Africa steadily declined as a percentage of the world total. Through the 1960s, most of Britain's former colonies were members of the Sterling Area, linking the value of their national currencies to the British pound. In the early 1970s, however, the Sterling Area effectively collapsed, and with it some of Britain's investment advantages in Africa. Nonetheless, the oil giants Royal-Dutch Shell (40 percent British), British Petroleum, and more recently Tullow Oil still have major investments in Africa's oil and natural resource–producing countries; otherwise, Britain's investments are rather modest.

As a donor, Britain's contributions to African development increased only very moderately between 1960 and 1990, as shown in Table 11.1, though Britain also contributed to the foreign aid granted by EU institutions after its entry into the organization in 1973.[6] Over these three decades, Britain went from being the second leading donor to Africa to only a minor contributor. By 1990, its aid contributions were below those of the Netherlands (which has a much smaller economy) and Japan (which does not have a historical interest in Africa). From the mid-1970s to the mid-1990s, Germany was a more generous donor than Britain. Since that time, however, Britain has rebounded, increasing its contributions to Africa nearly eightfold between 1990 and 2014. After 1997 in particular, Britain's aid to Africa increased rapidly under Prime Minister Tony Blair, who expressed a moral duty to assist Africa and created a Commission for Africa to promote its development. Whereas British aid had been focused on its former colonies during the 1960s and 1970s, with an eye toward maintaining influence, its aid after the end of the Cold War was distributed more widely, and with more humanitarian purposes (Cumming 1996).

La Françafrique: *Franco-African Relations After Independence*
France has arguably been the most important external actor in Africa's postcolonial international relations. During the Cold War, the two superpowers acted as major patrons to a half dozen or so African client states each (see Chapter 3). During this time, however, France was a major patron (donor and security guarantor) to nearly all of its former African colonies. These included eight of the nine members of the former French West Africa group (Benin, Burkina Faso, Côte d'Ivoire, Mali, Mauritania, Niger, Senegal, and Togo); the four members of the former French Equatorial Africa group (the Central African Republic, Chad, Congo-Brazzaville, and Gabon); as well as Cameroon, Comoros, Djibouti, Madagascar, and Togo. Guinea was the only former French colony to break its most important ties with France. All of the former French West and Equatorial Africa countries except Guinea continue to

Table 11.1   Aid Disbursements to Sub-Saharan Africa by Donor, 1960–2016 ($ millions)

	United Kingdom (% of total)	France (% of total)	Germany (% of total)	United States (% of total)	EU Bodies (% of total)	OECD DAC Total
1960	124 (21)	308 (53)	5 (1)	38 (7)	3 (>1)	578
1970	124 (15)	285 (34)	80 (9)	156 (18)	130 (15)	847
1980	446 (9)	1,054 (23)	645 (14)	583 (13)	627 (14)	4,529
1990	534 (5)	3,129 (27)	1,394 (12)	1,002 (9)	1,513 (13)	11,463
2000	1,124 (14)	1,209 (15)	766 (9)	1,139 (14)	1,101 (15)	8,156
2010	2,882 (11)	3,472 (13)	1,561 (6)	7,425 (28)	4,718 (18)	26,493
2016	3,345 (14)	1,455 (6)	2,280 (10)	9,906 (41)	4,255 (18)	24,014

Source: Organization for Economic Cooperation and Development 2018.

use the CFA franc, as do non-francophone Guinea-Bissau and Equatorial Guinea. France also gained important influence in the francophone former colonies of Belgium: Burundi, Congo-Kinshasa, and Rwanda. To a lesser extent, France pursued commercial interests elsewhere in Africa, notably in the oil fields of Angola and Nigeria. France even has attempted to extend its cultural influence into anglophone Africa, mostly in vain. Most significant of all, however, France has made more unilateral military interventions in African countries since independence than all other foreign powers combined.

As constructivists would readily agree, identity is crucial to understanding both why France has sought to maintain a major role in Africa and why it has been able to do so. Unlike Britain, France has never given up on the idea of itself as a "great power," capable and willing to determine outcomes in the developing world, even as it has declined economically (Profant 2010).[7] In turn, there is only one continent in the world where France can still be credibly considered a great power: Africa. Charles de Gaulle's concept of *grandeur* (greatness) in foreign policy can only apply there, and after independence "sub-Saharan Africa emerged as a privileged arena for the projections of French power" (Chafer 2014: 514). France's historical ties to Africa, its geographic proximity to the continent, and the lack of interest of other great powers to dominate Africa have served as permissive conditions for the enduring and substantial French role in Africa.[8] More controversially, the willingness of francophone African political elites to allow France to play such a role has been equally important. France has cultivated many collaborators in its African projects. Even many ordinary francophone African citizens continue to perceive France to be a great power and thereby inadvertently facilitate France's self-perception as a major world actor. Many such francophone African citizens are fierce critics of France's paternalistic role in Africa. Some implausibly attribute various political developments to the hidden influence of France. Paradoxically, many of the same individuals desire to travel to or live in France in order to improve their personal life prospects.

Other analysts would put far more emphasis on France's economic interests in Africa (e.g., Harel 2006). This perspective serves to frame perhaps the most important debate about why France continues to remain so involved in African affairs. The question is whether France is primarily motivated by the economic benefits of neocolonialism in Africa, or whether it is more driven by the desire to maintain its self-identity as a great power.

Less controversial is the notion that French strategies have evolved, even as its pursuit of French-constructed interests in Africa has been steady (Charbonneau 2008). As the moment of decolonization approached, France had to shift its institutional mechanisms for maintaining influence in Africa. Later, as relative French power declined in Africa and in the world, it had to retrench and focus its efforts on key African partners. Still later, as France became more deeply enmeshed in the EU institutions, it more often sought to get multilateral mandates—or at least "cover"—for its operations in Africa. Yet through all of these adaptations, France's robust engagement with francophone Africa in pursuit of (constructed) interests has been a constant.

France's political linkages with its African colonies were initially at the center of its efforts to maintain its influence on the continent. France moved from the formal to the informal as these political relationships evolved. After World War II, in October 1946 (under the Fourth Republic), France adopted a new constitution that formally set up the French Union to replace the prewar political order. Under this new dispensation, France's African colonies officially became overseas territories and gained representation through the Union's little-used institutions, the High Council of the Republic and the Union Assembly. Also in 1946, the penal code and forced labor were abolished. The French Union institutions reflected the ideology of assimilation, under which French colonial subjects were to be gradually integrated as full citizens into the French republican system. The Union constitution permitted territorial assemblies elected by a limited (but gradually expanding) franchise. Real power continued to lie with the French National Assembly, however, and not with the Union institutions (Mortimer 1969). Under the 1946 constitutional order, two citizens from each of twelve

French African colonial states represented their territories in the French National Assembly. Only those whom the French deemed to be "evolved" (*évolué*)[9] could stand for these seats. Among those elected were Félix Houphouët-Boigny and Léopold Senghor, future presidents of Côte d'Ivoire and Senegal, respectively, as well as other nationalist figures. Houphouët-Boigny held several cabinet posts in three French governments beginning in 1956.

Rather than quelling the thirst for freedom, the limited reforms and enfranchisement of the French Union of the Fourth Republic further whetted appetites for liberty. In response to the onset of the Algerian war for independence and political agitation elsewhere, the French Assembly adopted a reform act (*loi cadre*) in June 1956. The act was initially conceived to expand self-government in the trust territories of Cameroon and Togo (formerly German) but was then widened to include the French West and Equatorial Africa confederations (Manning 1988). The act eliminated the old system of dual assemblies, for black native and white colonial populations, and created unicameral territorial assemblies; it provided for universal adult suffrage, and it gave the assemblies the right to enact local policies executed by locally chosen ministers (Manning 1988). The act also opened the way for the French Community, the institutional framework that briefly succeeded the French Union. The Community was like the British Commonwealth of the 1950s, in that it was to grant full local autonomy but reserve ultimate executive authority to the European metropole. The reform act also paved the way for the dissolution of the two territorial confederations, in that each autonomous territory was given the choice of joining the French Community (Manning 1988). Throughout 1958, the twelve member territories of French West and Equatorial Africa, along with Madagascar, voted in individual referendums on the question of joining the Community. All except Guinea, led by Sékou Touré, voted by significant majorities to join. Snubbed by Guinea, France granted immediate independence and quickly left, "taking with them everything they could carry" (Manning 1988: 149). France subsequently cut off all cooperation with Guinea and even abstained when the country was admitted to the United Nations. Despite this well-remembered drama, all of the autonomous members of the Community claimed and were granted full independence a mere two years later, in 1960.

Once French efforts to assimilate black Africans into the republic, and then to incorporate them into a political community, had failed, France turned to informal and often secret means of maintaining political influence in Africa. A system established by Charles de Gaulle in 1958 at the advent of the Fifth Republic has persisted, in modified form, well into the twenty-first century. De Gaulle created a presidential office on African affairs (later called the *cellule Africaine*) in the French presidency headed by a secretary-general, reporting directly to the president. Under de Gaulle and then President Georges Pompidou (1969–1972), Jacques Foccart headed this African office. According to Douglas Yates, Foccart did more than prepare presidential papers on Africa and organize visits; he also "created a clandestine network of agents and spies, placed in every port and capital city of the former French Empire in Africa—the infamous *réseau Foccart* ('Foccart network')—to report disturbing developments that might challenge French supremacy in these countries, and promising discoveries that might enrich French businesses" (2012: 319). Foccart was succeeded by like-minded French public servants with a similarly neocolonial outlook, and with similarly close ties to successive French presidents. Notably, the Africa adviser for President François Mitterrand was his son, Jean-Christophe.

France negotiated a set of bilateral cooperation accords, often with secret protocols, with its former African colonies (Yates 2012). Through these accords and the secret networks of the *cellule Africaine,* France maintained influence in francophone Africa, including former Belgian Africa after 1960. France helped keep in place a number of long-term francophile African dictators, including Albert-Bernard (Omar) Bongo (1967–2009), Paul Biya (1982–present), Blaise Compaoré (1987–2014), and Felix Houphouët-Boigny (1960–1993). France's clandestine networks helped such rulers to surveil political opponents, fabricate election results, and deploy other authoritarian techniques of political control. Houphouët-Boigny used the term *Françafrique* to describe the close relationship between France and its former colonies in the 1950s, and the expression has since become both a shorthand for Franco-African relations and also a term of criticism (see, e.g., Verschave 1999). Since 1973, France has staged annual Franco-African summits, alternating between French and African locations, at which France and its African "partners" publicly rehearse their mutual commitments.

When all else failed for France in maintaining its political influence in Africa, it has resorted to military force. Upon independence, France maintained military bases in five of its former colonies: Chad, Côte d'Ivoire, Djibouti, Gabon, and Senegal (Yates 2012). France also later stationed troops at its old colonial base at Bouar and at Bangui in the Central African Republic in 1975, when it temporarily was forced out of Chad (Rouvez 1994). France has temporarily deployed its military forces to many other African countries with the concurrence of governing regimes for various purposes from 1960 to the present. On numerous occasions French troops have intervened to protect loyal francophile clients in power.[10] The first such occasion occurred in February 1964, when troops in Gabon staged a coup against Gabonese president Leon Mba, a loyal ally of France. Within two days after the start of the coup, French military forces forcibly put down the military rebellion and released President Mba from his captivity (Reed 1987).[11] French intervention in this coup sent a powerful message that France would support its African clients. It is important to note that France did not intervene everywhere in its former colonies to prevent coups: it had taken no action to protect Beninese president Hubert Maga against a coup in October 1963, only months before the coup in Gabon. In the strange case of David Dacko of the Central African Republic, France apparently helped orchestrate a coup *against* him in 1965, only to return him to power in 1979 through a military invasion (Douglas-Bowers 2015). These examples inclined the presidents of former French colonies to stay in the good graces of France at all costs, and even to willingly enter into security agreements when they had France's confidence. Aside from using its military forces to keep order, and to protect friendly regimes, France also has used them to evacuate its nationals and those of other North Atlantic Treaty Organization countries in times of civil war. France's much-studied intervention in Rwanda (Operation Turquoise) in 1994 had the putative purpose of protecting civilians near the end of that country's genocide, but it had the side effect of allowing many of the perpetrators of the genocide to escape into Zaire (McNulty 1997).

Since the mid-1990s there has been considerable discussion in France about scaling back the country's military presence in Africa, both as a cost-saving measure and as a way of blunting criticisms about French interventionism. In 1998, the French withdrew from their bases in the Central African Republic, but they have maintained their other bases. Radio France International (2010) announced with fanfare in 2010 that France was at last closing its base in Senegal, but these plans were quietly dropped. President Nicolas Sarkozy reportedly intended to reduce French bases in Africa to two in 2012, but this plan was sidelined by the al-Qaeda in the Maghreb rebellion in Mali in 2012, and France's intervention there in 2013 (*The Economist* 2014). President François Hollande similarly promised to reorient French policy in Africa (Chafer 2014), but again with little effect. Indeed, Africa was at the center of French foreign policy for some time after the country's interventions in Mali and the CAR (see later). Even so, France has been sensitive to African and international criticism of its unilateral interventionism and influence-seeking in Africa. As a result, it has sought EU, UN, or NATO sanction for all of its overt military interventions in Africa since the end of the Cold War, including the controversial Operation Turquoise in Rwanda.[12] There are signs that President Emmanuel Macron, a young leader with few African connections, is seeking to modernize Franco-African relations and finally move beyond *Françafrique,* but only time will tell.

Although France's interventions are always suspected and sometimes resented by Africans, France has also proved indispensable to international peacemaking and peace enforcement exercises. In many cases, no other capable military power is able and willing to take action on behalf of the African and international communities. For instance, in June 2003, France took the lead in a UN-authorized peacekeeping mission to the Ituri region of the DRC where disorder erupted after the withdrawal of Ugandan troops. More dramatically, France sent 4,000 troops to Mali in January 2013 to help that country avert a near takeover by al-Qaeda-inspired militants based in the north of the country under mandates of UN Security Council Resolutions 2071 and 2085.[13] When France intervened in the Central African Republic later in the same year to stem violence between two warring militia groups, even critical outsiders recognized that France had become a "reluctant interventionist" (Darracq 2014). Yet, humanitarian (and burdensome) peacemaking and influence-seeking are not incompatible with one another: France often seems to be doing both at the same time. This Janus-faced quality of French intervention is explored later in the case study of the French role in Côte d'Ivoire.

France has maintained strong aid and cooperation agreements with most of its former colonies and, less consistently, with other francophone African countries. For most of these African countries during most years, France has been the largest external donor. French aid to Zaire/DRC even far surpassed that of the United States from the mid-1970s through the end of the Mobutu regime in 1997, despite perceptions that the Mobutu regime was a US client (see Chapter 3) (Organization for Economic Cooperation and Development 2018). From independence until 2000, France was the single most generous Western donor to all of sub-Saharan Africa (see Table 11.1). Since then it has been surpassed by the United States, but France is also a major contributor to the growing EU budget for African assistance, as well as a bilateral donor. French aid has typically been delivered with the help of thousands of French technical assistants, or *coopérants,* who remained in Africa at independence or went there afterward. Thousands of French expatriates have worked in technical positions within the ministries of francophone African governments. During the 1980s, over 100,000 Africans were studying in France, while France was supporting the work of dozens of universities in francophone Africa (Gardinier 1997). According to David Gardinier, "French aid and assistance to education and culture underpin all other efforts to maintain and perpetuate the French presence and influence in these countries" (1997: 13). Indeed, French cultural centers are typically among the most popular meeting places for those interested in European and African art, drama, and music in many African capital cities. France makes robust efforts to encourage the continued use of the French language in Africa, both through school programs and through television and radio broadcasts, especially Radio France International.

The linchpin of French financial influence in Africa is the CFA franc zone. The CFA franc zone is a collection of partially contiguous West and Central African states that use the Communauté Financière Africaine franc as their national currency. France established the currency in 1945 to facilitate commerce with its West and Central African federations, as well as in its North African colonies and Madagascar.[14] The currency was pegged to the French franc at a rate of fifty CFA francs per French franc from 1958 to 1994 and was guaranteed by the French treasury. The currency survived the transitions from the French Union, to the French Community, and to independence for France's former colonies. In 1994, France abruptly devalued the CFA franc by half, reflecting the fact that the franc had become overvalued and franc zone exports uncompetitive. Since the advent of the euro in 1999, the CFA franc has been pegged to the euro, with its value floating with that currency but backed only by France.[15] The member states forego sovereign control over their own national currencies but gain a stable and convertible currency for international trade. The fact that they have not withdrawn from the franc zone suggests that national leaders consider it in their interest to remain. For France, the currency has greatly reduced the transaction costs of trade and investment in the franc zone.

Despite what some observers have maintained, Africa has not been central to the welfare of the French economy. Like Britain, France has frequently run trade deficits on its international accounts, but it has not made up those deficits with large trade surpluses in Africa. France's balance of trade with Africa often has been negative, and when it has been positive, its surpluses have done little to mitigate its overall trade deficits. France has had chronic surpluses with some countries (like Senegal) but deficits with oil exporters (like Gabon). France's trade with Africa in 1960 was almost exactly the same percentage as that of British-African trade. Also like Britain, France's trade with sub-Saharan Africa as a percentage of the total has declined steadily since independence, though not quite as steeply. The percentage of overall French trade conducted with sub-Saharan Africa shrunk by three-quarters between 1960 and 2015, from 8.7 percent to 2.2 percent (International Monetary Fund 2016a). French trade has remained much more important to several of its African trade partners: until 1980, some of France's former colonies still conducted about one-third of their foreign trade with France, including Côte d'Ivoire, Gabon, and Senegal (International Monetary Fund 2016a). French trade in Africa has been historically linked to the country's investments on the continent. The French oil company Total (previously Elf-Aquitaine) played a key role in developing the oil industries of the Gulf of Guinea states of Cameroon, Congo-Brazzaville, and Gabon. Other French industrial companies have invested in forestry and wood products, mining, fishing, shipping and ports, banking, insurance, and retailing throughout francophone Africa.

Despite France's historical investments in Africa dating to the colonial period, the countries of francophone Africa have greatly diversified their trading partners. China has supplanted France as the leading trading partner for most. France remained the leading world exporter to Senegal and second leading exporter (after China) to Côte d'Ivoire in 2015 (International Monetary Fund 2016a). Globalization has greatly mitigated the extent to which France now dominates the economies of its former colonies, despite the persistence of the CFA franc zone and other historical ties. Neither France nor any other foreign power any longer has a stranglehold on the economies of francophone Africa. These countries choose among (non-French) European, North American, South Asian, and East Asian trading partners and receive foreign investments from companies and states located in all of these regions.

Other European Countries in Africa

In contrast to Britain and France, the economies of Belgium, Portugal, and Spain were all too small to have much of an impact on African trade or investment. None was inclined or able to play a significant role as a donor. Belgium did try to maintain influence in its former colonies for some time: it spent more than half of its official aid budget between 1960 and 1972 on its three former African colonies (Burundi, Congo-Kinshasa, and Rwanda), maintaining political ties as well. In general, despite its small economy and aid budget, Belgium gave more generous aid to its former colonies than did France or the United States in most years through the 1990s (Organization for Economic Cooperation and Development 2018). One can see the influence of politics on the relative aid budgets, however. After the Mobutu regime was essentially abandoned by the United States in 1990 (see Chapter 3), France became a more important patron than either Belgium or the United States. Likewise, Rwanda became a major ally for the United States in the late 1990s, and US aid to Rwanda jumped accordingly, surpassing that of Belgium. Nonetheless, Belgium has sometimes acted as an important mediator in the serial crises that have wracked the DRC and Rwanda (Schraeder 2006a).

Because Portugal made a last-ditch effort to keep its African colonies into the 1970s, it had no possibility of maintaining a residual relationship with its erstwhile colonies. Portugal was led by fascist rulers until 1974 and fought bitter wars to maintain control of its African colonies. Interestingly, however, when Portugal later emerged as a donor, it concentrated its bilateral aid on its former African colonies (Angola, Cape Verde, Guinea-Bissau, Mozambique, and São Tomé and Príncipe). In the twenty-six years between 1990 and 2016, Portugal gave more than two-thirds of its bilateral aid to these countries (Organization for Economic Cooperation and Development 2018). When oil prices spiked in the mid-2010s, and when Portugal's economy slumped during the Great Recession of 2008, Angola's gross domestic product reached approximately 60 percent of that of Portugal. At that time, the Angolan capital was having a much larger impact on Portugal than the reverse (Ames 2015). Spain lacked the resources and interest to maintain any special relationship with Equatorial Guinea and Western Sahara, the latter of which was controversially incorporated into Morocco (see Chapter 8).

Another European metropole, Germany, had its colonial experience in Africa cut short by World War I. Germany was briefly the colonizer of Burundi, Cameroon, Rwanda, Tanganyika, and Togo until the end of that war. With Germany's economic recovery after World War II, it gradually became a major donor among the countries of the OECD. As suggested by the data in Table 11.1, Germany was often a larger donor to sub-Saharan Africa than either Britain or the United States during the 1980s and 1990s. Further, Germany has the largest economy in the EU and hence contributes the most to the EU institutions that provide increasing multilateral support in Africa. Between its EU contributions and bilateral aid, Germany has been the second most important European donor after France in Africa. Germany's political and security influence in Africa, on the other hand, has been minimal. Germany has tended to concentrate its bilateral aid on a few countries, including Tanzania and Ethiopia.

Several other Western countries became substantial donors to sub-Saharan Africa beginning in the 1960s. Among the most generous donors, particularly on a per capita basis, were the Netherlands and the Scandinavian countries. The Nordic countries were the strongest opponents in Europe of both Portuguese colonialism and South African apartheid (Hammerstad 2012). With the partial exception of the Netherlands (in South Africa through the eighteenth century), these European states did not have a historical stake in Africa or constructed interests there. As a result, there is a strong case to be made that they were more motivated by humanitarianism and less by financial concerns (Stokke 1989). The Scandinavian countries took a special interest in the Afro-socialist states of Tanzania and Zambia, beginning in the 1970s. Several of these countries have had a significant impact on human development in selected African countries where they have aid programs.

African Responses to European States After Independence

African states faced a painful dilemma in their relations with the former metropoles and with Europe in general upon achieving their independence. On the one hand, newly independent African states were anxious to assert and to realize their sovereign independence from former European colonizers. Indeed, for most, the job of achieving independence for the remaining colonies and majority rule for South Africa and Zimbabwe was at the very top of their foreign policy agendas. It was humiliating for some new regimes (like that of Nyerere in Tanzania) to rely on a former colonizer to prevent successful military seizures of power. Continuing economic dependency was similarly galling. Yet on the other hand, the former metropoles were best placed to supply the continuing security, economic, and technical assistance that African states needed. Here we present a typology for describing how African states negotiated this dilemma. It corresponds broadly to the different "ideologies of development" that categories of African states chose after independence (Young 1982). Although these patterns emerged in the 1960–1990 period, they retain considerable value into the second decade of the twenty-first century.

One set of African states came to be ruled by what one could best call collaborative regimes. These regimes engaged in fulsome collaboration with the former metropoles and other European partners. These regimes muted their criticisms of the former metropoles for the ravages of colonialism, even though they generally joined the African consensus about the imperative of ending Portuguese colonialism and white rule.[16] They accepted fully European technical and security assistance, making it convenient for European expatriates to remain in Africa. In some cases, European officers remained behind for more than a decade, holding command positions in new African armies. Such regimes generally accepted and even encouraged new European investments in their economies. Among former British colonies, the regimes of Jomo Kenyatta (Kenya), Hastings Banda (Malawi), and Sereste Khama (Botswana) manifested this behavior; among former French colonies, most were in this category, but notable examples include the regimes of Houphouët-Boigny (Côte d'Ivoire), Leon Mba and Omar Bongo (Gabon), Étienne

Eyadéma (Togo), and Paul Biya (Cameroon); among Belgium's former colonies, the regimes of Grégoire Kayibanda (Rwanda) and Mobutu Sese Seko (Zaire) generally took pro-Western and pro-market (in theory) stances. The regimes of William Tubman and William Tolbert (Liberia) allowed the United States to set up a CIA listening post in Monrovia and welcomed US capital investments. The poorest and least-secure African regimes (the francophone regimes of the African Sahel, Central African Republic, Botswana, Sierra Leone, and Liberia) had virtually no choice but to embrace cooperation with their former metropoles, whereas for Kenya and Côte d'Ivoire, this orientation was largely the choice of ruling presidents.

A second set of regimes adopted what one could usefully describe as an autonomous relationship with their former colonizers and the West more broadly. These regimes accepted Western assistance and investments, but they did so on their own terms. They put restrictions on the nature of existing Western economic activities and restrictions on new investments. In the late 1960s these regimes were more likely to be critical of the US war in Vietnam and to recognize the regime in Beijing as the legitimate government of China.[17] In some cases, they accepted economic military assistance from China or the Soviet bloc, as well as from the West. On the African continent, they were generally more openly supportive of the anticolonial and anti-apartheid projects of the OAU, and more critical of US, British, and French interventionism. The regimes that adopted this autonomous position ranged across the ideological spectrum in their domestic political orientation, though some of the best examples adopted what Crawford Young (1982) called "African socialist" positions. In anglophone Africa, the regimes of Julius Nyerere (Tanzania) and Kenneth Kaunda (Zambia) were exemplary cases, continuing trade and cooperation with Britain while also embracing robust cooperation with the People's Republic of China. These regimes broadened their aid partners to the Scandinavian states, then also "socialist" in orientation. Tanzania was the main host of the African National Congress for several years in the 1960s and 1970s. But pro-market Nigeria also falls into this category; during the Nigerian civil war (1967–1970), Nigeria depended on neither the West nor the Eastern bloc to defeat Biafra's secession. In 1979, after previously putting restrictions on British investment in Nigeria, the government nationalized the operations of British Petroleum and BP-Shell, the two largest oil companies operating there (Genova 2010). On the other end of the ideological spectrum, the nominally Marxist-Leninist regimes of Dennis Sassou-Nguesso (Congo) and Mathieu Kerekou (Benin) could also be described as autonomous. Throughout the 1970s and 1980s, these two regimes maintained relations with France, their leading donor, even as each signed treaties of friendship and cooperation with the Soviet Union.

Even collaborative regimes had to take some steps to establish their nationalist credentials vis-à-vis their own populations. For example, in Zaire, Mobutu Sese Seko's "authenticity" and nationalization campaigns were a method of distancing his regime from the colonial West. Mobutu also maintained an element of autonomy by cultivating good relations with the People's Republic of China, even adopting a form of the Mao jacket (the *abacos*) as a form of national dress. Most important, Mobutu nationalized (and renamed) the giant Belgian mining concern, the Union Minière de Haut Katanga (UMHK), in December 1966. Other collaborative regimes took similar substantive and symbolic steps to give the appearance of autonomy.

A third set of regimes that emerged soon after independence could be labeled defiant regimes. The exponents of such regimes vocally criticized the West for its alleged imperialism and neocolonial agenda in various international forums, such as the UN and the OAU. Kwame Nkrumah (1965), the ruler of independent Ghana, even wrote a book condemning the West's neocolonialism as the dying gasp of imperialism. Among the other defiant regimes of the immediate postcolonial period were those of Sékou Touré (Guinea, 1958–1982),[18] and all those that arose in the former Portuguese colonies. Having fought long wars against a brutal colonizer, the emergent regimes in lusophone Africa all adopted stridently anti-Western rhetoric. In any case, Portugal was in no position to serve as a useful postcolonial collaborator, as noted earlier. The two regimes in Angola and Mozambique were confronted by apartheid South Africa immediately after independence, reinforcing their anti-Western orientations. The position of Robert Mugabe (in power in Zimbabwe from 1980 to 2017) was similar, as he had fought a bitter battle against the white minority regime of Ian Smith.

Other examples include Muammar Qaddafi (Libya, 1969–2011) after Libya was nominally independent but still under Western influence; Mengistu Haile Mariam (Ethiopia, 1974–1991), who replaced his country's aging pro-Western emperor, Haile Selassie; and Omar al-Bashir (Sudan, 1989–present), a power-hungry coup-maker who turned against the West for pragmatic reasons. Defiant regimes of the 1960s and 1970s mostly decried the West's alleged economic imperialism, whereas those of recent decades have protested against the West's attempt to impose its standards of human rights and multiparty democracy. Mugabe expressed disdain for the sanctions placed upon his regime, and for Zimbabwe's suspension from the Commonwealth, just as al-Bashir has for his indictment by the International Criminal Court.

Both Mugabe and al-Bashir cultivated ties with China, receiving substantial Chinese economic assistance in order to avert Western pressures against their respective regimes (see Chapter 12).

This range of responses demonstrates that African regimes have had options with regard to their postcolonial relations with the former European metropoles, even if the scope of choice was limited. In any case, similar constraints apply to powerful and industrialized countries, as well: they seldom achieve their aims without considerable effort and they often fail. African regimes of all ideological stripes nationalized European and white-owned commercial enterprises during the 1960s and 1970s. They established diplomatic relations around the world, including with countries quite hostile to their erstwhile colonizers. They effectively pursued the most critical aims outlined in the OAU Charter, namely, the liberation from white rule in the remainder of Africa. On the domestic front, most postcolonial African states established one-party states, quickly shedding the hastily assembled multiparty systems that most inherited at independence. At the continent level, the new rulers chose close cooperation on certain matters while foregoing the full-scale unification dreamed of by some pan-Africanists. All of these choices were made by Africans themselves, for better and for worse, demonstrating that postcolonial African states forged international relations of their own choosing.

The European Union's Engagement with Africa

As noted in the introduction of this chapter, the EU as a collective body has gradually taken a larger and larger role in addressing European preferences in African affairs. Both Britain (Williams 2012) and France (Yates 2012) have expressed a desire to channel more of their aid and influence through the EU machinery. This has long been the desire of most other European states. As Table 11.1 shows, British and French bilateral aid as a percentage of total OECD aid accorded to Africa has shrunk over the passing decades; meanwhile, the percentage of aid that passes through EU institutions jumped between 1960 and 1970 and has slowly increased since that time. Another major trend is that the scope of Afro-European engagement and cooperation has widened considerably over the years, beginning with a focus on trade and development and gradually expanding into other areas. For its part, the African Union also has begun to engage with the EU as an institutional body (Mangala 2013b). Although Europe inevitably remains a senior partner in the relationship, Africa recently has asserted its right to negotiate with Europe on more equal terms, and Europe has broadly accepted those demands.

The Yaoundé Agreements and Lomé Conventions

The initial formulation for Afro-European cooperation was embodied in the Yaoundé Agreement of July 1963 between the original six members of the European Economic Community (EEC) and eighteen African countries. In fact, cooperation between the soon-to-be independent African states and the EEC had been established in the 1957 Rome Treaty,[19] but the Yaoundé Agreement was foundational in that independent African states were parties to it. The African participants included fourteen former French colonies, the three former Belgian colonies, and newly unified and independent Somalia (European Community Information Service 1966). The agreement contained two major parts. First, the agreement (later "convention") provided for preferential trade for the African participants. Second, the agreement provided for $800 million in economic and social assistance to be allocated over the next five-year period (1964–1969) (European Community Information Service 1966) through the European Development Fund (EDF) and the European Investment Bank. In 1969 the agreement was renewed, coming into force only on January 1, 1971, as the Yaoundé Convention but with a slightly increased aid and investment budget.

The Yaoundé framework was succeeded by four follow-on agreements, known as the Lomé Conventions. The first three Lomé Conventions covered five-year periods, and the fourth ten years, with the first coming into force on April 1, 1976. With each successive iteration of the convention, the original African participants were joined by other African, Caribbean, and Pacific countries. The total increased from forty-six under Lomé I to seventy by the time Lomé IV came into force (Montana 2003). The aid budget, not including investment, for the EDF increased over sixteenfold from Yaoundé I to Lomé IV (Montana 2003). The conventions generally allowed agricultural exports to enter the EEC zone duty-free, though not necessarily other goods. They also included an instrument that attempted to stabilize the earnings from volatile commodity exports. With each passing iteration of Lomé, the provisions became more complicated and qualified. Meanwhile, the EEC was also forging economic partnerships with other countries and blocs on its peripheries, including a Mediterranean group and later with Eastern European countries after the end of the Cold War. In general, trade was becoming freer around the world, and thereby Lomé became less significant economically.

If the main purpose of the Yaoundé and Lomé Conventions was to stimulate development in Africa or trade between European countries and Africa, they must be judged a failure. Rates of economic growth in Africa through the end of the 1990s were remarkably low, particularly in light of population growth. Further, the percentage of Europe's trade with less developed countries represented by the ACP group perpetually fell from the late 1950s to the late 1980s (Montana 2003). In general, the conventions did not lead to greater integration between Africa and Europe, either. On their face, the Yaoundé and Lomé Conventions appear to be a liberal scheme, creating mutual benefits for Africa and Europe through free trade and cooperation. Yet Kwame Nkrumah (1965) and others condemned them as a neocolonial scheme to perpetuate European dominance over Africa following formal independence. In either case, Africans realized that the results were unimpressive.

The Cotonou Agreements, the Africa-EU Partnership, and Nonstate Actors

Since the end of the Cold War, the EU has sought to broaden significantly its engagement with Africa. In particular, it became more interested in human rights and democracy with the failure of the one-party state model in Eastern Europe. Internally, of course, the EU has always been committed to democracy: no nondemocracy is permitted to join the Union. Following the adoption of the Maastricht Treaty in 1992, the European Parliament launched the European Initiative for Democracy and Human Rights in 1994. This action made funds available to support justice and the rule of law, a culture of human rights, tolerance, and democratic processes beyond Europe (EUR-Lex 2016). It led to the embodiment of Europe's goals in the European Instrument for Democracy and Human Rights, which monitors elections and promotes human rights around the world.[20] The EU also launched its first Common Foreign and Security Policy following the organization's revitalization in 1992.

These post–Cold War changes led to a wholesale replacement of the old Lomé regime with a new one embodied in the Cotonou Agreement of 2000. Compared to the old regime, the Cotonou order put development aid squarely in the foreground and recognized the diminished possibilities for trade preferences to bring about development in the era of the WTO and freer trade everywhere. The agreement blandly states that "economic and trade cooperation shall be directed at enabling the ACP States to manage the challenges of globalization and to adapt progressively to new conditions of international trade" (Article 34).[21] The agreement attempts to transfer "ownership" of the development process from Europe to the seventy-eight ACP parties. Namely, the agreement aid protocols emphasize budget support for the priorities of the ACP states rather than project support for priorities of the EU donors. The agreement was updated in 2005 and 2010 and has included new protocols that have increased aid.

Cotonou attempts to forge a new political relationship as well. The agreement's first article covers "The Political Dimension" and commits the parties to "regularly engage in a comprehensive, balanced and deep political dialogue leading to commitments on both sides" (Article 8). Several passages emphasize the equal responsibilities of all signatories, including EU members. Unlike the Lomé regime, the Cotonou Agreement also explicitly requires good governance, the observation of human rights, respect for the rule of law, and even democratization from the parties (Article 9). In extreme cases, members may be suspended for flagrant human rights violations or extreme indifference to the rule of law (Article 96). Another innovation of the Cotonou Agreement is that it claims important roles for subregional organizations, civil society groups, "decentralized authorities," parliaments, and the private business sector, unlike the old agreements. For instance, parliaments and nonstate actors have been drawn into the process of organizing and observing free elections in Africa.

The realization of both African and European actors that development can be achieved only in conjunction with other goals led to a great widening in the remit of the Cotonou Agreement compared to that of its predecessors. Most notable, all parties realized that development is impossible in the absence of peace and security, as recorded in the very first sentence of the agreement. To address the proliferation of civil wars in Africa, the AU created a new African Peace and Security Architecture (see Chapter 6), but it lacked the funding to make this institution functional. Accordingly, the EU created an African Peace Facility (APF) in 2004, at the behest of AU leaders. The APF primarily funds African peacekeeping missions, including those in Somalia, the Central African Republic, Sudan, and the Comoros, but it also funds capacity-building and early warning mechanisms (Africa-EU Partnership 2016). Between 2004 and 2016, the EU provided about $1.5 billion through the APF, which was 90 percent of the AU's peacekeeping budget (Anyadike 2016).[22] Beyond security, the Cotonou Agreement also refers to the environment, climate change, the welfare of migrants, gender equality, regional integration, and "questions related to cultural heritage" as concerns of the partners. Cotonou thus goes far beyond the previous order in what it hopes to achieve.

A closely related political initiative to the Cotonou Agreement is the Africa-EU Strategic Partnership, officially launched following the 2007 Africa-EU Summit in Lisbon. The first meeting at which EU and African leaders discussed a partnership took place in Cairo in 2000. Following that summit and subsequent dialogue, the EU Council adopted an EU Strategy for Africa in 2005. More behind-the-scenes discussions followed, leading to the 2007 Lisbon summit and the public issuance of a Joint Africa-EU Strategy (JAES), along with an action plan for implementation. A follow-on summit at Tripoli, Libya, in 2010 achieved relatively little. A more fruitful summit at Brussels in 2014 led to a tightening of the focus of the JAES. In 2015, an emergency meeting of African and EU leaders held in Malta led to a commitment of leaders from both continents to manage jointly the migration crisis in Europe (see Chapter 9). Thus far, the impact of the JAES has been limited. It remains to be seen whether it will evolve into the kind of substantive partnership that can make a difference for people on the ground in Africa.

Indeed, the grossly unwieldy institutional architecture of the JAES and its apparent lack of focus raise the question of precisely what the initiative has achieved. At the Tripoli summit in 2010, South African president Jacob Zuma complained that "we have very little to show in terms of tangible implementation of the undertaking we made in both Cairo and Lisbon" (cited in Mangala 2013a: 24). Like the UN, the JAES is really a forum for grappling with issues that affect the two neighboring continents. The extent to which that forum has stimulated economic development is surely slight. Likewise, whether African conflicts have been avoided, mitigated, or ended specifically through the mechanisms of the JAES is unknowable. Yet it is sensible that such institutions like those embodied in the JAES should exist. To some extent, Brussels and Addis Ababa, seats of the EU and AU, respectively, have been centers of decisionmaking and power, alongside national capitals. It, therefore, seems not only appropriate but also inevitable that a forum for cooperation at the continental level should exist.

Case Study: French Interventions in Côte d'Ivoire

Repeated French interventions in Côte d'Ivoire demonstrate the continuing importance of France's unilateral influence in sub-Saharan Africa. Yet they also demonstrate the increasing importance that France places on acquiring multilateral sanction and context for its activities in Africa. Despite what ideological purists might believe, France had multiple and changing reasons over time for its initial (2002) intervention in Côte d'Ivoire, for the evolution of its policies, and for its later intervention in 2011. This case shows that whether and how France intervenes in Africa depend both on international alignments and agreements and on the current state of French domestic politics. France has continued to take forceful action to determine political outcomes, for better or worse, in many of its former colonies in recent years, including the Central African Republic and Mali. Its intervention has often been decisive in these officially francophone countries.[23] It is remarkable that a former colonizer in Africa remains so influential over political outcomes in North, West, and Central Africa.

Before a series of crises unfolded in Côte d'Ivoire in the 1990s and 2000s, France had a historical and large presence in the country. As noted earlier, Félix Houphouët-Boigny was a French minister before becoming Côte d'Ivoire's first president in 1960. His regime took a collaborative stance at independence and became a critical partner in the *Françafrique* network that emerged in the 1960s. He maintained close relations with a succession of French presidents until his death in December 1993. Côte d'Ivoire has had a military cooperation agreement with France and has hosted a French military base since independence. These relationships encouraged French investors to increase their investments in the country after independence. As many as 700 French companies, including big ones like Total, Société Générale, Colas, and Castel, are involved in Côte d'Ivoire's energy, agro-industry, transport, and banking sectors, accounting for perhaps half of the government's tax revenues (ABAX 2015). Many companies have operated in Côte d'Ivoire since independence, while others have come and gone. Some 16,000 French citizens were living in Côte d'Ivoire on the eve of French intervention in 2002 (Chirot 2006), while past numbers had been even higher. According to Marco Wyss, they represented "the largest expatriate community south of the Sahara" (2013: 90). French technical cooperation with the Ivorian government has been continuous, and France has been the leading donor to Côte d'Ivoire since independence.

Following Houphouët-Boigny's death in 1993, Franco-Ivorian relations continued much as they had before. The country's founding president was succeeded by Henri Konan Bédié, a former ambassador and minister who at the time served as president of the Ivorian National Assembly. As a longtime Ivorian official educated in France, Bédié was as firmly embedded in the *Françafrique* networks as his predecessor had been. Bédié, however, operated in an entirely different domestic political context: in line with other African countries, Côte d'Ivoire had become a multiparty polity in 1990, when Houphouët-Boigny faced an opposition candidate in his successful reelection contest. Moreover, revenues from the sale of cocoa and coffee declined with the fall of commodity prices in the early 1990s, hindering Bédié's ability to dole out patronage to potential rivals and imperiling the security of his regime. To ensure his election in October 1995, Bédié embraced the ultranationalist concept of *Ivoirité*, defined as southern and Christian, and supported a law that required candidates for political office to be native-born citizens whose parents also were born in the country (Whitaker 2005, 2015). The primary target of this law was the well-known former prime minister Alassane Ouattara, a northern Muslim whose father allegedly came from Burkina Faso. The other main opposition leader, Laurent Gbagbo, boycotted the 1995 elections, and Bédié won with 96 percent of the vote. France, under the new leadership of the Gaullist Jacques Chirac after May 1995, offered no real criticism of Bédié's xenophobic policies and electoral manipulation.

Bédié proved himself to be an inept ruler, alienating southern opposition politicians as well as northerners of real or alleged foreign origin. His regime was ineffective and corrupt, as well as authoritarian. On Christmas Eve of 1999, Ivorian troops who had been denied bonuses for service in a UN mission abroad mutinied against the regime, deposing Bédié and creating a power vacuum (Chirot 2006). General Robert Guéï was soon brought out of retirement to head an interim government. Guéï, neither a northern Muslim, nor from the traditional southern ruling elite (the Baoulé), initially enjoyed popular support from most of the (non-Baoulé) Ivorian public. Again, France refrained from intervention in Côte d'Ivoire at the moment of another illegitimate change of power, despite the fact that Chirac and his ambassador in Abidjan were favorably inclined to Bédié (Wyss 2013). Two considerations seem to have guided the (in)action of the French president: first, Ivorian financial and political interests in Côte d'Ivoire did not seem to be threatened at this time, and second, the French government was then undergoing one of its periods of "cohabitation," with the Gaullist president sharing power with a Socialist prime minister (Lionel Jospin). One analyst claims that Jospin "blocked President Jacques Chirac's wish to maintain the old pattern" (Chirot 2006: 70), whereas another argued more subtly that Chirac "did not seem willing to risk cohabitation with Lionel Jospin, who was against intervention, to save a controversial president," meaning Bédié (Wyss 2013: 89).

In October 2000, Guéï attempted to legitimate himself in power by staging a competitive election, albeit one in which the electoral law disfavoring northerners remained in place. Accordingly, Gbagbo was Guéï's only major opponent; Gbagbo apparently won the vote handily, at around 60 percent, including most southerners. As the result of the vote became apparent, Guéï attempted to disband the electoral commission, sparking massive public demonstrations, this time rhetorically supported by France (Chirot 2006). Gbagbo thus became president, initially enjoying French support, especially from the French Socialist Party, with which Gbagbo was aligned. Unfortunately for Côte d'Ivoire, Gbagbo continued the xenophobic policies of his predecessors with respect to the disenfranchised populations of the north. Unemployed youths loyal to him were allowed to attack and loot the homes and businesses of northern Dioula residents of Abidjan after he came to power, for instance (Bovcon 2009). Gbagbo attempted to purge northerners from the civil service, police, and army while also creating his own political militia (Chirot 2006). These policies led to a mutiny and coup attempt by northern Ivorian soldiers against the Gbagbo regime, beginning in the early morning of September 19, 2002. Massacres of northerners living in the south and of southerners living in the north ensued; some 10,000 persons died, and 1 million fled their homes (Chirot 2006). General Guéï was murdered on the night that the conflict began, and Ouattara had to seek refuge. The country was quickly divided between forces loyal to Gbagbo and those of the New Forces of Côte d'Ivoire, the northern rebels.

On this occasion, France intervened in the conflict quickly. Its 600 troops already at Port-Bouët immediately went into action on the night of September 19 to protect French expatriates (French Ministry of Defense 2015). Three days later, on September 22, France began Operation Licorne (Operation Unicorn), gradually bringing 4,000 French troops into the country from other African bases and France. According to France's official explanation, the initial goal of the mission was to protect or evacuate French citizens, but then, "in response to mounting violence and tension in the country, and [notably] in response to the appeals from ECOWAS and the United Nations the mission evolved over several weeks into a peacekeeping force between the armed forces of the government and the rebellion" (French Ministry of Defense 2015). In early October, President Gbagbo asked France to use its forces to help him defeat the rebels under the terms of a bilateral Franco-Ivorian security agreement, some of whose clauses are confidential. France declined to play such a role, however, insisting that its forces would be neutral in the conflict (Bovcon 2009; Wyss 2013). France continued to justify Operation Licorne in terms of the appeals that went out—after France's initial intervention—from ECOWAS, the AU, and the UN. According to Wyss (2013), France's internal political situation also made the mission possible: Chirac had won reelection and regained a majority from his party in the French National Assembly earlier in the year.

France moved quickly after its (unilateral) intervention to reinforce domestic and international legitimacy for Licorne. Internationally, France was initially helped by ECOWAS, which broadly supported the French intervention and cooperated with France to bring about a ceasefire on October 17. ECOWAS ministers created their own African, multilateral mission for the country (ECOWAS Mission in Côte d'Ivoire [ECOMICI]), but the first ECOMICI forces arrived only in late 2002 (Bovcon 2009). President Chirac then organized a roundtable conference with both sides of the Ivorian conflict in January 2003, which led to the Linas-Marcoussis Accords. The accords provided for a transitional government, with opposition representation, and removed the controversial clause on *Ivoirité* (Article 35) from the Ivorian constitution (Bovcon 2009).[24] They disallowed partisan intervention from abroad (aimed at Burkina Faso) and promised free elections after a transitional period. Some of Gbagbo's supporters complained of France's "neocolonial" attitude and failure to support a legitimate African government at this point (Bovcon 2009). Two UN missions implicitly justifying French and then ECOWAS intervention in an ex post facto fashion followed. In May 2003, a UN Security Council resolution provided for a UN political mission to facilitate the implementation of the Linas-Marcoussis Accords. The following year, UN Security Council Resolution 1528 authorized the establishment of a full-fledged military mission, the United Nations Operation in Côte d'Ivoire (UNOCI), with 6,900 troops and other UN personnel. Although France helped initiate these UN resolutions (Wyss 2013), it never put its own troops under ECOWAS or UN command.

In 2004, the French role in Côte d'Ivoire underwent a major reorientation due to events on the ground. The Ivorian unity government, nominally composed of government, civilian opposition, and rebel leaders, never coalesced, and it began to fall completely apart in March 2004. Meanwhile, a pro-Gbagbo regime militia group was allowed to terrorize populations thought to favor opposition parties or the rebels (Pike 2017). All-out fighting between government and rebel forces resumed in June when the government used helicopter gunships to attack rebel positions along the front lines in an attempt to seize key towns (notably Bouaké) in the center of the country. This area was precisely where French Licorne troops were stationed to keep government and rebel troops apart. Finally, on November 6, 2004, an Ivorian jet fighter attacked a French base near the rebel front lines, killing nine French soldiers and wounding thirty-one others (French Ministry of Defense 2015). In response, reportedly under direct orders from President Chirac, the French military effectively destroyed Côte d'Ivoire's air force (Pike 2017). In Abidjan, French helicopters from Port-Bouët were used to prevent pro-Gbagbo protestors from crossing two key bridges in the city, causing two leading analysts to proclaim that "France had lost its [*sic*] Africa" (Glaser and Smith 2005: 11).[25] In the context of growing anti-France protests, some 8,000 French citizens were soon evacuated by the French military (French Ministry of Defense 2015).

For the next six years, Côte d'Ivoire was the scene of negotiations and political maneuvering but little fighting among local belligerents or between them and the peacekeepers. In early 2007, Guillaume Soro, the leader of the FNCI, and President Gbagbo "shocked the world" (Wyss 2013: 94) with an agreement mediated by the president of Burkina Faso (and not French diplomats) cementing the ceasefire and promising competitive elections in 2008. Although the elections were repeatedly delayed as the politicians maneuvered, the peace held. After perpetual negotiations, a competitive election pitting Gbagbo against both Bédié and Ouattara was finally organized on October 31, 2010. The results were disappointing for Gbagbo, who won only 38.3 percent of the vote. Ouattara finished second with 32.1 percent, and Bédié third with 25.2 percent (Banegas 2011). Following Ivorian electoral law, Gbagbo and Ouattara then faced each other in a runoff the following month. Former president Bédié threw his support behind Ouattara, who prevailed with 51.1 percent of the vote, as announced by the country's independent electoral commission. An analysis of vote by ethnicity and region shows clearly that Bédié's supporters had indeed largely supported Ouattara (Bassett 2011). Gbagbo, however, refused to recognize the result, and his presidentially appointed Constitutional Council invalidated the results and declared him the winner. Most outside states and organizations, including the African Union, ECOWAS, the EU, the United States, and France, believed that Ouattara had won the elections and called upon Gbagbo to step aside. A few other states, notably Angola and South Africa, sided with Gbagbo in the dispute (Banegas 2011).

At this point, fighting again broke out in Abidjan between the respective partisans of Gbagbo and those loyal to either the FNCI or to Ouattara; during the first four months of the crisis, Gbagbo's militias "committed the lion's share of urban violence" (Straus 2011: 483). In this context, France and the United States sponsored a successful Security Council resolution reinforcing the UNOCI mission. It passed unanimously. In response, Gbagbo demanded that French and UN troops leave Côte d'Ivoire, while the leader of his political militia declared that the UN was "preparing a genocide" in the country (Wyss 2013: 96). The Security Council then passed more resolutions, putting sanctions on the Gbagbo regime and further reinforcing its mission in Côte d'Ivoire. France remained militarily neutral into early 2011 but reiterated its view that Ouattara had won the election. In March 2011, the AU's Peace and Security Committee "recognized without reserve" Ouattara's electoral victory; in the same month, the UN Security Council passed yet another resolution, again calling upon Gbagbo to step down.

Meanwhile, Gbagbo was losing support within the country, and rebel forces were gaining control over more territory. By late March, they had taken control of Côte d'Ivoire's nominal capital, Yamoussoukro, and surrounded the de facto capital, Abidjan. Under these circumstances,

Gbagbo's forces became increasingly desperate and violent against unarmed civilians as well as rebel forces. In response, both UN and French forces essentially joined the rebel side in the fighting, first seizing control of the airport on April 3, 2011, and then attacking other strategic positions, including the presidential palace and Gbagbo's residence (Wyss 2013). Finally, on April 10, UN and French forces fought a decisive battle against Gbagbo's remaining forces, defeating them and allowing the rebels to arrest Gbagbo the following day. Later that year, Gbagbo was extradited to the International Criminal Court in The Hague to face charges of crimes against humanity. As of 2018, his trial in The Hague was ongoing.

The forceful actions of France in the dénouement of Côte d'Ivoire's civil war demonstrate unequivocally that the country still perceives both interests and responsibilities in many parts of Africa.[26] France's role in Côte d'Ivoire underscores the continuing moral ambiguity of France in Africa. On one hand, France was definitely acting with the broad support of the international and African communities, as represented by the UN and the AU, respectively. On the other, France was also pursuing its own perceived and constructed interests. As Maja Bovcon (2009) notes, French businesses were actually increasing their investments in Côte d'Ivoire during the years of the military standoff. A succession of Ivorian leaders perceived France to be either a serious threat or a powerful bulwark to the security of their regimes as circumstances evolved. After Ouattara took power, he traveled to Paris the following January to express his thanks to French president Nicolas Sarkozy (Wyss 2013) and to sign new defense agreements between Côte d'Ivoire and France. Meanwhile, it is notable that the EU did not play a particularly great role in this "high politics" affair, confirming that it is not yet in the business of resolving crises through the use of force. Instead, bilateral European actors, and particularly France, continue to play major roles in (selected) African crises. On the global stage, the United States is often called upon to intervene in various international crises but also widely resented when it does so. The same is true for France in Africa. French bilateral intervention, even under international mandates, seems far from ideal to either the French or the Africans. And yet, for the short term, no other outside power is willing to play roles that all parties deem indispensable.

Notes

1. One of the most ubiquitous books in social science departments in anglophone African countries is Walter Rodney's *How Europe Underdeveloped Africa* (1972).

2. In Tanzania, Kiswahili is also an official language, and South Africa has eleven official languages (including English). Some other African countries, like Equatorial Guinea and Rwanda, use multiple European languages as official languages.

3. The figure is given in the source as 1.33 billion euros and converted at a rate of $1.38 per euro, the rate on January 1, 2014.

4. Liberia was exceptional because it was not colonized by any European country, and Zaire because it became a client of the United States after the Congo crisis of 1960–1964 (see Chapter 3).

5. The figure in the text is 800 British pounds, converted here at a rate of $2.80 per pound, the approximate value on January 1, 1965.

6. Britain voted to leave the EU in June 2016 and is scheduled to complete its withdrawal from the organization in 2019.

7. For Britain, the Suez crisis marked the last gasp of Britain's efforts to maintain the empire, after which it was ready to liquidate the remainder of its colonial holdings as soon as practicable (Nielsen 1969; see also Chapter 3). Perhaps Britain was more sanguine about its decline as a great power because the United States, an anglophone country and progeny of Britain, had become a superpower and the world's economic hegemon after World War II.

8. Certain neo-Marxists have sometimes claimed that the United States wanted to dominate Africa. Yet the evidence from the Cold War is that the United States was more interested merely in keeping the Soviet Union *out* of Africa.

9. This paternalistic French term described those Africans who had learned French, gained an education, and adopted European social habits.

10. Bruno Charbonneau (2008) claimed that there was approximately one intervention per year between 1960 and 1990.

11. Upon his death by natural causes in 1964, Mba was succeeded by one of France's most loyal clients in Africa, Omar Bongo.

12. The case of intervention authorized only by NATO was that in Libya. UN Security Council Resolution 1973 did authorize the establishment of a no-fly zone over Libya to protect civilians, but there is general agreement that the NATO intervention exceeded what was authorized.

13. This intervention also had the sanction of the AU, ECOWAS, and the government of Mali.

14. One accessible summary of the CFA franc zone can be found in *African Business Magazine* (2012); some details in this paragraph come from that summary.

15. There has been some fluctuation in the membership of the franc zone. France's former North African colonies, Guinea, Mauritania, and Madagascar, all left the CFA franc zone between 1958 and 1973, but Equatorial Guinea (1985) and Guinea-Bissau (1997) later joined the zone, bringing membership to fourteen West and Central African states.

16. There were exceptions to this general rule. At least two of Africa's most "conservative" regimes, Malawi under Hastings Banda and Zaire under Mobutu Sese Seko, continued trade and cooperation with apartheid South Africa.

17. Taiwan was the official representative of China at the UN until 1971. For more on this issue in Africa, see Chapter 12.

18. Touré's regime was punished by France, whose net foreign assistance to Guinea was negative during the 1960s (Organization for Economic Cooperation and Development 2018). This is possible because France would demand the repayment of existing loans while offering no new assistance to the country.

19. Article 131 of the Rome Treaty recorded the intention of the new EEC to promote the development of the associated African dependencies, then all still colonies, of the original six members of the organization. Further, it established the European Development Fund with an initial investment of $581 million to be disbursed over a five-year period between 1958 and 1962 (European Community Information Service 1966).

20. The organization has a website at http://ec.europa.eu/europeaid/how/finance /eidhr_en.htm_en. We thank Markus Thiel for helping sort out this complicated history.

21. The text of the Cotonou Agreement can be found at http://www.europarl .europa.eu/document/activities/cont/201306/20130605ATT67340/20130605ATT67 340EN.pdf.

22. The source indicates a figure of 1.1 billion euros, or approximately $1.5 billion, converted at a rate of $1.33 per euro.

23. France also played a leading role in the NATO intervention in Libya in 2011, deploying the first NATO aircraft over Libya to enforce a no-fly zone in the country against Qaddafi's forces.

24. As Maja Bovcon (2009) notes, however, the accords hardly settled the issue of "alien" participation in Ivorian elections, and she provides details on the aftermath.

25. Although these two analysts are quite critical of France, and sympathetic to Africa, this language reveals the deep-seated paternalism that so often creeps into French establishment attitudes about francophone Africa.

26. Even as the 2011 crisis in Côte d'Ivoire was unfolding, France also was playing a leading role in the NATO operation that led to Qaddafi's demise in Libya.

12

Africa and the Emerging Powers

Even as African countries continue to interact with the traditional Western powers, their relations with the emerging powers of Asia, Latin America, and the Middle East are increasingly significant. Of the emerging powers that have escalated their engagement with Africa, none is as important as China overall. Accordingly, much of the analysis of this chapter examines Sino-African relations since the Cold War. India is another emergent power also having a major impact on developments in Africa. Russia might be considered a "reemerging" power, at least politically and militarily, whose political ties to Africa are again becoming stronger following their lapse at the end of the Cold War. In Latin America, Brazil is the most important regional power, also with growing ties in Africa. Together, Brazil, Russia, India, and China have been treated as a set, along with South Africa, under the acronym BRICS. Somewhat less visibly, other regional powers like Turkey and Iran also are engaging Africa in new ways. Collectively, the activities of the BRICS and other emerging powers have opened up the scope of possibilities for Africa in a rapidly globalizing world. At the same time, these activities have had a far more ambiguous impact on the trajectory of democratization and respect for human rights in Africa.

For the emerging powers, Africa provides a variety of new opportunities not available elsewhere in the world. Economically, Africa offers a source of energy and other raw materials for rapidly industrializing states like China and India. African economies also provide markets for the low-tech industrial goods produced by the newly industrializing economies. As wages begin to rise in East and South Asia, Africa is also beginning to provide a source of comparatively cheap labor for Asian

321

manufacturers. Moreover, Africa contains significant amounts of under-utilized farmland for agricultural investors. Politically, Africa's fifty-four independent states represent a large source of votes in international bodies such as the United Nations. These votes can potentially provide support for the emerging powers in their quests for international status or influence. Likewise, African support could be crucial to the BRICS in their disputes with the status quo powers of Europe and North America. Finally, the Africa policies of the BRICS countries and other regional powers like Turkey and Iran can contribute to the domestic legitimacy of ruling regimes. The fulfillment of international missions in Africa bolsters the claims of these regimes that they matter, at home and abroad, and that they are independent of the world's global great powers.

For African states, the BRICS and other emerging powers are invaluable sources of trade, aid, and investment. China has been the leading outside trading partner for Africa as a whole since 2009, while India is the leading trading partner for a few African states, like Tanzania. China is on a trajectory to surpass the entire euro zone[1] as Africa's leading trading partner within a decade. Although aid and investment are far harder to track, China also is clearly a leading source of capital for African countries. The investments of China and other emerging economies have helped fuel Africa's remarkable economic growth that began to climb after 2000, following two decades of stagnation. Politically, the emerging powers give African states more space for maneuver in international relations generally, and more leverage against the West in particular. African states are far less vulnerable to Western pressures or sanctions when they can plausibly turn to China and other emerging partners to meet their economic needs. When necessary, African regimes also can turn to the emerging powers for sources of arms and other security equipment needed to fight rebels or suppress dissent. Broadly speaking, the emerging powers allow African states to ignore or renegotiate the preferences of the industrial West in the conduct of their international relations.

In examining the impact of the emerging powers on Africa's international relations, one cannot ignore the role of private business and individuals. In India and Brazil, private companies have long operated independently of official government policies, even if government incentives were important to their behavior. The same is increasingly the case with Chinese business enterprises and investors as China privatizes its state-owned companies and liberalizes the flow of capital abroad. Meanwhile, African subsidiaries of emerging market companies have begun to export goods and services to the rest of the world, a remarkable development. At the individual level, both Africans and emerging-power citizens are "voting with their feet." Chinese and Russian citizens are much freer to travel than in past decades. Perhaps as many as 1 million Chinese have emigrated to Africa to take up long-term residence and commercial activity (French 2014), while about half a million Africans are living in China, centered in the city of Guangzhou (Bodomo 2015). Most of these individuals have been engaged in local commerce. Tens of thousands of Africans have traveled to China and India to undertake university studies or technical training. Thousands of others go to India and other Asian locations for medical treatment each year. These contacts at the personal level ultimately have consequences for state-level interactions between African states and emerging powers.

This chapter expands upon these aspects of Afro–emerging power relations since the end of the Cold War. The following section takes up Africa's burgeoning economic relations with several emerging powers. It presents some data on the nature of these relations, discusses the benefits to the respective sets of partners, and reflects on the debate over the effects of these relationships. The subsequent section follows the same line of analysis for political relations between African and emerging-power states. Clearly, diplomatic and political ties between African states and emerging powers have framed the opportunities for economic partnership, and vice versa. The final section offers some theoretical reflections on the meaning of Africa's increasingly vibrant engagement with emerging powers. The case study at the end of the chapter examines how China's long-term engagement with Zambia has affected the latter country's politics and economic development.

Economic Relations Between African States and Emerging Powers

In many ways, Africa's ties with emerging powers are its most important foreign relations of the twenty-first century. This claim is supported by the burgeoning Sino-African and Indo-African economic relations that have developed in the past twenty years. These ties include traditional activities of trade, aid, and investment, though it is difficult to separate the three. International organizations have more ability to measure trade accurately, and trade patterns reflect much of the aid and investment that the two emerging Asian powers have put into Africa, so we begin with that metric. Table 12.1 displays trends in sub-Saharan Africa's trade relations with the emerging powers compared with the subcontinent's continuing economic ties with the West.

The table reveals much about Africa's foreign trade, which increased nearly fourfold between 2000 and 2015. Clearly, China's trade relations with Africa are escalating at a breathtaking pace. According to International Monetary Fund (2017a) statistics, China's trade with Africa

Table 12.1   **Sub-Saharan Africa's Trade with Selected Partners as a Percentage of Its World Trade, 2000–2015**

Partner	2000	2005	2010	2015
Euro zone countries	48	25	20	20
United States	16	17	13	6
China	3	8	14	18
India	4	2	5	7
South Africa	3	3	3	3
Brazil	1	2	2	2

Source: Calculated from International Monetary Fund 2017a.

increased more than twentyfold between 2000 and 2015, from $5.7 billion to over $118 billion. The pace of the increase has been steady, along with the overall rise of China's economy. Although the euro zone countries remain important trading partners with Africa, China is rapidly overtaking them. India's trade with sub-Saharan Africa also is increasing steadily, from $6.2 billion in 2000 to $46.3 billion in 2015, surpassing that of the United States. Finally, the table also shows that South Africa's trade with its African neighbors, and Brazil's trade with the subcontinent, rose on pace with the average growth of Africa's trade. That is, their trade with sub-Saharan Africa rose about fourfold over the fifteen-year period, giving them a steady but modest percentage of Africa's trade with the entire world. In comparison, Russia's trade did not reach the 1 percent threshold during any of the years covered in the table.

Sino-African Economic Relations
China's remarkable increase in trade with sub-Saharan Africa bears more scrutiny. During the decade up to 2005, a continuing pattern in Chinese trade was established: by that date China was importing mainly fuel (especially oil and gas, at 71 percent of total sub-Saharan African exports to China) and crude materials like minerals (16 percent of the total) (Taylor 2009). Meanwhile, China was exporting various consumer goods and some capital goods, notably for use in the oil industry, to Africa. The exports to Africa in the first category tended to compete with more expensive products manufactured within Africa (Taylor 2009). These continuing patterns are reflected in China's leading trading partners in more recent years. In 2014, China imported more than $2 billion worth of goods from only eight sub-Saharan African states: South Africa ($44.7 billion), Angola ($31.1 billion), the Republic of Congo ($5.5 billion), South Sudan ($4.3 billion), Equatorial Guinea

($3.2 billion), Zambia ($3.1 billion), the DRC ($2.8 billion), and Nigeria ($2.7 billion) (International Monetary Fund 2017a). China's main imports from these states were oil and minerals. By contrast, Kenya ($4.9 billion), Ghana ($4.2 billion), Benin ($3.5 billion), and Ethiopia ($2.9 billion) were among the leading importers of Chinese goods (in addition to Angola, Nigeria, and South Africa). These countries were mainly importing manufactured consumer and capital goods. By 2015, China was enjoying a large trade surplus with sub-Saharan Africa ($45 billion), with its exports to the subcontinent more than double its imports. Trade relations with the euro zone, India, and the United States were all roughly balanced, though South Africa also enjoyed a trade surplus with the rest of Africa (about $6.7 billion) (Taylor 2009).

Of the five BRICS countries, China has also been the most impressive provider of "foreign aid," especially since the end of the Cold War.[2] China's aid to Africa can be divided into two distinctive periods, the first extending from 1960 to 1978, and the second from the early 1980s to the present. During the first period, China was still a profoundly impoverished country, but it was motivated by ideological commitments to help African countries following a socialist path. The first major recipient of Chinese aid was Guinea, which had broken with France in 1958 over its membership in the French Community (see Chapter 11). In 1960, China offered Guinea a no-interest loan of about $25 million to revitalize the country's stalled economy (Bräutigam 2009). The loan financed food, bamboo, and cigarette-processing enterprises; tea and rice plantations; a cinema; and a new "People's Palace" for the country. By 1967, there were approximately 3,000 Chinese aid workers in the country (Bräutigam 2009). Meanwhile, Chinese foreign minister Zhou Enlai had engaged in a high-profile tour of ten independent African countries between December 1963 and February 1964. Following the end of the tour, China made further commitments of nearly $120 million to five additional African countries (Bräutigam 2009). Over the next decade, China built numerous sports stadiums, parliament buildings, hospitals, and other highly visible structures across Africa. China also provided arms to the liberation movements in southern Africa fighting Portuguese colonialism and white minority rule.

China's biggest and most emblematic aid project was the 1,200-mile-long Tanzania-Zambia Railway (TAZARA) linking the Copper Belt of central Zambia with the Tanzanian port of Dar es Salaam. In 1967, China signed an agreement with Tanzania and Zambia to provide a $500 million ($3.7 billion in 2018 dollars) interest-free loan to finance the project. About 50,000 Chinese workers and technicians came to work on the project from its inception to its completion in 1975, and about 60,000

Africans participated (Monson 2009). The political significance of the effort was that it allowed Zambia to export its copper through a friendly, independent African state (Tanzania) rather than through white-ruled South Africa (see case study at the end of this chapter). Chinese and Africans alike took enormous pride in the TAZARA railway, the most impressive infrastructure project completed anywhere in Africa during the 1970s. Meanwhile, China continued to extend aid for a host of less spectacular projects. By 1978, "China had aid programs in more African countries than did the United States" (Bräutigam 2009: 42).

Following the death of Chinese leader Mao Zedong in 1976, a group of reform-minded communist Chinese leaders gradually consolidated power. They arrested the Gang of Four, who supported Mao's legacy, and put them on trial in 1980. In the same year, Deng Xiaoping consolidated his own power in China. Also in 1980, a top Chinese policy group completed an extended study of China's aid programs abroad. The policy group was stunned to learn that foreign aid had consumed an astounding 5 percent of government spending between 1967 and 1976 (Bräutigam 2009). China gradually began to both scale back and reorient its new aid programs while keeping its existing commitments. In 1982, Deng's premier Zhao Ziyang embarked on a month-long trip to Africa. Near the end, Zhao detailed four principles that were to guide Chinese economic relations thereafter: "equality and mutual benefit; stress on practical results; diversity in form; and common progress." Notably, he did not use the word "aid" in this description (Bräutigam 2009: 53). Over the next fifteen years or so, China focused on "consolidating" its aid projects in Africa. Rather than launch new projects, it mostly repaired, renovated, or reconditioned facilities that it had previously constructed. It also committed itself to not intervene in the internal affairs of its foreign partners. This policy demonstrated China's long-term commitment to its African partners, sacrificing the glamour of the new projects started during the years of China's Cultural Revolution.

In the new practical era of Sino-African relations that began in the 1980s, China's early economic relations with Japan became its model. Starting in 1973, during the first oil shock, Japan began to invest in Chinese oil through low-interest loans. Japan helped China develop its oil infrastructure, and China repaid it through the transfer of oil (rather than in scarce hard currency). Japan later began to transfer some of its low-technology capital goods, notably textile manufacturing equipment, to China; in return, it was repaid with the products that this equipment produced. In Japan, this pattern of mutually beneficial economic relations between developed and developing countries is known as the "flying geese" model, with the developed country playing the role of the leading goose. China applied this philosophy to its economic relations with Africa in the 1980s. China occupied a middle position between the industrial countries and underdeveloped Africa in the "formation" (Bräutigam 2009).

These general considerations raise the key question of how much aid China has provided to African countries since its great era of industrialization began. There are several answers to this question, but none are precise or very satisfying. The first and most honest answer is that we simply do not know how much China gives, partly because official aid figures are a state secret, even if China is gradually becoming more transparent (Bräutigam 2009). Second, the overall levels of Chinese aid by the Western definition have been comparatively quite low. In 2008, Chinese premier Wen Jiabao estimated that the entire amount of Chinese aid given to Africa in the fifty years between 1956 and 2006 was only $6 billion (Bräutigam 2009). This is a trivial amount compared to that given by the West during the same period. Deborah Bräutigam (2009) estimated that Chinese aid to Africa for 2009 would reach almost $2.5 billion. In 2010, the OECD countries on the Development Assistance Committee provided an amount approximately ten times greater than that (see Table 11.1).[3] In late 2015, China made a pledge of $60 billion in loans and export credits to Africa, but analysts calculated that only $5 billion of this sum would meet the Western definition of "aid" (Robertson and Benabdallah 2016). The usual time frame for realization of some pledges would be three years. Thus, China's aid to Africa continues to be a small fraction of that accorded by the OECD states. Third, as these examples suggest, it is quite difficult to compare Western and Chinese aid to Africa. For instance, some significant portion of Chinese aid to Africa comes in the form of the labor of Chinese workers and technicians. How is the value of this work to be calculated? European, African, and Chinese wage levels are quite different. The value of Chinese labor contributed to the TAZARA railway, for instance, cannot be meaningfully calculated.

The key fact to understand about Chinese aid to Africa is that it underwrites larger Chinese investments in Africa. In turn, most officially backed Chinese investments in Africa are designed to facilitate trade. Indeed, since 1995, it has been official Chinese policy to link aid, investment, and trade together. This is reflected in the fact that the vast majority of China's concessional loans to African states flow through its export-import bank (Bräutigam 2009). The China Development Bank also has begun more recently to make concessional loans in Africa. The main purpose of these loans is to facilitate investments in such areas as infrastructure (roads, railways, and power grids), power generation (especially dams), mining, urban construction, communications, industrial plants, and agriculture. The interest that China foregoes on these low- or no-interest loans is properly considered aid. The ultimate purpose of the investments is to facilitate trade, particularly in commodities needed in China.

A closer look at the leading African countries to which China has provided the most aid and investment is useful. This analysis illustrates how China uses these tools to build Sino-African economic relations. According to one skilled journalist (Constantaras 2016), drawing on extensive data, the seven African countries receiving the most Chinese "aid" (including funds better described as investment) between 2000 and 2013 were Angola ($12.1 billion), Sudan ($10.4 billion), Ghana ($10.1 billion), Ethiopia ($10.0 billion), Nigeria ($9.1 billion), the DRC ($8.9 billion), and Kenya ($7.8 billion). During this period, China financed a total of nineteen hydroelectric dams in six of these seven countries (all except Kenya) (Bräutigam, Hwang, and Wang 2015). Chinese construction companies built the majority of these dams. Further, for Angola, Sudan, and Nigeria, a major portion of the investment was in the oil industry and transportation. For the DRC, China financed and constructed a major road rehabilitation project in mineral-rich Katanga province, as well as financing the construction of four hydroelectric facilities. For Ethiopia, China funded seven hydroelectric projects and a 470-mile railway from Addis Ababa to the coast (Schemm 2016).

It is easy to imagine what China has reaped from its investments in Angola, Nigeria, and Sudan: access to oil, which all three exported in large amounts to China. In the cases of the DRC and Ghana, China is seeking access to other minerals, including copper, cobalt, and gold, though Ghana also now exports oil (see Chapter 4). Electric power and transport systems are necessary to produce and export such commodities. As for Ethiopia, it has the second largest population (more than 100 million) and the sixth largest economy in sub-Saharan Africa, while Nigeria, Angola, Sudan, and Kenya have even larger economies. All of these countries are importers of Chinese manufactured goods, with China ranked as the first or second largest source of imports for all (International Monetary Fund 2017a). Thus, in China's leading partners, as for the continent as a whole, trade, investment, and aid are all closely linked.

Indo-African Economic Relations

Turning to India, South Asia's economic giant has emerged as sub-Saharan Africa's second leading emerging-market trading partner. As Table 12.1 shows, India's trade with sub-Saharan Africa was greater than that of China as recently as 2000. Although India's trade with sub-Saharan Africa grew tenfold between 2000 and 2014 (from $6.2 to

$63.6 billion), it has not kept pace with China's twentyfold increase. India is the leading trading partner for Mauritius and Tanzania and the leading source of imports for Kenya and Uganda (International Monetary Fund 2017a). Sub-Saharan Africa generally enjoyed small trade surpluses with India for most years between 2000 and 2015. India's trade with sub-Saharan Africa surpassed that of the United States by 2015 and was gradually catching up with that of the euro zone.

Africa's trade mix with India has largely mirrored that with China in the past twenty years: Africa has mostly exported mineral fuels and other commodities to India, and it has mostly imported manufactured goods, though the mix of the latter differs from those imported from China. In the 2010–2014 period, mineral fuels composed 70.3 percent of Africa's exports to India, and precious mineral and stones, iron, and other ores composed another 5.8 percent (KPMG 2015). The countries with the greatest percentages of sub-Saharan Africa's total trade with India were Nigeria (34.6 percent), South Africa (19.5 percent), Angola (16.1 percent), and Egypt (5.7 percent). Coal was the leading export of South Africa to India, whereas the others exported primarily crude oil. India's exports to African countries were more evenly dispersed, and the nature of its exports more diversified, compared to those of China. The leading categories of Indian exports to Africa between 2010 and 2014 included refined mineral fuels (26 percent of Indian exports to sub-Saharan Africa), vehicles (10.3 percent), pharmaceuticals (8.4 percent), and machinery (5.6 percent). The leading consumers of India's exports to Africa were South Africa (18.1 percent), Kenya (11.6 percent), Nigeria (9.8 percent), Egypt (9.6 percent), and Tanzania (8.2 percent) (KPMG 2015).

India's aid programs in developing areas are surprisingly old but minimal in scale. India began extending some development assistance to its neighbors in 1951, four years after independence. In 1964, India launched the Indian Technical and Economic Cooperation (ITEC) program as its first "development cooperation instrument" through which it channeled foreign assistance (Sinha 2010: 77). The ITEC has more recently been responsible for the training of approximately 8,500 civilian and 1,500 military personnel from foreign countries (Indian Ministry of External Affairs 2016). Between its 1999–2000 budget year and its 2008–2009 budget year, India's total foreign assistance grew from about $200 million to about $600 million (Sinha 2010).[4] During this era, Indian aid and technical assistance were directed chiefly to its South Asian neighbors, however, and Africa received a paltry $2.2 million in 2008–2009 (Sinha 2010). On the other hand, a healthy 60 percent ($2.27 billion) of Indian credit lines offered through its export-import bank were allocated to Africa. In 2012, India revamped and rationalized the structure of its aid bureaucracy, creating a development partnership administration within which all foreign aid programs were housed. By the next year, India's foreign aid increased to $1.3 billion (Piccio 2013). The portion accorded to Africa expanded but remained small compared to India's strategic neighbors, including Bhutan. India's aid is as closely intertwined with trade and investment as is that of China.

India's foreign investments in Africa are significantly smaller than those of China but are rising quickly.[5] According to one source, Africa accounted for 16 percent of India's foreign investments in 2013 (United Nations Economic Commission for Africa 2015). Like China, India uses its export-import bank as a fundamental mechanism to encourage national (Indian) investment in Africa. Also like Chinese investment in Africa, Indian investment is difficult to track because the statistics are so inconsistent. For instance, the United Nations Economic Commission for Africa (UNECA) (2015) estimated that India had only $13.6 billion of investment in Africa as of 2013. Yet other sources suggest the figure is far higher. Bharti Airtel alone made a $10.6 billion purchase of a local cellular phone network in 2010 (*The Economist* 2013). India's export-import bank signed an agreement to provide $3.4 billion to the African Development Bank in 2009 (KPMG 2015). Another source reported that India's government made pledges of $5 billion in investment funding through its export-import bank in 2008, and a further $10 billion in 2015 (Ndiaye 2016). A third source reported over $5 billion of Indian investment in Mozambican oil and gas projects in 2013 alone (*The Economist* 2013). This selection of figures suggests that the total level of fixed Indian investment in Africa over decades is certainly higher than that reported by the UNECA, though the exact amount is unknown. Since much of Indian investment in Africa goes through private, nonstate companies, some portion is certainly not captured by official data.

One distinctive feature of Indian investment (and trade) in Africa compared to that of China is its relative concentration in eastern and southern Africa. India has a historical diaspora population in the eastern African countries of Kenya, Tanzania, and Uganda, dating back to the British colonial period. These communities maintain many ties with India while engaging in commerce in their African countries of residence (McCann 2010). One source (KPMG 2015) claims that India is the largest foreign investor in Ethiopia as well. Some Indian policies tend to reinforce these historical investment links. India's International Trade Centre launched a six-year program in 2014 to encourage investments and transfer skills to Ethiopia, Kenya, Rwanda, Tanzania, and Uganda through 2020 (KPMG 2015). The goal of the program is to increase two-way trade through strategic Indian investments. India also has a historical diaspora in South Africa, owing again to the legacy of British colonialism. This historical tie has led to substantial mutual investments. More recently, India has made major investments in the emergent hydrocarbons industry in Mozambique, thus connecting the countries from Ethiopia to South Africa that have received the most Indian investment. India has also made some investments in other oil-rich countries in West Africa (Gabon and Nigeria) and North Africa (Egypt and Libya). One particularity of Indian investment in Africa is that more than 95 percent of it flows through the island nation of Mauritius. This curiosity owes to the double-tax avoidance agreement between India and Mauritius, which provides a huge tax incentive for investments to and from Africa to take this route (Ndiaye 2016). This financial arrangement also complicates the calculation of Indian investment in Africa.

India's traditional areas of investment in Africa have been somewhat more diverse than those of China, with its strong emphasis on infrastructure and power. Some areas of Indian investment have included cellular phone networks (Bharti Airtel), agriculture and horticulture, food processing, hospitality and tourism, automobiles (Tata Group), mining (Vedanta Resources), retailing, and construction (Larsen & Toubro) (Murali 2013; *The Economist* 2013). One recent trend is for Indian investors to buy land in African countries, including over $1 billion worth in Ethiopia, on which plantations are developed; similarly, India's Karuturi Global operates a large cut-flower operation in Kenya (*The Economist* 2013). More recently, India's two public hydrocarbons giants have begun major investment operations in Africa, including oil exploration, oil production, natural gas development and liquefaction, and pipeline management. The two parastatals, Oil and National Gas Corporation (ONGC India) and Oil India Limited (OIL), have jointly and separately undertaken oil exploration or investments in Gabon, Libya, Mozambique, Nigeria, and Sudan/South Sudan (*Business Standard* 2015; Dutta 2013). Since 2013, OIL has been operating is first production site at the Shakthi bloc in Gabon, with a 45 percent stake in the operation (Dutta 2013). ONGC has interests in oil and gas assets in Mozambique, Libya, Sudan, and South Sudan, and it is exploring for oil in Angola, Algeria, and Equatorial Guinea (*Business Standard* 2015). In 2015, the company announced that it would double its investments in Africa from $8 billion to $16 billion by 2018. Increasingly, then, India's hydrocarbons companies are competing with those from China to develop energy assets in Africa.

South Africa, Brazil, and Russia's Economic Relations with Africa

South Africa is the next most important economic partner among developing countries for the other countries of sub-Saharan Africa, as Table

12.1 shows. South Africa is also the subcontinent's leading trading economy globally (and second leading economy, after Nigeria), and, therefore, the structure of its trade bears closer study. As Table 12.1 also shows, South Africa's share of global trade with the rest of sub-Saharan Africa remained stable as Africa's overall trade volume grew fourfold between 2000 and 2015; South Africa's trade with the rest of sub-Saharan Africa grew just slightly faster than the global average, though its (rounded) percentage did not change.

Three features of South Africa's trade with the rest of sub-Saharan Africa stand out. First, the structure of South Africa's trade with sub-Saharan Africa is different from that with its other partners and critical for South Africa's status as an industrial country. In its interactions with the industrialized countries and China, South Africa's trade patterns seem to be those of a developing economy: it imports manufactured and capital goods and exports mostly gold, diamonds, minerals, coal, and other commodities. In relationship to sub-Saharan Africa, however, South Africa exports chiefly finished cars and trucks, military weapons, chemicals, refined petroleum products, consumer goods, and other light manufactures. Its trade with sub-Saharan Africa, then, maintains and reinforces South Africa's industrial capacity and economic status in comparison to other countries in the region.

Second, sub-Saharan Africa's trade with South Africa and vice versa are of critical importance, but this becomes more obvious when the trade data for sub-Saharan Africa are aggregated. Most trade data websites merely state that South Africa's leading trading partners are China, India, the United States, Germany, Japan, and the United Kingdom (e.g., Global Edge 2017). If one reasonably aggregates the trade data for the euro zone countries, the Middle East, and sub-Saharan Africa, however, a somewhat different picture emerges. Prepared this way, the data show that South Africa's leading trading partners in 2015 were, in order, the euro zone countries, sub-Saharan Africa, and China. The next leading trading partner, the United States, had barely more than half of China's trade with South Africa, with only three others accounting for 4 percent or more of South Africa's total trade. Trade with Britain was only 3.5 percent of South Africa's total trade, and that with Brazil was only 1.3 percent in 2015. Thus, South Africa trades more with sub-Saharan African countries combined than with any other trading partner except the euro zone countries.

Table 12.2 reveals a third feature of South Africa's global and continental trade: South Africa had a large trade surplus with sub-Saharan Africa, almost $14 billion in 2015, whereas it had a considerable overall trade deficit of $12 billion (International Monetary Fund 2017a). South

Africa ran large trade deficits with China ($10 billion) and the euro zone countries ($8.5 billion) and a smaller but significant deficit ($3 billion) with the Middle East and North Africa (due to oil imports). South Africa's smaller trade volumes with the United States, India, and Japan were relatively balanced. Without its trade surplus with the rest of sub-Saharan Africa, South Africa would have had a massive trade deficit, and thus sub-Saharan Africa is a very important export market for South Africa. South Africa, then, benefits from its large trade with sub-Saharan Africa in two ways: the structure of the trade benefits its continuing industrialization, and the large surplus greatly reduces its overall trade deficit.

Given the small size of South Africa's economy, only one-fifth the size of the next smaller BRICS economy (Russia), South Africa cannot and does not provide much foreign aid. South Africa receives far more foreign assistance than it provides to others. South Africa did begin to slowly increase its foreign aid in 2001, when it established the African Renaissance and International Cooperation Fund (ARF). This new program complemented the New Partnership for Africa's Development (see Chapter 6), largely the brainchild of former South African president Thabo Mbeki. Yet by 2014, South Africa's total foreign assistance had grown to only $183 million for that year (Global Humanitarian Assistance 2017b). This level of aid was clearly insignificant compared to that of India and China, although it was largely targeted (90 percent) to other countries in sub-Saharan Africa. In general, South African aid did not seem to have the same direct ties to investment and trade as did the aid of the larger BRICS economies.

South Africa's foreign direct investment, on the other hand, is enormous for the size of the country's economy. According to the United Nations Conference on Trade and Development (UNCTAD) (2017), South Africa's total stock of FDI was $163 billion in 2015. By way of

Table 12.2   South Africa's Trade with Leading Partners, 2015 ($ billions)

Partner	Total Trade	Exports To	Imports From
Euro zone countries	34.39 (19.7%)	12.97 (15.9%)	21.42 (22.9%)
Sub-Saharan Africa	32.34 (18.5%)	23.05 (28.3%)	9.29 (9.9%)
China	24.70 (14.1%)	7.47 (9.2%)	17.23 (18.4%)
United States	12.87 (7.4%)	6.22 (7.6%)	6.65 (7.1%)
Middle East and North Africa	9.23 (5.3%)	3.02 (3.7%)	6.21 (6.6%)
India	7.89 (4.5%)	3.22 (4.0%)	4.67 (5.0%)
Japan	7.46 (4.3%)	3.99 (4.9%)	3.47 (3.7%)

Source: International Monetary Fund 2017a.

comparison, the total FDI stocks of the other BRICS were $1.01 trillion for China, $252 billion for Russia, $181 billion for Brazil, and $139 billion for India. Reliable data on the locations for the FDI of the BRICS are not available, but by a generous measure, not more than 14 percent of China's stock of FDI was invested in Africa in 2013 (Zhou and Leung 2015). This would amount to only $140 billion of China's 2015 stock of FDI. Similarly, Brazil, Russia, and India have only small investments in Africa compared to other locations. On the other hand, a large percentage of South Africa's FDI was invested elsewhere in Africa, and thus South Africa was almost certainly the second largest BRICS investor in Africa in 2015.

In sum, although South Africa has a much smaller economy than any of the other BRICS, its contiguous geography with other sub-Saharan African countries makes them an ideal location for South African trade and investment. The historical ties of the ruling African National Congress party with the former Frontline States (see Chapter 9) also give the country a natural affinity for intensive economic engagement with the rest of Africa.

Sub-Saharan Africa's trade with Brazil was only slightly more than half its trade with South Africa in 2015, though the percentage rounds up to 2 percent (see Table 12.1).[6] Using the more complete 2014 figures, Brazil exported only $4.9 billion to sub-Saharan Africa in that year and imported $13.4 billion. This amount represented about 4 percent of Brazil's world trade, approximately $478 billion in 2014 (International Monetary Fund 2017a). As the figures suggest, Brazil had a large deficit with sub-Saharan Africa, unlike South Africa. In 2014, nearly all of Brazil's imports came from four African countries: Nigeria ($10.1 billion), Angola ($1.2 billion), Equatorial Guinea ($1.2 billion), and South Africa ($776 million). The bulk of Brazil's much smaller exports went back to three of the same countries: Angola ($1.3 billion), South Africa ($1.2 billion), and Nigeria (1.0 billion) (International Monetary Fund 2017a). As the sources might suggest, Brazil's main import from sub-Saharan Africa was crude petroleum. This may seem puzzling since Brazil's own petroleum production roughly tripled between 1995 and 2005. The problem for Brazil is that about 70 percent of its crude oil production is of the heavy and sulfur-laden variety, and Brazil's refineries are incapable of refining this variety of oil into useful consumer products. Accordingly, Brazil both exports and imports significant quantities of oil (Duran 2013). Brazil's exports to Africa are quite varied, including foodstuffs and some manufactured goods.

Brazil's foreign investment and small foreign aid programs also have had less impact in Africa than those of South Africa. As noted earlier, Brazil's total stock of FDI was barely larger than that of South Africa in 2015, despite the much larger size of Brazil's economy (United Nations Conference on Trade and Development 2017).[7] According to one source (Muggah 2015), Brazil's Bank for Social and Economic Development invested $2.9 billion in Africa between 2007 and 2015. One major example of Brazilian investment in Africa is Petrobras Africa, the African division of Brazil's national oil company. Petrobras finalized a major exploration and production financing agreement in July 2013 to support its operations in five African countries (Angola, Benin, Gabon, Nigeria, and Tanzania) (Helios Investment Partners 2017). Brazil's National Economic and Social Development Bank and the Brazilian Agricultural Research Corporation have financed a host of smaller projects across Africa in recent years. The Brazilian construction giant Odebrecht has undertaken a number of infrastructure projects on the continent (Muggah 2015). These include Angola's largest dam and multiple housing projects in South Africa.

Like South Africa, Brazil historically was not a significant foreign donor. Under Brazilian president Luiz Inácio da Silva (2003 to 2010), however, things began to change. Brazil's impressive economic growth that had begun under his predecessor continued. Meanwhile, Lula, as he was known, took a great interest in Africa, just as he did in racial reform within Brazil. During Lula's time in office, Brazil's overall foreign aid budget rose from less than $25 million per year to over $400 million per year (Stolte 2015; cf. Trolio 2012). Moreover, the portion of that aid directed to Africa increased dramatically to over half of Brazil's total aid by 2010 (Stolte 2015). Although small in comparison to other donors, the aid of Brazil signaled the country's growing interest in Africa. The largest African recipient of Brazilian foreign aid was Mozambique, followed by other lusophone countries (Apolinário 2016). Since Lula left office, though, Brazil's foreign aid seems to have withered down to levels of the pre-Lula period (see Global Humanitarian Assistance 2017a).[8]

Russia's economic activity in sub-Saharan Africa is comparatively negligible and can be summarized more quickly. Russia's substantial aid programs, largely military, that existed during the Cold War (see Chapter 3) began dissipating even before the Soviet Union's collapse in 1991. Russia's economic chaos in the 1990s and other preoccupations precluded the revival of such programs. As for trade, there is little complementarity between Russia and Africa, given that both are mainly national resource exporters. Russia's total trade with all of sub-Saharan Africa barely surpassed $3 billion per year in 2014 and 2015 (International Monetary Fund 2017a), or about 0.5 percent of the continent's total. When oil and gas prices spiked in the late 2000s, oil-exporting

Russia did enjoy a brief economic revival, and many of Russia's quasi-state companies were infused with fresh cash. In that context, Russia began to make major new investments in oil, gas, mining, steel production, and banking in at least seventeen African countries in the late 2000s and early 2010s (Carmody 2013). Whether this investment trend will survive over the longer term remains to be seen, but new investment has recently declined as oil prices have dropped once again.

Africa's Economic Relations with Other States

Although this chapter focuses on sub-Saharan Africa's relationships with the BRICS, sub-Saharan Africa has quite significant economic relations with many other developing countries as well. In fact, these relationships are often far more important than those between Russia and Africa. Total trade between sub-Saharan Africa and several Middle Eastern partners in 2014, for example, far exceeded Russia's trade with the subcontinent: $17.4 billion worth of trade with the United Arab Emirates (UAE) (including $7.3 billion in African exports); $13 billion with Saudi Arabia ($11 billion in African exports, mostly oil); $4.7 billion with Turkey; and $3.2 billion with Kuwait ($2.3 billion in African exports) (International Monetary Fund 2017a).[9] It is important to note that these figures do not include the five North African states, where the Persian Gulf states engage in even greater trade. Overall, the trade of these Middle Eastern countries with sub-Saharan Africa exceeded that of Russia, and trade between the UAE and sub-Saharan Africa surpassed even that of Brazil.

As is evident from the preceding discussion, trade and investment are often closely linked. Thus it is no surprise to learn that many of the oil-rich states of the Gulf Cooperation Council (GCC)[10] have been investing heavily in sub-Saharan Africa, as well as North Africa. The bulk of this investment is quite recent, beginning with the global oil price spike that occurred in 2008, putting billions into the national accounts of the GCC states. Examples of investments include the $300 million stake that the Investment Corporation of Dubai took in Dangote Cement of Nigeria; Etihad Airline's 40 percent stake in Air Seychelles; Rani Investment's (Dubai) large investments in the tourism industry in Mozambique; Saudi Arabia's 75 percent stake in a South African cell phone company; the Qatari National Bank's investments in banks across Africa; and the Omani state Reserve Fund's investment in the port of Bagamoyo, Tanzania (GN Focus Team 2016).

One of the more fascinating bilateral investment relationships is between Ethiopia and the UAE. Since 2008, the UAE has invested vigorously in Ethiopian infrastructure (roads), agribusiness, light manufacturing, and pharmaceuticals, among other areas. Notably, the UAE-based firm Julphar built a $9.2 million pharmaceutical plant in Addis Ababa in 2012 and announced in 2015 that it would build a second plant there (Bacha 2015). In 2016, Ethiopia opened an embassy in the UAE (GN Focus Team 2016), and in December of that year the Ethiopian foreign affairs ministry announced that the two countries had signed an investment promotion and protection agreement. More recently, in 2017, the government of Somaliland[11] announced that it had agreed to allow the UAE to open a military base in its port of Berbera (Abdi 2017). The UAE company DP World gained the rights to run the port at Berbera for thirty years as part of the agreement. The deal would allow Berbera to become a major hub for trade from the entire Horn region. Since Ethiopia and Somaliland are allies, the port of Berbera may become a major route through which landlocked Ethiopia will execute its international trade, including trade with the UAE. A related arrangement is for the UAE government to finance the reconstruction of the road between Berbera and Ethiopia's free trade zone (Abdi 2017).

Aid passing from the Middle East to sub-Saharan Africa is hard to measure since no Middle Eastern states are members of the OECD, and they do not record their aid systematically. This aid is based in large part on Islamic solidarity with Africa's large Muslim communities but is not limited to majority-Muslim countries. For instance, the Organization of Islamic Cooperation (OIC) provides poverty relief, disaster assistance, and development financing to projects throughout sub-Saharan Africa. More typically, the OIC also provides financing for a number of universities in Africa, notably for the Islamic University in Uganda, with its multiple campuses.

Much more quietly, Iran also has provided some aid to African countries, particularly in the area of agriculture, though Iran's trade with Africa is exceedingly modest. After the Islamic Revolution of 1979, the new government of Iran mobilized groups of young people to do internal development work within the country under the label "Construction Jihad." After the revolutionary government became more institutionalized, Construction Jihad was turned into a bureaucracy called the Ministry of Agricultural Jihad (MAJ) (Lob 2016). After Iran was attacked by the Sunni-dominated Iraqi government of Saddam Hussein in 1980, Iran began to compete with Sunni-dominated Arab countries within the Middle East and elsewhere, including Africa. Iran's activities in Africa included such tactics as religious proselytization and clandestine operations against hostile governments but also an economic aid program run through the MAJ. According to Eric Lob (2016), the MAJ provided aid to at least a dozen African countries in the areas of fishing, farming, vehicle assembly, and vocational training in the late 2000s. Overall, "development, rather than arms or ideology, served as the most effective and promising means for Iran to make deep inroads into Africa" (Lob 2016: 327–328). Thus, the Muslim world has developed an aid competition in Africa, though on a much smaller scale than that between the United States and the Soviet Union during the Cold War.

The Debate over Africa's Economic Engagement with Emerging Powers

The economic relationships described in this section raise a crucial question from the African perspective: Does Africa's escalating economic engagement with other emerging powers contribute to Africa's economic development or impede it? Scholars and diplomats have raised this question about China's engagement with Africa with increasing frequency. During an earlier era, most scholars sympathetic to Africa assumed that "South-South" trade was a good thing, but this assumption is no longer so clear. A number of factors make the question virtually impossible to answer. First, the complexities of trade, investment, and aid make the overall effect of these quite hard to judge. As we saw in analyzing China's activities in Africa, the line between aid and investment is difficult to discern. What starts as a Chinese investment, backed by loans that are intended to be repaid, essentially turns into an aid project when the loans are not repaid and are later "written off." Second, the data on Africa's engagement with emerging powers are poor, much weaker than that on Africa's relations with OECD countries. Indeed, many of these economic activities are intentionally obscured to avoid political controversy.

Third, the broader forces of globalization pose even greater hurdles to answering this question. The emphasis in this section has been on the activities of official state organizations and business linked with states (state-owned enterprises). Increasingly, however, the business organizations in the emerging powers are operating autonomously of their host-state governments (Carmody 2013). When the scope and scale of their activities go uncaptured by the official figures, it is impossible to say what the impact of their activities is. The same is even more true for the activities of individuals. As noted at the outset of this chapter, some 1 million Chinese have moved to Africa (French 2014), not as agents of the Chinese state or as officials of Chinese companies but simply as human beings in search of better fortunes, personal and economic. Many tens of thousands of Indians, Arabs (particularly Lebanese), and individuals from other parts of the developing world also have moved to Africa in recent decades. They typically bring with them modest amounts of financial capital but enormous human capital, or expertise in launching and running business enterprises. The impact they have on African development is surely incalculable.

Despite these obstacles to determining the net effect of emerging-market countries' economic engagement with Africa, one can easily discern several patterns that bear on African development. Let us begin with the positive side of the ledger. Emerging countries not only have provided some modest amounts of aid to Africa, but they may also have stimulated OECD countries to increase their aid. Arguably, they have improved the quality of aid by drawing attention to the failures of OECD assistance in an earlier era. With respect to trade, the recent successes of emerging markets have stabilized or even driven up commodity prices, on which most African countries depend for their foreign exchange. China and India have consumed enormous quantities of African commodities for which prices generally have been higher. The purchases of these commodities have infused tens of billions of dollars into African economies. Looking at African imports, the manufactured goods produced in emerging markets, from housewares to capital goods, are far cheaper than those produced in OECD countries, where labor costs are higher. Finally, the investments of the BRICS and other emerging countries in Africa have been a tremendous economic boon to Africa. In particular, Africa's infrastructure, fragile and failing in the early 1990s, has been partly rebuilt and expanded. Thousands of miles of roads that had not been repaired since independence have finally been rebuilt thanks to Chinese investment; electricity output also has been hugely expanded, thanks to Chinese-built dams and other power generation projects; hundreds of miles of railways have been built or repaired; and medical infrastructure is much improved.

On the negative side of the development ledger, the emerging-market countries have little to contribute to Africa in untied aid; as we saw earlier, most of the transfers from China are not aid but investments. In turn, most of these investments work to cement Africa globally in the role of commodities producer. Also as we saw earlier, much of the BRICS's investment is in Africa's oil and mineral-rich countries; in turn, much of the infrastructure they have created or restored is aimed at the extraction of those mineral resources. Meanwhile, very little of the BRICS's investment has been in manufacturing so far, though this is slowly changing. In fact, Africa saw a massive deindustrialization from the early 1980s when structural adjustment took hold (see Chapter 4) through the early 2010s. Cheaply produced imported manufactures from China, and to a lesser extent India, made most African factories uncompetitive. Some scholars (e.g., Holslag 2007) have claimed that China was actively pursuing neomercantilist trade relations with Africa. Whatever China's intentions, the outcome could aptly be described as neomercantilist: China ran large trade surpluses with Africa, exporting mostly manufactured goods and importing mostly commodities (see Taylor 2009). Africa has exported almost no manufactured goods to China. South Africa has similar trading patterns with the rest of Africa. Such patterns surely do not speak well for the potential of autonomous development in Africa.

Identifying such patterns tells us little, however, about the net effects of the recent economic engagement between Africa and emerging powers. For what it is worth, many of the keenest observers of Sino-African relations (e.g., Bräutigam 2009; Taylor 2009) generally have concluded that the net effect of Chinese economic engagement with Africa has been positive. Although the complexity of Africa's economic relationships makes an objective analysis of this question impossible, Africa's economic trajectory since the mid-1990s supports the idea of a positive relationship. During the "high tide" of structural adjustment in the 1980s and early 1990s, and before the onset of major debt relief, almost all of Africa's economies were stagnant or contracting (see Chapter 4). Between 1994 and 2014, however, African economies took off and grew by an impressive average of 4.3 percent per year for twenty years; per capita incomes on average rose approximately 50 percent during these two decades; extreme poverty, as defined by the IMF, dropped from 61 percent to 43 percent; and infant mortality fell by more than half (Radelet 2016). Given that Africa's impressive economic growth spurt coincided with the rise of the BRICS in Africa, it would be hard to prove that the economic impact of their new engagement with the continent has been negative. Thus, for the interim, one must conclude that the net impact of increased South-South cooperation has been positive in terms of Africa's economic development.

Political Relations Between African States and the BRICS

Do not let the organization of this chapter suggest that the increasing economic engagement of emerging powers in Africa discussed earlier is somehow separated from their political interests and ambitions. Indeed, the pursuit of resources and markets by countries such as China, India, and Brazil is very much intertwined with their desire to gain influence and power on the global stage. Moreover, as even China has discovered in recent years (Carmody and Taylor 2010), increasing involvement in Africa's economies inevitably has political consequences at the domestic and international levels that cannot simply be ignored. This section thus explores the political motivations behind and consequences of the increasing economic engagement of emerging powers in Africa. We begin by discussing the underlying principles that have informed Africa's relations with the emerging powers; then we present an overview of the kinds of diplomatic and political activities in which Africa and its partners have engaged; and finally we discuss the distinctive benefits to the respective partners of the politico-diplomatic relations that have evolved since the 1950s.

In large measure, the same principles of friendship and cooperation that nominally govern relations among African states, as embedded in the OAU Charter and the AU Constitutive Act (see Chapter 6), also govern those between Africa and the emerging powers. In turn, these principles reflect the normative language in the opening articles of the UN Charter. Chinese Premier Zhou Enlai reaffirmed five of these principles with respect to Sino-Indian relations in the 1950s, including mutual respect for sovereignty and territorial affairs; mutual nonaggression; noninterference in internal affairs; equality of relations and mutual benefits; and peaceful coexistence. As one Chinese scholar fairly observed, "These principles have stood the test of time and very much underpin current Chinese foreign and aid policy toward African countries" (Haifang 2010: 55). Indeed, China, India, and Brazil have all lived up to these principles more consistently than have Africa's other partners. The superpowers intervened frequently in the internal affairs of African states during the Cold War (see Chapter 3), as did the former colonizers in the decades after independence (see Chapter 11). Even intra-African relations have not been guided as strongly by these principles (see Chapter 7).

Thus, one could say that relations between Africa and emerging powers have been surprisingly principled. Yet in a different sense they have also been pragmatic. With respect to mutual economic benefit, for instance, Africa has sought the best deals that it could get with its emerging-market partners. Leaders from both the BRICS and African states have frequently expressed solidarity with one another in various global forums. When specific issues are at stake, however, the same leaders tend to follow their regime security interests, and sometimes national interests. As noted earlier, most of China's "aid" to Africa is actually a disguised form of investment. Further, respect for the principle of noninterference is in fact a form of pragmatism: consistently good business relations preclude ideological stands on domestic politics. Neither China nor Russia evinces interest in human rights in Africa, and the record of the other three BRICS is mixed. Nor does any stand up against even egregious human rights abuses. Unconstitutional changes of government rarely interrupt relations between the BRICS and their African partners for very long. Arguably, South Africa has been surprisingly disengaged from many important issues for the continent, including the fight against AIDS, the proliferation of regional wars, and the uneven spread of democracy (Clark 2016; cf. Alden and Schoeman 2013).[12]

Another qualification on the theme of "principled" relations between Africa and the BRICS, including South Africa, is that all parties are perfectly capable of employing the seamier tactics of statecraft. That is, there is every reason to conclude that the more powerful representatives of the global South employ the timeworn practices of spying, bribery, and covert intervention to gain influence in Africa. For example, it was revealed publicly in 2017 that China had secret access to the computer network used by African diplomats at the African Union headquarters in Addis Ababa (Allison 2018). The Chinese had constructed the new AU headquarters as a "gift" to Africa and installed its computer systems to allow themselves access to the confidential documents of AU diplomats. It would hardly be surprising to learn that any of the other BRICS countries were doing the same. Nor is there any reason to think that African states eschew such tactics, though they often have fewer resources with which to do so.

These considerations bring us to the question of how Africa's relations with the leading states of the global South have evolved since the 1950s. In general, emerging powers gradually began to establish diplomatic relations with African states in the early years of the independence of the latter. Often, the first step was a bilateral visit by a senior African or BRIC-country representative (before South Africa joined the bloc), sometimes followed by a reciprocal visit. In the early days, such visits were exciting, heady affairs. For instance, Sékou Touré's visit to the PRC in September 1960, the first of a black African ruler to China, stimulated great interest. This first visit was returned by Zhou Enlai, who visited Guinea and thirteen other African countries in 1964, signaling China's political entry into the continent (Haifang 2010). Following Zhou's inaugural visit, Chinese premiers, vice premiers, and eventually presidents have regularly visited African states—typically many in the same trip—in every decade since. Likewise, independent African rulers followed the example of Touré: Kwame Nkrumah was in China in 1966 when the military coup that overthrew him unfolded back home (Woronoff 1972).

India's first prime minister, Jawaharlal Nehru, began making state visits to Africa (Egypt) in 1955, later visiting Nigeria in 1957 and again in 1963. One of his successors, Indira Gandhi (also his daughter), made even more trips to a variety of African states. State visits by Russian leaders were rarer but not unheard of: Khrushchev visited Egypt in 1956 and then Guinea in 1962, following Touré's earlier visit to the Soviet Union. State visits from Brazilian leaders to Africa became common only under

Brazilian president Lula da Silva, who made thirty-five visits to twenty-nine African states on twelve trips between 2003 and 2010 (Stolte 2015).

Many of these high-level state visits led to the signature of bilateral friendship or investment treaties, especially in the early years. For instance, Guinea signed treaties of friendship with the Soviet Union and China during or shortly after Touré's respective trips to the two countries. Each carried modest aid provisions. The Soviet Union's standard "Twenty-Year Treaty of Friendship and Cooperation" was a staple of the Cold War and applied to several Afro-Marxist states (see Chapter 3). Such treaties codified the rhetorical statements of mutual solidarity. China's standard treaty with African states, on the other hand, eventually became the "Bilateral *Investment* Treaty." China's first such treaty was signed with Ghana in 1989, and thirty-four more such bilateral treaties between China and African states followed by 2016 (Kidane 2016). India and later Brazil likewise signed scores of bilateral treaties with African countries, often following high-level visits.

Initial visits by heads of state or senior officials between African states and emerging powers gradually led to the establishment of embassies in the respective host countries. This establishment of permanent missions allowed the partners to develop or follow up on all forms of mutual cooperation. As importantly, they sent signals to the international community of commitment by the respective partners. During the Cold War, the United States quickly established missions in most African countries, whereas the Soviet Union took longer and worked harder to establish diplomatic relations with many African states. In 2017, Russia had embassies in forty African states, omitting several of the smaller, poorer, or island African states, while India had embassies in twenty-nine African countries. As part of Lula da Silva's outreach to Africa, Brazil opened twenty new embassies in Africa, bringing the total to thirty-seven. Although some of these were barely staffed (Stolte 2015), they boosted Brazil's symbolic presence in Africa.

Embassies are established only after formal diplomatic recognition, of course, and in this regard, China's challenge in Africa has been unique. Due to the ongoing dispute between the governments in Beijing and Taipei (i.e., Taiwan) over which legitimately represents the Chinese people, Africa became a diplomatic battleground in the 1960s.[13] African countries could only maintain diplomatic relations with one or the other of the two Chinese governments. Taiwan got an early start in Africa, securing diplomatic relations with nineteen African states by 1963, whereas the PRC had relations with only thirteen (Haifang 2010). Using the lure of its much greater economic and military aid, though, the Beijing government secured the recognition of thirty-seven African states by the early 1970s; twenty-six of these supported the PRC's replacement of Taiwan on the UN Security Council in 1971 (Haifang 2010). Afterward, the Beijing government continued to push for recognition by African states, and most succumbed to the allure of the PRC's trade, aid, and investment. As of 2017, only two African states (Burkina Faso and Swaziland) continued to maintain relations with Taiwan instead of China (*South China Morning Post* 2017).

A more recent innovation in African relations with two of the BRICS has been high-level, multilateral summitry. The Chinese led the way in this area, instituting the Forum on China-Africa Cooperation (FOCAC) at a grand meeting in Beijing in October 2000. The meetings of the forum every three years have become the signature event at which existing and new Chinese commitments to Africa are announced (Taylor 2011). The location of the forum alternates between Beijing and an African venue, with those of 2003, 2009, and 2015 taking place in Addis Ababa (Ethiopia), Sharm el-Sheikh (Egypt), and Johannesburg (South Africa), respectively. Almost all African countries have participated since the beginning. By tradition, China announces a doubling of its existing aid/investment commitments to Africa at each event. At the 2015 meeting in Johannesburg, however, China tripled its commitments to $60 billion for the 2015–2018 period. The mix of grants, buyer credits, low-interest loans, and investments in these commitments has been variable and rather vague (Yun 2015). At the most recent meeting, China reinforced its commitment to "industrial capacity cooperation" and downplayed its interest in natural resources (Yun 2015).

Beginning in 2008, India has followed China's lead with its own India-Africa Forum Summit, and the inaugural meeting took place in New Delhi. Like FOCAC, the India-Africa meetings take place once every three years and alternate between New Delhi and an African venue. Whereas the first two meetings only attracted fourteen and fifteen African representatives, respectively, the 2015 summit back in New Delhi attracted forty-one African representatives, including the Nigerian, South African, and Egyptian heads of state.[14] Although the rhetoric of solidarity and partnership is quite similar to that expressed at the FOCAC meetings, the commitments of the Indian Technical and Economic Cooperation Program pale in comparison with those extended by China.

Arms sales and security cooperation are another key element of BRICS-African relations. Arms transfers from the BRICS countries to African states have two distinctive purposes for the providers: profit and the maintenance of political influence. Among the BRICS, Russia and China have been the two big players in arms transfers to Africa, though the other three also have sold arms in smaller quantities. Selling mainly for profit, Russia specializes in heavy equipment. From 2011 to 2015, Russia accounted for 27 percent of the heavy weapons provided to sub-Saharan African countries; it was the first-ranked provider of armored vehicles and the second leading provider of military helicopters (Gorka 2017). Since 2010, Russia has signed major arms deals with Algeria, Angola, Egypt, Nigeria, Rwanda, Sudan, and Uganda. In 2013, it established a helicopter repair center in South Africa (Gorka 2017). China also sells heavy weapons to African states for profit, but it specializes more in small arms and light weapons. Infamously, China sold more than $1 billion to both sides during the Ethiopian-Eritrean war of 1998–2000 (Alden 2005). In the early 2000s, China sold combat aircraft and naval patrol boats to Nigeria essentially as a profit-making activity (Ogunsanwo 2008).

Although arms sales may be troubling in general, arms transfers in the midst of domestic conflict or repression are especially so. China is guilty of both practices, and two cases have garnered particular attention. China has built a strong and durable relationship with Sudan, partly based on oil sector cooperation but also solidified through arms transfers. While the government of Sudan was fighting rebels in South Sudan and Darfur (see Chapter 2), the Chinese were both transferring arms to Sudan and helping Sudan to build its own arms factories at home (Taylor and Wu 2013). During the early years of the Darfur conflict especially, China also used its role on the UN Security Council to protect Sudan from international intervention. Starting in 2006, though, widespread criticism of China's ties with Sudan, and particularly its complicity in Darfur, prompted calls by human rights activists to label the 2008 Olympics, to be hosted in Beijing, the "Genocide Olympics." Concerned about its international reputation, China launched a public relations campaign to emphasize its constructive role in Sudan and openly pressured Sudan to accept a proposal for a hybrid African Union–United Nations peacekeeping mission in Darfur, which it finally did in 2007. This apparent shift in Chinese policy indicated the possibility of a more flexible approach to its engagement in Africa (Carmody and Taylor 2010).

The second highly problematic case is that of Zimbabwe. China made deal after deal to supply arms to the former regime of Robert Mugabe after 2000 (Taylor and Wu 2013). Some of these deals were concluded on barter terms, with the Mugabe regime transferring (illegal) ivory or minerals as payment. Mugabe's forces used these Chinese arms to secure the regime in general and to quell dissent during a succession of elections campaigns (see Chapter 5). The situation reached a low point as violence escalated ahead of the 2008 presidential elections, when Chinese troops were said to be assisting Mugabe's security forces against dissidents (Evans 2008). Around that time, China sent a shipload of seventy-seven tons of arms to Zimbabwe, but port workers in Durban, South Africa, refused to offload the shipment for fear of how the weapons would be used by Mugabe's forces; after subsequently being refused entry to ports in Mozambique, Namibia, and even Angola, the ship returned to China (Munnion 2008). Also in 2008, China joined Russia in vetoing a UN Security Council arms embargo against Zimbabwe. Although Sudan and Zimbabwe are the most infamous cases of Chinese arms being transferred at moments of violence and repression, many other similar examples could be cited;[15] China also has rapidly recognized new regimes in Africa after military coups d'état (Holslag 2011).

A final linkage between Africa and the BRICS has been through the contributions of some BRICS countries to peacekeeping or peacebuilding missions in Africa. In this area, India has been the most consistent contributor, beginning with the UN mission to Congo between 1960 and 1963. India remains a top-three contributor to UN peacekeeping, most of which is in Africa. Yet Chinese activity in African peacekeeping has drawn far more attention lately, due to its arguably political nature. From the 1970s through the 1990s, China was either indifferent to, suspicious of, or even hostile to most UN peacekeeping activity. But China reached a turning point with the Kosovo War in 1999, after which it began gradually to provide more and more support to UN peacekeeping in Africa (Taylor 2009). In recent years, China has been the biggest contributor to UN peacekeeping among the permanent five members (P5) of the UN Security Council. As of 2017, China had about 2,500 peacekeepers deployed in ten UN missions, including those in Darfur, the DRC, Liberia, Mali, South Sudan, and Western Sahara. By far its largest commitment was that of a 1,050-strong battalion in South Sudan, which deployed in 2015 (Chin-Hao 2017). In July 2017, China opened its first military base in Africa, intriguingly not far from the US military's Camp Lemmonier in Djibouti. According to the Chinese government, the naval/ground forces facility was designed to support China's peacekeeping and anti-piracy operations in Africa (Liang 2017). China's escalating peacekeeping commitments in Africa have naturally raised questions about its motives. Whereas some believe that China is reluctantly accepting a leadership role that has been thrust upon it, others suspect that China is trying to expand its influence in Africa through the guise of humanitarianism (Taylor 2009). The two explanations are not mutually exclusive, however.

This overview of politico-diplomatic relations between emerging powers and Africa raises the question of what the partners on each side gain from their growing ties. A large part of the answer lies in the previous section: the respective partners are pursuing economic gains for their own countries. It is useful in this sense to think not of states but of regimes. Both regimes in the emerging powers and those in African countries, "democratic" or otherwise, seek to boost their legitimacy. One direct way to do so is by increasing employment, the availability of consumer goods, and access to infrastructure. In turn, mutually beneficial trade and investment relations provide these goods, in respective measure, to the economic partners. China and India need energy and raw materials to keep their economic engines revving. Brazil, Russia, and South Africa need markets for their arms and other manufactured goods. The regimes that rule these countries thus gain by cultivating their economic relationships in Africa. African regimes, likewise, love to tout the benefits of their partnerships with their partners of the global South. Once again, regime security seems to be one key to understanding Africa's international relations.

Emerging powers also seek direct diplomatic benefits from their African partnerships. In the past, Beijing sought support for its bid to take over the Chinese seat at the UN, and then it sought to gain global recognition as the only true representative of all of the Chinese people. Its successful efforts to gain recognition from Africa's governments reflect this goal. In the current context, China's most acute disputes are with its Asian neighbors (Japan, the Philippines, Vietnam, etc.) with overlapping claims to islands and mineral rights in the South China Sea. If these disputes ever make it to the United Nations as a matter of international peace and security, China will surely draw upon the influence it has gained in Africa over the past three decades.

Russia needed exactly this kind of diplomatic "cover" after its annexation of Crimea, previously Ukrainian national territory, in March 2014. As a permanent member of the UN Security Council, Russia repeatedly blocked attempts by that body to take action on the issue. In lieu of a binding resolution, Ukraine, Poland, and four other countries introduced a symbolic resolution in the UN General Assembly condemning the annexation. It passed on March 27, 2014, with 100 votes in favor, including those of the United States and all EU member states. Among the African delegations, though, twenty-seven abstained, six were absent, and two (Sudan and Zimbabwe) voted against the resolution. Thus, overall, Russia had far more support for its illegal annexation of Crimea in Africa than it did elsewhere.

Brazil and India have a different reason for seeking support of African states in the UN: the two states are part of the so-called Group of Four (G4) (also including Germany and Japan) that has sought permanent membership on the UN Security Council. In the event that the

P5 were ever to permit a serious consideration of adding members to the ranks of the Security Council's permanent membership, Brazil and India would surely like to have broad African support.

Aside from their specific aims in the UN and other bodies, the BRICS are arguably seeking to elevate their status in the international community in general. China, with the world's largest population and second largest economy, is a potential second superpower. India has the world's seventh largest economy, and one of the fastest-growing; it also has aspirations of a greater global role. Support from African states is crucial to these aspirations. Likewise, Christina Stolte boldly argues that Brazil's new activism in Africa that began under Lulu "is motivated by the aspiration to gain recognition as a Great Power" (2015: 7). For South Africa, support from its continental peers is crucial to its aspirations to maintain its status as an African leader, as well as one of the global South more broadly (Alden and Schoeman 2013).

For African states and regimes, too, relationships with emerging powers are about identity, autonomy, and status, as well as economic development. The dream of development through South-South cooperation, rather than Western aid, is alive and well in Africa. Many if not most African leaders find it more appealing to cooperate with their "brothers" from the global South than with former colonizers and perceived imperialists. Most significant, the BRICS and other emerging states represent an alternative to the politico-economic regime represented by the international financial institutions and Western states. The IFIs have insisted since the era of constructive engagement that the role of the state in African development must necessarily be minimal (see Chapter 4); none of the BRICS take such a view. On the contrary, all consider the role of the state to be crucial in development. Since both democratically chosen and authoritarian African rulers depend upon state patronage to secure their political fortunes, they generally prefer the more state-centric development model of the BRICS.

Second, as a matter of status, the BRICS simply have paid more attention to Africa than have the traditional great powers. Among European states, only France has consistently attempted the kind of multilateral summitry now being practiced by China and India (see Chapter 11). (The 2014 United States–Africa Leaders Summit discussed in Chapter 10 was likely a one-off event in US diplomacy.) Unlike France, however, China and India do not share the burden of a colonial past (even if some African leaders have treated Indians as collaborators in the British imperial project). Rather, they were also victims of European colonialism.

Finally, the BRICS have generally had little to say about democracy or human rights, unlike the Western powers (see Chapter 5); none "seek to apply political conditionality" (Carmody 2013: 133). China's nonin-terference policy with respect to domestic policies translates into qui-etude about gross human rights violations and unconstitutional changes of power, as even China's sympathetic observers admit (Chan 2013). Meanwhile, even Africa's democracies, and African states with improv-ing human rights records, detest the perceived paternalism of the West-ern states and groups that criticize their shortcomings. For instance, there has been an intensive African backlash against the International Criminal Court's habit of indicting mostly African political and military figures for their war crimes and crimes against humanity. In February 2017, the AU passed a nonbinding resolution calling for a mass African withdrawal from the Court (see Chapter 6). Further, African states that have come under Western sanctions, notably Sudan and Zimbabwe, have assiduously cultivated their relationships with the emerging states, particularly China. As a result, China has developed close relations with some African "defiant regimes" (see Chapter 11). African regimes that engage in gross human rights violations enjoy a certain degree of pro-tection from both China and Russia in the UN Security Council, where binding international sanctions are passed and monitored.

Interpreting the New Salience of Relations Between Emerging Powers and Africa

What are we to make of the escalating engagement of the emerging powers with sub-Saharan Africa? Such engagement brings both benefits and dangers to Africans and the states they inhabit. The growing inter-est of the BRICS in Africa disrupts and complicates the stagnant and neocolonial relationships that existed from the 1960s into the 1980s, and beyond in some cases. The multiplicity of potential partners and investors surely gives African governments more options than they had in the past. Africa's rising economic fortunes of the 2000s and 2010s appear to be linked, at least in part, to mounting investments from the emerging powers. On the other hand, the wave of enthusiasm for democratization that swept Africa in the early 1990s has now been tem-pered. Serious human rights abuses, even to the level of genocide in western Sudan, continue to curse the continent. Despite the rise of Chi-nese peacekeeping in Africa, and Chinese diplomacy in South Sudan and some other places, none of the BRICS has an easy formula for help-ing African countries deal with their civil or regionalized conflicts.

Economic realists expect states to engage in neomercantilist behav-ior, and when they do so successfully, they will enjoy economic devel-opment. This is how realists would explain the rise of China and India. When important powers enjoy long-term economic development, this redounds to their domestic power and makes them more assertive on the global stage. Realists from Morgenthau to Mearsheimer have expected rising powers to seek both economic advantage and greater status in other parts of the world. Hence, realists are not surprised by the rise of the BRICS in Africa or by the fact that Brazil's engagement with Africa has faltered since its economy contracted in 2011. They are unlikely to take South Africa's claims to leadership within the continent seriously, either, while its economy remains stagnant and its domestic politics unsettled. Realists are unmoved by the influence of Africa's historical solidarity with South Africa's black majority during the depressing decades of apartheid. In the escalating engagement between the BRICS and African states, realists do not expect real unity, or collective engagement, on either side: states will continue to be the main agents, and the representatives of those states will try to get the best deals they can for those whom they rule and represent.

Liberals in the economic sense are both more excited and alarmed by the escalation of emerging-power investment in Africa. They value economic competition and open trade among countries as a catalyst of economic development. The expansion of Africa's trading partners and investors seems to have produced precisely that result. Liberals also are concerned with human welfare and believe that it can best be achieved through economic growth. Investments by the BRICS and other emerging powers are part of the explanation for Africa's recent growth spurt. On the other hand, among international relations theorists, political liberals are also the most consistent advocates for the advance of human rights and democracy. Since none of the BRICS, including the three democracies, have contributed much to this cause in Africa, they are alarmed. China's seemingly indifferent embrace of the al-Bashir (Sudan) and the former Mugabe (Zimbabwe) regimes is only the most salient example of support for Africa's more ruthless leaders. Political liberals decry these politics, as they did the West's earlier indifference to apartheid and colonialism on the continent.

Constructivists inevitably see the power of a common identity at play in relations between Africa and emerging powers. Since at least the Bandung Afro-Asian Summit of 1955,[16] China has tried to position itself as a global leader for the former victims of European colonialism (Chan 2013). China has a moral commitment to Africa based on this shared identity as well as economic interests there. India, too, has a shared colonial history with Africa that is intertwined with its economic interests (Roy 2013). As for Brazil, unlike his Eurocentric predecessors, President da Silva embraced for the first time the country's African roots. He viewed Africa as "a cradle of Brazilian civilization" (Carmody 2013: 115) and evoked a common racial heritage to engage the continent for geopolitical ends. South Africa's common historical, cultural, and identity stake in the rest of the continent is far more obvious. Constructivists are likely to assert the importance of South Africa for Africa's future, however limited its economic means and internal disarray (Alden and Schoeman 2013).

Neo-Marxists are deeply ambivalent about the escalation of emerging power involvement in Africa. Many are nostalgic about China's past commitments to economic equality and anticolonialism and its efforts at African development in an earlier era. Many viewed India under the Congress Party with somewhat similar affection. In the 1970s, radicals dreamed that South-South trade would help overcome the residual economic dominance of former colonizers. Today, though, India and China have embraced private capital as the major driver of investment. Even the ruling ANC party of South Africa, once allied with communists, has reluctantly accepted the transformative power of private capital. Observing China's splurge of investment in Africa, some neo-Marxists like Tukumbi Lumumba-Kasongo have accused China of having "an instinct of acting as a neo-colonialist power in Africa" (2011: 259). At the same time, the dream of South-South trade has finally come true, though not exactly as envisioned in the 1970s. Moreover, the results seem to be positive for African growth, if not for the distribution of income. As a result, many radicals are deeply conflicted about the rise of the BRICS in Africa.

For African rulers of all political stripes, the BRICS represent above all another opportunity to reinforce their regime security. As noted earlier, authoritarian regimes are apt to rely upon Chinese and Russian arms and security equipment to confront dissenters. Likewise, the funding attained through natural resource exports can be channeled into the patronage networks that mute dissent. Elected regimes need to deliver the economic goods to their voters, who can either retain them in office or send them packing at election time. The aid and investments of the BRICS often make life better and thus make voters kinder to those in power.

Case Study: Sino-Zambian Relations

Relations between China and Zambia illustrate many of the broader patterns of China's engagement with African states over the past sixty years. The exuberance of the early independence period in Africa coincided with a radicalization in China that led to the Cultural Revolution in 1966. African rulers and citizens urgently needed to establish themselves as truly independent of their erstwhile colonizers, and to support others still enduring colonization or white minority rule. Meanwhile, China wished to position itself as a great power independent of the

Soviet Union, as well as the "imperialist" United States. It thus took a leading role in the Non-Aligned Movement that had emerged in the 1950s. China, then still very poor, made relatively large commitments of development aid in Africa from the early 1960s until the death of Mao Zedong in 1976. Afterward, there was a lull in Chinese investment in Africa over the next twenty years as China focused on internal development and partially liberalized its state-run economy. Beginning in the late 1990s, China again ramped up its investment in Africa but this time on a much more pragmatic—and arguably selfish—basis. Although the transparently self-interested nature of Chinese engagement in this second period created many tensions and resentments, Africans, including Zambians, have largely concluded that the benefits of Chinese investment outweigh the costs, perceived and real.

At the moment of Zambia's independence in October 1964, it was in substantial need of external assistance from a neutral source. The first president of Zambia, Kenneth Kaunda, followed a philosophy of African socialism that avoided both the Marxism-Leninism of the Soviet Union and unfettered capitalism. But his country was almost entirely dependent upon European capital; at that time, Zambia's economy was dominated by copper exports produced in mines still controlled by the British South Africa Company, founded in 1890 by imperialist Cecil Rhodes. Moreover, landlocked Zambia was nearly surrounded by European colonies or pro-Western independent states: Portuguese Angola and Mozambique, British Rhodesia (soon to be ruled by its white minority), and pro-Western Congo and Malawi. The only like-minded regime in a neighboring state was that of Julius Nyerere in Tanzania. During colonial times, Zambia's copper exports, and most other trade, had gone by rail through Southern Rhodesia and South Africa. At independence, this situation became intolerable to Kaunda and his fellow Zambians.

This context perfectly explains the need for the construction of the TAZARA railway. The railway allowed Zambia to export its copper and conduct other trade through friendly Tanzania, whose President Nyerere shared Kaunda's Afro-socialist ideology. It also allowed Zambia to avoid conducting its trade through white-ruled Rhodesia and South Africa. Zambia soon became a major supporter of Nelson Mandela and the ANC and thus the object of hostile acts by the government of apartheid South Africa. Thousands of Zambian workers gained new skills while building the railway. For its part, China pulled off a coup of ideological solidarity with two key African allies. The great Afro-Chinese achievement was made possible because the World Bank had previously studied the feasibility of a railway from the copperbelt to Dar es Salaam and found it wanting. The United States belatedly decided to fund a Tan-Zam highway project beginning in 1968 (Monson 2009), but this effort received almost no international attention. By contrast, the TAZARA railway was intensively celebrated, within China, Tanzania, and Zambia and around the nonaligned world. Indeed, the construction of the railway is remembered in those countries as a heroic achievement to this day, even if the recollections of the Chinese and African workers on the railway are variable and contested (Monson 2013).

The official handover of the TAZARA railway in July 1976 preceded the death of Mao Zedong by two months. Deng Xiaoping, a liberalizing reformer, only gradually consolidated his power thereafter. In the meantime, Chinese authorities undertook a prolonged review of China's aid policies and their results around the world (Bräutigam 2009). This review ultimately led to a reduction in the levels of Chinese aid and investment, and a refocus on the maintenance and repair of existing projects, rather than the launching of grand new ones. This pattern held in Zambia; whereas Chinese grants and loans to Zambia associated with TAZARA exceeded 600 million yuan, total Chinese support over the next twenty-five years did not reach that level (Mwanawina 2007, cited in Mutesa 2010). This retrenchment by China did not imperil the "all-weather friendship" that characterized Sino-Zambia relations after TAZARA, but it reflected China's effort to focus on internal economic development during this period. In the mid-1990s, Zambia belatedly began to undertake its own economic reforms, privatizing many state-owned companies that had been nationalized in the 1960s, including the mining sector. At the same time, the end of apartheid in South Africa in 1994 raised the possibility of renewed Zambian trade through that country. Transport on TAZARA fell drastically, as the railway fell into disrepair and old trade routes reopened. China's trade with Zambia in 1995 was only $3.5 million, or just 0.2 percent of Zambia's total international trade of $1.77 billion (International Monetary Fund 2017a).

In 1998, China undertook its first new major investment in Zambia in more than twenty-five years. In that year, the China Non-Ferrous Metals Corporation (CNMC) purchased an 85 percent stake in a defunct copper mine at Chambishi, closed since 1988, for $20 million (Bräutigam 2009). The CNMC then invested $132 million in the mine before reopening it in 2003 (Human Rights Watch 2011a). In the next several years, the CNMC launched three further mining-related operations in Zambia, including a copper ore processing plant, a copper smelter, and one further mining operation. In 2007, China announced the opening of two multifacility economic zones (MFEZs) in Zambia, one at Chambishi and the second in Lusaka ("Lusaka East"). The MFEZs are essentially free trade zones, where China can import equipment and other goods free of Zambian tariffs for five years. Companies operating in them receive tax reduction incentives over the first ten years that they make a profit, including no taxes for the first five years (Zambian Ministry of Commerce, Trade, and Industry 2017). In principle, other foreign companies can invest in the MFEZs, but so far only Chinese companies have done so. In 2012, Zambia and China opened a third MFEZ, "Lusaka South." Chinese firms accelerated their push to make investments in Zambia beyond mining through these zones after 2007. By March 2017, China had invested $1.6 billion in the three MFEZs through forty-eight companies, creating 8,630 jobs (*Zambia Daily Mail* 2017). In 2015, China was Zambia's second largest trading partner, importing over $1 billion (mostly in Zambian commodities) and exporting nearly $700 million (mainly in mining equipment and consumer goods) (International Monetary Fund 2017a).[17]

China's increased involvement in Zambia has not gone without criticism, however. Unlike in the 1960s, China's investment in Zambia since 1998 has been almost entirely on a commercial basis. Chinese firms have invested in Zambia to make profits. The Chinese government has supported them to ensure a flow of commodities to China but also to facilitate the capitalization of these firms. Since they operate on a profit-making basis, Chinese investors have sought to minimize their costs, including expenses on local labor and safety equipment. They have frequently skirted Zambian and international law in their treatment of workers. As a result, Zambian laborers at Chinese-run facilities and their sympathizers have developed deep grievances over the past two decades. These include very low wages paid to Zambian workers, sometimes even lower than the official minimum wage; differentials in wages paid to Chinese expatriates and Zambian workers doing similar jobs; often-brutal working conditions inside the mines and factories, and the inattention of Chinese firms to safety needs; and the violence periodically used against Zambian workers who protest deplorable wages and conditions (Human Rights Watch 2011a; Carmody and Hampwaye 2010; Mutesa 2010). A low point came in 2005 when forty-nine Zambian workers were killed at an explosives factory affiliated with the Chambishi mine; the following year, Chinese security guards shot and wounded six Zambian workers protesting at the mine (Bräutigam 2009). Sympathy for the miners was widespread, and Zambians also resented the repatriation of profits by Chinese firms. Beyond the industrial sector, Chinese merchants were accused of selling cheap clothing and other products, undercutting Zambian producers and sellers (Carmody and Hampwaye 2010). On the other hand, most Zambian analysts recognized the great value and impact of Chinese investments; they called not for a reduction in Chinese activity, but for more regulation and channeling of Chinese investment by the Zambian government (Ndulo 2008).

As Zambian resentment of Chinese investment in the country escalated, the issue increasingly factored into domestic political debates. In 2006, presidential candidate Michael Sata, leader of the opposition Patriotic Front, publicly condemned Chinese labor and commercial practices during his campaign. Running on a populist anti-Chinese platform, he argued that "Zambia has become a province of China" and "we need investors, not infesters" (quoted in Fitzgerald 2008). As Sata's popularity rose, China broke its long-standing practice of staying out of a country's domestic politics and threatened to suspend diplomatic ties if he became president. Although Sata garnered the majority of votes in areas with a heavy Chinese presence, he lost the election, prompting anti-Chinese riots in Lusaka (Carmody and Taylor 2010). In 2008, following the unexpected death in office of President Levy Mwanawasa, Sata again ran for president and again criticized Chinese practices. After the election, which he also lost, however, he clarified that he welcomed Chinese investments in Zambia and would protect them if ever elected president, while still condemning the abuses of Chinese bosses (Shacinda 2008).

Finally, in 2011, Sata was elected president of Zambia on his fourth attempt, defeating incumbent Rupiah Banda, who had continued to work closely with the Chinese during his time in office. Although Sata's campaign once again involved harsh anti-Chinese rhetoric, his message softened quickly after coming into office, presumably with the realization of the importance of Chinese investment to the Zambian economy. Concerned about ties between the two countries, China sent its ambassador to congratulate Sata on his victory and promised to hold Chinese investors in Zambia accountable for their business practices (Leslie 2016). For his part, just one month after being inaugurated, Sata hosted a luncheon at State House for Chinese investors, prompting criticism that he had made a U-turn from his preelection promises (*Lusaka Times* 2011). Even as Sata's government increased the minimum wage, China and Zambia maintained close economic relations and launched a third free trade zone the next year. When Sata died in office three years after his election, Chinese investments in Zambia were greater than ever.

Relations between China and Zambia reflect a broader pattern of Sino-African relations. After China's reengagement with Africa in the late 1990s, now with a bigger and more market-oriented economy, both Africans and Chinese had to adjust to new realities. This time, China's investments would be through partially privatized firms, with less direction from the Chinese state. These firms operated according to the logic of the market and frequently exploited African workers for profit. Such practices brought protests by some workers and criticism by members of the political class, particularly civil society representatives and opposition leaders. Both Africans and Chinese have become more realistic about their new economic partnerships, unlike the ideologically driven relations of the past. Meanwhile, more grassroots and organic relationships are taking hold. Indeed, "recent Chinese arrivals have implanted themselves in almost every lucrative sector of the economy" (French 2014: 13). Although the number of Chinese in Zambia is disputed,[18] China's influence there is not. The influence of China and the Chinese in Zambia is not likely to diminish in the decades to come, though it will continue to be a subject of political debate. More generally, Africa's relations with the BRICS and all of the developing world have become far more important since the end of the Cold War.

Notes

1. The term *euro zone* refers to the nineteen European Union countries that use the euro as their common currency.

2. During the Cold War, the Soviet Union had more capacity to provide aid, notably military aid (see Chapter 3), but Russian aid has since been minimal.

3. Both sets of figures count debt relief and the interest savings on concessional loans in the definition of aid.

4. The figures in the table in this source are given in Indian rupees and total 9.24 billion for the former year and 26.99 billion for the latter year. These figures were converted into US dollars at a rate of $1 to 45 Indian rupees; the rupee fluctuated around this value in each of the respective years.

5. We feel confident in making this assertion, though UNECA reported that China's total stock of foreign investment was only $9 billion, whereas that of India was $13.6 billion in 2013.

6. Sub-Saharan Africa's trade with Russia is even less and is not analyzed here. Its trade with Russia was only one-third that of its trade with Brazil in 2015 (International Monetary Fund 2017a).

7. Brazil has fewer globally integrated multinational companies than South Africa, owing to the latter's historical relationship with Britain. As a result, Brazil ranks lower on DHL's "global connectedness index," at 57, than does South Africa, at 47 (Ghemawat and Altman 2016).

8. References to Brazil's foreign aid in the media diminished rapidly after the Brazilian economy began to decline. Brazil's economy actually contracted in size in 2009, and then again in 2014 and 2015.

9. Figures for 2015 appeared to be incomplete at the time of research, so 2014 was selected as the year for comparison.

10. The GCC includes Bahrain, Kuwait, Oman, Qatar, Saudi Arabia, and the UAE. The three of these countries not discussed in the previous paragraph also have substantial, though smaller, trade relations with sub-Saharan Africa.

11. Somaliland has enjoyed de facto, though not internationally recognized, independence since the early 1990s and is generally regarded as a well-functioning state, especially compared to Somalia proper, which has not had an effective government for nearly that entire period (see Chapter 10).

12. For an alternative view, see Alden and Schoeman 2013.

13. Following the victory in 1949 of the Chinese Communist Party in the Chinese civil war, the leaders of the Chinese National Party (Kuomintang) fled to Taiwan and set up a separate government there. The Kuomintang government in Taipei, with Western support, was then able to gain recognition at the UN as the representative of the Chinese people until 1971.

14. The website, including an overview of the third summit, may be found at http://mea.gov.in/india-africa-forum-summit-2015/index.html.

15. For instance, China transferred anti-riot equipment to a new regime installed in Madagascar by a coup d'état in 2009 (Holslag 2011).

16. The Bandung conference was the first large meeting of the independent African and Asian states in 1955. Among the African states participating were Egypt, Ethiopia, Ghana, Liberia, Libya, and Sudan. The PRC attempted to position itself as the leader of the emergent group of countries from the developing world, many of which had only recently attained independence.

17. Zambia's leading trade partner was Switzerland, whose Glencore International mining company owns a 73 percent stake in Zambia's biggest mine, the Mopani mine.

18. President Sata's figure of 80,000 Chinese in Zambia was often cited in the press, though estimates range from as high as 100,000 (French 2014) to a more modest 13,000 (Postel 2016).

PART 5

Conclusion

13

International Relations and Domestic Politics Entwined

Africa's international relations are remarkably complex and involve a wide range of actors with multiple, often competing motivations. Within the continent, international relations are shaped most importantly by states and their leaders but also by regional and subregional bodies, civil society organizations, businesses, militant groups, and individual Africans, both elite and nonelite, a point to which we return later. Outside actors include other governments, especially those of the United States, European countries, and emerging powers like China and India, as well as nongovernmental organizations, international financial institutions, corporations, private foundations, criminal networks, and others. These actors have been involved to varying degrees in the topics covered throughout this book, from the historical context of Africa's international relations to more recent economic, political, and security challenges.

At independence in the 1960s, African countries were relics of the colonial system that created them. Having been formed with little regard to existing cultural and political realities, the states that African leaders inherited were inherently weak, lacking legitimacy and popular support. The state often was seen as a source of wealth whose resources could (and should) be used to enrich leaders' personal networks. African countries also emerged from colonialism as exporters of raw materials and importers of finished goods, with infrastructure designed accordingly, which perpetuated their position of weakness in the global economy. Despite the arbitrary nature of colonial borders, postcolonial leaders opted to preserve these boundaries to protect their own carved-out domains while avoiding the need to establish more legitimate authority and services. Independence also came to Africa at the peak of the Cold War, putting pressure on leaders to choose a side. While some tried to avoid alignment, the need for economic and military aid drove many to establish close relations with either the United States or the Soviet Union. These external alliances fueled violent conflicts in various parts of Africa, further complicating the quest for stability in the postcolonial era.

Africa's weak position in the global economy and great need for development left its states heavily dependent on foreign aid and thus subject to conditions imposed by donors. Western economists initially advocated state-centric approaches, including substantial investment in infrastructure and social services as well as tariffs and subsidies to encourage domestic production of industrialized goods. After the global economic crises of the 1970s and the resulting debt crisis, though, the World Bank and the International Monetary Fund started pressuring countries around the world to implement a process of structural adjustment that would extricate the government from the economy and rely on free market forces to generate development. Even as that process failed to bring about renewed economic growth in Africa, due in part to a lack of foreign investment, Western donors added political conditions to their foreign aid, first demanding "good governance" and later calling more directly for political liberalization. In the 1990s, as this international pressure converged with long-standing domestic demands, governments throughout Africa loosened political restrictions and permitted multiparty competition, though the extent to which this represented true democratization varied widely. Political changes in many countries also created an opportunity to inject new energy into the continent's intergovernmental organizations, including the African Union from 2002, with a goal of promoting greater regional and subregional cooperation around shared interests.

A key factor hindering the realization of dreams for greater freedom and development in Africa has been insecurity in many countries. Instead of declining after the Cold War, as many had hoped, the number and severity of African conflicts increased in the 1990s. Many conflicts started as a result of failures in domestic governance, often including the marginalization of one group or another, but became broader regional wars involving multiple state and nonstate actors. The wars in the eastern Democratic Republic of Congo are rooted in the predatory nature of the state over several decades, for example, but were triggered in part by the influx of refugees and militants from neighboring Rwanda and ultimately came to involve troops from at least five African countries. Although details vary, civil conflicts in Liberia, Sierra Leone, Sudan, and Somalia, among others, have undergone a similar process of regionalization. The international community has responded to most conflicts by providing humanitarian assistance and sponsoring peace negotiations; in some cases, the United Nations has authorized peace-keeping operations. Even when international action has been humanitarian in nature, warring parties often have sought to manipulate the situation for their own benefit, at times exacerbating conflicts. Protracted violence in some countries and poor governance in others have contributed to an increase in the number of Africans migrating within the region and beyond, creating added challenges and fueling political debates in many host communities.

Externally, the United States and European countries, especially the former colonizers, are still very important actors in Africa, providing significant foreign aid and trade opportunities. But their relations with African states are necessarily burdened by their past histories in the region, including decades of colonialism and neocolonialism and disruptive interventions during the Cold War. The fickleness of Western interest in Africa, in part due to vacillations in these countries' own domestic politics, and the emphasis on natural resource exploitation have done little to diminish long-standing suspicion and distrust toward these countries among many Africans. The recent rise of emerging-power interest in Africa, especially from China, but also from India, Brazil, and various Middle Eastern countries, has created a new dynamic, providing an alternative source of aid and investment that most African governments have welcomed and allowing them to avoid Western conditionality. Even so, the familiar focus on natural resources, especially oil, and concerns about the economic and political effects of emerging-power engagement have started to generate a new round of debate about the extent to which African countries can truly benefit from their relations with external actors.

This book has focused on these aspects of Africa's international relations, though we have inevitably neglected other relevant topics that warrant consideration elsewhere. Several crosscutting themes emerge from our examination of these topics. The first is the strong interconnection between domestic and international politics. Even as the foreign relations of African states cannot be fully understood without examining the domestic political contexts in which they take place, those domestic politics also are shaped by broader regional and global dynamics. This theme is most obvious in our examination of African conflicts that became regionalized through the cross-border movement of militants and weapons. An analysis of the civil war in Liberia, for example, is not complete without considering any number of international factors: the support of regional actors such as Libyan leader Muammar Qaddafi for Charles Taylor's rebels; taxes paid to Taylor's movement by the US-based Firestone company; Taylor's involvement in smuggling diamonds out of neighboring Sierra Leone; the departure (and later repatriation) of hundreds of thousands of Liberian refugees; and the Nigerian-led ECOMOG military intervention into the country, to name just a few. Such conflicts clearly must be examined and addressed within their broader global context.

Africa's dependence on foreign aid also bridges domestic and international politics, with leaders typically seeking external support not only to pursue economic goals but also (and often more importantly) to keep themselves in power. When external support drops, as it did in many African countries in the early 1990s, leaders have a hard time sustaining patronage networks and find their domestic legitimacy undermined, at times leading to instability. Foreign donors often explicitly push for domestic political change as well, as when Western governments started promoting multiparty competition in Africa after the Cold War. The emergence in Africa of alternative donors beyond the traditional Western sources again has implications for domestic politics, both by allowing some authoritarian governments to survive despite Western sanctions and by provoking debates among political actors within Africa about how to manage these new connections. The distinction between Africa's comparative politics and its international relations is thus a false one, as they are inextricably intertwined.

A second theme is that the recent rise in engagement by China and other emerging powers has significantly altered the landscape of Africa's international relations. Although a specific focus of Chapter 12, emerging-power interest in Africa has affected nearly every topic discussed throughout the book. The availability of alternative sources of aid and investment, for example, has undermined the use of conditionality by traditional donors. African leaders who want to avoid implementing free market economic reforms or embracing multiparty competition, as required by many Western donors, can instead seek support from China, as Zimbabwe, Sudan, and Angola have done. The influence of China is apparent in regional relations too, as the Chinese have worked closely with the African Union, even constructing a huge new headquarters building in Addis Ababa that opened in 2012. When it comes to Africa's security challenges, emerging powers' interest again plays a role. On the one hand, increased demand for Africa's natural resources, including everything from oil and diamonds to ivory and rhinoceros horns, fuels competition that can turn violent, especially when armed actors exploit such resources to fund their operations. External support of warring parties often sustains conflicts once they start. On the other hand, China, India, and other emerging powers also have supported ceasefire negotiations and provided peacekeeping troops to the continent, seeking to play an increasing role in conflict resolution. Even when it comes to migration, there has been a sharp increase in the number of people from China and other emerging states living in Africa, just as the numbers of Africans living in those countries also have risen. While China certainly is the most prominent of the emerging powers in Africa, the engagement of India, Brazil, and various Middle Eastern countries is expected only to rise in the decades to come.

Third, African regional organizations are doing more to address the continent's political and security challenges than ever before. Driven by eminent personalities such as Thabo Mbeki, Olusegun Obasanjo, Desmond Tutu, Graça Machel, and others, regional bodies have launched various programs to promote conflict resolution and good governance. Freed from its predecessor's focus on nonintervention, the African Union has authorized peacekeeping operations in several countries, though it has been slow to respond in others. Despite faults in the process, the peer review mechanism of the New Partnership for Africa's Development has established the concept of African leaders evaluating their own peers on various political and economic criteria. Subregional organizations such as ECOWAS, the EAC, and SADC have sought to address security challenges in member states even as they ramp up economic integration efforts. This is not to say that the African Union and subregional organizations have dramatically transformed themselves or the states they represent; indeed, the jury is still out on many of these initiatives. But these bodies have demonstrated more willingness to intervene to address internal political and security issues than in the past, which suggests the possibility of a more proactive role in the future. The challenge moving forward is to turn initiatives developed by Africa's diplomatic elite into true economic, political, and security cooperation that can make a substantive difference in the lives of everyday Africans.

This leads to the fourth theme weaving its way throughout this book, which is that Africa's international relations are not solely the domain of states. Relations among African countries and with the rest of the world are shaped by a huge number of nonstate actors: aid agencies, religious groups, commercial enterprises, foreign investors, rebel groups, criminal networks, refugees, migrants, diaspora populations, and the list goes on. Many of these nonstate actors have explicitly sought to encourage positive change in Africa. Nongovernmental organizations such as the Mo Ibrahim Foundation, for example, have promoted good governance by publicly criticizing authoritarian leaders and rewarding democratic ones. Numerous think tanks and independent media outlets on the continent publish detailed analyses of conflicts, corruption scandals, and other problems, often proposing policy solutions. Various private companies have adopted fair trade standards to try to improve living conditions for farmers and miners. The influence of other nonstate actors has been more controversial, though. This may be obvious when it comes to militant groups and criminal networks, but even outside groups that are presumed to be less nefarious can have malign effects in Africa. To take one example, Western evangelical groups with distinctly homophobic agendas recently have encouraged politicians in several African countries to pursue domestic legislation criminalizing "nonconforming" sexual activities, fueling an environment of hate that has led to violence against gays, lesbians, and their allies. In this era of instantaneous global communication through the Internet and social media, international relations are conducted not just by states and established organizations but also by individual people and their personal networks interacting through countless channels.

Finally, the fifth theme emerging from this book is that no single theory can explain Africa's international relations. Protecting regime security is certainly a central motivating factor for many African leaders, as realists would expect, and the same can be said for leaders of other countries around the world. But this prioritization of staying in power does not mean that African states do not cooperate to pursue common interests through international organizations such as the African Union, as liberal-institutionalists highlight, at times ceding some control in order to do so. In their interactions, African leaders also are influenced by the spread of international norms, from self-determination to democracy; moreover, the ways in which these norms are constructed, or understood, have evolved over time. And it is clear that Africa's international relations have been shaped by its position of dependence in the global economy, even as its resources have attracted considerable foreign attention. Thus, many factors influence Africa's international relations, including, but not limited to, power, interests, ideas, and wealth. Because of this wide range of possible explanatory variables, the field of international relations has largely moved beyond the search for a single theory. Instead, as we have done in this book, most present-day scholars seek to understand international relations by examining a combination of relevant factors that vary depending upon the outcome being examined.

In the end, Africa's international relations have implications not only for those living within the continent but also for people around the world. Outsiders are connected to Africans in myriad ways they often do not even realize. Consider, for example, a white male in his twenties living somewhere in the midwestern United States. Why should he care about what is going on in Africa? For one, his consumption habits influence economic and political patterns in the region, whether he eats chocolate made from cocoa picked by a child laborer in Côte d'Ivoire, drinks coffee harvested in Rwanda, or buys a workout shirt manufactured in Botswana. He probably has a cell phone or laptop computer (or both) made with gold, tantalum, and other minerals from eastern Congo, and may be saving up to buy a ring with a diamond from the Central African Republic. When his demand for these products increases, higher prices can fuel competition for land and resources within Africa. And when conflicts emerge or supplies are cut off, the prices he pays may rise. Perhaps this American comes from a farming family that sells beans and maize to the US government to provide as food aid in Niger. At the same time, they benefit from subsidies that allow them to sell their products below cost, driving down prices paid to farmers in Burkina Faso. This well-intentioned American may hear about the conflict in South Sudan and decide to donate to an aid agency, not realizing that militants there are stealing humanitarian assistance to benefit their own side. The point here, of course, is that we are all connected to Africa in some way, even if we do not realize it. It is only through closer examination of the actors and factors shaping Africa's international relations that we can make sense of these interconnections and seek to harness them toward positive change.

Acronyms

ACOA	American Committee on Africa
ACOTA	African Contingency Operations Training Assistance (United States)
ACP	African, Caribbean, and Pacific
ACRI	Africa Crisis Response Initiative (United States)
ADF	Allied Democratic Forces (Zaire)
AEC	African Economic Community
AFDL	Alliance of Democratic Forces for the Liberation of Congo (DRC)
AFISMA	African-led International Support Mission in Mali
AFRICOM	US Africa Command
AGOA	African Growth and Opportunity Act
AMIB	African Union Mission in Burundi
AMIS	African Union Mission in Sudan
AMISOM	African Union Mission in Somalia
AMU	Arab Maghreb Union
ANC	African National Congress (South Africa)
APF	African Peace Facility
APRM	African Peer Review Mechanism
APSA	African Peace and Security Architecture
AQIM	al-Qaeda in the Islamic Maghreb
ARC	African Risk Capacity
ARF	African Renaissance and International Cooperation Fund
ASEAN	Association of Southeast Asian Nations
ASF	African Standby Force
AU	African Union
BRICS	Brazil, Russia, India, China, and South Africa
CAR	Central African Republic
CBO	community-based organization
CCM	Chama cha Mapinduzi (Party of the Revolution) (Tanzania)
CEAO	Economic Community of West Africa
CFA	Communauté Financière Africaine

CIA	Central Intelligence Agency (United States)
CJTF-HOA	Combined Joint Task Force–Horn of Africa
CNMC	China Non-Ferrous Metals Corporation
COMESA	Common Market for Eastern and Southern Africa
CPA	Comprehensive Peace Agreement (Sudan)
CSO	civil society organization
CUF	Civic United Front (Tanzania)
DAC	Development Assistance Committee (OECD)
DDR	disarmament, demobilization, and reintegration
DRC	Democratic Republic of Congo
EAC	East African Community
ECCAS	Economic Community of Central African States
ECOMICI	ECOWAS Mission in Côte d'Ivoire
ECOMIL	ECOWAS Mission in Liberia
ECOMOG	ECOWAS Ceasefire Monitoring Group
ECOWAS	Economic Community of West African States
EDF	European Development Fund
EEBC	Eritrea-Ethiopia Boundary Commission
EEC	European Economic Community
EIDHR	European Instrument for Democracy and Human Rights
EPLF	Eritrean People's Liberation Front
EU	European Union
FAC	Congolese Armed Forces
FARC	Revolutionary Armed Forces of Colombia
FCCD	Fund for Cooperation, Compensation, and Development (ECOWAS)
FDI	foreign direct investment
FIB	Force Intervention Brigade
FLS	Frontline States
FNCI	New Forces of Côte d'Ivoire
FNLA	National Front for the Liberation of Angola
FOCAC	Forum on China-Africa Cooperation
FRELIMO	Mozambique Liberation Front
G4	Group of Four (Brazil, Germany, India, Japan)
GCC	Gulf Cooperation Council
GDP	gross domestic product
GPOI	Global Peace Operations Initiative (United States)
HIPC	Heavily Indebted Poor Country Initiative
ICC	International Criminal Court
ICRC	International Committee of the Red Cross
ICU	Islamic Courts Union (Somalia)
IDA	International Development Association (World Bank)
IDP	internally displaced person
IFI	international financial institution
IGAD	Intergovernmental Authority on Development
IGO	intergovernmental organization
IMET	International Military and Education Training (United States)
IMF	International Monetary Fund
INGO	international nongovernmental organization
IR	international relations
IRC	International Rescue Committee
ISI	import substitution industrialization

ISIS	Islamic State of Iraq and Syria
ITEC	Indian Technical and Economic Cooperation
JAES	Joint Africa-EU Strategy
KANU	Kenyan African National Union
LRA	Lord's Resistance Army (Uganda)
LURD	Liberians United for Reconciliation and Democracy
M23	March 23 Movement (DRC)
MAJ	Ministry of Agricultural Jihad (Iran)
MDC	Movement for Democratic Change (Zimbabwe)
MDRI	Multilateral Debt Relief Initiative
MEND	Movement for the Emancipation of the Niger Delta
MFEZ	multifacility economic zone
MINURSO	United Nations Mission for the Referendum in Western Sahara
MINUSMA	United Nations Multidimensional Integrated Stabilization Mission in Mali
MJP	Movement for Justice and Peace (Côte d'Ivoire)
MLC	Movement for the Liberation of Congo
MNC	National Congolese Movement
MNLA	National Movement for the Liberation of Azawad
MODEL	Movement for Democracy in Liberia
MONUC	United Nations Organization Mission in the Democratic Republic of the Congo
MPCI	Patriotic Movement of Côte d'Ivoire
MPIGO	Ivorian Popular Movement of the Great West
MPLA	Movement for the Popular Liberation of Angola
MUJAO	Movement for Unity and Jihad in West Africa
NAFTA	North American Free Trade Agreement
NAM	Non-Aligned Movement
NARC	National Rainbow Coalition (Kenya)
NATO	North Atlantic Treaty Organization
NDC	National Democratic Congress (Ghana)
NEPAD	New Partnership for Africa's Development
NGO	nongovernmental organization
NIDO	Nigerians in Diaspora Organisation
NPFL	National Patriotic Front of Liberia
NPP	National People's Party (Ghana)
OAU	Organization of African Unity
OCHA	Office for the Coordination of Humanitarian Affairs (United Nations)
ODA	official development assistance
ODM	Orange Democratic Movement (Kenya)
OECD	Organization for Economic Cooperation and Development
OIC	Organization of Islamic Cooperation
OIL	Oil India Limited
ONGC India	Oil and National Gas Corporation
ONUB	United Nations Operation in Burundi
ONUC	United Nations Operation in the Congo
ONUMOZ	United Nations Operation in Mozambique
OPEC	Organization of Petroleum Exporting Countries
P5	permanent five members of the United Nations Security Council
PEPFAR	President's Emergency Plan for AIDS Relief (United States)

PRC	People's Republic of China
PREACT	Partnership for East Africa Regional Counterterrorism
PRS	poverty reduction strategy
R2P	responsibility to protect
RCD	Rally for Congolese Democracy
REC	regional economic community
RENAMO	Mozambican National Resistance
RGB	Rwandan Governance Board
ROC	Republic of China
RPF	Rwandan Patriotic Front
RUF	Revolutionary United Front (Sierra Leone)
SACU	Southern African Customs Union
SADC	Southern African Development Community
SADCC	Southern African Development Coordination Conference
SAP	structural adjustment program
SPLM/A	Sudan People's Liberation Movement/Army
SWAPO	South West African People's Organization (Namibia)
TAZARA	Tanzania-Zambia Railway
TSCTP	Trans-Sahara Counterterrorism Partnership
UAE	United Arab Emirates
UDI	Unilateral Declaration of Independence (Rhodesia)
UEMOA	West African Economic and Monetary Union
UK	United Kingdom
UMHK	Union Minière de Haut Katanga (Zaire)
UN	United Nations
UNAIDS	Joint United Nations Programme on HIV and AIDS
UNAMID	United Nations–African Union Mission in Darfur
UNAMIR	United Nations Assistance Mission in Rwanda
UNAMSIL	United Nations Mission in Sierra Leone
UNAVEM	United Nations Angola Verification Mission
UNCTAD	United Nations Conference on Trade and Development
UNECA	United Nations Economic Commission for Africa
UNHCR	United Nations High Commissioner for Refugees
UNICEF	United Nations Children's Fund
UNITA	National Union for the Total Liberation of Angola
UNITAF	Unified Task Force (Somalia)
UNMIL	United Nations Mission in Liberia
UNMISS	United Nations Mission in South Sudan
UNOCI	United Nations Operation in Côte d'Ivoire
UNOSOM	United Nations Operation in Somalia
UNSC	United Nations Security Council
USAID	US Agency for International Development
WFP	World Food Programme
WHO	World Health Organization
WTO	World Trade Organization
YALI	Young African Leaders Initiative
ZANU	Zimbabwe African National Union
ZANU-PF	Zimbabwe African National Union–Popular Front
ZAPU	Zimbabwe African People's Union

Bibliography

ABAX. 2015. "Côte d'Ivoire-France: Historically Strong Economic Ties." October 1. http://www.abaxservices.com.

Abdi, Mohamed Farah. 2017. "UAE Military Base Will Boost Somaliland-Ethiopia Relations." February 14. http://hornaffairs.com.

Abdullah, Ibrahim. 1998. "Bush Path to Destruction: The Origin and Character of the Revolutionary United Front/Sierra Leone." *Journal of Modern African Studies* 36(2): 203–235.

Abdullah, Ibrahim, and Ismail Rashid. 2004. "Rebel Movements." In *West Africa's Security Challenges: Building Peace in a Troubled Region,* ed. Adekeye Adebajo and Ismail O. D. Rashid. Boulder: Lynne Rienner, 169–193.

Aborisade, Oladimeji, and Robert J. Mundt. 2002. *Politics in Nigeria.* 2nd ed. New York: Longman.

Abrahams, Mark. 2008. "Accountability, Autonomy, and Authenticity: Assessing the Development Waltz Conducted to a 'Kwaito' Beat in Southern Africa." *Development in Practice* 18(1): 40–52.

Achebe, Chinua. 2012. *There Was a Country: A Personal History of Biafra.* New York: Penguin.

Adamson, Fiona B. 2006. "Crossing Borders: International Migration and National Security." *International Security* 31(1): 165–199.

Adebajo, Adekeye. 2002a. *Building Peace in West Africa: Liberia, Sierra Leone, and Guinea-Bissau.* Boulder: Lynne Rienner.

———.2002b. *Liberia's Civil War: Nigeria, ECOMOG, and Regional Security in West Africa.* Boulder: Lynne Rienner.

———. 2004. "Pax West Africana? Regional Security Mechanisms." In *West Africa's Security Challenges: Building Peace in a Troubled Region,* ed. Adekeye Adebajo and Ismail O. D. Rashid. Boulder: Lynne Rienner, 291–318.

———. 2016. "Ghosts at the AU Summit." *The Guardian* (Nigeria), February 8. http://www.ngrguardiannews.com.

Adebajo, Adekeye, and Ismail O. D. Rashid, eds. 2004. *West Africa's Security Challenges: Building Peace in a Troubled Region.* Boulder: Lynne Rienner.

Adem, Seifudein. 2010. "The Paradox of China's Policy in Africa." *African and Asian Studies* 9(3): 334–355.

Adida, Claire L. 2011. "Too Close for Comfort? Immigrant Exclusion in Africa." *Comparative Political Studies* 44(10): 1370–1396.

————. 2014. *Immigrant Exclusion and Insecurity in Africa*. New York: Cambridge University Press.

Adler, Emmanuel. 1997. "Seizing the Middle Ground: Constructivism in World Politics." *European Journal of International Relations* 3(3): 319–363.

Africa Confidential. 2008. "Déby—Caught Between Paris and Khartoum." February 15, 49(4): 6–7.

Africa-EU Partnership. 2016. "The African Peace Facility." http://www.africa-eu -partnership.org.

Africa Research Bulletin. 2013. "AFRICA-ICC: AU Special Summit." *Political, Social, and Cultural Series* 50(10): 19901–19902.

————. 2017. "Senegal: Parliament Seats for Diaspora." *Political, Social, and Cultural Series* 54(1): 21283A.

African Business Magazine. 2012. "A Brief History of the CFA Franc." February 19. http://africanbusinessmagazine.com.

African National Congress. 2017. "Declarations and Resolutions of the Organization of African Unity, 1963–1994." http://www.anc.org.za.

Ake, Claude. 1996. "Rethinking African Democracy." In *The Global Resurgence of Democracy,* 2nd ed., ed. Larry Diamond and Marc F. Plattner. Baltimore: Johns Hopkins University Press, 63–75.

Akindès, Francis. 1996. *Les Mirages de la Démocratie en Afrique Subsaharienne Francophone*. Paris: Codesria-Karthala.

————. 2004. *The Roots of the Military-Political Crisis in Côte d'Ivoire*. Research Report no. 128. Uppsala: Nordiska Afrikainstitutet.

Akyeampong, E. 2000. "Africans in the Diaspora: The Diaspora and Africa." *African Affairs* 99(395): 183–215.

Alden, Chris. 2000. "From Neglect to 'Virtual Engagement': The United States and Its New Paradigm for Africa." *African Affairs* 99(396): 355–371.

———. 2005. "China in Africa." *Survival* 47(3): 147–162.

Alden, Chris, and Maxi Schoeman. 2013. "South Africa in the Company of Giants: The Search for Leadership in a Transforming Global Order." *International Affairs* 89(1): 111–129.

Allison, Simon. 2018. "How China Spied on the African Union's Computers." *Mail & Guardian* (South Africa), January 19. https://mg.co.za.

Ames, Paul. 2015. "Portugal Is Becoming an Angolan Financial Colony." *Politico,* April 28. http://www.politico.eu.

Amin, Samir. 1974. *Accumulation on a World Scale: A Critique of the Theory of Underdevelopment*. 2 vols. New York: Monthly Review.

————. 1992. "Thirty Years of Critique of the Soviet System." *Monthly Review* 44(1): 43–51.

————. 1997. *Capitalism in the Age of Globalization: The Management of Contemporary Society*. London: Zed.

Amnesty International. 2012. *"We Can Run Away from Bombs, but Not from Hunger": Sudan's Refugees in South Sudan*. June 7. https://www.amnestyusa.org.

Anderson, David M., and Jacob McKnight. 2015. "Kenya at War: Al-Shabaab and Its Enemies in Eastern Africa." *African Affairs* 114(454): 1–27.

Anderson, Mary B. 1999. *Do No Harm: How Aid Can Support Peace—or War*. Boulder: Lynne Rienner.

Andrew, Christopher. 2006. *The World Was Going Our Way: The KGB and the Battle for the Third World*. New York: Basic.

Anyadike, Obi. 2016. "Who Should Pay for African Peacekeeping?" *IRIN,* June 24. http://www.irinnews.org.

————. 2017. "Foreign Military Intervention in Africa Is Controversial When It Happens, and Occasionally Controversial When It Doesn't." *IRIN,* February 15. http://www .irinnews.org.

Anyanwu, John C., and Andrew E. O. Erhijakpor. 2010. "Do International Remittances Affect Poverty in Africa?" *African Development Review* 22(1): 51–91.

Apolinário, Laerte. 2016. "Foreign Aid and the Governance of International Financial Organizations: The Brazilian-Bloc Case in the IMF and the World Bank." *Brazilian Political Science Review* 10(3). http://dx.doi.org.

Apuuli, Kasaija Phillip. 2006. "The ICC Arrest Warrants for the Lord's Resistance Army Leaders and Peace Prospects for Northern Uganda." *Journal of International Criminal Justice* 4(1): 179–187.

Asiwaju, Anthony Ijaola. 1985. *Partitioned Africans: Ethnic Relations Across Africa's International Boundaries, 1884–1984.* London: Hurst.

Associated Press. 2015. "Nigeria Recalls Senior Diplomats from South Africa over Attacks on Immigrants." April 26. http://www.foxnews.com.

———. 2017. "UN Chief Commends African Countries for Accepting Refugees." *New York Times,* January 30. https://www.nytimes.com.

Austen, Ralph A. 1988. "The 19th Century Islamic Slave Trade from East Africa (Swahili and Red Sea Coasts): A Tentative Census." *Slavery and Abolition* 9(3): 21–44.

———. 1992. "The Mediterranean Islamic Slave Trade Out of Africa: A Tentative Census." *Slavery and Abolition* 13(1): 214–248.

Autesserre, Séverine. 2009. "Hobbes and the Congo: Frames, Local Violence, and International Intervention." *International Organization* 63(2): 249–280.

———. 2010. *The Trouble with Congo: Local Violence and the Failure of International Peacebuilding.* Cambridge: Cambridge University Press.

———. 2012. "Dangerous Tales: Dominant Narratives on the Congo and Their Unintended Consequences." *African Affairs* 111(443): 202–222.

———. 2017a. "The Right Way to Build Peace in Congo." *Foreign Affairs,* April 6. https://www.foreignaffairs.com.

———. 2017b. "What the Uproar over Congo's Elections Misses." *Foreign Affairs,* March 1. https://www.foreignaffairs.com.

Azam, Jean-Paul, and Flore Gubert. 2006. "Migrants' Remittances and the Household in Africa: A Review of Evidence." *Journal of African Economies* 15(supp. 2): 426–462.

Bach, Daniel C. 1983. "The Politics of West African Economic Co-operation: C.E.A.O. and E.C.O.W.A.S." *Journal of Modern African Studies* 21(4): 605–623.

———, ed. 1999. *Regionalisation in Africa: Integration and Disintegration.* Oxford: Currey.

Bacha, Alemayehu. 2015. "Ethiopia: Julphar to Construct Injectable Medicine Plant." January 21. http://www.2merkato.com.

Bachmann, Max O., and Frederick L. R. Booysen. 2003. "Health and Economic Impact of HIV/AIDS on South African Households: A Cohort Study." *BMC Public Health* 3: 14.

Bailer, Seweryn, and Michael Mandelbaum. 1989. *The Global Rivals: The Soviet-American Contest for Supremacy.* London: Tauris.

Bakker, Jan David, Christopher Robert Parsons, and Ferdinand Rauch. 2016. "Migration and Urbanisation in Post-Apartheid South Africa." IZA Discussion Paper no. 10113. https://ssrn.com.

Balakian, Sophia. 2016. "'Money Is Your Government': Refugees, Mobility, and Unstable Documents in Kenya's Operation Usalama Watch." *African Studies Review* 59(2): 87–111.

Baldé, Yéro. 2011. "The Impact of Remittances and Foreign Aid on Savings/Investment in Sub-Saharan Africa." *African Development Review* 23(2): 247–262.

Banegas, Richard. 2011. "Post-Election Crisis in Côte d'Ivoire: The Gbonhi War." *African Affairs* 110(440): 457–468.

Barkan, Samuel. 2003. "New Forces Shaping Kenyan Politics." *CSIS Africa Notes* 18(May): 1–5.

Barnes, Cedric, and Harun Hassan. 2007. "The Rise and Fall of Mogadishu's Islamic Courts." *Journal of Eastern African Studies* 1(2): 151–160.

Barnes, Sam. 1998. "Humanitarian Assistance as a Factor in the Mozambican Peace Negotiations: 1990–2." In *War and Peace in Mozambique,* ed. Stephen Chan and Moisés Venâncio. London: Palgrave Macmillan, 117–141.

Barnett, Michael. 2002. *Eyewitness to a Genocide: The United Nations and Rwanda.* Ithaca: Cornell University Press.

Barnett, Michael, and Thomas G. Weiss. 2013. *Humanitarianism Contested: Where Angels Fear to Tread.* New York: Routledge.

Barnett, Thomas. 2007. "The Americans Have Landed." *Esquire,* June 27. http://www.esquire.com.

Bassett, Thomas J. 2010. "Slim Pickings: Fairtrade Cotton in West Africa." *Geoforum* 41(1): 44–55.

———. 2011. "Winning Coalition, Sore Loser: Côte d'Ivoire's 2010 Presidential Elections." *African Affairs* 110(440): 469–479.

Bates, Robert H. 1974. "Ethnic Competition and Modernization in Contemporary Africa." *Comparative Political Studies* 6(4): 457–484.

———. 1981. *Markets and States in Tropical Africa: The Political Basis of Agricultural Policies.* Berkeley: University of California Press.

———. 2015. *When Things Fell Apart: State Failure in Late-Century Africa.* Cambridge: Cambridge University Press.

BBC News. 2011. "South Sudan Referendum: 99% Vote for Independence." January 30. http://www.bbc.com.

———. 2012. "Charles Taylor 'Worked' for CIA in Liberia." January 19. http://www.bbc.com.

———. 2015. "South Africa Xenophobia: Africa Reacts." April 17. http://www.bbc.com.

Beah, Ishmael. 2007. *A Long Way Gone: Memoirs of a Boy Soldier.* New York: Sarah Crichton.

Beinart, William. 2001. *Twentieth-Century South Africa.* 2nd ed. New York: Oxford University Press.

Bercovitch, Jacob. 2007. "A Neglected Relationship: Diasporas and Conflict Resolution." In *Diasporas in Conflict: Peace-Makers or Peace-Wreckers?*, ed. Hazel Anne Smith and Paul Stares. Tokyo: United Nations University Press, 17–38.

Berman, Bruce J. 1998. "Ethnicity, Patronage, and the African State: The Politics of Uncivil Nationalism." *African Affairs* 97(388): 305–341.

Beswick, Stephanie. 2016. "Precolonial History of South Sudan." In *Oxford Research Encyclopedia: African History.* New York: Oxford University Press.

Betts, Alexander, Louise Bloom, Josiah Kaplan, and Naohiko Omata. 2017. *Refugee Economies: Forced Displacement and Development.* Oxford: Oxford University Press.

Betts, Richard K. 1994. "The Delusion of Impartial Intervention." *Foreign Affairs* 73(6): 20–33.

Bodomo, Adams. 2015. "Africans in China: Guangzhou and Beyond—Issues and Reviews." *Journal of Pan African Studies* 7(10): 1–9.

Bond, Patrick. 2006. *Looting Africa: The Economics of Exploitation.* London: Zed.

Bovcon, Maja. 2009. "France's Conflict Resolution Strategy in Côte d'Ivoire and Its Ethical Implications." *African Studies Quarterly* 11(1): 1–24.

Bowden, Mark. 1999. *Black Hawk Down: A Story of Modern War.* New York: Atlantic Monthly.

———. 2000. *African Atrocities and the "Rest of the World."* Hoover Institution Policy Review. http://www.hoover.org.

Brader, Ted, Nicholas A. Valentino, and Elizabeth Suhay. 2008. "What Triggers Public Opposition to Immigration? Anxiety, Group Cues, and Immigration Threat." *American Journal of Political Science* 52(4): 959–978.

Branch, Adam. 2009. "Humanitarianism, Violence, and the Camp in Northern Uganda." *Civil Wars* 11(4): 477–501.

———. 2011. *Displacing Human Rights: War and Intervention in Northern Uganda.* Oxford: Oxford University Press.

Branch, Daniel. 2014. "Violence, Decolonisation, and the Cold War in Kenya's North-Eastern Province, 1963–1978." *Journal of Eastern African Studies* 8(4): 642–657.

Bratton, Michael. 1998. "Second Elections in Africa." *Journal of Democracy* 9(3): 51–66.

Bratton, Michael, and Nicolas van de Walle. 1997. *Democratic Experiments in Africa: Regime Transitions in Comparative Perspective*. Cambridge: Cambridge University Press.

Bräutigam, Deborah. 1998. "Economic Takeoff in Africa?" *Current History* 97: 204–208.

———. 2009. *The Dragon's Gift: The Real Story of China in Africa*. Oxford: Oxford University Press.

Bräutigam, Deborah, Jyhjong Hwang, and Lu Wang. 2015. "Chinese-Financed Hydropower Projects in Sub-Saharan Africa." SAIS-CARI Policy Brief no. 8: 1–7.

British Army. 2017. "The British Army in Africa." http://www.army.mod.uk.

Brown, Stephen. 2001. "Authoritarian Leaders and Multiparty Elections in Africa: How Foreign Donors Help to Keep Kenya's Daniel arap Moi in Power." *Third World Quarterly* 22(5): 725–739.

———. 2005. "Foreign Aid and Democracy Promotion: Lessons from Africa." *European Journal for Development Research* 17(2): 179–198.

———. 2009. "Donor Responses to the 2008 Kenyan Crisis: Finally Getting It Right?" *Journal of Contemporary African Studies* 27(3): 389–406.

Brownell, Josiah. 2010. "'A Sordid Tussle on the Strand': Rhodesia House During the UDI Rebellion (1965–80)." *Journal of Imperial and Commonwealth History* 38(3): 471–499.

Bull, Hedley. 1977. *The Anarchical Society: A Study of Order in World Politics*. London: Macmillan.

Burchfield, Amy, and Andrew Dorchak. 2017. "UPDATE: International Criminal Courts for the Former Yugoslavia, Rwanda, and Sierra Leone: A Guide to Online and Print Resources." Hauser Global Law School Program, New York University School of Law. http://www.nyulawglobal.org.

Bures, Oldrich. 2005. "Private Military Companies: A Second Best Peacekeeping Option?" *International Peacekeeping* 12(4): 533–546.

Burgess, Stephen F. 2009. "In the National Interest? Authoritarian Decision-Making and the Problematic Creation of US Africa Command." *Contemporary Security Policy* 30(1): 79–99.

Burnside, Craig, and David Dollar. 2000. "Aid, Policies, and Growth." *American Economic Review* 90(4): 847–868.

Bush, President George W. 2001. "Presidential Address to a Joint Session of Congress and the American People." https://www.theguardian.com.

Business Standard. 2015. "ONGC Videsh to Double Africa Investments to $16 bn in 3 Years." October 28. http://www.business-standard.com.

Buzan, Barry, and Ole Wæver. 2004. *Regions and Powers: The Structure of International Security*. Cambridge: Cambridge University Press.

Cain, Kenneth L. 1999. "The Rape of Dinah: Human Rights, Civil War in Liberia, and Evil Triumphant." *Human Rights Quarterly* 21(2): 265–307.

Callaghy, Thomas M. 1993. "Political Passions and Economic Interests: Economic Reform and Political Structure in Africa." In *Hemmed In: Responses to Africa's Economic Decline,* ed. Thomas M. Callaghy and John Ravenhill. New York: Columbia University Press, 463–519.

Callaghy, Thomas M., and John Ravenhill, eds. 1993. *Hemmed In: Responses to Africa's Economic Decline*. New York: Columbia University Press.

Campbell, Eugene K. 2003. "Attitudes of Botswana Citizens Toward Immigrants: Signs of Xenophobia?" *International Migration* 41(4): 71–111.

Campbell, Horace. 2008. "China in Africa: Challenging US Global Hegemony." *Third World Quarterly* 29(1): 89–105.

Carmody, Pádraig. 2010. *Globalization in Africa: Recolonization or Renaissance?* Boulder: Lynne Rienner.

———. 2013. *The Rise of the BRICS in Africa: The Geopolitics of South-South Relations*. London: Zed.

Carmody, Pádraig, and Godfrey Hampwaye. 2010. "Inclusive or Exclusive Globalization? Zambia's Economy and Asian Investment." *Africa Today* 56(3): 84–102.

Carmody, Pádraig R., and Francis Y. Owusu. 2007. "Competing Hegemons? Chinese Versus American Geo-Economic Strategies in Africa." *Political Geography* 26(5): 504–524.

Carmody, Pádraig, and Ian Taylor. 2010. "Flexigemony and Force in China's Resource Diplomacy in Africa: Sudan and Zambia Compared." *Geopolitics* 15(3): 496–515.

Carr, E. H. 1946. *The Twenty Years' Crisis: An Introduction to the Study of International Relations*. 2nd ed. New York: Harper and Row, 1964.

Carter Center. 2011. "DRC Presidential Election Results Lack Credibility." December 10. http://www.cartercenter.org.

Castagno, A. A. 1964. "The Somali-Kenyan Controversy: Implications for the Future." *Journal of Modern African Studies* 2(2): 165–188.

Ceuppens, Bambi, and Peter Geschiere. 2005. "Autochthony: Local or Global? New Modes in the Struggle over Citizenship and Belonging in Africa and Europe." *Annual Review of Anthropology* 34(1): 385–407.

Chafer, Tony. 2014. "Hollande and Africa Policy." *Modern and Contemporary France* 22(4): 513–531.

Chan, Stephen. 2013. "The Middle Kingdom and the Dark Continent: An Essay on China, Africa, and Many Fault Lines." In *The Morality of China in Africa: The Middle Kingdom and the Dark Continent,* ed. Stephen Chan. London: Zed, 3–43.

Charbonneau, Bruno. 2008. *France and the New Imperialism: Security Policy in Sub-Saharan Africa*. New York: Routledge.

Chazan, Naomi. 1988. "Ghana: Problems of Governance and the Emergence of Civil Society." In *Democracy in Developing Countries: Africa,* ed. Larry Diamond, Juan Linz, and Martin Lipsett. Boulder: Lynne Rienner, 93–139.

Chin-Hao, Huang. 2017. "Peacekeeping Contributor Profile: The People's Republic of China." http://www.providingforpeacekeeping.org.

Chirot, Daniel. 2006. "The Debacle in Côte d'Ivoire." *Journal of Democracy* 17(2): 63–77.

Claassen, Christopher. 2016. "Group Entitlement, Anger, and Participation in Intergroup Violence." *British Journal of Political Science* 46(1): 127–148.

Clapham, Christopher. 1996. *Africa and the International System: The Politics of State Survival*. Cambridge: Cambridge University Press.

———. 1998. "Rwanda: The Perils of Peacemaking." *Journal of Peace Research* 35(2): 193–210.

Clapp, Jennifer. 2015. *Hunger in the Balance: The New Politics of International Food Aid*. Ithaca: Cornell University Press.

Clarence-Smith, William Gervase. 1988. "The Economics of the Indian Ocean and Red Sea Slave Trades in the 19th Century: An Overview." *Slavery & Abolition* 9(3): 1–20.

———. 2006. *Islam and the Abolition of Slavery*. Oxford: Oxford University Press.

Clark, John F. 1992. "The Evaluation of Superpower Intervention and Competition in Several Conflicts of Sub-Saharan Africa, 1960–1990." PhD diss., University of Virginia (August).

———. 1994. "The National Conference as an Instrument of Democratization in Francophone Africa." *Journal of Third World* Studies 11(1): 304–335.

———. 1997. "The Challenges of Political Reform in Sub-Saharan Africa: A Theoretical Overview." In *Political Reform in Francophone Africa,* ed. John F. Clark and David E. Gardinier. Boulder: Westview, 23–39.

———. 1998. "The Nature and Evolution of the State in Zaire." *Studies in Comparative International Development* 32(4): 3–23.

———. 2001a. "Explaining Ugandan Intervention in Congo: Evidence and Interpretations." *Journal of Modern African Studies* 39(2): 261–287.

———. 2001b. "Foreign Policy Making in Central Africa: The Imperative of Regime Security in a New Context." In *African Foreign Policy: Power and Process,* ed. Gilbert Khadiagala and Terrence Lyons. Boulder: Lynne Rienner, 67–86.

———. 2001c. "Realism, Neo-Realism, and Africa's International Relations in the Post Cold-War Era." In *Africa's Challenge to International Relations Theory,* ed. Kevin C. Dunn and Timothy M. Shaw. New York: Palgrave Macmillan, 85–102.

——. 2002. "The Neo-Colonial Context of the Democratic Experiment of Congo-Brazzaville." *African Affairs* 101(403): 171–192.

——. 2005. "The Collapse of the Democratic Experiment in the Republic of Congo: A Thick Description." In *The Fate of Africa's Democratic Experiments: Elites and Institutions,* ed. Leonardo Villalón and Peter VonDoepp. Bloomington: Indiana University Press, 96–125.

——. 2008. *The Failure of Democracy in the Republic of Congo.* Boulder: Lynne Rienner.

——. 2011. "A Constructivist Account of the Congo Wars." *African Security* 4(3): 147–170.

——. 2016. "South Africa: Africa's Reluctant and Conflicted Regional Power." *Air and Space Power Journal: Africa and Francophonie* 7(1): 30–47.

Clark, John F., and David E. Gardinier, eds. 1997. *Political Reform in Francophone Africa.* Boulder: Westview.

Claude, Inis L. 1962. *Power and International Relations.* New York: Random.

Cliff, Julie, and Abdul Razak Noormahomed. 1988. "Health as a Target: South Africa's Destabilization of Mozambique." *Social Science & Medicine* 27(7): 717–722.

Cliffe, Lionel, and Basil Davidson, eds. 1988. *The Long Struggle of Eritrea for Independence and Constructive Peace.* 1st American ed. Trenton: Red Sea.

Cline, Lawrence E. 2013. *The Lord's Resistance Army.* Santa Barbara: Praeger.

Clinton, William Jefferson. 1998. "Text of Clinton's Rwanda Speech." http://www.cbsnews.com.

Clough, Michael. 1992. *Free at Last? US Policy Toward Africa and the End of the Cold War.* New York: Council on Foreign Relations.

Collier, Paul. 2007. *The Bottom Billion: Why the Poorest Countries Are Failing and What Can Be Done About It.* New York: Oxford University Press.

Collier, Paul, and David Dollar. 2002. "Aid Allocation and Poverty Reduction." *European Economic Review* 46(8): 1475–1500.

Collier, Paul, and Jan Willem Gunning. 1999. "Why Has Africa Grown Slowly?" *Journal of Economic Perspectives* 13(3): 3–22.

Collier, Paul, Anke Hoeffler, and Dominic Rohner. 2008. "Beyond Greed and Grievance: Feasibility and Civil War." *Oxford Economic Papers* 61(1): 1–27.

Collier, Paul, Anke Hoeffler, and Måns Söderbom. 2004. "On the Duration of Civil War." *Journal of Peace Research* 41(3): 253–273.

Collins, Robert O. 2008. *A History of Modern Sudan.* Cambridge: Cambridge University Press.

Collins, Robert O., and James M. Burns. 2014. *A History of Sub-Saharan Africa.* Cambridge: Cambridge University Press.

Comaroff, Jean, and John L. Comaroff. 1991. *Of Revelation and Revolution: Christianity, Colonialism, and Consciousness in South Africa.* Chicago: University of Chicago Press.

Connah, Graham. 2001. *African Civilizations: An Archaeological Perspective.* 2nd ed. Cambridge: Cambridge University Press.

Connell, Dan. 2017. "Refugees, Migration, and Gated Nations: The Eritrean Experience." *African Studies Review* 59(3): 217–225.

Conrad, Justin, and Kevin Greene. 2015. "Competition, Differentiation, and the Severity of Terrorist Attacks." *Journal of Politics* 77(2): 546–561.

Constantaras, Eva. 2016. "Visualizing China's Aid to Africa: China Aid Map Reveals Nearly $100 Billion Infrastructure Investment Boom in Africa." *Chinafile,* June 30. http://www.chinafile.com.

Council on Foreign Relations. 2017. "Global Conflict Tracker: Civil War in South Sudan." https://www.cfr.org.

Crisp, Jeff, and Karen Jacobsen. 1998. "Refugee Camps Reconsidered." *Forced Migration Review* 3(December): 27–30.

Cronin-Furman, Kate. 2015. "Is the International Criminal Court Really Targeting Black Men?" *The Monkey Cage,* June 17. https://www.washingtonpost.com.

Crush, Jonathan S. 2001. "The Dark Side of Democracy: Migration, Xenophobia, and Human Rights in South Africa." *International Migration* 38(6): 103–133.

Crush, Jonathan S., and Wade Pendleton. 2004. *Regionalizing Xenophobia? Citizen Attitudes to Immigration and Refugee Policy in Southern Africa.* Cape Town: Idasa and Southern African Migration Project.

Cumming, Gordon. 1996. "British Aid to Africa: A Changing Agenda?" *Third World Quarterly* 17(3): 487–502.

———. 2001. *Aid to Africa: French and British Policies from the Cold War to the New Millennium.* Aldershot: Ashgate.

Curtin, Philip D. 1969. *The Atlantic Slave Trade: A Census.* Madison: University of Wisconsin Press.

Dale, Richard. 1987. "Not Always So Placid a Place: Botswana Under Attack." *African Affairs* 86(342): 73–91.

Dalgaard, Carl-Johan, Henrik Hansen, and Finn Tarp. 2004. "On the Empirics of Foreign Aid and Growth." *Economic Journal* 114(496): F191–F216.

Dallaire, Romeo. 2009. *Shake Hands with the Devil: The Failure of Humanity in Rwanda.* Cambridge, MA: Random House of Canada.

Damman, Erin. 2015. "Rwanda's Strategic Humanitarianism: Lessons from a Janus-faced State." *African Security* 8(1): 20–55.

Darracq, Vincent. 2014. "France in Central Africa: The Reluctant Interventionist." Al Jazeera, February 11. http://www.aljazeera.com.

Dau, John Bul, and Michael S. Sweeney. 2008. *God Grew Tired of Us: A Memoir.* Reprint ed. Washington, DC: National Geographic.

Davenport, T. R. H., and Christopher Saunders. 2000. *South Africa: A Modern History.* 5th ed. New York: St. Martin's.

David, Steven. 1991. "Explaining Third World Alignment." *World Politics* 43(2): 233–256.

Davidson, A. B. 1968. "African Resistance and Rebellion Against the Imposition of Colonial Rule." In *Emerging Themes of African History,* ed. Terence O. Ranger. Nairobi: East Africa Publishing House, 177–188.

Davidson, Basil. 1969. *A History of East and Central Africa to the Late Nineteenth Century.* New York: Doubleday/Anchor.

———. 1998. *West Africa Before the Colonial Era: A History to 1850.* London: Longman.

de Goede, Meike, and Chris van der Borgh. 2008. "A Role for Diplomats in Postwar Transitions? The Case of the International Committee in Support of the Transition in the Democratic Republic of the Congo." *African Security* 1(2): 92–114.

de Haas, Hein. 2007. "Turning the Tide? Why Development Will Not Stop Migration." *Development and Change* 38(5): 819–841.

———. 2008. "The Myth of Invasion: The Inconvenient Realities of African Migration to Europe." *Third World Quarterly* 29(7): 1305–1322.

de Jonge Oudraat, Chantal. 2000. "Humanitarian Intervention: The Lessons Learned." *Current History* 99(641): 419–429.

de Maio, Jennifer L. 2010. "Is War Contagious? The Transnationalization of Conflict in Darfur." *African Studies Quarterly* 11(4): 25–45.

de Waal, Alex. 1997a. "Democratizing the Aid Encounter in Africa." *International Affairs* 73(4): 623–639.

———. 1997b. *Famine Crimes: Politics and the Disaster Relief Industry in Africa.* Oxford: James Currey/Indiana University Press.

———. 2002. "What's New in the 'New Partnership for Africa's Development'?" *International Affairs* (Royal Institute of International Affairs) 8(3): 463–475.

———. 2003. "How Will HIV/AIDS Transform African Governance?" *African Affairs* 102(406): 1–23.

———. 2007. "The Politics of a Health Crisis." *Harvard International Review* (Spring): 20–24.

———. 2008. "Chad: Civil War, Power Struggle, and Imperialist Interference." *Green Left Weekly,* February 8. http://www.greenleft.org.au.

———. 2013. "Sizzling South Sudan." *Foreign Affairs,* February 7. https://www.foreignaffairs.com.

de Witte, Ludo. 2002. *The Assassination of Lumumba*. London: Verso.

Decalo, Samuel. 2008. *The Stable Minority: Civilian Rule in Africa*. Gainesville: Florida Academic Press.

del Biondo, Karen. 2015. "Donor Interests or Developmental Performance? Explaining Sanctions in EU Democracy Promotion in Sub-Saharan Africa." *World Development* 75: 74–84.

Deng, Alphonsion, Benson Deng, Benjamin Ajak, and Judy A. Bernstein. 2005. *They Poured Fire on Us from the Sky: The True Story of Three Lost Boys from Sudan*. New York: PublicAffairs.

Deng, Francis M. 2011. *War of Visions: Conflict of Identities in the Sudan*. Washington, DC: Brookings Institution.

Deng, Francis M., and I. William Zartman. 2002. *A Strategic Vision for Africa: The Kampala Movement*. Washington, DC: Brookings Institution.

Dercon, Stephan, and Roxana Gutierrez-Romero. 2012. "Triggers and Characteristics of the 2007 Kenyan Electoral Violence." *World Development* 40(4): 731–744.

des Forges, Alison L. 1999. *Leave None to Tell the Story: Genocide in Rwanda*. New York: Human Rights Watch.

——. 2000. "Shame." *Foreign Affairs* 79(3): 141–144.

Devlin, Larry. 2007. *Chief of Station, Congo*. New York: PublicAffairs.

Diamond, Larry. 1988. "Nigeria: Pluralism, Statism, and the Struggle for Democracy." In *Democracy in Developing Countries: Africa,* ed. Larry Diamond, Juan Linz, and Martin Lipsett. Boulder: Lynne Rienner, 33–91.

Diamond, Larry, Juan Linz, and Martin Lipsett, eds. 1988. *Democracy in Developing Countries: Africa*. Boulder: Lynne Rienner.

Dionne, Kim Yi. 2011. "The Role of Executive Time Horizons in State Response to AIDS in Africa." *Comparative Political Studies* 44(1): 55–77.

——. 2012. "Local Demand for a Global Intervention: Policy Priorities in the Time of AIDS." *World Development* 40(12): 2468–2477.

Dionne, Kim Yi, Patrick Gerland, and Susan Watkins. 2011. "AIDS Exceptionalism: Another Constituency Heard From." *AIDS and Behavior* 17(3): 825–831.

Dixon, Simon, Scott McDonald, and Jennifer Roberts. 2002. "The Impact of HIV and AIDS on Africa's Economic Development." *British Medical Journal* 324(7331): 232–234.

Dogbevi, Emmanuel K. 2017. "Ghana, Rwanda, and Kenya Introduce 0.2% Import Tax to Fund African Union." *Ghana Business News*, June 12. https://www.ghana businessnews.com.

Douglas-Bowers, Devon. 2015. "Colonialism and Foreign Intervention: Coups, Conflict, and Sectarian Violence in the Central African Republic." February 6. http://www .globalresearch.ca.

Dowd, Caitriona, and Clionadh Raleigh. 2013. "The Myth of Global Islamic Terrorism and Local Conflict in Mali and the Sahel." *African Affairs* 112(448): 498–509.

Doyle, Michael W. 2011. *Liberal Peace: Selected Essays*. New York: Routledge.

Dumo, Denis. 2016. "South Sudan, Sudan Agree to Peg Crude Pipeline Fees to Oil Price." Reuters, February 3. http://af.reuters.com.

Dunn, Kevin. 2002. "A Survival Guide to Kinshasa: Less of the Father, Passed Down to the Son." In *The African Stakes of the Congo War,* ed. John F. Clark. New York: Palgrave Macmillan, 53–74.

Dunning, Thad. 2004. "Conditioning the Effects of Aid: Cold War Politics, Donor Credibility, and Democracy in Africa." *International Organization* 58(2): 409–423.

Duran, Rebecca. 2013. "Importation of Oil in Brazil." *Brazil Business,* August 26. http://thebrazilbusiness.com.

Dutta, Pullock. 2013. "Oil Hits First Reserve Abroad—Black Gold Find in Africa." *The Telegraph* (Calcutta), July 27. https://www.telegraphindia.com.

Easterly, William. 2003. "Can Foreign Aid Buy Growth?" *Journal of Economic Perspectives* 17(3): 23–48.

——. 2006. *The White Man's Burden: Why the West's Efforts to Aid the Rest Have Done So Much Ill and So Little Good*. New York: Penguin.

Ebiede, Tarila Marclint. 2017. "Community Conflicts and Armed Militancy in Nigeria's Niger Delta: Change and Continuity?" *Society & Natural Resources* online first: 1–15. https://www.tandfonline.com.

Economic Community of West African States (ECOWAS). 1999. "Protocol Relating to the Mechanism for Conflict Prevention, Management, Resolution, Peace-Keeping and Security." Lomé.

The Economist. 2011. "Africa's Impressive Growth." January 6. http://www.economist.com.

———. 2013. "Elephants and Tigers." October 26. http://www.economist.com.

———. 2014. "France in Africa: We Can't Help Coming Back." July 15. http://www.economist.com.

Ekeh, Peter P. 1975. "Colonialism and the Two Publics in Africa: A Theoretical Statement." *Comparative Studies in Society and History* 17(1): 91–112.

el-Khawas, Mohamed A., and Julius Ndumbe Anyu. 2014. "Cote d'Ivoire: Ethnic Turmoil and Foreign Intervention." *Africa Today* 61(2): 41–55.

Elkins, Caroline. 2005. *Imperial Reckoning: The Untold Story of Britain's Gulag in Kenya.* London: Holt Paperbacks.

Ellis, Andrew, Alan Wall, International Institute for Democracy and Electoral Assistance, and Instituto Federal Electoral (Mexico), eds. 2007. *Voting from Abroad: The International IDEA Handbook.* Stockholm: International IDEA and Federal Electoral Institute of Mexico.

Engel, Ulf, and João Gomes Porto, eds. 2010. *Africa's New Peace and Security Architecture: Promoting Norms, Institutionalizing Solutions.* New York: Routledge.

Englebert, Pierre. 2009. *Africa: Unity, Sovereignty, and Sorrow.* Boulder: Lynne Rienner.

Englebert, Pierre, and Rebecca Hummel. 2005. "Let's Stick Together: Understanding Africa's Secessionist Deficit." *African Affairs* 104(416): 399–427.

Epstein, Marc. 1990. "France-Afrique: L'Heure de Vérité." *L'Express,* June 22. http://www.lexpress.fr.

Ernst and Young. 2014. *Africa Attractiveness Survey 2014.* http://www.ey.com.

EUR-Lex. 2016. "European Initiative for Democracy and Human Rights (EIDHR) (2000–2006)." http://eur-lex.europa.eu.

European Community Information Service (ECIS). 1966. "Partnership in Africa: The Yaoundé Association." EU Commission, Community Topics Brochure no. 26. http://aei.pitt.edu.

European Instrument for Democracy and Human Rights (EIDHR). 2017. "What Is EIDHR?" European Commission. http://www.eidhr.eu.

Evans, Ian. 2008. "Chinese Troops Are on the Streets of Zimbabwean City, Witnesses Say." *The Independent* (London), April 18. http://www.independent.co.uk.

Evans-Pritchard, Ambrose. 2002. "EU Imposes Sanctions on Mugabe Inner Circle." *The Telegraph* (London), February 19. http://www.telegraph.co.uk.

Fanon, Frantz. 1963. *The Wretched of the Earth.* New York: Grove.

Fatton, Robert, Jr. 1990. "Liberal Democracy in Africa." *Political Science Quarterly* 105(3): 455–473.

———. 1995. "Africa in the Age of Democratization: The Civic Limitations of Civil Society." *African Studies Review* 38(2): 67–99.

Fauvelle-Aymar, Christine, and Aurelia Segatti. 2011. "People, Space, and Politics: An Exploration of Factors Explaining the 2008 Anti-Foreigner Violence in South Africa." In *Exorcising the Demons Within: Xenophobia, Violence, and Statecraft in Contemporary South Africa,* ed. Loren B. Landau. Johannesburg: Wits University Press, 58–89.

Fayissa, Bichaka, and Christian Nsiah. 2010. "The Impact of Remittances on Economic Growth and Development in Africa." *American Economist* 55(2): 92–103.

Fessy, Thomas. 2012. "Hissene Habre: Senegal MPs Pass Law to Form Tribunal." *BBC World News,* December 19. http://www.bbc.com.

Finkel, Steve, and Amy Smith. 2011. "Civic Education, Political Discussion, and the Social Transmission of Democratic Knowledge and Values in a New Democracy: Kenya 2002." *American Journal of Political Science* 55(2): 417–435.

Fitzgerald, Mary. 2008. "Zambia Becomes Shorthand for What Can Go Wrong." *Irish Times,* August 25. http://www.irishtimes.com.

Flint, Julie, and Alex de Waal. 2005. *Darfur: A Short History of a Long War.* London: Zed.

Foltz, William J. 1965. *From French West Africa to the Mali Federation.* New Haven: Yale University Press.

Ford, Robert. 2011. "Acceptable and Unacceptable Immigrants: How Opposition to Immigration in Britain Is Affected by Migrants' Region of Origin." *Journal of Ethnic and Migration Studies* 37(7): 1017–1037.

Forest, James J. F., and Rebecca Crispin. 2009. "AFRICOM: Troubled Infancy, Promising Future." *Contemporary Security Policy* 30(1): 5–27.

Forsberg, Erika. 2008. "Polarization and Ethnic Conflict in a Widened Setting." *Journal of Peace Research* 45(2): 283–300.

Frank, André Gunder. 1967. *Capitalism and Underdevelopment in Latin America.* New York: Monthly Review.

———. 1998. *ReOrient: Global Economy in the Asian Age.* Berkeley: University of California Press.

Freedman, Jane. 2016. *Gender, Violence, and Politics in the Democratic Republic of Congo.* New York: Routledge.

Freedom House. 2014. *Freedom in the World 2014.* Washington, DC.

———. 2015. "Regional Trends." In *Freedom in the World 2015.* Washington, DC. https://freedomhouse.org.

French, Howard. 2014. *China's Second Continent: How a Million Migrants Are Building a New Empire in Africa.* New York: Knopf.

French Ministry of Defense. 2015. "Fin de l'Opération Licorne." http://fr.calameo.com.

Fridell, Gavin. 2007. *Fair Trade Coffee: The Prospects and Pitfalls of Market-Driven Social Justice.* Toronto: University of Toronto Press.

Fukuyama, Francis. 1991. *The End of History and the Last Man.* New York: Free Press.

Gaddis, John Lewis. 1998. *We Now Know: Rethinking Cold War History.* Oxford: Oxford University Press.

Gaffey, Conor. 2017. "South Africa: Xenophobic Attacks Prompt Angry Backlash in Nigeria." *Newsweek,* February 23. http://www.newsweek.com.

Gallup, John Luke, Jeffrey D. Sachs, and Andrew D. Mellinger. 1999. "Geography and Economic Development." *International Regional Science Review* 22(2): 179–232.

Galser, Antoine, and Stephen Smith. 2005. *Comment la France a Perdu l'Afrique.* Paris: Calmann-Lévy.

Gardinier, David E. 1997. "The Historical Origins of Francophone Africa." In *Political Reform in Francophone Africa,* ed. John F. Clark and David E. Gardinier. Boulder: Westview, 9–22.

Gaviria, Marcela, Will Lyman, Jonathan Jones, and T. Christian Miller. 2014. "Firestone and the Warlord." *Frontline,* November 18. http://www.pbs.org.

Gazibo, Mamoudou. 2005. "Foreign Aid and Democratization: Benin and Niger Compared. *African Studies Review* 48(3): 67–87.

Geda, Alemayehu, and Atnafu Meskel. 2010. "China and India's Growth Surge: The Implications for African Manufactured Exports." In *The Rise of China and India in Africa,* ed. Fantu Cheru and Cyril Obi. London: Zed, 97–106.

Genova, Ann. 2010. "Nigeria's Nationalization of British Petroleum." *International Journal of African Historical Studies* 43(1): 115–136.

Geschiere, Peter. 2009. *The Perils of Belonging: Autochthony, Citizenship, and Exclusion in Africa and Europe.* Chicago: University of Chicago Press.

Ghana Diaspora Homecoming Summit. 2017. "GDHS—About Us." http://www.ghana diasporahs.org.

Ghana Web. 2017. "Ghanaians Abroad to Vote Now." https://www.ghanaweb.com.

Ghemawat, Pankaj, and Steven A. Altman. 2016. "DHL Global Connectedness Index 2016: The State of Globalization in an Age of Ambiguity." http://www.dhl.com.

Gibbs, David. 1991. *The Political Economy of Third World Intervention: Mines, Money, and US Policy in the Congo Crisis.* Chicago: University of Chicago Press.

Gilkes, Patrick. 1999. "The Somali Connection." *BBC News*, July 23. http://news.bbc .co.uk.

Glaser, Antoine, and Stephen Smith. 2005. *Comment la France a perdu l'Afrique*. Paris: Calmann-Lévy.

Gleditsch, Kristian Skrede, Idean Salehyan, and Kenneth Schultz. 2008. "Fighting at Home, Fighting Abroad: How Civil Wars Lead to International Disputes." *Journal of Conflict Resolution* 52(48): 479–506.

Gleijeses, Piero. 2013. *Visions of Freedom: Havana, Washington, Pretoria, and the Struggle for Southern Africa, 1976–1991*. Chapel Hill: University of North Carolina Press.

Global Edge. 2017. "South Africa: Trade Statistics." https://globaledge.msu.edu.

Global Firepower. 2015. "African Countries Ranked by Military Power (2015)." http://www.globalfirepower.com.

Global Humanitarian Assistance. 2017a. "Brazil." http://www.globalhumanitarian assistance.org.

———. 2017b. "South Africa." http://www.globalhumanitarianassistance.org.

Global Witness. 1999. "A Rough Trade: The Role of Companies and Governments in the Angolan Conflict." https://www.globalwitness.org.

GN Focus Team. 2016. "Annual UAE-Africa Trade Is Dh64 Billion but Opportunities Abound: ECA." *Gulf News,* April 10. http://gulfnews.com.

Godehardt, Nadine, and Dirk Nabers, eds. 2011. *Regional Powers and Regional Orders*. New York: Routledge.

Goldsmith, Arthur. 2001. "Foreign Aid and Statehood in Africa." *International Organization* 5(1): 123–148.

Golooba-Mutebi, Frederick. 2013. "Why Tanzania Drags Its Feet in the EAC." *The East African,* August 31. http://www.theeastafrican.co.ke.

Gonzalez-Garcia, Jesus, et al. 2016. *Sub-Saharan African Migration: Patterns and Spillovers*. Washington, DC: International Monetary Fund.

Good, Kenneth. 2008. *Diamonds, Dispossession, and Democracy in Botswana*. Suffolk: Currey.

———. 2010. "The Illusion of Democracy in Botswana." In *Democratization in Africa: Progress and Retreat*, ed. Larry Diamond and Marc F. Plattner. Baltimore: Johns Hopkins University Press, 280–294.

Good, Kenneth, and Ian Taylor. 2007. "Mounting Repression in Botswana." *Round Table* 96(390): 275–278.

Goody, Jack. 1971. *Technology, Tradition, and the State in Africa*. Cambridge: Cambridge University Press.

Gordon, Steven. 2015. "Xenophobia Across the Class Divide: South African Attitudes Towards Foreigners, 2003–2012." *Journal of Contemporary African Studies* 33(4): 494–509.

———. 2017. "A Desire for Isolation? Mass Public Attitudes in South Africa Toward Immigration Levels." *Journal of Immigrant & Refugee Studies* 15(1): 18–35.

Gordon, Steven, and Brij Maharaj. 2015. "Neighbourhood-Level Social Capital and Anti-Immigrant Prejudice in an African Context: An Individual-Level Analysis of Attitudes Towards Immigrants in South Africa." *Commonwealth & Comparative Politics* 53(2): 197–219.

Gorka, Alex. 2017. "Russia Makes Big Strides to Expand Arms Sales in Africa." May 18. https://www.strategic-culture.org.

Greenhill, Kelly M., and Solomon Major. 2007. "The Perils of Profiling: Civil War Spoilers and the Collapse of Intrastate Peace Accords." *International Security* 31(3): 7–40.

Greste, Peter. 2010. "Could a Rusty Coin Re-Write Chinese-African History?" *BBC News,* October 18. http://www.bbc.co.uk.

Guéhenno, Jean-Marie. 2009. *Robust Peacekeeping: The Politics of Force*. New York: Center on International Cooperation, New York University.

Guimarães, Fernando A. 1998. *The Origins of the Angolan Civil War: Foreign Intervention and Domestic Political Conflict*. New York: Palgrave-Macmillan.

Gupta, Sanjeev, Catherine A. Pattillo, and Smita Wagh. 2009. "Effect of Remittances on Poverty and Financial Development in Sub-Saharan Africa." *World Development* 37(1): 104–115.

Gyimah-Boadi, E., and H. Kwasi Prempeh. 2012. "Oil, Politics, and Ghana's Democracy." *Journal of Democracy* 23(3): 94–108.

Haifang, Liu. 2010. "China's Development with Africa: Historical and Cultural Perspectives." In *The Rise of China and India in Africa,* ed. Fantu Cheru and Cyril Obi. London: Zed, 53–62.

Hainmueller, Jens, and Dominik Hangartner. 2013. "Who Gets a Swiss Passport? A Natural Experiment in Immigrant Discrimination." *American Political Science Review* 107(1): 159–187.

Hammerstad, Anne. 2012. "The Nordics, the EU, and Africa." In *The EU and Africa: From Eurafrique to Afro-Europa,* ed. Adekeye Adebajo and Kaye Whiteman. New York: Columbia University Press, 385–403.

Hancock, Graham. 1989. *Lords of Poverty: The Power, Prestige, and Corruption of the International Aid Business.* New York: Atlantic Monthly.

Hanlon, Joseph. 1986. *Beggar Your Neighbors: Apartheid Power in Southern Africa.* Bloomington: Indiana University Press.

Hansen, Ketil Fred. 2011. "Chad's Relations with Libya, Sudan, France, and the US." Norwegian Peacebuilding Resource Centre. http://www.peacebuilding.no.

Hansen, Stig Jarle, and Mark Bradbury. 2007. "Somaliland: A New Democracy in the Horn of Africa?" *Review of African Political Economy* 34(113): 461–476.

Hansen, Thomas Obel. 2013. "Kenya's Power-Sharing Arrangement and Its Implications for Transitional Justice." *International Journal of Human Rights* 17(2): 307–327.

Harbeson, John, Donald Rothchild, and Naomi Chazan, eds. 1994. *Civil Society and the State in Africa.* Boulder: Lynne Rienner.

Harel, Xavier. 2006. *Afrique Pillage à Huis Clos: Comment un Poignée d'Initiés Siphonne le Pétrole Africain.* Paris: Fayard.

Hartzell, Caroline, and Matthew Hoddie. 2003. "Institutionalizing Peace: Power Sharing and Post–Civil War Conflict Management." *American Journal of Political Science* 47(2): 318–332.

Hassim, Shireen, Tawana Kupe, and Eric Worby, eds. 2008. *Go Home or Die Here: Violence, Xenophobia, and the Reinvention of Difference in South Africa.* Johannesburg: Wits University Press.

Heinisch, Elinor Lynn. 2006. "West Africa Versus the United States on Cotton Subsidies: How, Why, and What Next?" *Journal of Modern African Studies* 44(2): 251–274.

Helios Investment Partners. 2017. "Petrobras Africa." Helios Investment Report. http://www.heliosinvestment.com.

Hempstone, Smith. 1997. *Rogue Ambassador: An African Memoir.* Sewanee, TN: University of the South Press.

Henderson, Errol A. 2015. *African Realism? International Relations Theory and Africa's Wars in the Postcolonial Era.* Lanham: Rowman and Littlefield.

Herbst, Jeffrey. 1989. "The Creation and Maintenance of National Boundaries in Africa." *International Organization* 43(4): 673–692.

———. 1990. "War and the State in Africa." *International Security* 14(4): 117–139.

———. 2000a. *States and Power in Africa: Comparative Lessons in Authority and Control.* Princeton: Princeton University Press.

———. 2000b. "Western and African Peacekeepers: Motives and Opportunities." In *Africa in World Politics: The African State System in Flux,* ed. John Willis Harbeson and Donald S. Rothchild. Boulder: Westview.

Hildebrandt, Timothy, Courtney Hillebrecht, Peter M. Holm, and Jon Pevehouse. 2013. "The Domestic Politics of Humanitarian Intervention: Public Opinion, Partisanship, and Ideology." *Foreign Policy Analysis* 9(3): 243–266.

Hirt, Nicole. 2015. "The Eritrean Diaspora and Its Impact on Regime Stability: Responses to UN Sanctions." *African Affairs* 114(454): 115–135.

Hochschild, Adam. 1998. *King Leopold's Ghost: A Story of Greed, Terror, and Heroism in Colonial Africa.* Boston: Houghton Mifflin.

Holslag, Jonathan. 2007. "China's New Mercantilism in Central Africa." *African and Asian Studies* 5(2): 133–169.

———. 2011. "China and the Coups: Coping with Political Instability in Africa." *African Affairs* 110(440): 367–386.

Hook, Steven W. 1998. "'Building Democracy' Through Foreign Aid: The Limitations of United States Political Conditionalities, 1992–1996." *Democratization* 5(3): 156–180.

Hoskyns, Catherine. 1965. *The Congo Since Independence: January 1960–December 1962*. Oxford: Oxford University Press.

Human Rights Watch. 2008. *"Why Am I Still Here?": The 2007 Horn of Africa Renditions and the Fate of Those Still Missing*. October 1. https://www.hrw.org.

———. 2011a. *"You'll Be Fired If You Refuse": Labor Abuses in Zambia's Chinese State-Owned Copper Mines*. November 4. https://www.hrw.org.

———. 2011b. *Zimbabwe: No Justice for Rampant Killings, Torture*. March 8. https://www.hrw.org.

———. 2017. *South Africa: Events of 2016*. https://www.hrw.org.

Huntington, Samuel. 1991. "Democracy's Third Wave." *Journal of Democracy* 2(2): 12–34.

Hyden, Goran. 1980. *Beyond Ujamaa in Tanzania: Underdevelopment and an Uncaptured Peasantry*. Berkeley: University of California Press.

Iliffe, John. 2017. *Africans: The History of a Continent*. 3rd ed. Cambridge: Cambridge University Press.

Indian Ministry of External Affairs. 2016. "Development Partnership Administration." http://www.mea.gov.in.

Inglehart, Ronald, and Christian Welzel. 2005. *Modernization, Cultural Change, and Democracy: The Human Development Sequence*. Cambridge: Cambridge University Press.

Institute for Economics and Peace. 2015. *Global Terrorism Index 2015*. New York. http://economicsandpeace.org.

Integrated Regional Information Network (IRIN). 1997. "Background Brief on Congo-Brazzaville." United Nations Office for the Coordination of Humanitarian Affairs (UNOCHA), October 22. http://reliefweb.int.

———. 2005. "Interim Government Starts Relocation." United Nations Office for the Coordination of Humanitarian Affairs (UNOCHA), June 13. http://www.irinnews.org.

International Criminal Court (ICC). 2015a. "Al Bashir Case: *The Prosecutor v. Omar Hassan Ahmad Al Bashir*." https://www.icc-cpi.int.

———. 2015b. "Situation in Republic of Kenya." https://www.icc-cpi.int.

International Crisis Group (ICG). 2016. *The African Union and the Burundi Crisis: Ambition Versus Reality*. https://www.crisisgroup.org.

International Monetary Fund (IMF). 2010. "IMF and World Bank Announce US$12.3 Billion in Debt Relief for the Democratic Republic of the Congo." July 1. https://www.imf.org.

———. 2016a. "Direction of Trade Statistics (DOTS): External Trade by Counterpart." http://data.imf.org.

———. 2016b. "Heavily Indebted Poor Countries (HIPC) Initiative and Multilateral Debt Relief Initiative (MDRI): Statistical Update." http://www.imf.org.

———. 2017a. "Direction of Trade Statistics (DOTS): External Trade by Counterpart." http://data.imf.org.

———. 2017b. "Factsheet: Debt Relief Under the Heavily Indebted Poor Countries (HIPC) Initiative." http://www.imf.org.

International Rescue Committee (IRC). 2007. "Mortality in the Democratic Republic of Congo: An Ongoing Crisis." https://www.rescue.org.

Isaacman, Allen, in collaboration with Barbara Isaacman. 1976. *The Tradition of Resistance in Mozambique*. Berkeley: University of California Press.

Isaacman, Allen, and Barbara Isaacman. 1977. "Resistance and Collaboration in Southern and Central Africa, c. 1850–1920." *International Journal of African Historical Studies* 10(1): 31–62.

Jackson, Robert H., and Carl G. Rosberg. 1982. "Why Africa's Weak States Persist: The Empirical and the Juridical in Statehood." *World Politics* 35(1): 1–24.

Jackson, Stephen. 2006. "Sons of Which Soil? The Language and Politics of Autochthony in Eastern DR Congo." *African Studies Review* 49(2): 95–123.

Jacobsen, Karen. 1996. "Factors Influencing the Policy Responses of Host Governments to Mass Refugee Influxes." *International Migration Review* 30(3): 655–678.

———. 2002. "Can Refugees Benefit the State? Refugee Resources and African State-building." *Journal of Modern African Studies* 40(4): 577–596.

James, Laura M. 2011. "The Oil Boom and Its Limitations in Sudan." In *Sudan Looks East: China, India, and the Politics of Asian Alternatives,* ed. Daniel Large and Luke A. Patey. Suffolk: Currey, 52–69.

Jaulin, Thibaut, and Étienne Smith. 2016. "Généralisation et Pratiques du Vote à Distance." *Afrique Contemporaine* (256): 11–34.

Jennings, Kathleen M. 2007. "The Struggle to Satisfy: DDR Through the Eyes of Ex-Combatants in Liberia." *International Peacekeeping* 14(2): 204–218.

———. 2009. "The Political Economy of DDR in Liberia: A Gendered Critique." *Conflict, Security & Development* 9(4): 475–494.

Jiggins, Janice. 1989. "How Poor Women Earn Income in Sub-Saharan Africa and What Works Against Them." *World Development* 17(7): 953–963.

Jordaan, Eduard. 2006. "Inadequately Self-Critical: Rwanda's Self-Assessment for the African Peer Review Mechanism." *African Affairs* 105(420): 333–351.

———. 2014. "South Africa and the United Nations Human Rights Council." *Human Rights Quarterly* 36(1): 90–122.

Kainz, Lena. 2016. "People Can't Flood, Flow, or Stream: Diverting Dominant Media Discourses on Migration." Border Criminologies, Oxford Law Faculty. https://www.law.ox.ac.uk.

Kalb, Madeleine. 1982. *The Congo Cables: The Congo War in Africa from Eisenhowever to Kennedy.* New York: Macmillan.

Kamei, Seraphina. 2011. "Diaspora as the 'Sixth Region of Africa': An Assessment of the African Union Initiative, 2002–2010." *Diaspora Studies* 4(1): 59–76.

Karlsrud, John. 2015. "The UN at War: Examining the Consequences of Peace-Enforcement Mandates for the UN Peacekeeping Operations in the CAR, the DRC and Mali." *Third World Quarterly* 36(1): 40–54.

Kazeem, Yomi. 2017. "Nigeria's First Ever Diaspora Bond Has Raised $300 Million." *Quartz Africa,* June 26. https://qz.com.

Keen, David. 1994a. *The Benefits of Famine: A Political Economy of Famine and Relief in Southwestern Sudan, 1983–1989.* Princeton: Princeton University Press.

———. 1994b. "The Functions of Famine in Southwestern Sudan: Implications for Relief." In *War and Hunger: Rethinking International Responses to Complex Emergencies,* ed. Joanna Macrae, Anthony B. Zwi, Mark Duffield, and Hugo Slim. London: Zed, 111–124.

———. 2008. *Complex Emergencies.* Cambridge: Polity.

Kennedy, David. 2011. *The Dark Sides of Virtue: Reassessing International Humanitarianism.* Princeton: Princeton University Press.

Kennes, Walter. 1999. "African Regional Economic Integration and the European Union." In *Regionalisation in Africa: Integration and Disintegration,* ed. Daniel C. Bach. Oxford: Currey, 27–40.

Kenyan Ministry of Foreign Affairs and International Trade. 2014. "Kenya Diaspora Policy." https://www.kenyaembassy.com.

Keppler, Elise. 2012. "Managing Setbacks for the International Criminal Court in Africa." *Journal of African Law* 56(1): 1–14.

Kessler, Glenn, and Colum Lynch. 2004. "US Calls Killings in Sudan Genocide." *Washington Post,* September 10.

Kibreab, Gaim. 1985. *African Refugees: Reflections on the African Refugee Problem.* Trenton: Africa World.

Kidane, Won. 2016. "China's Bilateral Investment Treaties with African States in Comparative Context." *Cornell Journal of International Law* 49: 141–176.

Kigozi, David. 2017. "The Reality Behind Uganda's Refugee Model." *Refugees Deeply,* May 30. https://www.newsdeeply.com.

Klinghoffer, Arthur J. 1980. *The Angolan War: A Study in Soviet Policy in the Third World.* Boulder: Westview.

Klotz, Audie. 1999. *Norms in International Relations: The Struggle Against Apartheid.* Ithaca: Cornell University Press.

Konadu-Agyemang, Kwadwo. 2000. "The Best of Times and the Worst of Times: Structural Adjustment Programs and Uneven Development in Africa: The Case of Ghana." *Professional Geographer* 52(3): 469–483.

Koremenos, Barbara, Charles Lipson, and Duncan Snidal, eds. 2003. *The Rational Design of International Institutions.* Cambridge: Cambridge University Press.

Kpessa, Michael, Daniel Béland, and André Lecours. 2011. "Nationalism, Development, and Social Policy: The Politics of Nation-Building in Sub-Saharan Africa." *Ethnic and Racial Studies* 34(12): 2115–2133.

KPMG. 2015. "India and Africa: Collaboration for Growth." https://assets.kpmg.com.

Kriel, Robyn, and Briana Duggan. 2015. "Al-Shabaab Faction Pledges Allegiance to ISIS." *CNN News,* October 22. http://www.cnn.com.

Kuperman, Alan J. 2000. "Rwanda in Retrospect." *Foreign Affairs* 79(1): 94–118.

———. 2008. "The Moral Hazard of Humanitarian Intervention: Lessons from the Balkans." *International Studies Quarterly* 52(1): 49–80.

Kyle, Keith. 1991. *Suez: Britain's End of Empire in the Middle East.* London: I. B. Taurus.

Lacassagne, Aurélie. 2012. "Cultures of Anarchy as Figurations: Reflections on Wendt, Elias, and the English School." *Human Figurations* 1(2). http://hdl.handle.net.

Lafleur, Jean-Michel. 2015. "The Enfranchisement of Citizens Abroad: Variations and Explanations." *Democratization* 22(5): 840–860.

Laïdi, Zaki. 1990. *The Superpowers and Africa: The Constraints of a Rivalry, 1960–1990.* Trans. Patricia Baudoin. Chicago: University of Chicago Press.

Lake, Anthony. 1976. *The "Tar Baby" Option: American Policy Toward Southern Rhodesia.* New York: Columbia University Press.

Lancaster, Carol. 1999. *Aid to Africa: So Much to Do, So Little Done.* Chicago: University of Chicago Press.

———. 2000. *Transforming Foreign Aid: United States Assistance in the 21st Century.* Washington, DC: Institute for International Economics.

Landau, Loren B. 2003. "Beyond the Losers: Transforming Governmental Practice in Refugee-Affected Tanzania." *Journal of Refugee Studies* 16(1): 19–43.

———. 2005. "Urbanisation, Nativism, and the Rule of Law in South Africa's 'Forbidden' Cities." *Third World Quarterly* 26(7): 1115–1134.

———. 2006. "Transplants and Transients: Idioms of Belonging and Dislocation in Inner-City Johannesburg." *African Studies Review* 49(2): 125–145.

———. 2010. "Loving the Alien? Citizenship, Law, and the Future in South Africa's Demonic Society." *African Affairs* 109(435): 213–230.

———, ed. 2011. *Exorcising the Demons Within: Xenophobia, Violence, and Statecraft in Contemporary South Africa.* Johannesburg: Wits University Press.

Langan, Mark. 2016. *The Moral Economy of EU Association with Africa.* New York: Routledge.

Lavelle, Kathryn C. 2004. *The Politics of Equity Finance in Emerging Markets.* New York: Oxford University Press.

Lawson, Letitia. 1999. "External Democracy Promotion in Africa: Another False Start?" *Commonwealth and Comparative Politics* 37(1): 37–58.

Leblang, David. 2017. "Harnessing the Diaspora: Dual Citizenship, Migrant Return Remittances." *Comparative Political Studies* 50(1): 75–101.

Lebow, Richard Ned. 2003. *The Tragic Vision of Politics: Ethics, Interests, and Orders.* Cambridge: Cambridge University Press.

Legvold, Robert. 1970. *Soviet Policy in West Africa.* Cambridge: Harvard University Press.

Leibfritz, Willi, and Gebhard Flaig. 2013. "Economic Growth in Africa: Comparing Recent Improvements with the 'Lost 1980s and Early 1990s' and Estimating New Growth Trends." CESifo Working Paper no. 4215. https://ideas.repec.org.

Leo, Christopher. 1978. "The Failure of the 'Progressive Farmer' in Kenya's Million-Acre Settlement Scheme." *Journal of Modern African Studies* 16(4): 619–638.

Leonhardt, Alec. 2006. "Baka and the Magic of the State: Between Autochthony and Citizenship." *African Studies Review* 49(2): 69–94.

Lesch, Ann Mosely. 1987. "A View from Khartoum." *Foreign Affairs* 65(4): 807–826.

Leslie, Agnes Ngoma. 2016. "Zambia and China: Workers' Protest, Civil Society, and the Role of Opposition Politics in Elevating State Engagement." *African Studies Quarterly* 16(3–4): 89–106.

LeVan, A. Carl. 2010. "The Political Economy of African Responses to the U.S. Africa Command." *Africa Today* 57(1): 3–23.

Lewsen, Phyllis. 1971. "The Cape Liberal Tradition: Myth or Reality?" *Race* 13(1): 65–80.

Liang, Meichen. 2017. "China's First Overseas Military Base Opens in Djibouti." August 2. http://www.ecns.cn.

Licklider, Roy. 1995. "The Consequences of Negotiated Settlements in Civil Wars, 1945–1993." *American Political Science Review* 89(3): 681–690.

Lindberg, Staffan. 2006. *Democracy and Elections in Africa*. Baltimore: Johns Hopkins University Press.

Lindenmayer, Elisabeth, and Josie Lianna Kaye. 2009. "A Choice for Peace? The Story of Forty-One Days of Mediation in Kenya." International Peace Institute. https://www.ipinst.org.

Linz, Juan L., and Alfred Stepan. 1978. *The Breakdown of Democratic Regimes*. Baltimore: Johns Hopkins University Press.

Lischer, Sarah Kenyon. 2003. "Collateral Damage: Humanitarian Assistance as a Cause of Conflict." *International Security* 28(1): 79–109.

———. 2005. *Dangerous Sanctuaries: Refugee Camps, Civil War, and the Dilemmas of Humanitarian Aid*. Ithaca: Cornell University Press.

Lob, Eric. 2016. "The Islamic Republic of Iran's Foreign Policy and Construction Jihad's Developmental Activities in Sub-Saharan Africa." *International Journal of Middle East Studies* 48(2): 313–338.

Lochery, E. 2012. "Rendering Difference Visible: The Kenyan State and Its Somali Citizens." *African Affairs* 111(445): 615–639.

Lodge, Tom. 1987. "State of Exile: The African National Congress of South Africa, 1976–86." *Third World Quarterly* 9(1): 1–27.

Lofchie, Michael F. 1993. "Trading Places: Economic Policy in Kenya and Tanzania." In *Hemmed In: Responses to Africa's Economic Decline,* ed. Thomas Callaghy and John Ravenhill. New York: Columbia University Press, 398–461.

Longman, Timothy. 2002. "The Complex Reasons for Rwanda's Engagement in Congo." In *The African Stakes of the Congo War,* ed. John F. Clark. New York: Palgrave Macmillan, 129–144.

Lovejoy, Paul E. 2012. *Transformations in Slavery: A History of Slavery in Africa*. 3rd ed. Cambridge: Cambridge University Press.

Lumumba-Kasongo, Tukumbi. 2011. "China-Africa Relations: A Neo-Imperialism or a Neo-Colonialism? Reflection." *African and Asian Studies* 10(2–3): 234–263.

Lusaka Times. 2011. "Sata U-Turns on China." October 30. https://www.lusakatimes.com.

Lüthi, Lorenz M. 2010. *The Sino-Soviet Split: Cold War in the Communist World*. Princeton: Princeton University Press.

Lyman, Princeton. 2009. "The War on Terrorism in Africa." In *Africa in World Politics: Reforming Political Order,* ed. John W. Harbeson and Donald S. Rothchild. Boulder: Westview, 276–304.

———. 2017. "Sudan and South Sudan: The Tragic Denouement of the Comprehensive Peace Agreement." In *Africa in World Politics: Constructing Political and Economic Order,* ed. John W. Harbeson and Donald Rothchild. Boulder: Westview, 156–175.

Lyons, Terrence. 2006. "Diasporas and Homeland Conflict." In *Territoriality and Conflict in an Era of Globalization,* ed. Miles Kahler and Barbara Walter. Cambridge: Cambridge University Press, 111–130.

——. 2007. "Conflict-Generated Diasporas and Transnational Politics in Ethiopia." *Conflict, Security & Development* 7(4): 529–549.

——. 2016. "The Importance of Winning: Victorious Insurgent Groups and Authoritarian Politics." *Comparative Politics* 48(2): 167–184.

Lyons, Terrence, and Ahmed I. Samatar. 1995. *Somalia: State Collapse, Multilateral Intervention, and Strategies for Political Reconstruction*. Washington, DC: Brookings Institution.

Macdonald, Alastair. 2015. "EU Launches $2 Billion Emergency Fund for Africa to Combat Migration." Reuters, November 15. http://www.reuters.com.

MacGaffey, Janet, ed. 1991. *The Real Economy of Zaire: The Contribution of Smuggling and Other Unofficial Activities to National Wealth*. Philadelphia: University of Pennsylvania Press.

Makumbe, John Mw. 1998. "Is There a Civil Society in Africa?" *International Affairs* 74(2): 305–319.

——. 2002. "Zimbabwe's Hijacked Election." *Journal of Democracy* 13(4): 87–101.

Malik, Aditi. 2016. "Mobilizing a Defensive Kikuyu-Kalenjin Alliance: The Politicization of the International Criminal Court in Kenya's 2013 Presidential Election." *African Conflict and Peacebuilding Review* 6(2): 48–73.

Mallik, Girijasankar. 2008. "Foreign Aid and Economic Growth: A Cointegration Analysis of the Six Poorest African Countries." *Economic Analysis and Policy* 38(2): 251–260.

Manby, Bronwen. 2009. *Citizenship Law in Africa: A Comparative Study*. New York: Open Society Institute.

Mandela, Nelson. 1994. *Long Walk to Freedom: The Autobiography of Nelson Mandela*. Boston: Little, Brown.

Mangala, Jack. 2013a. "Africa-EU Strategic Partnership: Historical Background, Institutional Architecture, and Theoretical Frameworks." In *Africa and the European Union: A Strategic Partnership,* ed. Jack Mangala. New York: Palgrave Macmillan, 15–45.

——. 2013b. "Africa-EU Strategic Partnership: Significance and Implications." In *Africa and the European Union: A Strategic Partnership,* ed. Jack Mangala. New York: Palgrave Macmillan, 3–14.

Manning, Patrick. 1988. *Francophone Sub-Saharan Africa, 1880–1985*. Cambridge: Cambridge University Press.

Mappa, Sophia. 1995. "L'Injonction Démocratique dans les Politiques Européennes de Développement." In *Développer par la Démocratie? Injonctions Occidentales et Exigences Planétaires,* ed. Sophia Mappa. Paris: Karthala, 121–178.

Marcum, John. 1978. *The Angolan Revolution: Exile Politics and Guerilla Warfare, 1962–1976*. Vol. 2, *The Anatomy of an Explosion*. Cambridge: Massachusetts Institute of Technology Press.

Martin, David M., and Phyllis Johnson. 1989. *Apartheid Terrorism: The Destabilization Report*. London: Currey.

Martin, Guy. 1995. "Continuity and Change in Franco-African Relations." *Journal of Modern African Studies* 33(1): 1–20.

Mashindano, Oswald, Dennis Rweyemamu, and Daniel Ngowi. 2007. "Deepening Integration in SADC: Tanzania: Torn Between EAC and SADC." In *Regional Integration in Southern Africa*. Gaborone: Friedrich Ebert Foundation Botswana Office.

Mays, Terry M. 2002. *Africa's First Peacekeeping Operation: The OAU in Chad, 1981–1982*. Westport: Praeger.

Mbali, Mandisa. 2004. "AIDS Discourses and the South African State: Government Denialism and Post-Apartheid AIDS Policy-Making." *Transformation: Critical Perspectives on Southern Africa* 54(1): 104–122.

Mbeki, Thabo. 1998. "The African Renaissance, South Africa, and the World." Presented at the speech by South African deputy president Thabo Mbeki, United Nations University. http://archive.unu.edu.

McCann, Gerard. 2010. "Ties That Bind or Binds That Tie? India's African Engagements and the Political Economy of Kenya." *Review of African Political Economy* 37(126): 465–482.

McDonald, David A., and Sean Jacobs. 2005. "(Re)Writing Xenophobia: Understanding Press Coverage of Cross-Border Migration in Southern Africa." *Journal of Contemporary African Studies* 23(3): 295–325.

McNamara, Francis T. 1989. *France in Black Africa*. Washington, DC: National Defense University Press.

McNulty, Mel. 1997. "France's Role in Rwanda and External Military Intervention: A Double Discrediting." *International Peacekeeping* 4(3): 24–44.

Mehler, Andreas. 2005. "The Shaky Foundations, Adverse Circumstances, and Limited Achievements of the Democratic Transition in the Central African Republic." In *The Fate of Africa's Democratic Experiments: Elites and Institutions,* ed. Leonardo Villalón and Peter VonDoepp. Bloomington: Indiana University Press, 126–152.

———. 2009. "Peace and Power Sharing in Africa: A Not So Obvious Relationship." *African Affairs* 108(432): 453–473.

Melvern, Linda. 2000. *A People Betrayed: The Role of the West in Rwanda's Genocide*. London: Zed.

Menkhaus, Ken. 2006. "Governance Without Government in Somalia: Spoilers, State Building, and the Politics of Coping." *International Security* 31(3): 74–106.

———. 2009. "False Start in AFRICOM." *Contemporary Security Policy* 30(1): 53–57.

———. 2012. "No Access: Critical Bottlenecks in the 2011 Somali Famine." *Global Food Security* 1(1): 29–35.

Milanovic, Branko. 2012. *The Haves and the Have-Nots: A Brief and Idiosyncratic History of Global Inequality*. New York: Basic.

Milburn, Josephine. 1970. "The 1938 Gold Coast Cocoa Crisis: British Business and the Colonial Office." *African Historical Studies* 3(1): 57–74.

Miller, Gina Lei, and Emily Hencken Ritter. 2014. "Emigrants and the Onset of Civil War." *Journal of Peace Research* 51(1): 51–64.

Mills, Kurt. 2005. "Neo-Humanitarianism: The Role of International Humanitarian Norms and Organizations in Contemporary Conflict." *Global Governance: A Review of Multilateralism and International Organizations* 11(2): 161–183.

———. 2012. "'Bashir Is Dividing Us': Africa and the International Criminal Court." *Human Rights Quarterly* 34(2): 404–447.

Mirus, Rolf, and Nataliya Rylska. 2001. "Economic Integration: Free Trade Areas vs. Customs Unions." Western Centre for Economic Research. https://www.ualberta.ca.

Mkutu, Kennedy. 2008. *Guns and Governance in the Rift Valley Pastoralist Conflict and Small Arms*. London: Currey.

Mohan, Giles. 2006. "Embedded Cosmopolitanism and the Politics of Obligation: The Ghanaian Diaspora and Development." *Environment and Planning A* 38(5): 867–883.

———. 2008. "Making Neoliberal States of Development: The Ghanaian Diaspora and the Politics of Homelands." *Environment and Planning D: Society and Space* 26(3): 464–479.

Monson, Jamie. 2009. *Africa's Freedom Railway: How a Chinese Development Project Changed Lives and Livelihoods in Tanzania*. Bloomington: Indiana University Press.

———. 2013. "Remembering Work on the Tazara Railway in Africa and China, 1965–2011: When 'New Men' Grow Old." *African Studies Review* 56(1): 45–80.

Montana, Ismael Musa. 2003. "The Lomé Convention from Inception to the Dynamics of the Post–Cold War, 1957–1990s." *African & Asian Studies* 2(1): 63–97.

Moorehead, Alan. 1960. *The White Nile*. London: Hamish Hamilton.

Morgenthau, Hans J. 1951. *In Defense of the National Interest*. New York: Knopf.

———. 1973. *Politics Among Nations: The Struggle for Power and Peace*. 5th ed. New York: Knopf.

Morphet, Sally. 2004. "Multilateralism and the Non-Aligned Movement: What Is the Global South Doing and Where Is It Going?" *Global Governance* 10(4): 517–537.

Mortimer, Edward. 1969. *France and the Africans 1944–1960: A Political History*. London: Faber and Faber.

Moss, Todd. 2004. "The Politics of Aid: A Marshall Plan Is Not What Africa Needs." *New York Times,* December 29.

Moss, Todd J., and Danielle Resnick. 2018. *African Development: Making Sense of the Issues and Actors*. 3rd ed. Boulder: Lynne Rienner.

Mosselson, Aidan. 2010. "'There Is No Difference Between Citizens and Non-Citizens Anymore': Violent Xenophobia, Citizenship, and the Politics of Belonging in Post-Apartheid South Africa." *Journal of Southern African Studies* 36(3): 641.

Moyo, Dambisa. 2009. *Dead Aid: Why Aid Is Not Working and How There Is a Better Way for Africa*. New York: Farrar, Straus, and Giroux.

Mueller, Susanne D. 2014. "Kenya and the International Criminal Court (ICC): Politics, the Election, and the Law." *Journal of Eastern African Studies* 8(1): 25–42.

Muggah, Robert. 2015. "What Is Brazil Really Doing in Africa?" *Huffington Post*, January 4. http://www.huffingtonpost.com.

Munnion, Christopher. 2008. "China's Zimbabwe Arms Ship Turned Away by African Nations." *The Telegraph* (London), April 24. http://www.telegraph.co.uk.

Murali, Krishnan. 2013. "Indian Investment in Africa Soars." July 15. http://www.dw.com.

Murdie, Amanda. 2014. *Help or Harm: The Human Security Effects of International NGOs*. Redwood City: Stanford University Press.

Museveni, Yoweri Kaguta. 1997. *Sowing the Mustard Seed: The Struggle for Freedom and Democracy in Uganda*. London: Macmillan.

———. 2011. "The Qaddafi I Know." *Foreign Policy*, March 24. http://foreignpolicy.com.

Mutesa, Frederick. 2010. "China and Zambia: Between Development and Politics." In *The Rise of China and India in Africa*, ed. Fantu Cheru and Cyril Obi. London: Zed, 167–178.

Mutisi, Martha. 2016. "SADC Interventions in the Democratic Republic of the Congo." http://www.accord.org.za.

Mwanawina, Inyambo. 2007. "An Assessment of Chinese Development Assistance in Africa: Zambia." Study commissioned by the Africa Forum and Network on Debt and Development (AFRODAD).

Mwangi, Oscar Gakuo. 2010. "The Union of Islamic Courts and Security Governance in Somalia." *African Security Review* 19(1): 88–94.

Nattrass, Nicoli. 2007. *Mortal Combat: AIDS Denialism and the Struggle for Antiretrovirals in South Africa*. Scottsville: University of KwaZulu-Natal Press.

Ndiaye, Alioune. 2016. "India's Investment in Africa: Feeding Up an Ambitious Elephant." *Bridges Africa* 5(7). http://www.ictsd.org.

Ndulo, Muna. 2008. "Chinese Investments in Africa: A Case Study of Zambia." In *Crouching Tiger, Hidden Dragon? Africa and China*, ed. Kweku Ampiah and Sanusha Naidu. Pietermaritzburg: University of KwaZulu-Natal Press, 138–151.

Negash, Tekeste. 1997. *Eritrea and Ethiopia: The Federal Experience*. Stockholm: Nordic Africa Institute.

Neocosmos, Michael. 2008. "The Politics of Fear and the Fear of Politics: Reflections on Xenophobic Violence in South Africa." *Journal of Asian and African Studies* 43(6): 586–594.

———. 2010. *From "Foreign Natives" to "Native Foreigners": Explaining Xenophobia in Post-Apartheid South Africa*. Dakar: Council for the Development of Social Science Research in Africa (CODESRIA).

Newbury, Catharine. 1995. "Background to Genocide: Rwanda." *Issue: A Journal of Opinion* 23(2): 12–17.

Newbury, David. 1997. "Irredentist Rwanda: Ethnic and Territorial Frontiers in Central Africa." *Africa Today* 44(2): 211–221.

Nielsen, Waldamar. 1969. *The Great Powers in Africa*. New York: Council on Foreign Relations.

Nigerians in Diaspora Organisation UK. 2016. "About Us." http://nidouksouth.org.

Nkrumah, Kwame. 1965. *Neocolonialism: The Last Stage of Imperialism*. New York: International Publishers.

Noah, Trevor. 2016. *Born a Crime: Stories from a South African Childhood*. New York: Spiegel and Grau.

Novak, Andrew. 2009. "Face-Saving Maneuvers and Strong Third-Party Mediation: The Lancaster House Conference on Zimbabwe-Rhodesia." *International Negotiation* 14(1): 149–174.

Nuba Reports. 2016. "75 Trips to 22 Countries in 7 Years: An Indicted War Criminal's Travels." March 7. https://nubareports.org.

Nwaubani, Ebere. 2001. *The United States and Decolonization in West Africa, 1950–1960*. Rochester: University of Rochester Press.

Nyamnjoh, Francis B. 2006. *Insiders and Outsiders: Citizenship and Xenophobia in Contemporary Southern Africa*. London: Zed.

Nzongola-Ntalaja, Georges. 2002. *The Congo: From Leopold to Kabila—A People's History*. London: Zed.

OANDA. N.d. "Historical Exchange Rates." http://www.oanda.com.

Obadare, Ebenezer, and Wale Adebanwi. 2009. "Transnational Resource Flow and the Paradoxes of Belonging: Redirecting the Debate on Transnationalism, Remittances, State, and Citizenship in Africa." *Review of African Political Economy* 36(122): 499–517.

O'Brien, Conor Cruise. 1962. *To Katanga and Back: A UN Case History*. New York: Simon and Schuster.

Oguine, Ike. 2000. *A Squatter's Tale*. Oxford: Heinemann.

Ogunsanwo, Alaba. 2008. "A Tale of Two Giants: Nigeria and China." In *Crouching Tiger, Hidden Dragon? Africa and China*, ed. Kweku Ampiah and Sanusha Naidu. Pietermaritzburg: University of KwaZulu-Natal Press, 192–207.

Ojo, Olatunde B. J. 1999. "Integration in ECOWAS: Successes and Difficulties." In *Regionalisation in Africa: Integration and Disintegration*, ed. Daniel D. Bach. Oxford: Currey, 119–124.

Okpalaobi, Nkechi. 2014. "Globalization and Conflict: The African Experience." *International Journal of Arts and Humanities* 3(3): 35–46.

Omach, Paul. 2010. "Regionalisation of Rebel Activities: The Case of the Lord's Resistance Army." In *Militias, Rebels, and Islamist Militants: Human Insecurity and State Crises in Africa*, ed. Wafula Okumu and Augustine Ikelegbe. Pretoria: Institute for Security Studies, 287–312.

O'Mahony, Angela. 2013. "Political Investment: Remittances and Elections." *British Journal of Political Science* 43(4): 799–820.

Onimode, Bade, ed. 1989. *The IMF, the World Bank, and the African Debt: The Economic Impact*. London: Zed.

Onishi, Norimitsu. 2017. "South Africa Reverses Withdrawal from International Criminal Court." *New York Times*, March 8. https://www.nytimes.com.

Oppong, Richard Frimpong. 2010. "The African Union, the African Economic Community, and Africa's Regional Economic Communities: Untangling a Complex Web." *African Journal of International and Comparative Law* 18(1): 92–103.

Organization for Economic Cooperation and Development (OECD). 2015. *Development Aid at a Glance: Statistics by Region—Africa*. http://www.oecd.org.

———. 2018. "Query Wizard for International Development Statistics." http://stats.oecd.org.

Organization of African Unity (OAU). 1964. *Resolution on Border Disputes Among African States*. AHG/Resolution 16(I).

———. 1980. *Lagos Plan of Action for the Economic Development of Africa, 1980–2000*. Addis Ababa.

O'Rourke, Kevin H., and Richard Sinnott. 2006. "The Determinants of Individual Attitudes Towards Immigration." *European Journal of Political Economy* 22(4): 838–861.

Ottaway, Marina. 1982. *Soviet and American Influence in the Horn of Africa*. New York: Praeger.

———. 1999. *Africa's New Leaders: Democracy or State Reconstruction?* Washington, DC: Carnegie Endowment for International Peace.

Oyebade, Adebayo. 2002. "Colonial Political Systems." In *Africa*, ed. Toyin Falola. Durham: Carolina Academic Press, 71–86.

Page, Matthew T. 2017. "Donald Trump Could Be Getting His US-Africa Policy Right by Simply Not Having One." *Quartz,* August 9. https://qz.com.

Pailey, Robtel Neajai, and Thomas Jaye. 2016. "The UN Had to Go, but Is Liberia Ready to Keep Its Own Peace?" *African Arguments,* July 13. http://african arguments.org.

Pallotti, Arrigo. 2009. "Post-Colonial Nation-Building and Southern African Liberation: Tanzania and the Break of Diplomatic Relations with the United Kingdom, 1965–1968." *African Historical Review* 41(2): 60–84.

Parks, Miles. 2017. "World Faces Largest Humanitarian Crisis Since 1945, U.N. Official Says." National Public Radio, March 11. http://www.npr.org.

Patton, Anna. 2016. "Is Uganda the Best Place to Be a Refugee?" *The Guardian* (London), August 20. https://www.theguardian.com.

Pazzanita, Anthony G. 1991. "The Conflict Resolution Process in Angola." *Journal of Modern African Studies* 29(1): 83–114.

Peberdy, Sally. 2001. "Imagining Immigration: Inclusive Identities and Exclusive Policies in Post-1994 South Africa." *Africa Today* 48(3): 15–32.

Peil, Margaret. 1971. "The Expulsion of West African Aliens." *Journal of Modern African Studies* 9(2): 205–229.

———. 1974. "Ghana's Aliens." *International Migration Review* 8(3): 367.

Pella, John Anthony. 2014. *Africa and the Expansion of International Society: Surrendering the Savannah.* New York: Routledge.

Persaud, Randolph B. 2001. "Re-envisioning Sovereignty: Marcus Garvey and the Making of a Transnational Identity." In *Africa's Challenge to International Relations Theory,* ed. Kevin C. Dunn and Timothy M. Shaw. New York: Palgrave, 112–128.

Peters, Krijn. 2010. "Local Communities, Militias, and Rebel Movements: The Case of the Revolutionary United Front in Sierra Leone." In *Militias, Rebels, and Islamist Militants: Human Insecurity and State Crises in Africa,* ed. Wafula Okumu and Augustine Ikelegbe. Pretoria: Institute for Security Studies, 389–416.

Piccio, Lorenzo. 2013. "India's Foreign Aid Program Catches Up with Its Global Ambitions." *Devex,* May 10. https://www.devex.com.

Pike, John. 2017. "Ivory Coast Conflict." http://www.globalsecurity.org.

Piombo, Jessica, ed. 2015. *The US Military in Africa: Enhancing Security and Development?* Boulder: First Forum.

Polack, Peter. 2013. *The Last Hot Battle of the Cold War: South Africa vs. Cuba in the Angolan Civil War.* Oxford: Casement.

Pool, David. 2001. *From Guerrillas to Government: The Eritrean People's Liberation Front.* Athens: Ohio University Press.

Posel, Dorrit. 2004. "Have Migration Patterns in Post-Apartheid South Africa Changed?" *Journal of Interdisciplinary Economics* 15(3–4): 277–292.

Posner, Daniel N. 2006. "African Borders as Sources of Natural Experiments." Unpublished manuscript. http://www.polisci.ucla.edu.

Postel, Hannah. 2016. "We May Have Been Massively Overestimating the Number of Chinese Migrants in Africa." *African Arguments,* December 19. http://african arguments.org.

Power, Samantha. 2001. "Bystanders to Genocide." *Atlantic Monthly* 288(2): 84–108.

———. 2002a. *"A Problem from Hell": America and the Age of Genocide.* New York: Basic.

———. 2002b. "Raising the Cost of Genocide." *Dissent* (Spring): 85–96.

Premium Times Nigeria. 2014. "Nigeria to Contribute $17 Million to AU Budget in 2015." June 28. http://www.premiumtimesng.com.

Prendergast, John. 2009. "Can You Hear Congo Now? Cell Phones, Conflict Minerals, and the Worst Sexual Violence in the World." April. http://www.enoughproject.org.

Profant, Tomáš. 2010. "French Geopolitics in Africa: From Neocolonialism to Identity." *Perspectives* 18(1): 41–62.

Prunier, Gérard. 1997. *The Rwanda Crisis: History of a Genocide*. New York: Columbia University Press.
———. 2005. *Darfur: The Ambiguous Genocide*. Ithaca: Cornell University Press.
———. 2009. *Africa's World War: Congo, the Rwandan Genocide, and the Making of a Continental Catastrophe*. Oxford: Oxford University Press.
Prys, Miriam. 2010. "Hegemony, Domination, Detachment: Differences in Regional Powerhood." *International Studies Review* 12(4): 479–504.
Quinn, Ben. 2016. "South Sudan Peacekeeping Commander Sacked over 'Serious Shortcomings.'" *The Guardian* (London), November 2. https://www.theguardian.com.
Radelet, Steven. 2016. "Africa's Rise: Interrupted?" *Finance and Development* 52(2). http://www.imf.org.
Radio France International. 2010. "Senegal 'Takes Back' French Military Bases." April 5. http://en.rfi.fr.
Ramphele, Mamphela, and Francis Wilson. 1987. *Children on the Front Line: The Impact of Apartheid, Destabilization, and Warfare on Children in Southern and South Africa*. New York: United Nations Children's Fund.
Ranger, Terence O. 1967. *Revolt in Southern Rhodesia 1896–1897: A Study in African Resistance*. Oxford: Heinemann.
———. 1983. "The Invention of Tradition in Colonial Africa." In *The Invention of Tradition*, ed. Eric Hobsbawm and Terence Ranger. Cambridge: Cambridge University Press, 211–262.
Rawlence, Ben. 2005. "Briefing: The Zanzibar Election." *African Affairs* 104(416): 515–523.
Raynolds, Laura T., Douglas Murray, and John Wilkinson. 2007. *Fair Trade: The Challenges of Transforming Globalization*. New York: Routledge.
Reed, Holly E. 2013. "Moving Across Boundaries: Migration in South Africa, 1950–2000." *Demography* 50(1): 71–95.
Reed, Michael C. 1987. "Gabon: A Neo-Colonial Enclave of Enduring French Interest." *Journal of Modern African Studies* 25(2): 283–320.
Rees, Jonathan. 2015. "What Next for the African Standby Force?" December 2. https://issafrica.org.
Regan, Patrick M. 2002. "Third-Party Interventions and the Duration of Intrastate Conflicts." *Journal of Conflict Resolution* 46(1): 55–73.
Regan, Patrick M., and M. Rodwan Abouharb. 2002. "Interventions and Civil Conflicts: Tools of Conflict Management or Simply Another Participant?" *World Affairs* 165(1): 42–54.
Reno, William. 2011. *Warfare in Independent Africa*. Cambridge: Cambridge University Press.
Renwick, Danielle. 2015. "Peace Operations in Africa." May 15. http://www.cfr.org.
Reynolds, Edward. 1985. *Stand the Storm: A History of the Atlantic Slave Trade*. New York: Alison and Busby.
Reyntjens, Filip. 2009. *The Great African War: Congo and Regional Geopolitics, 1996–2006*. Cambridge: Cambridge University Press.
———. 2013. *Political Governance in Post-Genocide Rwanda*. Cambridge: Cambridge University Press.
Richburg, Keith B. 1997. *Out of America: A Black Man Confronts Africa*. New York: Basic.
Riddell, Roger. 1987. *Foreign Aid Reconsidered*. 3rd ed. Baltimore: Currey.
Rieff, David. 2002. *A Bed for the Night: Humanitarianism in Crisis*. New York: Simon and Schuster.
Robertson, Winslow, and Lina Benabdallah. 2016. "China Pledged to Invest $60 Billion in Africa—Here's What That Means." *The Monkey Cage*, January 7. https://www.washingtonpost.com.
Rodney, Walter. 1972. *How Europe Underdeveloped Africa*. London: Bogle-L'Ouverture.

Roessler, Philip. 2011. "The Enemy Within: Personal Rule, Coups, and Civil War in Africa." *World Politics* 63(2): 300–346.

———. 2013. "Why South Sudan Has Exploded in Violence." *The Monkey Cage*, December 24. https://www.washingtonpost.com.

Rothchild, Donald. 1997. *Managing Ethnic Conflict in Africa: Pressures and Incentives for Cooperation*. Washington, DC: Brookings Institution.

Rouvez, Alain. 1994. *Disconsolate Empires: French, British and Belgian Military Involvement in Sub-Saharan Africa*. Lanham: University Press of America.

Roy, Sumit. 2013. "And What About India and Africa? The Road Ahead." In *The Morality of China in Africa: The Middle Kingdom and the Dark Continent*, ed. Stephen Chan. London: Zed, 131–139.

Rugalema, Gabriel. 2000. "Coping or Struggling? A Journey into the Impact of HIV/AIDS in Southern Africa." *Review of African Political Economy* 27(86): 537–545.

Runde, Daniel. 2015. "African Risk Capacity: Insurance for African Development." *Forbes*, December 22. https://www.forbes.com.

Russett, Bruce. 1993. *Grasping the Democratic Peace: Principles for a Post–Cold War World*. Princeton: Princeton University Press.

Rutsch, Poncie. 2015. "Guess How Much of Uncle Sam's Money Goes to Foreign Aid—Guess Again!" National Public Radio, February 10. http://www.npr.org.

Rwanda Governance Board. 2015. "Mission, Vision, and Core Values." http://www.rgb.rw.

Sachs, Jeffrey. 2009. "Aid Ironies." *Huffington Post*, June 24. http://www.huffington post.com.

Sachs, Jeffrey, and John W. McArthur. 2009. "Moyo's Confused Attack on Aid for Africa." *Huffington Post*, May 27. http://www.huffingtonpost.com.

Salehyan, Idean. 2008. "The Externalities of Civil Strife: Refugees as a Source of International Conflict." *American Journal of Political Science* 52(4): 787–801.

Salehyan, Idean, and Kristian Skrede Gleditsch. 2006. "Refugees and the Spread of Civil War." *International Organization* 60(2): 335–366.

Schatzberg, Michael. 1988. *The Dialectics of Oppression in Zaire*. Bloomington: Indiana University Press.

———. 2001. *Political Legitimacy in Middle Africa: Father, Family, Food*. Bloomington: Indiana University Press.

Schedler, Andreas, ed. 2006. *Electoral Authoritarianism: The Dynamics of Unfree Competition*. Boulder: Lynne Rienner.

Schemm, Paul. 2016. "Ethiopia Has a Lot Riding on Its New, Chinese-Built Railroad to the Sea." *Washington Post*, October 3. https://www.washingtonpost.com.

Schmidt, Elizabeth. 2013. *Foreign Intervention in Africa: From the Cold War to the War on Terror*. Cambridge: Cambridge University Press.

Schraeder, Peter. 1994. *United States Foreign Policy Toward Africa: Incrementalism, Crisis, and Change*. Cambridge: Cambridge University Press.

———. 2000. "Cold War to Cold Peace: Explaining US-French Competition in Francophone Africa." *Political Science Quarterly* 115(3): 395–419.

———. 2001. "'Forget the Rhetoric and Boost the Geopolitics': Emerging Trends in the Bush Administration's Policy Towards Africa, 2001." *African Affairs* 100(400): 387–404.

———. 2006a. "Belgium, France, and the United States in the Great Lakes Region." In *Security Dynamics in Africa's Great Lakes Region*, ed. Gilbert Khadiagala. Boulder: Lynne Rienner, 163–186.

———. 2006b. "Why the United States Should Recognize Somaliland's Independence." December 16. https://www.csis.org.

———. 2012. "Beyond the 'Big Man': Democratization and Its Impacts on the Formulation and Implementation of African Foreign Policies." Paper presented at the Nordic Africa Days Conference, Reykjavik, October 18–19.

Schünemann, Julia. 2014. "Africa Needs More Than Just the Silencing of Guns." June 17. https://issafrica.org.

Scott, Ridley. 2001. *Black Hawk Down*. Columbia Pictures.

Scott, Rob. 2011. "EAC: Rhetoric and Reality 07-11." Economist Corporate Network. https://www.slideshare.net.

Searcey, Dionne, and Jaime Yaya Barry. 2017. "Why Migrants Keep Risking All on the 'Deadliest Route.'" *New York Times,* June 22. https://www.nytimes.com.

Seay, Laura. 2012. "What's Wrong with Dodd-Frank 1502? Conflict Minerals, Civilian Livelihoods, and the Unintended Consequences of Western Advocacy." Center for Global Development Working Paper no. 284. http://papers.ssrn.com.

Shacinda, Shapi. 2008. "Sata Warms to Chinese Investment in Zambia." https://www.iol.co.za.

Shain, Yossi. 2002. "The Role of Diasporas in Conflict Perpetuation or Resolution." *SAIS Review* 22(2): 115–144.

Sheffer, Gabriel. 2003. *Diaspora Politics: At Home Abroad.* Cambridge: Cambridge University Press.

Shefte, Whitney. 2015. "Western Sahara's Stranded Refugees Consider Renewal of Morocco Conflict." *The Guardian* (London), January 6. https://www.theguardian.com.

Signé, Landry. 2013. "The Tortuous Trajectories of Democracy and the Persistence of Authoritarianism in Africa." CDDRL Working Paper no. 147. http://cddrl.fsi.stanford.edu.

Simiyu, Vincent. 1988. "The Democratic Myth in the African Traditional Societies." In *Democratic Theory and Practice in Africa,* ed. W. O. Oyugi and A. Gitonga. Portsmouth, NH: Heinemann.

Simmons, Beth. 2009. *Mobilizing for Human Rights: International Law in Domestic Politics.* Cambridge: Cambridge University Press.

Sinha, Pranay Kumar. 2010. "Indian Development Cooperation with Africa." In *The Rise of China and India in Africa,* ed. Fantu Cheru and Cyril Obi. London: Zed, 77–93.

Smith, Hazel Anne, and Paul Stares, eds. 2007. *Diasporas in Conflict: Peace-Makers or Peace-Wreckers?* Tokyo: United Nations University Press.

Smith, Robert Sydney. 1989. *Warfare and Diplomacy in Pre-Colonial West Africa.* 2nd ed. Madison: University of Wisconsin Press.

Socpa, Antoine. 2006. "Bailleurs Autochtones et Locataires Allogènes: Enjeu Foncier et Participation Politique au Cameroun." *African Studies Review* 49(2): 45–67.

South China Morning Post. 2017. "Taiwan Thanks African Ally for Rejecting Diplomatic Advances from Beijing." January 26. http://www.scmp.com.

Southall, Aidan W. 1970. "The Illusion of Tribe." *Journal of Asian and African Studies* 5(1–2): 28–50.

Spears, Ian S. 2000. "Understanding Inclusive Peace Agreements in Africa: The Problems of Sharing Power." *Third World Quarterly* 21(1): 105–118.

Stearns, Jason, Koen Vlassenroot, Kasper Hoffmann, and Tatiana Carayannis. 2017. "Congo's Inescapable State." *Foreign Affairs,* March 16. https://www.foreignaffairs.com.

Stedman, Stephen John. 1997. "Spoiler Problems in Peace Processes." *International Security* 22(2): 5–53.

Stokke, Olav, ed. 1989. *Western Middle Powers and Global Poverty: Determinants of the Aid Policies of Canada, Denmark, the Netherlands, Norway, and Sweden.* Uppsala: Nordic Africa Institute.

Stolte, Christina. 2015. *Brazil's Africa Strategy: Role Conception and the Drive for International Status.* New York: Palgrave.

Straus, Scott. 2011. "'It's Sheer Horror Here': Patterns of Violence During the First Four Months of Côte d'Ivoire's Post-Electoral Crisis." *African Affairs* 110(440): 481–489.

Stultz, Newell M. 2006. "African States Experiment with Peer Reviewing: The ARPM, 2002 to 2007." *Brown Journal of World Affairs* 13: 247–257.

Sturman, Kathryn. 2003. "The Rise of Libya as a Regional Player: Commentary." *African Security Review* 12(2): 109–112.

Sun, Yun. 2015. "The Limits of U.S.-China Cooperation in Africa." April 6. https://www.brookings.edu.

Tarabrin, E. 1980. *USSR and Countries of Africa: Friendship, Cooperation, Support for the Anti-Imperialist Struggle.* Moscow: Progress.

Tardy, Thierry. 2011. "A Critique of Robust Peacekeeping in Contemporary Peace Operations." *International Peacekeeping* 18(2): 152–167.

Taylor, Adam. 2015. "Why So Many African Leaders Hate the International Criminal Court." *Washington Post,* June 15. https://www.washingtonpost.com.

Taylor, Ian. 2003. "Conflict in Central Africa: Clandestine Networks and Regional/Global Configurations." *Review of African Political Economy* 30(95): 45–55.

———. 2009. *China's New Role in Africa.* Boulder: Lynne Rienner.

———. 2010. "Governance and Relations Between the European Union and Africa: The Case of NEPAD." *Third World Quarterly* 31(1): 51–67.

———. 2011. *The Forum on China-Africa Cooperation (FOCAC).* New York: Routledge.

———. 2013. "African Unity at 50: From Non-Interference to Non-Indifference." June 25. http://www.e-ir.info.

Taylor, Ian, and Gladys Mokhawa. 2003. "Not Forever: Botswana, Conflict Diamonds, and the Bushmen." *African Affairs* 102(407): 261–283.

Taylor, Ian, and Zhengyu Wu. 2013. "China's Arms Transfers to Africa and Political Violence." *Terrorism and Political Violence* 25(3): 457–475.

Terry, Fiona. 2002. *Condemned to Repeat? The Paradox of Humanitarian Action.* Ithaca: Cornell University Press.

Teshome-Bahiru, Wondwosen. 2013. "Democracy Promotion and Western Aid to Africa: Lessons from Ethiopia (1991–2012)." *International Journal of Human Sciences* 10(1): 993–1049.

This Is Africa. 2016. "Botswana Reiterates Support for the ICC While Saying It 'Regrets' South Africa's Decision to Leave the Court." October 25. https://thisisafrica.me.

Thompson, Leonard Monteath. 2001. *A History of South Africa.* New Haven: Yale University Press.

Thomson, Alex. 2010. *An Introduction to African Politics.* 3rd ed. New York: Routledge.

Thomson Reuters Foundation. 2014. "Darfur Conflict." July 31. http://news.trust.org/.

Thornton, John. 1998. *Africa and Africans in the Making of the Atlantic World, 1400–1800.* Cambridge: Cambridge University Press.

Tieku, Thomas Kwasi. 2004. "Explaining the Clash and Accommodation of Interests of Major Actors in the Creation of the African Union." *African Affairs* 103(411): 249–267.

Timmer, Ashley S., and Jeffrey G. Williams. 1998. "Immigration Policy Prior to the 1930s: Labor Markets, Policy Interactions, and Globalization Backlash." *Population and Development Review* 24(4): 739–771.

Toft, Monica Duffy. 2010. "Ending Civil Wars: A Case for Rebel Victory?" *International Security* 34(4): 7–36.

Torbati, Yeganeh. 2017. "Republicans Push Back Against Trump Plan to Cut Foreign Aid." Reuters, May 23. https://www.reuters.com.

Totten, Samuel. 2015. "The World's Unexplained Silence over Human Tragedy in the Nuba Mountains of Sudan." *The Conversation,* May 20. http://theconversation.com.

Touval, Saadia. 1966. "The Shifta Warfare." *East Africa Journal* 3(2): 7–10.

Trefon, Theodore. 2011. *Congo Masquerade: The Political Culture of Aid Inefficiency and Reform Failure.* London: Zed.

Tripp, Aili Mari. 1994. "Gender, Political Participation, and the Transformation of Associational Life in Uganda and Tanzania." *African Studies Review* 37(1): 107–131.

———. 2000. "Political Reform in Tanzania: The Struggle for Associational Autonomy." *Comparative Politics* 32(2): 191–214.

Trolio, Pete. 2012. "Setting Its Own Course, Brazil Foreign Aid Expands and Evolves." July 9. www.devex.com.

Tull, Denis M. 2009. "Peacekeeping in the Democratic Republic of Congo: Waging Peace and Fighting War." *International Peacekeeping* 16(2): 215–230.

Tull, Denis M., and Andreas Mehler. 2005. "The Hidden Costs of Power-Sharing: Reproducing Insurgent Violence in Africa." *African Affairs* 104(416): 375–398.

Turcu, Anca, and R. Urbatsch. 2015. "Diffusion of Diaspora Enfranchisement Norms: A Multinational Study." *Comparative Political Studies* 48(4): 407–437.

Turner, Thomas. 2002. "Angola's Role in the Congo War." In *The African Stakes of the Congo War,* ed. John F. Clark. New York: Palgrave Macmillan, 75–92.

Turse, Nick. 2015. "AFRICOM's New Math, the US Base Bonanza, and 'Scarier' Times Ahead in Africa." November 17. http://www.truth-out.org.

UK Department for International Development. N.d. "Elections in the Democratic Republic of Congo in 2006." Government of the United Kingdom. https://www.gov.uk.

United Nations Conference on Trade and Development (UNCTAD). 2017. "UNCTAD STAT Data Center." http://unctadstat.unctad.org.

United Nations Department of Economic and Social Affairs (UNDESA). 2015. "Trends in International Migrant Stock: Migrants by Destination and Origin." Population Division. http://www.un.org.

United Nations Department of Public Information (UNDPI). 1997. "United Nations Operation in Somalia I." March 21. http://www.un.org.

United Nations Economic Commission for Africa (UNECA). 2015. "Africa-India: Facts & Figures 2015." October. http://www.uneca.org.

United Nations High Commissioner for Refugees (UNHCR). 2017. "More Than 6,000 Flee Fresh South Sudan Violence into Uganda." *Refworld,* April 7. http://www.refworld.org.

United Nations News Service. 2017. "South Sudan Refugees in Uganda Exceed One Million; UN Renews Appeal for Help." UN News Centre, August 17. https://www.un.org.

United Nations Office of the High Commissioner for Human Rights (OHCHR). 2010. "Democratic Republic of the Congo, 1993–2003: Report of the Mapping Exercise Documenting the Most Serious Violations of Human Rights and International Humanitarian Law Committed Within the Territory of the Democratic Republic of the Congo Between March 1993 and June 2003." http://www.securitycouncil report.org.

US Agency for International Development (USAID). 2017. "U.S. Overseas Loans and Grants: Obligations and Loan Authorizations, July 1, 1945–September 30, 2015." https://explorer.usaid.gov.

US Committee for Refugees and Immigrants. 2001. "Crisis in Sudan." Arlington, April.

US Department of State. 2008. "Somaliland." Taken Questions, January 17. https://2001-2009.state.gov.

US Embassy–Harare. 2015. "US Sanctions Policy: Facts and Myths." http://harare.usembassy.gov.

US Federal Budget. 2015a. "Compare United States Foreign Aid: Grants and Loans." http://us-foreign-aid.insidegov.com.

———. 2015b. "US Overseas Loans and Grants to Kenya." http://us-foreign-aid.insidegov.com.

US Government Printing Office. 2003. "Executive Order 13288 of March 6, 2003: Blocking Property of Persons Undermining Democratic Processes or Institutions in Zimbabwe." *Federal Register* 68(46): 11457–11562. http://www.gpo.gov.

van de Walle, Nicolas. 2001. *African Economies and the Politics of Permanent Crisis, 1979–1999.* New York: Cambridge University Press.

Vansina, Jan. 2012. *How Societies Are Born: Governance in West Central Africa Before 1600.* Charlottesville: University of Virginia Press.

Varadarajan, Latha. 2010. *The Domestic Abroad: Diasporas in International Relations.* Oxford: Oxford University Press.

Verschave, Francois-Xavier. 1999. *La Françafrique: Le Plus Long Scandale de la République,* Paris: Stock.

Villalón, Leonardo, and Peter VonDoepp, eds. 2005. *The Fate of Africa's Democratic Experiments: Elites and Institutions.* Bloomington: Indiana University Press.

Vines, Alex. 2013. "A Decade of the African Peace and Security Architecture." *International Affairs* 89(1): 89–109.

Volman, Daniel. 2007. "US to Create New Regional Military Command for Africa: AFRICOM." *Review of African Political Economy* 34(114): 737–744.

VonDoepp, Peter. 1996. "Political Transition and Civil Society: The Cases of Kenya and Zambia." *Studies in Comparative International Development* 31(1): 24–47.

Wallerstein, Immanuel. 1979. *The Capitalist World Economy.* Cambridge: Cambridge University Press.

Waltz, Kenneth N. 1959. *Man, the State, and War: A Theoretical Analysis.* New York: Columbia University Press.

———. 1979. *Theory of International Politics.* New York: McGraw-Hill.

Wassara, Samson S. 2010. "Rebels, Militias, and Governance in Sudan." In *Militias, Rebels, and Islamist Militants: Human Insecurity and State Crises in Africa,* ed. Wafula Okumu and Augustine Ikelegbe. Pretoria: Institute for Security Studies, 255–286.

Watkins, Kevin. 2002. "Cultivating Poverty: The Impact of US Cotton Subsidies on Africa." *Oxfam Policy and Practice: Agriculture, Food, and Land* 2(1): 82–117.

Weigert, Stephen. 2011. *Angola: A Modern Military History, 1961–2002.* New York: Palgrave Macmillan.

Weiss, Thomas G. 1999. "Principles, Politics, and Humanitarian Action." *Ethics & International Affairs* 13(1): 1–22.

Welch, Claude E., Jr. 1966. *Dream of Unity: Pan-Africanism and Political Unification in West Africa.* Ithaca: Cornell University Press.

Wellman, Elizabeth Iams. 2016. "Le Vote de la Diaspora en Afrique du Sud." *Afrique Contemporaine* (256): 35–50.

Wendt, Alexander. 1992. "Anarchy Is What States Make of It." *International Organization* 46(2): 391–425.

———. 1999. *Social Theory of International Politics.* Cambridge: Cambridge University Press.

Wesseling, Hendrik Lodewijk. 1996. *Divide and Rule: The Partition of Africa, 1880–1914.* Westport: Praeger.

Wheeler, Nicholas J. 2000. *Saving Strangers: Humanitarian Intervention in International Society.* Oxford: Oxford University Press.

Whitaker, Beth Elise. 1999. "Disjunctured Boundaries: Refugees, Hosts, and Politics in Western Tanzania." Chapel Hill: University of North Carolina at Chapel Hill.

———. 2001. "Creating Alternatives: Refugee Relief and Local Government in Western Tanzania." In *The Charitable Impulse: Relief, Development, and Non-Governmental Organisations in North East Africa,* ed. Ondine Barrow and Mike Jennings. Oxford: Currey, 81–93.

———. 2002. "Refugees in Western Tanzania: The Distribution of Burdens and Benefits Among Local Hosts." *Journal of Refugee Studies* 15(4): 339–358.

———. 2003. "Refugees and the Spread of Conflict: Contrasting Cases in Central Africa." *Journal of Asian and African Studies* 38(2–3): 211–231.

———. 2005. "Citizens and Foreigners: Democratization and the Politics of Exclusion in Africa." *African Studies Review* 48(1): 109–126.

———. 2007. "Exporting the Patriot Act? Democracy and the 'War on Terror' in the Third World." *Third World Quarterly* 28(5): 1017–1032.

———. 2008. "Reluctant Partners: Fighting Terrorism and Promoting Democracy in Kenya." *International Studies Perspectives* 9(3): 254–271.

———. 2010a. "Compliance Among Weak States: Africa and the Counter-Terrorism Regime." *Review of International Studies* 36(3): 639–662.

———. 2010b. "Soft Balancing Among Weak States? Evidence from Africa." *International Affairs* 86(5): 1109–1127.

———. 2011. "The Politics of Home: Dual Citizenship and the African Diaspora." *International Migration Review* 45(4): 755–783.

———. 2013. "Why It's Hard for the U.S. to Fight Terrorism and Promote Democracy in East Africa." *The Monkey Cage,* October 8. https://www.washingtonpost.com.

———. 2015. "Playing the Immigration Card: The Politics of Exclusion in Côte d'Ivoire and Ghana." *Commonwealth & Comparative Politics* 53(3): 274–293.

———. 2016. "The Politics of Closing Refugee Camps." *Political Violence at a Glance,* June 22. https://politicalviolenceataglance.org.

———. 2017. "Migration Within Africa and Beyond." *African Studies Review* 60(2): 209–220.

Whitaker, Beth Elise, and Jason Giersch. 2015. "Political Competition and Attitudes Towards Immigration in Africa." *Journal of Ethnic and Migration Studies* 41(10): 1536–1557.

Whitaker, Beth Elise, and Salma Inyanji. 2016. "Vote de la Diaspora et Ethnicité au Kenya." *Afrique Contemporaine* (256): 73–89.

White, George. 2005. *Holding the Line: Race, Racism, and American Foreign Policy Toward Africa, 1953–1961.* Lanham: Rowman and Littlefield.

White, Luise. 2015. *Unpopular Sovereignty: Rhodesian Independence and African Decolonization.* Chicago: University of Chicago Press.

Whitehouse, Bruce. 2012. *Migrants and Strangers in an African City: Exile, Dignity, Belonging.* Bloomington: Indiana University Press.

Whitfield, Lindsay. 2009. "'Change for a Better Ghana': Party Competition, Institutionalization and Alternation in Ghana's 2008 Elections." *African Affairs* 108(433): 621–641.

Williams, David. 1961. "How Deep the Split in West Africa?" *Foreign Affairs* 40(1): 118–127.

Williams, G. Mennen. 1969. *Africa for the Africans.* Grand Rapids: Eerdmans.

Williams, Paul D. 2001. "Fighting for Freetown: British Military Intervention in Sierra Leone." *Contemporary Security Policy* 22(3): 140–168.

———. 2008. "Keeping the Peace in Africa: Why 'African' Solutions Are Not Enough." *Ethics & International Affairs* 22(3): 309–329.

———. 2009. "The African Union's Peace Operations: A Comparative Analysis." *African Security* 2(2–3): 97–118.

———. 2011. *War and Conflict in Africa.* Malden: Polity.

———. 2012. "Britain, the EU, and Africa." In *The EU and Africa: From Eurafrique to Afro-Europa,* ed. Adekeye Adebajo and Kaye Whiteman. New York: Columbia University Press, 343–364.

Windrich, E. 1978. *Britain and the Politics of Rhodesian Independence.* London: Croom Helm.

Wing, Susanna D. 2016. "French Intervention in Mali: Strategic Alliances, Long-Term Regional Presence?" *Small Wars & Insurgencies* 27(1): 59–80.

Wolpe, Howard. 2011. *Making Peace After Genocide: Anatomy of the Burundi Process.* Washington, DC: US Institute of Peace.

World Bank. 1981. *Accelerated Development in Sub-Saharan Africa: An Agenda for Action.* Washington, DC: International Bank for Reconstruction and Development/World Bank.

———. 2000. *Kenya: Country Assistance Evaluation.* Report no. 21409. http://site resources.worldbank.org.

———. 2012. *Global Development Finance: External Debt of Developing Countries.* Washington, DC: International Bank for Reconstruction and Development.

———. 2015. "World Databank: World Development Indicators: Kenya." http://databank.worldbank.org.

———. 2017a. "Remittances to Developing Countries Decline for Second Consecutive Year." April 21. http://www.worldbank.org.

———. 2017b. *World Development Indicators.* http://data.worldbank.org.

World Health Organization (WHO). 2015. "Official Development Assistance for Health to the Democratic Republic of the Congo." http://www.who.int.

World Trade Organization (WTO). 2015. *International Trade Statistics 2015.* Geneva.

World Values Survey. 2017. "World Values Survey." http://www.worldvaluessurvey.org.

Woronoff, Jon. 1972. *West African Wager: Houphouet Versus Nkrumah*. Metuchen, NJ: Scarecrow.

Wyss, Marco. 2013. "The Gendarme Stays in Africa: France's Military Role in Côte d'Ivoire." *African Conflict and Peacebuilding Review* 3(1): 81–111.

Yates, Douglas. 2012. "France, the EU, and Africa." In *The EU and Africa: From Eurafrique to Afro-Europa,* ed. Adekeye Adebajo and Kaye Whiteman. New York: Columbia University Press, 317–342.

Yihdego, Zeray W. 2007. "Ethiopia's Military Action Against the Union of Islamic Courts and Others in Somalia: Some Legal Implications." *International and Comparative Law Quarterly* 56(3): 666–676.

Young, Crawford. 1982. *Ideology and Development in Africa*. New Haven: Yale University Press.

——. 1994. "The Shattered Illusion of the Integral State in Zaire." *Journal of Modern African Studies* 32(2): 247–263.

Yun, Sun. 2015. "Xi and the 6th Forum on China-Africa Cooperation: Major Commitments, but with Questions." *Africa in Focus,* December 7. https://www.brookings.edu.

Zambia Daily Mail. 2017. "Economic Zones to Create over 8,000 jobs." March 7. https://www.daily-mail.co.zm.

Zambian Ministry of Commerce, Trade, and Industry. 2017. "Multi-Facility Economic Zones (MFEZ)." http://www.mcti.gov.zm.

Zartman, I. William. 1989. *Ripe for Resolution: Conflict Resolution in Africa*. New York: Oxford University Press.

Zhou, Lihuan, and Denise Leung. 2015. "China's Overseas Investments, Explained in 10 Graphics." January 28. http://www.wri.org.

Zimbabwe Human Rights NGO Forum. 2001. "Politically Motivated Violence in Zimbabwe 2000–2001: A Report on the Campaign of Political Repression Conducted by the Zimbabwean Government Under the Guise of Carrying Out Land Reform." http://hrforumzim.org.

Index

Addis Ababa Agreement (1972), 41
Addis Ababa summit (1963), 12, 61
Africa Action, 276, 284*n*24
African Americans, 218–219, 276–277, 283*n*12
African Development Bank, 111, 288, 330
African Economic Community (AEC), 147–148, 158, 166*n*22
African Growth and Opportunity Act (AGOA), 97, 261–263, 276, 283*nn*5–7
African National Congress (ANC), 55, 169, 248–249, 351
African Peace and Security Architecture, 139, 174, 311
African Peer Review Mechanism (APRM), 140–141
African Risk Capacity (ARC), 141, 165*n*8
African Standby Force, 139, 174, 208
African Union (AU), 4, 10, 17, 289, 312; China surveillance of, 342; conflict resolution of, 138–139, 142, 158–159, 174–175, 195*n*9, 208, 311; diaspora population recognized by, 240; economic and political reform efforts of, 126, 139–141, 365; electoral mediation by, 131; EU relations with, 308; goals in forming of, 138–139, 362; leadership of, 141–142, 164, 175; membership in, 126, 285; natural disaster relief of, 141; OAU transition to, 135, 137–139, 158, 163
African Union Mission in Somalia (AMISOM), 139, 281–282, 284*n*28

African unity, 33–34, 135–138, 143–146, 308, 350. *See also* Organization of African Unity
Afrikaner nationalism, 244–245, 250*nn*12–13
Agriculture/farmers, 157–158, 222*n*4, 367; development models impact on, 81–84; fair trade impact on, 98–99; privatization of, 89; SAPs impact on, 91; under-utilization of, 322
Aid Worker Security Database, 224*n*26
Aidid, Mohammed, 279
Algerian war (1954), 30, 298
Amin, Idi, 150, 165*n*15, 166*n*16
Amnesty International, 107, 112
Angola, 65, 164*n*2, 195*n*12; civil war in, 17, 49–50, 53, 64, 68–73, 75*n*22, 169, 172, 177; military interventions in, 49–50, 69–73, 177; military power of, 173; oil production in, 62, 73; Portugal relations with, 304; superpower rivalry over, 56; UNITA in, 38, 69–74, 83, 98, 104*n*3, 177, 193, 215
Angola-Namibia Peace Accord, 72–73
Annan, Kofi, 131
Apartheid, 1, 6, 31, 70–71, 165*n*5, 276; migration with, 239, 245–246; OAU against, 63, 136, 306, 308; origins and class structure of, 245–246, 251*n*15; Soviet stance on, 64–65; violence, 156, 169; violence after, 247–248. *See also* White minority rule
Arab Maghreb Union (AMU), 3

70, 75*n*14, 307; Mugabe regime support from, 120, 308, 345–346, 350; peacekeeping support from, 346, 364–365; relations with, 51, 54, 61, 64, 69–70, 75*n*14, 173, 185, 284*n*22, 306–308, 321–328, 341, 343–346, 349–356, 357*n*16, 357*n*18, 364–365; Soviet relations with, 54; Sudan relations with, 173, 185, 345; surveillance practices of, 342; trade policy and relations with, 15, 19, 322–324, 324*tab*, 328, 332, 333*tab*, 339, 353–355; UN Cold War representation of, 50–51, 74*n*4, 319*n*17, 344, 357*n*13; US rivalry in Africa with, 9; Zambia relations with, 325–326, 351–356, 357*n*18. *See also* BRICS; Republic of China

China Non-Ferrous Metals Corporation (CNMC), 353–354

Chirac, Jacques, 314–316

Christianity, 28, 186, 276

Citizenship, 141, 151, 241–242, 247

Civil liberties, 112, 122, 125, 274

Civil wars: Cold War influence on, 17, 49–50, 53; migration and, 185–186; regionalized conflicts instigated with, 176–178, 187–188, 362–363. *See also specific civil wars*

Clark Amendment, 71–72

Class structure, 74*n*8, 229; of apartheid, 245–246, 251*n*15; from colonization, 81–82

Clinton, Bill, 257–258, 260–261, 266, 275, 278

Cold War, 1, 74*n*8, 363; aid decline after, 255; aid during, 52, 295, 356*n*2; China/PRC influence during, 64; China's UN representation during, 50–51, 74*n*4, 319*n*17, 344, 357*n*13; civil wars impacted by, 17, 49–50, 53; conflict and violence increase after, 169–170, 172–173, 182–184, 255–256; in decolonization motivations, 31, 47–49; development models during, 52–53; divisions and alliances during, 50–55, 57, 351–352, 362; end of, in Africa, 256; Marxist-Leninist movements during, 48, 53, 55–57, 65–66, 352; 1956 to 1965 era of, 55–61; 1965 to 1974 era of, 56, 61–64; 1975 to 1988 era of, 56–57, 64–66; Soviet policies toward Africa during, 56, 61–62, 64, 66–68, 343; US policies toward Africa during, 52, 56, 62–65, 67, 74*n*2, 126–127, 172, 289, 319*n*3, 343; Zaire-US relations during, 172, 289, 319*n*3. *See also* Superpower rivalries and interventions

Colonialism/colonization, 3, 17, 32, 165*n*14; border legacy from, 27, 31, 33–38, 40, 43, 45–46, 144; BRICS shared history with, 350–351; under Britain, 28–29, 244–245, 319*n*7; China position with, 350–352; cooperation with, 16, 27–28; end of formal, 1, 361–362; European-African relations impacted by, 286–288, 305–308; under France, 29–30, 57, 195*n*19, 298, 313; natural resources impetus for, 27–28, 81; OAU goal of ending, 136; political leadership during, 29–30, 34; under Portugal, 28–29, 62–63; poverty ties to, 14; in South Africa, 244–245; state-run economy from, 81–82; World War II impact on, 28–31. *See also* Decolonization; Precolonial era

Communauté Financière Africaine franc. *See* CFA franc

Communism, 50–51, 54–57, 63–64

Community-based organizations (CBOs), 96–97

Compaoré, Blaise, 109, 166*n*18, 299

Conflict and violence, 29; apartheid, 156, 169; BRICS response to, 346, 349; decolonization, 30–31, 65, 67–70, 287, 291; diaspora impact on, 242–243; electoral, 121–122, 131–132, 134*n*21, 165*n*10, 216–217; facilitators of, 181–182; migration ties to, 185–186, 227, 232; peacekeeping impact on, 206, 209–211, 220, 256, 279, 282; post-apartheid, 247–248; post-Cold War increase of, 169–170, 172–173, 182–184, 192, 255–256; with religious and ethnic groups, 179–180, 184–187, 193, 219. *See also* Civil wars; Congo conflicts; Darfur conflicts; Genocide; Military interventions; *specific locations, conflicts*

Conflict and violence, regionalized: alliance systems impacting, 178–179; causes and interpretations of, 170–183, 363–364; civil wars influence on, 176–178, 187–188, 362–363; Congo as case study of, 188–195, 362; examples/impacts of, 169–170, 183–188; global/external actors impact on, 170–173, 182, 188, 192; political leadership role in, 178–181, 194; refugees in, 182, 184, 193

Conflict resolution, 217; of AU, 138–139, 142, 158–159, 174–175, 195*n*9, 208,

rights abuses in, 161–162; military power of, 173; remittances initiatives in, 240; terrorist threat in, 273

Nile river, 27

Nimeiri, Jaafar, 41

9/11 terrorist attacks, 42, 165*n*17, 258, 269, 280

Nixon, Richard, 56, 62–64, 75*n*14

Nkrumah, Kwame, 135, 291; anti-imperialist stance of, 51, 57, 307, 310; coup on, 62, 101; diplomatic relations under, 342

Noah, Trevor, 251*n*15

Non-Aligned Movement (NAM), 47, 54, 74*n*1, 352

Nongovernmental organizations (NGOs), 4–5, 95–97, 112, 199, 365–366

North Africa, 19*n*2, 333, 333tab

North Atlantic Treaty Organization (NATO), 48, 54, 300, 319*n*12, 320*n*23, 320*n*26

Nyerere, Julius, 36, 90, 125, 149–150, 166*n*16, 213, 352

Obama, Barack, 222*n*4, 260, 265, 284*n*24; African support for, 275; AFRICOM under, 268–269; counterterrorism policy in Africa under, 272; visits to Africa, 103, 119, 132, 283*n*17

Obasanjo, Olusegun, 137–138, 162–164, 166*n*24

Obote, Milton, 149–150

Odinga, Raila, 130–132

Ogaden War, 56, 75*n*17

Oil production: in Angola, 62, 73; Brazil investments in, 335; British investments in, 295; Chinese investments in, 328; cost/benefit of, 98; economic crisis ties to, 85; French role in, 303; India investment/trade in, 329, 331; in Nigeria, 160; Russian investments in, 335–336; in Sudan, 41–43; US policy towards Africa and, 62, 219, 267, 276–278

Operation Licorne/Unicorn, 315–316

Operation Restore Hope, 278

Operation Turquoise, 300

Orange Democratic Movement (ODM), 130–131

Organization for Economic Cooperation and Development (OECD), 112, 126, 133*n*6, 296tab, 327, 337, 339

Organization of African Unity (OAU), 10, 17, 164, 164*n*2, 165*n*3, 341; anti-apartheid focus of, 63, 136, 306, 308;

AU formation and divergence from, 135, 137–139, 158, 163; colonial border durability and, 34; conflict resolution efforts of, 136–137, 174, 222*n*7; on economic crisis of 1980s, 85; founding and goals of, 61, 63, 67, 135–137, 306, 308; noninterference role of, 137, 159, 165*n*4; refugee definition under, 250*n*2, 250*n*4

Organization of Petroleum Exporting Countries (OPEC), 85

Orphans, 263, 283*n*10

Ouattara, Alasane, 185–186, 314–315, 317–318

Pan-Africanism. *See* African unity

Paris Club, 93, 95

Passports and visas, 141, 151

Paternalism, 107, 286, 297, 319*n*9, 320*n*25, 349

Peacebuilding: elites role in, 215–216; justice concerns in, 216–217; in Liberia, 220–222; peace agreement sustainability in, 214–217, 221–222; power-sharing emphasis in, 213, 215; process and negotiations for, 212–214; sites for, 214

Peacekeeping missions, 121, 136, 198; AU, 139; BRICS contributions to, 346; to Burundi, 138–139, 142, 208–209; challenges/risks of, 209–212, 224*n*26, 279; China's role in, 346, 364–365; conflict ignited or prolonged by, 206, 209–211, 220, 256, 279, 282; in Congo conflicts, 210–211, 301; in Darfur, 44, 211; economic integration focus shift to, 153–154, 157; in Lesotho, 157; in Liberia, 206, 219–220; in Mali, 209–210, 301; misconduct associated with, 211–212; political leadership manipulation of, 207–208, 211; for political reform, 116–117; sovereignty debates and, 205–206; subregional organizations to "Africanize," 208; troops allocation and training for, 206–208, 220, 223*n*12, 266–267; withdrawal of, 208–210. *See also* United Nations

People's Republic of China (PRC). *See* China

Polisario Front, 165*n*3, 214

Political leadership/parties, 8, 15–16, 19, 363–365, 367; aid manipulated to benefit, 201–203; Clinton support of, 257–258; during Cold War, 51, 56; colonial era, 29–30, 34; credibility shift

Southern African Customs Union (SACU), 157, 166*n*22
Southern African Development Coordination Conference (SADCC), 3, 155–158, 223*n*13, 365
Soviet Union. *See* Russia/Soviet Union
Spain, 28, 304
Stalin, Joseph, 47, 54
Stock market, 89–90, 97
Structural adjustment programs (SAPs): conditions and outcomes of, 14–15, 81, 87–88, 90–93, 340; currency devaluation with, 87–88, 102; debt worsened with, 92–93; Ghana adoption of, 102–103
Subregional integration. *See* Regional integration/organizations
Sudan, 9, 182, 195*n*11; aid to, 41, 45, 173, 201; Chinese relations with, 173, 185, 345; civil wars in, 40–41, 45, 53, 176, 180, 183–184, 195*n*16; colonial system in, 40; oil production in, 41–43; rebels support in, 177, 216; refugees from, 41, 44; South Sudan independence conflicts with, 37, 40–46, 152, 183–184, 195*n*16, 243; South Sudan power-sharing deal with, 41–42, 45–46, 215; terrorists in, 42, 165*n*17, 179; US relations with, 42, 173, 178–179, 184. *See also* Darfur conflicts; South Sudan
Sudan People's Liberation Movement/Army (SPLM/A), 41–44, 176–177, 180, 183–184, 195*n*10
Suez Canal crisis (1956), 55, 319*n*7
Superpower rivalries and interventions, 8–9, 17, 31, 33; alliances and rejections of, 47–50, 52–57, 66–67, 362; in Congo conflicts, 57–61, 192; motivations in, 47–49, 67–68, 319*n*8; security issues with withdrawal of, 172–173, 183–184, 192, 255–256
Surveillance, 130, 271, 342
Swaziland, 166*n*19, 292
Switzerland, 357*n*17
Syria, 237

Taiwan, 50–51, 74*n*4, 319*n*17, 343–344, 357*n*13
Tanganyika, 36, 165*n*14
Tanzania, 3, 90, 149–150, 152, 233; Chinese railway project partnership with, 325–326, 352–353; creation of, 36; European relations with, 287, 305; political stability and human rights

in, 125; Rwandan refugees in, 202–203
Tanzania-Zambia Railway (TAZARA), 325–326, 352–353
Taylor, Charles, 118, 186, 224*n*30, 224*n*32; CIA relations with, 224*n*29; Liberian conflict role of, 187–188, 219–222, 224*n*31, 293, 363–364; war crimes of, 187–188, 224*n*29
Territorial Assembly, 30, 57, 298
Terrorists/terrorism, 165*n*15; of Boko Haram, 163–164; in Kenya, 129–130, 187, 283*n*18; in Mali, 272–273; in Nigeria, 273; 9/11 attacks of, 42, 165*n*17, 258, 269, 280; regionalized conflict arising from, 170–171; of al-Shabaab, 130, 187, 281–282, 284*n*27, 284*n*29; in Somalia, 130, 187, 280–282; in Sudan, 42, 165*n*17, 179; UNITA, 73; US embassy, 133*n*20; US policy toward Africa and, 129–130, 258–259, 267–275, 284*n*27
Tolbert, William, 219, 306
Touré, Sékou, 51, 62, 101, 307, 319*n*18; diplomatic relations under, 342–343; Guinea independence under, 30, 287, 298
Trade policy and relations, 4, 10, 20*n*10; with Brazil, 324, 324*tab*, 332, 334; with BRICS, 322; with Britain, 294, 332; with China, 15, 19, 322–324, 324*tab*, 328, 332, 333*tab*, 339, 353–355; consumerism and African, 366–367; EU framework for, 309–310; fair trade programs in, 98–99; foreign aid debates with, 97–98, 261; with France, 302–303; global comparisons of, 324, 324*tab*; imbalances in, 32–33, 81–82, 339–340; with India, 324, 324*tab*, 328–329, 333*tab*, 339; Kenyan post-Cold War, 127; with Middle East, 336; precolonial, 26; regional integration for free, 143, 145–146, 148, 152, 157, 166*n*22; with Russia, 324, 324*tab*, 356*n*6; SAPs conditions on, 88–89; with South Africa, 324, 324*tab*, 332–333, 333*tab*, 334; with US, 97, 222*n*4, 261–263, 276, 283*nn*5–7, 324, 324*tab*, 332, 333*tab*, 367; US farmers impacted by, 222*n*4, 367; Zambia-China, 353–355
Transportation, 33, 149, 325–326, 352–353
Tripartite Accord, 72–73
Trump, Donald, 237, 260, 265, 272, 274–275
Tshombe, Moïse, 59–60

Waltz, Kenneth, 8
War crimes/crimes against humanity, 138, 165*n*11, 274, 349; of al-Bashir, 42, 44, 118–119, 121, 143; in Burundi, 165; foreign judiciary role for, 117–119, 121, 133*n*13; of Gbagbo, 318; of Taylor, 187–188, 224*n*29
Warlord politics, 187–188, 280
Wars. *See* Civil wars; Conflict and violence; *specific wars*
Weah, George, 221
Weapons. *See* Armament
Wen Jiabao, 327
Wendt, Alexander, 12
West Africa, 146; Ebola outbreak in, 163, 221, 224*n*33, 269; fair trade programs in, 99; migrant relations in, 234; precolonial, 24; Soviet aid in, 62; warlord politics in, 187–188
West African wager, 57
Western Sahara, 2, 214
White minority rule, 1; decolonization and, 30–31; OAU goal of ending, 63, 136, 306, 308; Soviet response to, 52; US response to, 62–64; in Zimbabwe, 62–64, 75*n*15
Wight, Martin, 11
Women, 86, 99
World Bank, 14, 85, 87–91, 94, 111, 362
World Food Programme (WFP), 198–199, 222*n*4

World Health Organization (WHO), 199
World Trade Organization (WTO), 262, 310
World War I, 28, 36, 63, 70, 165*n*14, 290, 304
World War II, 6, 28–31, 37, 52, 80, 290

Xenophobia, 38, 232, 235–236, 247–248, 314–315

Yaoundé Agreement, 309–310

Zaire, 86, 172, 289, 319*n*3. *See also* Congo/DRC
Zambia, 183, 305, 357*n*17; British relations with, 291; Chinese relations with, 325–326, 351–356, 357*n*18; democratization efforts in, 108
Zanzibar, 36, 46*n*2
Zenawi, Meles, 184, 258
Zhao Ziyang, 326
Zhou Enlai, 341–342
Zimbabwe (Rhodesia), 1, 183; British relations with, 291–293; Chinese armament of, 345–346; political reform in, 114, 119–120, 157–158; Soviet-China rivalry in, 54; white minority rule in, 62–64, 75*n*15
Zimbabwe African National Union–Popular Front (ZANU/ZANU-PF), 54, 74*n*9, 114
Zuma, Jacob, 251*n*17, 312

About the Book

Comprehensive and engaging, this timely introduction to Africa's international relations explores how power, interests, and ideas influence interactions both among the continent's states and between African states and other actors in the global arena.

How has history shaped the international relations of African states and peoples? What role does identity play? How are foreign policies linked to domestic political dynamics, and especially to the pursuit of regime security? How are states grappling with the tensions between sovereignty and external pressures? These are among the questions answered as the authors address a wide range of ongoing and emerging challenges, all in historical and theoretical context. In addition, a case study at the end of each chapter illustrates key concepts and reflects an ongoing debate. The result is an ideal text for students, as well as an invaluable resource for researchers and policymakers.

Beth Elise Whitaker is associate professor of political science at the University of North Carolina at Charlotte. **John F. Clark** is professor of politics and international relations at Florida International University.